The
AMERICAN HERITAGE
COOKBOOK
❖ and Illustrated History of ❖
American Eating & Drinking

Moses Marcy, a Massachusetts merchant, savors a goblet of punch.

The

AMERICAN HERITAGE

COOKBOOK

and Illustrated History of
American Eating & Drinking

BY THE EDITORS OF AMERICAN HERITAGE, THE MAGAZINE OF HISTORY

WITH CHAPTERS BY

CLEVELAND AMORY · LUCIUS BEEBE · GERALD CARSON · PAUL ENGLE
MARSHALL FISHWICK · EVAN JONES · LEONARD LOUIS LEVINSON
RUSSELL LYNES · ARCHIE ROBERTSON · GEORGE F. WILLISON

HISTORICAL FOODS CONSULTANT: HELEN DUPREY BULLOCK
RECIPES EDITOR: HELEN McCULLY · ASSOCIATE: ELEANOR NODERER

PUBLISHED BY

AMERICAN HERITAGE PUBLISHING CO., INC.

BOOK TRADE DISTRIBUTION BY

SIMON AND SCHUSTER, INC.

TABLE OF CONTENTS

PART 1

PART 2

AMERICAN HERITAGE

The Magazine of History

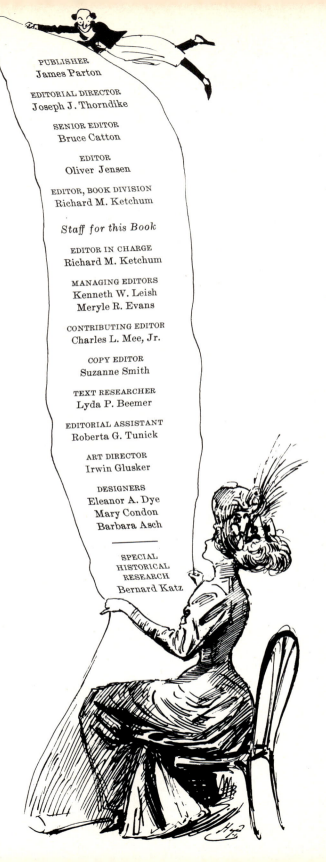

PUBLISHER
James Parton

EDITORIAL DIRECTOR
Joseph J. Thorndike

SENIOR EDITOR
Bruce Catton

EDITOR
Oliver Jensen

EDITOR, BOOK DIVISION
Richard M. Ketchum

Staff for this Book

EDITOR IN CHARGE
Richard M. Ketchum

MANAGING EDITORS
Kenneth W. Leish
Meryle R. Evans

CONTRIBUTING EDITOR
Charles L. Mee, Jr.

COPY EDITOR
Suzanne Smith

TEXT RESEARCHER
Lyda P. Beemer

EDITORIAL ASSISTANT
Roberta G. Tunick

ART DIRECTOR
Irwin Glusker

DESIGNERS
Eleanor A. Dye
Mary Condon
Barbara Asch

SPECIAL
HISTORICAL
RESEARCH
Bernard Katz

PART 1
Illustrated History of American Eating & Drinking

INTRODUCTION

"Kissing don't last," George Meredith once wrote. "Cookery do!" Or, as Thomas Wolfe put it (more romantically), "There is no spectacle on earth more appealing than that of a beautiful woman in the act of cooking dinner for someone she loves." In this day of frozen and precooked foods, when entire meals may require no more preparation than flicking on an electric oven, is it any wonder that the thoughts of an older generation sometimes stray wistfully to the dim memory of a farm kitchen, alive with rich, savory smells, to a fond recollection of foods prepared as Mother—or Grandmother—used to make them?

Since the dreadful "Starving Times" of Jamestown and Plymouth, American women have fed their husbands and their children remarkably well. With ingenuity and determination, they have taken the myriad food-stuffs of a new land and turned them into a tempting array of dishes ranging from baked beans bubbling in earthenware pots to the American classic, apple pie.

Pioneer wives, moving westward to transform a wilderness into a cornucopia, gritted their teeth, rolled up their sleeves, and cooked everything from buffalo tongue to beaver tail; their cuisine could be as adventurous as the life they led. They baked bread in makeshift ovens dug into hillsides, used buffalo chips as fuel, and learned to make use of anything that was available; even the rocking of the covered wagon, they discovered, could be put to use: it was helpful in making butter.

Once settled on farms and plantations, with a growing variety of foods at hand, American wives were able to cook dishes that were tasty as well as nourishing. They became experts at creating corn bread, pumpkin soup, and hasty puddings; hush puppies, fried chicken, and spicy hams; shoo-fly pie, apple butter, and pepper pot soup; sausages, chicken potpie, and persimmon pudding. Busy from dawn to dusk, and buying nothing that could be raised, grown, or cooked at home, they gave their menfolk strength to plant a nation's roots in fertile soil, and left a heritage of tastes and aromas that still provokes nostalgia.

On quite another level, food and drink have played a key role in the history of the United States. As Arthur M. Schlesinger wrote in *Paths to the Present*, "The very discovery of the New World was the by-product of a dietary quest." Europe wanted spices from the Orient to season and preserve its meats; this need brought Columbus inadvertently to America. Later, British taxes on tea and molasses raised patriot tempers to the boiling point. ("I know not why we should blush to confess that molasses was an essential ingredient in American independence," John Adams observed.) And surely the knowledge that they could survive without imported foods gave added confidence to the colonists who rebelled against England.

During the Civil War, the bountiful farms of the North were of crucial importance; before the war and afterward, the vision of a land where hunger seemed to be unknown drew millions of immigrants to these shores and enriched American cookery with hundreds of new dishes, from cheese blintzes to *panettone*. The land's incredible abundance, augmented by hard-working men and modern machinery, helped propel the United States to the forefront of world powers.

What men eat, and how, is a reflection of the society they live in, but food can do more than mirror a way of life. It helps—it is said—to shape the character of both men and nations. As Jean Anthelme Brillat-Savarin noted in the nineteenth century, "The destiny of nations depends on how they nourish themselves." America has nourished itself uncommonly well.

—The Editors

NATIVE
BOUNTY

By George F. Willison

Good cooking is a high art, a form of wonder-working magic, a source of ever-fresh delight. It has a high moral value, too. As that much-quoted authority Anon. once sagely observed:

"Bad dinners go hand in hand with total depravity, while a man properly fed is already half-saved."

American cookery, although not of the longest lineage, has a proud tradition. The people of many lands and cultures have contributed to it. It is a

The sixteenth-century engraving at left, from a painting by John White, shows life in the Indian village of Secotan in North Carolina. Depicted are a pumpkin garden (I), a ceremonial feast (D), a deer hunt (upper left), and several cornfields, including one with a human scarecrow (F).

rich and varied cuisine, having a wealth of foods to work with, many of them indigenous to the hemisphere and not generally known until recent centuries.

Much has been sung in praise—and rightly—of the great discoveries made in the New World by European explorers. But a really great American discovery, perhaps the greatest, had been made thousands of years before by the originals, the Indians. It was they who, in a real sense, discovered or "invented" corn.

Finding it growing as a wild grass (to scientists, *Euchlaena mexicana*) that had apparently originated in the southern Mexican highlands, the Indians cultivated it, learned by trial and error its particular requirements for

11

best growth, developed it into *Zea mays* (Indian corn, or maize), and gave the world one of its finest foods and most valuable crops.

Corn proved a most adaptable plant, making itself at home in many kinds of soils and conditions. In their widely varying languages and dialects, the Indians gave corn different names. But no matter how different, all meant the same, "Our Life."

Corn was life, too, to the first white settlers. In her charming *Singing Valleys: The Story of Corn*, Dorothy Giles has said: "So corn provided infant America with a backbone while it was

*And those who came were resolved
    to be Englishmen
Gone to the World's end,
    but English every one,
And they ate the white corn-kernels,
    parched in the sun,
And they knew it not,
    but they'd not be English again.*
        —Stephen Vincent Benét,
            "Western Star"

developing the use of its legs. America was growing, quite literally, up the cornstalk."

The immigrants who crossed the Atlantic, whether to North or South America, "found in the red man's maize a food which sustained them while they conquered those who gave it them to eat. They rose up refreshed, and built the cities of the New World on the cornfields." (To Europeans and the more precise, "corn" is any kind of

edible grain; "maize" specifies a particular variety—the grain Americans call "corn." It will be so called here, without any useless pedantry.)

Christopher Columbus was the first European to make mention of corn, referring to it in the journals of his voyage to the Caribbean in 1492. The first Englishman to take note of the grain was Thomas Hariot, who came to Roanoke Island (North Carolina) in 1585 with Sir Walter Raleigh's company. This ill-fated colony later got lost, vanishing without a trace in a great unsolved mystery, but Hariot, fortunately, returned home before that occurred and published, in 1588, *A Briefe & True Report of the New Found Land in Virginia*. It was republished in 1590 in Germany with splendid illustrations based on paintings and drawings by his friend John White, who had also been at Roanoke. The book aroused great interest throughout western Europe.

"*Pagatowr*, a kinde of graine so called by the inhabitants, the same in the West Indies is called *Mayze*," wrote Hariot. "English men call it *Guinney wheate* or *Turkie wheate*." Its kernels were "of divers colours: some white, some red, some yellow, and some blew. All of them yeelde a very white and sweete flowre . . . [which] maketh a very good bread. Wee made of the same in the countrey some mault, whereof was brued as good ale as was to bee desired . . . It is a graine of marvelous great increase: of a thousand, fifteene hundred, and some two thousand fold.

Of these graines besides bread, the inhabitants make victuall eyther by parching them; or seething them whole untill they be broken; or boyling the floure with water into a pappe."

Hariot and the other early comers were astonished at the highly sophisticated pattern of agriculture developed by the Indians. By experimenting, the latter had learned that corn grew best if four seeds were planted close together in a circle, in small hillocks a yard or more apart, with the hillocks running in rows about the same distance apart. They timed their planting of corn so that they had three crops of it each year, and they used the cleared ground around the hillocks to grow other vegetables simultaneously.

Along with corn, Hariot observed, the Indians planted *"Okindgier,* called by us *Beanes,"* the vines of which caught hold of the cornstalks and used them as bean poles to climb up into the sun. They also planted *"Wickonzówr,* called by us *Peaze* . . . far better then our English peaze" and *"Macócqwer . . .* called by us *Pompions* [pumpkins and squash of many varieties], *Mellions* [watermelon and others] . . . and very good." And with all these, "another great hearbe in forme of a Marigolde, about six foot in height. . . . Some take it to bee *Planta Solis* [sunflower]: of the seedes heereof they make both a kinde of bread and broth."

The intertillage system developed by the Indians, with single seeds carefully planted, was new to Europeans. The latter, in general, planted field

Pounding acorns

crops by scattering seed at random, hoping some would catch and root. Fields planted Indian-fashion with corn, beans, peas, squash, melons, and sunflowers yielded, as Hariot noted admiringly, "at the least two hundred London bushelles" an acre, whereas in England, "fourtie bushelles of our wheate [an acre] . . . is thought to be much."

The Indians had contrived many imaginative ways to use the produce from their fields. From them the whites learned how delicious young corn is when freshly picked, boiled immediately (before the sugar in the ears turns to starch), and eaten off the cob. They learned what tasty dishes can be made of corn, beans, and peas "by boyling them all to pieces into a broth; or boyling them whole untill they bee soft . . . eyther by themselves or mixtly together. . . . Sometime, also beeing whole sodden, they bruse or pound them in a morter, & thereof make loaves or lumps of dowishe bread."

These were not "dowishe" at all, despite Hariot's description. The Indians made crisp and delicious *appones* (pones), ashcakes, and hoecakes, and the settlers praised, enjoyed, and learned to make their maize bread, baked in an oblong shape, which contained dried huckleberries.

To this day our corn recipes largely follow Indian ways of making *misick-quatash* (succotash), corn and beans cooked together, with or without meat; *rockahominy* (hominy, or grits); and *nasaump* (samp), "a kind of meal pottage" made of unparched corn. For generations, samp served the colonists as both breakfast and supper, with milk and a pat of butter added. It was sweetened with cane sugar or with molasses or – far better – with maple syrup.

In the wilds beyond the tilled fields abounded eatables of all kinds, to be had for the gathering. There were wild fruits and berries, to be eaten fresh-picked or stewed or dried or made into jams, jellies, wines, brandies, and cordials. The more plentiful and more generally used varieties were blackberries, blueberries, raspberries, whortleberries, elderberries, mulberries, cranberries, and, above all, "fine and beautifull Strawberries, foure times bigger and better than ours in England," according to Captain John Smith.

Of wild fruits, there were cherries, plums ("being almost as good as a Damsen," said Edward Winslow),

grapes (fox, scuppernong, and others), and the *"Putchamin,"* or persimmon, which, when eaten green, "will drawe a mans mouth awrie with much torment," as John Smith discovered, but which, when ripe after the first hard frost, "is as delicious as an Apricock."

When men went into the woods to gather persimmons on the ground or to shake down more from the tree, they often found—far out on a limb, enjoying the luscious fruit—another native American, the opossum, described by Captain Smith as having *"an head like a Swine,* and a taile like a *Rat* . . . and the bignes of a Cat."* The foragers always tried to add him to their bag, for in the phrase of Negro field hands: "Possums and 'simmons comes together, an' bofe is good fruit."

To the south, in Florida, grew a wild orange in groves so thick a man could not get through them. Though these oranges were small and very sour, the Seminole ingeniously made a great delicacy of them, as John Bartram observed. Slicing off the top of the orange, they made a hole in the middle of the fruit, filled it up with wild honey, let this stand a bit, and then scooped out the innards with horn or wooden spoons. "Delicious," said Bartram. Both Indians and whites carefully watched and plotted the flight of wild bees, hoping for a clue that would lead to a store of honey, usually in a dead, hollow "bee tree."

There were also other sources of sweetness and sugars. Indians extracted syrup and sugar from the corn-

Buffalo-horn spoon

stalk and made it into a kind of candy. Cutting it up, they chewed small bits of the stalk, sucking out the sweet juice and spitting out the fiber. In more northerly parts a wonderful sweet came from the beautiful sugar maple. Cane sugar and molasses did not begin to arrive from the West Indies until 1650, not in quantity till the 1700's, and the former remained very expensive, not to be used lightly.

Wild roots helped Indians and early settlers to keep body and soul comfortably together. One that was used widely was the so-called groundnut (*Apios tuberosa*), a member of the pea family. Strung along its lengthy root, like beads on a necklace, grew a series of tubers about the size of hens' eggs. Indians dug up the tubers in the fall, storing them in baskets kept in a dry and relatively warm place to prevent rot, a practice the settlers adopted. During their first hungry winters at Plymouth, the Pilgrims made large use of the groundnut.

Other edible wild roots included the sweet potato, commonly called a yam, though it is not a yam. Curiously, it belongs to the morning-glory family and was found, for the most part, south of what became the Mason-Dixon Line. Then, there was the *tockawhonghe (Peltandra virginica)*, known as the tuckahoe to the whites. It grew thickly in swampy places along the larger rivers from Virginia south. Powhatan's braves and the Jamestown settlers ate a lot of tuckahoe root, either boiled or pounded into flour and baked as bread.

Both Indians and whites made much use of the yellow pond-lily, eating its seeds and blooms and particularly its roots. Squaws would wade hip-deep in quiet waters to pull up the lilies, the roots of which, when boiled long enough, became very tender—"with the flavour of Sheep's liver," according to the seventeenth-century naturalist John Josselyn.

From the forests came a great plenty of nuts, an important food supply — chestnut, hickory, black walnut, white walnut, chinquapin, beechnut, and acorns. These were eaten out of the shell or roasted or broken up to be added to bread or to give extra flavor and body to succotash and other spoon meats. Nuts also served another need. The Indians had no domesticated animals except their wolfish dogs — no cows, goats, or sheep — so they boiled chestnuts and hickories, as well as corn, to make a milk that was drunk cold or hot and used in general cooking and in making such particular dishes as custards and puddings. "Verie good" it was, said the Pilgrims.

As for meat, there were deer ("great store," according to Hariot), red and fallow and the distinctive Virginia white-tailed; elk; moose in the northern woods; and bear (chiefly black, but some cinnamon). Among smaller animals providing meat for the pot were hares and rabbits, found almost everywhere, possums, coons, and squirrels —the big gray, the red squirrel (known in the colonies as Red the Boomer), and the somewhat smaller flying squirrel. For generations, squirrel pie was a mainstay in the diet of woodsmen and of families in outlying farmsteads along the westward-moving frontier.

There were birds by the millions, by the billions — waterfowl, shore birds, land birds. During their seasonal migratory flights, ducks and geese covered sheltered coastal waters, lakes, and larger rivers. Wedges of feeding waterfowl often extended miles across, with scarcely a glint of water to be seen through the bright multicolored mass. Shore and wading birds included curlew, plover, sandpipers, and snipe. In the fields and woods were grouse, quail, woodcock, and that wonderful bronzed American native, the wild turkey, some reportedly weighing as much as fifty pounds.

Above all, there was the passenger pigeon, a beautiful bird about sixteen inches long. During their migrations, these birds flew in great clouds that darkened the sky to the horizon in all directions. Watching such a flight, the ornithologist Alexander Wilson noted, "It was then half past one [when the first birds appeared in the sky]. About four in the afternoon, the living torrent above my head seemed as numerous and extensive as ever." Wilson estimated that, in less than three hours, he had seen more than two billion birds. Later, in 1813, Audubon witnessed a similar "torrent" of life that lasted for three days. If anyone had suggested to him at the time that the passenger pigeon would be extinct a century later, he would have laughed aloud. Yet so enor-

mous and stupid was the slaughter of the birds that none remain, the last having died in 1914.

The pigeons by their habits facilitated the slaughter. At sunset they would roost in the trees, piling up on one another to such a height and with such weight that they frequently brought down main branches of the largest trees, after which they rested on the ground. Little short of a cannon boom could frighten them; men simply went among them with a stick and knocked them on the head. During the flights, country families had pigeon every day in as many different ways as housewives could contrive. In 1760, when a flight was on, a man journeying from Virginia to Boston noted that in the taverns along the way he was served, as the main dish at every meal, almost nothing but pigeon.

Even more countless were fish in the sea and in fresh waters — in the latter, largemouthed and smallmouthed bass, trout, perch, roach, chub, sturgeon (some twelve feet long), and others. Along the seashore could be found soft-shelled and hard-shelled clams, huge oyster beds, scallops, mussels, and other shellfish — as well as giant crabs and lobsters. Some crabs were a foot long and about half as wide, providing delicious meat sufficient to feed four persons. Lobsters six feet long were taken from the waters off New Amsterdam by the Dutch, but as Adriaen Van der Donck remarked: "Those a foot long are better for serving at table." Also to be found were turtles and their eggs, both "choice eating," according to John Bartram.

Deeper waters in bays and open ocean were alive with fish of all kinds. In his *New England's Rarities,* published in 1672, John Josselyn listed more than two hundred fishes caught for eating purposes in northern waters —among the more important, cod (the "Sacred Cod" became—and remains— the totem of Massachusetts), mackerel, haddock, hake, flounder, mullet, and sheepshead.

That engaging scapegrace Thomas Morton of Merry Mount, one of the most joyous communities America has ever known, where there was good food and drink for all, even for the sour Pilgrims in neighboring Plymouth, declared that on his section of Massachusetts Bay he had seen, "at the turning of the tyde . . . such multitudes of sea bass [striped bass] that it seemed to me that one might goe over their backes dri-shod."

One day in 1608, while exploring Chesapeake Bay, Captain John Smith and his men ran into a massive school of fish, "lying so thicke with their heads above the water," that their boat could scarcely get through. Being hungry, a chronic state in early Jamestown, they decided to fish. Having no hooks, nets, or seines, they got out a frying pan and tried to use that. "But we found it a bad instrument to catch fish with," said Smith sadly. The fish simply did not jump into the skillet.

What may be called the frying-pan technique characterized much of the firstcomers' attempts to get settled. The ways of the wilderness were utterly foreign to them, and in their ignorance they failed to provide themselves with proper gear and equipment. With an assist from the Indians, they had to learn the hard way — by experience — and the road was very rough indeed for the pioneers at Jamestown and Plymouth.

The gallants who founded Jamestown, too many of them being "gentlemen" who had never done a day's work

And can any bee so simple as to conceive that the fountains [of New England] should streame forth Wine, or Beare, or the woods and rivers be like Butchershops, or Fish-mongers stalles, where they might have things taken to their hands. If thou canst not live without such things, and hast no meanes to procure the one, and wilt not take paines for the other . . . rest where thou art . . .
—Edward Winslow, 1624

and had no desire to begin, were among the worst frontiersmen the world has ever known. After the landing in May, 1607, things went steadily from bad to worse, leading to the terrible "Starving Time" in the awful winter of 1609-10, when four out of five died.

"All was fish that came to net to satisfy crewell Hunger," wrote a survivor, George Percy, recalling those harrowing days. With supplies exhausted, the starving were "glad to make shift with vermin as doggs, catts, ratts, and myce . . . to feede upon Serpents and Snakes, and to digg for wylde and unknown Rootes." One man, his mind unhinged by slow starvation, killed his wife, "powdered [salted] her, and had eaten part of her before it was knowne," for which he was hanged. "Now whether shee was better roasted, boyled or carbonado'd, I know not," quipped Captain John Smith, "but such a dish as powdered wife I never heard of."

Virginia grew up to be a great beauty, the mother of many distinguished men, but she suffered a childhood so frightful that only the firsthand records make it credible. Things took a sudden sharp turn for the better in the mid-1620's, largely because the colonists ceased to be plagued by foolish directives from London. Faced with rising revolutionary tides at home, Charles I had no time to think about Virginia. Left to their own devices, the colonists began to dig in and really make themselves at home.

By the 1630's, Virginians (then numbering some 2,500) were, in general, "well housed . . . and well stored with cattle, as likewise with goats and swine in abundance, and great store of poultrie"; enjoyed "plentie" of bread (corn, wheat, and rye); brewed "good ale, both strong and small," and distilled quantities of corn liquor.

Meantime, another experiment was well under way. On November 11, 1620, the *Mayflower* swung around the tip of Cape Cod and anchored in the sheltered harbor there (now Provincetown Harbor). The ship, crowded to the gunwales, held 102 passengers — fifty men, twenty women, and a simply preposterous number of children, thirty-two in all.

For more than three months, the company had been living on the usual ship's fare of the day — hardtack, salt horse (salted beef), dried fish, cheese, and beer, with an occasional hot dish — not only a monotonous but an upsetting diet, which often brought on scurvy and other serious disorders.

Ravenous for fresh food, the Pilgrims came ashore and prowled the beach for shellfish. Happily, they found toothsome soft-shelled clams and tender young quahogs, and had a great

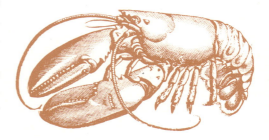

Lobster

feast on these. They also devoured many large mussels — "very fat," according to *Mourt's Relation*, an account of the Pilgrims' first year in America, written by Edward Winslow and William Bradford. This was a mistake, for the mussels made them sick, causing all "to cast and scoure."

Exploring the neighborhood, the Pilgrims chanced to find, buried in the ground, a number of large Indian baskets, all filled with corn. This was to them, they said, "a verie goodly sight, haveing never seen any such before."

The local Indians, the Pamet, had buried the corn for winter supply and for seed in the spring. The Pilgrims realized this, but stole all the corn they could find, condoning their larceny by arguing their necessity and by promising themselves that they would recompense the "locals"—which, at their first opportunity, they did. Meantime, the Pamet went hungry.

After deciding to settle on Plymouth Bay, on the north bank of a "very sweete brooke" (Town Brook), with many cleared fields around, the Pilgrims began building on Christmas Day. Progress was slow, and daily the rations from the common stores brought on the *Mayflower* grew shorter and shorter. Captain Myles Standish went out hunting one day and brought back an "eagle" (probably a fish hawk). The hungry ones at Plymouth boiled and ate it, pronouncing it "excellent . . . hardly to be discerned from Mutton."

It was also a memorable occasion when a sailor picked up on the beach a live herring, "which the Master [kindly Captain Christopher Jones, skipper of the *Mayflower*] had to his supper." This put the Pilgrims in hope that they would have plenty of fish shortly. As yet, according to *Mourt's Relation,* they had "got but one Cod." They had said that they wished to become fishermen, but being naïve landlubbers all, they had not brought what they needed most — small hooks and nets.

With great good sense, the Pilgrims early made a firm treaty of peace with Massasoit (Big Chief), head of the strong Wampanoag Confederacy that ruled southeastern New England. This was a master stroke. The peace treaty was not broken or even seriously strained for more than a half century, and enabled the Pilgrims to give their entire attention to affairs more constructive than warfare.

Some months after the peace treaty, word came by Indian messenger that Massasoit was dying. This greatly upset the Pilgrims; the loss of their new friend and powerful ally would be a heavy blow. Edward Winslow was sent posthaste to the principal Wampanoag village, where he found that the Big Chief was neither dead nor dying, but obviously very sick, and groaning that he had lost his sight, that everything was black before his eyes, that his jaws were almost locked, that he was feeling miserable all over.

Though Winslow knew nothing about doctoring, his offer to help was quickly accepted. Having brought from Plymouth a pot of jam or jelly — in Winslow's words, "a confection of many comfortable conserves" — he put some on the point of his hunting knife and fed it to the patient, having the greatest difficulty in forcing it between the clenched teeth — a very delicate operation in every respect. If there had been a slip and the Big Chief had been cut, there might have been all hell to pay. But all went well. Shortly, to everybody's amazement, Massasoit's "sight began to come [back] to him."

Now the sachem wanted soup, some of that "good English pottage" he had enjoyed so much at Plymouth. Winslow brewed up corn, wild strawberry leaves, and sassafras roots into something so palatable that the patient wanted more — but this time with a duck or goose in it. To humor him, Winslow went out and shot a duck, put that in the pot, and when the brew was ready, directed that the fat be skimmed off before serving.

Massasoit, however, would not hear of this and in spite of every warning "made a gross meal of it," quickly had

[An Indian] lately pledged ... that he would bring me a turkey, but in its place he brought an eagle and wished to persuade me that it was a turkey. When however I showed him that I had seen many eagles he acknowledged to a Swede who stood by that he had done it out of deception, in the belief that because we had lately come into the land I should not know such birds so accurately.
—Francis Pastorius, 1684

a violent relapse, again lost his sight, retched, and began to bleed profusely at the nose—which was regarded by the Indians as an almost certain sign of death. Again Winslow took charge and persuaded him to lie down and get some sleep — and the next day, again to everybody's surprise, the Big Chief was "able to sit upright of himself." One wishes that Winslow, or someone, had kept the Pilgrims' recipe for their magical "comfortable conserves."

Another Indian, of lesser rank but equal posthumous fame, helped the Pilgrims almost beyond measure—Tisquantum, or Squanto, as he was known. By strange circumstances, he had lived in England for a time before the Pilgrims arrived in America and had learned the language. He was truly a Plymouth local, having been born and brought up along Town Brook. Squanto taught the baffled Pilgrims the ways of the wilderness, for they were literally babes in the woods. He showed them how to plant their corn — the pilfered Pamet seed corn — in properly spaced hillocks. He told them the corn would come to no good "in these old grounds" unless fertilized with fish. He assured them that they could catch fish aplenty when the herring began their spring run up Town Brook, and he helped them build weirs and traps of vines. He showed them how, on each corn hillock, three fish should be laid out spokewise, with their heads toward the center.

Squanto was invaluable, too, as a guide on foraging and trading expeditions and as the Pilgrims' adroit ambassador-at-large among the Indians. Without his nature lore and native skills, without his undeviating loyalty and sound advice, the Pilgrims would have starved, or at least would have been forced to abandon "Plimoth Plantation." As it was, they just barely managed to pull through.

After the paralyzing "General Sickness" which killed half the company by spring, the Pilgrims mustered what strength they had and went into the fields to plant their first crops. They worked very hard on these, but the harvest was disappointing. Thanks to Squanto, their twenty acres of corn did well enough, but their more familiar crops failed miserably. Six or seven acres of wheat, barley, peas, and other things — planted with seed brought from home — came to nothing, either from "ye badnes of ye seed, or latenes of ye season, or both, or some other defecte" — an explanation by Governor Bradford that certainly covers the ground quite thoroughly.

Although the harvest was disappointing, it enabled Plymouth to increase its ration of a peck of meal a week per person. To this was now added a peck of corn, and the Pilgrims decreed a holiday, a day of Thanksgiving, that all might, according to Edward Winslow, "after a more speciall manner rejoyce together."

Four men were sent to hunt waterfowl and brought back enough to supply the town for a week. Massasoit had been invited to attend, and came with ninety brightly painted braves, some of whom went out and brought in five deer and other good things from field and forest. It was a gala occasion, enlivened with games of chance and skill, and it went on for three days with the Pilgrims and their guests gorging themselves on venison, duck, goose, and probably turkey, clams and other shellfish, smoked eels, corn breads, leeks and watercress and other greens, with wild plums and dried berries as dessert —

Tilling and planting

all washed down with wine made of the wild grape.

This Thanksgiving holiday was a great success, and the Pilgrims repeated it down the years. In time, it became a New England tradition to enjoy the harvest feast with Pilgrim trimmings—a tradition carried to other parts of the country as restless Yankees moved westward. But it remained an unofficial local or regional holiday until 1863, when President Abraham Lincoln proclaimed the first national Thanksgiving, setting aside the last Thursday in November for the purpose.

The now-hymned first landing of the Pilgrims passed without any public notice for a century and a half — until 1769, when about a dozen fashionable young gentlemen of Plymouth, most of them *Mayflower* descendants, organized themselves in a very exclusive club, the Old Colony. Their first purpose was to elevate the social tone of the town; their second, to honor their ancestors.

Inviting a few others of the first families of Plymouth to join them, the Old Colony members raised "an elegant silk flag," fired a salvo of cannon, and then repaired for the *pièce de résistance* (for club members only) to the popular tavern kept by Thomas Southworth Howland, another *Mayflower* descendant but not eligible for the Old Colony because he was a barkeeper.

In accord with old Pilgrim traditions, the Club had directed that the banquet board at Howland's be "dressed in the plainest manner, with all appearances of luxury and extravagance being avoided." The dinner itself, however, was anything but plain. If the ghosts of the hungry first settlers were present, they must have smiled and sighed on reading the menu. There were nine courses:

First, a large, baked Indian whortleberry pudding, followed by a steaming dish of succotash, which at Plymouth was a soup containing fowl, lean pork, and corned beef; a dish of clams (probably on the half shell, but perhaps steamed); a dish of oysters and codfish; a haunch of venison, "roasted on the first jack brought to the Colony"; a dish of waterfowl; a dish of "frost-fish" (tomcod) and eels; apple pie; cranberry tarts and cheese — with plenty of beer, hard cider, wines, and rum to enliven proceedings, inspire toasts and speeches, and aid digestion.

By the time the Old Colony Club was formed, all the colonies from New Hampshire to Georgia were well rooted and growing larger and stronger. Along the seaboard were some sizable port towns, thriving on coastal and ocean trade and on off-shore and deep-sea fisheries. Already there was some lifting of eyebrows about the luxury, extravagance, and general high-living of city people who were taking to indulgence in unheard-of things, such as eating elaborate French dishes (containing God knew what), in place of plain, honest roast beef, and drinking Irish whisky, or *usquebaugh* (from the Celtic "water of life"), instead of good old New England rum. Inland, some smaller towns and a growing number of villages stretched along the narrow Atlantic watershed.

But nine out of ten people, or even more, lived and worked on family-operated and largely family-owned small farms — the basic living and economic unit of seventeenth- and eighteenth-century America. Rich virgin lands were so cheap as to be had almost for the asking, but it cost plenty of back-breaking labor to clear them and bring them into cultivation. Still, the almost herculean effort was worth it and had high rewards. A man could be independent, his own master, beholden to no one and to nothing but the good green earth and his own industry and skills to provide his family with an ever-more-comfortable manner of life.

From every farm, if managed and stocked reasonably, came plenty of good things to be eaten raw or cooked—corn, wheat, rye, and oats from the fields; vegetables, salad greens, and herbs from the kitchen garden; berries from cultivated patches; fruits of many kinds from the orchard. Apple, plum, and peach trees, grown from European stock, flourished.

Every farmstead had poultry furnishing eggs and fowl for spit or oven. Out of the barn came milk to be drunk, used on cereals and other dishes, churned into butter, or pressed into cheese. In the pastures were sheep, providing lamb, mutton, and fleece to be woven for warm winter clothing. In the pigpen, or foraging in the woods for acorns and other mast, were fat porkers promising hams, bacon, hogback, pig's knuckles and feet, and lard for cooking. On the farm, or in the neighborhood, were waters to fish and woods to hunt. In the kitchen, about the only "boughten" things were salt, spices, molasses, cane sugar, and, for occasional inspiration, a demijohn of New England rum.

Thanks to the natural bounties of the New World, and to their own energies and skills, the colonists had grown well up the cornstalk and felt themselves strong enough for new adventure — one with consequences soon felt and still resounding round the world. By the middle 1770's, proclaiming their unalienable right to "life, liberty, and the pursuit of happiness," they were ready to challenge the mighty British lion, monarch of the globe — and they triumphed, for they had not misjudged their strength.

Conquering their initial weaknesses, Americans had come a long way since the awful Starving Time in early Jamestown and the first hungry years at Plymouth, so graphically described by Governor William Bradford. It was thought wonderful and beyond match-

It is an unhappy thing that in later years a Kind of Drink called Rum has been common among us. They that are poor, and wicked too, can for a penny or twopence make themselves drunk.
—Increase Mather, 1686

ing, he noted, that Spanish *conquistadores* could endure such hunger as they did, often leading *"a miserable life for 5 days togeather, with the parched graine of maize only."*

But the Pilgrims often had no maize at all, Bradford remarked, and when they had even a few grains, they "thought it as good as a feast," going "some time for 2 or 3 months togeather, and neither had bread nor any kind of corne," keeping themselves alive largely by feverishly digging clams and prowling the woods for groundnuts. Referring to the Pilgrims, the Spaniards, and other courageous and indomitable firstcomers, the Governor concluded eloquently and truly: "That with their miseries they opened a way to these new lands; and after these stormes, with what ease other men came to inhabite in them, in respecte of ye calamities these men suffered; so as they seeme to goe to a bride feaste wher all things are provided for them."

William Bartram, by Charles W. Peale

THE BARTRAMS

By George F. Willison

*A father and son, eighteenth-century naturalists, jour-
neyed into America's wilderness; their writings vividly
depict the wonders and the exotic foods they found*

Sharing a passionate interest in
the world of nature, a genius
for accurate observation, and a
flair for clearly and often beautifully
recording their observations, John
Bartram and his son William won international recognition and acclaim as
America's first great native-born naturalists.

John (1699-1777) was regarded as
the greatest "natural botanist" in the
world by his Swedish contemporary
Linnaeus, the father of modern sys-
tematic botany. The vast knowledge,
penetrating insights, artistic skills, and
inspired writing of William (1739-
1823) gained him immortality as the
author of a still widely read classic,
*Travels through North & South Caro-
lina, Georgia, East & West Florida,* etc.

Both father and son had an immense
range of interests, which included
good food.

Wholly self-educated except for a
bit of cursory elementary schooling,
John Bartram became a farmer, establishing himself in 1728 at Kingsessing,
a few miles outside Philadelphia, on a
fertile and beautiful tract that sloped
down to the Schuylkill River. He took
as much pride as George Washington
in what the latter liked to call "knowl-
edgeable husbandry," and the Kingsessing farm soon became a showplace.

No one grew corn, wheat, berries,
fruits, vegetables, melons, salad greens,
herbs, and other crops as "Master
Bartram" did, so neighbors said, and
many distinguished visitors agreed.
No one served better cider, either soft

or hard, than that which came from the ingenious stone press that Bartram had designed and fashioned with his own hands. Benjamin Franklin, his good friend, took great pleasure in riding out from Philadelphia to hoist a tankard or two of Bartram's cider and enjoy an "honest country dinner."

Bartram early decided that he wished to be more than what might be called a bread-and-butter farmer. He laid out a special five-acre plot running down from his large stone house, which he built himself, to the river and made it into a remarkable botanical garden. He explored neighboring fields and forests, searching for new plants, useful and ornamental, to transplant in his garden, and gradually he began making longer and longer explorations —into western Pennsylvania, New Jersey, New York, Maryland, Virginia, and the Carolinas. Traveling on horseback, with several large leather pouches strapped behind his saddlebags to hold the seeds, seedlings, curious rocks, and whatever else of interest he found, he lived off the country as he went along —and lived very well indeed, for he was an expert woodsman, fine shot, skilled fisherman, and accomplished cook.

Through a friend, Bartram began a long correspondence with a man who greatly helped him and whom he came to love—Peter Collinson, a rich London woolen merchant and an ardent amateur naturalist. For more than forty years, from 1734 till his death in 1777, Bartram sent each year to Collinson and others in London hundreds of packets of seeds, and boxes and boxes of living roots and seedlings.

Bartram first gained wide international recognition in 1751 with the publication in London of *Observations . . . made by John Bartram in his travels from Pensilvania to . . . Lake Ontario*. He and a small party had traveled through the back country, by wilderness trails, and Bartram had kept a journal. Franklin urged him to publish the gist of his notes, remarking later that "many people are fond of accounts of old buildings, monuments, etc., but there is a number, who would be much better pleased with such accounts as you could afford them . . ."

As for himself, added Franklin, "I confess that if I could find in any Italian travels, a receipt for making Parmesan cheese, it would give me more satisfaction than a transcript of any inscription from any old stone whatever."

Though ignorant about Parmesan cheese, John could tell his friend Ben how the Indians cooked eels. "Their way of roasting eels is thus: They cut a stick about three foot long, and as thick as one's thumb. They split it about a foot down, and when the eel is gutted, they coil it between the two sides of the stick and bind the top close, which keeps the eel flat, and then stick one end in the ground before a good fire . . ." "Delicious," he added.

Bartram noted that as soon as a white traveler dismounted in an Indian village, the people brought him food, a hospitality "agreeable to the honest simplicity of ancient times." They brought "not only what is already dressed . . . but the most pressing business is postponed to prepare the best they can get for him, keeping it as a maxim that he must always be hungry."

In upper New York State, after a conference with the chiefs of the Iroquois Confederacy, Bartram's party dined on a repast consisting "of three great kettles of *Indian* corn soop, or thin homony, with dry'd eels and other fish boiled in it, and one kettle full of young squashes and their flowers boiled in water, and a little meal mixed." To Bartram's taste, this was "but weak food." Other courses were better, and the last was very good: ". . . a great bowl, full of Indian dumplings, made of new soft corn, cut or scraped off the ear, then with the addition of some boiled beans lapped well up in Indian corn leaves; this is good hearty provision "

In 1765, through Collinson's efforts, Bartram was appointed Botanist Royal in America by His Majesty George III, and decided to undertake a long-desired journey to Florida. Sixty-six, but hale and strong, John was eager to be off, immediately writing his son William urging him to come along. The son, though exceptionally gifted, had been a sore disappointment to his father. He seemed to have no ambition.

"Botany and drawing are his darling delight," his father told Collinson; "am afraid he can't settle to any business else." When only in his teens, accompanying his father on longer field trips, William had made many fine drawings of flora and fauna that entranced Franklin, Collinson, and other exacting critics. But botany and drawing were not a paying business, as the older Bartram well knew. He had been enabled to carry on his explorations and studies only because of his prosperous farm and funds from England. William had to get an economic base, a way of earning a living. Before he was twenty, the youth had been an apprentice in a Philadelphia store. Not liking that, he went to North Carolina and set up his own small business, and there, at Cape Fear, he spent what others regarded as many wasted years, becoming "poor Billy Bartram" to his father and the latter's many friends.

Billy, it is plain, did not attend to business. He did only such things as he wanted to do, and in his own good time. Letters to him went unanswered, or replies were long delayed, which exasperated his father. Although he signed himself "thy loving father," the latter sharply complained: "And yet I have not received one single seed from my son who glories so much in the knowledge of plants, and whom I have been at so much charge to instruct therein. I don't want thee to hinder thy own affairs to oblige me; but thee might easily gather a few seeds, when thee need not hinder half an hour's time to gather them, or turn twenty yards out of thy way to pluck them."

Still, as Bartram contemplated his Florida assignment he decided that poor Billy, for all his faults, would be an invaluable aide. Would he come along? Yes, came the prompt reply, and they were off together for St. Augustine, spending several months in purposeful wandering, exploring the St. Johns River to its source. Here the older Bartram noted a food he had never sampled before—the top of the palm known as the cabbage tree.

The top, about a foot long, three or four inches wide at the base, and tapering to a point, "cuts as white and tender as a turnip," he discovered; "this [the Indians] slice into a pot and stew with water, then, when almost tender, they pour some bear's oil into it, and stew it a little longer, when it eats pleasant and much more mild than cabbage."

Returning to Kingsessing, John Bartram was in ill health, still feeling the effects of jaundice, fever, and other ailments that had struck him in Florida. He felt out of sorts, too, because his salary as Botanist Royal did not begin to pay expenses. He was further out of pocket through helping his son.

William had decided that he was done with merchandising and such business. He was going to stay in Florida, which he had found a land of "enchantment." To support himself, he would become a planter and grow indigo—and find time to explore, botanize, paint,

draw, and laze to his heart's content. Financed by his father, he bought a lonely plantation along the St. Johns River near St. Augustine. This venture soon collapsed, and poor Will became a field hand to earn his keep.

John Bartram's Florida expedition was his last long one. During his later years, he stayed rather close to home. Busy with his farm and botanical garden, with his many friends, with his voluminous correspondence on all kinds of things, he was at peace with himself and the world when he died in 1777, at the age of seventy-eight.

One of the dying man's chief concerns had been William, whom he had not seen in years. He suspected that his son might have been killed by Indians, but he need not have worried, for the gifted William had found himself at last—if, indeed, he had ever really been lost. Poor Billy now had a sponsor, a rich patron, Dr. John Fothergill of London, to finance him in doing what he had always wanted to do. In 1773 he had agreed to send Fothergill rare seeds and seedlings and drawings of "birds, reptiles, insects, or plants," made "on the spot." As soon as he had received this commission he had begun a trip which was to last four years, as he slowly prowled his way through the Carolinas, Georgia, and Florida, with a sally westward along the Gulf Coast to the Mississippi.

"This world, as a glorious apartment of the boundless palace of the sovereign Creator," wrote William, who was as profoundly religious as his father, "is furnished with an infinite variety of animated scenes, inexpressibly beautiful and pleasing, equally free to the inspection and enjoyment of all his creatures."

The book he wrote on his travels abounds in animated scenes. If Indians were making "milk" by boiling hickory nuts, he watched and recorded every step of the process. He came upon peach and fig trees, "loaded with fruit . . . affording a very acceptable dessert after the heats and toil of the day," and upon "three young racoons . . . which are excellent meat." He was fond of trout "stewed in the juice of Oranges, which, with boiled rice, afforded me a wholesome and delicious supper," and he dined often with the Indians, enjoying with them many "a delightful repast," some "consisting of venison, stewed with bear's oil, fresh corn cakes, milk and homony, and our drink honey and water, very cool and agreeable."

William Bartram liked the Indians, and they liked him; the Seminole affectionately named him Puc-puggy, Flower Hunter. He made a notable number of discoveries in his journeying, finding and collecting specimens of a great many new plants.

But he was happiest when his travels took him back to Florida to relive the enchantment he had known years before. He revisited the "fountains," or sinks, he had found with his father. In these great wide fountains, boiling up merrily "like a pot," water rose swiftly and with bubbling force from wells or caverns in the rock below. Fish of all kinds in "unspeakable numbers" came out of the rocky vents and swam into them to be "conducted and carried away by secret subterranean conduits and gloomy vaults to other distant lakes and rivers."

Sampling the fish, he tried the large mailed gar; the Indians liked it, but he did not. Nor did he care for mudfish ("meat white and tender, but soft and tastes of the mud"). His favorite was the blue bream, "a large, beautiful, and delicious fish."

A hunter in the party shot and brought back one of the sonorous "savanna cranes . . . We had this fowl dressed for supper, and it made excellent soup; nevertheless, as long as I can get any other necessary food, I shall prefer his seraphic music in the etherial skies . . ."

Bartram loved birds and had a fine appreciative ear for their language and their calls. Making drawings of many of them, he drew up a list of American birds, with notes on their migratory and breeding habits, the most complete list of its kind at the time. At last, having completed his "collections," Bartram "took leave of these Southern regions," never to return.

Unaware of his father's death, he did not return to Kingsessing for several months. His brother John had inherited the estate and generously made

William his partner. The latter lived his remaining years in the large stone house where he had been born. His brother ran the farm while William added to and tended the botanical garden, when he was not in his father's study working up into a moving narrative the thousands of notes he had made in the South—a work of love that resulted about fifteen years later in publication at Philadelphia of his *Travels*.

Without sacrificing any scientific accuracy, the book was wonderfully poetic, full of the joy and wonder of life. It won immediate critical acclaim and was surprisingly popular. Within a decade, there were three American and seven foreign editions. A young poet, Samuel Taylor Coleridge, picked up a copy in London and exclaimed, "The latest book of travels I know, written in the spirit of the old travelers, is Bartram's account of his tour in the Floridas. It is a work of high merit every way."

There are many echoes of Bartram's singing prose and many reflections of his graphic images in Coleridge's poems—in "The Rime of the Ancient Mariner," for one. For another, Bartram's description of the boiling cavernous Florida fountains probably inspired in the poet's "Kubla Khan" the often-quoted opening lines:

In Xanadu did Kubla Khan
A stately pleasure-dome decree:
Where Alph, the sacred river, ran
Through caverns measureless to man
    Down to a sunless sea.

There are also echoes of Bartram in the works of William Wordsworth and several others of the Romantics. Later, the irascible Thomas Carlyle wrote his friend Ralph Waldo Emerson: "Do you know Bartram's *Travels*? . . . treats of *Florida* chiefly, has a wonderous kind of floundering eloquence in it; and has also grown immeasureably *old*. All American libraries ought to provide themselves with that kind of book, and keep them as a kind of *biblical* article."

Characteristically, Bartram did nothing to exploit the success of his book or of his enormous reputation. He was content to tend the garden, keep a journal about what he saw and did, draw, and write letters when he felt like it. One day, in his eighty-fifth year, he was walking into the garden when he suffered a massive lung hemorrhage and died within a few minutes.

In a quiet way, William's life had been a paean to the joys of nature, a "shout," like that of the Florida turkey cocks he once described so eloquently:

". . . I was awakened in the morning early, by the cheering converse of the wild turkey-cock . . . saluting each other, from the sun-brightened tops of the lofty Cupressus disticha and Magnolia grandiflora. They begin at early dawn and continue till sun rise, from March to the last of April. The high forests ring with the noise . . . of these social centinels, the watch-word being caught and repeated, from one to another, for hundreds of miles around; insomuch that the whole country, is for an hour or more, in a universal shout."

NATIVE BOUNTY

A Picture Portfolio

John James Audubon painted the wild turkey, in which the East abounded; the early settlers wrote of great flocks that "sallied by our doors."

"*Everything in Great Plenty*"

In 1789, the impoverished Mohegan Indians of Connecticut applied to the state assembly for help. They recalled, in their petition, the days before the white man decimated their once-abundant food supply: "Our Fore-Fathers . . . had everything in Great plenty. When they Wanted meat they would just run into the Bush a little ways with their Weapons and would Soon bring home good venison, Raccoon, Bear, and Fowl. If they choose to have Fish, they wo'd only go to the River or along the Sea Shore and . . . presently fill their Cannoons With Variety of Fish, Both Scaled and shell Fish, and they had abundance of Nuts, Wild Fruit, Ground Nuts and Ground Beans . . . it lay in Common to them all, and they had but one large dish and they Cou'd all eat together in Peace."

Billions of passenger pigeons, like these painted by Walter Thorp, once darkened the skies. The Indians simply knocked the fledglings off the trees with poles. The tasty birds, now extinct, were sold at six for a penny in 1736.

Bighorn sheep

Virginia opossums

American elk

These animals (painted by John James Audubon) made good eating and were hunted by Indians and whites alike. Except for the bighorn sheep, which lived in mountainous regions, they were all found in the East. Bear meat, naturalist John Bartram wrote, was "very mild and sweet."

Eastern gray squirrels

Black bears

Fruits
and
Vegetables

The fruit of the pawpaw (above) had a rich, custardy taste and was quite nutritious. Below is the indispensable corn, called Our Life by the Indians.

Some Indians believed that a naked squaw, walking in the garden under a bright moon while dragging her clothes behind her, would keep cutworms from destroying the vegetables. Despite such superstitions, the first Americans were often excellent farmers. Particularly successful were the Cherokee and the Seneca, who cultivated a dozen types of corn, several varieties of beans, squashes, and pumpkins, plus melons and sunflowers, all supplemented by the nuts, roots, fruits, and berries that grew wild in such profusion. The clearing of the communal fields was done by the men, but the farming itself was usually the work of the squaws, to whom the French explorer Samuel de Champlain once ungallantly referred as "the Indian's mule."

Pumpkins were grown by tribes in the Southwest, as well as in the East.

NEW YORK BOTANICAL GARDEN

A New World

The Spanish conquistadors, the first white men to penetrate North America, often starved to death in the midst of plenty. Always on the march in search of gold, yet fearful of detaching hunting parties because of Indians, the greedy transients ate dogs, roots, and sometimes each other. Even so, Europe heard tales of the New World's fabulous abundance. The journals of de Soto's expedition referred to fish "so plentiful ... that they were killed with blows of cudgels," and reported that "the Indians never lacked meat." David Ingram, who wandered from the Gulf of Mexico to New Brunswick in Canada in 1568, told of "Vines which beare Grapes as big as a mans thumbe." And Cabeza de Vaca piqued Old World imaginations with his references to "wild hunch back cows" — buffalo.

The shaggy beast above was sixteenth-century Europe's idea of a buffalo. At left is a painting by Jacques le Moyne, member of a French expedition to Florida in 1564. The Indians in it are worshiping a pillar, at the base of which they have placed corn and vegetables. Below, a fanciful German engraving depicts a lush Virginia scene.

The manner of their fishing.

Cannow

Hunting and Cooking

Weapons used by the Indians for hunting included the familiar bow and arrow, lances, and blowguns, used by natives of the South. Traps, pits, slings, and nets were among the other devices employed. In fishing, weirs and traps were used, as well as nets, hooks, spears, poisons, and arrows. Food was cooked by three basic methods: broiling, roasting, or boiling. Lacking implements, the women often used earth ovens: wrapping the raw meat in leaves, they placed it in a hole filled with hot stones and covered it with dirt until cooked. Heated stones were also placed in liquids that native chefs wanted to boil.

In the Theodore de Bry engraving at left (after a painting by Jacques le Moyne), three Indians disguised in deerskins sneak up on five deer. This deception permitted hunters to get close to their prey without frightening them away.

The natives in the painting at left (made by John White in the 1580's) are using nets, spears, and traps built of reeds and sticks to catch fish.

Fish, reptiles, and small animals are dried on a platform made of stakes in this De Bry engraving, after a painting by Le Moyne. Fish were also boiled and sometimes were eaten raw.

The Buffalo Hunt

When a herd of buffalo was spotted near a cliff, the Indians adopted the hunting method shown in this painting by Alfred Jacob Miller. "The riders," Miller wrote, driving the beasts between themselves and the canyon, "now urge their horses at full speed, yelling like so many demons; the unsuspecting animals . . . reach the ledge, topple down one after another, until they form a huge compound hecatomb at the bottom." With such a large kill, the Indians sometimes took only the tongues from the buffalo; one witness reported a band of Sioux trading 1,400 fresh tongues for a few gallons of whiskey. 41

Squash

Camas

Nutmeg

"It Did Very Well"

Winnebago Indians, depicted by George Catlin, fill their canoes with seeds of wild rice.

Vegetables that pleased the Indians did not always suit the white man. Lewis and Clark, for instance, complained that the camas, a bulbous root, caused them severe dysentery, and John Bartram, served a "bowl of boiled squashes, cold" in Pennsylvania, thought it "poor entertainment." On the other hand, Peter Pond, a fur trader, wrote of Wisconsin's wild rice: "When it is Cleaned fit for youse thay Boile it as we Due Rise and Eat it with Bairs Greas and Suger ... we yoused it in the Room of Rise and it Did very well as a Substatute for that Grane. . . ."

The restored mural above, painted by Arizona Indians in the early 1600's, was used as a background for ceremonies propitiating the spirits. It depicts bowls of corn and squash and a body of water filled with fish, frogs, and tadpoles.

Below is George Catlin's drawing of the Green Corn Dance, performed by the Creeks during their annual festival celebrating the first harvest.

Rituals and Taboos

44

To appease the supernatural powers and assure themselves of food, the Indians observed taboos, rules, and ceremonies that varied from tribe to tribe. Animals, some believed, were magical and should not be offended. It was all right to kill them (their spirits went to heaven), but certain hunting rituals had to be followed, and respect paid to the dead creatures. Dogs were not allowed to gnaw their bones, and no mourner or murderer could touch fresh meat. Each tribe had its forbidden foods. The Zuñi ate nothing that lived in water; one tribe of Omahas shunned the shoulder of the buffalo; and the Navaho eschewed bear meat.

This ceremonial wooden deer mask, made prior to 1600, was found in an Oklahoma mound.

The Indians of the Northwest had their own version of the Jonah legend. As this painting of an old carving shows, a salmon replaced the whale.

45

2

SOURDOUGH
and
HARDTACK

By Evan Jones

D own the winding Ohio and up the Mississippi for a hundred miles, five convoys of keelboats brought—a decade before the Revolution—the first bulk supplies from England to the American heartland. Almost every item known to Indians or white settlers was on board, along with not less than twenty-two men to row each boat, "two of whom," young George Morgan specified, "should be good hunters."

Morgan, the first English merchant to establish himself in the Illinois country after the French and Indian War, set up business at the junction of the

With his muzzle-loader at the ready, a westward-bound pioneer, who has already shot one bird, keeps watch for more, in Something for Supper *by Harvey Dunn.*

Mississippi and Kaskaskia rivers, site of an old French settlement. His original provisions included beef and flour and kegs of salt, with which a crew might "cure their meat when they come into the Buffaloe country . . ." He also brought kettles, knives and forks, tablecloths, milk and pudding pans, tinware packed in barrels of coffee beans, English cheeses, mustard to enhance the taste of venison, chocolate, and two kinds of tea. Soon the post, a branch of a Philadelphia firm, had a stock of 8,000 gallons of alcohol, including West Indian rum, Madeira, and wines from Lisbon.

Morgan dealt in large quantities of buffalo meat; one team of hunters brought him 18,000 pounds of wild beef, plus fifty-five buffalo tongues, sixty venison hams, and a vast amount of tallow. And although Morgan was at first convinced that the salt for curing his meat would have to be imported from Philadelphia, he soon began to boast of the fine quality of his roasts,

---

My fare is really sumptuous this evening; buffaloe's humps, tongues and marrow- bones, fine trout parched meal pepper and salt, and a good appetite; the last is not considered the least of the luxuries.
—From the journals of Lewis and Clark, Thursday, June 13, 1805

---

lightly seasoned (a bushel-and-a-peck per thousand pounds of meat) with the product of the saltworks on the nearby saline deposits.

Salt, indeed, was more important on the early frontier than anything except food itself. And it was expensive, too. In the beginning of the tramontane frontier the cost of salt per pound was as much as four times the price of beef, and not until 1801 did it drop as low as $2.50 per bushel. Yet its use was mandatory for keeping domestic animals healthy, and the location of salt licks was so urgent that Daniel Boone's knack for finding licks added much to his frontier reputation. In fact, Boone's last land grant, on the Missouri River, is known as Boone's Lick, sometimes spelled Booneslick.

Salting meat was the commonest method of preserving it, but no matter how it was kept, meat in some form was eaten in such daily abundance that many Europeans who visited the frontier did not refrain from comment. Poverty—as it existed among European peasants who had to survive almost solely on bread—was unknown in the new land so lush in wildlife. Spices like ginger, mace, nutmeg, and cinnamon were not hard to get for cash or by swap from a transient trader (at least not for a Cumberland housewife who could pay thirty-five cents for two whole nutmegs or twenty-five cents an ounce for cloves).

This southern frontier was visited in 1837 by the outspoken pre-Victorian novelist Captain Frederick Marryat, who wrote in his *Diary in America,* "The English will agree with me that there are plenty of good things for the table in America; but the old proverb says: 'God sends meat and the devil sends cooks.'"

Nonetheless Marryat took issue with James Fenimore Cooper, who had commented tartly, "The Americans are the grossest feeders of any civilized nation known. . . . Their food is heavy, coarse and indigestible. . . ." Marryat thought Cooper unnecessarily harsh, and he corrected him, adding, "The cookery in the United States is exactly what it is and must be everywhere else—in ratio with the degree of refinement of the population."

Seldom could there be found anything akin to refinement among pioneers, in spite of the goods sold by such men as George Morgan. From the trappers who stayed on when the English took over the Old Northwest to the sourdoughs of the Klondike, men always outnumbered the women. French woodsmen escaped civilization to live as Indians; so did the mountain men.

These pathfinders lived off the land or, like the backwoodsmen of William Byrd's well-known survey of the Carolina-Virginia border in 1728, carried hard biscuit and, as Byrd said, counted on "Providence for meat." A kettle and sometimes a skillet were the only necessary cooking tools, and hit or miss, Byrd's men turned out savory stews by tossing several kinds of game into the pot along with wild vegetables. What they may have lacked in delicacy of palate, they made up for in lusty imagination—fried bacon, its grease included, was sometimes covered with rum and, as Byrd said, served "at once for meat and Drink."

On the other hand, *voyageurs* of the Old Northwest had a trail diet so basic that they were called pork eaters throughout the fur frontier. "The tin kettle in which they cooked their food,"

Dining on buffalo ribs

a trader wrote, "would hold eight or ten gallons. It was hung over the fire, nearly full of water, then nine quarts of peas—one quart per man, the daily allowance—were put in; and when they were well bursted, two or three pounds of pork, cut into strips, for seasoning, were added, and all allowed to boil or simmer till daylight, when the cook added four biscuits, broken up, to the mess, and invited all hands to breakfast. The swelling of the peas and biscuit had now filled the kettle to the brim, so thick that a stick would stand upright in it.... The men now squatted in a circle, the kettle in their midst, and each one plying his wooden spoon or ladle from the kettle to mouth, with almost electric speed, soon filled every cavity."

Wildlife offered variety for these Frenchmen skimming the early-nineteenth-century waters of Michigan, Minnesota, and Wisconsin in search of beaver and other pelts. Their appetite for fish and game was such that some of them rationalized what religious scruples they maintained by classifying beaver as fish when they ate it during Lent (an animal living so much of the time underwater was logically not to be considered as forbidden meat).

Beaver tail was accepted as a great delicacy by almost everyone who ever ate it, as were several cuts of buffalo, described by Zebulon Montgomery Pike in his 1806 journal as "equal to any meat I ever saw, and we feasted sumptuously on the choice morsels." As late as the 1870's, when organized hunts were reducing buffalo herds almost to the point of extinction, the hide hunter Dick Bussell said he "would not eat anything but buffalo meat if I could get it," and he told how he dried and aged buffalo hams by hanging them in mesquite trees. After several months, he said, "I would trim off about a quarter of an inch of the outside. It would be as nice and red as could be. Then I'd slice it and throw it in a skillet of hot grease and make a lot of gravy with it. It was surely fine."

Whatever the method of cooking meat (and sometimes it was eaten raw), the frontiersman's appetite for it was prodigious. The English adventurer George Frederick Ruxton said that "voyageurs and hunters in the consumption of [buffalo] meat strike the greenhorn with wonder and astonishment, and are only equalled by the gastronomical capabilities exhibited by Indian dogs, both following the same plan in their epicurean gorgings." Ruxton asserted that the delicacy most enjoyed was the *boudin,* the French word for intestine.

Once seasoned to the frontier, a man could eat almost anything, but there is more than one reference to *mal de vache,* the disease that laid up some newcomers to the buffalo diet. As early as 1700, when Pierre Le Sueur built a fort west of the Mississippi, his men had trouble getting used to the new meat. "In the beginning," one of Le Sueur's company wrote, "...we had diarrhea and fever and became so squeamish that we could not taste it;

but little by little our bodies became so accustomed to it that after six weeks there was not one of us who did not eat more than ten pounds of it daily and drink four bowls of the broth....it made us quite fat, and there were no more sick among us." In fact, twentieth-cen-

A ferry crossing

tury scientists have declared buffalo meat to be a complete diet.

So complete was frontier dependence on the buffalo that thirsty travelers even drank the contents of the paunch. Setting out from the Missouri early in the nineteenth century, a band of traders got lost and came so close to dying of thirst that they were saved only when a lone buffalo was killed; then, as the incident was reported, "an invigorating draught [was] procured from its stomach. I have since heard one of the parties to that expedition declare that nothing ever passed his lips which gave him such exquisite delight as his first draught of that filthy beverage." This was no isolated instance; the green and gelatinous juice was welcomed by many who found themselves a long way from water.

But it was the meat, of course, that

counted most. When the slain buffalo had been stretched out on his belly, the tongue was the butcher's first trophy, and many agreed with Ruxton that this part especially had "exquisite flavor." When the tongue had been extracted, the hunter drew his knife along the spine and cut away the skin to be used as a tablecloth for the cuts to follow. He carved out the small hump at the base of the neck, the large hump ribs, the "fleece" (the flesh between the spine and the ribs), the side ribs, and the tender belly fat. Sometimes each ham was cut into four or five pieces, and always the marrowbones were put aside, for these provided "hunter's butter," in which the tongues were often fried. "We pushed the marrow out with a stick," an expert on buffalo recalled. "We poured it into a barrel . . . We used it to season biscuits. Sometimes we stuck the bones in the fire and roasted them, then used the marrow as butter."

Fresh meat was always preferable, but frontiersmen quickly accepted the Indian method of turning the dried meat called jerky into pemmican, and thus discovered one of the best portable foods ever devised. In fact, pemmican so extended the fur trade's field of operations, in an era when canoes and a man's feet were the most practical means of transportation, that every beaver stream in the West became accessible to trappers who stayed away from home base for many months.

The making of pemmican was an art, the foundation of which was butchering. "I have seen meat jerkers," a pio-neer recalled, "who could cut a whole hind quarter into one big sheet of meat." Buffalo served almost exclusively as the principal ingredient of pemmican. It was cut into strips about an inch thick, then dried (often it was smoked), and pounded fine. Sometimes called beat meat at this stage, the pounded jerky always was mixed with fat and, as often as possible, with pulverized berries, then packed in skin bags. The best pemmican, according to the great Nor'wester David Thompson, was a mixture of fifty pounds of beat meat and twenty each of two kinds of fat, plus a goodly quantity of maple sugar or of dried berries "as sweet as the best currants."

"Meat is meat" was a favorite expression among the mountain men who dominated the fur trade in the Rockies, and cannibalism in the fur country has been reported more than once. One starving *voyageur* is said to have killed and eaten one of his colleagues and an

> *I go for days without eating, & am pretty well satisfied if I can gather a few roots, a few Snails, or, much better Satisfied if we can affod our selves a piece of Horse Flesh, or a fine Roasted Dog. . . .*
> —Jedediah Smith, letter to his brother, 1829

Indian as well. Mountain men frequently escaped starvation by bleeding their horses and drinking the blood, and there are innumerable stories of trappers who ate the ears of their pack mules or boiled leather thongs for what broth might be produced. Joe Meek, one of several mountain men who told their adventures in print, said that he had held his hands in an anthill until they were covered with ants, "then greedily licked them off." He said that he and his mates considered crickets "fair game." They would toss the insects into boiling water "and when they stopped kicking, eat them."

But there also were frontiersmen who, though they escaped famine, never had a diet of meat. Away from the roaming buffalo of the plains, men were sometimes forced to an all-fish diet, year after year. "*Toujours le poisson!*" is an anguished cry in a trader's journal. And yet Alexander Mackenzie, first white man to cross the continent north of the Isthmus, said that men who had not even vegetables to relieve their diet of fish were healthier than those who lived on venison.

Bread was almost unknown among men who lived alone, an exception being *voyageurs* who sometimes were

I wish some of the feble ones in the States could have a ride over the mountains, they would say like me, victuals even the plainest kind never relished so well before.

—Narcissa Whitman, 1836

lucky enough to get a kind of primitive cake. "This *galette*," a report of a visit with French trappers says, "is the only form of bread used on a voyage, that is

when voyageurs are so fortunate as to have any flour at all." Such bread was sometimes made with the eggs of wild birds but more often it was prepared "in a very simple style:—the flour bag is opened, and a small hollow made in the flour, into which a little water is poured, and the dough is thus mixed in the bag; nothing is added, except, perhaps some dirt from the cook's *unwashed* hands, with which he kneads it into flat cakes, which are baked before the fire in a frying pan, or cooked in grease."

Hardtack, not bread, was the lot of the mountain man, even when he gathered at the trappers' rendezvous, once defined by Bernard De Voto as "the annual season of supply, trade, and saturnalia." Like a raucous county fair to which no white women were invited, the rendezvous was the occasion for the trapper to turn in his pelts and for the fur company to bring in its pack trains carrying liquor, bacon, hardtack (sometimes called sea bread or ship's biscuit or pilot bread but always a dehydrated mixture of flour and water which, though never tempting, would stay edible for months), sugar and coffee, powder and blankets —all at exorbitant prices. Alcohol, usually raw and diluted by as much as seventy-five per cent, often cost five dollars a pint, and two dollars a pound was the fixed price for coffee, sugar, pepper and other spices, none of which sold for more than fifteen cents in St. Louis. Indeed, flour selling for two dollars a pound at the rendezvous was marked up exactly one hundred times the current market price.

But after all, in California during the Gold Rush, flour cost up to four hundred dollars a barrel — reason to wonder how many miners could afford

Hardtack

to make the sourdough bread that began to gather fame in 1849 and fifty years later found lasting renown as the nickname for Klondike miners. Real sourdough bread required—aside from a gold-stuffed poke—a substitute for yeast called emptings (or emptins), a lump of dough that had been allowed to ferment. A son of an Alaskan sourdough (and incidentally a neighbor of Robert W. Service, who enshrined the Klondike in memorable doggerel) wrote that every miner's cabin had hanging over its red-hot stove just such "a tin full of fermented dough, used in place of yeast in making bread, biscuits, and flapjacks."

Another sourdough might have been happier had the Klondike, like the trappers' rendezvous, been restricted to native females. He was "Swift-

water Bill" Gates, dubbed the "Knight of the Golden Omelette" after an incident involving his inamorata, Gussie Lamore. Eggs were a lot scarcer than gold around the city of Dawson in 1897, but Gussie had an unfailing appetite for them. The story goes that one day during the food shortage Swiftwater found Gussie and a well-known gambler tête à tête over plates of fried eggs, the most expensive dish on the restaurant menu. In passionate jealousy Swiftwater set about buying up every egg he could find. A writer who called himself an eyewitness said that Swiftwater had the eggs fried one at a time and tossed them out the window to a pack of famished dogs. Like most incidents that develop into legend, there are many versions of this tale of a mining-camp egg monopoly, but most of them agree that Gussie was thus persuaded to accept her extravagant suitor, even though she neglected to mention, somehow, that she had one husband already.

Legendary characters like Swiftwater Bill strode every frontier horizon, and even in 1801 the lumberjack had evolved into an American species that caused European travelers to take note. "The strength and execution of his arm almost exceed belief," an English reporter wrote. So did his appetite. It was said that a logger would eat anything, even hay, if only it had been sprinkled with whiskey. Such lusty trenchermen were, however, subject to the violent moods of the dictatorial camp cook, who might blast a man from his seat at the table for violating the rule of mealtime silence. But there was seldom silence in the bunkhouses, and lumberjacks, migrating with the shifting frontier, embellished the early American penchant for tall talk to one of its high points in the creation of Paul Bunyan and his kitchen chief, Hot Biscuit Slim.

Paul's cookhouse was said to be "like another Mammoth Cave," with ranges so huge that they were greased by men who strapped sides of bacon to their feet. On these ranges Paul one day instructed Hot Biscuit Slim to create a Sunday dinner to make logging history, and Paul promised to supply the viands. Spotting an enormous flock of black ducks in moonlight flight, Paul

Flipping pancakes

lured the birds into mistaking a vast tarpaulin for open water. The giant lumberjack grasped the four corners of the canvas so quickly that not a duck got away, and he strode home to the cookhouse with food aplenty. The story of that historic feast was told to James

Floyd Stevens, a Bunyan biographer, at a lumber camp near Blackduck, Minnesota.

"And great as the plates were," a lumberjack told Stevens, "by the time one was heaped with a brown, fried drumstick, a ladle of duck dumplings, several large fragments of duck fricassee, a slab of duck baked gumbo style, a rich portion of stewed duck, and a mound of crisp brown dressing, all immersed in golden duck gravy, a formidable space was covered." The menu was not all duck. There was creamed cabbage, mashed potatoes, potato cakes, stewed tomatoes, baked beans, peas, applesauce, corn bread, hot biscuits. Cream Puff Fatty, the pastry chef, also had outdone himself with the specialty that had given him his sobriquet. Yet other "enchantments still kept [the loggers] in their seats: lemon pies with airy frostings, glittering cakes of many colors . . . ," desserts ad infinitum. Paul Bunyan's feast was the stuff of dreams belonging to men who live in a womanless world, who entertain themselves by piecing together legends like that of Bunyan and his blue ox, Babe.

Just as the real counterparts of Hot Biscuit Slim and Cream Puff Fatty were despots in the cookhouse and never turned out meals of which a man could dream, the rulers of cowboy kitchens were laws unto themselves. Range cooks were paid fifteen to twenty-five dollars a month more than cowpunchers, and a ranch boss often put a cook on the payroll weeks in advance of work to keep him from being hired by someone else. Chuck-wagon fare was often far closer to potluck, and the usual rule was that anyone who complained about the food had to do the cooking himself.

"The grub consisted of some [corn] meal and salt," an old-time cowman said, adding, "We would kill a fat animal when we wanted meat, dry what we couldn't eat fresh, and save the tallow. That tallow, mixed up with meal, water and salt, made good corn bread." Like the mountain man who preceded him, the cowboy thrived on meat, the principal ingredient in many a recipe for long life. "Try to get your beefsteaks three times a day, fried in taller," an ancient Texan told author J. Frank Dobie. "Taller is mighty healing, and there's nothing like it to keep your stumich greased-up and in good working order."

Frontiersman Charles Goodnight is given credit for helping to keep cowhands in good working order by devising the first of the famous chuck wagons when he adapted an Army wagon in the 1850's. When mealtime came on Goodnight's spread, the cook unhitched his team, propped up the canvas cover for shade, and tapped the water barrels lashed to the sides of the wagon. If he was without other means to light his fire, he could pour a little gunpowder into the muzzle of his pistol, holding it close to the kindling as he fired. But the range cook was less ingenious about menus. There were no fresh vegetables to be had, and the *pièce de résistance* was always stew. Cowboys used their

pocketknives to stab out pieces of meat from the pot and saturated biscuit or corn bread with gravy, eating with their fingers like the Indians. Goodnight, for his own part, wanted to be sure that his meat was buffalo, which he considered a necessity for longevity,

> *Endless thickets of the wild plum and the blackberry, interlaced and matted together by the young grape-vines streaming with gorgeous clusters, were to be seen stretching for miles along the plain. Such boundless profusion of wild fruit I had never seen before. Vast groves of the ruby crab-apple, the golden persimmon, the black and white mulberry, and the wild cherry, were sprinkled with their rainbow hues in isolated masses over the prairie. . . .*
> —**Edmund Flagg in Illinois, 1837**

and he kept a herd of wild beef until his death, insisting that the finest elixir ever concocted was his mixture of an extract of buffalo meat and whiskey.

Equally certain that his own tonic was invincible was John Chapman, whose prescription for health was milk and honey, which he was disposed to call "heavenly food." This man who became the legendary figure known in folklore as Johnny Appleseed would touch neither tea nor coffee, and his friends said that he would turn down real bread in preference for beebread (the yellowish substance in the honeycomb upon which bees feed) and buttermilk. In fact, some who knew him said that he ate foods intended for the slop pail. Yet in spite of such casualness about his diet, Johnny was credited with doing more than anyone else to grace the land between the Alleghenies and the Mississippi with apple orchards. Walking barefoot much of the time, wearing a coffee sack for a shirt, and at least in legend, crowning

---

Thurs. 11 Fried two big pans of cakes. Baked two ovens full of bread & plenty of tarts. Hope husband will smell them & come where they are.
—Mrs. Mary Walker, whose husband was away preaching the gospel to the Indians; in Oregon, 1841

---

his head with a visored tin vessel that served not only as a hat but as a pan in which to cook his corn mush, he moved westward with the frontier in the early decades of the nineteenth century. "Among the pioneers," an Indiana historian wrote in 1864, "was an oddity called Johnny Appleseed. . . . The trees from his nursery are bearing fruit in a dozen different counties in Indiana, and thousands are enjoying the fruit who never heard of Johnny Appleseed."

The frontier demand for apples was more basic than it might seem today. No fruit crop was as simple to get started, and none served so many purposes. Bushel after bushel was dried and hung in strings from rafters, waiting to be cooked in puddings and pies for a winter's meal. Other bushels sim-

mered in outdoor kettles on brisk autumn days to make apple butter, a preserve that could be kept easily in kitchens that seldom had ice. Bushels more went to the nearest cider press, for it was, as many have said, the "cider age" in American history, a period when more applejack than corn whiskey was available to the frontiersman. And although Johnny Appleseed became legendary, he was far from the only one to visit the cider mill for seeds that could be had for the asking.

Indeed, in 1836 when Narcissa Whitman and Eliza Spalding became the first white women to cross the continent, they found at Dr. John McLoughlin's famous Fort Vancouver a spectacular cuisine that included apple pies made from the fruit of trees brought from London by a sailing master. Though Narcissa had baked most evenings on the long trek west, formally serving tea to mangy mountain men in the party, she was in no way prepared for the opulent life of McLoughlin's fur post. Here roast duck was an everyday dish, along with fresh salmon, sturgeon, pork, and a profusion of fresh vegetables from the gardens of the fort. On the trail Narcissa had said that she could eat buffalo steaks every meal, and she did not balk at cooking over fires made from *bois de vache*, the dried buffalo droppings that were to serve as fuel for thousands of other women. She learned to make do. "To supply our men and visitors," she wrote, "we have killed and eaten ten wild horses . . . This will make you pity us, but you had better save your pity for more worthy subjects." Narcissa would not complain of eating horse-flesh, but could "eat it very well when we have nothing else."

Hundreds of the accounts of west-ward migration speak either of near-starvation or of having to make do with whatever might be at hand. A forty-niner, writing in his journal, described a meeting with another wagon train: "Their sugar, rice, beans, & flour were also out & they had been living on nothing but hard tack & coffee, & coffee and hard tack. They had no shot guns & of course took no game. This recon-ciled us, I assure you, & we censured ourselves for our past time growling, & find, instead of suffering, we have been feasting." His group, in fact, had been varying a diet of salt pork with "Jack Ass" rabbits on which, the journal says, "we fared sumptuously."

Perversely, some early emigrants ran out of food on the trail because they had overloaded their wagons in the first place. Many followed the ad-vice of *The Emigrant's Guide to California* by Joseph E. Ware. Each per-son, this book suggested, would need a barrel of flour to see him through to the mining fields, plus 150 to 180 pounds of bacon, 25 pounds of coffee, 40 pounds of sugar, 25 pounds of rice, 60 pounds of peas or beans, and 30 to 40 pounds of dried peaches, as well as molasses, vinegar, and a keg of beef suet as a substitute for butter.

As a result of this somewhat irre-sponsible advice, hundreds of forty-niners so overloaded their wagons that before they had traveled six hundred miles a choice had to be made between loss of goods and loss of oxen and mules, which simply did not have the energy to last the distance under such heavy burdens. Hence at Fort Laramie there grew a stockpile of abandoned supplies that one traveler said included "not less than 30,000 lbs. bacon." Many others noted the great quantities of dried beef, salt, and hardtack that had been tossed aside.

Misleading advice and extravagant propaganda found many a gullible audience. According to a writer who followed "the tracks of Lewis and Clarke," Oregon had lured him because it had been described as a place where "pigs are running about under the great acorn trees, round and fat, and

We have laid in every possible mitigation of the fatigues and discomforts of the long ride. There are rifles and revolvers for Indians and game; sardines for those who cannot digest bacon; segars for the smoking Speaker; black tea for the ner-vous newspaper men; crackers for those fastidious stomachs that reject saleratus biscuit; and soap for those so aristocratic as to insist on washing themselves en route.

—Samuel Bowles in Atchison, Kansas, 1865

already cooked, with knives and forks sticking in them so that you can cut off a slice whenever you are hungry." The hard facts for most who crossed the mountains, however, were that domestic animals had to be herded for long miles in "cow columns," and as families began to move westward with all their worldly goods many of the tribulations of the trail fell on the women.

"They could hardly be called housewives in etymological strictness," an emissary of President James K. Polk wrote of the women in his party; "but it was plain that they had once been such. . . . They learned to make butter on the march by the dashing of the wagon, and so nicely to calculate the working of barm [yeast] in the jolting heats that, as soon after the halt as an oven could be dug in the hill-side and heated, their well-kneaded loaf was ready for baking, and produced good leavened bread for supper. . . ."

Nancy Wilson Ross, who has likened these mobile kitchens to modern trailer homes, quotes one pioneer wife's memoirs: "On the center cross-piece was placed a little round sheet-iron stove, about the size of a three-gallon bucket, with a little tea-kettle, a boiler and fry-

A pair of mugs

ing pan. On this little stove cooking was done with great ease and satisfaction. Mrs. Van Dusen says that many times she sat in her cozy little kitchen on wheels and cleaned and cooked a bird while the wagon moved along. On cold nights their little stove made their house very comfortable."

Memories, however, sometimes make conditions sound easier than they actually were. At the end of the trail, on whatever frontier, the transformation into a home of a cabin or a house made of blocks cut from the hard prairie sod was always a challenge to a woman's taste and ingenuity. Her husband cleared fields, planting corn and potatoes among the stumps, but the garden belonged to her and on it depended her reputation as a cook. "Seed swappin'" was a February pastime, and early March a good time to burn a brush pile and to sow the seeds of squash, cucumbers, cabbage, and turnips in the mingled soil and ashes. A pot of cabbage boiled with fat meat was just the thing when a man came in from the fields "hog hungry."

A Midwest pioneer recalled that her husband "raised the first wheat on the Des Moines River. We put the sacks in the bottom of the wagon, then our featherbeds on top of them. The children were put on these and we started for the mill . . . one hundred and thirty miles away. . . . As I was walking beside the oxen while my husband slept, I started up a flock of very young geese [and] I caught them all. . . . When we got home, we had a regular jubilation over that flour. Twenty of our neighbors came in to help eat it. They were crazy for that bread. I made three loaves of salt rising bread and they were enormous, but we never got a taste of them."

Yet it was corn—corn, the gift of the Indians—that played the biggest role in every frontier diet from the thirteen colonies to the Rockies and beyond. Corn had served its great purpose in the woodlands because a crop could be planted before the ordeal of stump pulling. And just as wheat was to take corn's place as homesteads were gradually fashioned into efficient farms, wildlife as a source of meat was replaced by domestic animals when the game diminished in the first few seasons after settlement. The era soon passed when a settler could bring down "during one forenoon alone . . . forty-two blue-winged teal," when families could find it "cheaper to have pheasant, prairie chicken, wild duck, or venison on the table than to buy meat at a butcher shop." Wild sweet potatoes, wild turnips, artichokes, beans, nuts, berries, plums, apples, grapes, wild tea, and wild rice were soon exhausted.

Steamboat traffic, which brought in foods from the East, began to return burdened with frontier crops for urban markets, and at last the boats, in turn, were replaced by railroads. Such commerce brought civilization to the frontier—and changed the character of the family table. Hardtack and sourdough gave way to wheaten bread as yeast became readily available.

Few pioneer recipes have remained unmodified in today's cookbooks, and of them all perhaps it is johnnycake, the flat corn-meal cakes of the moving frontier, to which the aroma of nostalgia clings most. In one version of the origin of its name, given by some long-ago pioneer, is a hidden reminder of a much broader debt in terms of frontier food: "The trappers followed the In-

---

A party recently left Joe's store at Mormon Bar for the Valley, and a friend of the *Star* furnishes the following statistics — showing the amount of " the necessaries of life" which is required for an eight day's trip in the mountains :

    8 lbs potatoes.
    1 bottle whisky.
    1 bottle pepper sauce.
    1° bottle whisky.
    1 box tea.
    9 lbs onions.
    2 bottles whisky.
    1 ham.
   11 lbs crackers.
    1 bottle whisky.
    ½ doz. sardines.
    2 bottles brandy, (4th proof.)
    6 lbs sugar.
    1 bottle brandy, (4th proof.)
    7 lbs cheese.
    2 bottles brandy, (4th proof.)
    1 bottle pepper.
    5 gallons whisky.
    4 bottles whisky (old Bourbon.)
    1 small keg whisky.
    1 bottle of cocktails, (designed for a
        " starter.")

—From *Hutchings' California Magazine*, 1860

dians' example in the baking of Shawnee-cakes, as they called them [after the Algonquian tribe] and the lapse of a few years was sufficient to corrupt the term into that of Johnny Cake. . . ." As civilization swept westward it survived on the culinary tricks of the Indians, who always before had been first on every American frontier.

59

Mark Twain, by Carroll Beckwith

MARK TWAIN

By Evan Jones

"Tastes are made, not born," said this son of the frontier. Even while he dined with Europe's royalty, his thoughts turned wistfully to the plain home-cooked meals of his Missouri boyhood

He was a meat and potatoes man, a milk and hoecake man, a watermelon and clabber man. He was, after all, as American as the food he liked best, and in more than one book he paused in the course of his story to interject his enthusiasm. "A man accustomed to American food and American domestic cookery would not starve to death suddenly in Europe," he wrote nostalgically in *A Tramp Abroad,* "but I think he would gradually waste away, and eventually die."

The writer of such words would not have been Mark Twain had he not resisted the blandishments of cuisines he considered too exotic for sanity. "There is here and there an American who will say he can remember rising from a European table d'hôte perfectly satis-fied; but we must not overlook the fact that there is also here and there an American who will lie."

However, Mark Twain himself would not lie when he discovered the gustatory solace of a British mixed drink. "Livy my darling," he wrote his wife in 1874, "I want you to be sure to have in the bathroom, when I arrive, a bottle of Scotch whisky, a lemon, some crushed sugar, & a bottle of *Angostura bitters.* Ever since I have been in London I have taken in a wine-glass what is called a cock-tail (made with those ingredients) before breakfast, before dinner, & just before going to bed....To it I attribute the fact that up to this day my digestion has been won-derful—simply *perfect*....Now my dear, if you will give the order *now,* to have

61

those things put in the bath-room & left there till I come, they will *be* there when I arrive. Will you?...I love to picture myself ringing the bell, at midnight—then a pause of a second or two —then the turning of the bolt, & 'Who is it?'—then ever so many kisses—then you & I in the bath-room, I drinking my cock-tail and undressing, & you standing by—then to bed, and—everything happy & jolly as it should be."

In those post-bellum years he was to label the Gilded Age, Sam Clemens of Hannibal, Missouri, matured from a connoisseur of wild fruit to a Yankee *bon vivant*. "I know the look of an apple that is roasting and sizzling on a hearth on a winter's evening," he wrote in his sixties, "and I know the comfort that comes of eating it hot, along with some sugar and a drench of cream....I know how the nuts taken in conjunction with winter apples, cider, and doughnuts, make old people's old tales and old jokes sound fresh and crisp and enchanting....I know the look of Uncle Dan'l's kitchen as it was on the privileged nights, when I was a child...."

Especially when he was traveling in foreign countries was he haunted by the tastes and smells of kitchens he remembered, and in Paris during the summer of 1879 he turned his memory back over four decades to compile a bill of fare (appearing in this book's epilogue) that includes dozens of "nourishing" dishes— a modest, private dinner, which he said he would have "all to myself" and which must "be hot when I arrive."

Mark Twain, his wife, and children once spent a year and a half in Europe, and paterfamilias, at least, was literally fed up. He said that after a few months' exposure to the coffee served in a European hotel a man's mind was apt to weaken. Even the bread was "unsympathetic" because it was cold, and the butter, "made of goodness knows what," had no salt. Asserting that the commonest American breakfast consisted of coffee and beefsteak, he stormed over the inadequacy of European meat, calling it dry, insipid, and usually "as overdone as a martyr."

Sam Clemens began complaining about food when he was a fifteen-year-old apprentice on a weekly newspaper in Hannibal. The invariable diet of thin stew and boiled cabbage drove him and a fellow apprentice to steal onions and potatoes from the editor's cellar and to cook them at night on the print-shop stove. When offered a job on another newspaper, owned by his brother, he readily accepted. But with subscribers paying in cordwood and turnips rather than in cash, the paper failed, and Sam left home for good.

Much of his life was to be spent in travel—to New York when he was seventeen, up and down the Mississippi as a steamboat pilot, roughing it in western mining camps. From his first overseas voyage to Hawaii in 1866 to his last to Bermuda just before his death in 1910, he spent much of his time on the road as a lecturer—perforce in hotels and restaurants—and he was never persuaded that home-cooked food, southern style, could be outmatched.

He grudgingly admitted that European provincial fare was better than that to be had in "our minor cities." But even in lunching with Andrew Carnegie and other tycoons who were his friends, he preferred to take his companions to his family dining room. "The main splendor," he once said in some rapture, was in the way that food was cooked at home. And at the mention of beef he could work up a fine disdain for European notions about preparing and serving a piece of meat.

"Then there is the beefsteak. They have it in Europe, but they don't know how to cook it. Neither will they cut it right. It comes on the table in a small, round, pewter platter. It lies in the centre of this platter, in a bordering bed of grease-soaked potatoes; it is the size, shape, and thickness of a man's hand with the thumb and fingers cut off. It is a little overdone, is rather dry, it tastes pretty insipidly, it rouses no enthusiasm.

"Imagine a poor exile contemplating that inert thing," he sniffed scornfully; "and imagine an angel suddenly sweeping down out of a better land and setting before him a mighty porter-house steak an inch and a half thick, hot and sputtering from the griddle; dusted with fragrant pepper; enriched with little melting bits of butter of the most unimpeachable freshness and genuineness; the precious juices of the meat trickling out and joining the gravy, archipelagoed with mushrooms; a township or two of tender, yellowish fat gracing an outlying district of this ample county of beefsteak; the long white bone which divides the sirloin from the tenderloin still in its place; and imagine that the angel also adds a great cup of American home-made coffee, with the cream a-froth on top, some real butter, firm and yellow and fresh, some smoking hot biscuits, a plate of hot buckwheat cakes, with transparent syrup—could words describe the gratitude of this exile?"

When the Clemens family first went to live in London they took Katy Leary with them to supervise the children and to pinch-hit occasionally for the English cook. As the Clemens housekeeper for a quarter-century, Katy had her troubles with the food, "because the English," she said in her own story of Mark Twain, "they didn't half cook things through, specially the vegetables." She added that she was able finally to educate a London cook to some extent, but that there was no one in England who could be taught to make creamed potatoes—a regular Sunday-night treat for the Clemenses. Katy grumbled at the beer that had to be kept on tap for all the English servants, to say nothing of the weekly bottle of whiskey exacted by the cook. But Twain grumbled over the five weeks it took to find the English cook in the first place and over the taste of the simplest products of her cuisine. "English Toast!" an entry in his notebook exclaims. "Execrable!"

He even dreamed about food, and his notebook records a somnolent fancy of buying a pie, "a mush apple pie—hot." Huckleberry, another pie that appealed to him, was used by Katy to lure her master into breaking his habit of going without lunch. She ordered a pie every morning, she said, recalling a period in which Twain was depressed. "Then I'd get a quart of milk and put it on the ice, and have it all ready—the huckleberry pie and the cold milk— about one o'clock. He'd eat half the huckleberry pie, anyway, and drink all the milk."

Katy was not the only one who worried about Mark Twain's eating habits. In her own account of the family, Clara Clemens described an unsuccessful effort "to prevail on Father to return to the house at noon and eat his favorite 'dishes' cooked in the old Southern way. . . ." But Sam Clemens remained a stubborn individualist, and spasmodic culinary enthusiasms were not the least of his idiosyncrasies. Once he wrote to his wife: "I take only one meal a day just now and would keep this up if you permitted it. It consists of four boiled eggs and coffee. I stir in a *lot* of salt and then keep on dusting and stirring in black pepper till the eggs look dirty—then they're booming with fire and energy and you can taste them all the way down and even after they get there."

His disregard for food when he himself was not hungry caused much talk in the family on the occasion of the first visit of Rudyard Kipling. As an unsung young journalist writing about the United States for an Indian newspaper, Kipling had pursued Twain from his home in Elmira, New York, to his nearby summer farm, and back to his mother-in-law's house, where Kipling arrived just as the Clemens family was sitting down to lunch.

The trouble, as Katy Leary remembered it, "was that Kipling had heard the sound of dishes in the dining-room and knew it was lunch time and there was something to eat, and I suppose it made him hungry as a bear to hear them." If so, Kipling became so engrossed in talking to the American author that he seems to have forgotten the absence of food. "A big darkened drawing room," he wrote for his readers in India; "a huge chair; a man with eyes, a mane of grizzled hair, a brown mustache covering a mouth as delicate as a woman's, a strong, square hand shaking mine, and the slowest, calmest, levelest voice in the world. . . . I was smoking his cigar and hearing him talk—this man I had learned to love and admire fourteen thousand miles away. . . . Blessed is the man who finds no disillusion when he is brought face to face with a revered writer."

Mark Twain was deeply loved and extravagantly admired at home, but in the unfinished biography begun by his daughter Susy when she was only thirteen, he is not quite perfect. "Papa uses very strong language," the little girl wrote, "but I have an idea not nearly so strong as when he first maried mamma." Indeed his behavior at meals was such that his wife made a habit of reprimanding him for his misdemeanors in a way that his children called "dusting Papa off." During a season in Paris in which the Clemenses entertained frequently, the harassed father told his wife that she might dust him off after every dinner for a year and still not eliminate all his bad habits. The solution, he thought, lay in a system of signals and the use of colored cards as a family code.

"The children got a screen arranged so that they could be behind it during the dinner and listen for the signals and entertain themselves," Twain recalled. "At a hint from behind the screen, Livy would look down the table and say, in a voice full of interest, if not of counterfeited apprehension, 'What did you do with the blue card that was on the dressing table———?'

"That was enough. I knew what was happening—that I was talking the lady on my right to death and never paying any attention to the one on my left. . . . [The system] headed off crime after crime all through dinner, and I always came out at the end successful, triumphant, with large praises owing to me, and I got them on the spot."

Sam and Livy Clemens had come a long way to those dinners given in Paris, or those in London, or at any of their several homes in the United States. Describing their lack of culinary education on the day of their marriage in 1870, Mark Twain wrote that at about midnight they were left alone in their new quarters. "Then Ellen, the cook, came in to get orders for the morning's marketing—and neither of us knew whether beefsteak was sold by the barrel or by the yard." He was joking, of course, but it was true that neither Sam nor Livy knew much about housekeeping.

In spite of such beginnings, when the Clemenses built a house in Hartford, Connecticut, soon after their marriage, they swiftly became noted among the literati for their hospitality. The house itself was an oddity of geometrically patterned red and white bricks that had a balcony like a pilothouse and a porch like a Mississippi steamboat deck. Although newspapers gibed at the bizarre design, the Clemens home became a stopping place for traveling authors and publishers and was famous for dinner parties that were said to produce "an incomparable hilarity."

Over the library mantel Sam had set a brass plate inscribed with a line from Emerson: "The ornament of a house is the friends who frequent it." Sam so meant these words that he had ordered a guest room built on the ground floor, a revolutionary idea in those days. There were other precedent-breakers, among them the fact that all the rooms were free of the usual Victorian clutter because Sam liked to move as he talked, and he never freed himself of his compulsion to stride around the dining table between courses.

Bret Harte came more than once to drink Sam's whiskey, and frequent dinner guests included Charles Dudley Warner, Harriet Beecher Stowe, and Thomas Wentworth Higginson. William Dean Howells said Livy was a hostess "without a touch of weakness. . . . I suppose she had . . . her female fears of etiquette and conventions, but she did not let them hamper the wild and splendid generosity with which Clemens rebelled against the social stupidities and cruelties. . . ." Sam entertained so many people, and was wined and dined himself by so many others, that his daughter Jean said with enough inherited wit to make up for the irreverence: "Papa, the way things are going, pretty soon there won't be anybody left for you to get acquainted with but God."

Books poured from his pen; during the Hartford years Mark Twain created Tom Sawyer, Huck Finn, the Prince and the Pauper, and many other characters to delight his growing audience. Many friends shared in the birth of Twain's creations, whether he was at home or away, for it was his custom to give dinners, following which he would read his most recent manuscript.

He described one such event at which "we had a gay time. . . . Shandy-gaff [beer and ginger ale] for the gentlemen & buttermilk & seltzer-lemonades for the ladies."

Living gaily was Mark Twain's nature, and so was living well. Yet, cosmopolitan as he became, he remained at heart the original of Tom Sawyer, the frontier boy whose great nostalgia was for the summer days he had spent on the Missouri farm of his Uncle John Quarles. Working on his autobiography at the age of sixty-two, he recalled the look of the dinner table and ticked off thirty-eight dishes that came from that farm kitchen—from roast pig to hot corn pone to peach cobbler. "Well," he wrote, "it makes me cry to think of them." When he wrote of the dinner given for him by Kaiser Wilhelm II it was not the royal menu in general that interested him; it was the kind of potatoes served, only because they reminded him of the midnight feasts in the Hannibal print shop. White-tie-and-tails did not change Sam Clemens, nor did the decades of what he called "banqueteering." As Mark Twain he was loved in every civilized part of the world, and to himself he seemed, as Bernard De Voto has put it, "a proof of the American Dream." So he was—and so he lived.

SOURDOUGH
AND HARDTACK

A Picture Portfolio

The trappers in this Alfred Jacob Miller painting are cooking a hump rib, the part of the buffalo that artist Miller called "that most glorious of all mountain morsels."

An Artist on the Trail

Leaving home   *Arrival in California*

J. Goldsborough Bruff, a draftsman for the Bureau of Topographical Engineers, was one of the thousands of easterners who traveled to California in search of gold in 1849. His sketches, some of which are shown here with his own amusing captions, are a wry record of life along the overland trails. But his diaries are even more vivid, recalling the tribulations of the westward journey and the hardships of life in the Sierra Nevada, where miners were sometimes grateful if they could ease their hunger pangs with a tainted piece of venison, a scrawny bluebird, or a tallow candle. Bruff's report of a happier moment, an Independence Day celebration on the plains in 1849, is excerpted on the facing page.

"After a hearty supper, we slept well, excepting the usual disturbance of our lupine serrenaders."

Eat a hearty supper, boys! To-morrow you'll have to try Shank's mare!

A FOURTH OF JULY
CELEBRATION
IN THE WILDERNESS

This occurred near the "Court House Rock," on the banks of the Platte.... The banquet hall, was formed of 4 wagons—2 on each side, and parallel about 8 feet apart — covered over with tent cloths. The ground was covered with gum tent-carpets: on the two sides were arranged, along the edge of the carpet, tin platters and iron spoons: (Knives & forks for the ladies) Down the centre, the *luxuries of the season* were placed, at convenient distances, in tin pans,—viz:—boiled beans and salt pork, bean broth, middling bacon, ship bread, and *hot rolls of wheat bread. Dessert* — pies, of dried apples and peaches, and stewed dried apples. In the centre, on one side, a raised seat was formed, of bags of flour, covered neatly, with red blankets, for the ladies.... The Star-spangled banner, floated through an opening in the *roof*.

—*J. Goldsborough Bruff, 1849*

The Buffalo are not quite so green as some folks think

Buffalo hunting, Bruff wrote, often resulted in lost horses, "and many a poor fellow, after a hard day's hunt...has a long & tiresome walk" back to his camp.

Milk man, Sacramento

A Day's Shooting

"Many of the most *distinguished* guns acquire names of the most fearful import . . . and small bets are sometimes made on *Black Snake, Cross Burster, Hair Splitter, Blood Letter,* and *Panther Cooler.*" So wrote contributor "Moss Bucket" in a Boone's Lick, Missouri, newspaper in 1825. He was describing the popular shooting-for-beef contests, in which frontier marksmen vied for the quarters of a fat steer. To the victorious sharpshooter went the valuable "fifth quarter," the hide and the tallow. Except for these contests, however, meat on the frontier was gained by shooting at moving game, not at a stationary target. As the photograph at right illustrates, it was the trusty gun that provided the antelope for dinner.

Shooting for the Beef, *above, was painted in 1850 by George C. Bingham.*
The intrepid Colorado ladies below used a bicycle for hunting in the 1890's.

Using chairs for his table, a Nebraska bachelor prepares supper in 1886.

"Signs of Progress"

The first buildings to spring up in the towns where miners struck it rich were the general store and the saloon. In the former, prices were incredibly high, with a jar of pickles selling for eleven dollars in some California boom towns. In the bars the price of a glass of whiskey was often a pinch of gold dust, so saloon owners made a point of hiring bartenders with large fingers. As for the liquor, it was, to quote Horace Greeley, "dubious." Greeley visited Denver, Colorado, in 1859, when its only hotel had an earth floor and a cloth roof. The basic diet, he noted, "was bread, bacon, and beans," but there were some "signs of progress-improvements—manifest destiny :—there was a man about the city yesterday with lettuce to sell—and I am credibly assured that there will be green peas next month—actually peas!—provided it should rain soakingly meantime . . ."

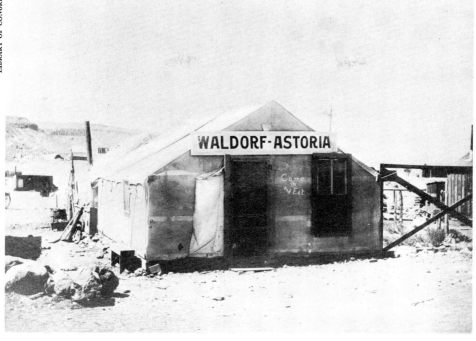

Hotels and restaurants on the frontier had little enough to recommend them, so occasionally, in a nostalgic mood, a proprietor might conjure up a posh eastern establishment (above). Shown below is the main thoroughfare of Deadwood, South Dakota, in the year 1877.

The Sizzler's Domain

Since silence at mealtime was the rule in most lumber camps, it must have been a special occasion that prompted a concert (right) in a poster-bedecked cookhouse in Minnesota. But if the men ate their meals without conversation, they talked about them at length afterward, using a colorful vocabulary of their own. Griddlecakes were a "string of flats," and an inferior cook was a "boiler" or a "sizzler." Assistants to the cooks were "flunkeys" or "cookees," and companies that had lunch brought to the men in the woods instead of letting them return to camp were derisively called "nosebag shows." Camps providing bad food were dismissed as "hardtack outfits."

A new cook is welcomed by jubilant cowboys in this Frederic Remington painting.

His lap and the ground were the cowboy's dining table (above). The chuck wagon at right had a canvas fly to make a covered cooking area.

Home on the Range

Highly paid, the cowboy cook earned every cent of his salary. With ashes and dust from an open-pit fire blowing in his face, as well as in the food, he prepared three meals daily for twenty to thirty hungry cowhands who expected plenty of beans, fried beef, and stew, and coffee strong enough to float a horseshoe. Up before dawn on roundup days to build his breakfast fire, often with wet wood or cow chips, the cook did not end his day until after dark, when he put a last pot of coffee on for the nighthawks. Sometimes he even worked as he slept: many a cook took his sourdough starter to bed with him to keep the cold night air from stopping the crucial fermenting process.

Meanwhile, Back at the

Homestead...

Newcomers to the prairies lived in homes made of sod cut in squares, until something more permanent was built. In 1886, this Nebraska family posed for the camera before eating the melons on the table. Everyone but the cow watched the birdie.

3

The
YANKEE
KITCHEN

By Gerald Carson

"When I die you will find engraved upon my heart 'New England,'" wrote Boston-bred Thomas Hutchinson, the last royal governor of Massachusetts, from his exile in England.

Perhaps only a sturdy race of fishermen-farmers and freeholders could have subdued the glaciated, rock-strewn Yankee land and flourished in the robust climate. Yet they formed there a pattern of civilization which has been dominant in the social development of the northern parts of the United States, determining not only how we think and feel but also what we eat. Rejecting English authorities unsuited

In The Dinner Horn *(left), painted by Winslow Homer, a New England farm wife summons the men in the fields to dinner.*

to the new environment and climate, the wives of the colonists followed "rules" for cooking which they carried in their heads. They levied upon the Indians for new foodstuffs and invented dishes of their own which have become a cherished part of our tradition of cookery: brick oven baked beans and brown bread, corn or maize in all of its delectable forms, the Thanksgiving turkey-and-cranberry-sauce combination, maple syrup, the fish chowders, hot biscuits, and the manipulation of the codfish, affectionately known as Cape Cod turkey.

Codfish balls, indeed, have been extolled in the most exclusive gentlemen's club in the world—the United States Senate—where Senator George Frisbie Hoar rose during a debate upon a pure food bill to praise "the exquisite flavor of the codfish, salted, made into balls, and eaten on a Sunday morning by a person whose theology is sound, and who believes in the five points of Calvinism" and where the

> *No where is the stomach of the traveller or visitor put in such constant peril as among the cake-inventive housewives and daughters of New England. Such is the universal attention paid to this particular branch of epicurism in these states, that I greatly suspect that some of the Pilgrim Fathers must have come over to the country with the Cookery book under one arm and the Bible under the other.*
> —Charles Joseph Latrobe, 1836

magnetic voice of Daniel Webster was raised to champion a recipe for fish chowder. And, on a humbler level, history fortunately has not ignored Aunt Joanna Dyer's applesauce cake or Mrs. Georgia Grindle's tomato relish from East Blue Hill, Maine.

Although there was game to be taken in the forests, fresh-water fish leaping in brooks and ponds, and over two hundred varieties of fish in the seas which washed the coast of Massachusetts, the Pilgrims very nearly starved to death. But they pulled through on the Indians' immortal maize and the clams they could tread out of the mud on the tidal flats—"the treasures hid in the sands" which Elder William Brewster thanked the Lord for when the pot hung empty from the lug pole.

English shallops had been coasting along American shores for more than a century. But the fishermen were not Pilgrims. And the Pilgrims were not fishermen. They were tradesmen, craftsmen, and farmers, unfamiliar with the skills developed in upper-class sporting life, which might have served them well in their Starving Time. They lacked seines and tackle. Their hooks were too large, their bait wrong, their luck bad. And they were not marksmen. So they pounded the Indian corn to a coarse powder called samp or *nasaump*, after the Algonquian word for corn mush. Fortunately, as Roger Williams wrote, "Nasaump ...boil'd and eaten hot or cold with milke or butter...is a dish exceeding wholesome for the *English* bodies."

Wheat was not a major crop in early New England, but rye prospered to provide, along with corn, the staple dark bread known colloquially as rye 'n' Injun—rye flour and corn meal mixed. Pigs thrived on the nuts of the woodlands. With the passage of time, our grandsires became superb fishermen. The Yankee farmer learned to cultivate the black honey bee and slashed the sugar maple for sweetening to pour over his hasty pudding. It is a common error to suppose that the first settlers embraced discomfort and privation as being per se a good thing. They took their ease when they found it, ate bountifully when they could. Well before the first hundred years had passed, the Puritan homemakers understood thoroughly the use of the new foodstuffs of the western hemisphere. Firelight danced on pewter porringers. There was plenty of cider with a spike in it to wash down the salty diet of fish and pickled pork.

The heart of colonial life was the common room, or kitchen, with its great fireplace, often eight feet or more across and five feet high, an immense recess large enough, in the seventeenth century, for a person to sit inside the jambs, or side walls. Such "chimneys," to call them by their old English name, used up fuel extravagantly, and since the scientific principle involved was not understood, they drew poorly and smoked abominably. In the late 1700's,

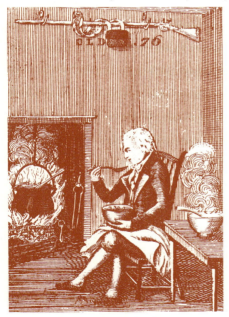

Eating hasty pudding

Benjamin Thompson, better remembered by his patent of nobility, Count Rumford, called the smoky chimney "that greatest of all plagues" and, like Dr. Franklin, considered the design of more efficient fireplaces a subject worthy of serious study. Through the study of the physics of heat, Count Rumford became, as we would express it today, a heating engineer, and went on to invent a cooking range and the drip coffeepot.

Long-legged skillets were thrust into the hot coals of maple for cooking griddlecakes and frying meats. Spits for roasting and broiling were common. But most of the food New Englanders ate for more than two hundred years came out of heavy black iron pots. The large "dinner pot," in which meat was boiled with the suet pudding, hung on stout pot chains from wooden lug poles or later from the crane, a Yankee invention. Bean porridge was made in this pot, as were the fish stews of the daily bill of fare. The famous and succulent New England boiled dinner—corned beef and root vegetables that would keep until dandelion-green time—was a triumph of art over the limitations of fireplace cookery and owed some of its popularity, among the wives at least, to the fact that it could simmer for hours with little attention. Accompanied by mixed mustard pickles and horse-radish and a dessert like baked apple dumplings, a boiled dinner could be counted upon to keep a man putting up a stone wall well-fueled until his afternoon snack.

On the hearth stood the Dutch oven, a broad, flat-bottomed kettle with long legs and a lid that turned up all around the rim. This oven, being charged with bread dough or potatoes for roasting, was set in the coals, and more coals were heaped over the top. At the table wooden trenchers, the plates of the period, were piled high with smoking spoon meat — hashes, thick stews, salted venison — with pompion (pumpkin) sauce or pie for the dessert course. The trenchers were often used for two courses by the simple expedient of turning them over. Thus they spoke, upcountry, of "the dinner side and the pie side." Usually two ate from the same trencher. If a youth and maiden shared a plate, they were considered to be engaged. The table was, literally, a board. The husband and his wife sat on stools or benches or, like the children, ate standing. There was some pewter but little silver in seventeenth-century New England, no glass, no china, no saucers, no forks.

John Winthrop, governor of the Massachusetts Bay Colony, brought over a fork, which came carefully preserved in its own case. It was unique. Fingers or a clam shell and plenty of napery met the demands of domestic manners among the early colonists and their immediate descendants. A vivid sense of the times comes through in the maxims of the New England schoolteacher Eleazar Moody. His *School of Good Manners* (circa 1715) includes such advice as: "Take not salt with a greasy knife. Blow not thy meat. Smell not of thy meat, nor put it to thy nose. Foul not thy napkin all over, but at one corner."

Two forms of oven developed around the fireplace, the built-in brick oven and a portable reflector, or "tin kitchen," that stood on the hearth and caught the heat radiated from the fire. They turned out johnnycake, roasts, puddings, pies, and cakes of delicate lightness and toothsome flavor. Brick-oven pork and beans must have been invented very early, for Judge Samuel Sewall, probably the greatest of American diarists, writing in the period of the Mathers, mentions a stop he made at Andover in 1702, "and there din'd on Pork and Beans."

The menu expanded as the century wore on. Court records mention, to name some of the food materials available in the period, bacon, beef, butter,

Seesaw butter churn, 1808

cheese, eggs, lamb, fowl, milk, mutton, suet, veal, wild game, many varieties of fish, Indian beans, cabbage, parsnips, peas, honey, pumpkins, and an abundance of fruits and berries. The white, or Irish, potato, a native of South America, came to New England by way of Europe and appears to have found its first permanent home in North America at Londonderry, now Derry, New Hampshire, in 1719. But like the tomato, which also came to us from South America through Europe, the white potato was not commonly used until the nineteenth century.

The colonists relished condiments and used ginger and pepper generously, as well as cloves, mace, cinnamon, and allspice. Seasonings also served a special purpose in those iceless days by making tainted foods tolerable in a pinch. There was more than a touch of gourmet cookery, at least in upper-class homes, where herbs were cultivated: pennyroyal, sage, savory, and sweet marjoram dried in the tin kitchen and hung in the fireplace cupboard.

During the "six weeks' want," the early spring when the vegetables in the root cellar were wilted or mildewed or eaten up, the salty diet was supplemented with native potherbs—milkweed, marsh marigolds, or the common nettle—a low-calorie diet with a vengeance!

We can conclude that food during the remainder of the year was sufficiently abundant and sometimes even epicurean. Yet there were limits. The loaf sugar was saved for guests, the white bread for the minister's visit, since the brown bread *du pays* was said to give him heartburn and inhibit his preaching. Caramelized grain often substituted for coffee. "Tea" was often made from raspberry leaves or dittany.

Sometimes the meal barrel stood empty.

During the years before the American Revolution the fireplaces began to be reduced in size as fuel grew scarcer. But the kitchen was still the most

Our too liberal entertainment of our countrymen here has been reported at home by our guests, to our disadvantage, and has given offence. They must be contented for the future, as I am, with plain beef and pudding. The readers of Connecticut newspapers ought not to be troubled with any more accounts of our extravagance. For my own part, if I could sit down to dinner on a piece of their excellent salt pork and pumpkin, I would not give a farthing for all the luxuries of Paris.

**—Benjamin Franklin,
writing from Paris, August, 1784**

cheerful and most used room in the house. Beside the fireplace hung the ancestral salt box, a colonial symbol of good cooking and provident domestic management, fashioned from black cherry wood. Over the fireplace hung the father's musket, the old "queen's arm," and powder horn. Strings of dried apples, peppers, and pumpkins looped across the room. The colonial goodwife ate not the bread of idleness, for the spinning wheel whirred and the loom clacked while the farmer took his after-supper pipe and toddy on the settle or fashioned a butter paddle with his jackknife.

A block of wood stood inside the

Nineteenth-century coal stove

well, relatively—to clean. Yet there is clear evidence that the change-over was gradual. One of Miss Eliza Leslie's cookbooks, written in the light of the eighteenth century, was still in print in 1870, still carried instructions which took it for granted that cooking was done in the fireplace; and in 1872 Marion Harland noted that some housekeepers were using a spit and the tin kitchen.

Many good cooks believed that the cookstove worsened the American cuisine. Mrs. Harriet Beecher Stowe articulated what others felt when she wrote that "an open fireplace is an altar of patriotism. Would our Revolutionary fathers have gone barefooted and bleeding over snows to defend air-tight stoves and cooking-ranges? I trow not. It was the memory of the great open kitchen-fire . . . its roaring, hilarious voice of invitation, its dancing tongues of flame, that called to them through the snows of that dreadful winter . . ."

Indubitably there were social gains and losses. The simple board disappeared from the kitchen. The quality of the ventilation declined. There was no handy place to throw trash and refuse. And it was not dainty when the man of the house spat on a hot stove. More happily, the smelly dye pot on the hearth, with its yarn floating in indigo, goldenrod, butternut, and urine, was withdrawn from service at about the same time as the fireplace; and the stove, raised up on legs, provided a convenient place for laying wet socks out to dry and increased the com-

jamb, on which a child could sit and look upward through the throat of the great stack and watch the stars winking and swinging in the sky. Between the andirons, as Whittier wrote, "The mug of cider simmered slow, The apples sputtered in a row . . ."

Few greater changes ever took place in the American household than occurred around the time Whig gentlemen in broadcloth were lifting their hats slightly when Mr. Clay's name was mentioned. About that time, that is, 1840-50, the old fireplaces were boarded up, the last ham taken down from the chimney hooks. The new source of heat for cooking was a simple cast-iron box with two stove lids at the top. But the prototype was rapidly improved. After 1850 the compilers of cookbooks generally assumed that a woman who could buy a book would be using a wood range that was economical in its fuel consumption and easy—

forts of the family cat. As the kitchen shrank the dining room appeared, and the Victorian parlor, replete with its heavy, ornate horsehair and black-walnut furnishings, was just around the corner. But the old common room should never be forgot, with grandma gently rocking in her Boston rocker, the children doing their sums from Thompson's *Higher*, the relaxed chat and gossip.

Rustic life in New England was not markedly different from that of countrymen in New York, Pennsylvania, New Jersey, or any of the northern states, many of which were the children of New England. John Adams wrote in his diary of a visit he made in New York State: "The Manners of this Family are exactly like those of the New England people. A decent Grace before and after Meat — fine Pork and Beef and Cabbage and Turnip." New York, it should be noted, contributed sweet corn to the pleasures of American dining. The Indian corn of the Northeast was hard and flinty, but in 1779 one Richard Bagnal, an officer in General John Sullivan's expedition against the Iroquois, allegedly found sweet corn among the Indians of western New York. He carried seeds back to his home in Plymouth, but field corn, not sweet corn, remained prevalent on American tables until the 1850's.

Farming in the Northeast was carried on for subsistence, to supply the necessities of life rather than to produce a surplus in a cash economy. Before 1800, one must recall, there were very few towns or cities in the United States with a population exceeding ten thousand inhabitants. Manners, customs, and ways of thought were established for the whole country by rural people who produced their own food and fiber and followed the agricultural procedures of seventeenth-century England. There was little incentive to do better. Markets beyond the town line did not exist except in limited areas — near the towns with wharves and ocean traffic, along the Connecticut and Hudson rivers. With the family the economic unit, producer and consumer were practically identical.

Plowing his rocky lots with a wooden plow, sowing his seed broadcast like the sower of biblical times, threshing his grain with the flail, his labors in the fields supplemented by the domestic arts practiced by wives and daughters, a New England farmer could, as the records show, at one time live comfort-

Pray how does your asparagus perform?
—**John Adams,**
in a letter to his wife, Abigail

ably by laying out from ten to one hundred dollars in cash in a year.

The exchange of commodities took place at the crossroads store. And it *was* an exchange — goose feathers for molasses, potatoes for salt, cherry boards for tropical dyes, hemlock bark for tea and bean coffee. And there was a social aspect to a visit at the store. Under the blackened ceiling sat the common man's parliament, where public issues were disposed of and merry tales were told of mighty liars and sexual mischances; and there the broken soldier shouldered an Indian broom and showed how Louisbourg was won. Such men did not lay their money on the barrelhead casually.

"Many a one parting with a silver dollar," wrote a historian of Fairfield County, Connecticut, "would squeeze

---

The corned beef is exquisitely done, and as tender as a young lady's heart, all owing to my skilful cookery; for I consulted Mrs. Hale [Sarah Hale's cookbook] at every step, and precisely followed her directions. To say the truth, I look upon it as such a masterpiece in its way, that it seems irreverential to eat it. Things on which so much thought and labor are bestowed should surely be immortal . . .
— **Nathaniel Hawthorne, 1844**
(while Mrs. Hawthorne was away)

---

it so hard the eagle would holler, or parting with a silver half-dollar, the Goddess of Liberty would turn pale."

In the era of town economy, such manufacturing as was done was handled by small enterprisers and craftsmen, the tanner, the wheelwright, the combmaker, and the cooper. Nailer Tom Hazard, for example, was a blacksmith who turned out handmade nails and was so-called to distinguish him from College Tom, his cousin; Pistol-Head Tom, his son; Shepherd Tom, who raised sheep; and some forty other

Toms who also lived nearby in Rhode Island. Nailer Tom also made trammels, gridirons, mink traps, eelspears, ladles, shovels, and once a pair of handcuffs for a crazy woman.

The cobbler came to the farmstead once a year and stayed as long as was necessary to outfit the whole family, though sometimes the versatile head of the family could "whip the cat," or do the chore himself. Often under the handicraft system the specialized worker gave up his touring to become a merchant-manufacturer with a shop of his own. Conditions varied according to geography. An industrial society developed first in the coastal region because of water transportation and the rapid expansion of cotton culture. There factory-made yarn was woven in the cottages of the workers as "put out" work and returned as finished cloth.

A measure of prosperity beyond mere subsistence came to those producers who lived near tidewater. Merchants were sending their sloops and schooners to the West Indies and Surinam loaded with horses, boards, masts, hoops, barrel staves, and salted fish to trade for molasses, coffee, white cones of loaf sugar, and good old Demerara rum. Quintals of "merchantable" (the highest grade) fish went to Spain for the fast days; the proceeds were invested in goods that did not reach Aunt Nabby back in the hills but gave a touch of urbanity to the coastal region —lemons and raisins, olive oil from Lisbon, almonds from Cadiz, Madeira and Canary wines.

The great New England food resource was fish. After clams ceased to be the Pilgrims' bread, the Reverend Francis Higginson, apparently full up to bursting, wrote of the cod, the mackerel, the bass, and lobsters: "... I was soon cloyed with them, they were so great, and fat, and luscious." He goes on to mention similarly in his *New-Englands Plantation* (1630), the herring, haddock, eels, crabs, and oysters, expressing the hope that New England would prove to be a good country for making salt. The fish, in turn, stimulated shipbuilding. By the dawn of the eighteenth century, bold skippers of pinkies with names like *Good Intent, Harvester,* the *Miranda,* and the *Open Sea* knew the Grand Bank, Cape Sable, Labrador, and the waters of the Arctic Circle as intimately as the quiet coves of their home ports and "wet down their salt" with many a "trip" of fish from Nova Scotia.

The preservation of food was accomplished by heat—as in the instance of canned foods; by drying—apples, corn, and pumpkins; by smoking or brine in the case of meats; and by the coolness of the root cellar. In the economy of New England's farmer-mechanics, ice was an unknown luxury. It is very possible, indeed, that more ice was used in the southern states than in New England, for it was harvested in the early nineteenth century from Massachusetts ponds and sent to Charleston, Cuba, and Jamaica. Ice from the ponds of Cambridge could be had at retail in Boston in the early years of the same century. There was plenty more in Maine and New Hampshire, but it could not stand the high freighting charges. Frederic Tudor, an indomit-

LEVEE AND SUPPER
OF THE
MAMMOTH COD

ASSOCIATION.
AT GLIDDEN'S HOTEL, IN NEWPORT,
On Friday Eve., Feb'y 16th, 1855,
Your company, and Lady, is respectfully solicited.

able merchandising genius of Boston, became known as the "Ice King," designed a successful icehouse, pioneered the business of shipping ice, and eventually created for the home icebox as significant a role in the history of American cookery as that of the cookstove.

In the Dutch farm areas of New York the cellar and garret were great storehouses of substantials. Hams, sides of bacon, smoked beef, sausages hung by the attic chimney. Great bins of apples, turnips, beets, and other coarse vegetables filled the cellar, along with tonnekens of salt shad and mackerel, firkins of butter, kegs of pigs' feet, kilderkins of lard, barrels of cider, hogsheads of rum and molasses.

Some of the activities connected with the production of food were carried on in an atmosphere of social relaxation and gaiety, such as sugaring off and the apple-paring bees. The discovery of maple sugar was the high moment of gastronomic invention in the Indian culture, fortunately passed on to "the old sirs" at a very early date. About the time the wild geese went honking north, our forebears gashed the sugar maple, inserted the spile, and boiled down the delectable sap for syrup or crystalline sugar. A ladleful of syrup, thrown on a snowdrift or poured over cracked ice, quickly congealed into sugar-on-snow, or "jack wax," a half-warm, chewy kind of taffy. Poured into a flat dish, stirred for fifteen or twenty minutes, with butternuts cut in, transferred to buttered tins, the confection became maple cream. Sugaring off called for a party, with refreshments of hot soda biscuits baked in the camp and dunked in the new syrup, which was sometimes bright, clear, and delicate, sometimes dark and robust with a faint hint of smoke in it. It is impossible to say which kind was better.

In Orange County, New York, as St. John de Crèvecoeur, the "American Farmer," author of a famous series of letters on rural life in the eighteenth century, observed, the neighbor women gathered in October to peel, quarter, and core the ripe pippins and greenings while learning who was to be married, who had had a baby, and what man was drinking too much. And many a maiden got a mate. For after the sharp knives and rapid hands dispatched the work came cider and doughnuts, the fiddle and the dance, for those whom Joel Barlow called "brown,

Pressing apples for cider

corn-fed nymphs, and strong, hard-handed beaux." Soon there was a wedding in the front room. The community's good wishes were extended over blackberry cordial and pound-cake, and the happy couple departed with a kettle full of coals to light a new Yankee hearth down the road.

New England could scarcely have survived without the apple. Tradition has it that at Yale College every supper served for more than one hundred years included apple pie. The custom of eating apple pie for breakfast, at which lesser men have quaked and blanched, has seemed natural, inevitable, and pleasurable to New Englanders. "What is pie for?" Emerson exclaimed, and the matter was settled.

"We liked apple pie early in the autumn but got tired of it before pumpkin pie took its place," wrote U. P. Hedrick, the late, great pomologist of New York State, recalling his Michigan farm boyhood. A good tangy piece of cheese went wonderfully well with apple pie; as a folk saying put it: "Apple pie without cheese is like a kiss without a squeeze." The Reverend Henry Ward Beecher, who esteemed the good things of this life as well as the next, declared that an apple pie should be made with Spitzenburgs, anointed with sugar and butter and spices to form "a glorious unity," and baked with a crust "that lies upon the tongue, so as to let the apple strike through and touch the *papillae* with a mere effluent flavor." The pie should be eaten, he wrote, "while it is yet florescent, white or creamy yellow, with the merest drip of candied juice along the edges, (as if the flavor were so good to itself that its own lips watered!) of a mild and modest warmth, the sugar suggesting jelly, yet not jellied, the morsels of apple neither dissolved nor yet in original substance, but hanging as it were in a trance between the spirit and the flesh of applehood . . . then, O blessed man, favored by all the divinities! eat, give thanks, and go forth, *'in apple-pie order!'"*

For beverages the merchant and professional class and, in colonial times, the small court circle surrounding the royal governor drank port, Madeira, claret, and the Burgundies. The middle classes relied upon fruit cordials, wines, and ciders of native growth. The yeoman farmers made their own spruce beer, elderberry and dandelion wine, metheglin, and applejack. Almost everybody took rum as a form of cen-

tral heating. Rum mixed with molasses was known as blackstrap; compounded with cider, the resulting potion was a "stone-wall." Either way, it was a necessity at hog-killing time, when the stem and stern posts were raised in a shipyard, at the ordination of ministers, or at the ceremonies at Harvard College. At the militia trainings it was more necessary than gunpowder. Charles Francis Adams sadly observed the New England attachment to ardent spirits, attributing it to the constant use of salt meats. Children got thoroughwort tea when they were ailing.

Cider was, next to water, the most abundant and the cheapest fluid to be had in New Hampshire, while I lived there,—often selling for a dollar per barrel. In many a family of six or eight persons, a barrel tapped on Saturday barely lasted a full week.... The transition from cider to warmer and more potent stimulants was easy and natural; so that whole families died drunkards and vagabond paupers from the impetus first given by cider-swilling in their rural homes . . .

—Horace Greeley

Milk, scarce at first, became so plentiful that John Cotton remarked that milk and ministers were the only things cheap in New England.

By the 1870's a colonial wife, if she could have visited a Yankee kitchen, would have found it a place of marvels. The heavy, unwieldy iron vessels of fireplace cookery days had been replaced by lighter ware of coated steel. The housewife, in a full-gathered gingham apron tied over a many-gored skirt, shot a dollop of kerosene onto the crumpled pages of the Boston *Transcript,* as Kenneth Roberts has related, put six sticks of kindling and three of stove wood into the firebox, and she was ready to make toast, boil the coffee, and coddle the eggs. A pan of potatoes, sliced the night before, stood ready on

---

In our private room the cloth could not, for any earthly consideration, have been laid for dinner without a huge glass dish of cranberries in the middle of the table; and breakfast would have been no breakfast unless the principal dish were a deformed beefsteak with a great flat bone in the centre, swimming in hot butter, and sprinkled with the very blackest of all possible pepper . . .

—Charles Dickens in Boston, 1842

---

the back of the stove. A reservoir of heated water awaited the "redding up" after the meal. Soon enticing aromas mingled with the smell of geranium leaves.

The homemaker still needed four boards—one for kneading the bread dough, one for slicing the loaf, one each for the preparation of vegetables and meats. City wives had already dispensed with the churn, the cheese press, the equipment for making soft soap. Scales, steamers, waffle irons, gem pans, long-handled spoons, choppers and chopping bowls, the coffee grinder,

colander, and flour cabinet were still familiar sights. A pantry or storeroom held jellies, homemade relishes, pickled peaches with the pointed ears of cloves dotting their amber sides.

Clam chowder was a first-of-the-week dish. Toward the end of the week leftovers made a platter of red flannel hash, colored by beets and accompanied by sour-milk biscuits, applesauce sprinkled with nutmeg and dotted with butter, a custard so light it hardly counted, gooseberry pie, and a curd cheese flavored with tansy. Saturday was baking day. It was also fish day, to distinguish it from the Friday fast of the papists. Codfish as cakes or balls reigned at the Sunday breakfast table, and dinnertime brought the traditional pork and beans, which had been on the fire since early Saturday. The brown bread was made, according to the recollection of one New England food authority, in a five-pound lard pail with the word "Swift" on the side in raised letters, which referred, she decided as a child, to the speed with which the bread disappeared. After sundown, with the Sabbath over, the kitchen was apple-fragrant with the aroma of great, yellow-green Pound Sweets as Mother cut them, still baking hot, into bowls of johnnycake and milk.

Life in the provinces quickened as the rail network was completed. The trains hauled out New England farm products—the brown eggs for Boston, the white for New York, the milk for both—and brought back the horse rake, mowing machine, flowered wallpaper, ingrain carpets, women's fashions from the National Cloak and Suit Company, and ruffled curtains from Sears, Roebuck. The simple old ways of hamlet and farm were merged into an intricate civilization. Food processing moved from the home to food factories. The family marketer could no longer candle every egg or vouch personally for the milk supply. And so, for a period around the beginning of the present century, technology ran ahead of conscience. The small state of North Dakota alone consumed ten times as much "maple syrup" as Vermont produced, and the familiar Maine herring was dressed up like a hussy as "imported French sardines" and came in fancy boxes labeled in the French language. The federal Food and Drug Act, which became law in 1906, regulated commerce in misbranded and adulterated foods and beverages. Subsequently strengthened by legal interpretations and amendments, the law produced a revolution in factory food-processing and effectively redressed the balance between manufacturer and consumer.

Today there is no question about the general integrity of our food supply. We enjoy a variety and a quality of food materials which would have astounded the victualers of old New England. To this abundance we have added the graces, a belated appreciation of what the great nutritionist Dr. Harvey W. Wiley called the "social function of food"—the charm of service and setting. We are heirs of the past, masters

if we choose to be, of the lore of blackberry grunt, of Indian pudding, sweet corn caramelized in its own husks, Vermont bean soup eaten with Montpelier crackers—of, in short, the Americana of the kitchen. Cranberry sauce pleases the imagination as well as the taste, bringing to mind the reds of September. Steamed clams remind one of the tang of the spray on Nauset Beach. Baked cod conveys the indefinable flavor of the days of long ago, perpetuates the memory of the captains who sleep on the hill behind the silver-gray meetinghouse.

Come—move the coffeepot to the back of the range and close the damper. Squeeze the genealogical section of the *Transcript* into the pot's spout. The baked beans are waiting for a rendezvous in the earthenware pot—those plump, shiny yellow-eyes, molasses-dark, their skins fairly bursting with goodness, the slashed salt pork peeking provocatively through the crusted surface. Before the beans have fairly stopped bubbling, lace them with grandma's old-fashioned ketchup. Here's the brown bread, warm, sliced thin, lightly dappled with cow's butter.

Let those who will, sigh for their duck bigarade and Rock Cornish hens. Let them sound the praises of their entremets and *vol-au-vents*. To the Yankee race, from Maine to California, there are dearer glories—blueberry slump and the small-mouthed pot of baked beans. It is a simple style of cookery perhaps. But it has integrity and there are those who love it.

Catharine Beecher

CATHARINE BEECHER

By Gerald Carson

Daughter of a famous New England family, this cookbook authoress, teacher, and pioneer home economist urged every housewife to "regard her duties as dignified, important, and difficult"

"Why," George B. Emerson, New England educator and author of *A Lecture on the Education of Females,* was asking in the 1830's and 40's, "may not the healthiness of different kinds of food and drink, the proper modes of cooking . . . be discussed as properly as rules of grammar, or facts in history?"

Emerson found an affirmative answer to his rhetorical question in a book published in 1841 by Miss Catharine Esther Beecher, a pioneer herself in the field of women's education, able, witty, dedicated, and a member of the formidable clan of New England Beechers. The then-novel idea that women's "sacred duties" should be treated as an academic subject was advanced so persuasively in Catharine Beecher's *A Treatise on Domestic Economy for the use of Young Ladies at Home and at School* that Emerson endorsed the book and used it as a text in his own private school in Boston.

The *Treatise,* later supplemented by *Miss Beecher's Domestic Receipt-Book* (1846), a collection of recipes and practical procedures, broke new ground in presenting the household arts in a setting of general principles. From the time when the first colonial goodwife had placed her bannock cakes on a board before the glowing coals or improvised a whisk to beat up a syllabub, until almost two hundred years later, there was no printed guide to cookery which took into account her situation in the New World. The colonial cook depended upon tradition, memory, and manuscript "receipt" books.

A small number of English works on housewifery were brought over, but the literature of cookery which the American homemaker could tap was slight—a judgment based upon what knowledge we have of colonial private libraries. Women read, if they read at all, works of piety, the novels of Samuel Richardson, occasionally "bookes of cookerie." The circumstances of life and heavy executive responsibilities did not encourage the chatelaine of a colonial household to consult books.

W illiam Parks, public printer of Williamsburg, Virginia, issued in 1742 the first work on the art of cookery that was relevant to American needs. The publication was a revision of E. Smith's *The Compleat Housewife,* which appeared in England in 1727. Parks excluded recipes calling for food materials not available here, but added nothing native to our coasts. Indeed, it was not until the late eighteenth century that corn, our American maize, showed up in a printed recipe. This happy event occurred when Amelia Simmons, who described herself as an American Orphan, appeared as author of a modest, paper-covered little volume of forty-seven pages. It was entitled *American Cookery,* and in 1796 it came off a press in Hartford, Connecticut. Little is known of Amelia Simmons except that her education was so slight that she employed another person to put her "receipts" in form for publication.

Although Amelia did some borrowing from English works, as she herself was later plundered, her cookbook was American in spirit, written in a muscular vernacular – slapjack for griddle-cakes, molasses for treacle – and Miss Simmons enjoys the distinction of printing *five* recipes calling for corn meal. She also introduced recipes for Jerusalem artichokes and spruce beer and gave instructions for making *soft* gingerbread. (European gingerbread was hard and thin, like a modern cooky.) When a second edition of her book was required, Amelia added new features which were completely American—such as Election Cake and that staff of New England life, rye 'n' Injun. Election Cake was a New England institution, a fruity, spiced, rich, and highly flavored cake with a bread-dough base, served only on "town meetin'" days, when the male members of the family were suitably rewarded for their labors in making history at the polls. Rye 'n' Injun was a dark bread made from a mixture of rye flour, the meal of white flint corn, molasses, and yeast.

The best rye 'n' Injun came from the seacoast counties of Rhode Island, according to Shepherd Tom Hazard of the Narragansett Hazards, and was water-ground by millstones of Rhode Island granite; the bread was baked in a fireplace, not in an iron stove. It was because Nathanael Greene was nourished on genuine Rhode Island corn meal,

Shepherd Tom averred in his delightful *Jonny-Cake Papers*, that Greene became our Number Two general in the war for independence; and if he had been born in Washington or Newport counties instead of Kent and had grown up on their more genial and delicious grains, he would undoubtedly have gotten ahead of George Washington, who ate hoecake made from inferior Virginia corn, baked on the blade of a hoe.

In Amelia Simmons one encounters for the first time cranberry sauce, pumpkin pies and New England mince pie, watermelon-rind pickles, and pearlash—purified potash—as a leavening agent, precursor of baking powder. Here at last was a start toward an "American mode of cooking." The American Orphan was reprinted in various editions for thirty-five years, and appeared frequently in unacknowledged versions.

Cooking practices began to be codified during and after the late 1820's by the writings of Lydia Maria Child, Miss Eliza Leslie of Philadelphia, Sarah Josepha Hale (Nathaniel Hawthorne once cooked corned beef "exquisitely" by faithfully following Mrs. Hale's instructions), Esther Allen Howland, the wife of a Worcester bookseller, and Mary Randolph, who wrote *The Virginia Housewife* in 1824. This was the first American regional cookbook, to be followed by countless others recording gustatory glories with a local character—Block Island corn chowder, roast oysters Savannah, New Orleans bouillabaisse, fried Mexican beans. Mrs. Randolph dealt authoritatively with such southern delicacies as turtle soup, Virginia ham, and gooseberry fool, a sort of custard made of crushed berries mixed with whipped cream and sugar.

Catharine Beecher's *Treatise* lifted the subject of woman's role in the kitchen to a new level and marks the beginning of the movement toward serious education in the household arts. In her *Receipt-Book,* Miss Beecher discussed ovens, utensils, the buying and storing of foodstuffs, meat cookery, yeast and breadmaking, the preparation of "temperance drinks," baking and pickling. She offered suggestions on child feeding and directions for making butter and cheese in the home, obtained, she wrote with evident relish, from a man in Goshen, Connecticut, "a place distinguished all over the nation for the finest butter and cheese." Miss Beecher added significantly that she did not copy her material out of other books and that her recipes had been tested by "superior housekeepers."

Catharine Esther Beecher was born September 6, 1800, daughter of an eminent Presbyterian clergyman, the Reverend Lyman Beecher, in East Hampton, Long Island. She was the eldest child in a large family which included the famous Harriet and the Reverend Henry Ward Beecher. Her girlhood was passed in Litchfield, Connecticut, where the cultivated Beechers found a congenial and "elegant" society. There, Catharine attended Miss Sarah Pierce's school for young ladies, learned "the primary branches," and acquired the polite accomplishments—drawing, piano—suited to the social position, if not necessarily the talents, of well-placed young ladies. Drilled in household tasks by a careful mother, later by an orderly stepmother, educated by independent study in "the higher branches," filled with an inchoate desire to be useful in the world—Catharine fell in love.

But the dream of domestic happiness was tragically shattered when Catharine's fiancé, brilliant, young Professor Alexander Metcalf Fisher of Yale College, was lost in a shipwreck off the coast of Ireland. Stricken with grief made more cruel by her father's opinion that Professor Fisher's soul was in eternal torment because he presumably died too suddenly to have made a settlement with the God of Calvinism, Catharine turned to "living to do good." Spinsters in the 1820's could run a boardinghouse or teach. Catharine started a small school in Hartford, where her sister Harriet was one of the scholars. This successful enterprise was repeated in Cincinnati, with Harriet as assistant principal, when their father was called west to become president of Lane Theological Seminary.

It was as a result of her Cincinnati experiences that Catharine wrote her influential books. Pursuing her mission, Catharine undertook what proved to be an insuperable task—obtaining endowments for schools to instruct young women in homemaking techniques, along with the liberal arts subjects taught in men's colleges. Catharine recruited teachers in the East, organized and staffed schools in Burlington, Iowa; Quincy, Illinois; and Milwaukee, Wisconsin. None attained the permanence she hoped for.

Yet Catharine's writings and ideas were read and discussed, serving to create a new climate of opinion. She and Harriet, the latter having become Mrs. Stowe and a world celebrity as author of *Uncle Tom's Cabin*, collaborated on *The American Woman's Home; or, Principles of Domestic Science . . .* (1869), an expansion of the original *Treatise*. Other enlargements of Catharine's 1841 material followed: *The New Housekeeper's Manual* in 1873, and *Housekeeper and Healthkeeper*, issued the same year. These books were sold by the door-to-door method. Catharine Beecher noted with satisfaction that the canvassers carried her books into every state in the Union.

The deficiencies of the cookbooks of the period came under shrewd appraisal from Catharine. They had an English background. The recipes were stated too generally to be useful. The dishes and menus were rich and fussy. "Half of the recipes in our cook-books," Miss Beecher said, "are mere murder to such constitutions and stomachs as we grow here." The English dishes, she explained, were all right for a foggy, chilly island in the North Sea. But, "in America, owing to our brighter skies and more fervid climate, we have developed an acute, nervous delicacy of temperament far more akin to that of France than of England."

In 1877 Catharine Beecher went to make her home with her half brother, the Reverend Thomas K. Beecher, affectionately known as Father Tom, in Elmira, New York. While living in this household Catharine was stricken with apoplexy and died, May 12, 1878. One can grasp something of her character and personality from pictures that have come down to us: the strong face set off demurely by corkscrew curls, a prim headdress, and white fichu, the eyes wonderfully intelligent, humorous, and filled with the light of purpose. Her abounding faith in humanity, and specifically, in the future promise of American life, was unshakable. In her last days, Catharine was still forming committees, still writing, still in touch with civic leaders, teachers and educational administrators, bishops and statesmen, singing in a quavering voice to her own tinkling accompaniment in the parlor at Elmira, "It's better farther on."

As a reformer and thinker who kept a sound balance between general theory and practical detail, Miss Beecher saluted the nineteenth-century homemaker with a touch of Churchillian eloquence as "the sovereign of an empire" who "should regard her duties as dignified, important and difficult." Her writings in the field later known as domestic science were best sellers for over a generation and were, wrote her grandnephew Lyman Beecher Stowe in his entertaining *Saints, Sinners and Beechers,* "almost as omnipresent in American homes as was in an earlier day, Benjamin Franklin's *Poor Richard's Almanack.*"

Yet history has neglected the woman who occupies first place among the founders of the homemaking movement in America. Was Catharine simply overwhelmed by a father who was the embodied conscience of the evangelical middle classes and lived with a lively sense that the ages were looking down upon him? By Harriet and God, who she said helped her write *Uncle Tom's Cabin?* By the spectacular Henry Ward Beecher, who sold slaves from his Brooklyn pulpit to people who would set them free? Harriet, after all, could cook as well as write; and Henry's tribute to hot apple pie and ripe cheese is still enough to set man or boy to drooling. A more likely hypothesis tends in this direction: the woman's rights movement became absorbed, as a practical matter, in the suffrage question, and its rationale came to rest upon the proposition that women are not only equal to but identical with men in their capacities. This represented a turning away from Miss Beecher's whole body of thought that women occupied a special place in the world *as women.* The freedom the old leaders fought for has long been won, yet women still make homes, still reign over families. Perhaps now we can appreciate better than did the generation that followed her, how much Catharine Esther Beecher did to make life easier for the ordinary homemaker.

Cookery literature became more exact in the 1870's as ladies' cooking classes in eastern cities developed a new body of data. Miss Juliet Corson opened the New York Cooking School in 1876. (The Plain Cook's class, incidentally, was the most popular.) In Boston, Miss Maria Parloa and Miss Johanna Sweeney were associated with Mrs. Mary Johnson Bailey Lincoln in the establishment of the Boston Cooking School, its fame made imperishable by a later principal, Fannie Farmer (*see* page 293). The cooking schools, while improving the cookery books, also turned out capable young girls, "whom young men want to marry," as Henry T. Finck observed, in his *Food and Flavor*.

By this time the United States did indeed have a New Woman, the urban wife who tended no home garden, cherished no family cow or pig, and made no more soap out of her grease and ashes but cooked over gas and purchased foods processed in food factories. She needed a new kind of information to meet new trends in eating and in food preservation, new guidance as to diet and food values. But women could not be pushed too fast. The reason appears in an anecdote often told by Mrs. Ellen H. Richards, chemist and pioneer home economist, when she was director of the New England Kitchen, an experiment in the scientific feeding of workingmen and their families. Mrs. Richards quoted one of her clients as saying: "I don't want to eat what's good for me; I'd ruther eat what I'd ruther."

One hopes that there is an all-electric, experimental kitchen in heaven with gleaming work surfaces of thermosetting resins, where Amelia Simmons, Mrs. Randolph, Catharine Beecher, yes, and Fannie Farmer, too, may compare their experiences which span a century—from trivet and trammel to the gas range. Surely they would find common ground with each other and with that still earlier authority on the pleasures of the table, William Shakespeare, whose Macbeth declared, "Now good digestion wait on appetite And health on both!"

THE YANKEE KITCHEN

A Picture Portfolio

All the pig had to do in this nineteenth-century trade sign was to pull a steaming pot of baked beans. In real life, however, the pig's role was more integral: pieces of salt pork were cooked with beans and molasses for several hours, then served with brown bread.

Coastal Bounty

"But when that smoking chowder came in, the mystery was delightfully explained. Oh! sweet friends, hearken to me. It was made of small juicy clams, scarcely bigger than hazel nuts, mixed with pounded ship biscuits and salted pork cut up into little flakes! the whole enriched with butter, and plentifully seasoned with pepper and salt . . . we despatched it with great expedition."

The clam chowder that so enraptured Ishmael in Herman Melville's *Moby Dick* was standard fare along the New England coast, where the Yankee needed only his bare hands—or at most a net and a boat—to obtain a variety of tempting foods. Lobsters (colonial diarists reported some weighing twenty-five pounds) and crabs; bass, cod, and scrod; berries of all sorts—these were available, as Winslow Homer's pictures show, to anyone desiring them.

In The Herring Net, *above, a pair of slickered fishermen seine on a choppy sea.*

Clambakes were invented by the Indians and adopted quickly by New Englanders.

t left, berries for pies and puddings are gathered on a coastal hilltop.

Horse-drawn sleds carried the sap to the sugaring camps.

Constant attention and frequent stirring were required.

Inside the sap-house, the boiling off went on for days.

When
the Sap
Ran

The gaiety of a sugaring party was captured by Eastman Johnson in this 1865 painting.

Sugaring time was a festive period in New England, with the cold air permeated by the sweet smell of boiling sap, with sugar-on-snow parties delighting the youngsters. But it was also a time for hard work. The maple trees had to be tapped, and each day's accumulation of clear sap transported over the snow to the sugar camps. It took about thirty-five gallons of sap to produce just one gallon of syrup. The boiling process was long and arduous, and the impurities had to be removed by straining the syrup through pieces of cloth or blankets. But from this annual labor came the crystallized maple sugar and the amber syrup that sweetened a family's food until the sap ran once more.

The wooden mold above was used to make decorative maple-sugar candy. The mold is shown closed (at left) and separated in halves.

A Maine "Pic Nick"

J. B. Thompson's idyllic painting of a "pic nick" (the artist's spelling) was probably done near Camden, Maine, in the 1850's. It suggests that such festive outings were marked not only by good eating and drinking but also by music and flirtations.

Apple parer

Coffee mill

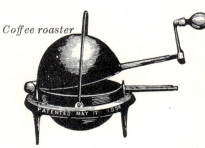

Coffee roaster

Egg beater

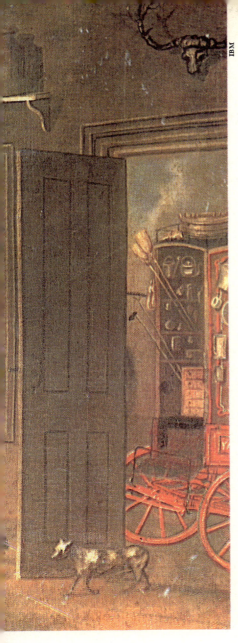

IBM

The Yankee Peddler

The day the peddler called was a bright one for the housewives of rural New England. These itinerant hawkers brought with them not only labor-saving kitchen devices like the ones shown below and a myriad of other items ranging from shoelaces to cloth, but also news and gossip, which they were more than willing to exchange for a cup of apple cider or a potluck supper. At first the Yankee peddlers carried their wares on their backs; later, in wagons filled to overflowing, they traveled to the Far West and South. Their prices were sometimes higher than their ethics, but it was a rare woman who did not welcome them.

At left, two women find it hard to concentrate on preparing dinner while the peddler shows his goods.

Jelly molds

Teakettle

Lemon squeezer

Cherry pitter

109

"Such a Vegetable"

In 1835, in Massachusetts, the English visitor Harriet Martineau was first introduced to corn on the cob. "The greatest drawback," she wrote, "is the way in which it is necessary to eat it. . . . It looks awkward enough: but what is to be done? Surrendering such a vegetable from considerations of grace is not to be thought of." To resident New Englanders, however, corn was not a delicacy but a staple, appearing at almost every meal in breads, porridges, or puddings. And after each harvest, neighbors gathered at husking bees, events marked by songs and dances and by the blushes of the girls who found red ears of corn and thereby earned the right to demand a kiss from the young man of their choice.

The metal device above was employed to remove the husks from the corncob. In the Eastman Johnson painting at left, a farmer pours corn onto a cloth so that the wind will carry off the chaff. At right is a husking bee, as pictured in a Harper's Weekly *of 1858.*

Harper's Weekly, NOVEMBER 13, 1858

Apples and Cider

One box of Pettit's Preservative (forty cents) kept fifty gallons of cider from fermenting.

In the 1830's, when the temperance movement flourished in America, fanatic teetotalers took up axes and flailed away at whole orchards of apple trees. With no thought for the delights of apple pie or syrupy baked apples, they were bent on eliminating the evil of hard cider. From colonial times, cider had been the most popular drink in New England. Served at meals and offered to all guests, it was also used for barter, as indicated by this entry in an 1805 diary: "one-half barrel of cider for Mary's schooling."

The cider-making process is illustrated in the painting at left by William M. Davis. The ripe apples were first shoveled into a round trough, where they were crushed by a horse-drawn roller. Then the pulp was carried to a press (right), where the juice was extracted.

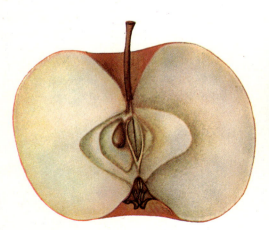

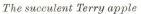

The succulent Terry apple

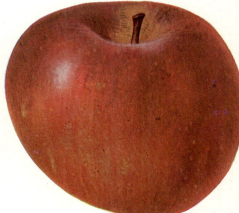

NOTICE

Step up ye gallant fair and brave!
  Step up, Tom, Jake and Kate,
Unto my store in Norwalk town,
  In Main Street, number eight!

In Main street, number eight, good folks
  Things very cheap are sold,
To fat and lean, to rich and poor,
  And to the young and old.

It is the cheap Cash Store, my friends:
  At J. W. Renoud's, please call,
And find things sold at reason's fee,
  To one, to ten, to all!

Yes, find things sold at reason's fee,
  Bread, butter, candles, cheese,
Salt, Onions, Crackers, Coffee, Brooms,
  And choicest, best of Teas!

Sugar and Alspice, Flour and Pork,
  And *matches,* not the kind
The young folks often, often make,
  So pleasing to the mind;

Theirs will light up their future hopes
  And gratify desire!
While mine on a cold winter's day,
  Will soon light up a fire.

There's Yeast, Molasses, Eggs & Ham
  Not *Ham* of olden days,
Who lived with Noah in the ark,
  And sang sweet sacred lays!

No, this is Ham that fills us up,
  And gives us strength to work,
And flog the French, the Spanish and
  The Russian and the Turk.

I've fine Codfish, Mackerel & Starch,
  Tobacco, choicest brand,
And Ginger, Pepper, Chocolate,
  As good as in the land.

And Blue and Oats, & Colgate's Starch,
  Made from good Indian Corn,
And fit for Shirts of any man,
  Of any woman born.

But oh to name all things I keep
  Would puzzle even Mars,
But I must not forget to state
  I sell the best Segars.

And come my friends my goods are
    cheap,
  True, true, what I relate,
All kinds of Groceries you'll find
  In Main Street, number eight!

J. W. RENOUD.
Norwalk, August 16th, 1859.

Villagers line up for mail in the painting above by Thomas Wood. At left is an 1859 advertisement. Below, desire outweighs discretion.

The Country Store

The typical rural store boasted a wide variety of goods, with little or no system in their arrangement. Kegs of nails stood beside barrels of whale oil; harnesses and hardware hung from the rafters. On the long shelves, built often at the expense of windows, items ranging from licorice to mirrors were stored side by side. The rich odors of coffee, molasses, and tobacco merged into one pungent aroma. Here farmers bartered for what they could not grow themselves. Eggs were exchanged for buckshot, butter for tea and salt, maple sugar for frying pans. Post office and meetinghouse as well as market, the country store also served to tie the surrounding farms together into a single community.

Feeding the chickens

Churning butter

Pumping water

Cleaning vegetables

A Woman's Work...

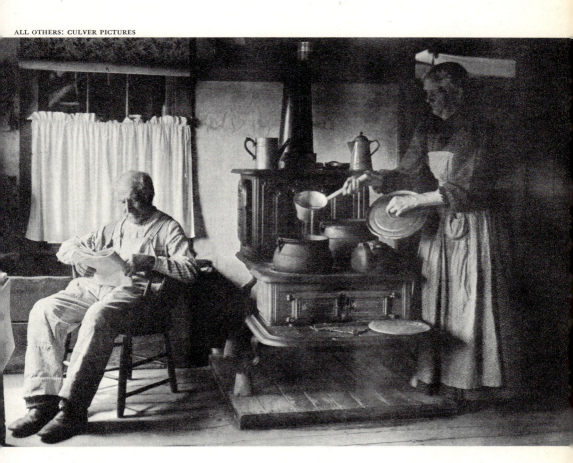

When Chansonetta Stanley Emmons took these photographs of rural Maine in the late nineteenth century, housewives had become used to many new conveniences. By then, they had stoves (above) instead of skirt-singeing fireplaces, and unlike their grandmothers, they had matches to light fires. They had Mason jars and newfangled revolving egg beaters. But the New England wife did not exult in her good fortune. She was too busy cooking, baking, and doing the other chores illustrated here, and perhaps recalling a poem that began: "Here lies a poor woman, who always was tired; She lived in a house where help was not hired."

After a day spent preparing food for immediate and future use, the hard-working Maine women above finally sat down to the fruits of their labors: supper.

Suppertime

4

SOUTHERN COOKING

By Marshall Fishwick

Whatever else southerners may have lacked, they have rarely been short on appetite, or regional delicacies to appease it. Drenched in sunlight, soaked in memory, their land has been well-loved, and their children well-fed.

No one should try to separate what men eat from what they think and what they are. Southern culture is strongly traditional and highly flavored, and so too is southern cookery. In the Confederate states, three cultural and gastronomic styles blended: Latin, Anglo-Saxon, and Negro — romance, tradition, and primitive strength.

In the water color at left, painted by Benjamin Latrobe in 1796, Martha Washington serves tea to the General and their guests on the portico of Mount Vernon.

The Spanish and the French came first, but the seaboard South was settled mainly by Elizabethans. Ill-prepared for the New World, these early Englishmen seldom ate well; in fact, they often starved to death.

From the beginning, however, grim reality was played against a glorious legend of abundance and plenty. *Eastward Hoe,* a 1605 play by George Chapman, John Marston, and Ben Jonson, contained the first European description of the South's standard of living. Says a character named Seagull: "[In the New World] all their dripping Pans . . . are pure gold . . . for Rubies and Diamonds they goe forth on holydayes and gather 'hem by the Seashore, to hang on their children's Coates." Writing a century later, the

121

Virginia historian Robert Beverley indicated how far settlers had come in their efforts to turn such wistful thinking into actuality: ". . . they have a great Plenty and Variety of Provisions for their Table," he reported in 1705, "and as for Spicery, and other things that the Country don't produce, they have constant supplies of 'em from England. The Gentry pretend to have their Victuals drest, and serv'd up as Nicely as at the best Tables in *London.* Their richer sort generally brew their Small-Beer with Malt, which they have from *England,* though they have as good Barley of their own, as any in the World. . . . Their Strong Drink is Madera Wine, which is a Noble strong Wine; and Punch, made either of Rum from the Caribbee Islands, or Brandy distilled from their Apples, and

Icehouse at Mount Vernon

Peaches; besides *French-Brandy,* Wine, and strong Beer, which they have constantly from *England."*

General morale improved with the diet. The valedictory address made by a youth at the 1699 May Day exercises at the College of William and

Mary bears this out. "Methinks," he said, "we see already that happy time when we shall surpass the Asiaticans in civility . . . the Egyptians in geometry, the Phoenicians in arithmetic, and the Chaldeans in astrology! Oh happy Virginia!"

Long before this balmy rhetoric, the days of Sir Walter Raleigh's sack posset (ale, sherry, eggs, boiled milk, seasoned to taste) had passed, and the Syllabub Era had arrived. A delightful concoction in which cream and wines are brought into a sensuous symbiosis, the syllabub existed long in folklore before it was described in the first cookbook published in this country: *The Compleat Housewife, or accomplish'd gentlewoman's companion* (Williamsburg, 1742). Colonists of high and low estate had by then become admirers of rich food and devotees of Bacchus. Governor Alexander Spotswood of Virginia had staged one of the all-time great "for men only" outings in connection with a trek to the top of the Blue Ridge. Though the country gentlemen who went along complained because "they had not good beds to lie on," they perked up immediately when they stood a-tiptoe on the crest of the mountains and drank a toast to King George. Lieutenant John Fontaine, who kept the official diary, reported: "We drank the King's health in champagne, and fired a volley; the Prince's health in Burgundy, and fired a volley; and all the rest of the royal family in claret, and a volley; we drank the Governor's health, and fired another volley."

All this was possible because these self-styled Knights of the Golden Horseshoe had included in their provisions "several sorts of liquor, viz.: Virginia red wine and white wine, Irish usquebaugh, brandy shrub, two sorts of rum, champagne, canary, cherry punch, cider, etc." One can only surmise that the explorers were prepared to float the Shenandoah Valley into the British Empire.

Gradually the South acquired a full-blown mythology, with food and drink to sustain it. People always live by the mythology of their time. The medievalists had their saints, the *philosophes* their reason, the British their empire. The South had its plantation. Here the alluring Garden of Eden myth found a local habitation and a name. Rural life (to quote Francis P. Gaines's *The Southern Plantation*) was "less hurried, less prosaically equalitarian, less futile, richer in picturesqueness, festivity, in realized pleasure that recked not of hope or fear or unrejoicing labor." And it was full of good things to eat and drink.

Planters managed the Garden—men like John Randolph of Roanoke, who could say: "I am an aristocrat. I love liberty. I hate equality." Men like Robert Toombs, who summed up the South's way of life in six words: "We are a race of gentlemen." Here dwelt (said William Alexander Caruthers) "that generous, fox-hunting, wine-drinking, duelling and reckless race of men which gives so distinct a character

to Virginians wherever they may be found." Southern gentlemen were to society what the mint is to the julep: they dwelt triumphantly on top.

Planted in the seventeenth century, plantation society took root throughout the South in the eighteenth and flowered in the nineteenth. General no-

I rose at 5 o'clock in the morning and read a chapter in Hebrew and 200 verses in Homer's Odyssey. *I ate milk for breakfast. I said my prayers. Jenny and Eugene [servants] were whipped. I danced my dance. I read law in the morning and Italian in the afternoon. I ate tough chicken for dinner.*

—From the diary of William Byrd, 1709

tions of British squires were bolstered by thoughts from French physiocrats and recipes from French kitchens. In manor houses like Nomini Hall, Westover, Mount Vernon, Holly Hill, Monticello, Hermitage, Mulberry Plantation, Dunleith, Drayton Hall, Belle Grove, and Shadows-on-the-Teche, American cookery and hospitality reached a peak which has seldom if ever been surpassed.

Such places were not merely houses, but little planetary systems around which a whole set of people and buildings orbited—schoolhouse, stables, hen house, dairy, dovecot, smokehouse, springhouse, slave quarters, icehouse, kitchen. Usually a short distance from the manor, the kitchen was full of the cook's wares: pots, kettles, waffle irons, swinging cranes, bake ovens, scales, iron firedogs holding rotating spits. This was the spot in which southern cooking had its inspiration and con-

---

Yesterday we had ninety persons to dine with us at one table,—put up on the lawn, under a thick arbor. The dinner was profuse and good, and the company very orderly. —Dolley Madison, July 5, 1820

---

summation. The demand was great: often as many as fifty, or even seventy, people would be on hand for a meal.

Conjuring up mental pictures of such lordly estates, we inevitably confront the plantation lady—fluttering her fan and filling guests' wineglasses —forgetting that she also managed a huge kitchen and staff with responsibilities that would floor the modern can-opening housewife. The plantation became a kind of matriarchy; the real focus was not the planter but his wife, whose benevolent rule extended over the entire household, white and black. Even if dalliance destroyed a planter's initiative, the need to serve countless meals and to assume unending responsibilities increased the woman's status and dignity. No wonder Thomas Nelson Page called her "mistress, manager, doctor, nurse, counsellor, seamstress, teacher, housekeeper, slave, all at once." She kept the keys and the recipes.

Records of the Virginia plantation Nomini Hall show that the annual food consumption included, among many other things, 27,000 pounds of pork, 20 beeves, 550 bushels of wheat (excluding corn eaten by servants), 4 hogsheads of rum, and 150 gallons of brandy. Philip Vickers Fithian, the Yankee tutor there in the 1770's, reported that after dark Mrs. Carter, the mistress, could be found in the yard, "seeing to the Roosting of her Poultry."

Such capable ladies held sway north of Tidewater Virginia as well as south. The plantation pattern thrived in Maryland and Delaware, where country gentlemen drew succulent treats from the rivers, inlets, and bays. Has anyone ever dealt more triumphantly with the oyster and the crab? Think of southern-fried oysters, pickled oysters, oysters *farcis*, pan-broiled oysters, scalloped oysters, oysters wrapped in bacon ("little pigs in blankets"), or deviled imperial crab, baked crab meat, crab salad, creamed crab, and crab cakes. With them one might well serve Miss Sallie's Maryland beaten biscuits. (For the uninitiated, Miss Sallie Cromer of Washington County achieved such heights in the kitchen that her name stuck to her recipe. She beat her batter with a wooden mallet until blisters appeared on the dough. It was indeed beaten—then each biscuit was stuck four times with a silver fork, for ritual as well as flavor.) Add to such regional specialties the standard items of plantation diet, and you know why one distinguished English traveler declared it worth a voyage across the Atlantic to have a Maryland feast and why the aged Hero of Two Worlds, General Lafayette, ate like a hungry young man on his 1824 visit to Baltimore. The culmination of his enthusiasm, a member of the welcoming committee reported, was reserved for the unsurpassed canvasback and hominy: "The consumption of a whole duck [was] the tribute paid by him to the excellence of our unequalled Southern winged delicacy . . ."

But people didn't have to come across the Atlantic to wax ecstatic about southern cooking. Many a north-

Fruit stand

erner was as impressed as Henry Barnard, who graduated from Yale in the 1830's, toured the Southland, and kept a diary of all he did. "I think you would delight to visit this region," he wrote home to his sister from Tidewater Virginia, "merely to observe the differ-

ence of manners and habits, from what you have been accustomed to, aye and to experience the princely hospitality of the *gentle* born families." He then described a succession of feasts like the dinner at Shirley: Mrs. Hill Carter was at one end of the table, with a large dish of rich soup; Mr. Carter at the other, with a saddle of fine mutton, buttressed by ham, beef, turkey, duck, and innumerable vegetables. The visitor had never seen such cooking. Barnard took pains to describe hominy—"made of their white corn and beans—a very fine dish." This part of the meal was followed by sparkling champagne. "After that off passes the things, and the *upper* table cloth, and upon the next one is placed the dessert, consisting of fine plum pudding, pies, tarts, etc. etc.—after this comes ice cream, West India preserves, peaches preserved in brandy, etc. When you have eaten this, off goes the second table cloth, and then upon the bare mahogany table is set the figs, raisins, and almonds . . . Madeira, Port, and a sweet wine for the ladies . . . after the first and second glass the ladies retire, and the gentlemen begin to circulate the bottle pretty briskly."

Novels, as well as the diaries of the time, give detailed accounts of the country gentleman at the table. A memorable example is Chapter 33 of John Pendleton Kennedy's *Swallow Barn,* that archetypal novel in which the streams of charm and verisimilitude merged in a broad meadow of episode. Swallow Barn was the name of a fictional plantation—an aristocratic old edifice which sat on a riverbank like a brooding hen. It was not merely a conglomeration of sticks and stones, but a storehouse of memory and tradition. The great dinner table seemed to be laden not in relationship to the guests' capacity but to its own dimensions. At the head, in the customary pride of place, was a goodly ham, rich in its own perfections, as well as in the endemic honors that belong to it. On it the cook had carved fanciful figures. Opposite was a huge roasted saddle of mutton which seemed, from its trim and spruce air, ready to gallop off the dish. In between was an enticing diversity of poultry, including fried chicken (sworn brother to the ham), another "must" for every country gentleman's table. Well-seasoned, rolled in flour, and sizzled in hot lard, this unjointed fowl was a regional triumph. So were the hot biscuits: a mixture of flour, lard, soda,

Oyster advertisement

and buttermilk, lightly kneaded, rolled, cut out, baked in an oven till brown, and served piping hot. Interspersed between oysters, crabs, and fish was a multitude of vegetables.

Southern cooks perfected their own way of seasoning and passed the secret on to their children. That made for an unbroken continuity of good eating. This was especially true in the rice country of the Carolinas, that narrow belt of land near the coast where the tides could be used to flood and drain the fields. Here men like William Aiken, who cultivated 1,500 acres of rice and 500 acres of corn, lived like feudal barons. Another rice planter, John Berkley Grimball, kept a diary from 1832 to 1880, which is a treasure-trove for historians. In July, 1833, he bought 200 bushels of corn, 15 pounds of bacon, and 100 pounds of tobacco for his people at Slann's Island—since they had all the fish, molasses, rice, and sweet potatoes they could eat. A little later Grimball was serving far different food to aristocratic friends at a plantation dinner: turtle soup, ham, boiled mutton, scalloped oysters, roast turkey, a haunch of venison, and—needless to say—mountains of rice. (Favorite recipes were boiled rice, Charleston red rice, South Carolina dry rice, and various pilaus.) All this was polished off with plum pudding, apple pie, floating island, blancmange, cheese, fruit, sherry and Madeira and claret wines. Let those who study the rise and fall of prices note that in 1833 such a dinner, for eight, cost Grimball twenty-seven dollars.

Local fish were highly prized, too. A paragraph from William Gilmore Simms's novel *The Forayers*, set in 1781 South Carolina, emphasizes this point: "The greatest delicacy of a fresh-water river, this is the Edisto blue cat—for very nice people a most discouraging name. Gentlemen, look to yourselves. Here is boiled fish, such as George the Third can not procure; dressed in a style which would not discredit the table of our great ally, the king of France."

The passage also hints at another important fact: politics can have a profound effect not only on the mind but on the stomach.

After the French alliance of 1778 many southern aristocrats adopted the fashionable cuisine of America's European ally. French soups, salads, bonbons, and fricassees were the order of the day. General Washington was served by a steward of French extraction; later on, Jefferson brought a French cook to the White House. During Monroe's administration the food-minded French minister Baron Hyde de Neuville delighted to have southern planters try his inventions: celery shaped like oysters, puddings in the form of fowl, codfish disguised in a salad, for instance. So pervasive was this Francophilia that in the 1830's the German visitor Francis Lieber observed that Americans had "somewhat engrafted" French cookery upon the English. Some of the fancy dishes did not hold up well, however, in the days before refrigeration. At one of the Washingtons' lordly presidential dinners, Mrs. Robert Morris found that the cream had soured in the dessert. When she whispered the news to the President, he immediately changed his plate. "But Mrs. Washington," the visitor noted, "ate a whole heap of it!"

If French cuisine made important advances in the upper South, it never lost its supremacy in parts of the Deep South. Northern visitors and foreigners seldom failed to marvel at this fact.

We have now not infrequently had mutton at table, the flavor of which is quite excellent...but it is invariably brought to table in lumps or chunks of no particular shape or size, and in which it is utterly impossible to recognize any part of the quadruped creature sheep...I at length inquired why a decent usual Christian joint of mutton...was never brought to table: the reply was that the carpenter always cut up the meat...
—Frances Anne Kemble,
on a Georgia plantation, 1839

"Here was Old France again!" wrote the visiting Englishman William Howard Russell when he toured Louisiana just before the Civil War. "One might imagine a lord of the seventeenth century in his hall, but for the black faces of the servitors and the strange dishes of tropical origin. There was the old French abundance, the numerous dishes and efflorescence of napkins, and the long-necked bottles of Bordeaux, with a steady current of pleasant small talk . . ." Reading details of what Russell did and ate, we fully understand his enthusiasm. Awakened early by a wonderful chorus of riotous mockingbirds and by a servant's assurance that *"Le seigneur vous attend,"* he went from one happy meal to another. Early coffee and biscuits made up a sort of preliminary breakfast. After a ride in the fields, where the Negroes were eating molasses, hominy, and boiled Indian corn, he returned to have his real breakfast, which included fish, prawns, and red meat. A later Deep South breakfast outdid this one: grilled fowl, prawns, eggs and ham, fish from New

---

I was so exceedingly surprised at seeing on the table a great variety of beautiful-looking bread, made both from fine wheaten flower and Indian corn, that I exclaimed, "Bless me, we must be in Virginia!"

—George Featherstonhaugh, 1834

Orleans, potted salmon, preserved meats from France, claret, ice water, coffee and tea, varieties of hominy, mush, African vegetable preparations, and "other delicate things." Here, on a single table, the three cultures blended into a single breakfast.

But even this epicurean delight was surpassed by morning meals served on those posh floating palaces, the Mississippi river boats, which opened service in 1835. Their history still brings tears to the eyes of nostalgic gourmets. Where can one go, now that they sail no more, for his *coquetier* (a mixed drink named for the tiny egg cup in which it was served to the ladies)? And where now can one sit down to a breakfast of beefsteak plain or with onions, à la Creole, Bordelaise, with mushrooms, or with tomatoes; ham, pork

chops, calves' liver, mutton chops, mackerel, and various assorted meats; and twelve kinds of hot breads? The current gastronomic hardships inflicted by the Jet Age are frightful to contemplate. The historically minded look back to the days when they could enjoy special treats that few of the new generation have ever tasted—such items as:

Hush puppies—golden-brown puffs invented to hush up the barking puppies at an outdoor feast; made by putting corn-bread batter into deep fat.

Corn dodgers—pone-shaped corn sticks so hard when first baked that if they were thrown, the intended victim dodged to keep from being hit.

Caillette—cabbage stuffed with bread crumbs, eggs, cheese, and seasoning; a delicacy brought over to North Carolina by Italian Waldensians after the Revolution. From the French word *cailler,* meaning "to curdle."

Chicken shortcake—creamed chicken served between squares of corn bread sliced in half like a hot biscuit; a favorite in the cotton belt.

Burgoo—a stew made in iron pots and usually served in enormous quantities. Gus Jaubert, one of General John Hunt Morgan's Confederate cavalrymen, used to take whatever "makings" Morgan's foragers brought into camp (including blackbirds on at least one occasion), put them into a huge saltpeter kettle, and produce a meal that Morgan's men never forgot. One old recipe called for "800 pounds of lean beef with no bones or fat, one dozen squirrels for each 100 gallons, and 240 pounds of fat hens or roosters, besides potatoes, cabbage, tomatoes, carrots, and other vegetables."

Hopping John—black-eyed peas combined with rice; a type of jambalaya, probably of Spanish origin. Some think the name is a tribute to a famous and lively waiter who brought the dish to customers at a fashionable Charleston hotel.

Hoecake—a small piece of hot bread made of biscuit dough and so named because it was originally cooked on a hoe. The accepted technique was to throw the cake from one hand to the other, slap it down on the hoe blade, and turn it once to brown the other side. *Ashcakes* were baked in hot ashes between two cabbage leaves. *Scratch backs* were corn pones dropped from a spoon on a buttered tin. Because they retained their rough tops, they could "scratch" the mouth.

Poke salad—a bowl of what southerners often called the wild greens (dandelion, pigweed, cowslip, turnip tops, and land cresses). Turnip greens especially have long been associated with southern home cooking.

Chitterlings (or chitlins)—the small intestines of swine, which were usually dipped in batter, then fried in deep fat until golden brown.

Such dishes were never typical of the whole South. The grain on which southern culture rests is corn; the indispensable meat is pork. They are, to most southerners, *food,* as the English traveler Harriet Martineau discovered

when she visited America in the mid-1830's. In the South, she wrote, corn was more valuable than gold. "A man who has corn may have everything. He can sow his land with it; and, for the rest, everything eats corn from slave to chick."

Unlike many crops, corn cannot reproduce itself; there is no such thing as a "wild" ear of corn. If the man dies, the cornfield perishes with him. But all over Dixie the corn lives. Stand in a Carolina or Georgia cornfield in Au-

Cutting sugar cane

gust and listen to the corn rustling and growing in the blazing sun. And, if you are a southerner, anticipate the multiple delights which are to follow.

Corn meal is one of the rich and savory products of our heritage. For breakfast it can be turned into light luscious battercakes; syrup-drenched waffles; muffins into which a pad of yellow butter has been absorbed forever; or grits, in which the butter is taking an early-morning swim.

For dinner try corn pone—golden-brown and hot from the oven, ready to be washed down with freshly churned buttermilk. (The word is derived from Indian *appone,* meaning "corn cake.") Or one might have corn dumplings, boiled with a mess of greens. Suppertime is ideal for hoecake, which cries out for gravy distilled from the juices of a country-cured ham; popcorn; or green sweet corn in its husks. The versatility of corn meal has intrigued southerners like Joel Chandler Harris. "Pot pie and chicken fixings . . ." Harris admitted, "are very good for a Sunday dinner, they fit the day, and tend to breed thought. . . . But they do not fit in well with hard work and practical business propositions. . . . But corn meal . . . lends itself to all days and all meals." Harris also formulated a basic axiom of southern life: "Real democracy and real republicanism, and the aspirations to which they give rise, are among the most potent results of corn meal, whether in the shape of the brown pone or the more delicate ash-cake, or the dripping and juicy dumpling."

With corn meal the southerner has traditionally eaten what the rest of the country calls pork, but which he calls meat, fat back, salt pork, sowbelly, or middlin'. Though most of the early English settlers were mutton eaters, they soon found that the pig prospered and sustained them better than the sheep. Pigs picked up their own living in all seasons and required no attention. The flavor of pork actually improves as a result of preservative processes. No other animal shares the pig's ability to increase its weight one-hundred-and-fifty-fold in the first eight months of life.

The frontier housewife in James Fenimore Cooper's *The Chainbearer* spoke for most southern families when she said: "I hold a family to be in a desperate way when the mother can see the bottom of the pork barrel. Give me the children that's raised on good

Southern barbecue

sound pork afore all the game in the country. Game's good as a relish and so's bread; but pork is the staff of life."

All parts of the hog were relished. Spareribs, backbones, ribs, and sausage were eulogized by southerners. Plain people were content with chitterlings, cracklings, pig's feet, and jowls. Bacon was used to supply the flavor for string beans, black-eyed peas, turnip tops, poke, mustard, and collards. Juice left in the container after the vegetables were removed—called "pot likker"—was said to have magical nutritive values. A whole line of politicians, including Huey Long, publicly extolled the unmatched virtues of corn pone and pot likker.

No self-respecting southern pig can imagine a higher distinction than becoming, in due course, a Virginia ham —spicy as a woman's tongue, sweet as her kiss, as tender as her love. The Virginia (or Tidewater) ham dates back to the mid-seventeenth century, when English piglets got loose and began to savor the local products—especially peanuts. Called earth chocolate, peanuts had been transplanted to Africa as a cheap food on slave ships; back in Virginia they were excellent fodder for pigs turned out to root in the sandy fields, and they gave hams a unique and unforgettable flavor. Let those who prefer Tennessee country ham backed with pickled peaches, Texas ham with corn-meal coating, Georgia country ham, glazed sugar-coated ham with champagne sauce, fried Kentucky ham with red gravy, Alabama ham loaf with mustard sauce, or Florida ham with cayenne pepper argue their cases. All one has to do to be completely won over to Virginia ham is to *eat* it.

Anyone who has read this far (let alone slipped off to sample a thin slice of Virginia ham) must be thirsty by now. Consider, for a moment, southern drinking habits. As has already been broadly hinted, drinking is both a favorite indoor and outdoor sport in the Four Kingdoms (tobacco, cotton, rice, and sugar). Hot weather, tradition, and natural inclination all point the way. No less a figure than the Father of our Country capitalized on this fact

They say that you may always know the grave of a Virginian as, from the quantity of juleps he has drunk, mint invariably springs up where he has been buried.
—Frederick Marryat, 1839

when he ran for the House of Burgesses. During the 1758 elections in Frederick County, Washington's agent supplied 160 gallons to the 391 qualified voters and "unnumbered hangers-on." The supporters of Washington were asked to choose not only between candidates but between spirits. Rum, punch, wine, beer, and cider royal flowed. Washington won handily.

Eschewing the smoother and lighter drinks of outlanders, southerners have remained true to corn whiskey and its sophisticated cousin, bourbon. The distillers in Maryland and Kentucky are generally considered proper sources, although in periods of great stress (Prohibition, for example) mountain stills are considered adequate. Hardly a man in the back country fails to respond with a wink if you ask him where you can get a little corn likker, moonshine, white lightnin', or rotgut.

The fame and flavor of bourbon have won many outside the region, but some mixed drinks are inextricably bound with the South. The most famous is the mint julep. At this high shrine it is time for us to do homage.

Historians say the julep (or *gulab*) originated in Persia, where it was a minted, nonalcoholic, fruit drink. Med-

Mint julep

ical people still use the word to refer to a sweet, demulcent mixture—but southerners reserve it for livelier and more potent occasions. For them it must be, as a *sine qua non,* alcoholic and delectable. There is no agreement among them on how a "proper" mint julep should be made, but those who smacked their lips at concoctions served at the Pearl Street House in ante-bellum Louisville put up an impressive case. Having done considerable research on this whole matter, in books and bottles, I am casting my lot with their prescription:

"Take a large and deep cut-glass tumbler, fill it with sufficient sugar and ice to the brim—half of the ice shaved into snow and the rest in lumps of moderate size. Lay on the top of it three fresh leaves of mint without any part of the stem attached. Pour on just half a glass of fine, unimpeachable cognac brandy, then just half a glass of fine old Jamaica rum; then add half a glass of old ripe port wine. Then pour the mass rapidly for some time, back and forth in two tumblers; the longer this action continues the better. Then plant a small bunch of mint on one side of the tumbler by putting the stems down into the ice, and having the leaves up about as high as the nose of the drinker should come." Now—drink up!

Even as I put the words to paper I can hear the contentious uproar. Kentuckians will be gathering to swear that the insult just done to their bourbon whiskey calls for revenge. The julep must be prepared only in a *silver* goblet. The mint leaf must be crushed gently between the thumb and forefinger, the goblet nearly filled with shaved ice. Then add all the bourbon the goblet will hold. A few mint sprigs should decorate the top, after it has been frappéed with a spoon. A straw is strictly forbidden. It must be *sipped*.

"Nonsense!" advocates of Alabama mint juleps will shout. "Anyone knows you take a double handful of mint leaves and crush them until well bruised. These you drop into a saucepan of boiling water, adding sugar to make a syrup. This mint syrup is poured over the ice—*then* the glass is filled with whiskey. And, of course, a sprig of mint is stuck into the ice." So it goes.

Another approach might be to analyze the mint juleps which turn up in southern literature and travel accounts. When William Russell got ready to take his morning bath in Mississippi, he was given a mint julep as an adjunct. The main ingredients were brandy, sugar, and peppermint beneath an island of ice. Soon the servant came in with a second one, announcing: "Massa say fever very bad this morning—much dew." After a respectable time he returned with mint julep number three: "Massa says, Sir, you had better take this, because it'll be the last he make before breakfast!"

But even as Russell was drinking up, time was running out for the plantation South. The Civil War was approaching, with its insurrection and invasion, hunger and chaos. The country gentlemen would fight hard, and for a while they would talk of victory. Wounded Rebel soldiers would be carried to Richmond where (wrote Caroline Harrison in 1861) "residents of . . . houses standing back in gardens full of roses set their cooks to work . . . to compound delicious messes . . . after the appetizing old Virginia recipes." White-jacketed Negroes carried "silver trays with dishes of fine porcelain under napkins of thick white damask, containing soups, creams, jellies, thin biscuit . . . chicken, etc., surmounted by clusters of freshly gathered flowers." The flowers withered; the fancy foods disappeared. In 1865 Sheridan's well-fed cavalry finally cut off Lee's starved tatterdemalions at Appomattox. For the plantation South, the power and the glory disappeared.

No matter how great the cataclysm, history always preserves old fragments to adorn the new order. The remnants remain. South of the Potomac memories and recipes endure—thanks often to wealthy outsiders entranced by the "southern way of life." Unhurried cooks still measure by hand and taste. Hams are cured slowly by hickory smoke. Some anachronistic souls still like the lettuce in their salad and the

You are very fortunate to be assigned to duty at Fortress Monroe [on Chesapeake Bay]; it is just the season for soft-shelled crabs, and hog fish have just come in, and they are the most delicious pan fish you ever ate.

—General Winfield Scott, May, 1861,
to General Benjamin Butler

mint in their julep fresh from their garden, not from the supermarket. The world beyond their picket fences has a radically different tone and tempo. A raucous new band plays revolutionary music. They prefer to listen to the sweeter, slower songs of the past, to reminisce with Thomas Nelson Page's Old Sam: "De voice soundin' low like bees, and the moon sort of meltin' over the lawn . . . soft music floatin' out from de open window, and all de ladies laughin'. Laws, de old times done come back again!"

Thomas Jefferson, by Charles W. Peale

THOMAS JEFFERSON

By Marshall Fishwick

Gourmet, gracious host, and enthusiastic farmer, the Sage of Monticello brought recipes and delicacies from France to America, only to be accused of having "abjured his native victuals"

During the Jeffersonian years almost everybody who was anybody visited Monticello. Reactions to the man and the manor varied greatly; but research shows that no one who went there ever came away hungry.

Thomas Jefferson's admirers and biographers cite endlessly three achievements (the Declaration of Independence, Virginia's Statute for Religious Freedom, the University of Virginia), which the Sage himself suggested for his epitaph. Some go further, noting that he could design a plow, translate an ode, play a violin, found a political party, or calculate an eclipse. But how many acknowledge that the savant was a gourmet—not only a leading one in his day, but in all American history?

Not one puritanical pang pulled at Jefferson's heartstrings as he savored an exquisite meal and a vintage wine. "I am an Epicurean," he wrote to his friend and protégé William Short—who, having purchased in Europe for Jefferson such items as Parmesan cheese, boned anchovies, tarragon vinegar, Dijon mustard, and a pipe (126 gallons) of Madeira, had no reason to doubt the claim. The Jefferson he knew could season a salad, cure a ham, write a definitive evaluation of Burgundy or Rhine wines, or stock the wine cellar for the White House.

His interest in good food and drink rested on three pillars: inheritance, personality, and philosophy. Jefferson's leisure was made possible by three generations of slaves. As a youth he enjoyed fine cooking at plantations like Tuckahoe, Dungeness, Ampthill, and Eppington; later on, in towns like Annapolis, Philadelphia, and New York. As a student at Williamsburg, he often dined with urbane Governor Francis Fauquier. He fell naturally into the expected social pattern of the gentry. Hospitality was his heritage.

So were a convivial personality and a passion for social amenities. "Man was destined for society," Jefferson wrote. He hated to be or to eat alone and felt that without good talk and good wine, men would sour and lose their vitality. His whole philosophy favored the enjoyment of the fruits of a benevolent Creator. The brave new world had been put here, he reasoned, for men to toast and enjoy.

Small wonder, then, that Jefferson rejoiced at the prospect of a reduction on wine duties by the federal government—for moral as well as for personal reasons. "No nation is drunken where wine is cheap," he wrote, "and none sober, where the dearness of wine substitutes ardent spirits as the common beverage . . ."

All that Jefferson was and aspired to be combined to make him an eminent and dedicated gourmet. That his career centered around law and politics was more accidental than deliberate. His lifelong ambition was to be a gentleman planter. The goals of such a person he expressed with characteristic precision and clarity: "His estate supplies a good table, clothes himself and his family, furnishes a surplus to buy salt, sugar, coffee, and a little finery for his wife and daughters, enables him to receive and visit his friends, and furnishes him pleasing and healthy occupations."

Admitted to the bar at twenty-four, Jefferson took his seat in the House of Burgesses two years later. Married at twenty-nine, he embarked upon a task which continued for the rest of his life: to make the estate named Monticello ("Little Mountain" in Italian) a worthy place—intellectually, socially, gastronomically—for himself, his family, and his friends.

Incredibly detailed records and letters tell the story. His garden books, for example, begun when he was a boy at Shadwell, covered half a century. No vegetable was too exotic, none too commonplace, for this agrarian-epicure. Succory, endive, Spanish onions, savoy, turnips, various beans, sugar beets: he insisted on having them all in his garden. Later on he experimented with cucumbers, cabbage, spinach, sprouts and squash, salsify, potatoes, artichokes, lettuce, cauliflower, eggplant—and was never too busy to make careful tables of their appearance and departure. The original ground plans for Monticello were meant to assure the availability of game to match the "succulents." "Keep it in deer, rabbits, peacocks, guinea, poultry, pigeons, etc.," he instructed his overseer. "Let it be an asylum for hares, squirrels, pheasants, partridges, and every other wild animal (except those of prey). Court them to it by laying food for them in proper places."

One of Jefferson's passions was to produce fine local wine. Through the efforts of an Italian named Philip Mazzei and a group of Tuscan vignerons, portions of Jefferson's vineyard prospered. He also tried orange trees with "new shoots from old roots brought from Italy." In his 1774 *Garden Book* he gives instruction for a garden 686 feet long, 80 feet wide, "and at each end forms a triangle . . . of which the legs are 80 feet and the hypothenuse 113 feet." Then he outlines the day-by-day planting schedule for the last week in March.

On the first day, carrots from Pisa, Salmon radishes, Lattuga lettuce, Windsor beans, cluster peas, spinach, and vetch were to be put out. The next day would center on a major culinary item: peas. The third day would see the green lentils and black-eyed peas in the ground; then followed the *grano estivo* (summer wheat) from Tuscany (in seven rows), celery, radishes, cress, nasturtium (in thirty-five hills). After this, an orchard of apples, cherries, almonds, and olive slips must be put out. Later on there would be greengage plums, plum peaches, carnation cherries, French chestnuts, and English mulberries. The overseer, Edmund Bacon, recalled: "I have never seen such a place for fruit . . . He [Jefferson] always knew all about everything in every part of his grounds and garden. He knew the name of every tree, and just where one was dead or missing."

The young planter loved every growing thing at Monticello, and every meal produced by his cooks. Yet he was to be constantly away from home for the next forty years. While he was planting unusual vegetables, Bostonians were having an extraordinary Tea Party. Soon Jefferson left for the Continental Congress, then took on a wartime governorship — committing his heart and mind to the cause of freedom. This didn't mean there was no time for fancy food. In Philadelphia he explored fine dining rooms with such good eaters as Benjamin Franklin and John Adams. The latter gentleman recalled one unforgettable encounter with "Ducks, Hams, Chickens, Beef, Pigg, Tarts, Creams, Custards, gellies, fools, Trifles, floating Islands, Beer, Porter, Punch, Wine." To appease his conscience Adams labeled such superb meals "sinful feasts." His friend from Monticello was content to eat and record the recipes for later use.

Patriots' souls were tried and not found wanting. The war was won. In 1785 Jefferson went to France to serve as American minister—and to wed Virginian and French cooking in one of the happiest unions recorded in the history of cookery.

He went, he saw, France conquered. The glories of French cuisine never had a stouter defender. Whenever he could, the Minister turned his attention from treaties to recipes, recording memorable ones like this for making meringues: *"12 blanc d'oeuf, les fouettes bien fermes, 12 cueillerres de sucre en poudre,* put them by little and little into the whites of eggs, *fouetter le tout ensemble, dresser les sur un papier avec un cueiller de bouche, metter les dans un four bien doux,* that is to say an oven after the bread is drawn out. You may leave there as long as you please."

After Paris, the provinces. He was not above advising the native Lafayette on how to tour France. "You must be absolutely incognito," he advised the General in a letter dated April 11, 1787. "You must ferret people out of their hovels, as I have done, look into their kettles, eat their bread, loll on their beds under pretense of resting yourself, but in fact to find if they are soft. . . . [Later on] you shall be able to apply your knowledge to the softening of their beds, or the throwing a morsel of meat into their kettle of vegetables." En route Jefferson noted everything: the seedless grapes at Marseille, the strawberries at Castres, cheeses in Provence, wild gooseberries at Beaujolais, blooming almonds at Lyons. He looked for plums at Brignoles, stopping to measure a mule. His comments on French wines filled pages.

When the day of his departure arrived, a sad but well-fed Jefferson went to the docks loaded down with cookbooks and plants. A new job, as President Washington's Secretary of State, awaited him; one of his first duties would be to order French wines for state dinners. Exasperated nativists spoke out against such carryings-on. Jefferson came home from France so Frenchified, complained Patrick Henry, "that he abjured his native victuals."

When he became President, Jefferson set culinary standards which have never been matched in the White House. Among those who begrudged him this distinction was his immediate predecessor—that good eater but bad loser, John Adams. "I dined a large company once or twice a week," he wrote. "Jefferson dined a dozen every day. I held levees once a week. Jefferson's whole eight years was a levee." He served such novelties as "French fries" with beefsteak, desserts flavored with vanilla, and macaroni, and even managed to serve ice cream inside hot pastries, to everyone's amazement.

Even the godly Mr. Manasseh Cutler, who spoke often of the next world, spoke enthusiastically of this after attending a White House dinner on February 6, 1802. That night the preacher and other guests had rice soup, round of beef, turkey, mutton, ham, loin of veal, cutlets of veal, fried eggs, fried beef, and "a pie called macaroni." Desserts followed. "Ice cream very good, crust wholly dried, crumbled into thin flakes; a dish somewhat like a pudding—inside white as milk or curd, very porous and light, covered with cream sauce—very fine. Many other jim cracks, a great variety of fruit, plenty of wine, and good."

Eleven servants came up from Monticello, two of them for the specific purpose of learning French cookery. Bacon, his Monticello overseer, also came and noted: "Mr. Jefferson's steward was a Frenchman named Lamar. . . . He would get out the wagon early in the morning and Lamar would go with him to Georgetown to market . . . it often took fifty dollars to pay the marketing they would use in a day. Mr. Jefferson's salary," Bacon observed, "did not support him while he was President."

Bacon described the "very long dining room," and a table "chock-full" of "Congressmen, foreigners, and all sorts of people to dine with him." The main meal was served at four o'clock; talk continued into the night. His French chef's concoctions, such as "Pannequaiques," so delighted Jefferson that he sent the recipes home to his daughter. Let anyone who wonders whether wine was prominent at the table of the founder of the Democratic party scrutinize an 1801 wine order. It included five pipes (630 gallons in all) of Madeira; one pipe of sherry; 540 bottles of sauterne; and 400 bottles of claret.

Finally he returned to his plantation; but the world followed him there. "They would always be a great many carriages coming to Monticello," Isaac, a Negro slave who lived there, recalled.

"[Jefferson] never would have less than 8 covers at dinner . . . plenty of wine, best old Antigua rum and cider; very fond of wine and water. Isaac never heard of his being disguised in drink." Visitors came "in gangs," Edmund Bacon said, "and they almost ate him out of house and home. . . . I have killed a fine beef and it would all be eaten in a day or two. There was no tavern in all that country that had so much company."

Some guests left detailed accounts. One of these, George Ticknor, visited Monticello during February, 1815. The first bell for breakfast rang at eight; the meal itself was served at nine. A typical half-Virginian half-French breakfast might be served – braised partridges, Capitolade of fowl on toast, eggs, bacon, fried apples, cold meats, tansy pudding, hot breads, and battercakes. At 3:30 P.M. the warning bell rang again, and at four o'clock the main meal was served. "The dinner was always choice," Ticknor wrote, "and served in the French style, but no wine was set on the table till the cloth was removed. The ladies sat until about six, then retired, but returned with the tea-tray a little before seven, and spent the evening with the gentlemen. . . ."

The overseer commented on Jefferson's personal eating habits. "He was never a great eater, but what he did eat he wanted to be very choice," recounted Bacon. "He never ate much hog-meat. He often told me, as I was giving out meat for the servants, that what I gave one of them for a week would be more than he would use in six months . . . I knew mighty well what suited him. He was especially fond of Guinea fowls, and for meat he preferred good beef, mutton, and lamb. . . . Merriweather Lewis' mother made very nice hams. And every year I used to get a few from her for his special use. He was very fond of vegetables and fruit, and raised every variety of them."

On March 21, 1819 (when he was seventy-six), Jefferson wrote to Dr. Vine Utley: "I have lived temperately, eating little animal food, and that not as an aliment, so much as a condiment for the vegetables, which constitute my principal diet. I double, however, the Doctor's glass and a half of wine, and even treble it with a friend . . . Malt liquors and cider are my table drinks, and my breakfast . . . is of tea and coffee. I have been blest with organs of digestion which accept and concoct, without ever murmuring, whatever the palate chooses to consign to them, and I have not yet lost a tooth by age."

In his late years Jefferson was constantly exchanging plants, roots, cuttings. He literally scattered seed broadcast throughout the state, and asked his friend John Hartwell Cocke: "If you have any Sea-Kale seed to spare I will thank you for some to replenish my bed." With his grandchildren Jefferson loved to invent fanciful names for various plants: Marcus Aurelius, Psyche, Queen of the Amazons, King of the Gold Mine. "How eagerly we watched the first appearance of the shoots above ground . . ." a granddaughter recalled; "what joy it was for one of us to discover the tender green breaking through the mould, and run to grandpapa to announce that we really believed Marcus Aurelius was coming up, or the Queen of the Amazons was above ground!"

Earlier in his life Jefferson had inconvenienced and even endangered himself to find and to bring home seeds that would help his native land. He had smuggled Lombardy rice out of Italy in his pockets, for example—at a time when the exporting of the rice was punishable by death. Livestock was another passion with him. Jefferson imported Calcutta hogs and the first broad-tailed Merino sheep to America.

His endless experiments and boundless generosity led inevitably to financial problems for the Sage of Monticello. "We are looking at the taxes coming on us as an approaching wave in a storm," he wrote in 1814. "Still I think we shall live as long, eat as much, and drink as much, as if the wave had already glided under our ship. Somehow or other these things find their way out as they come in." Our nation should not, and has not, forgotten the man who faced life with that grace and spirit.

John Adams' last words were correct. Jefferson still survives.

SOUTHERN COOKING

A Picture Portfolio

A turkey, a duck, and a basketful of fruits and vegetables await the attention of the cooks in this plantation kitchen, painted by Samuel B. Palmer just before the Civil War.

Tidewater Kingdom

*The prosperity and abundance of the plantation South are evident in
this primitive view of an estate in Tidewater Virginia. The vines are
laden with grapes, a tobacco ship sets sail for England, and the
great house reigns supreme over the slave cabins and warehouses.*

143

Time of Sacrifice

During the Revolution, General Francis Marion, leader of a band of southern irregulars, allegedly invited a British officer to dine with him under a flag of truce. The meal consisted solely of sweet potatoes and a beverage of vinegar and water. So impressed was the redcoat with the Spartan courage of his opponents that he resigned his commission and went home. True or not, the oft-told story illustrates how the war for independence deprived Americans of many foods imported from abroad. Tea was forsworn even before the war because of the hated tax; instead patriots quaffed coffee and a beverage made from dried raspberry leaves—"a detestable drink," one foreign visitor observed, which Americans "had the heroism to find good."

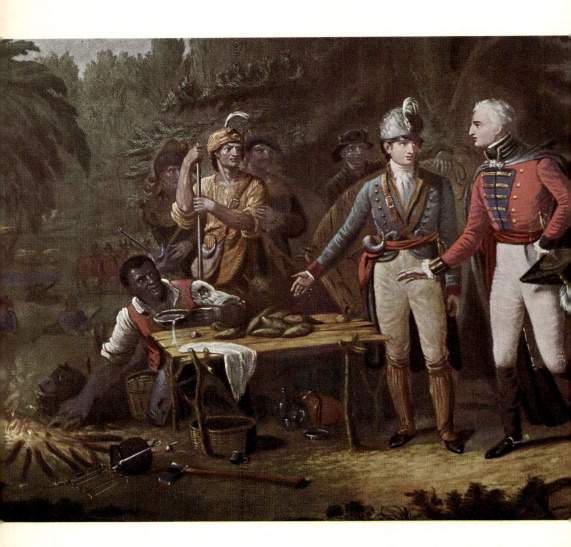

arion offers potatoes to the
ritish officer in the John B.
hite painting below. The
tirical engraving at right,
inted in London in 1775, por-
ayed "A Society of Patriotic
idies" from Edenton, North
irolina, signing a pledge to
jure tea. Below it is an anti-
a poem that appeared in
veral American newspapers
ortly before the Revolution.

>>>->>>->>>->>>->>>->>>->>>->>>->>>->>>->>>->>>->>>->>>->>>->>>

A Lady's Adieu to Her Tea-Table

FAREWELL the Tea-board with your gaudy attire,
Ye cups and ye saucers that I did admire;
To my cream pot and tongs I now bid adieu;
That pleasure's all fled that I once found in you.
Farewell pretty chest that so lately did shine,
With hyson and congo and best double fine;
Many a sweet moment by you I have sat,
Hearing girls and old maids to tattle and chat;
And the spruce coxcomb laugh at nothing at all,
Only some silly work that might happen to fall.
No more shall my teapot so generous be
In filling the cups with this pernicious tea,
For I'll fill it with water and drink out the same,
Before I'll lose LIBERTY that dearest name,
Because I am taught (and believe it is fact)
That our ruin is aimed at in the late act,
Of imposing a duty on all foreign Teas,
Which detestable stuff we can quit when we please.
LIBERTY'S The Goddess that I do adore,
And I'll maintain her right until my last hour,
Before she shall part I will die in the cause,
For I'll never be govern'd by tyranny's laws.

<<<-<<<-<<<-<<<-<<<-<<<-<<<-<<<-<<<-<<<-<<<-<<<-<<<-<<<-<<<-<<<

Mount Vernon Hospitality

Mount Vernon, George Washington once wrote, was a "well-resorted tavern." A constant stream of guests visited the plantation, and were served elaborate meals in the southern style. Washington himself usually ate only one dish at dinner, accompanied by a cup of beer and two glasses of wine. Among his favorite foods were mutton, shad, shrimp, and oysters; for breakfast he liked salt herring, corncakes, honey, and tea. Always hospitable to callers, he nevertheless wrote with relief to a friend in 1797: "I am alone at *present*, and shall be glad to see you this evening. Unless someone pops in unexpectedly — Mrs. Washington and myself will do what I believe has not been done within the last twenty years by us — that is to set down to dinner by ourselves."

146

The silver and the pieces of Chinese export porcelain shown here were all used at Mount Vernon. At left are a coffeepot created by a Philadelphia artisan and a knife and fork imported from London. Above is a punch bowl, decorated in enamel and gilt. The platter and tureen at right bear a Fitzhugh border around motifs of the Society of the Cincinnati, the order formed by officers of the Continental Army. Below are a cup and saucer decorated with Martha's initials and the names of the states.

The Carolina Rice Fields

THRESHING MILL.

DITCHING.

A RICE FIELD

FLOOD GATE

THE RICE BIRD

These scenes of a rice plantation on Georgia's Ogeechee River appeared in *Harper's Weekly* in 1867. One acre of fertile land could produce thirty bushels of rice, unless the birds and rodents were permitted to decimate the crop.

MAIN FLOOD GATES

REAPING

THE RICE FLOODED

"A Jolly Existence"

During his visit to White Sulphur Springs in the 1830's, the English traveler George Featherstonhaugh discovered a genteel inn that served "Champagne, Madeira, claret, bottled ale, rum, brandy, gin . . . and indeed all the appliances of a jolly existence." A rival establishment, less refined, sold "cock tails, gin slings, gum ticklers, mint juleps, phlegm cutters, and other American sherbets" to the "smoking and stinking *reel* gentlemen that passed their time there." Obviously, southerners enjoyed a wide variety of potables. Most of them agreed, however, on the virtues of the one great American contribution to the liquors of the world: bourbon. Made from corn, rye, and malted barley and aged in new barrels of charred white oak, bourbon first appeared in and around Kentucky in the quarter century after the Revolution. It was the pride of Kentuckians, one of whom wrote that "one Small drink would Stimulate the whole Sistom. . . . It Brot out Kind feelings of the Heart . . ."

Liquor manufacturers decorated their barrels with pictures of their distilleries (above).

These glass flasks, blown in two-part molds in the 1840's, depict William Henry Harrison, the log cabin that was his campaign symbol, and, at right, George Washington. Below, a Charleston gentleman entertains his friends after dinner in the 1750's. The guests, evidently playful after many toasts, are passing one man's wig (right) around the table.

The Charleston Market

"It is long, perhaps four inches, and crooked like a long-necked squash; it has a sweetish, insipid taste, and it grows in clusters upon a small twig. . . ." Thus did Mrs. Anne Royall, a visitor to the Charleston market in the 1820's, describe that exotic fruit from the West Indies, the banana. Charleston, South Carolina's great port city, was the commercial center of the South, and to its market came "astonishing quantities" of oranges and "all the nuts of the globe," as well as local produce. In stalls, on heavily laden shelves, were fish, meat (mutton cost twelve cents a pound), and every sort of vegetable. "But I did not dream," Mrs. Royall wrote after her visit, "that such a variety of sweet potatoes, peas (dried), and beans existed on the globe, as I saw in Charleston market."

The Roman-style building above is Charleston's Market Hall, erected in 1840. Hovering overhead in this painting by C. J. Hamilton are buzzards, which were protected by law and which kept the market area clean. At the right, a pie vendor makes a sale.

"*What Angels Eat*"

Justifiably, southerners and their guests waxed ecstatic over the glories of such delicacies as turtle soup, crab cakes, and hams made from peanut-fed hogs. Some exaggerated slightly, like Henry Knight of New England, who wrote in 1818 that southern potatoes "grow so large, that you may sit on one end, and roast and eat the other." But Mark Twain was sincere in his praise of the watermelon. "It is chief of this world's luxuries. . . . When one has tasted it," he said, "he knows what angels eat. It was not a Southern watermelon that Eve took; we know it because she repented."

Peanut

Turtle

Watermelon

Sweet potato

Land crab

Plantation Memories

The memoirs of white men and women who grew up on plantations are filled with references to good foods and to the servants who prepared them. Letitia Burwell, for instance, writing of her childhood in Virginia, recalled "the queen of the kitchen, Aunt Christian," and "the incomparable rice waffles and . . . lady's fingers constantly brought by relays of small servants. . . ." More poignant, however, is a story told by Booker T. Washington, born a slave. Seeing his mistresses eating ginger cakes, "the most tempting and desirable things that I had ever seen," he resolved that "if I ever got free, the height of my ambition would be reached if I . . . could secure and eat ginger-cakes in the way that I saw those ladies doing."

The cook above poses proudly with a dish of rolls, fresh from the oven. At right is the "battercake express"— hot food is rushed from the kitchen to the main house at Tuckahoe, a plantation on the James River in Virginia.

The two men above are grinding corn in a hand-operated gristmill, which crushed the kernels between a revolving stone and a stationary one. At left, a girl leans against a shock of peanuts drying in the Virginia sun.

5

PLAIN
and
FANCY

By Archie Robertson

At the close of the nineteenth century, Rudyard Kipling saw southeastern Pennsylvania as a land of "little houses and bursting big barns, fat cattle, fat women, and all as peaceful as Heaven might be if they farmed there." This is the home of the Pennsylvania Dutch, and even today, when the face of rural America elsewhere has changed drastically in appearance, the Pennsylvania Dutch region still looks much the same.

It is a country of "fatness," in the fine, Old Testament phrase. Its well-watered farms, fertilized and guarded against soil erosion for centuries, are

In the detail at left from Outdoor Scene with Feasting and Dancing, *guests enjoy a back-yard picnic. Some drink and flirt as others sample the array of tempting foods.*

the most valuable nonirrigated farmland in the United States. From the same rich soil the towns and cities of mellow red-brick houses draw their own character. At the food stalls in the farmers' markets of Lancaster, Mennonite and Amish ladies in trim bonnets preside over the most appetizing array of food to be found anywhere—fresh butter, elegantly stamped by a mold which is a family treasure, bursting white cauliflowers, mountains of golden pumpkins, and stacks of gay cakes and cookies, shoo-fly pies, smoked hams, and sausages. A glorious army of glass jars contains the homemade condiments—including pickled oysters, corn relish, fox-grape jelly, apple butter, and ginger pears—from which a Pennsylvania housewife selects the "seven sweets and seven sours" which traditionally accompany a meal.

Here, over a period of nearly three hundred years, has grown up the most enduring American regional cuisine. Well into the age of advanced homogenization, Pennsylvania Dutch cooking has held its own. It has done even better. As billboards along the highways attest, it has become a major tourist attraction. From all over America, as they have been doing for a long time, people come here just to eat.

It is interesting to speculate why. The Pennsylvania Dutch are predominantly German in origin — with a strong admixture of Swiss, Moravians, and some Hollanders among them — and many of their favorite dishes, like sauerkraut and pickled pig's feet, are available anywhere that Germans have foregathered. Others which the Pennsylvania Dutch can take credit for introducing, like scrapple, waffles, apple butter, and Philadelphia pepper pot, have long since joined the nationwide menu. Still others, of course, like chicken corn soup or *schnitz-un-gnepp* (made with slices of dried apple soaked back to original size, dumplings, and ham or pork), are available only here. No one else seems to know how to make a shoo-fly pie from molasses, brown sugar, flour, and spices. (The name may have come from the fact that a cook working with these ingredients on a hot summer day would have winged visitors.) But the genius of this cuisine lies not so much in its unique dishes as in the fresh touch which these people give to the conventional American food obtainable anywhere. They have quite a way with common things.

They are gifted pancake cooks, for instance. Their buckwheat cakes may contain — besides buckwheat flour — corn meal, potato water, and a touch of molasses. The Pennsylvania Dutch know how to bring to greatness a simple meal like the classic breakfast of fried mush, fried apples, and sausages. They are connoisseurs of corn-meal mush, to begin with, always choosing yellow meal, preferably from corn that has been roasted for extra flavor before grinding. And unlike New Englanders with their "hasty pudding," the Pennsylvania Dutch like to let mush bubble happily away in a big iron pot for hours. They may eat it hot with cold milk or cold with hot milk, but always with a puddle of melted butter in the middle. When it is

> Q. *"Mr. Delp: . . . My daughter thought it wasn't polite to serve schnitz-un-gnep to her boyfriend for dinner, and wanted us to kill a chicken. But I made the schnitz-un-gnep anyway, and that Bucks County chap ate three plates full. Now, where was anything wrong? A Farmer's Wife"*
> A. *". . . The next trip I would give that fellow schnitz-un-gnep again . . . Then, slyly, I would give him to understand that my daughter made the schnitz-un-gnep. I'll bet there will be a wedding at your house inside of seven weeks. Dory Delp."*
> —Letters from a column in the *Daily Argus* (Easton, Pennsylvania), 1898

fried, they pour all sorts of good things over it — old-fashioned dark molasses from a country store, comb honey, pure maple syrup, or their own apple butter, which is dark and spicy with cloves, cinnamon, or sassafras, and quite different from that found elsewhere.

They choose the tastiest kind of apples for frying, depending on the season, for they have a choice of many kinds on the orchard slopes of their misty blue hills. The apples, of course, are lightly sprinkled with powdered sugar and cinnamon before serving. The sausage is homemade, delicately seasoned and smoked.

This is a cuisine of abundance, created by thrift and hard work. "Fill yourself up, clean your plate," is a popular motto. Like the people themselves, their cooking can be either plain or fancy—parsnip fritters or oysters and caviar. All will be good, and all, whatever the more exquisite type of gourmet may think, could well appear on the same table. This cuisine is completely without class consciousness. What is good—and not what is novel, fashionable, or easy to fix—determines what the Pennsylvania Dutch eat and serve to their guests. "No trouble," they always say politely to appreciative visitors. By this, they do not really mean that good cooking is no trouble. They mean simply that the results are worth it, in terms of human happiness.

Appetite is the basis of any good cuisine, but the roots of Pennsylvania Dutch cooking go even deeper than

this, into a background of suffering and privation which drove them from the Old World to the New. Here they created on free soil an authentic, distinct culture, of which their food is only one —although a very important—element. This particular regional cookery is like living history. So, in some ways, are the people themselves—especially the

Going to market

Plain People. (Outstanding among these are the Amish, who still wear black hats and long beards, drive their gray buggies along the roads of Lancaster County, and fasten their clothes with hooks instead of buttons, for buttons were associated with the nobility and the military.) Their ancestors first began to come to southeastern Pennsylvania in the seventeenth century. Conditions in the Palatinate—a province of the Rhineland in Germany— had been nothing less than dreadful. Beginning with the Thirty Years' War in 1618, there were persecutions of Protestants by Catholics, of Catholics by Protestants, and — most bitterly sometimes — of Protestants by Protestants. Toward the end of the century, an especially vindictive army from France invaded the Palatinate and took pains to cut down the fruit trees, dig up the vineyards, burn the farmhouses, and turn the people out in the dead of winter. Their sufferings were observed with sympathy by William Penn, who was planning a commonwealth in the New World devoted to religious liberty—and peace. He circulated his prospectus throughout the Rhineland and twice visited the region in person to invite the distressed survivors to join him. The Mennonites—followers of Menno Simons, an early sixteenth-century religious reformer—were the first to accept. In 1683, at Germantown, near Philadelphia, they made the first German settlement in America.

The Mennonites were Plain People, members of the radical wing of the Reformation which disavowed all established churches, Protestant as well as Catholic, sought to recover the simplicity of New Testament Christianity, practiced pacifism, and, to emphasize their separateness from the world, dressed in plain, dark clothes. They were, of course, pleased to learn that their new Quaker neighbors also "dressed plain," were pacifists, and held religious views not unlike their own. Other Mennonites soon came, and other Plain People of various kinds— the Dunkers, or Brethren, who baptized by total immersion three times; Moravians from Bohemia, followers of John Huss, who was burned at the stake in 1415; and a small group called Schwenkfelders, who, like the Moravians, had been persecuted for centu-

ries, driven from one country to another across the map of Europe.

They all arrived hungry, if only from the long sea voyage. The Schwenkfelders, when their ship dropped anchor in 1734 near New Castle, Delaware, obtained their first fresh water in months, along with apples and fresh bread. They still commemorate this occasion each September, sharing, after church service, a

Kneading bread dough

meal of the same basic ingredients— apple butter, fresh bread, butter, and water, "spiced," as a Quaker observer noted, "with cheerful talk."

In one way or another food became a sort of religious symbol with all of the Plain People. After worship, the Dunkers held love feasts, suppers at which the main dish was a lamb stew commemorating the paschal lamb. The House Amish, fundamentalist Mennonites who felt that their brethren were backsliding, held services in each other's homes and followed them with a memorable dinner for all. The Moravians, at Bethlehem, became famous for their baking. Their love feasts consisted of rolls and a beverage, served in church and shared in a spirit of devotion and brotherhood.

The Plain People were followed to America in the early eighteenth century by many of the "church people," members of the Reformed and Lutheran churches, with some Catholics, too, who had remained behind in the Rhineland. (These, of course, were the "gay" or "fancy" Dutch, and their descendants in southeastern Pennsylvania came to outnumber the "plain" Dutch by ten to one.)

Conditions in the Palatinate had not much improved. In the terrible winter of 1709, it was so cold that birds allegedly froze in the air, and wild beasts in the forest. Men looked into each other's eyes, one historian reported, and said, "Let us go to America; and if we perish, we perish." Pennsylvania, however, was not their original destination. Queen Anne of England invited the Lutherans and Reformed to go to New York, which the English had taken over from Holland.

This frightfully mismanaged project provided the gay Dutch with an episode of suffering almost equal to anything the Plain People had known. On shipboard, with inadequate food and no sanitation and no light or air below decks, they died by the hundreds. By the time they reached New York Harbor, typhus had broken out; installed in tents on Governors Island, hundreds more died of disease and as the result of the rigors of the voyage. The survivors were sent up the Hudson, told to build their own villages, and fed salty meat and short rations of bread. A minister among them wrote home that "they boil grass and ye children eat the leaves of the trees." When a letter of invitation reached them from Pennsylvania, one hardy band accepted. After that the church people emigrated from the Rhineland direct to Pennsylvania.

Now the plain and the fancy, reunited on the rich soil in the valleys of the Susquehanna, the Lehigh, and the Schuylkill north of Philadelphia, began to build the culture that became known as Pennsylvania Dutch, because to their eighteenth-century neighbors anyone speaking any variant of the German language was a Dutchman. And it was in fact their particular dialect that did most to unite them and keep them separate

Although this far-distant portion of the world consisted of nothing but wildernesses ... it is truly matter for amazement how quickly, by the blessing of God, it advances, and from day to day grows perceptibly. For although in the beginning we were obliged to have our victuals brought from Jersey, and to pay somewhat dearly for them with money, yet we are now able, praise be to God! to serve other neighboring communities.

—Francis Pastorius, founder of Germantown, writing in 1700

from other Americans. That dialect, which can still be understood in parts of the Rhineland today, is neither the

"Low Dutch" of Holland nor the "High Dutch," or classical German, in which their Bibles were printed. Thus, it distinguished them both from other German immigrants who came later and from their Low Dutch neighbors in New York, as well as from the English-speaking Quakers, Episcopalians, and Presbyterians all around them. It was a language without a written literature, and for centuries they lived in a world apart, continuing to paint hex signs on their barns and observing many other Old World customs long after they died out elsewhere. Several of their own words, of course — like "dunking," for a local custom with doughnuts which became widespread —joined the American language.

In a strange, wonderful way Pennsylvania Dutch—as Englished—makes

When I was making mush one night,
My true love he came in,
And I was put in such a fright,
I got my mush too thin.
—Pennsylvania Dutch rhyme

very good sense. "My off is on," for instance, means "My vacation has started." "Do you think it will make down?" is "Will it rain?" Or, "the cream is all,"—gone, of course—"the milk is yet." And there is the classic story of a sign on a front door, "Bell don't make—Bump." But all these are the trivial aspects of this culture. Its mainspring, which set it going, was the common memory of the fertile,

lovingly cared for farms and orchards of the Rhineland, and as rapidly as they could clear the forests the Pennsylvania Dutch set out to reproduce these in their new homeland and to stock their larders.

In anything pertaining to food they were especially inventive. To bring home more game, they designed a longer, more accurate rifle, mistakenly called the Kentucky rifle after Daniel Boone took it there from Pennsylvania. The first American cookstove was cast here, at Mary Ann Furnace in 1765. They made a long-handled waffle iron, imprinting a tulip design, for use on the open hearth. Instead of diamonds, which were notably scarce, young men gave their sweethearts handsomely carved rolling pins as engagement presents.

In fact, a notably rich folk art grew up around their cooking and eating. Many of their early stoves were so beautifully decorated with biblical scenes that they have been called "The Bible in Iron." Henry William Stiegel's glassware, a treasure today, was blown here. And inevitably, from this fertile soil and these busy kitchens a surplus of food began to emerge. Therefore the Pennsylvania Dutch invented the great Conestoga wagon, a ship on wheels, to transport their produce to fairs and farmers' markets. Since good food knows no language barrier, their own diet became the standard for the region. For example, the bachelor President James Buchanan, a Lancaster man, was famous for his sauerkraut suppers after he left office; he won the hearts of a Dutch family with whom he sheltered one night by insisting that the big bowl of corn-meal mush, which was all they had planned for supper, was exactly what he wanted.

By the time of the American Revolution, Philadelphia had become famous as the capital of a land of good eating, and one of its Pennsylvania Dutch bakers became famous for his usefulness to the American cause.

Christopher Ludwick, who had emigrated from Germany to become the city's first gingerbread baker, was commissioned by Congress as baker general of the Continental Army. He must have been a good baker. Washington, who called him "my honest friend," often had him to dine. Somehow he kept the ovens going even at Valley Forge. After the Revolution, in which Ludwick lost his property, he built another estate from the profits of his baking and left it to be shared by all the churches of Germantown, Catholic and Protestant, and to start public schools.

This admirable citizen was also the first American on record to employ food as a weapon in psychological warfare. Learning that the British had quartered German mercenaries on Staten Island, Ludwick — who was a Hessian — obtained permission from Congress to go there as a secret propaganda agent. He did not discuss ideologies, in which one assumes the Germans were not much interested. In-

stead he told them, as Fredric Klees has written in *The Pennsylvania Dutch,* "of the wonders of Philadelphia, of the mile-long market in the High Street with counters laden with

Making sausages

plump chickens and sausages, with crisp fresh bread and buns fragrant with cinnamon, with cherries and sparrowgrass and peas and other vegetables in season; of the snug inns where a man could sit at ease before the fire and down his pot of liquor, or turn in between fresh, lavender-scented sheets." At the first opportunity, dozens of Germans deserted to the American lines. Many of their descendants are in Pennsylvania still, but they are not usually counted among the Pennsylvania Dutch. That title is generally reserved for those who had emigrated before the Revolution and had already created this abundant fare.

Throughout the nineteenth century the life of the region changed surprisingly little. The railroad came to replace the Conestoga wagon. Lean and hungry Confederate armies invaded several times, the Southerners writing home their astonishment at such peace and plenty. In the latter part of the century, as commerce began to rival agriculture in importance, many of the Reformed and Lutheran families began to move to town. But many others, along with nearly all the Plain People, stayed on the farm. No group of Americans has ever loved the land more intensely. Well into the twentieth century these farms were still food factories such as have never been excelled.

One historian of the region, J. George Frederick, has recorded in detail his memories of his grandparents' farm in the 1880's. His grandmother bought almost nothing from the store except sugar, salt, pepper, and coffee. From clay on their farm they even baked their own earthen pots, crocks, and pie plates — in the winter, when farm work was light. Every day after milking, of course, there was cream to be separated by hand. Making butter and cheese went on steadily and so did baking. The oven, in this home as in most, stood outside the house. It was breast-high, fired by loads of brushwood burned to ashes, which were then raked out. Loaves of bread, pies, cookies, and crumb cakes were placed on the hot brick hearth, and when these were done the remaining heat was used for drying fruit.

In the spring there was a big garden to plant, allowing a surplus for the market. Dandelions were made into wine, and raspberries and blackberries

were picked for pies or for drying. For most of the year fruit was constantly being dried, in the sunshine or in the oven. From these dried fruits the Pennsylvania Dutch baked probably the world's greatest variety of pies the year round. But the universal favorite, of course, was *Schnitz* (a German word that means "cut"), which is dried apple slices and which even today is still among the basic facts of life in Pennsylvania Dutch country. ("What do I get if I slice an apple in half?"

Shaking down fruit

asks the arithmetic teacher. "Halves," the children reply. "And if I slice the halves?" "Quarters," they say. "And if I slice the quarters?" "SCHNITZ!" cry the children.)

Schnitz, which was also used as chewing gum before the arrival of the store-bought variety, is even on the map. A farmer on his way to market once upset a wagonload in a creek; the slices swelled up in the water to flood the whole valley, and today this is Schnitz Creek.

The Pennsylvania Dutch also made cider, for sale, for home consumption, for vinegar, and for cooking the rich, dark apple butter that they ate with cottage cheese *(schmierkäse)* on slices of homemade bread. They made apple soup, too, and they dried corn, which they often called "Shaker dried corn," since it was one of the many ingeniously preserved foods which the Shakers used to sell.

The Shakers, who believed in the Second Coming, lived only in their own settlements, and practiced celibacy and community of goods, were a very special variety of Plain People. They were not among the Pennsylvania Dutch, being of English origin and living chiefly in New York, New England, Kentucky, and Ohio, but they did at one time have a colony in Philadelphia, which probably accounts for the presence in their recipe books of such Pennsylvania Dutch foods as scrapple and apple butter.

Their motto was "Give your hands to work and your heart to God," and they were surpassingly inventive, both in machinery and in the products which they sold to help support their colonies. They are best remembered, perhaps, for their exquisitely simple furniture, but they were also pioneers in scientific agriculture and in the sanitary preparation and preservation of food. Their packaged garden seeds, medicinal and culinary herbs, vegetable extracts, and preserved fruits and vegetables were famed for their high quality. And in an age when too much dirt and carelessness attended not only the production of food but its consumption, the Shaker brethren and sisters demanded good table manners from all those who dined with them:

> *What we deem goodly order we're*
> *willing to state,*
> *Eat hearty and decent and clean*
> *out our plate;*
> *Be thankful to heaven for what*
> *we receive,*
> *And make not a mixture or*
> *compound to leave.*

The Shakers shared with the Plain Dutch a belief in separateness from the world, in pacifism and piety, and in hard work. But their chief kinship lies in their attitudes toward food, in which both were ahead of their times. Shaker cuisine, revived in contemporary cookbooks, has survived the sect, which has now passed into history. And in Shaker dried corn, esteemed a delicacy by the Pennsylvania Dutch, their memory is still alive. Made by baking fresh kernels in the sun for five days or in an oven for two, the dried corn is soaked in lukewarm water for twelve hours, then salted and simmered, and served with butter and cream. Pennsylvania Dutch housewives, many of whom make Shaker

Be not angry or sour at table; whatever may happen put on a cheerful mien, for good humor makes one dish a feast.
—From a Shaker manual, *Gentle Manners*

dried corn each fall, also believe that it is better than fresh corn for making fritters, puddings, and that great stand-by, chicken corn soup.

Another fall activity among the

Pennsylvania Dutch was the storing of vegetables for the winter: beets, turnips, potatoes, and pumpkins. Mr. Frederick's grandmother took prizes for pumpkins at the county fair. Before frost she cut off the best, leaving a tail of vine which she stuck in a jar of milk, through which the thirsty

Seed-package label

pumpkin continued to grow. Fall was also the time for gathering chestnuts for stuffing fowls, and walnuts for pickling or cookies. And of course sauerkraut was made in the autumn. An unnamed Pennsylvania Wordsworth once sang:

All my soul is in delight

When mommy fixes kraut just right.

Kraut, in the early days, was made by men who "stomped" the cabbage with their bare feet, like peasants pressing grapes for wine. It is now, of course, made by quite sanitary methods, and the Pennsylvania Dutch, who adore it, try to give it an aristocratic background, pointing out that it was reputed to be the favorite food of Charlemagne. It is, in any case, a fav-

orite of theirs. And it is best accompanied by pig meat. The home-grown poet quoted above continued:

Calm my troubled, sinful mood—

Oh, but pork is always good!

He had ample nourishment for his spiritual aspirations after hog butchering and meat packing on the farm early in December. For this season the men of the family joined the food factory. They brought in specially selected woods for the smokehouse, each chosen to give the best flavor to sausages, tongues, bacon, pork, and ham. (Pennsylvania Dutch country smoked ham was perhaps the inspiration for the saltier "country hams" of the South, for the Dutch early began to spread from Pennsylvania down through Maryland and the Valley of Virginia deep into the southern mountains, where they are found today.) Nobody has ever made more thorough use of the pig, not even the great meatpacking houses. The feet, of course, were put up in jelly, and the boys even saved the hog bristles, which they were allowed to sell in town to buy Christmas candy. From the tiniest scraps of hog meat, unusable elsewhere, they made scrapple, one of their truly great contributions. And when the butchering was all over, each respectable family set aside some of the choicest cuts of the hogs, or perhaps some sausages or a side of bacon, as presents for neighbors who had helped or as gifts to the poor at Christmas—a time when nobody in the Pennsylvania Dutch country was allowed to be hungry.

At Christmastime, too, cookies were baked by the bushel in every home, using the treasured old cooky cutters, shaped like animals, brought from the Old World. Also baked for Christmas were sand tarts, doughnuts, *Lebkuchen* (a honey cake usually containing almonds, citron, or orange peel), and mince pies—called Christmas pies. The Moravians, those highborn cousins of the Pennsylvania Dutch who were finally settled by Count Nikolaus Ludwig von Zinzendorf, their leader, at Bethlehem, outdid themselves at Christmas. They erected a four-sided structure on tables to form a cooky pyramid — a forerunner of the Christmas tree, which the Pennsylvania Dutch unquestionably introduced to America.

The first Christmas tree of record appeared in the upper Rhineland in 1608; for two centuries thereafter it remained a local custom in this region of Germany, and was brought by the emigrants to America. An issue of the *Saturday Evening Post* for 1825 described what a lovely sight the trees made, hung with cookies and candies, glimpsed through Philadelphia windows. Such jollifications were not usually the doings of the stern Plain People. It was mostly the gay Dutch who—at a time when Puritan sentiments predominated in this country, and the great festival was largely ignored — made the American Christmas merry. Until the twentieth century, in fact, one day was hardly enough. They celebrated the day after, too. In the towns of the gay Dutch, Second Christmas

was even livelier than Christmas Day. The local hotel might serve free drinks all day; there would be greased-pig races, shooting matches, and fireworks; a cannon might be fired; and Santa Claus — who is partly a Pennsylvania Dutch invention — might arrive from a neighboring town on a special train. Even the sober Amish, who delight in visiting, ate a great many cookies and took a glass or two of wine at Christmastime.

Special foods followed the cycle of the Christian year. For example, doughnuts called fastnachts were prepared in abundance for Shrove Tuesday, a day when even the women ceased work. (To sew on Shrove Tuesday, some believed, might sew up the hens and keep them from laying eggs.) The fastnachts — still baked in large quantities at this season — might be round or square, and a hole in the middle was optional. But they were very powerful medicine. The last person out of bed on Shrove Tuesday morning was called the Fastnacht; he had to do extra chores and was teased and tormented about it all day long. If you wanted to grow large heads of cabbage it was essential to eat lots of fast-

No Better And good Cooks Can be found no where...
--Lewis Miller, on the York Hotels

nachts. And the lard in which they were fried was kept to heal sores or grease wagon wheels.

Ash Wednesday, of course, was not a feast day (ashes were scattered over garden and livestock), but with the approach of Holy Week many preparations had to be made. Dandelion greens had to be gathered to be eaten as a salad on Maundy Thursday, sometimes called Green Thursday. (The favorite dressing was a hot cream gravy made with bacon, and if this sounds strange for use on a green salad the only advice can be to try it.) The dandelion salad would help to keep fevers away all year, and in fact its vitamins were good to have at this season. But the great culinary activity centered around eggs.

The Pennsylvania Dutch introduced the Easter egg and its proud parent,

the Easter bunny. (To make the point entirely clear they used to bake a big cooky rabbit in the act of laying an egg, until the squeamish objected.) All winter long, housewives had been saving red onionskins and other natural dyes. For a fancy design, eggs could be boiled in tightly wrapped flowered calico. Each worshiper at the Moravian Easter service received an egg marked "The Lord is Risen."

Eggs were important all week long. An egg laid on Good Friday was a real treasure and could advantageously be eaten on that day and its shell saved to drink water from on Easter morning. On that day, as soon as the children had found the bunny's nest, eggs appeared in enormous quantities. Some were made into "Easter birds"— charming, toothpick creatures; others were stuck on an Easter-egg tree. But most were eaten. The winner of one egg-eating contest was reported—dubiously—to have consumed fifty-six. All day long, boys meeting on the street "picked eggs"; that is, each would thump his egg, at the base, against the other's. The egg with the weaker shell would crack and be claimed and eaten by the winner.

The Easter egg and the Christmas tree will no doubt always survive (along with Santa Claus, if he can be rescued from the Chamber of Commerce). But most of the holiday customs which the gay Dutch introduced with their feasts have long since disappeared. And looking ahead, it seems clear that it is their more self-denying relatives, the Plain People, who will do most to keep alive the Pennsylvania Dutch cuisine in its full glory for generations to come. For this, there are reasons.

The Amish, in particular, make it part of their religion to farm. They are not allowed, except under rare circumstances such as physical disability, to make a living in any other way. With a tenacious judgment—and it is hard to see how they are mistaken—they realize that if their way of living is to survive, it must almost totally exclude the twentieth century. They discourage educating their children above the eighth grade and prefer them to attend their own one-teacher schools with a privy in the yard. They have no telephones in their homes, indeed no electricity at all, and no tractors on their land. ("The tractor, it don't give no manure.") It is almost unheard-of

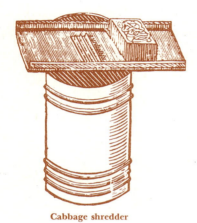

Cabbage shredder

for an Amish family to purchase food from the store. Frozen foods would not keep, and no Amish housewife would think of feeding her man "outen a can." Their own products are far better anyway. Just as in the old days, an Amish farm is a food factory, preparing good foods the whole year through. Any surplus will bring a good price from "the fancy" at a farmers' market.

To enforce their separateness from the world, the Amish will not only excommunicate a backslider but "shun" him completely — even in the marital relationship. (It was over the necessity for this stern point of discipline that the Amish separated from the other

Mennonites in Switzerland, some 270 years ago.) However, they have other, more genial methods for helping each generation in turn to keep in the old paths. A newly married couple, for example, will not take a wedding trip "into the world," but will embark in their buggy on a series of honeymoon visits throughout the neighborhood. In each house they are made welcome and feasted, and from each housewife in turn the bride learns more and more of the arts which go into preparing a feast. In Amish hands the old-fashioned Pennsylvania Dutch cuisine should be safe for many years to come.

Yet it is only fair to say that, as of this writing, many gay Dutch still cherish this heritage, too. A few miles north of Lititz, for example, a venerable log tavern can be found filled with neighborhood families eating nothing but Pennsylvania Dutch food and drinking beer, both in substantial amounts. A visitor will be warmly welcomed and invited to come back next day for an "all-day raffle." (The prizes will be live turkeys and Black Angus cattle; the price of one dollar will include raffle ticket, Dutch soup, and free beer with eggs pickled in beet vinegar.) And in a store window a sign advertising a church fair recommends, "Bring container to take home soup." Such soups there will be! Corn soup with popcorn floating on top, pretzel soup, calf's liver soup, pea soup "thick enough to stand on."

This is still a country of abundance, and the good food of good people.

Sylvester Graham

SYLVESTER GRAHAM

By Gerald Carson

Although the Pennsylvania Dutch saw no conflict between religion and good eating, Graham and the food faddists cited Scriptures as well as science in their attack on the American diet

At a gala, meatless banquet held at Roswell Goss's boardinghouse in Barclay Street, New York City, a company of earnest intellectual experimenters, mystics and utopians, abolitionists, Sabbatarians, Perfectionists, whiskeyphobes, comeouters, phrenologists, and the editor of *Zion's Watchman,* gathered late in 1839 to enjoy "nature's luxuries" without the assistance of shortening, flesh foods, pepper and other condiments, coffee, or alcohol. Among the guests the commanding figure of Gerrit Smith, wealthy New York State philanthropist, was conspicuous. One lady studied Smith's ruddy cheeks with suspicion.

"I think they indicate high living," she observed with disapproval.

"I do live high," replied the reformer. "I live on the Graham system."

The reference was to the Reverend Sylvester Graham, a former Presbyterian preacher, temperance lecturer, self-styled doctor of medicine, and dietetic expert. Graham came to public notice in a time of dynamic social change. Yeasty new ideas were bubbling—ideas about women and prisons and peace; about health, exercise, eating, and drinking; about the millennium and the perfectibility of man; and about cookery. Harriet Beecher Stowe, in her *Household Papers,* praised "the great abundance of splendid [food] material we have in America," but found it in sharp contrast with the "poor cooking." She itemized the latter: "green biscuits with acrid spots of alkali; sour yeast-bread; meat slowly simmered in fat till it seemed like grease itself . . . and above all, that unpardonable enormity, strong butter! . . . The frying-pan has awful sins to answer for."Mrs. Frances Trollope, the middle - aged, middle - class English woman whose fantastic mission to America—to establish a department store in Cincinnati—produced a never-forgotten commentary upon our domestic scene, found us lacking in appreciation of soups, our sauces unskillfully made, rolls half-baked, the corn breads ever-present "but in my opinion all bad." Mrs. Lydia Maria Child wrote disapprovingly of our "gravies and gout," while Professor Edward Hitchcock of Amherst College blamed our style of cookery for the common national ailment, dyspepsia, and Mrs. Ellen Gould White, who was the inspired prophetess of the Seventh-day Adventists, invoked divine authority from her headquarters at Battle Creek, Michigan, against dietary sin.

In this climate of opinion the Reverend Graham became the propagandist of a regimen in which bread made from coarse, unbolted flour and eaten when slightly stale occupied a central position. The Yankee race had been steadily deteriorating for three generations, Graham declared; or, as he cast the idea in vivid metaphor, the miller's bolting cloth was fast becoming the shroud of the American people. Graham became the center of a dietetic storm, his eccentricities the butt of many a witticism. Some of his contem-

poraries listened and believed, and many persons prominent in the national life for two generations after Graham were known as followers of Grahamism.

A sampling of such names would include the founders of Oberlin Collegiate Institute, John J. Shipherd and Philo Penfield Stewart (also the inventor of the Oberlin stove); the revivalist Charles Grandison Finney; the popular biographer James Parton; Bronson Alcott, the sage of "Apple Slump"; Joseph Smith and Amelia Bloomer; the Fox sisters, famous mediums who produced the "Rochester Rappings"; and, intermittently, Horace Greeley and Thomas A. Edison. Dr. James Caleb Jackson, a hydropathic physician, planted the Grahamite doctrines in western New York State and invented a new food, Granula, which led on to Granola, Granose, Grano, Grape-Nuts, and the vast modern breakfast-food industry which C. W. Post, the Seventh-day Adventists, and the Kelloggs—Will K. and Dr. John Harvey Kellogg—created in Battle Creek.

By a connection that can be clearly traced, then, one's morning bowl of bran or corn flakes is linked with radical health and dietary doctrines of the nineteenth century, backed by the sanctions of revealed religion. The ready-to-eat cereals of Battle Creek in their infinite variety, one remembers gratefully, exist because dedicated and ingenious men once tried to save men's souls in a novel way—through their stomachs. The master's memory is preserved today in the still-familiar phrases "Graham bread" and "Graham crackers." His prolix writings are kept in print and reverently read by naturopaths, theosophists, and food faithists.

Sylvester Graham was born July 5, 1794, in West Suffield, Connecticut, the last child of a man then seventy-two years old, John Graham, a clergyman and physician, who died when the son was still an infant. Young Graham was farmed out among relatives, worked at various casual jobs, and finally got to college, entering Amherst Academy when he was twenty-nine years old. There he first demonstrated his prodigious flow of language, an extraordinary egotism, contrariness, and a faculty for stirring people up. Graham left Amherst under a cloud, and after a bout with ill health—almost the hallmark of a leader in food radicalism—he married his nurse, Miss Sarah Earl, in 1826. Following his marriage, the future food philosopher entered the Presbyterian ministry, preaching at various points in New Jersey. In the early 1830's he became a temperance lecturer, traveling extensively as general agent for the Pennsylvania State Society for the Suppression of the Use of Ardent Spirits.

In connection with his lectures attacking alcohol as a beverage, the Reverend Graham made a study of human physiology, looking for arguments to use against those who liked to take a belt of the Old Sinner. Without in the least relaxing his aversion to strong drink, Graham shifted gears and soon became the censor of American recklessness at the dinner table, where he found another variety of intemperance, equally in need of correction and even more widespread than addiction to the Serpent. While continuing the crusade against alcohol, Graham developed his bill of particulars against the American cuisine and a positive program of dietary reform and improved personal hygiene. Its most notable feature was an assault upon meats and fats—in general, the vegetarian position—and the insistence upon the use of bread made from unbolted, or unsifted, whole-wheat flour. This was a startling posture—to square off thus against white bread, the long-established symbol in Western civilization of the joys of good living.

By 1835-36, the newspapers were full of Graham's preachments, often poking fun at the master's oracular dogmatism, yet spreading the knowledge of his regimen, too. Graham hotels sprang up in various cities. Graham societies were formed, all drawing popular attention to the consequences of piggery at the table. Specialized shops, forerunners of the modern "health food" stores, stocked the foods which Graham approved. There were sympathetic links between the Grahamites and the Anti-

Tobacco Society, the Anti-Vivisection Society, the American Society for Promoting Observance of the Seventh Commandment, and the water-cure movement, as well as with the large and vocal public which was demanding a milder system of treating stomach disorders than the orthodox reliance upon calomel.

Coterie periodicals of various organizations, such as the *Water Cure Journal and Herald of Reform* and the *Graham Journal of Health and Longevity,* helped to diffuse Graham's ideas on food, nourishment, and physical and moral well-being. The new philosophy of food was especially well received in Boston. The *Hampshire Gazette,* of Northampton, Massachusetts, explained this: "The Bostonians are a dyspeptic variety of the human family ... The surest way of approaching most men is said to be through a dinner, but you must secure a Bostonian by telling him how to digest one."

Graham and his disciples were conscious of crusading against moral, as well as physiological, error. Their reasoning may seem daft, but it was strictly logical if their premises are accepted. God is the author of physical laws. So it is not only unwise to violate them, but it is an offense against true religion. Graham relied heavily upon scriptural authority, especially those passages which fitted his thesis, such as Genesis 1:29: "And God said, Behold, I have given you every herb bearing seed, which *is* upon the face of all the earth, and every tree, in the which *is* the fruit of a tree yielding seed; to you it shall be for meat."

The meals must have been tedious enough—the oatmeal gruel, the beans and boiled rice without salt, the daily procession of puddings eaten when tepid or stone cold, the bread at least one day old. Condiments were proscribed because they inflamed the thirst for the Red Stuff. Fats, gravies, and seafood were also out of bounds. Soups were not permitted, since they provided no opportunity for chewing. Graham insisted that the teeth get a thorough workout—a teaching later carried on by Horace Fletcher, who required his followers to chew every bite thirty-two times, one chew for each tooth in man's natural complement of masticators. Little or no water was allowed at meals to help the faithful swallow Graham crackers, a kind of unleavened biscuit made from unbolted or whole-grain flour.

Other voices were raised in America in favor of the dark wheat bread, fruits, bulk foods, a more restrained approach to dining. But Graham was the prime mover. With the passion of a flagellant or an Old Testament prophet, he called upon men to stop digging their graves with their teeth. One of his lecture topics had a rather spicy title, "Chastity." Its message was that men could curb sexual sin by a shift from meat eating to the cereal diet. In view of the age-old search for aphrodisiac foodstuffs, one may speculate on whether the denunciations by the excitable lecturer against meat as a source of sexual vigor produced the effect he had in mind.

One of the Reverend Graham's public appearances in Boston became the occasion for a civil commotion remembered as "the Bakers' Riot." Graham's view of the commercial bakers was not charitable. He considered them all cheats and adulterators. The family's bread, he preached, should be baked in the home, where its preparation was a kind of rite or sacred office. He dwelt fondly in his printed *Lectures on the Science of Human Life* upon the image of the good New England matron and mother of early federal days, telling how she stood long over her dough trough kneading the dough, shaping the loaves with loving hands, then watching over the baking with a vigilant eye. On the occasion of the attempted violence against Graham, it had been announced that he would deliver a lecture at Amory Hall in Boston, urging the women of New England to bake their own bread and boycott the "public bakers." Threats made against the proprietors of the hall were effective, and the Doctor found himself without a forum. The owner of the not-quite-finished Marlborough Hotel, first "temperance house" in the United States, offered the use of his dining room, and when the mayor warned that he could not protect the meeting with city constables, the resourceful Graham recruited his own police from the ranks of his disciples. When the mob appeared at the front of the hotel, a loyal "shovel brigade" stationed in the upper stories dumped slaked lime on the rioters until the bakers appeared to be covered with flour, "whereupon the 'eyes' having it," according to a jovial account of the episode, "the rabble incontinently adjourned."

In 1837, Graham purchased a home in Northampton, Massachusetts, and lived there until his death in 1851. Many stories have been told of the eccentricities of the spare, sprightly, scholarly-looking food fighter. Since it was his opinion that there was no need of one's being sick, he once published an apology in the local newspaper for having taken to his bed during a brief indisposition. Graham bathed daily in Mill River, summer and winter, cutting a hole in the ice when necessary. He dabbled in Whig politics, strolled on Main Street in his old dressing gown, expounding the true inwardness of whatever aspect of nutrition, cookery, hygiene, or theology he was currently pursuing. To the end he was a soapbox man. Gradually failing in health for about a year, Dr. Graham died at his residence after a dose of Congress water and a tepid bath, hailed by the *Hampshire Gazette* as a remarkable man and the author of a system of dietetics "in which his peculiar views were advocated ably and well."

For all his rusticity of manner and method, Sylvester Graham left a heritage of valuable health ideas—about bathing, exercise, brushing the teeth, the ventilation of sleeping chambers, the importance of moderation in eating. Long before food chemistry demonstrated that refining white flour took out the minerals and vitamins, Graham arrived at the truth of the matter by observation and intuition as set forth in his *Treatise on Bread and Bread-making* in 1837. Graham performed a service in showing that muscular strength was not dependent upon a high protein diet; he also opened the way to wide use of the coarser cereals and the latter-day cereal breakfast foods, enlarged the place of fruits and vegetables in the American diet, and so helped to introduce a more attractive table into the homes of the United States. Yet for all his pioneering work, Graham is known to history as something of a crank, barely tolerating the use of milk, eggs, honey, adamant against salt, shellfish, or pork. But Graham, perhaps more than any other man, made Americans, as Professor Frederick J. Stare of the Harvard University School of Public Health described them recently, "probably the most health conscious people in the world," which "has created a climate for nutritional quackery that has grown to alarming proportions." In general, the agitators of the "food pro-

test" who followed after Sylvester Graham carried on with such useful concepts as the lighter diet, new respect for the whole grains and the human body.

But along with the flowers came the weeds in the shape of commercialization: nut grinders, peanut roasters, and grain-puffing machines for the home; scare tracts based upon pseudo science. Thus the nutritional quack, often with a persuasive personality, cashing in on some form of dieto-mysticism, led the unwary down the primrose path of ground-up alfalfa, "natural" foods, inorganic salts, gimmicks for reducing weight, blackstrap molasses, mung bean sprouts, soy milk, and seaweed. Food fads flourish, in plain words, because people want them. A "cult satisfies some craving . . . to be in fashion . . . to attract attention . . . to *do something*," Dr. L. Jean Bogert concluded in *Diet and Personality*, a pioneering study which has lost nothing of its validity with the passing years.

Today our food supply is the best we have ever had in this land of plenty. All the nutrients are abundantly within reach to furnish an ideal diet for that omnivorous eater, the human animal. But as long as mankind finds satisfaction in being *avant-garde*, Sylvester Graham will undoubtedly continue to have his following.

PLAIN AND FANCY

A Picture Portfolio

This earthenware dish, made in Pennsylvania in 1786, was a gift from a beau to Katharine Raeder, whose name appears above the entwined doves.

Mush and Milk

Lewis Miller, a carpenter by trade, made almost two thousand drawings of nineteenth-century life in York, Pennsylvania, including the one below of "Dr. John Rause, and Family, at the dinner table Eating Nudelsup, and in the Evening meal, mush and milk." Mush, the porridge made from boiled corn meal, was daily fare among the Pennsylvania Dutch. Some of their neighbors, however, were not as adept at preparing it, as Robert Boyd, an itinerant preacher, pointed out in 1862: "Just look for a moment at the difference between a mess well salted, *long* and well cooked, and a *hasty*, thin splash, nearly raw . . . I would, therefore, advise the preacher not to extol the mush supper in a strange place, lest he should get into a trap."

In Lewis Miller's drawing of a hotel kitchen, top right, the cook uses a long-handled peel to put bread dough in the oven. In the center scene, a tavern keeper fries potatoes and sausages on an open hearth. At the bottom, a group of Pennsylvanians congregate outside a brewhouse, where they came to buy yeast.

The York Hotels, Kept In 1800.
No Better, And good Cooks Can be found no where
to prepare Victuals for the table, As these Taverns,
See the names - Mrs. Abraham Miller, Mrs. Polly Waltemyer,
Mrs. Gosler, Mrs. Laub, Mrs. Upp. Mrs. Kimel, Mrs. baltzers Spangler.
Mrs. George Hay, Mrs. Beard, and Mrs. Eichelberger, not far
from town, the two last names.
old Style Cooking,

The Bake oven, baking
Bread.

Smokeing Sausage
and Baltone

for the customers In her Tavern.

After - frying the Sausage -
the potatos put in the pan.

Little Sally.

Mrs. Lottman frying Sweetpotatos and give to Lewis Miller,
Some of them the first I ever tasted the where good Eating.
It was in her tavern South George Street. 1799.

The Old Brewhouse.
in the year 1801.
the made Good Beer.

Hearts and Flowers

Although Pennsylvania Dutch dress was usually sober, the household utensils were colorful and ornate. Their pottery was adorned with graceful tulips, birds, and hearts, applied either by trickling liquid clay onto the earthenware (the slip method) or by scratching out the design on a layer of clay (the sgraffito technique). In Lancaster County in the last half of the eighteenth century, the delicately enameled, engraved, or cut glassware of "Baron" Henry W. Stiegel was produced, and Pennsylvania Dutch artisans made from wood and iron items that were as attractive as they were functional. So well-known was the Pennsylvania Dutch love of beautiful everyday objects that a special toleware, called gaudy Dutch, was made in England solely for export to Pennsylvania.

A toleware coffeepot, made from tinned and painted sheet iron

A dough trough of poplar wood

A cast-iron device for baking waffles

A saffron box, made of pine

A Stiegel-type flip glass

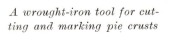

A wrought-iron tool for cutting and marking pie crusts

183

Using corncobs as fuel, the tireless housewife above dyes eggs for Easter. At left is an egg that was dyed in 1870. The design—a farm wagon and a shovel—was made by carefully scraping away the red dye with a pointed knife. At right, two Pennsylvania Dutch women make apple butter. Frequent stirring was necessary to prevent the mixture from sticking to the kettle.

Holiday Treats

The indefatigable Pennsylvania Dutch housewives, who prepared food for market, as well as for their families, nevertheless found time and energy to make the traditional treats at holiday time. Many evenings were spent cracking nuts, beating eggs, and grating chocolate for Christmas cookies, baked "by the washbucketful" so there would be enough for guests and *Belsnickels,* the Christmas Eve trick-or-treaters. For their special day of thanksgiving in September, the Schwenkfelder women pared and quartered apples, then stirred them all day in boiling cider to make apple butter. And no Pennsylvania Dutch mother, no matter how busy, would deny her children the joy of dyed Easter eggs, even though it meant standing over the stove for hours.

Tin cooky cutters, shaped like animals or people (above), were used by the Dutch, who sometimes put red sugar on the cookies "for pretty."

Apple Festival

The apple harvest was a jolly time in rural Pennsylvania, if this 1853 primitive painting by an unknown artist is any indication. Although a few people are paring and boiling apples for mead or butter, most of the guests are simply enjoying themselves, with the aid of musicians and an evidently high-powered beverage. One woman has removed her shoes and seems determined to wade in the stream. In the center, two men carry off their inebriated companion.

The Hard Way

The Arabs allegedly made the first butter by accident: skins filled with milk were loaded on camels, whose rolling gait turned the liquid into butter. Whether that story is true or not, the farm wives of Pennsylvania and other rural areas had no such four-footed help in making their butter. They had to skim the cream from each day's milk, and when enough was collected, churn it themselves. Then it had to be worked by hand until the water was removed and it was ready to be molded. Cheese making was even more time-consuming. First, rennet had to be made from the stomach of an unweaned calf. This was soaked in water, and the resultant liquid was then added to milk. Stirring, straining, separating the curd from the whey, and breaking up of the curds followed, until the salted, softened curds were placed in the press, which produced a wheel of cheese. Buttered and wrapped in cloth, the cheese was then stored away, until it was either used for barter or enjoyed by the family.

hese photographs were taken in
e late nineteenth century by
. Winslow Fegley of Hereford,
ennsylvania. Above, Schwenk-
lder men and women make liver-
urst and sausages. Meat hangs
om the rafters. At left, two girls
lp their mother make two-pound
aves of butter for sale in the city
arket. At right, an old woman
kes bread in an outdoor oven.

For Love of God

Other states besides Pennsylvania were havens for groups and sects wishing to follow distinctive ways of life. A band of religious dissenters from Sweden founded the Bishop Hill community in Illinois in 1846. Hearty eaters of traditional Swedish foods, they eschewed liquors in theory if not always in practice. Another group, the Perfectionists of New York's Oneida Community, practiced free love and preached that Christ's Second Coming had already occurred. Their meals were simple, consisting chiefly of bread, milk, potatoes, and beans, with a little meat. The Moravians, Protestants from Europe, settled in North Carolina and Pennsylvania in the eighteenth century. Their love feasts, which consisted of rolls and beverages served in the church, reflected their belief in the brotherhood of those who broke bread together.

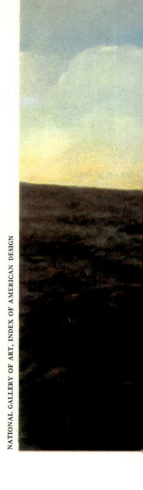

Harper's Weekly, APRIL 18, 1874

SERVING COFFEE.

LOVE FEAST IN THE CHURCH.

Food for the Moravian love feasts (above) was always prepared in advance, so that the solemn service could proceed without interruption. Hymns were sung as the baskets of rolls and mugs of coffee were passed around. At right is the dining room at Oneida.

Corn was planted at the Bishop Hill community by the method shown in the painting above by Olaf Krans. The prongs on the poles measured the distance between
rows, and the knots on the rope showed the women how far apart to plant the corn.

The Shakers

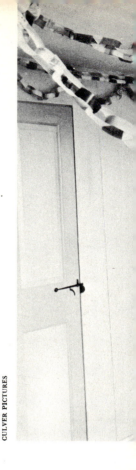

Work was sacred to the pious, celibate Shakers, and although they labored neither for spouse nor personal fortune, no group was ever more industrious. Visitors to their communal farms were always struck by their cleanliness, order, and prosperity. Their experiments with plants, soils, and fertilizers led to a profitable seed business, and the Shaker name on a can of vegetables was a sign of quality. Among the devices produced by Shaker ingenuity were a threshing machine, a revolving oven, and a machine for paring, coring, and quartering apples. Their efficient and sanitary methods of food processing were invaluable examples to their neighbors and customers. The Shakers themselves often ate in complete silence, and the sexes were always segregated in the dining rooms. From 1837 to 1847, the members of the sect were forbidden to eat meat. But even then their meals were appetizing and nutritious. Many of their delicious recipes have been preserved, though the pioneering Shakers no longer exist.

The Shaker sisters above are preparing herbs for cooking and medicinal use. They grew, dried, and ground the herbs themselves. At right, a Shaker lady cuts newly baked bread.

The Shaker dining room at Canterbury, New Hampshire (above), was decorated for the Fourth of July, 1898. Condiments hang from the ceiling. At right is part of a poem on table manners, used by a Shaker community in 1868.

We found of those bounties
  Which heaven does give,
That some live to eat,
  And that some eat to live —
That some think of nothing
  But pleasing the taste,
And care very little
  How much they do waste.

Tho' heaven has bless'd us
  With plenty of food;
Bread, butter and honey,
  And all that is good;
We loathe to see mixtures
  Where gentle folks dine,
Which scarcely look fit
  For the poultry or swine.

We often find left,
  On the same China dish,
Meat, apple-sauce, pickle,
  Brown bread and minced fish;
Another's replenish'd
  With butter and cheese;
With pie, cake and toast,
  Perhaps added to these.

6

The
BREADBASKET

By Paul Engle

Between the Midwest, that ocean of good grass, and the Pacific, that ocean of salty water, lies almost every landscape known to man. Those landscapes produce almost every form of food known to man.

The massive fields of Kansas ripen so much wheat that it has had to be stored in circus tents or on the streets of towns. In a green and growing Iowa June, not only the planted crops, but the trees, the pastures, the lush roadside weeds, the very plowed-up soil itself, look good enough to eat. And in California's Sacramento Valley, men have watched machines working across fields so rich and long that they seemed to disappear into the sky.

In the nineteenth-century poster at left, a pretty housewife trims her pie crust.

In regions that raise so much food in such dramatic abundance, it is natural that crops and harvests should be of intense concern to the people living there. This personal association with food was especially strong toward the close of the last century and the beginning of the twentieth, when men and women (children and dogs, too) were far closer to the planting, tending, gathering, and preparing of food than they are today. It was a time of close-up smells, of rich tastes, of food handled by the same person who would ultimately eat it.

Every autumn, when the cold weather came, I would appear at my Uncle Charlie Reinheimer's farm near Cedar Rapids, Iowa, on the weekend chosen for slaughtering. A great kettle would

195

be washed out under the windmill, and the fattened pig, squealing as if he knew just what miseries lay ahead, would be hauled up by a chain and tied to a tripod. I had watched that porker grow from a round blob I could hold in one hand to this 225-pound shoat. (There was always some distinguishing mark on the pig—three white feet and one black, or a belt of white around the belly.)

Then the knife would flash in Charlie's firm fist; the blood would be caught in a bucket; the carcass would be scalded in the kettle, eviscerated, split, then chopped into parts. A packing house might advertise that everything was used but the squeal; Charlie did better than that. He always said, when we sat down next morning to our first breakfast of fresh sausage, which was popping and crackling in the frying pan, "Now listen there, boy, you can hear the squeal if you've got good ears." I heard.

There would be the annual argument between Charlie and his wife over the amount of seasoning to be put in the sausage. He liked lots of black pepper, coarse-ground, and sage, but my Aunt Gertrude preferred milder tastes. "I don't want my sausage tasting like cactus," she would say with spirit. Charlie always won, and when the sausage was being fried down to be put in stone crocks and covered with a layer of fat from the same hog, the whole house would take on the tang of pepper and desert sage.

My job would be the ham. I would gouge holes in it with a steel knife-sharpener and fill them with salt, brown sugar, and a little saltpeter. Then the hams would soak in a tub of brine for a month or five weeks. Taken out and rubbed clean of salt, they were covered with pepper and more brown sugar and hung to drain for two days. The final step was to put them in the smokehouse over a fire of green hickory (the smoke itself was so rich I am sure a man could have lived on it alone). That ham had no water or quick-curing chemicals in it, just solid meat and natural flavors, with a juice which, when mixed with milk and maybe a pinch of flour, was transformed into gravy with an authority worthy of an appetite honestly earned by hard farm work in the open air.

Sausage making was a job for the kids. The intestines would be turned inside out and cleaned, then soaked in brine all night. In the morning, with smooth pieces of wood, we scraped them clean before helping to stuff them with spicy meat, taking a twist at regular intervals to make the individual sausage. Then they went to the smokehouse, that shrine of the mortal appetite, to join the slabs of bacon oozing fat and flavor.

It was a great time for children. In summer, when ice cream (and it really had cream, not thin milk) would be made at home, there was always the dividing-up of the labor between the kids, each doing a fixed number of turns with the crank. And afterward, there was the sharing of the ice cream left clinging to the dasher. Nothing in a dish, eaten with a spoon, was as full of flavor as that remnant, hardly five minutes old. Chances were that, licking the cold wonder with a hot tongue, we could look across from the back porch and see the cow that had given us the cream and the tree that had given us the nuts. The chances were just as good that we had milked that cow and gathered those nuts. Surely this enriched that ice cream far beyond the contribution of the ingredients which had not come from the farm, the artificial flavoring and the sugar.

Often enough, the butter would be churned by the children, too, and here again there was something to be scraped off and eaten, as well as the buttermilk to be taken into the milk house and cooled. Charlie would come up from threshing on a burning July day, his overalls soaked with sweat, chaff in his hair and eyebrows, dust in his nose and throat. From the can of fresh buttermilk, sitting deep in the tank of water drawn by the windmill out of a well which went 250 feet through solid stone, he would take a dipper and drink from it in long, grateful gulps. It cut the dust, he said, reaching for another. No vintage champagne could have rewarded a thirsty man as that buttermilk did. He had earned it.

On occasion, there were more potent drinks than buttermilk. On an especially cold night, another uncle might appear with a suspicious bottle which he pretended to hide under his coat. My aunt would have nothing to do with the hilarious preparations in the kitchen, but I would peer at the conspirators blending their ingredients: whiskey, maple syrup, nutmeg, boiling water. Charlie would give me a sip of

I have food and drink in abundance. . . . Supper is eaten at six o'clock, with warm biscuits, and several kinds of cold wheat bread, cold meats, bacon, cakes, preserved apples, plums, and berries, which are eaten with cream, and tea and coffee—and my greatest regret here is to see the superabundance of food, much of which has to be thrown to the chickens and the swine, and to remember my dear ones in Bergen, who like so many others must at this time lack the necessaries of life.

—Jannicke Saehle, a Norwegian immigrant in Wisconsin, 1847

the froth on top, and in spite of a doubtful life since, I never again tasted as uplifting a liquid.

Farmhouses at that time were poorly heated, but even this discomfort was helpful in storing food. The attic was hung with hams and sides of bacon, and there was usually a root cellar (in my Uncle Charlie's house, this was a cave dug into the cellar wall), sometimes lined with stone or brick. Below the frost line, it would keep apples, potatoes, carrots, squash, beans, turnips, and often the rows of canned berries and meat which were the winter reliance of the family.

Some root cellars had barrels set into the ground, filled with cabbages, and then covered with cornstalks, straw, and boards. In the spring, when all of the cabbages had been taken out and eaten, the stench of the rotten leaves was strong enough to lift the covering. Equally powerful was the smell of those cabbages that had been chopped up and put into stone jars, tamped down, salted, and covered with a cloth until they stopped "working."

In the west, when you stop at an inn, they say—

"What will you have? Brown meal and common doings, or white wheat and chicken fixings?"—that is, "Will you have pork and brown bread, or white bread and fried chicken?"

Also, "Will you have a feed or a check?" —A dinner or a luncheon?

—Frederick Marryat, A Diary in America, 1839

In the gloom of Charlie's cave, the jars had a sinister look, like cans of gunpowder waiting to explode. A good, deep sniff of the air rising out of the jars would hit a man like a shot of that "Taos Lightning" that Charlie's hired man, who had lived in the Southwest, would brag about. As a child, I would look on his face for the scars where the lightning had struck, but I never saw any. I believe this was the same wheat

whiskey that was called Nebraska Needle Gun in the Midwest.

In the midst of such abundance, it was hard to believe that there were once men who thought that the vast region west of the Mississippi could not support a population. What proved them wrong was that the Midwest was settled not by landlords but by men willing to work the land themselves. Yet hard work alone did not suffice; it had to be supported by an ingenuity greater than had ever before been applied to agriculture.

When the first settlers came into Iowa, they laboriously cleared land in the woods along rivers, intimidated by those broad, open spaces of the grassy prairies, so unlike the eastern countryside they had known. Gradually they moved out of their woods and onto that rich soil, but at once there was a problem. Their iron plows from back East would not cut through the dense roots of the grass, which had been growing there from immemorial time. The farmer could not hold a plow deep enough in the ground against the resistance of the matted roots.

The sod-breaking plow was devised, with a long and heavy beam to keep the share cutting steadily; it was pulled by six to eight oxen (sometimes horses). This broke the sod and turned it over, but at once another problem snarled at the diligent man who had just solved the first difficulty. Although a field would lie in fine furrows with the grass partly turned under, when he tried to plow it over and over before seeding, the heavy, damp soil clung to his plow so that it would not "scour," and he had to stop so often to clean the share that it was impossible to plow much in a day.

A young Vermont blacksmith, John Deere, who had come to the little village of Grand Detour in northwestern Illinois, listened to the complaints of the farmers about their iron plows and decided to try an experiment. Finding a steel sawmill blade, he knocked off the teeth, heated it, and reshaped it into a plowshare, with a high, curved moldboard. Taking it out one day in 1837, in the presence of a small crowd which came to sneer, stare, or hope, he put it in a field and plowed a straight furrow all the way across without stopping, and back again. The grass was turned completely under, and at the end of the furrow the steel plow was clean; the soil did not cling to its bright surface. It was that self-scouring, self-polishing plow (a similar one had been developed by John Lane in Illinois, but he did not then patent his idea) which made possible all of the later nineteenth century's great production of grain and meat in the Midwest and West.

That plow broke the prairies and turned them into fields of corn. Without the corn, there would not have been enough feed to turn western range cattle into finished beef, or locally raised hogs into rich pork. And it was that plow that helped to replace the shorter plains grass of the drier Dakotas, Nebraska, Kansas, Oklahoma,

and eastern Wyoming with an immensity of wheat.

But a big landscape needed big tools. With the new plow, a farmer still could manage only a small farm.

He could harvest only small crops—and slowly—always running the risk of weather destroying them before he could get them into the barn. He still cut his wheat and oats with a hand-swung cradle, essentially an ancient scythe with fingerlike rods added to catch the stalks. He still threshed by beating the grain on the barn floor with a flail or by driving horses or cattle back and forth over it. As a harvester, he was little beyond primitive man.

In 1832 Cyrus McCormick invented the reaper, whose blades severed the stalks while a rotating paddle wheel swept them back against a cutter onto a platform. Later a binder for making sheaves was added. Now the farmer could seize that moment when the grain was utterly ripe and get it cut and safely bound. Just as important as building the machine was McCormick's sales device. Few farmers could pay cash for a reaper—one cost $100 before the Civil War, but the price rose to $1,500 in the 1870's—so McCormick offered it on time payments, an invention of quite as much help to the farmer as the outfit itself.

The prairie farms, away from streams in many cases, needed water, so the windmill with a circle of blades, instead of the traditional cloth sails of Europe and New England, was built to draw water from wells—which were now drilled instead of dug. Because of these advances, the farmer could move his house and his operation nearly anywhere, and with the advent of wire fencing in 1874 he could mark off his own land and keep his cattle confined.

Wheat was the great cash crop. Unlike corn, most of which was fed back to the livestock on the farm where it was raised, wheat was sent away, to mills in the area or to other parts of the country and the world. The cattle also had to be moved, and long distances. In one of those far-seeing actions that Lincoln so often took despite the harrowing distractions and anxieties of the Civil War, he signed, on July 1, 1862, a bill for a transcontinental railroad. Soon the distance from the open range to the kitchen range was a short step.

Some big steps were now being taken on the farms. The portable thresher was built, replacing the quaint beating-on-the-floor and the winnowing of the grain from the chaff by hand. At first this thresher required six to eight men and several horses. Later, steam power took over, with five or six men running the machine and a large crew

of itinerants working with them. Rigs would work north from Texas through Oklahoma to Canada. Their arrival caused great excitement, for it was al-

J. I. Case thresher

ways an occasion for a debauch of food. There would be a "ring" of families in an area, all served by the same threshing outfit. A woman could make a handsome reputation (apart from her looks) by the sort of table she set for the men who put in those long days in which the heat of the sun joined with the heat of labor and of the steam boiler to produce a raging thirst and a solid appetite.

Days before the threshing crew actually arrived, preparations for feeding would begin with baking pies and cakes, washing off hams, slaughtering chickens (to be soaked in lightly salted cold water before cooking), bringing up jellies and jams from the cellar. Ripe berries and fresh vegetables were gathered from the garden. At sunrise, when the fire was started under the steam boiler of the threshing engine, a fire would also be started in the kitchen range. This took almost as much skill as the preparation of the food, itself, since there had to be a steady, even-burning heat. To achieve this with chunks of wood on iron grates called for skill as great as that required in blending the ingredients of the food.

The remarkable quality of those farm cooks was that, although they were accustomed to cooking for one family, perhaps four to eight people, they could plan and prepare food for as many as twenty to thirty men, all of whom consumed food as voraciously as the huge black range consumed wood. Neighbor women whose farms were also in the ring would come to help—and to admire, or sniff at, the meals served. There was great rivalry for the praise of the threshers. A casual comment, such as "Never saw baking-powder biscuits that light," from a satisfied man as he pushed his chair away from the table, could bring glory to a woman's day.

At such times, all normal standards of bulk and number vanished. Potatoes were prepared by the bushel, pies by the dozen; there were pickles in infinite variety: crab-apple, beet, red-cabbage, watermelon-rind, green-tomato, dill, sweet, bread-and-butter. A big ham would be boiled in a wash tub, but there was never only one kind of meat. Always an immense beef roast and fried chicken (it was sometimes alleged that frugal farmwives used the occasion to cull out their tough roosters), perhaps a platter of pork chops, would appear on the table. And there was cabbage in every form: fresh in coleslaw, boiled, in sauerkraut, pickled. Just as the steam engines could burn any fuel (coal, old fence posts or barn siding, elm chunks, straw), so the stomachs of the threshers could handle any item a cook served.

Of course milk in every form helped to hold those appetites in control until the evening meal: pitchers of it cold; pounds of butter (kept hard in the steamy kitchen by putting over them unglazed, porous earthenware crocks or even flowerpots, wrapped with thick cloth dipped in the chilly water from the milk house); cottage cheese, often with caraway seeds or chives; yellow "rat" cheese in thick slabs served with apple pie.

One of the fine things about planting, cultivating, and harvesting food is that it makes one hungry for food. But the cities were clamoring for food, too, and thousands of farmers were ready to provide it.

The first really large-scale wheat operation was managed by Oliver Dalrymple for the Northern Pacific Railroad, which had huge holdings in the Red River valley at the eastern edge of North Dakota. Totaling 75,000 acres, most of it in wheat, using masses of men and machines, horses and mules, this was called bonanza farming. There were 120 gang plows, 80 seeders, 200 binders, 53 steam-powered threshers, 30 steam engines. There was a special wagon for oil and grease, one with water for the engines, one with water for the men, one with twine for the binders. Grub wagons brought two meals out to the fields, in addition to the two served in the bunkhouse. Some of the bigger farms in the project had their own doctors, hospitals, and churches. Not only did the holdings of the Northern Pacific enterprise increase, but crowds of men rushed in to take over their own land. In 1877, homestead entries in the Dakota country totaled 213,000 acres; in 1885, 11,083,000 acres. Only the hope of large-scale plowing and threshing, even on the smaller farms, made this settlement possible.

One of the largest wheat farms of the times was owned by Dr. Hugh Glenn. By 1880, the crop on his Sacramento Valley ranch ran to a million bushels. Big teams pulling gang plows

DOES NOT HEAT THE BLOOD
Nourishing. Non-Stimulating. Delicate. Delicious.
NICEST SUMMER DISH
GRANULE OR MUSH
—MADE OF—
"EXCELSIOR MILLS" WHOLE WHEAT FLOUR.

Flour advertisement, 1883

would begin a straight furrow in the morning, never turning; at noon, they would stop for lunch at a halfway house and then go on in the same straight furrow until nightfall; one field ran sixteen miles. Some of the most enormous steam-powered combines ever built were constructed especially for reaping in the California valleys. Cutting a forty-two-foot swath, capable of doing 100 acres a day, they could harvest wheat for as little as twenty-five cents an acre. But horses

were still used for certain combines, and fourteen to forty were hitched together, with seven to eight men operating the massive machines. Extensions could be fitted to the rims of the wheels, giving them a six-foot width for travel over soft and rough ground. Chains drove the rear wheels, which could be twelve feet in diameter.

One man who had a decisive influence on nineteenth-century agriculture was Jerome I. Case (it is meaningful that his middle initial stood for Increase), who developed a steam thresher which would pour wheat out one side, straw and chaff out the other. He began with a rudimentary little thresher called a ground hog, operated by horse-tread power, and soon he was the leading builder of steam engines for farmers, advertising that all his engines needed to make steam was pure water, without any admixture of whiskey.

Machines powered by horses had made the first big break-through toward mechanization of farming, but the most profound changes came first with steam-powered, and then with gasoline-powered, equipment. In 1800, with the sickle, it required about 56 hours to harvest an acre of wheat. By 1880, with the horse-drawn reaper, it took some 20 man-hours. Today on the Great Plains, ten minutes will do the job and do it better. With corn, using the hand-hoe process of 1800, it took 344 man-hours to produce 100 bushels, but today the really efficient farmer can do the same in less than four hours.

Drillers, mowers, plows, spring-tooth harrows, and threshers were continually improved. The wind stacker was introduced: a fan forced air through a pipe which could be directed, the straw rising high in the air like a cloud of smoke. This added a new noise to the steady roar of the engine and the growl of the threshing cylinder, which men said they could hear, on a quiet morning, four miles away.

There were risks involved in progress. Fire from blowing sparks was so frequent that many insurance companies would not carry a policy if a steam engine was used for threshing. Boilers blew up and killed or maimed those close to them. Men could be caught in the many belts, levers, and knives in motion, losing arm, leg, life, or at least clothes.

Gay moments were more frequent, however. Demonstrations of agricultural machinery were common, and were attended by crowds, bands, and terrified horses. Case's firm sent out special red-white-and-blue trains with special flatcars fourteen feet longer than the usual, with flags running the length of the train, and with steam calliopes which began to play "In the Good Old Summertime" as the train neared a town. There were wonderful proofs of the delicacy with which the huge steam tractors—some thirty-seven feet long and weighing many tons—could be driven. One salesman drove his machine up a teeterboard and balanced it there. Backing down, he then approached an open watch hung on a stake and gently closed the case without scratching crystal or case.

The first gasoline tractors to be so named were built by Hart-Parr at Charles City, Iowa, in 1902. These machines resembled steam traction outfits without the boiler. Some weighed eleven tons and were so hard to start that farmers would let them run all night. By 1914 a small tractor was being manufactured, leading to the all-purpose "row" tractor of today which can perform almost any farm operation save washing the farmer's overalls while he is wearing them.

The development of machinery was paralleled by great changes in the handling of cattle. The Civil War had decimated livestock on southern farms, but in Texas the longhorns had increased so rapidly that they would not bring a dollar apiece. Before the War they had been "trailed" to New Orleans and once to Chicago; by 1867 the railroad reached Abilene, Kansas, and the northward drives were begun over the Chisholm Trail. Cattle had been driven over long stretches before and in other

> *Our country friends, who have not yet paid their subscription, are respectfully informed that we have to buy all the vegetables for table use, and those who have cabbage, potatoes, or anything of that kind to spare can pay their indebtedness in that way.*
>
> —Marshall, Missouri, *Democrat*, November 28, 1858

countries, but what was unique about the Texas drives was their great size. The total brought north between 1870 and 1890 has been estimated at over 10,000,000 animals. It took sixty to ninety days to go from San Antonio to Abilene at a rate of eight to ten miles a day. The lanky animals little resembled the yard-fattened steers of today; their long, spreading horns rose

Fencing was too costly to be obtained. No gardens could stand the herds of cattle, a thousand strong, which might come swooping over at any minute. Just as our corn was ripe, the bears would strip the ears; just as the pumpkins grew golden, herds of deer would hollow out the gourds. As we got more land, there was no transportation to carry away the crops. Butter was five cents a pound, eggs were three cents a dozen; corn was six cents a bushel, wheat twenty-five cents. A cow was worth five dollars, and a man's labor fifty cents a day. Do you wonder we clamored for railroads, lied for them, went in debt for them—did anything till we got them?

—William Henry Herndon, describing Illinois in 1826

over long thin legs and yellow, dun, red, or roan hides. It was said that a cow could be raised in Texas for less than the cost of a chicken in any other place in the United States.

This river of meat had to be utilized, and the means were being developed to do that. Originally the term "packer"

meant someone who packed meat in barrels with salt. Salt pork was the standard food of westward-bound Americans for many years, and Cincinnati was the first large packing city because of its location on the Ohio River — a convenient avenue for shipping cured meat downstream. But as the railroad pushed west it began to bring cattle closer to people.

The first slaughterhouses were in rural areas, and often hogs roamed underneath to eat the waste. Operations were usually conducted in winter, since meat would spoil in the summer. There was no great variety—hams and bacon were heavily smoked to preserve them —and the method of distributing fresh or salted meat was very slow.

The acceleration in meat packing came when many rail lines pushed into Chicago from east and west. The Union Stockyards were built in 1865, making it possible to ship in carloads of animals on any rail line and shuttle them directly to the yards. About this same time the great names of the packing business appeared on the scene—men like Swift, Armour, and Morris—some of them with ingenious ideas that would revolutionize meat packing.

Gustavus Franklin Swift came from Cape Cod (of all places in the United States the least productive of meat animals), and early in his career he began buying pigs at the big Brighton yards near Boston; he also slaughtered steers there and took the parts in a wagon to the Cape and sold them. When he arrived in Chicago, which he saw would be the meat center of the country, he was an experienced butcher and cattle buyer. P. D. Armour moved to Chicago the same year, 1875, but it was Swift, with his eastern background, who originated the shipping of dressed beef, rather than the live animal, to eastern markets.

The railroads opposed sending dressed beef east; not only were they equipped for shipping live cattle, but

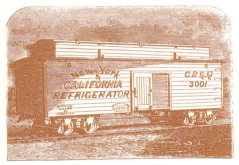

Refrigerator car, 1870

the heavier weights meant larger freight charges. (The roads also controlled the facilities for feeding and watering.) But Swift was true to his name, and soon was building his own refrigerator cars, with ice at both ends. Suddenly the modern way of bringing dressed meat quickly from packer to consumer had arrived. In 1885 the firm was incorporated as Swift & Company with a capital stock of $300,000; two years later the company was worth $3,000,000. The refrigerator car brought every city into the presence of good meat at a good price. The packing industry became the fresh-meat industry, adding the refrigerator ship to the refrigerator railroad car, and extending the market to Europe.

Thus pigs, cattle, and sheep entered Chicago on the hoof and left it as hams, roasts, and chops. Packers soon found that the by-products of the animal made the difference between profit and loss, so that liver was no longer given away to the dear old lady for her cats. Western range cattle were replaced by Shorthorns and Herefords and the stocky Black Angus, which had been finished on midwestern farms with corn and commercial feed.

While meat was thus turning into a finished product, the very character of the wheat grown on the plains was changing. The Mennonites seem to have brought into Kansas the hard winter wheat which replaced the soft eastern variety, and this ancestor of today's hybrid spring and winter wheats was ideally suited to the region.

Another event that was to affect the American diet occurred in 1862 when President Lincoln signed the so-called Land Grant Act, to establish colleges especially for the scientific development of agriculture. Since that time, such institutions as Iowa State University have improved the animal, grain, vegetable, and fiber crops of the country beyond anything seen in the world. They are in part responsible for the many advances in seeds, bringing fatter, more abundant, more disease-resistant products. One of these is hybrid corn, that astonishing end-result of an ancient grass. With its oils and starches, this yellow corn kernel is the most nourishing single item in the world. It is planted on more acres than any other crop and is worth more than any other. This is one of America's great gifts to the world.

Certainly that is only fair; we have taken so much in the way of food from other lands and other cultures—a fact that is nowhere so evident as in the Southwest, where Spanish and Mexican influences are alive today. The Spanish brought with them the first cattle, goats, horses, pigs, cats, fowl, the first hoes, spades, grinding stones, plows, files, the first wheels. They brought the seeds of peaches, figs, oranges, apples, lemons, grapes, apricots, pears, olives. For many years the only grape grown in California was the Mission grape. The first wheat planted in Colorado was known as Sonora wheat. Cooking was done on a *hornillo,* an open hearth built up three feet from

Nineteenth-century label

the floor. Baking and roasting were done in an outdoor oven, dome-shaped and made of adobe.

The tortilla was an unleavened corn pancake flattened by pounding between the hands and cooked on an earthenware plate. Chili con carne (chili with meat), chili *con huevos* (chili with eggs), and enchiladas (cheese rolled inside a tortilla, perhaps with chili) were, and still are, basic dishes for the southwestern family of Mexican descent. Frijoles, the cowboys' pinto beans, simmer for several hours; with chili peppers added, they are one of the standard daily foods of many southwesterners.

In the Southwest, as well as in the West, lamb and mutton are staples as in no other part of the country. The Spanish had an ancient sheep culture when they came here, and their ways of preparing the meat persist today. The Midwest is a beef and pork area, but to the West the sheep, which can live adequately from the sparse grazing of dry land, provides a desirable meat.

The Spanish also founded the great herds of cattle and pigs at the California missions. When the missions were secularized in 1834, the padres slaughtered the herds for hide and tallow, wasting the rest of the carcass because it could not be shipped. Sadly, only a few years later the gold fields brought in the forty-niners with their insatiable appetite for meat, but the great herds were gone.

The vast Irvine Ranch in Orange County, southern California, was the equivalent for that area of the Glenn wheat ranch on the Sacramento River. Everything was grown there—olives, vegetables, oranges, lemons—whatever could be raised by adequate water, warm sun, and the labor of men. And in 1895 some 31,000 acres were sown with barley for brewing purposes. Here in the Far West, as in the rest of the country, men had developed some notable thirsts. As was sometimes said of the old Midwest frontier, poor food and too little of it, poor whiskey and too much of it. At Galena, Illinois, for example, the favorite drink was lead-mine rye (I cannot certify that lead would dissolve in it, but I certainly will not argue that it would not). In Texas, a sick traveler was given a toddy which was guaranteed to make him forget his illness. After drinking it and feeling his interior break into flames, he finally gained enough breath to ask what it was — whiskey strained many times through layers of hot chili pods. There were many ordinary distilleries in the Midwest and West which provided the comfort required after prolonged periods of deprivation when cowboys, ranchers, and trappers were far away from the relief of any spirits save evil ones.

It was found after 1840 that Americans preferred lager beer to the heavier English ales and porters. The early beers had a high alcoholic content, to keep them from decomposing, but eventually finer beers were brewed. A New Orleans newspaper, in a story about a local brewery in 1865, described the latest way to make beer, proving that the steam engine had as powerful an impact on drink as it did on food:

"The engine is sixteen horse power.

It can, at the same time, grind the malt, sift it, throw it into the mash tub, let in boiling water that it has made to boil, stir up the malt and water, draw it off,

An unusually great number of pumpkins and melons are grown. On the slopes of the Sierra Nevada they sometimes grow so high up in some places that it takes several hours of driving before the fields are reached. It is a fine sight to watch the harvesting of such a field. The big fruits roll down the slopes just like golden balls. Men stand below, with sacks ready, to receive them. . . . At the annual California agricultural exhibition I saw a pumpkin weighing one hundred and thirty pounds.
—Alexandra Gripenberg, 1888

pump it upstairs and throw it into the kettle, heat the kettle of liquid until it boils, throw it out into the coolers, cool it, force and carry it off into vats, ferment it, chafe it, and draw it off beer. With a little practice the engine could be taught to drink the beer."

Yet the greatest distiller of them all is the humble cow. Dairying is, along with steel and the auto, one of the great industries of the country. Milk ranks with liquor as a fortifier of man, and is still preferred by the discriminating palate of the child. The kernel of corn and wheat, the fiber of beef and pork, the drop of milk—these and many other basic products of the Midwest and West nourish the country and give it some of their own flavor and richness.

George H. Hartford, by Ivan G. Olinsky

THE HARTFORDS

By Paul Engle

After a down-at-heels dry-goods salesman proved he could sell food at low prices, his sons followed him into the business and intensified its early slogan: "There's good news for the ladies"

As with so many revolutions, the one that had its beginnings on the New York City water front in 1859 started with two young men talking to each other.

Unlike other great changes, this one was accompanied by no violence, and no report was published in the newspapers. Even its leaders did not know that what they began so casually would become a way of life and would affect more people than many more spectacular and bloody events.

The subject the two young men were discussing was not an act of social protest; it was not a shipment of arms, but of tea. This country has a tradition of associating tea with violence, but in this case George Huntington Hartford and his partner, George Gilman, watched tea being unloaded from ships at the New York docks and decided that a great improvement could be made in the handling of those delicate leaves from an Asian shrub. Their solution was not to throw the tea into the harbor, in the great Boston tradition, but rather, in the practical American tradition of the nineteenth century, to devise ways of selling it more cheaply.

Hartford, then twenty-six, had been born in cautious Maine, but had proved that he had an adventurous streak by leaving it while he was still young. He had had a steady lack of success in dry goods and like Gilman was looking for some way to get ahead. Watching tea being unloaded, they knew that it would pass through the hands of several middlemen before the customer bought it for one dollar a pound. Why not, they asked themselves, buy directly off the ship and retail the tea at thirty cents a pound?

The solution had the sort of simplicity, and the instantaneous originality, associated with inventions. These young men conceived a retailing process, rather than a machine, but it was still a new thing with a strong impact on American life. And they invented new ways of selling to go with their new concept of handling food.

After testing their idea by buying a shipload of tea and selling it at dockside, the two men bought their first store—at 31 Vesey Street in New York City. There, salesmanship was accompanied by showmanship. The store was painted a startling red and gold, and large blue, white, and red globes glittered in the windows. A huge letter *T* was put up outside the store and lit with gas, one of the early illuminated signs.

Inside, the red and gold bins of tea and the cashier's cage, built in the shape of a Chinese pagoda, were illuminated by Japanese lanterns and chandeliers. On Saturday nights, a band was hired to attract customers, and while lithographs of babies were passed out to the ladies, the musicians tootled a popular song of the day: "Oh, this is the day they give babies away, with a half a pound of tea."

Eight dapple-gray horses pulled a big wagon, painted fireman's red, through the streets of the City, announcing the store's unique qualities. The astonishing sum of $20,000 was offered to anyone who could guess the combined weight of the harness, wagon, and horses.

This store was called grandly The Great American Tea Company. Its advertisements proclaimed cheerfully and prophetically, "There's good news for the ladies." The good news was, of course, the low prices resulting from direct buying. And the news was equally good for The Great American Tea Company, as the ladies flocked to the store in great numbers.

New ways were devised to bring in further profits. Advertisements appeared in national magazines, offering tea at bargain prices by mail. Circulars (part of one issued in 1869 is shown at right) were sent out, urging people to band together in "tea clubs" and thus receive weekly or monthly shipments at special rates and suggesting that "any person out of employment can make good wages peddling our Great Sun-Sun Chop, and Wootang Oolong Teas—and it takes but little capital to start with."

Soon coffee was being sold, too. "Our Coffee Department is very extensive—the largest perhaps, in the country," boasted a Great American Tea Company circular. "We run three engines constantly, and sometimes four and five, in roasting and grind-

210

ing our Coffee ... We sell none but the fully ripe, rich flavored Coffee." Prices ranged from thirty-five cents a pound for the Sultana brand ("cannot be excelled") to a quarter per pound for the "healthy and strong" Eight O'Clock Breakfast Coffee.

As transportation systems improved, so did business. When the transcontinental railroad line was built in 1869, George Hartford was quick to announce that this would permit the company to "distribute teas to their customers in 30 or 40 days from China and Japan." Meanwhile, wagons with tea and spices continued to be driven out to the open country for the benefit of rural housewives.

Photographs of George H. Hartford reveal a black hat, black eyebrows, black necktie, black coat, and a white beard. His shrewd and intense eyes look as if they could penetrate not only the details of business but the wrappings on a package and identify the quality of the contents. The nose is broad, and the mouth obstinate, suggesting that here was a man who, once possessed of an idea, would bull it on to completion. Since Gilman had sold out soon after the expansion began, it is obvious that Hartford's was the resourceful mind at work, the mind that began modern chain-store retailing.

The typical food store of the time was very small-scale, and the items sold were in small quantities. By the time food reached the customer's hand, many other hands had carried it, measured it, and wrapped it—each one adding its cost and markup to the final price. Tea of very romantic names—spider leaf, gunpowder, souchong—was weighed out in little packages. Coffee was ground on the spot, according to the customer's taste. Salt mackerel came in tubs, herring in handsomely tapered little kegs, as did sweet and sour pickles. Many items, such as beans, came in bushel baskets. Vinegar arrived in heavy barrels, and once the spigot had been pounded in and the barrel rolled into its cradle, customers could get a whiff of the sharp tang as their container was filled. Crackers came in barrels; cheese in large wheels or bricks. The purchase of any of these involved not only all the previous distributors but also the store's clerks, who measured out small amounts for each sale. The process increased not only the price but the time expended in selling the food. But all this was to change with the entrance of two more Hartfords upon the scene.

In 1880, George L. Hartford, the founder's fifteen-year-old son, joined the company as a cashier. By that time there were 95 stores in the chain, reaching as far west as Milwaukee. It was George who suggested that they produce their own baking powder, which could be sold for a fraction of the price of other brands. This was the first item other than tea, coffee, and spices to be sold by the company, and with it the concern began a manufacturing operation. Peas and tomatoes were being canned by the time of the Spanish-American War, followed a few years later by other products which were prepackaged.

Another Hartford son, John Augustine, began working in 1888, when he was sixteen, as office boy for what had by then been renamed The Great Atlantic & Pacific Tea Company, although it had not yet spread to the west coast.

Out of respect for the red of his father's original store, John always had a red carnation in his buttonhole after he became an executive. But at first he filled inkwells and learned the trade. Like his father, however, he found the current situation in need of change.

As John and George began to manage the company with their father the number of stores grew to four hundred. Yet the methods of operation were still old-fashioned, and in 1912 John took a hard look at them. There was an elaborate system of orders by telephone, endless charges on credit, and tedious deliveries by horse and wagon. The cost of giving away premiums was high, the paper work was enormous, the displaying and locating of food was inefficient.

John must have figured that the United States was the first nation in history dedicated to the notion that work was dignified, that it was proper for men, and even women, to do things for themselves. With typical Hartford ingenuity, he argued: Why not let the customers themselves participate in the distribution of food, and in return share in the saving which resulted? Thus was created that most American scheme— having the customer carry the food out of the store in his own arms and take it home himself. When he paid, a little money remained in his pocket as a just return for his effort in delivering his own food to his own house.

John proposed to his father and his brother that they try an experiment: do away with charge accounts, orders by telephone, premiums, deliveries, credit. Let every transaction be cash-and-carry. Keep the volume large, the profit small, and the price low.

It was an imaginative concept which shattered all retailing principles; furthermore, the existing stores were doing well and increasing in number. Why change? This was not a mere shift in policy. It was not simply changing horses in the middle of the stream. It was changing the course of the stream itself. The elder Hartford and brother George looked at these proposals with suspicion. They had a going operation. Why alter it? And yet they decided to give John a modest chance. He could have $3,000 to risk in the reckless venture.

John opened his first "economy store" at 794 West Side Avenue in Jersey City. The location was just around the corner from the most profitable A & P store. Operated by one man, with no clerks to help, with the merchandise readily available on the shelves, within six months the new store had run the older and much larger store out of business. Thus, in 1912, through a single family's vision, the retailing of food in the United States entered the twentieth century.

There followed one of the most spectacular episodes in the history of food and in the history of the free-enterprise system that a country accustomed to the spectacular had ever seen. Within five years, more than 3,000 economy stores were opened by the Hartfords. That represented a building rate of nearly three stores for every working day in the year, and the surge continued until in 1925 the rate had reached the unbelievable total of seven new stores a day. Such momentum will probably never be repeated in the future of American stores.

The unbeautiful store that John A. Hartford planned in Jersey City was as revolutionary as the new idea for handling tea that George H. Hartford had conceived on a New York wharf back in 1859. It proved that people— above all the housewife — would certainly give up the convenience of credit and delivery if convinced that money could be saved. Because every A & P store was laid out in the same way, someone who had never been in a newly opened one could find whatever he wanted; it was sure to be in the precise place where he had seen it at another A & P store. This was good news for the ladies, and in a subtle way it made the stores seem a little like home, with each article in place. (Admittedly, there may have been a few homes from the Atlantic to the Pacific in which a few things may *not* always have been in place—but surely these disorderly housewives were all the more grateful for the orderliness of the place where they traded.)

Since the U.S.A. was a country on the move, with families packing up and traipsing to other states for other jobs and tearing up roots perhaps several times in a single career, the fact that the identical A & P store could be found in every city, with the same merchandise available, gave an unexpected feeling of security to the housewife. She might not know one living soul in the new city, but the A & P was a familiar place.

When new stores were being opened at so rapid a rate, John A. Hartford commented later with a humor not always associated with executives, "We went so fast that hobos hopping off the trains got hired as managers." But it was not only the retailing of food that concerned the A & P; it was buying cheaper, which helped make possible selling cheaper. What began as a tea company became one of the great coffee enterprises of the world. Factories were set up to make many more of the products sold under the A & P's own brand names. The American Coffee Corporation was organized to buy direct from growers in Brazil and Colombia. An Atlantic Commission Company was created to buy produce for the stores. Baked goods and pastries were manufactured in their own shops.

But as before, the A & P continued to be a highly personal Hartford operation. At 2:30 P.M. every day George Hartford drank samples of various coffee blends, always including the standard three from A & P stocks, to make sure they were exactly as intended. In one year John visited 3,000 stores. (Once he candled all the eggs in a Chicago store to check their freshness.) The push into mass marketing of food was in great part accomplished by men who kept in close touch with all aspects of the business.

The A & P began as a horse-drawn affair. In his later years, John A. Hartford kept alive that affection for the antique, the handmade, and the old-fashioned that has been so marked a characteristic of men who have successfully created modern mass-production. It was his pleasure to leave his office and its business bustle and drive in a fringe-topped, horse-drawn surrey through his own roads on his Westchester estate. He and his family had altered a nation's food habits, but he wanted to keep unchanged this symbol of that handcrafted, small-scale, neighborly America he had helped to change.

THE BREADBASKET

A Picture Portfolio

Life on the farm was idealized by this poster, published in 1873. It implies that any man who earns his living by tilling the soil is bound to embody all the virtues.

This enormous cabbage was taller
than the midwesterner who grew it.

"The very Tails of the American Sheep are so laden with Wooll, that each has a little Car or Waggon on four little Wheels, to support & keep it from trailing on the Ground." That hyperbolic story, told by Benjamin Franklin, was outdone in the Midwest, where the rich soil was tilled by men with equally fertile imaginations. In Kansas, for instance, a popular anecdote concerned a farmer who climbed up a cornstalk to look over his acreage. When he decided to descend, he realized that the stalk was growing faster than he could climb down it. Subsisting on raw corn until the plant finally stopped its ascent, he returned to the ground and found forty bushels of corncobs, the remains of what he had eaten while perched on the stalk. Incredible as such stories were, they did have some basis in fact. Vegetables in the Midwest often grew to phenomenal sizes, as attested by the photograph at left.

THE ENORMAL STRAWBERRY
THE ONLY STRAWBERRY EVER PRODUCED THAT WILL GROW SUCCESSFULLY OUT OF A BARREL

The poster above advertised strawberries from Iowa. Below is a painting based on an 1869 cartoon by a Kansas artist who wanted to refute the eastern impression that his state was a desert.

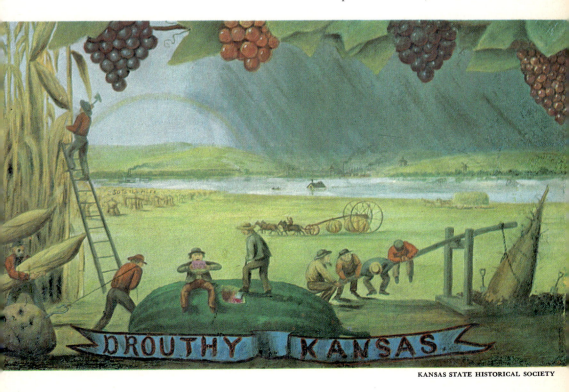

DROUTHY KANSAS.

Summer Outings

A fishing party in Missouri

Like their eastern counterparts, westerners enjoyed alfresco dining. Their special favorite was the barbecue. "In the strict definition of the term," William Allen White wrote, "Barbecue is any four-footed animal—be it mouse or mastodon — whose dressed carcass is roasted whole. . . . at its best it is a fat steer, and it must be eaten within an hour of when it is cooked. For if ever the sun rises upon Barbecue, its flavor vanishes like Cinderella's silks, and it becomes cold baked beef—staler in the chill dawn than illicit love."

The beef barbecue in the photograph above took place in Hugoton, Kansas, in 1913. At right, four girls pose for the camera while eating corn on the cob.

220

Rolling Farm Land

In 1864, a farmer in Walla Walla, Washington, discovered to his surprise that the hills nearby could produce thirty-three bushels of wheat per acre. Soon the uplands that stretch from Pendleton, Oregon, to the Palouse prairie of Idaho and eastern Washington became one of the nation's most productive breadbaskets, its wheat harvested by horse-drawn combines like those shown above.

The Minneapolis Grain Exchange, seen at right as it appeared in 1895, was established seven years earlier by the Chamber of Commerce. It enhanced the city's importance as a grain and flour center.

The poster above emphasized the lightness of bread made from one brand of flour. The one at right is more subtle: the cook making bread has left her hand prints on the gentleman's coat—to the wife's surprise.

MINNESOTA HISTORICAL SOCIETY

Knead for forty-five minutes...

Although it was cheaper to buy bread than to make it (the fuel for the stove cost more than the flour at the end of the nineteenth century), most American housewives still preferred to make their own loaves. It was a time-consuming process, as indicated by a warning from a popular cookbook, *Practical House-keeping:* "Knead for from forty-five minutes to one hour . . . Any pause in the process injures the bread." In Minneapolis, which became the capital of the nation's flour industry, a "middlings purifier" was invented; it removed the bran from spring wheat and resulted in the production of a superior white flour. Grain elevators were designed to store wheat; milling, farming, and transportation methods improved rapidly. By 1886, the Pillsbury company alone was turning out 10,000 barrels of flour a day, and Minnesota flour was regarded as the finest.

Cattle and Cowmen

At the end of the Civil War, some six million cattle were roaming the plains of Texas. These longhorns, descendants of animals brought to America by the Spaniards, commanded a high price in the North. Thus began the great cattle drives; thousands and thousands of cattle were driven over long, difficult trails to booming railheads like Abilene and Dodge City in Kansas, where they were freighted on to Chicago. At the same time, other cowmen began ranching in Montana, the Dakotas, and elsewhere on the endless miles of open grazing land on the Great Plains. In time, the rangy longhorn gave way to meatier cattle which were produced by crossbreeding. As settlers moved west and as the railroads expanded, ranching became less mobile, more scientific. Old-timers lamented the passing of an adventurous era, but for most Americans it meant more and better meat, available everywhere.

When the drawing at left of Chicago's Union Stockyards was made in 1866, cattle were still being shipped to eastern markets alive. In 1875, Gustavus Swift's company began to slaughter the animals in Chicago and send the meat east. Below is a huge Hereford bull, imported from England.

WYOMING STATE ARCHIVES

Below is a variety of cans used at the turn of the century. They contained (from left to right) cough drops, string beans, coffee, allspice, tea, cinnamon, biscuits, and tobacco. The label on the can containing tea shows the Boston Tea Party.

ANTIQUE CAN COLLECTION OF THE CAN MANUFACTURERS INSTITUTE

esidents of Sunrise, Wyoming, ought groceries at the store shown t left, where they did their shopping beneath potted palms. Since esh foods were limited, most of the ems sold there were canned, bottled, ried, or salted. At right is an early n opener. In 1910, a government rvey showed that the average merican ate 17½ pounds of canned uits and vegetables each year.

The Ubiquitous Can

"The people must live on canned fruits and vegetables," Samuel Bowles wrote in 1865 while visiting Virginia Dale, Colorado. "Corn, tomatoes, beans, pine apples, strawberry, cherry and peach, with oysters, and lobsters are the most common. . . . They range from fifty cents to one dollar a can of about two quarts. Families buy them in cases of two dozen each at twelve to fifteen dollars a case; while away up in Montana, they are sold at only twenty-seven dollars a case . . ." Food has been canned in America since about 1820, when reports of French and British research on airtight preservation reached this country. Not until 1847, however, was a stamping process invented that allowed tin cans to be made cheaply. Canned milk was used extensively during the Civil War, and by 1870 some thirty million cans of food were being sold annually. Advances in technology, and the passage of the Pure Food and Drug Act in 1906, alleviated lingering distrust of canned products. Thereafter, it was a rare housewife who did not consider a can opener essential.

Spanish friars brought the Mission grape to California and made the first wine there, but not until the 1850's did the state, whose dry summers were ideal for grapes, start to become an important wine-producing area. The most influential figure in the growth of the industry was Agoston Haraszthy de Mokcsa, a Hungarian who came to California and devoted himself to the improvement of its wines. Importing hundreds of varieties of roots and cuttings from Europe and planting them on his Sonoma Valley farm, he also studied and adapted European methods and proved that redwood could be used for casks. In 1850, California had produced only about 58,000 gallons of wine. In 1869, the figure rose to 4,000,000, and in the 1890's it soared to 23,000,000. It was no longer true, as Richard Henry Dana had observed of California in 1835, that "the country abounds in grapes, yet they buy, at a great price, bad wine made in Boston..."

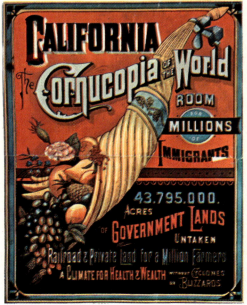

In the engraving above, Chinese laborers, who worked for eight dollars a month, press grapes with their feet on a California farm. Indians had performed the same chore for the mission padres. At right is a railroad poster, meant to attract settlers to fertile California.

Chili and Tortillas

"When they have to pay for their meat in market, a very little is made to suffice a family; it is generally cut into a kind of hash with nearly as many peppers as there are pieces of meat—this is all stewed together." J. C. Clopper, an American visiting San Antonio in 1828, thus described chili con carne, a dish invented by Mexican residents of Texas. It was eaten, he said, with thin circles of dough made from corn meal and called tortillas, "with which they all dip into the same dish of meat & peppers prepared as above, one spoon not lasting longer than to supply with two mouthfuls when a new one is made use of." Northern reactions to chili con carne varied. Edward King, writing in 1874, complained that the "fiery pepper . . . biteth like a serpent." But in his short story "The Enchanted Kiss," O. Henry wrote of "delectable *chili-con-carne* . . . composed of delicate meats minced with aromatic herbs and the poignant *chili colorado*—a compound full of singular savor and a fiery zest . . ."

Chili peppers

At top right, a vendor sells tamales (layers of crushed corn and minced meat, wrapped in cornhusks and steamed) on a Texas street. He was painted in 1850 by Théodore Gentilz. Below him is the same artist's La Cocina ("the kitchen"), which shows Mexican women making tortillas. At left is a beehive oven, made of adobe.

Animals outnumber people in this view of San Antonio's Military Plaza, painted about 1879 by Thomas Allen. Chili, cooked in cauldrons, is being sold to the passers-by.

Before:

During:

After:

'Sweet and Juicy"

Watermelons were commonplace to the midwesterners who partook of the feast depicted here. But for Gro Svendsen, a Norwegian woman who migrated to Iowa in the 1860's, they were something new. "I must tell you about a fruit called 'watermellon,'" she wrote. "We have an enormous quantity of them; I can't compare them to anything I ever saw in Norway. They are as big as a child's head; some are larger. They are round, and the inside is red or yellow. The melons are sweet and juicy."

"Zuzzarete"

L. Castellanos May

7

COSMOPOLITAN TASTES

By Leonard Louis Levinson

With the exception of the full-blooded Indians among us, we are all relatively recent immigrants to America. And with the exception of succotash and other dishes made from corn, the basis of most of our recipes came from the Old World, many of them as part of that great migration from Europe to the United States that began in 1820.

This century-long movement of peoples created not only a melting pot, out of which has emerged the composite American, but also a cooking pot, from which is slowly emerging

At left is the cover of a manuscript cookbook made for a New Orleans family in the early 1900's. It was bound in the colors of their cook's apron. She was called Zouzoute, and she is portrayed on the cover.

what promises to be one of the world's finest eating cultures.

Into this cooking pot has gone not only the overflowing cornucopia of American raw materials but the finest foreign foodstuffs and the best recipes of a dozen nations, brought here by immigrants, many of whom were driven from their homelands by famine.

Aside from language difficulties, fear of hunger often kept the immigrants pinned down in their own ghettos in the fast-growing American cities. "Distrust of unfamiliar food and the need to stick close to the source of what they were accustomed to eating was the reason the newcomers clustered together," said Preston Sturges, who was a food expert as well as a playwright and film director. "They feared that if they ventured out into the country by themselves, they would starve to death."

This was doubly true of immigrants of the Hebrew faith, who had to cope with dietary laws, including the kosher slaughtering of meat. Many an itinerant pioneer peddler lived a vegetarian life except when he could dine at the home of a coreligionist or get back to the city.

The result of urban concentration was the forming of colorful quarters, ethnic pockets, and cities-within-cities, spiced not only with mouth-watering, strange smells and loud, boisterous

But what was most remarkable, Broadway being three miles long, and the booths lining each side of it, in every booth there was a roast pig, large or small, as the centre attraction. Six miles of roast pig! and that in New York City alone; and roast pig in every other city, town, hamlet, and village in the Union. What association can there be between roast pig and independence?

—Frederick Marryat, describing a Fourth of July celebration in 1837

foreign sounds but with colorful, lively sights—all adding up to teeming streets full of shouting vendors of cheap merchandise of every description, customers haggling with heat and wit, and an air of excitement that was fascinating to the third- and fourth-generation American.

Beginning with the Dutch traders who wintered in 1613 on what is now lower Broadway, New York has been host to almost every known foreign group. Boston had its Irish enclaves and later Italian and even Chinese, colonies. In Newport, Rhode Island, two hundred years ago there was a group of Jews large enough to form a congregation and support a synagogue, which is still active. Philadelphia welcomed many Germans, who introduced sauerbraten and sauerkraut and helped create pepper pot soup and scrapple. Other Germans settled in Baltimore, which was also influenced by incoming French planters and their cooks, who had been driven from Hispaniola by the slave revolt at the beginning of the nineteenth century. To the southern cities came Africans and West Indians, cooks who made a unique contribution to the cuisine of that area. Charleston received an influx of French Huguenots; to the Florida Keys came Spaniards, Cubans, and the Cockney English. Ever since 1813, San Antonio has had a huge square filled with alfresco Mexican eating places; the Olvera Street district in Los Angeles has them, too, and not far away are two different Chinatowns. The largest, oldest, and most famous Chinatown in America is around San Francisco's Grant Avenue, while the nearby junction of Broadway and Columbus is the axis of a wonderful Little Italy. Fisherman's Wharf in San Francisco, the largest Italian fishing village outside of Italy, has a concentration of fish restaurants

Irish immigrants at a party

that rivals the Santa Lucia district of Naples.

German neighborhoods sprang up a century ago in Chicago, Milwaukee, St. Louis, and Cincinnati, and most other midwestern cities have their *Turnvereine, Bierstuben,* and breweries, around which has revolved the cult of the knackwurst, the coffeecake, the pretzel, and the potato dumpling. The Austrians blended into this milieu, except that their pastry shops have always been something special. Hungarians and Bohemians maintained their own little principalities, with paprika and Pilsener their respective trademarks.

In the century between 1820 and 1920, the population of the United States increased more than tenfold, from less than ten million to more than one hundred and five million. During those years, more than thirty-three million immigrants came to this country, over eighty per cent of them from ten countries: Germany, about 5 million; Ireland, 4⅓ million; Italy, 4⅕ million; Austria, 3½ million; Russia, 3¼ million; Great Britain, including Scot-

land, 3 million; Canada, 2 million; Sweden, 1 1/10 million; Norway and Denmark, another million.

The French, who influenced our cooking so markedly, sent only half a million immigrants, while tiny Switzerland was the source of a quarter million. An equal number arrived from Portugal, while the Netherlands' 225,000, Poland's 170,000, and Spain's 135,000 slowly made their native dishes a part of our heritage. During the same period, over 360,000 Greeks emigrated to the United States, bringing the ubiquitous Greek restaurant to these shores.

While the nations of Europe were pouring these masses, with their infinitely varied tastes and customs, into the United States, there was developing, at the mouth of the Mississippi River, another style of cooking—one so distinctive and popular that its vogue spread northward to the rest of the country and then across the Atlantic to be accepted at the very fountainhead of fine food, France. This was the Creole cooking of Louisiana and, more particularly, of New Orleans.

The word "Creole," often erroneously used to designate a person of mixed Caucasian and Negro blood, refers to the white descendants of the original French and Spanish settlers of Louisiana—the Frenchmen who came directly from the mother country, rather than from Acadia (Nova Scotia). Immigrants from the latter, a former French colony ceded to Great Britain in 1713, and their heirs are known as Cajuns.

Few cooking cultures in history have been derived from so many different sources as à la Creole. It combines the Spanish zest for highly seasoned dishes with the peasant cookery of early French immigrants, including the *filles à la cassette,* the girls who came on the bride ships carrying their dowries in little caskets. On this cuisine was superimposed the more delicate cookery of *émigrés* from the French Revolution and their trained chefs, then the natural skill of the Negro cooks they trained in turn, plus the native Indian contribution of wild herbs and vegetables—and American enthusiasm for the result.

Of all these elements, the one deserving the lion's share of credit, according to Charles Gayarré, an old-time gourmet, was the colored cook. Writing in

And if the stomach is the centre and origin of civilization, as some astute philosophers maintain, the French element of progress is still in the ascendency here.
—From an article titled "Sunday in New Orleans" in *Every Saturday* magazine, July 15, 1871

Harper's New Monthly Magazine in the 1880's, he tossed this laurel wreath:

"The Negroes are born cooks, as other less favored beings are born poets. The African ... gradually evolved into an artist of the highest degree of excellence, and had from natural impulses and affinities, without any conscious analysis of principles, created an art of cooking for which he should deserve to be immortalized. And how is it possible to convey to this dyspeptic posterity of our ancestors, to a thin-blooded population whose stomach has been ruined by kitchen charlatans, sauce and gravy pretenders, kettle and pot druggists, any idea of the miracles of the old creole cooking . . . ? It was not imitative; there was no traditionary lore about its origin; it had no ancestry; it sprang from itself. Pierre or Valentin, the colored cook . . . had not studied the records of roasting, baking, and boiling.... He could neither read nor write, and therefore he could not learn from books. He was simply inspired; the god of the spit and the saucepan had breathed into him; that was enough. . . . Who but Valentin knew how to bake rice in an iron pot? I say *iron,* because it must be nothing else, and that rice must come out solid, retaining the exact shape of the pot, with a golden crust round its top and sides. . . . Who but Pierre ever made *grillades de sang de dinde,* looking and tasting like truffles? What a sauce! Where did he get that sublime composition? But time and space do not permit me to continue. . . . I will content myself with saying that black Pierrot or yellow Charlotte, as a cook in the days of the Egyptian fleshpots in Louisiana, is not within the comprehension of any one born since the firing of the first gun against Fort Sumter."

No small part of the success of the New Orleans cuisine was due to the city's geographic position. It boasted a colorful food market, so lively and interesting that it has always been a sight-seeing attraction. To this market gravitated the widest range of foodstuffs. Down the Mississippi came the beef and pork of Kansas City, Chicago, and Cincinnati; the flour and grains of Minneapolis; the fruits and farm produce of the whole Midwest, from Ohio to Iowa. And from the lower river came garden greens and truck vegetables, while up to the port from the West Indies, Mexico, and Latin America came papayas and cactus fruit, cherimoyas and Surinam cherries, kumquats and loquats and limequats, oranges, nuts and pineapples from Brazil, ginger from Jamaica and onions from Bermuda, spicy sapodillas, mangoes and avocados, yellow and red bananas and plantains, tamarinds, tangelos, passion fruit, pomegranates, figs, yams, garlic, squashes, *garbanzos*, peppers, frijoles and egg plants, breadfruit and cassava . . . the list drools on.

Add to this the local game, such as snipe, quail, duck, rabbits, the many varieties of fish of the lakes and rivers, and the seafood of the Gulf, and New Orleans could boast a cupboard chockfull of a wider variety of foods to eat than almost any other city, anywhere —and all the year round.

These provisions provided the bases for a delicious array of dishes and even for several new drink concoctions, such as the Sazerac (a blend of bourbon, Penrod, Angostura and orange bitters, a twist of lemon peel, and

No money, no refreshments

sugar) and the Ramos gin fizz (crushed ice, lemon juice and lime juice, cream, powdered sugar, soda, orange-flower water, gin, and beaten egg white, shaken well, then shaken some more).

Of all Creole dishes, the gumbos were the most distinctive. They ranged from oyster, crab, and shrimp gumbo to chicken, which contained oysters, crabs, and shrimp; but no gumbo was ever complete without tomatoes and okra or filé, the powdered young leaves of the sassafras. Gumbo z'herbes, built of a choice of fifteen different greens and several herbs and seasonings from a list that included bay leaf, sage, borage, thyme, dill, tarragon, and chives, was a beautiful purée to which chicken, ham, or fried shrimp could be added for a main dish not only delicious and different but healthful.

Then there were delicate soups of the bisque family and hearty ones like black bean, which required sherry and a hard-boiled egg and a large lemon and allspice. Oysters were baked in the half shell "Bourguignonne," with chopped shallots, walnuts, anchovies, and a suspicion of garlic; or Grand

241

Island, with onion, celery, tomatoes, and mushrooms; or Rockefeller, with a blend of spinach, parsley, and anise—or with green lettuce or sorrel, or combinations thereof—plus butter and bread crumbs and Pernod. Shrimp and crab and lobster were served a dozen different ways, each more delicious than the other: jambalaya, ravigote, Newburg, remoulade, *piquante*, stuffed, au gratin, in omelettes, croquettes, as canapés, and as a pie. Chicken *Louisiane* was fried golden-brown and covered with a sauce of olives, mushrooms, and artichoke hearts. Ham Pontalba was stuffed with ground pecans, truffles, onion, seasonings, and Madeira, then boiled in a savory liquid and baked and glazed. These dishes were eaten with a variety of hot breads and biscuits, and it was a poor table that did not offer four different kinds.

While home cooking and cooks were responsible for most of the early Creole dishes, the fame of the cuisine was spread principally by the French Quarter restaurants in which the traveling public was exposed to New Orleans cookery, much to that public's

At a New York market

delight. Mouth-watering descriptions were first carried by visitors, and New Orleans, like San Francisco and New York, became a strong magnet for tourists.

Among the most famous of the restaurants were Antoine's, Galatoire's, Broussard's, La Louisiane, Vieux Carré, Bégué's, Maylié's, Tujague's, Léon's, and those of the old St. Charles and other hotels. Going to dine in the French Quarter, you found your appetite sharpened by an air of excited anticipation, and few native or visiting gourmets were so blasé that they did not share some of the feelings of the greenest gawking tourist.

You made your way through narrow, romantic streets that bubbled with traffic and trade to an almost disappointingly modest door and into a painfully plain, scrubbed set of rooms. Their appearance seemed to tell you that the only fancy interior décor was intended for the stomach. There were few distractions. The lights were low, the napery and silver immaculate. The entries on the menu were in French and were interpreted for the uninitiate by waiters with the dignity of foreign ministers, who negotiated between you and a distant sanctum where the chef presided. The service was deft but leisurely, and the waiters, like actors in a long-run musical show, were pleasantly confident as they presented you with the hit selections of the house. And the dishes—from the *bouillabaisse à la Nouvelle-Orléans* (Thackeray declared "a better was never eaten at

Marseilles") to the *pompano en papillote* (fish fit for a king, baked and served in a paper bag), to the *pommes de terre soufflées,* those beautiful little potatoes—each seemed to have some small mystery in its flavoring, a nagging reminder of some subtle ingredient just beyond your palate's memory.

Then, when you were ready to swear that you could not possibly swallow another morsel, you would slump back and contemplate the desserts, which had to be wonderful to get any attention after the rest of the meal. The list (including *crème brûlée,* pecan pie, praline ice cream, *baba au rhum,* Chess and Quadroon pies, watermelon ice) was always long, and the selection usually difficult.

Many an American had his initial formal experience with French wines at his first dinner in New Orleans and found to his delight and enjoyment that the marriage of different vintages with different foods was one that was successful not only in the mouth, but all the way down.

Crowning the dinner was *café brûlot* and often a liqueur sent over by the *patron.* Then, in a rosy daze, you got up, examined the old menus on the walls, paid a rather stiff *addition,* and floated out into the charming cobblestoned street.

Of all other foreign sections in American cities, the sharpest contrast to the Vieux Carré was to be found in the lower East Side of New York. Where the French Quarter was petite,

architecturally beautiful, clean, and romantic, Manhattan's principal foreign settlement, growing with the city, sprawled for miles. Filled with the filthiest slums and sordid tenements,

---

Today many of the passengers went ashore, and I tasted American food for the first time. It was white bread and fresh milk that I have yearned for so long.

—A Norwegian immigrant, 1862

---

it was a battleground for survival, day and night.

The first substantial wave of immigrants arriving in New York, just before 1820, consisted mainly of English factory workers who had lived on oatmeal, potatoes, and water and of Irish workmen, whole generations of whom were born, grew up, married, and died without ever having tasted meat. In America, even if they found no work, they felt that the worst fare dished up by New York's soup kitchens and poorhouses was better than the best at home.

By 1840, New York was the leading port of entry for immigrants. (Twelve times as many landed there as at Boston, the next busiest stop.) More Irish and some Germans were arriving, and the flow became a flood after the potato blight of 1846 in Ireland and the failure of the liberal-national revolution of 1848 in Germany.

Most of the Germans had to content

themselves with the most menial of jobs (there was a colony of trash collectors in "Rag-Picker's Paradise," a row of miserable shacks off Sheriff Street), but within a few years they prospered, and there sprang up "queer, dingy, rattle-trap dining-houses in which families of Teuton race—men, women and children —appear to pass a great deal of their time," according to Charles Dawson Shanly, writing in the *Atlantic Monthly* for May, 1867.

In these restaurants, he continued, there was a bar, "which is also a counter for the exposition . . . of a wonderful amount and variety of pungent viands, [and] looks like a breastwork thrown up by a regiment of gourmands to oppose the march of famine. It is piled with joints and manufactured meats adapted to the strong German stomach;—enormous fat hams, not thoroughly boiled, for the German prefers his pig undone; rounds of cold corned beef, jostled by cold roast legs and loins

---

Just order two seidels of lager, or three
If I don't want to drink it, please force
*   it on me,*
The Rhine may be fine
but a cold stein for mine,
Down where the Wurzburger flows.
—From "Down Where the Wurzburger
    Flows," popular song of 1902

---

of veal; pyramids of sausages of every known size and shape, and several cognate articles of manufactured swine-meat. . . . baskets full of those queer twisted briny cakes which go variously,

I believe, by the names of *Pretzel* and *Wunder;* sardine-boxes piled upon each other. . . . huge glass jars of pickled oysters, flanked by huge earthen jars of caviare. Raw onions in heaps give a tone to the combined odors of all these; and through this confusion of smells come powerful whiffs of the Limburger and Sweitzer cheeses, without which the *menu* of no German restaurant would be considered complete."

Most such German restaurants were on the Bowery, as were Irish and Italian eating and drinking gardens, theatres of every sort, clothing stores with "puller-inners" and $1.95 suits, saloons with free lunch day and night, and inexpensive hotels.

"Mulberry Bend had its 'stale beer' dives and 2¢ restaurants," reported Smith Hart in *The New Yorkers,* "where the privilege of sleeping on the floor or in a barrel was given with each purchase, ladies admitted free."

As the Irish and German immigrants improved their status and moved to Hell's Kitchen and Yorkville, newer arrivals took over the tenements. Polish, Hungarian, and Russian Jews jammed into the Tenth Ward, east of the Bowery, and the density rose to one-third of a million humans per square mile, the highest in the world. Hester Street became the center of the ghetto, and the already crowded tenements became sweatshops where $1.95 suits, "Havana" cigars, and artificial flowers were made.

From inside the stores out to the middle of the road, the sale of food was conducted on four separate levels. In the store, which was a permanent establishment, the highest-grade merchandise was offered. In front the merchant offered his bargains or rented out space to someone who had a stand with fruit and vegetables or candies or even bargains that undercut the store. At the curb, in the street, were pushcarts with bigger bargains—damaged cans, riper bananas. And moving along the street were hucksters with their wagons: the hokeypokey man with his box on wheels, the vendors of hot dogs, hamburgers, Italian ices, hot sweet corn, and taffy apples on a stick. From the store proprietor, standing in his doorway, to the high-hatted "chef" who seemed to be able to drive a horse and wagon, cook sugared waffles, and beat a large triangle simultaneously, they all "advertised" at the top of their lungs. The same performance went on in Maxwell Street in Chicago and, to a lesser degree, in Boston's Spring Street and along Pittsburgh's Logan Street, where it runs down into Fifth Avenue.

In Italian neighborhoods, carts with a bed of ice offered raw oysters, mussels, and clams on the half shell with half lemons to squeeze over the shellfish, just as they did in Trastevere, the comparable section of Rome. In summer the ice-cream and flavored-shaved-ice peddlers did a brisk business, and as winter approached the same men switched to hot chestnuts and "miggies"—charred Irish potatoes or yams. In the Chinese theatres around Chatham Square, the "butchers" sold sweets, nuts, and dumplings and tossed hot, damp towels to their customers in lieu of napkins. Little girls sold cold soda pop to Sicilians who attended the imported puppet shows, which had stories, like the Chinese entertainments, that were continued nightly for a week and sometimes longer.

The Neapolitan saints' day festivals and street fairs were occasions on which highly colored, highly seasoned, seasonal food was hawked. Special holiday sweets were dispensed from temporary stands lining the gaily decorated, garishly lit blocks of Mulberry or Bleecker streets. There were *sfinge di San Giuseppe* (St. Joseph's Day cream puffs), *torrone* (Christmas nougat), *pastiera di Pasqua* (Easter tart), and *panettone di Milano* (Christmas fruit bread).

In those times a boy with a penny and a sweet tooth was somewhat like J. P. Morgan in an art gallery with only a hundred thousand to spend. In each case the problem was how to get the most for the money. Candies came in an enormous variety of substances, sizes, shapes, colors, and flavors. And a penny was a respectable sum of money. Remember, there were hash houses for poor men where two cents would purchase a meal.

The boy could invest his penny in the equivalent of today's ten-cent candy bar or he could get a cupful of spice drops; five or—depending on the size—ten jawbreakers; a wide strip of paper a foot and a half long dotted with candy buttons; three or four licorice whips, pipes, or whistles; twenty little "tar

245

babies"; a package of ten candy cigarettes with gold tips and glowing ends; a big chocolate cigar which split down the middle; a small tin pan with candy ham and eggs and tiny spoon; fake plug chewing tobacco with tin label; a pack of five sticks of inferior chewing gum; a block of *halvah;* colored and flavored wax flutes; a sizable hunk of bubble gum or a larger chunk of Bonomo's Turkish Taffy; Tootsie Rolls; and chocolate coins wrapped in gold or silver foil. Then there were marshmallow confections in the shape of bananas, ice cream cones, and pistols; taffy bars with a peanut-butter center (if you found a colored strip of paper inside the wrapping, you got another bar free); and seasonal candies—chocolate and marshmallow rabbits and eggs at Easter, pumpkins and witches at Halloween, turkeys and axes at Thanksgiving, and Santas at Christmas.

Also at holiday time there would spring up white candy kitchens of Austrian and Swiss origin, selling marzipan in the shape and color of every other kind of food—sausages and hams, fruits and vegetables, eggs and chickens—but it all tasted of the grainy, sweet almond paste which was the basis for the sculptured and tinted confections.

There were many other immigrant candies: hard drops from England, Scotch toffee, Jordan almonds (called *confetti* in Italy), Turkish delight and sesame seed candy from the Near East, as well as stuffed dates and glazed cherries from around the Mediterranean,

sheets of apricot "leather" from the Balkans, smooth chocolate from Holland and Switzerland, French bonbons, and Austrian filled candies. The Greeks were quick to become candy-kitchen operators, and the invention of the electric fan enhanced their salesman-

Root beer dispenser

ship. In addition to the display of taffy-pulling in the window, the exhaust fan wafted the enticing sweet smell of cooking candy out onto the sidewalk in both directions, to whet the appetite and lower the resistance of the passer-by.

In the kaleidoscopic Land of Penny Candy, the native American youth and his immigrant counterpart met in mutual enjoyment, discarding their fears of the unknown in a common relish of the sugary confections which were frowned upon by all parents. As long as it was highly colored and bad for the teeth, the foreign-born boy and his native opposite number could bury their prejudices against *halvah, torrone,* jawbreakers, or gumdrops.

But there was a real prejudice

against foreign foods among Americans, a prejudice which rose as the social strata lowered. The sophisticated upper classes were quick to accept French cooking and English servants, but the common folk of Anglo-Saxon stock were so resentful of the acquired tastes of their superiors that this antipathy was used in politics against anyone suspected of being a dainty eater.

In the presidential campaign of 1840, the Whigs succeeded in picturing William Henry Harrison as an abstemious eater of unsalted raw beef, while accusing the Democrat, President Martin Van Buren, of using public funds to raise strawberries, raspberries, celery, and, horror of horrors, *cauliflower* for his table. A campaign song went:

Let Van from his coolers of silver drink wine,
And lounge on his cushioned settee,
Our man on his buckeye bench can recline
Content with hard cider is he.

Harrison won, but died a month later after consuming too much ice water and raw fruit on a sizzling hot day.

Twelve years after, Democrats were appealing to the same prejudices when they ridiculed General Winfield Scott's preference for foreign food. "He was fed on Hasty Plates of Turtle and Oyster SOUP," they claimed, "Which inspired him to Swim in the Sea of Society with Plumes."

It required many years of exposure to immigrant food to break down the resistance of the *hoi polloi,* who struggled much longer than the hoity-toity against strange smells and tastes and names. The garlic and onions of Mediterranean cooking, the strong cheeses and cooked cabbage of Germany's cuisine, the alleged zest of the French for frog's legs and snails, led to a whole literature of foreign-food jokes such as: "*Newspaperman:* And what is the secret of your longevity?

Ninety-year-old Italian: I eat a fist of garlic every day.

Newspaperman: Thank you . . . but what makes you think it's a secret?"

Little by little, foreign foods became more acceptable. For one thing, the strong tastes and odors were modified. (Beer, for example, has been transformed into a lady's drink; Swiss cheese has lost its strong aroma; the American onion is much milder than its Italian counterpart.) Then, closer contact led to acceptance. As Swedish, Irish, and Polish maids and nurses moved in, so did their cooking cultures. German cooks fixed pot roast and sauerbraten, and the combination of hunger and appetizing smells broke down finicky opposition. Hungarian women, especially, were prized as great cooks, thanks to their stuffed cabbage, goulashes, chicken and veal *paprikash,* and all kinds of strudel, including cabbage. On the West Coast, male Chinese were quick to achieve superiority with American dishes, as well as with Mexican specialties and their own fluffy version of rice. In the Southwest, Mexican cooks put their brand permanently on eating habits.

Next to servants, the greatest influences on American eating habits were ethnic restaurants and stores. Except for the superior French eating places, these were usually opened as havens for immigrants. Frequently a foreigner with a wife who cooked would take in fellow countrymen as boarders. Such enterprises would grow, by popular demand and dreams of wealth, into restaurants catering to other immigrants who yearned for home-country cooking. In the case of the Italian *trattorie* of Greenwich Village, the first Americans to invade their Latin exclusivity were the artists who had lived and studied in Italy and who were eager to enjoy the cuisine, not only because they were accustomed to the taste but because bountiful meals, with wine, were extremely inexpensive. Neighbors, schoolmates, business associates, and fellow workers were introduced by immigrants to German, Jewish, Hungarian, and Austrian as well as Italian restaurants, where they learned the delights of *pasta* and "Dago Red," blintzes and Russian tea, corned beef and celery tonic, gefilte fish, potato pancakes, *spumone,* noodle pudding (kugel), and kosher Concord grape wine.

The delicatessen, originally as German as its name, became in the United States a treasure house of many nations. Scandinavian delicatessens sprang up to satisfy the *smörgåsbord* (literally, "bread and butter table") trade. Italian delicatessens were festooned with many varieties of salami and strange-shaped cheeses, hanging overhead. They quickly produced the Latin version of *smörgåsbord:* the Hero, or Submarine sandwich. Hungarian delicatessens featured pungent pickles and red pepper meat.

But delicatessen reached its most glorious heights in the Jewish enterprise known as the appetizing store. This was the home of the overstuffed sandwich. Upon entering one of these pastrami palaces, one's nose was greeted by a thousand smells, coming from every kind of food (with the exception of the meat of the pig), prepared in all known ways.

Since the Jews in their many wanderings borrowed the best from every cooking culture they encountered, a well-stocked appetizing store would carry an international array of dainties to stagger the imagination and glut the appetite. Amid a clamor of demanding housewives and impatient clerks (who cried, "What else? What else? What else?" as they cut and weighed and wrapped) and over barrels, boxes, trays, and bins heaped with provender, a busy trade was carried on from early morning until far into the night. Only on Friday night and on the Sabbath was the place closed; it leaped to life again after sundown on Saturday for the most crowded, hectic session of the week.

It was a department store with sections for fish, pickled goods, preserved meats, salads, dairy goods, spices, staples, sweets, and baked products. In addition to the braided egg breads, the sour pumpernickels and ryes, and the soft rolls, the bakery department always featured those thick-dough, doughnut-shaped delicacies called bagels. There was the standard bagel, others of whole-wheat flour, some with onionskin sprinkled on top, and others with seeds. One enterprising bagel baker journeyed across the country, stopping at Jewish communities where he produced miniature "bagelettes" as long as the novelty lasted, before moving to the next stand.

Closely allied to the bagel was the *bialystoker* kuchen, a tasty onion roll which presumably originated in the Polish textile center of Bialystok. About 1910, the bearded patriarch Yonah Schimmel began producing knishes, pastry surrounding chopped meat or other stuffings. Today the family still carries on the tradition in two lower East Side stores, now featuring frankfurters-in-jackets, hot hors d'oeuvres, and cocktail-sized knishes.

One of the greatest immigrant contributions to the American table has been the variety of breads these people introduced. Every country that poured settlers into the United States has given us one or more kinds, from the Scandinavian *knäckebröd*, which we know as Ry-Krisp, to the Euphrates Bread of Asia Minor, which has become a bed for cocktail snacks. And among pastries and desserts are *gugelhupf* from Austria, pfeffernusse from Germany, *baklava* from Turkey, tutti-frutti, *spumone,* and biscuit *tortoni* ice creams from Italy, sweet puddings from England, the coffeecakes of Germany, *dobos*

torte from Hungary, Scotch shortbread, and the innumerable pastries of France, including the light circle of yeast pastry called savarin. The latter was named in honor of the celebrated French food philosopher and gourmet, Jean Anthelme Brillat-Savarin, who spent some two years in this country at the end of the eighteenth century.

> *In the matter of dining, the tastes of all nations can be gratified here. There are ... three Chinese houses, denoted by their long three-cornered flags of yellow silk. The latter are much frequented by Americans, on account of their excellent cookery, and the fact that meals are $1 each, without regard to quantity ... There the grave Celestials serve up their chow-chow and curry, beside many genuine English dishes; their tea and coffee cannot be surpassed.*
> **—Bayard Taylor in San Francisco, 1849**

Then there are the "foreign" foods that are unknown in the Old Countries, having seen the light of day in America. Cioppino, the savory fish stew of the Monterey peninsula and Fisherman's Wharf in San Francisco is one of several American-created Italian specialties. Ask for Swiss steak in Switzerland and all you get in return is your echo. A request for Russian dressing brings you *ryet* in Russia. And chop suey is viewed by most Chinese gourmets as a rather peculiar American hash. But one must be philosophical; after all, as someone has written, "What France admires is good enough for France."

John, Lorenzo, and Peter Delmonico

DELMONICO'S

By Leonard Louis Levinson

A family of Swiss immigrants ran an establishment whose cuisine and tone were unmatched. A London paper called it and Yosemite the "most remarkable bits of scenery in the States"

Why John Delmonico left the family vineyards in the Swiss canton of Ticino to become captain of a trading ship in the West Indies, and how he acquired the foresight, talent, and taste to establish a restaurant dynasty in New York that dominated the City for almost a century, are questions that remain unanswered. But his timing was right.

People were beginning to flock to New York in 1825, when John opened a hole-in-the-wall near the Battery to deal in European wines, which he bought by the cask and sold by the bottle. Over a period of about a hundred years, the tides of immigration swept thirty million strangers onto our shores; during that same time, the Delmonico family was transforming and improving the dining habits of the American upper class.

In the 1820's the American palate was still accustomed to the heavy, unadorned farm fare of colonial days, and the food offered in taverns and hotels of the period had little to recommend it either in taste, variety, or presentation. It was prepared to fill the belly and was served on a take-it-or-leave-it basis.

While he measured the potential appetite of New York, John Delmonico prospered, and within a year or two he went back home and persuaded his older brother, Peter, a confectioner, to return to New York with him. In 1827 they opened the first of more than a dozen eating establishments that brought the name Delmonico to pre-eminence in the creation and serving of fine food. In the 1880's the esteemed *Pall Mall Gazette* of London declared: "The two most remarkable bits of scenery in the States are undoubtedly Delmonico's and the Yosemite Valley, and the former place has done more to promote a good feeling between England and America than anything else in [that] country." And as James Grant Wilson, in his *Memorial History of the City of New York,* wrote: "Never had caterer such a field for his art, with the produce of every zone cheap and in bountiful profusion close at hand. And never did caterer better improve his opportunities, teaching the inhabitants of this new world the culinary habits of the old. . . ."

But the Delmonico success did not come overnight. Their first establishment was a narrow store on William Street, where they sold cakes, ices, and wine, either to be taken home or to be consumed at plain pine tables. In contrast to the careless conduct and sloppy linen of contemporary shops, the aprons and the manners of the brothers were immaculate; their pastry was delicate and delicious. Advertisements and announcements and menus were printed in both English and French, and with smart New York still clustered there at the toe of Manhattan Island, it became the fashion to drop in for a sweet and a glass of wine from Europe. Swiss-born Albert Gallatin, who had been

the Secretary of the Treasury from 1801 to 1814, was a lover of good cheer, and the Delmonicos "had his favor."

As "Del's" became a popular meeting place, it was quite the thing for students to save up for a Saturday spread there, and soon the stores on either side were taken over by the brothers. More foods were added to the menu, and a new restaurant opened on Broad Street. That same year, 1832, a nineteen-year-old nephew, Lorenzo, was summoned from Switzerland.

Lorenzo was destined to become the "great" Delmonico. Short, stocky, amiable, and eagle-eyed, he had foresight, daring, and a winning sense of taste in food, décor, and clientele. For almost fifty years he watched over every detail of the establishment. He went to market early every morning, purchasing the freshest and finest food. He organized the employees in the kitchens and dining rooms along military lines, so that there was no waste time, motion, or foodstuffs. And, because capacity was limited and because New York was peopled increasingly with the new rich, he became a powerful social arbiter, as well as confidant and consultant to old Knickerbocker society.

The transformation from a modest store to de luxe eating establishments did not come until after the disastrous fire of 1835, which destroyed the original place of business. In less than two years the Delmonicos opened a three-story restaurant with dining rooms, a lounge, and a ballroom. Situated on the corner of William and Beaver streets, it was a far cry from the ice-cream-and-cake parlor up the street, and it was destined to become the premier restaurant of the financial district. (In 1890 the building was replaced by one of eight stories, with even more elaborate dining and banquet rooms. It was sold by the family in 1916 and has continued as a Wall Street gathering place to the present time.)

A second great fire, in 1845, destroyed the Delmonico establishment on Broad Street, and to replace it Lorenzo built a new restaurant and hotel on Broadway, across from Bowling Green. This one played host to many notables, including Jenny Lind and Louis Napoleon. Indeed, almost everyone of fame or talent (including every President from Monroe to McKinley) who visited New York was feted at one or the other of the Delmonico caravansaries. These were not only sight-seeing attractions but places of entertainment. "The Delmonicos did something for New York which others could not have done," the New York *Sun* reported in 1901. "They have been public benefactors. It is not merely that the Delmonicos have had the biggest establishments of their kind in the world, not that they made a great deal of money out of them, but that they conferred a

positive benefit upon the community and helped to make New York take its place among the half dozen capitals of the world.... Their restaurants have been and are numbered among the institutions of the city, things perfect of their kind and at the same time peculiar to New York. They are places not merely to dine at, but to talk about, to take foreigners to, places to be proud of, places which make the city attractive the world over."

How Delmonico's fitted into the life of the upper-class New Yorker can be glimpsed in the diaries of George Templeton Strong, a prominent lawyer who grew up with the restaurants. One entry, written in 1837, when he was a student at Columbia College, had all the measured solemnity of a youth-about-town: "Evening...Went to Delmonico's...and drank some of the only good chocolate I ever tasted, as much superior to the stuff that ordinarily goes under that name as champagne to small beer."

Eleven years later, distributing announcements of his forthcoming wedding, he wrote: "Carried two round to Delmonico's and took his breath away with the news." Lorenzo was a friend who supplied French waiters for Strong's home and welcomed him at Christmas luncheons and after-concert suppers when his family was in the country and at innumerable banquets and committee dinners. "Haven't been very energetic this morning," Strong wrote on another occasion, "though I tried to get myself into working order by a stimulating cup of coffee at Delmonico's—the first time I've so sinned against my liver for some months . . ."

As the center of fashion moved up Manhattan Island, Lorenzo opened and closed restaurants up and down Broadway and Fifth Avenue. In 1861 he purchased the Grinnell mansion at 14th Street and Fifth, and when it opened it was acclaimed the finest café-restaurant in America.

"To lunch, dine or sup at Delmonico's," Abram C. Dayton wrote regarding the 14th Street restaurant, "is the crowning ambition of those who aspire at notoriety, and no better studio for character does the city afford than that expensive resort at almost any hour of the day." It was "beyond all question the most palatial café or restaurant on this continent."

After a particularly enjoyable dinner there, President Lincoln summoned Lorenzo and told him: "Mr. Delmonico, in my home in Washington, there are many mansions, but alas! we have no cooks like yours." Charles Dickens was also a visitor here, and it is recorded that he would drink two bottles of champagne with his luncheon, then a tumbler of brandy before embarking to deliver a lecture. William Thackeray was entertained so nobly that he insisted on reciprocating

with a supper of his own—and then screamed when he saw the bill. There were dinners for two hundred that cost $25,000, and others at $400 a plate. The night the Atlantic cable was put into operation, Samuel F. B. Morse was honored. He sent the first telegram from his table, and in forty minutes the answer came back and was read to the assembled 350 guests.

Foxhall Keene, son of the great Wall Street operator Jim Keene, supposedly suggested a way to prepare creamed chicken which became known at Delmonico's as chicken à la Keene—since twisted into chicken à la king. Another man-about-town, Ben Wenberg, showed the chef how he had seen lobster prepared in South America. As lobster Wenberg, this became one of the most famous Delmonico dishes—until Mr. W. made the mistake of brawling in the restaurant and was barred. Then the dish was renamed lobster Newburg.

Lorenzo and his staff had high standards of behavior, for their patrons as well as for themselves. Brawlers, fisticuffers, and those who were not capable of carrying their wine or whiskey well were shown the door they were never to darken again. Parties in private dining rooms had to leave their doors open; once when another couple failed to put in an appearance with the August Belmonts, Lorenzo refused to allow the Belmonts to dine by themselves in a private room, even though he knew very well that they were married to each other.

This strict attention to appearances and insistence on good behavior characterized the establishment in later years, too. In a New York newspaper article, one of Lorenzo's successors, Charles Crist Delmonico, was described as a small, slim man, neatly dressed in black, who "lingered unobtrusively near the doors, quietly turning his pale, keen face and quick, sharp eyes upon every visitor. He knew everybody. No tramps or beggars or bunco steerers or stool pigeons infested Delmonico's. It is as if the house were a club where none but gentlemen were allowed to enter. There is always the peace, order, comfort and elegance for which Delmonico's is famous."

Not long after the Civil War, New York began to move uptown again, and in 1876 Lorenzo sold the 14th Street place and created an even more resplendent Delmonico's on the triangle formed by Fifth Avenue, Broadway, and 26th Street, facing Madison Square. But Lorenzo enjoyed the prosperity and excitement of the new building for only five years; in 1881 he died of a stroke aggravated by gout.

In a tribute to him, the New York *Tribune* recalled that in 1860, at the height of the oil rush in western Pennsylvania, when petroleum was being hunted everywhere, Lorenzo was persuaded to invest in a company drilling for oil in Brooklyn and was made president. He went to Europe that year, leaving instructions with his brothers to supply any additional funds that might be needed. Debts of over a million dollars were contracted, the company failed, and Lorenzo's entire fortune was swept away. The Delmonico restaurants and hotels were put up at auction, but so great was the public confidence in Lorenzo that the creditors reinstated him, and subsequently he not only paid off all the debts but made another million.

There were nearly a thousand Delmonico employees at Lorenzo's funeral, but no direct heir, so once again the mantle of leadership was bestowed on a nephew. This time it was Charles, son of Lorenzo's brother Joseph. Charles was well-grounded in the family operation, but unfortunately he suffered a nervous breakdown, and less than three years after taking over, he wandered off, crossed into Orange, New Jersey, and died of starvation and cold during a snowstorm.

Next in line was *his* nephew, Charles Crist, who added Delmonico to his name by permission of the New York legislature and who made the last great move uptown. On November 15, 1897, sensing another northerly trend in the city, Charles Crist Delmonico opened, at the northeast corner of 44th and Fifth Avenue, the last and most elaborate Delmonico's. That night over a thousand guests flowed through the Ladies' Restaurant, the Palm Garden, the Gentlemen's Elizabethan Café, the private dining and banquet rooms, the ballroom ("lighted by electroliers screened by a mass of small glass beads"), and the Roof Conservatory.

Charles, who died in 1901, was the last male Delmonico kin to run the family business. He was succeeded by his aunt; then his sister assumed the management; but within five years competition from Sherry's, across the street, and from the Waldorf-Astoria and other hotels began to cut into the commanding position that Delmonico's had held for so long. The decline of leisured dining, lavish parties, and fine wines in favor of the quick meal and the cocktail, plus the devastating effects of Prohibition, are often given as reasons for the eventual death of Delmonico's in 1923. But Leopold Rimmer, a former waiter, gave another:

"The only mistake that ever was made against the interest of the Delmonicos' business was Mr. Charles Ranhofer's cook book [*The Epicurean,* written in 1894 by the man who had been Delmonico's chef for many years] which gave away all secrets of the house [so that] every Tom, Dick and Harry, who calls himself a chief cook, and had learned his trade in Delmonico's kitchen, can cook and make up the finest dinners on record, with that book, which tells him everything he don't know. There is hardly one hotel in New York to-day whose chef did not learn cooking at Delmonico's ...The book gave all the secrets to the world—the market, what is in season, where to get it, and what is the correct thing to eat every day, and all year around. And this is the error that was made by Mr. Delmonico."

One man who knew the secrets of Delmonico's had become the presiding genius at the Waldorf. He was Oscar Tschirky, a young Swiss whose career began at the Hoffman House, near Delmonico's Madison Square restaurant. One evening, while he was on his way home from work, he passed Delmonico's entrance and heard the doorman call: "Miss Russell's carriage, please!"

The door opened, and Miss Lillian Russell came out with a party of friends. Captivated by the beauty of her face, her golden hair, and rose-petal complexion, young Oscar vowed to get a job at the fabulous place where she dined three or four times a week. He applied for a position the next day, and not long after was working there. "Its food was the best in the city," Oscar later told his biographer, Karl Schriftgiesser. "Its service was not equalled elsewhere. But what really gave it its tone was the fact that Ward McAllister, creator of the Four Hundred and social arbiter to Mrs. Astor, had long since decided that if one must entertain outside one's home the *only* place to do so was at Delmonico's."

Following a series of promotions, Oscar was placed in charge of the private dining rooms, and at last his opportunity came to serve Miss Russell and her escort, "Diamond Jim" Brady, whose enormous appetite Oscar knew by reputation. But the young man's vision of romance was shattered. "I had the surprise and disillusionment of my lifetime. Lillian Russell ate more than Diamond Jim."

COSMOPOLITAN TASTES

A Picture Portfolio

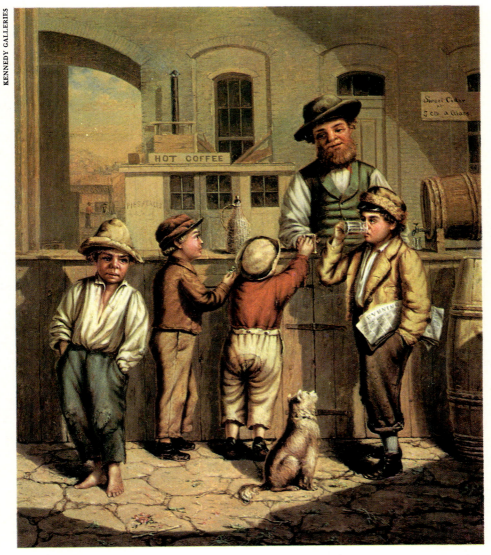

Three city boys, painted by John Magee in the mid-1800's, are buying sweet cider at five cents per glass. A less affluent waif, shoeless as well as nickel-less, stands by unhappily.

LENT BY ROBERT CARLEN, PHILADELPHIA, TO THE PHILADELPHIA MUSEUM OF ART

Victualers' Procession

"*The occasion that gave rise to this* SPLENDID PROCESSION [*in Philadelphia in 1821*] *was conveying the meat of the stock* **of** *exhibition Cattle to Market, which for number, quality, beauty and variety, has never been slaughtered at any one time in this, or probably any other country.*" *So says a contemporary account of this parade, painted by J. L. Krimmel.*

Even at $1.56 for twelve
pounds of mutton and $3.94 for
an "ordinary-hind
quarter veal, 21 lbs.," a
butcher (below) sometimes heard
complaints about his prices.

"Strawberries! Strawberries!
Fine, ripe, and red!" sang
this girl, who was painted,
with the others here, by
Nicolino Calyo in 1840.

The pipe-smoking woman at right sold beans,
peas, cucumbers, cabbage, onions,
and potatoes. A sign on the hydrant
advertises a doctor: "No Cure, No Pay."

"*Here Comes the Fishman*"

In the mid-nineteenth century, a city housewife was able to buy almost every kind of food from vendors who made the streets their market place. Some rode in horse-drawn wagons, while others, such as the oystermen who carried plates and condiments in case their customers wanted to eat their wares on the spot, used pushcarts. Many simply wandered around carrying their goods in baskets and singing or shouting the street cries that announced their arrival to all but the stone-deaf. These cries were often direct and to the point: "Here comes the fishman! Bring out your dishpan, Porgies at five cents a pound!" Some vendors, however, attempted to entertain, as well as sell. A Philadelphia peddler, for instance, used this cry: "My hoss is blind and he's got no tail, When he's put in prison I'll go his bail. Yed-dy go, sweet potatoes, oh! Fif-en-ny bit a half peck!"

The young man below dispenses refreshing glasses of Knickerbocker root beer to a drover and a pedestrian at three cents a glass.

The French Market

On assignment for *Every Saturday* magazine, artist Alfred R. Waud and writer Ralph Keeler visited New Orleans in 1871. Three of Waud's sketches appear here; the text that accompanied them was equally interesting. The French market was described as a place where "all races and nationalities are buying and selling all imaginable wares," from live fowl and strings of onions to coffee, macaroni, and shoes. Rows of stalls stretched for a quarter of a mile, and the shopper had to move "through the throng of women of all colors, shuffling about with their baskets on their arms." There were also Indian squaws, with tall baskets "filled with leaves, roots, herbs, and papooses . . . The scene in its fulness is simply indescribable."

Waud once wrote that New Orleans "abounds in the picturesque," and his drawings bear him out. At right is the outdoor kitchen of one of the French Quarter's many restaurants. The French market, crowded on a Sunday with vendors and shoppers of several races, is depicted at left below.

A woman walking on the levee caught Waud's eye.

Wonders
of the
Crescent City

Restaurant Antoine.

"Try our Specialties."

Tomates frappées à la Jules César.

Toste St. Antoine.   Canapée à la Russe.

Piment frappé, Rupinicoscoff.

Huitre en Coquille, Rockefellow.   Toast Rotschild.

Soupe.

Bisque d'Ecrevisse à la Cardinal.

"   de Crabes.

"   Crevette.

"   d'huitres.

Consommé à la Nilson.   Gombo Créole.

Poisson.

Terrapine à la St. Antoine.

Moules à la Parisienne.

Filets de Sole à la Marguery.

Chevrettes Marinière.

Ecrevisses Bordelaise.

Poisson a la Jules César.

Escargots Bordelaise.

Relevé.

Paté de foie gras a la gelée,

(Our own make)

At left is a nineteenth-century menu from the New Orleans restaurant Antoine's. Above are paintings of the okra plant (top) and the sassafras leaf. Okra and filé, a powder made from sassafras, are used in gumbos.

New Orleans, with its superb Creole cooking, captivated visiting gourmets, particularly foreigners who were surprised to find such delicious food in the United States. Sweden's Fredrika Bremer commented in 1850 that a dinner she ate in New Orleans was "remarkably good, and gumbo is the crown of all the savoury and remarkable soups in the world—a regular elixir of life of the substantial kind. He who has once eaten gumbo may look down disdainfully upon the most genuine turtle soup." And William Makepeace Thackeray summed up his affection for the great Gulf port this way: "As for New Orleans, in spring-time,—just when the orchards were flushing over with peach-blossoms, and the sweet herbs came to flavor the juleps—it seemed to me the city of the world where you can eat and drink the most and suffer the least."

These women of New Orleans were portrayed by Léon J. Frémaux in 1876. The turbaned woman above is "Rose: She who sells coffee in the French Market." At left, two Choctaw squaws, one carrying a papoose in a large basket, spread out the herbs they hope to sell.

Three for a Penny

In both city and country stores, the prime attractions for children were rows of gleaming glass jars containing candies. Gumdrops and peppermints, rock candy and chocolate drops, candy-coated peanuts (Boston Baked Beans) and Non-Pareils, taffy and licorice whips, chewable wax bottles filled with sweet liquids made a vast array of treats in countless shapes and colors. Among the favorites after 1866 were "conversation lozenges," or "cockles," shell-shaped candies made of sugar and flour, in which slips of colored paper were inserted. Printed on them were jokes ("Why is love like a canal boat? Because it's an internal transport"), fortunes ("Married in pink, He will take to drink"), and such titillating salutations as "Oh, you Kid!"

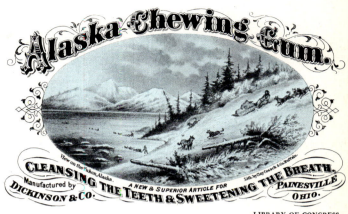

At left, the proprietress of the general store in Catskill, New York, berates some boys who had tried to steal an apple. Albertis D. O. Browere painted the scene in 1844. The chewing-gum and soft-drink advertisements are nineteenth-century seductions.

Reuben Reuben I've been thinking
What a good thing it would be
If the people all were drinking
Cherry Ripe like you and me

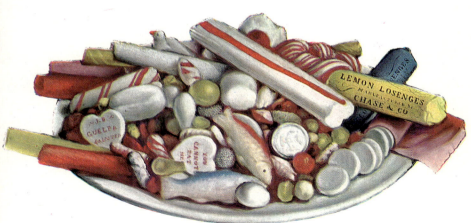

Peppermint sticks, lozenges, and other hard candies are depicted in this painting by J. B. Guelpa, whose name appears on the candy heart at the left of the full dish.

In the West, the Glories of the East

Visiting San Francisco in 1865, Samuel Bowles, a newspaper editor from Springfield, Massachusetts, was invited to a Chinese banquet. He was served, among other things, fried shark's fins, seaweed, bird's nest soup, stewed chicken with watercress, chestnuts, rice soup, and stewed pigeon with bamboo soup. "The dinner was unquestionably a most magnificent one after the Chinese standard," he said; "the dishes were many of them rare and expensive . . . But as to any real gastronomic satisfaction to be derived from it, I certainly 'did not see it.' " Before the dinner was two-thirds over, Bowles departed for a nearby American restaurant where, as he noted, he "got something to eat."

A San Francisco family whose home was destroyed by the earthquake dines alfresco (above). At right, a Chinese grocer poses before his store.

The Beer Gardens

From Germany, around 1840, came the special yeast that permitted the production of lager beer in the United States. Breweries prospered, and as thousands of German immigrants swelled the population of large cities like New York, St. Louis, San Antonio, and Milwaukee, beer gardens became favorite centers of relaxation. Describing those in New York City's Bowery, author James Dabney McCabe wrote in 1868: "These are immense buildings, fitted up in imitation of a garden.... They will accommodate from four hundred to twelve hundred guests. Germans carry their families there to spend a day, or an evening ... Beer and other liquids are served out at a small cost ... The music is a great attraction to the Germans. It is exquisite in some places."

The elegant interior of the German Winter-Garden (above) was painted by Fritz Meyer in the 1850's. The Winter-Garden, situated at 45 Bowery in New York, was one of the most ornate beer halls and was famed for its music and pleasant atmosphere. The lithograph at right, with slogan in both German and English, advertised a variety of potables in 1871.

THE BEST WINES, LIQUORS, ALES & LAGER BEER, WE ARE SELLING HERE.
Die besten Weine, Liquors, Ales und Lager-Bier, Sind zu haben hier.

America, America

After a hard voyage, often marked by hunger and illness, immigrant families arrived in the United States and found that the streets were paved neither with gold nor with bread. While the men, many of whom had been farmers in Europe, worked as laborers their wives learned to cope with new foods, with coal stoves and gas ranges, and with grocers who did not permit bargaining over prices. Possessing neither the money to buy, nor the room to store, large quantities of food, women shopped daily, purchasing small amounts from the peddlers who set up shop on the sidewalks.

The immigrant women and children seen at left are enjoying their first meal in the United States, on Ellis Island in 1906. At right, a new arrival carries a package of matzo, unleavened bread for Passover.

Harper's Weekly, FEBRUARY 11, 1871

This engraving from an 1871 issue of Harper's Weekly *depicts a dreary water-front restaurant, which sold hot coffee and butter cakes to the impecunious denizens of lower New York.*

Street Scene

Pushcarts laden with fruits and vegetables, horse-drawn wagons, and crowds of children and bargain-seekers fill the street in a 1906 photograph. This section of New York City was inhabited largely by immigrants. Another such area, around Hester Street, was populated chiefly by Jewish people and was known face-tiously as the Pig Market, since the only food not available there was pork.

In front of posters with Yiddish subtitles advertising vaudeville a movies, two peddlers wait for customers.

Some of these boys are nattily dressed, others appear bedraggled, but all are thoroughly enjoying the fresh fruit.

A pushcart vendor and his friend engage in a philosophical discourse Pushcarts were the city's cracker barrels.

A dirty-faced urchin
looks at the camera and
wins a smile from the
young girl who makes her
living by selling nuts.

Fresh oranges, wrapped
up and hung from a
long pole, were a
constant temptation for
fleet-footed boys.

Replete with fezzes and
a large samovar, two
Turkish immigrants sell
hot coffee to other
newcomers to the city.

8

DINING
at
HOME

By Russell Lynes

W e live in an age of what might be called creeping informality, and nowhere is this more evident than in our changing customs of eating and serving food. Each year seems to bring the disappearance of one more custom or one more appurtenance that not long ago was considered indispensable to "the right way of doing things." How often, for example, does one encounter a finger bowl today? Not that it has vanished entirely, but it was only a few years ago that it sat on hundreds of thousands of American dinner tables

The Dinner Party, left, was painted by Henry Sargent, who was also the host at the event depicted. It was a meeting of the Wednesday Evening Club, and it took place around 1825 in his home in Boston.

on a lace doily with a slice of lemon or a leaf of rose geranium floating in it, and its presence was taken for granted. How long since one has seen a silver table-crumber? It is decades since anyone waited on table wearing gloves, though they were once considered essential on the hands of servants in any respectable household. In fact it was not very long ago that ladies always wore their gloves to the table at a formal dinner and deposited them, along with their fans, in their laps.

Creeping informality reflects many changes in American attitudes toward ritual, particularly the rituals of the dinner table. The principal cause of this is, of course, the disappearance of servants from most households. Forty or so years ago, families with what might today be called "lower middle incomes" had at least one servant, and only slightly more prosperous families had a cook and a maid. In the middle of the last century at a formal dinner party, custom called for a minimum of one "waiter" for every four guests. At such parties the butler served no one; he merely supervised the other servants, dispatching them to their duties with an almost imperceptible nod of the head. Today the nearest thing to a butler in most households is a husband, though unlike a butler his activities are supervised by the cook, his wife.

Dining in the home, no matter how casual or how elaborate it may be, is always something of a ritual. It is ritual that turns the process of downing food into a meal, and as a nation of hearty (if often hasty) eaters, Americans have devised some very elaborate ways of satisfying their hunger and their taste for a feast. They have also devised very exacting rules (some of them borrowed from the French and the English) for how one must behave in the presence of food and other feeders, and they have stretched their imaginations to concoct dishes and complexes of dishes and settings in which to serve them that would do credit to Oriental potentates.

Basically there are just two ingredients that are indispensable to dining in, and they have received almost equal attention from mentors of the American household for the last century and a half. They are manners and menus. If to these you add friends, you have

The wrong way to carve

also added the ingredient of hospitality, and the formula for dining in is complete.

First let us look at manners; it is they that prescribe the rituals of eating, and it is ritual that makes the merely edible seem palatable, and the delicious, a feast.

In a society as mobile as ours, in which families are continually picking up and moving along both physically and socially, there is every reason why there should long have been an outpouring of books of etiquette to tell people how they should behave under every possible social circumstance. It is also reasonable that so many of our cookbooks and housekeeping manuals should have devoted chapters not only to foods and their preparation but to how to set a table; how to serve luncheons, teas, dinners, and suppers; how to behave at table; how to act toward the "help"; and even, in some cases, how to dress.

In the eighteenth century such books of manners as circulated in America were mostly translations of French books or importations from England, and when George Washington as a boy

...and the right

wrote out his own rules for how to behave at the table, he took them from a
well-known French manual. "Put not
another bit into your Mouth till the
former be Swallowed," the young
Washington wrote and added, "Cleanse
not your teeth with the Table Cloth
Napkin Fork or Knife." But in the
early years of the nineteenth century
Americans began to write their own
books of etiquette, and they poured
from the presses in a prodigious torrent. In the thirty years after 1830
more than ninety were published, and
found their ways to the homes of
farmers and merchants, diplomats and
lawyers. They were elegantly bound
and paper-bound; they were sold in
shops and by subscription and given
away as soap premiums and by soft-
drink bottlers and grocery stores. They
stole examples and anecdotes from one
another and copied each other's rules
verbatim. Sometimes they contradicted
each other about such matters as
whether the hostess should be the first
or the last to enter the dining room at
her dinner party. They went by such
names as *The Young Lady's Friend,*
The Illustrated Manners Book, and

How to Behave and How to Amuse.

The manners books coincided with
a wave of gentility in America, a wave
that, curiously enough, came along at
the same time as a new spirit of republicanism and a new emphasis on equality. When every man is as good as every
other man there is likely to be a scramble on the part of a good many people
to be better than other people or, anyway, to emulate the manners of those
whom they consider to be well established. To be genteel was the aim of
every young lady, and gentility led to
some exaggerated kinds of behavior
that were thought to be the very opposite of "vulgar." In her delightful and
worldly book of etiquette, *The Young
Lady's Friend,* Mrs. John Farrar in
1838 mentioned a young lady who
thought it was not "very refined and
pretty" to chew one's food. "I have
heard her speak," Mrs. Farrar wrote,
"with great disgust of some of her acquaintance, for chewing their food so
much."

Not everyone was equally impressed
by the new gentility, of course. When
Senator Thomas Benton of Missouri
visited President Martin Van Buren
after the latter retired to Kinderhook,
New York, he encountered finger bowls
for the first time. "I am very chary of
new customs," the Senator later reported, "but when I saw Mr. Van
Buren dip the tips of his fingers
in the bowl and wipe them daintily
on a napkin, I just raked back my
sleeves and took a good plain Republican wash."

Nearly every move one makes at a meal has a rule to cover it. Manners dictate not only how to get into a dining room (who follows whom) but how to pick up a fork, how to butter a piece of bread, how to sip a cup of coffee or wield a soup spoon. Conventions still limit the kinds of subjects that are considered suitable for conversation at the table, and other conventions have to do with dress, who is served what and when, how one sits, chews, and speaks.

A clumsy waiter

The nineteenth-century books of etiquette overlooked none of these niceties, though they did not, as I have said, always agree. Mrs. Farrar and the anonymous author of *The Perfect Gentleman* saw no reason why it was not reasonable to eat with a knife as long as one did not close one's lips over the blade, but the anonymous author had to admit that custom in this regard had changed; "it is doubtful," he said, "if you can afford to disregard it."

Most other books of etiquette were adamant on this point. One of the reasons why the custom had changed (and it was the same kind of reason that makes customs change so rapidly today) was a newfangled invention: the three- and four-tined forks, with which it was possible to pick up peas. They replaced the two-tined fork, which was useless for such a purpose. Another such change was brought about by the introduction of the butter knife. Once it became generally used, books of manners said that it was vulgar to employ one's own knife to cut butter from the butter dish. The custom "of turning tea or coffee from the cup into the saucer," formerly common and acceptable, had become definitely uncouth by 1870. The lengths to which advice on table manners went is best demonstrated by a statement in *The Laws of Etiquette; or Short Rules and Reflections for Conduct in Society*. Ladies, the author wrote, "may wipe their lips on the table cloth, but not blow their noses with it." There was no *gaffe* nor solecism that etiquette experts did not anticipate.

But the manners of dining in (or out, of course) were not only concerned with the behavior of the individual. They applied equally to the setting of the table, the seating of the guests, the gathering before dinner for what was generally considered to be the "dreadful ten minutes" of introductions. They applied also to the method by which the meal was served.

All of the rituals of the dining room met at their most conventional and elaborate on the occasion of a dinner party. It was then that the hostess rallied all of her forces, social and culinary, and all of her resources of silver and crystal and napery. There was a rule to cover almost every move she and her guests made and the placement of every object on the table.

Invitations to dinner were, of course, sent by letter or note or card even long after the telephone was a common household instrument. (In Chicago a century ago it was the custom for the hostess not only to write the invitations to any party, however large, in her own home but to deliver them herself. Invitations were too important to entrust to a paid messenger, and to send them by mail was considered rude.) The hour specified for dinner was precisely what it said it was, and the acceptance of an invitation was a commitment not to be taken lightly. Ward McAllister, one of the most determined social butterflies of the end of the last century and the inventor of the phrase "the Four Hundred" for New York society, declared in his memoirs: "If you intend to decline an invitation to dinner, do so at as early a date as possible. A dinner invitation, once accepted, is a sacred obligation. If you die before the dinner takes place, your executor must attend the dinner." That is not quite what he meant, and he added: "This is not to be taken literally, but to illustrate the obligation."

Not to be punctual was considered an "unpardonable rudeness." One was expected to arrive ten to fifteen min-

utes before the dinner hour so that the hostess might introduce the guests and assign escorts to accompany the ladies into the dining room. In the 1870's *Century Magazine* described what it

All the knives and forks were working away at a rate that was quite alarming; very few words were spoken; and everybody seemed to eat his utmost, in self-defence, as if a famine were expected to set in before breakfast-time to-morrow morning, and it had become high time to assert the first law of nature.

—Charles Dickens, on an American dinner in *Martin Chuzzlewit*

found to be a pleasant new custom: "... each gentleman [is given] in the dressing room a buttonhole bouquet tied with a ribbon, the color of which he finds, on reaching the drawing room, corresponds with that on the bouquet of the lady he is expected to attend to the dining-room."

The method by which the dinner itself was served changed radically in the middle of the last century. The traditional method (which was called English service) was to place the roast and vegetables, the breads and wines and water carafes and relishes on the table to be served by the host and hostess or for the guests to serve themselves. The new method, and we still use it today though its name has been forgotten, was called service *à la russe*. The Russian method of serving "from the side" introduced several innovations. The roast, instead of being carved by the host, was now carved in the kitchen. The vegetables were passed, as was the meat, by the waitress or waiter and so were the wines, the water, the bread (though bread was not served at formal dinners), and other delicacies. In a manual called *The Up-to-Date Waitress,* published in 1906, the author said that "this is not only the most elegant, but the simplest style of service . . ."

The setting of the dinner table, a topic that has consumed hundreds of millions of words of advice to the housewife over the years, changed basically with the introduction of service *à la russe.* It had been customary to have casters containing oil and vinegar, salt and pepper, meat sauces, and sometimes other condiments at regular intervals on the table, along with a wine bottle for every two or three guests and a water carafe not far from anyone's reach. With the exception of the basic condiments (salt and pepper), much of the other "furniture" disappeared from the table and turned up on the sideboard (now overelegantly called a buffet by many people), from which it could be served by the waitress or waiter. With fewer necessities on the table, there was room for more decorations, and as there were fewer evidences on the table of the food one was about to eat, it became fashionable to place a menu at the place of each guest. In more pretentious houses (and there were a lot of pretentious families) these

menus were commonly in French, in spite of the fact that books of manners were inclined to call such practices nonsensical. When the custom of providing each person at the table with a menu died away in the home, only the hostess had one at her place. She was, after all, the presiding chairman, and it behooved her to have the agenda at hand.

The decoration of the dinner table has called forth flights of delicate fancy, tidal waves of opulent expenditure, and even howls of political protest. "There is no pleasanter sight than an artistically set dinner table just before the guests are seated," wrote the author of *How to Behave and How to Amuse.* She was writing for the modest housewife in the 1890's, but her instructions could be expanded to any degree of richness. Basic to everything was a white tablecloth over a flannel table cover. The flannel made

President Hayes at a clambake

the tablecloth lie more smoothly and protected the finish of the table from the heat of the dishes. Tablecloths with white garlands woven into their whiteness were family treasures and became heirlooms as highly prized as crystal and silver. Modest families collected "solid spoons and forks" one by one; members of New York's Four Hundred and their counterparts in other cities bought twenty-four-piece silver services and gold services and had their tablecloths embroidered in Paris at the price, as one alarmed writer put it, "of a year's income."

Flowers on the table in the 1870's and 80's burgeoned lavishly. At rich New York parties florists let their fancy run; they "took possession of the table," McAllister wrote, "and made a flower garden of it, regardless of cost." There were bouquets for the ladies in little glass or silver flower holders, and boutonnieres for the gentlemen protruded from the folds of their napkins. The custom of expensive favors at the places of the ladies, which evidently originated in the South, became popular with northern society. But this kind of ostentation, which was considered excessive by those who were rich enough to set limits of delicacy on their vulgarity, gave way to more subtle refinements. Instead of a garden over which it was impossible to see who sat across the table, there would be merely a centerpiece of *gloire de Paris* roses abetted by silver epergnes of bonbons and *compotiers* of fruit.

Perhaps the epitome of the reaction against the overcolorful dinner table was the fad in the late eighties and nineties for what were then called white dinners. The *Illustrated American* described in detail one such party in Newport in July, 1890. The dining room was hung with white muslin; gaslight from a crystal chandelier filtered down upon the table through "huge silk tissue moths

> *When anyone desires to make a wide-spread impression that the President and family sit down to a four- or five-course breakfast, a six- or seven-course lunch, and a ten-course dinner, the President feels that a denial is not inappropriate.*
> —Theodore Roosevelt, replying to a magazine article labeling him a "gourmet"

that spread their silvery white wings.." The table was decorated with clusters of bridal roses, white carnations, and white poppies; the meal was served on pure white porcelain "with the hostess's monogram wrought in slender argent lettering." In the epergnes the confections were "colorless French dragees and almonds blanched and frosted with salt." The meal itself was white: "Clams and cream of celery soup... fish dressed with white sauce... fair breasts of young chickens... cauliflowers smothered in creams, Roman punch introduced in the chalice of a lily, and salads in beds of crisp celery." Over this repast presided the hostess "in white from top to toe." She was, of course, a blonde.

One of the most prominent hostesses of the last century, Mrs. William Astor (nee Caroline Schermerhorn), whose dinners have been described as "three-hour-long feats of endurance ... chiefly remarkable for a surpassing sterility in conversation and ideas," paid a special tribute to her friend Ward McAllister shortly after his death. "In a rare access of sensitivity and fine feeling," wrote Grace Mayer in *Once upon a City,* "Mrs. Astor gave a highly selective farewell feast ... at a table decked with mauve and pink orchids."

The most famous table setting ever to raise an American eyebrow was

---

The washing of dishes does seem to me the most absurd and unsatisfactory business that I ever undertook. If, when once washed, they would remain clean for ever and ever (which they ought in all reason to do, considering how much trouble it is,) there would be less occasion to grumble; but no sooner is it done, than it requires to be done again. On the whole, I have come to the resolution not to use more than one dish at each meal.

—Nathaniel Hawthorne, in 1844 (while Mrs. Hawthorne was away)

---

celebrated by the famous "Gold Spoon Speech" delivered in the House of Representatives by Congressman John Ogle, a Whig of Pennsylvania, on April 14, 1840. Mr. Ogle wound up

and let fly with about twenty thousand words of invective against President Van Buren, a Democrat, because of the extravagant manner in which he ornamented the White House and the lavishness of its appointments and its hospitality. Nothing moved Mr. Ogle to greater heights of oratorical contempt than the table service in the dining room of what he called "the palace" (Van Buren, according to Ogle, was about to make himself into a monarch) and the meals with which the President gorged his guests. In the state dining room there was a thirteen-foot centerpiece that had cost $1,125 in the days of President Monroe, but what got Ogle's dander bubbling was the fact that Van Buren had spent $75 of taxpayers' money on having it gilded. He was also exercised by a French "STERLING SILVER PLATE and GILT DESSERT SET, bought from a RUSSIAN NOBLEMAN" for the sum of $4,308.82. The flat silver, Ogle noted, was the sort "used in the palaces of kings and at the castles of wealthy noblemen in Europe."

The food that the President served on his state table with its elaborate ornaments and gilt tableware was harder for the Congressman to swallow *(in absentia)* than the decorations. It is too bad that the *Congressional Record,* which published Ogle's speech, did not also give his pronunciation of the items of the menu that so horrified him. Here is the menu that Ogle singled out to be printed in the *Record:*

"*For the first course.*—Potage au tortue, Potage à la Julienne, et Potage aux pois.

Second course.—Saumon, sauce d'anchois, Bass piqué à la Chambore.

Third course.—Suprême de volaille en bordure à la galée, Filet de boeuf piqué au vin de Champagne, Pate chaud à la Toulouse.

Fourth course.—Salade d'homard monté, Filets mignons de mouton en chevreuil, Cerveau, de veau, au suprême, Pigeons à la royal aux champignons.

Fifth course.—Bécassines, Canard sauvages, Poulet de Guinée piquée.

Patisserie.—Charlotte russe au citron, Biscuit à la vanille decoré, Coupe garnie de gelée d'orange en quartiers, Gelée au marasquin, Gelée au Champagne rose, Blanc mange, Sultane, Nougat, Petits gateaux varies.

Dessert.—Fruits, et glace en pyramide, et en petits moules, Toste d'anchois, Café et liqueur. Followed by Saturne, Hock, Champagne, Claret, Port, Burgundy, Sherry, and Madeira, 'choisest brands.' "

Congressman Ogle's speech dealt a smarting political blow to Mr. Van Buren (the "Log Cabin and Hard Cider" boys beat him at the polls), but it did nothing to curtail the dinner menus of the nineteenth century.

In the days before the introduction of service *à la russe,* dinner was likely to be just two courses. That is, the table was set with eight or nine different dishes that were then cleared away and replaced by another lot. When these two courses were con-

Headcheese

sumed, the dishes were taken from the table, the crumbs swept up, and finger bowls put before each person (Mrs. Farrar in *The Young Lady's Friend* warned her readers not to drink out of them nor to use the water for rinsing out their mouths). After this bit of ritual the tablecloth was removed, and dessert was put on the bare surface of the table, along with wine and wineglasses. Ladies did not consume more than a single glass of wine and left the table after so doing, so that the gentlemen might indulge in more sturdy drinking. "A dinner, well performed by all the actors in it," wrote Mrs. Farrar, "is very fatiguing and, as it generally occupies three hours or more, most persons are glad to go away when it is fairly done."

Dinners were not only long and exhausting; they were frequently a bore. The art of conversation was not highly prized by American men in the last century (any more than it is now). A Swedish writer, Fredrika Bremer, who visited America in the 1850's, wrote: "Is there in this world any thing more wearisome, more dismal, more intolerable, more indigestible, more stupefying, more unbearable, any thing more calculated to kill both soul and body, than a great dinner at New York? People sit down to table at half-past five or six o'clock; they are sitting at table at nine o'clock, sitting and being served with one course

---

Evening tea is a boring and monotonous ceremony. The mistress of the house serves it and passes it around, and as long as a person has not turned his cup upside down and placed his spoon upon it, just so often will he be brought another cup. You hear a thousand true and false accounts of Frenchmen who, in their ignorance of this peculiar custom, have been so inundated by tea that they have suffered intensely.

—Moreau de St. Méry,
writing in the 1790's

---

after another, with one indigestible dish after another, eating and being silent. I have never heard such a silence as at these great dinners."

As the century wore on the dinners became, if not necessarily less elaborate, at least shorter. Ward McAllister insisted that an hour and a half was long enough for any dinner, however festive, and in Washington it became a social *gaffe* to serve a dinner that kept the assembled guests at the table for more than two hours. The elegance of dinners, however, increased as the century wore on, and more and more hostesses imported European chefs for their kitchens and English butlers to preside over their dining rooms and

over the men in livery who served their guests. In 1900 a wealthy and socially aspiring couple named Mr. and Mrs. Pembroke Jones from North Carolina arrived in New York to establish themselves in society, and they were advised by Harry Lehr, a prominent member of the Four Hundred: "Feed New York well enough, and it will eat out of your hand." The Joneses, who could afford to heed such advice, decided that they would have not just one chef but two. In her memoirs Harry Lehr's widow, a famous beauty of her day, wrote: ". . . their table groaned under the weight of rare Southern delicacies, rice birds and Indian corn brought from their own estates, chicken and corn fritters, Sally Lunns and muffins cooked to perfection by their Negro cook who had his special little kitchen while their famous Russian chef, lured from the Czar's own household by a fabulous salary, prepared his elaborate menus in his own domaine."

Dinners were by no means the only means of entertaining one's guests. There were picnics (sometimes called frolics) and teas; there were breakfasts and luncheons and evening parties, sometimes called suppers and sometimes soirees, depending on the region and the pretentions of the hostess.

At Newport, where the palaces built by the fashionable architect Richard Morris Hunt were called cottages and nudged each other like a development of houses for Renaissance princes, the Vanderbilts and Astors and Goelets vied to outdo each other in hospitality, and Ward McAllister's picnics were famous.

For his gastronomic sweepstakes, McAllister managed to get his friends to provide the food and to compete with each other in offering up from their kitchens the greatest delicacies. Young men who had no facilities for providing cooked dishes or salads were encouraged to produce a bottle of champagne, a bunch of grapes, or a quart of ice cream from a confectioner. McAllister hired musicians and servants and had carpenters build a platform on which the guests might dance; he deployed men along the road to direct the guests to his farm, where the picnic was held, and he had his farmer and his family dressed up "in holiday attire."

"I had an army of skirmishers in the way of servants," he wrote, ". . . to take from each carriage its contribution to the country dinner. The band would strike up, and off the whole party would fly in the waltz, while I was directing the icing of the champagne and arranging the tables; all done with marvelous celerity. Then came my hour of triumph, when, without the slightest signal . . . I would dash in among the dancers, secure our society queen [Mrs. Astor] and lead with her the way to the banquet."

Before we quit the nineteenth century there are two other highly ritualistic forms of hospitality in which our forebears indulged that are worth remembering. One is the formal evening party at which home talent entertained and mountains of food appeared. The other is the progenitor of a modern institution (some call it a rat race): the cocktail party.

The evening party was a well-established custom even in the frontier cities, such as Cincinnati in the 1820's, when Mrs. Frances Trollope of London visited there and recorded her shocked impressions of the crude manners of Americans. Evening parties were not dinners (dinner then happened in the middle of the day or, as in Boston, at two in the afternoon); they were suppers, at which it was possible to entertain a great many more people than could be seated at a table. The feasts that were spread (and the gentlemen fetched the food for the ladies, presumably) were often rich and various. Mrs. Trollope recites with horror what might appear on such occasions: "tea, coffee, hot cake and custard, hoe cake, johnny cake, waffle cake, and dodger cake, pickled peaches, and preserved cucumbers, ham, turkey, hung beef, apple sauce and pickled oysters . . ."

It was, of course, customary for young ladies to perform on the spinet or sing a few songs for the edification of the company; it was also customary, except in the higher reaches of society, for the women to gather in one corner of the room and the men in another. "The gentlemen spit, talk of elections, and the price of produce, and spit again," Mrs. Trollope wrote. "The ladies look at each other's dresses till they know every pin by heart; talk of

Parson Somebody's last sermon on the day of judgment, on Dr. T'otherbody's new pills for dyspepsia, till the 'tea' is announced, when they all console themselves together for whatever they may have suffered in keeping awake" by diving into the food. "After [the] massive meal is over, they return to the drawing room, and it always appeared to me that they remained together as long as they could bear it, and then they rise

> *The way to a man's heart is through his stomach.*
> —Mrs. Sara Payson Parton (Fanny Fern)

en masse, cloak, bonnet, shawl, and exit." The elegant evening parties of Boston and Washington and New York, though different in the sophistication of the guests, were much the same in spirit.

The progenitor of the cocktail party, a relatively inexpensive method of paying off a great many social debts all at once, was the afternoon tea party, which was called in the 1870's and for several decades after that a kettledrum. All one needed to provide one's guests was sandwiches as thin as tissue paper and as dainty as lace doilies and tea. Tea cost practically nothing, and thin sandwiches were easily made in the days before bread became limp and pre-sliced. There are several conflicting accounts of why the parties were called kettledrums. One writer on manners in the 1870's said that it was because such parties had first been introduced by the

wives of British officers as a simple way of entertaining in the garrisons and that a drum was often used instead of a tea table. A more likely explanation is Mrs. M. E. W. Sherwood's, in her *Manners and Social Usages* (1887). She said that at tea parties in Victorian England "people talked so fast and so loud as to suggest the noise of a drum—a kettledrum, the most rattling of all drums." The analogy with the sound of the cocktail party is obvious.

One of the paradoxes in the history of dining in the American home is that as the means of preparing food have become more and more efficient, menus have become less and less elaborate and less demanding of skill in their preparation. When one considers that in 1800 lavish two-course dinners were cooked on an open fire, that meats were roasted on spits or by metal heat reflectors, that pies and breads were baked in brick ovens preheated with hot coals or by burning twigs in them, it seems to us nearly incredible. "It was a wonder," wrote a household expert in 1900, "that the women who ministered as cooks before those great altars were not devoured by the flames." It was not until about 1840 that wood- and coal-burning stoves began to appear in American kitchens, and gas ranges were not common until nearly fifty years after that. The first electric kitchen was displayed in America at the great World's Fair of 1893 (the Columbian Exposition) in Chicago, and people were astonished by it as a marvel of science. Twenty years went by, however, before reliable electric ranges were on the market.

Iceboxes were common more than a century ago, and they often sat with their drip pans under them on the back porch, so that the iceman could fill them without coming into the house. Electric refrigerators first were sold to American housewives in 1916, and they cost about $900 apiece. By 1941 the price had come down from the clouds, and they were considered indispensable in every household that could afford one. It was not until after the Second World War that the home freezer had such an extensive influence on what got put on the American table, and delicacies that were once attainable only by the rich (and others that even they could not buy because they were unpreservable) became everybody's provender.

The mechanical gadgets with which the kitchen is now filled are partly a result of the disappearance of domestic servants from so many households and partly a cause for their disappearance. If informality has crept into almost every crevice of American life, the principal reason for it is that there are fewer hands willing to undertake the elaborate rituals that were once identified with hospitality. Almost no one drops calling cards or pays "dinner calls" (which until about forty years ago one failed to pay on one's hostess within three days only at the risk of social ostracism), or sets tables with hundreds of pieces of silver that have to be polished—except, of course, on

Stirring the Christmas pudding

rare occasions. On Thanksgiving and some other feast days we revert to customs and menus that go far back into our past.

The remarkable thing about creeping informality is that it has not curtailed hospitality but has, I believe, spread it by making it more manageable. It has simplified the preparations, limited the menus (without diminishing their quality), and spread the responsibility for at least part of the ritual of service from host and hostess to their guests. We have come a long, relaxed way from the days when propriety was always identified with formality. We have discovered that the amiable rituals of informality, while they may not be as demanding as the rituals of our grandparents, sacrifice nothing in the far more important realm of personal dignity.

Fannie Farmer

FANNIE FARMER

By Russell Lynes

Insisting on exactitude, "the mother of level measurement"
brought order and accuracy to American cookery. Meanwhile,
over three million families were nurtured on her recipes

The year before the publication in 1896 of Fannie Merritt Farmer's celebrated *Boston Cooking-School Cook Book,* an expert on the household, Lillian W. Betts, complained that the trouble with cookbooks was that they were "not scientific." One could hardly trust a word they said, according to Miss Betts. They not only contradicted each other but they contradicted themselves. "The housekeeper," she advised, "must fit herself to separate the chaff from the wheat when reading them, and if she is wise she will cull the best into a book of her own, after experiment and investigation."

Fannie Farmer suffered under the very same inexactitudes, contradictions, and sloppinesses that bothered Miss Betts, and she did something about it. There probably has never been anyone in America who so disapproved of "a pinch" of salt or a "walnut" of butter as Miss Farmer or who looked so darkly on the dubious quantity of a "heaping" tablespoon. Guesswork. Never twice the same. Not even spoons are of consistent sizes, much less pinches and walnuts. How could you expect to tell somebody how to cook something when you could not even be precise about the ingredients?

Miss Farmer was a woman of iron character who, because of physical disability, had had to conserve her time and her strength. She was by no means impatient of pleasure, or even of fanciness and frippery, and certainly not of the subtleties of decoration and of taste,

293

but she would abide no waste of her energies or anyone else's because of inexactitude. She was thirty-nine when *The Boston Cooking-School Cook Book* was published by the Boston firm of Little, Brown and Company at her own expense, and she had already had a distinguished career.

Fannie was a red-haired Boston girl, the eldest of four daughters of an editor and printer, J. Frank Farmer, and of Mary Watson Farmer, who, according to one of Fannie's very few biographers, was "a notable housewife" at a time when housewifery was not regarded as one of the prime social female virtues. When Fannie was seventeen and a junior at the Medford High School she suffered a "paralytic stroke," the exact nature of which medicine in those days could not define. It was not, however, polio, as a second stroke later in her life caused even further curtailment of her physical mobility. The first stroke ended Fannie's high-school career and, as her doctors forbade her any further formal schooling, the aspirations that she and her family had had for her going to college. Fannie was confined to staying home and, as she gradually recovered, to helping her mother in such ways as her limited strength and agile mind would permit.

Eleven years after her first illness Fannie's family found it financially expedient to take in boarders. The boardinghouse as an American institution was then in its heyday, and taking in boarders was one of the few ways in which a family could supplement its income. During the nineteenth century nearly seventy per cent of all Americans lived at one time or another for an average of about three years in boardinghouses. Young couples frequently started married life in them, as they could afford to live more "genteelly" than they could in a home of their own, where they believed they would have to support several servants. Older people retired to them, and bachelors found in them permanent homes. The best ones, especially those where the cooking was known to be excellent, had long waiting lists. Fannie helped with the cooking in her family's boardinghouse and evidenced such skill and interest in it that one of her younger sisters suggested that she go to the Boston Cooking School and learn to be a teacher of cooking.

This was sound advice. Fannie was thirty-two when she graduated, and Mrs. Carrie M. Dearborn, the director of the school, was so impressed with Fannie's intelligence, skill, and executive abilities that she invited her to become her assistant. Just two years later Mrs. Dearborn died, and the board of trustees of the school elected the impressive young Miss Farmer to take over the school as its head in spite of her physical handicaps.

"Aunt Fannie," according to Mrs. Wilma Lord Perkins, Fannie's niece-in-law, who, since 1930, has been editing, revising, and modernizing the cookbook, "was a great executive, food detective, and gourmet, rather than a great cook herself."

While she was the head of the Boston Cooking School and later when she had a school of her own, Fannie spent as much time as she could going to the best restaurants that she could discover and sampling their dishes. Sometimes, when she encountered a sauce that baffled her, Fannie would take out a calling card, put a few drops of the sauce on it, fold it carefully, and take it away with her for future analysis and reference. Many of her pupils took delight in reporting their discoveries to her. One of her colleagues recalled, in an article in the *Woman's Home Companion* published shortly after Fannie's death, that the young ladies would come to her with such excitements as: "Ah, Miss Farmer, those rolls at the Holland House," or "They're serving a sausage at the Ritz-Carlton that you've nothing to match," and, the writer said, "Away would go Miss Farmer" to see for herself. Sometimes the entire faculty of the Boston Cooking School would experiment on the recipe of a baffling dish in the short snatches of time between classes.

The Boston Cooking School was primarily a teacher-training institution, and after eleven years of being its director Miss Farmer grew restless under the restraints of her trustees and decided to set up a school of her own that would be devoted primarily to teaching housewives and professionals to cook, rather than to instructing teachers to teach cooking. She founded the new institution, which she called Miss Farmer's School of Cookery, in Boston in 1902, with five assistant teachers and five full-time maids.

On Wednesdays Fannie gave demonstration lectures both morning and evening. In the mornings she lectured

Cookery means the knowledge of Medea and of Circe and of Helen and of the Queen of Sheba. It means the knowledge of all herbs and fruits and balms and spices, and all that is healing and sweet in the fields and groves and savory in meats. It means carefulness and inventiveness and willingness and readiness of appliances. It means the economy of your grandmothers and the science of the modern chemist; it means much testing and no wasting; it means English thoroughness and French art and Arabian hospitality; and, in fine, it means that you are to be perfectly and always ladies—loaf givers. —John Ruskin, quoted in the first edition of *The Boston Cooking-School Cook Book*

to homemakers and in the evenings to professional cooks. "She was too impatient to cook a whole meal," Mrs. Perkins has said. "Even when she lectured, someone else on stage did the actual cooking." Her lectures, which consistently had audiences of one hundred and fifty to two hundred hopeful and skilled cooks and chefs, were regularly reported in detail the next day in the Boston *Evening Transcript* and copied by papers all over the country.

One of Fannie's primary interests, not surprisingly, was in the special problems of cooking for invalids. In her school there were courses in "invalid cookery," and she lectured to nurses on this subject. During one year she gave a course in special invalid diets and in cooking for the sick at the Harvard Medical School. Fannie was a scientist at heart, but a practical scientist, not an abstract one.

Fannie Farmer's greatest contribution to the households of America was, of course, *The Boston Cooking-School Cook Book,* which has come to be known as just "Fannie Farmer." "Look it up in Fannie Farmer" is to the cook what "Look it up in Emily Post" is to the nervous hostess or to the mother of the bride. (Mrs. Post's book's real name was originally *Etiquette, the Blue Book of Social Usage.*)

When Miss Farmer went with her book in 1896 to Little, Brown and Company, an august and long-established firm of publishers, she was told firmly (and I have no doubt politely) that they were not interested in taking on her manuscript. It seemed most unlikely to them that the American housewife could possibly be persuaded to buy one more collection of recipes, and Miss Farmer's cookbook, unlike so many others of the nineteenth century, did not have advice on how to kill rats,

cure cancer, or make cold cream. (It did, however, offer hints on cleaning piano keys and removing dust from rattan furniture.)

The red-headed Fannie was not the sort of woman who would have offered a publisher a book to which she had not given her entire intelligence or behind which she was not willing to put her personal resources. She therefore persuaded Little, Brown to publish three thousand copies on the agreement that she would pay for the printing. It is unlikely that in the entire history of the American book business any unwilling publisher ever got talked by an author into so lucrative (and at the same time so safe) a deal. By the time the tenth revised edition of the book was published in 1959, more than three million copies of the book had been printed. As Inez Robb noted in her newspaper column at the time, ". . . millions of dollars later, the old publishing firm has the grace to blush for its little faith. The volume has been the equivalent of a license to steal."

In a preface to the first edition, Fannie wrote that she had prepared the book "at the earnest solicitation of educators, pupils, and friends . . . It is my wish that it may not only be looked upon as a compilation of tried and tested recipes, but that it may awaken an interest through its condensed scientific knowledge which will lead to deeper thought and broader study of what to eat."

In addition to recipes and suggested menus, *The Boston Cooking-School*

Cook Book gave definitions and chemical breakdowns of basic foods and stressed the need for a balanced diet. Also included were a special section of recipes for the sick and a chapter of "Helpful Hints to the Young Housekeeper." ("Before using a new Iron Kettle, grease inside and outside, and let stand for forty-eight hours; then wash in hot water in which a large lump of cooking soda has been dissolved.")

But as Kathleen Ann Smallzreid wrote in her splendid book *The Everlasting Pleasure,* Fannie's book was "more than a compendium of known rules, habits, recipes. She brought to the study of food a creative understanding which made cooking easier, and its results more reliable. . . . It is doubtful whether any home or any food company has escaped the influence of Fannie Merritt Farmer, indirect if not direct."

Often referred to as "the mother of level measurement," Fannie stressed in her book that "correct measurements are absolutely necessary to insure the best results." After she had been for several years the head of the Boston Cooking School, she was asked to judge a recipe contest by a flour company. To her dismay, she discovered that only five per cent of the recipes submitted used level measurements. An indication of the influence of her books and teachings is that when, eighteen years later, she judged a contest for gelatin recipes, ninety per cent of the entries specified level measurements.

Fannie also insisted on high standards of accuracy in other areas. Oven thermometers were on the market, and stoves were being made that had temperature indicators. Instead of saying "a moderate oven for as long as necessary," it became possible to say "350 degrees for ninety minutes." Fannie believed that a recipe should be as accurately reproducible in the kitchen as a formula in the laboratory. Cooking should and could be a precise and standardized procedure.

The vast sale of the cookbook was only one of the ways by which Fannie's influence spread. For ten years she wrote a regular column for the *Woman's Home Companion* on topics such as "Cooking the Cheaper Meats," "The Banana in Cookery," "Twenty Good Sandwiches" (including peanut butter mixed with orange juice, and toasted oyster sandwiches), and "The Thanksgiving Turkey." She lectured to a great many women's clubs as far from Boston as the Pacific Coast. She also wrote six shorter specialty cookery books, including *Food and Cookery for the Sick and Convalescent* (1904), *What to Have for Dinner* (1905), *Catering for Special Occasions, With Menus and Recipes* (1911), and *A New Book of Cookery* (1912).

Fannie Farmer spent the last seven years of her life in a wheel chair or on crutches. A second stroke had felled her, but she diligently followed the regime prescribed by her physicians and with the greatest exertion of will power managed to continue to lecture and spread the gospel in which she so fervently believed. "I certainly feel," she had said in the preface to the first edition of her cookbook, "that the time is not far distant when a knowledge of the principles of diet will be an essential part of one's education. Then mankind will eat to live, will be able to do better mental and physical work, and disease will be less frequent." She gave her last lecture from her wheel chair just ten days before she died at the age of fifty-eight on January 15, 1915, in Boston.

"This was Miss Farmer," wrote Mary Bronson Hartt in the *Woman's Home Companion*, "a practical, womanly, woman . . . deeply impressed with the importance of lifting cookery to its rightful place . . . as a science and an art."

But this was not all Miss Farmer was. She was a dignified woman who shunned personal publicity and, it is said, never saved a clipping about herself. She would not let her publisher use her picture in her famous book. She had a passionate determination not to permit her physical handicaps to stand in the way of her mission. Like Catharine Beecher she was a crusader for raising the sights (I almost said the level) of the American woman by increasing her womanly skills and by giving dignity to her profession, as Miss Beecher called it, of housewife. She was not a crusader for woman's rights, but she believed that intelligent planning and efficient use of time and equipment would mean that women could be freed from much of the drudgery by which they bound themselves. She was, in other words, for liberation.

But she was also for pleasure, and she gave it remarkably. Not many books published in America have given more people more pleasurable hours than the precise, voluminous, continually revised *Boston Cooking-School Cook Book*. It happens very rarely that when a woman dies she ceases to be a person but becomes a book. That is precisely what happened to "Fannie Farmer."

DINING AT HOME

A Picture Portfolio

Nineteenth-century housewives purchase choice cuts from two nattily dressed butchers.

Mother's Helpers

As the nineteenth century progressed, many changes took place in American kitchens. Wooden sinks were replaced first by iron and copper ones, later by enameled or porcelain models. The icebox, with the drip pan that had to be emptied daily, changed little between 1830 and 1910, but stoves evolved rapidly, as wood and coal ranges were refined and as other fuels were tried. (It took several decades for gas ranges, introduced in the 1850's, to become popular, since many women were afraid of blowing up themselves along with their stoves.) As equipment became more modern, kitchens became smaller and cleaner. "The sight of a tidy kitchen," phrenologist O. S. Fowler said in 1854, "is not so very disgusting, even to men of refined tastes."

The servant girl above wears a book harness, a device that purportedly allowed her to read while washing dishes. Below is an icebox from an 1882 catalogue. Prices ranged from thirteen to thirty-five dollars for the model, depending on the size.

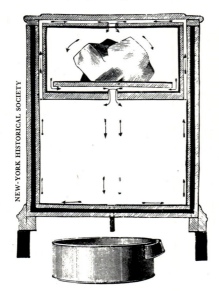

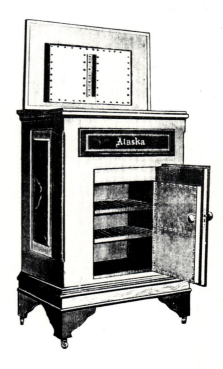

While fresh bread cools atop the coal stove, the housewife above attends to the turkey and the roast in the oven. Kitchens were usually in the basement or tacked on behind the house until the middle of the nineteenth century, when first-floor kitchens off the dining room began to be popular.

301

The Cooking Class

These aproned young ladies, posing demurely with egg beater, grill, grater, tea-kettle, and other kitchen utensils, were learning the art of housekeeping in the mid-1880's. They were all daughters of socially prominent families in Detroit.

Never, never, never...

The proper way to hold fork, knife, and teacup, according to Hill's Manual

"Never allow butter, soup or other food to remain on your whiskers. Use the napkin frequently."

That warning, and the three drawings on this page, appeared in the 1880 edition of *Hill's Manual of Social and Business Forms*, in the section on "Etiquette of the Table." Included also were these rules:

"Never allow the conversation at the table to drift into anything but chit-chat; the consideration of deep and abstruse principles will impair digestion."

"Never hesitate to take the last piece of bread or the last cake; there are probably more."

"Never hold bones in your fingers while you eat from them. Cut the meat with a knife."

"Never wipe your fingers on the table-cloth, nor clean them in your mouth."

BAD MANNERS AT THE TABLE

. Tips back his chair.
. Eats with his mouth too full.
. Feeds a dog at the table.
. Holds his knife improperly.
. Engages in violent argument at the meal-time.
. Lounges upon the table.
. Brings a cross child to the table.
. Drinks from the saucer, and laps with his tongue the last drop from the plate.
. Comes to the table in his shirt-sleeves, and puts his feet beside his chair.
. Picks his teeth with his fingers.
. Scratches her head and is frequently unnecessarily getting up from the table.

Errors of etiquette are graphically illustrated above. Oblivious to such rules, the guest in the photograph at right poses with her elbow on the tea table. The group below, however, at a dinner party in Brockton, Massachusetts, adheres to the laws of etiquette.

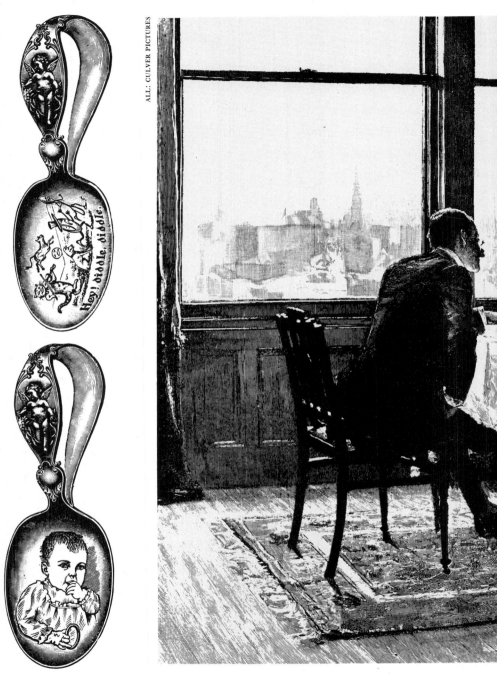

A child's first Thanksgiving is the subject of this engraving, made from a painting by W. T. Smedley. It appeared in Harper's Weekly *in 1889, accompanied by an article that cooed over the "two small dimpled hands tenderly held in place" while grace was said. The silver spoons at left were made with special handles, so that a child could grip them firmly.*

Bringing Up Baby

Holiday Time

Friends help a hostess prepare the dining room for her New Year's Day reception.

Christmas was a family occasion in New York City, but New Year's Day was time for open house. "Every woman, that *is* 'anybody,' stays at home, dressed in her best," authoress Lydia Maria Child noted in 1842. By the hostess's "side is a table covered with cakes, preserves, wines, oysters, hot coffee, &c; and as every gentleman is in honour bound to call on every lady, whose acquaintance he does not intend to cut, the amount of eating and drinking done by some fashionable beaux must of course be very considerable. The number of calls is a matter of . . . boasting among ladies, and there is . . . considerable rivalry in the magnificence and variety of the eating tables. This custom is eminently Dutch in its character, and will pass away before a higher civilization."

This congenial scene, and the others shown here, appeared in Leslie's Illustrated *in January, 1878.*

Hostess and guests watch in dismay as one caller concentrates on eating his fill.

The Servant Problem

"I cannot find a cook in the whole city but what will get drunk," Abigail Adams wrote in 1789. But her servant problem seems simple when compared with that of Mrs. Stuyvesant Fish, whose butler, Morton, became enraged one day when she invited an unusually large group to lunch at her Newport mansion. According to Mrs. Harry Lehr, wife of the social arbiter, Morton was dismissed the next day, "unfortunately on the eve of one of Mrs. Fish's biggest dinner parties. His revenge was subtle. With amazing ingenuity he unscrewed the whole of the gold dinner-service into three hundred separate pieces and mixed them in one heap on the . . . floor, so that they resembled the parts of a jigsaw puzzle. As none of his satellites had mastered the secret of putting them together a wire had to be sent to Tiffany's and two men dispatched . . . from New York to have the service in readiness for the dinner."

CORNING MUSEUM OF GLASS

*Glass sugar bowls, saltcellars, and celery vases like those above were
de rigueur on all proper dinner tables of the nineteenth century.*

*In the elegantly appointed dining room of their New York brownstone,
left, a wealthy couple named Mannering enjoy breakfast beneath a Tiffany chandelier. Attending them on that morning in 1901 were a maid,
a secretary, and the family dog. Below, in a drawing by Charles Dana
Gibson, a maid imitates her mistress, to the amusement of her co-workers.*

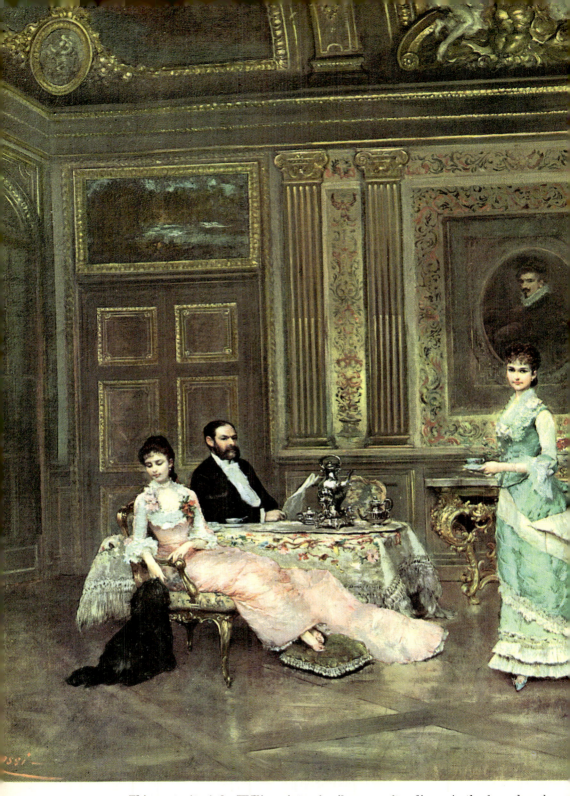

This portrait of the William Astor family, seen after dinner in the formal parlor of their New York City mansion, was made by Lucius Rossi in 1875. William, a grandson

f John Jacob Astor, is sitting with his daughter Helen at the table. Charlotte stands with coffee cup in hand; by Mrs. Astor (on the settee) are John Jacob IV and Caroline.

Place cards, from Newport, Rhode Island

Hints for the Hostess

A bible for many hostesses in the 1890's was *Practical Housekeeping,* a cookbook dedicated "to those Plucky Housewives who master their work instead of allowing it to master them." In a section on how to give a dinner, the book recommended an oval-shaped table as the most sociable, and suggested that stools or hassocks be supplied for the feet of lady guests. Describing a summer breakfast for ten (a diagram of the elaborate table setting appears opposite) the author outlined six courses: melon, fish, chicken with cream gravy, poached eggs on toast, fillets of porterhouse steak with tomatoes à la mayonnaise, and quartered peaches. Under "General Hints," *Practical Housekeeping* included the following warning: "The worst torture that survives the inquisition is a *bad* formal dinner. A worse torture than any known to the inquisition is *any* formal dinner . . . inefficiently served."

Napkins, said an 1898 cookbook, "may be folded in a variety of ways, which impart a style to a table, without adding much to the expense." Included in the book were the diagrams above, plus instructions for folding the napkins, which bore such names as the Flirt (top right) and the Favorite (bottom).

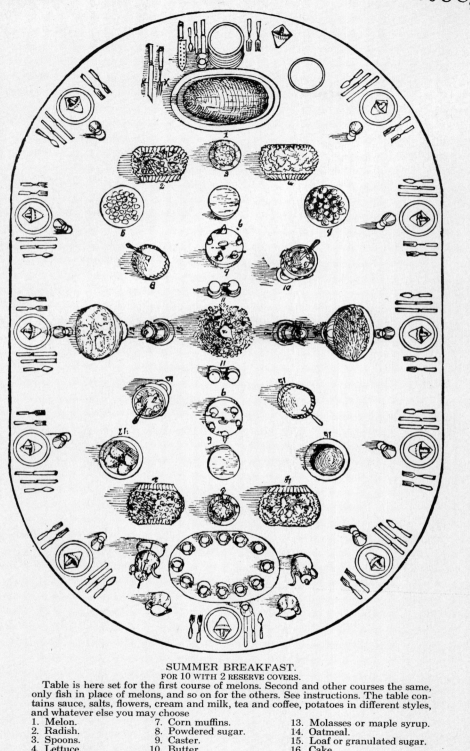

SUMMER BREAKFAST.
FOR 10 WITH 2 RESERVE COVERS.

Table is here set for the first course of melons. Second and other courses the same, only fish in place of melons, and so on for the others. See instructions. The table contains sauce, salts, flowers, cream and milk, tea and coffee, potatoes in different styles, and whatever else you may choose

1. Melon.	7. Corn muffins.	13. Molasses or maple syrup.
2. Radish.	8. Powdered sugar.	14. Oatmeal.
3. Spoons.	9. Caster.	15. Loaf or granulated sugar.
4. Lettuce.	10. Butter.	16. Cake.
5. Fancy biscuit.	11. Pickles.	17. Cold dry toast.
6. Dressing.	12. Dish Custard.	18. White syrup.

Whiskey braced these yachting gentlemen against the cold spray of San Francisco Bay.

These doughty ladies and their escorts are savoring a cookout in the woods of Maine.

Outings

Americans have always enjoyed outings on sea or on land, especially when the food was good. Few such occasions surpassed those put on by James M. Seymour, a New Yorker whose yacht *Radha* was the subject of an article in a culinary magazine, *The Cook*, in 1885. The dinners concocted by Seymour's chef ("a genius") ran to twenty courses; a typical breakfast, "without great preparation, consisted of fried halibut, clam fritters, veal cutlet, broiled English ham, cheese omelette, squab with tomato salad, fruit and coffee." Said Mr. Seymour: "The effects of rich foods and extensive dinners and wines are robbed of their terrors by the ocean breezes, and I know of no pleasanter place to enjoy a dinner, than on the water."

A mustachioed Harvard man and his companion enjoy lunch aboard a canal boat in 1892.

At Home in the White House

In 1837, Jackson invited the public to partake of a smelly, 1,400-pound cheese (above).

Some Presidents, including Thomas J[efferson and Martin Van Buren, were go[urmets]; others cared little for food. Ab[raham] Lincoln, for instance, was a li[ght] eater. He did, however, enjoy burnt sug[ar] cakes, corncakes, and gingerbread. ([He] often quoted a childhood friend who h[ad] said, "Abe, I don't s'pose anybody [on] earth likes gingerbread better'n I do—a[nd] gets less'n I do.") White House hostes[ses] varied, too, from the gracious to the a[us]tere. "Lemonade Lucy," the teetotal[ing] wife of Rutherford B. Hayes, locked [up] all the wineglasses in the Executive M[an]sion. After Hayes was elected in 1876 [a] wag remarked bitterly, "Buttermilk w[ill] flow like water."

At left is the state dining room, during a dinner given by President Grant. He disliked fowl ("I never could eat anything that goes on two legs") but enjoyed roast beef, boiled hominy, wheaten bread, and rice pudding.

e state dining room at the e of Benjamin Harrison's esidency is shown at top ht. In 1902, Teddy Roose- t (who liked plain food large quantities and used t from the White House dens to make juleps) en- ged the room and hung his ffed animal heads on the ls. At lower right is the chen, with an array of en- eled and copper pots and s, during McKinley's term.

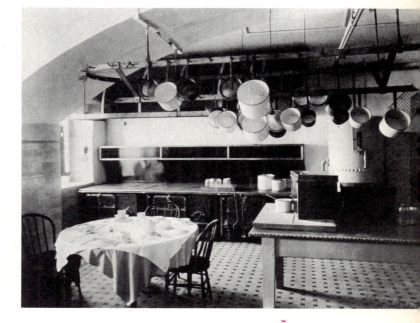

In 1885, the Buffalo *News* carried a story about a woman who had murdered her husband by putting arsenic in a pumpkin pie. The accused woman, added a whimsical editor, "lacked education. Had she only been a Vassar graduate, she might have rested all her hopes on the pie-crust." Such jokes about bad cooking were common, but to the magazines that catered to ladies, cooking was not a joking matter. "The young woman who does not learn cooking and housekeeping may grow to be an old maid and always live in boarding-houses," warned *The Cook*. If the girl should be lucky enough to marry, the article continued, she had better learn to cook posthaste. "There is no knowing how much domestic unhappiness and how many divorce suits . . . have been caused by the lack of such practical knowledge . . ."

Girl friends toast a bride-to-be in the 1905 photograph at left. In "Love in a Cottage," below, the cook has quit, the kitchen is in turmoil, and the loving husband says, "Never mind; don't cry, pet, I'll do all the cooking."

9

DINING OUT

By Lucius Beebe

"There are several restaurants in the city, on the model of those in the Palais Royal. The most superb of these, *but not by any means the most respectable,* is Taylor's, in Broadway. It combines Eastern magnificence with Parisian taste, and strangers are always expected to visit it."

Isabella Bird Bishop, an Englishwoman visiting New York City in 1854, was obviously impressed by the opulence of Taylor's, an establishment that served dinners and fancy ices to New York's beau monde. "It is a room about 100 ft. in length, by 22 in height; the roof and cornices richly carved and

Chez Mouquin, *painted by William Glackens in 1905, celebrates a famous old New York City restaurant and its chic patrons.*

gilded, the walls ornamented by superb mirrors, separated by white marble. The floor is of marble, and a row of fluted and polished marble pillars runs down each side. It is a perfect blaze of decoration. There is an alcove at one end of the apartment, filled with orange-trees, and the air is kept refreshingly cool by a crystal fountain. Any meal can be obtained here at any hour. . . . It might be supposed that Republican simplicity would scorn so much external display; but the places of public entertainment vie in their splendour with the palaces of kings."

Elegant though Taylor's was, the era of lavish restaurants and hotels had not fully flowered by the 1850's in the United States; it waited upon the prosperity that followed the Civil War.

In urban centers like New York and Boston, however, there were premonitions of the good public way of life to come.

In Boston, as early as 1794, a French refugee named Jean Baptiste Gilbert Payplat, known locally as Julien, had opened what he called a Restorator, or public ordinary, a cut above the general run of taverns (and a good cut at that, since it introduced to that city truffles from Périgord, cheese fondue, and soups so delicious that Julien became known as the Prince of Soups). So widely did the fame of Julien's Restorator spread that another distinguished Frenchman, the most celebrated professional epicure of all time —Jean Anthelme Brillat-Savarin, who was hunting wild turkey in Hartford —hurried to Boston and lent the establishment his influential blessing. It was the beginning of public dining in a community where innovation was regarded with distrust and where Bostonians, while accustomed to the good things of life, enjoyed them almost entirely in private.

To meet the growing demand for public accommodations at a more luxurious level than was offered by the purely functional taverns, a group of public-spirited Bostonians pooled their resources in 1828 to build the Tremont House, probably the earliest first-class hotel (by modern standards) in the United States. Daniel Webster and Edward Everett attended the inaugural banquet, served amidst Turkish carpets, crystal chandeliers, and French ormolu clocks. For years the Tremont House furnished all guests under its roof at New Year's with a free dinner and provided diners with felt slippers, free of charge, while their boots were being cleaned and polished.

In 1855, Harvey D. Parker, whose name was to be immortalized in a soft-crusted hot roll, opened, in Boston's School Street, a restaurant whose instant success was based on the notion, long entertained by the proprietor, that patrons might like meals at irregular hours. Hitherto, even at the Tremont, meals had been served only at fixed hours, the chief joint at dinner

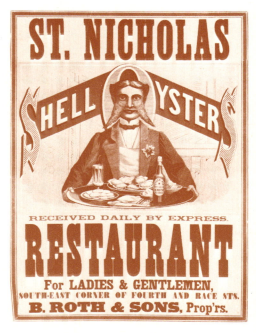

Nineteenth-century advertisement

usually being carved at the head of the table by the proprietor himself. Parker offered an à la carte menu available at all hours and made a fortune from it.

Pre-Civil War New York was by no means behind Boston in public elegances. Perhaps the most admired repository of comfort was the St. Nicholas Hotel, between Broome and Spring streets, where six hundred private rooms were serviced by a staff of more than three hundred. In its restaurant each dish was served over a spirit lamp, and forty liveried waiters functioned "harmoniously and at the word of command."

Foreigners were amazed at the profligate dining habits of New Yorkers and dismayed by the availability and consumption of alcohol at all hours and in every circumstance of life. The Scottish scientist William Ferguson reported that dinner at the St. Nicholas in 1855 included "two soups, two kinds of fish, ten boiled dishes, nine roast dishes, six relishes, seventeen entrées, three cold dishes, five varieties of game, thirteen varieties of vegetables, seven kinds of pastry, and seven fruits, with ice-cream and coffee." Another observer of the same period remarked that "gin-sling, brandy-smash, whisky-skin, streak of lightning, cock-tail, and rum-salad" were "consumed . . . morning, noon, and night, by persons who in a similar rank of life in England would no more think of going into a gin-shop than robbing the Bank."

By the late sixties, America was a nation on the move, impelled toward the far horizon and toward realization of its "manifest destiny." The vast fortunes accumulated in banking, coal, iron, railroads, and eventually cattle and mining in the Far West were making themselves felt in a new demand for luxury in every form then available.

To some degree, this new wealth made itself conspicuous in the form of vast mansions and opulent suburban residences, in clothes, jewelry (it was an age when gentlemen wore diamonds without reproach), fine horses and equipages, the Grand Tour of Europe, and seasonal appearances at the great pleasure resorts which were coming into being: Saratoga Springs, White Sulphur Springs, the New Jersey seacoast, and Newport, Rhode Island. But far and away the most accessible luxuries were travel and gastronomy, and as the sixties merged with the seventies, Americans began to see their desires amply gratified.

Hotels and restaurants that had been comparatively small-time ventures blossomed in florid extravagance, and such establishments as Willard's Hotel in Washington (long a popular rendezvous of high-living politicians), the Hoffman House in New York, the vast gingerbread splendors of the Grand Union and United States hotels in Saratoga, the St. Charles in New Orleans, the Palace in San Francisco, and Potter Palmer's eye-popping hotel in Chicago were firmly established as status symbols for their patrons and as resorts of exotic luxury.

Nor were ostentatious gastronomic displays confined to such static premises as the new hotels and restaurants. De luxe dining became mobile, at first upon the inland waters of the Mississippi and Ohio and along the coastal sea lanes, which were the principal avenues of travel and transport before the coming of the railroads, and then in the finest expression of dining-in-motion, upon the steam cars themselves.

Water-borne epicurism had its inception and first intimations of grandeur upon the floating palaces that plied the Mississippi in ante-bellum years between New Orleans and Memphis, Cairo, and St. Louis.

The abundance of plantation life and the culinary refinements that were the heritage of Creole New Orleans easily translated themselves to the river packets, which in the forties and fifties of the nineteenth century were being

Tell a country lady in these times that when she comes to New York she must eat and pass the evening in a room by herself, and she would rather stay at home. The going to the Astor and dining with two hundred well dressed people, and sitting in full dress in a splendid drawing room with plenty of company is the charm of going to the city!

—Nathaniel P. Willis, in the 1800's

built with ever-increasing splendor. Patrons of the Mississippi River boats were recruited almost exclusively from the well-to-do classes: planter-aristocrats and satraps of cotton and tobacco who, in increasing numbers, accompanied their families to northern resorts, such as Saratoga Springs, in the summer months, commission mer-

chants, well-heeled foreigners exploring the American scene, and, of course, the ever-present river-town gambler.

This was a clientele that demanded and could easily afford the best of everything, and the owners and masters of the great steamers in the New Orleans-St. Louis trade spared no cost or effort to see that it was made abundantly available.

The architecture and appointments of the floating palaces reflected the taste of the time, as well as the immense and widespread affluence which could finance and patronize them. The public rooms of such celebrated steamers as the *Rob't E. Lee,* the *Natchez,* the *Frank Pargoud,* the *Western World,* and the *Grand Republic* — usually painted white for a tropical climate— were amazements of fretwork and pilasters, decorated clerestories and myriad crystal lamps, which shone on elaborate Victorian sofas and armchairs, marble-topped tables, silver water coolers, bevel-edged mirrors, and thick Turkish carpets. The private cabins which opened off this grand *salon* were usually of more Spartan décor, the owner's resources having been reserved for the boat's public apartments, but the over-all impression of life and travel on such lordly conveyances was one of magnificence never hitherto present in a democracy.

Since the scenery was largely unvarying and the voyage often of four or five days' duration, amusement was at a premium. The gentlemen might, of course, patronize a splendidly furnished wine room, set apart from those portions of the ship available to ladies, where whiskey toddies and juleps and gambling for large sums provided ample excitement for men in skirted coats who could and did lose and win, at a single session of cards, plantations covering thousands of acres and served by hundreds of slaves. These recreations, with their occasional recourse to gunfire and the code duello, were exclusively masculine, so that the great common meeting ground of the sexes was at meals—three times a day, with late supper for those who wished.

On the most stylish packets, dinner was served at six in the evening, and it was the custom for the entire passenger list to be seated at a single long table which was set up in the grand *salon* and loaded with gleaming silver and spotless linen under the congenial glow of high, ornate chandeliers burning coal oil. On the truly sumptuous *J. M. White* as many as two hundred and fifty cabin passengers were served at a time off Sèvres china, each article of which bore the ship's likeness in full color. The napkins were of Irish linen worked with the initials *J.M.W.* Dishes of all sorts—soups, entrees, fish, roasts, relevés—were brought from the galley by a veritable army of colored waiters and eaten with solid silver flatware. The *White* was famous for its pyramids of nougat, its daubes *glacés,* and incomparable salads and desserts; the bill for fresh fruit and nuts alone came to seven hundred dollars a week, a tidy sum in hard gold currency.

Ladies' luncheon

The menu of the *M. S. Mepham* (a celebratedly hospitable boat in the St. Louis-Memphis-New Orleans service), aside from being a masterpiece of typographic and lithographic art, listed no fewer than fifty meat and fish entrees and thirty of the cold aspics and *pièces montées* of elaborate and fanciful design which were ranged down the center of the literally groaning board.

As if this bountiful bill of fare were insufficient, many of the more aristocratic passengers carried with them specialties from their own home kitchens which were brought to the common table by their personal servants. If an adjacent diner made the mistake of reaching for one of these, the politely modulated words "Private pie" or "Private gumbo" apprised him that he was trespassing on posted gastronomic land.

Although the *belle époque* of Mississippi River packets continued into the 1870's, their ultimate doom was implicit in the vast program of railroad construction which was inaugurated on a national scale at the conclusion of the Civil War.

As early as 1858, combined river-steamer-and-railroad connections with the North were being advertised, and a "card" in *The Crescent City Business Directory* for that year advertised "The Great Southern Route & U. S. Mail Line" via river packet from New Orleans to Memphis and thence overland via the Memphis & Charleston, the East Tennessee & Virginia, and the Orange & Alexandria railroads, with

---

It was a long extended oval table, and every inch of it was covered with flowers, excepting a space in the centre, left for a lake, and a border around the table for the plates. . . . it was an oval pond, thirty feet in length . . . four superb swans, brought from Prospect Park, swam in it . . . Then, all around the inclosure, and in fact above the entire table, hung little golden cages, with fine songsters, who filled the room with their melody, occasionally interrupted by the splashing of the waters . . . by the swans.

—Ward McAllister, at Delmonico's

---

a variety of facilities north from Washington for Boston, Philadelphia, and New York.

The first primeval railroad accommodations provided neither sleeping cars nor diners. Trains of day coaches, some of which were supplemented with private drawing rooms and parlor cars, halted at appropriate intervals while the passengers descended and ate in strategically located depot restaurants.

In the South especially, food was hawked through the cars by Negroes selling cold fried chicken, corn pone, and other regional delicacies, and it was not uncommon, in the relaxed spirit of the age, for a small bar to cater to a masculine clientele in the baggage car, a monopoly of enterprising members of the train crew.

But the traveling American public, already indoctrinated in luxurious accommodations by the great metropolitan hotels and the lavish tradition of Mississippi River table fare, was impatient with such arrangements, and as early as 1865 a Boston newspaper facetiously forecast the time in the not-too-distant future when hotel cars would be incorporated in the better trains, and long-distance passengers on overnight runs might actually sleep and eat while traversing the countryside at an incredible twenty miles an hour. The time was closer at hand than the editor imagined.

In 1858 George Mortimer Pullman, a cabinetmaker from Brocton, New York, had produced for the Chicago & Alton Railroad the first practicable sleeping cars; the secret of their economic success was a retractable upper berth which doubled the pay-load capacity of the car. A decade later, on the same railroad, Pullman inaugurated the first dining car, named *Delmonico* as a tribute to the dynasty of New York restaurateurs.

With the advent of the diner began the golden age of American railroad travel which lasted in mobile glory for nearly three-quarters of a century.

It was the age of savage competition for passenger traffic among carriers, and astute operating officials at once recognized that the dining car and its cuisine could be a matchless showcase for other services the railroads hoped to sell. An important shipper of merchandise could be influenced to divert hugely profitable freight consignments to a railroad on which he could enjoy terrapin Maryland on the dollar dinner or fillets of the best and tenderest aged Kansas City beef. Obsequious maîtres d'hôtel and waiters with just the right touch, working in harmony with a sympathetic chef, were as effective in soliciting business for the railroad as its most forceful salesmen.

As a result the dining car suddenly became, and remained until the dismal age of cost accounting, an incomparable agency for high living for very little money. All dining cars operated at a loss, and many carriers urged ever-greater deficits on their commissary departments, confident that the good will derived from offering the best of everything at a very modest price to the customer far outweighed the economic considerations involved. It is said that Fred Harvey, who almost singlehandedly brought civilization to the Southwest through his chain of excellent restaurants and his catering arrangements with the Santa Fe Railroad, fired a dining-car manager who had been losing five hundred dollars a month and replaced him with a man who upped the deficit to fifteen hundred with such expedition that he was made general superintendent.

By the early 1890's dining cars on even secondary lines offered such lavish table fare that foreigners, confronted with menus that would have done credit to the best European hotels, while rolling through prairies that only a decade or so before had crawled with hostile Indians, were incredulous.

Inevitably, certain roads became celebrated for regional specialties or for the preparation of uncommonly exotic dishes. The patriarchal Baltimore & Ohio was famous for terrapin stew and for Chesapeake Bay seafood, which was put aboard its cars fresh, and often live, at the beginning of each run. The Santa Fe (Fred Harvey again) was noted for its broiled sage hen, Mexican quail, prairie chicken, and charlotte of peaches with cognac sauce. The New Haven, serving a lordly clientele of Boston Brahmins, was celebrated for its scrod, Cotuit oysters, and Maine lobster, and for its wine and staple groceries, all of which came from the venerable firm of S. S. Pierce Company in Boston. The Wabash is to this day famous for a particularly succulent creamed chicken pie. And the Illinois Central, main line between the Great Lakes and New Orleans, was renowned for its Creole dishes, prepared according to secret recipes from the oldest families in the Vieux Carré. The Northern Pacific advertised itself as "The Line of the Great Big Baked Potato," while the Chicago & North Western, a Vanderbilt line for many years, regularly listed roast Canadian goose, rabbit stew, venison steaks, and mallard duck on its dollar dinners.

After the turn of the century, when the major carriers were inaugurating all-Pullman, extra-fare, de luxe limiteds and flyers between their terminals, prices aboard the cars began to rise, but only microscopically. When, in 1902, the New York Central placed in service the Twentieth Century Limited, probably the most famous train in the world, the line made dining aboard it a status symbol by raising the dollar dinner to a dollar and a half. To compensate for this extravagance, the management let it be known that all the butter served on the Century diners derived from the model dairy farm in Vermont of a Vanderbilt in-law, William Seward Webb, who also happened to be a director of the connecting Lake Shore & Michigan Southern Railroad.

But luxurious as they were, not even the railroad diners topped the florid effulgence of good living that attended the mining bonanzas of the Old

The Americans possess a most singular taste for marring the beauty of every place which can boast of any thing like scenery, by introducing a bar-room into the most romantic and conspicuous spot.
—E. T. Coke, 1833

West, beginning with the discovery of California gold in 1848 and coming to an end only with the decline of the Tonopah and Goldfield diggings in Ne-

vada in 1910. For six full decades the discovery by fortunate miners of vast material wealth in its most tangible forms, gold and silver, was immediately followed by a rush to acquire the symbols of the good life.

Grand pianos and diamond brooches, silk hats and frock coats, magnums of champagne, thoroughbred horses with silver-trimmed harnesses, stylish bonnets and dresses from the great houses of female fashion in Paris, and in some cases an urban style of living complete with grand opera and cotillions, suddenly flowered in lonely gulches and desolate deserts where only a year before the sagebrush and rattlesnake had held sway. Last year's slaving housewives, who had toiled to prepare meals of beans and sourdough biscuits for their menfolk, suddenly assumed the airs of *grandes dames* in Newport. Hornyhanded, hard-rock miners, who had spent their lives wresting unpromising specimens from the earth with pickaxe and blasting powder, now commanded vintage wines while playing poker with stacks of gold double eagles in sumptuous clubrooms. Fortunate speculators in mining shares and mining claims, who had been accustomed to sleeping in the halls in dubious rooming houses, demanded state apartments in hotels boasting diamond-dust mirrors in their barrooms and rode in private palace cars when they made the grand tour to San Francisco, Denver, or Chicago.

In Central City, a Colorado boom town fifty miles from Denver in an escarpment of the Rockies, the populace paved part of the sidewalk in front of a hotel with silver bricks in anticipation of a visit by President Grant. In Virginia City, Nevada—one year a sunblasted waste of desert mountainside and the next the setting of the incredible and almost inexhaustible Comstock Lode—there still stands a house, built by the town's first banker, with recessed seats inside its massive front doors for the night shift of footmen who awaited the return of the owner from the riotous saloons of C Street.

No aspect of rejoicing in this newfound wealth found expression in more passionate devotion to ostentation than the décor of hotels and restaurants which came into florid and rococo being amidst the headshafts and milltails of the proven diggings of Colorado, California, and Nevada.

In these stately sarabands of extravagance not only the pattern of established elegance in the cities of the East was slavishly followed; the very nomenclature was the same. Hotels were all named Waldorf, Windsor, Fifth Avenue, or Astor, with here and there a Vendôme or Grand Imperial. Restaurants, although they might be known locally as French Louie's, were formally christened Delmonico, Monte Carlo, or the Café de Paris.

Tinned oysters and vintage champagne were transported over lonely distances of mountain and desert by the dusty stages of Wells Fargo & Company or by the narrow-gauge railroads, which found a foothold where stand-

ard-gauge operations were unthinkable. In Leadville, Colorado, the archetype of gun-fighting frontier towns, the management of the Saddle Rock Res-

A precarious situation

taurant actually imported—at the behest of its best customer, E. A. W. Tabor, a multimillionaire who could scarcely write his own name—a *chef de cuisine* hired away from Delmonico's.

Denver, by the year 1880, had already appropriated for itself the title "Queen City of the Plains" and justified its royal pretentions by building the most effulgently sybaritic hotel anywhere between Potter Palmer's in Chicago and the Palace in San Francisco. The Windsor Hotel in Larimer Street was financed with English capital, for it was the golden noontide of the great English and Scottish financing of cattle baronies in Wyoming and Colorado.

In a direct throwback to the steamboat-Gothic ostentation of the Missis-

---

Orchestral music ushered in the guests, who took their seats at table; the major-domo raised his wand, and each waiter man advanced and stood back of the guests; at the second wave of the wand the waiters laid hands upon the dish-covers, and at the third wave every cover was lifted and laid upon small dumb-waiters, which other attendants carried away. Then the major-domo laid his hand upon his heart and bowed to the guests, the music struck up, and the waiters served the dishes.

—Mrs. E. S. Bladen's description of a dinner at the United States Hotel in Saratoga Springs, in 1902

---

sippi packets, the Windsor's architecture included giant bevel-edged mirrors, twenty feet tall, into which diamond dust had been liberally blown. The effect at night, when the countless crystal chandeliers were illuminated, was one of sparkling and iridescent magnificence.

The Windsor menus were perhaps the most complete catalogue of edible wildlife on the western plains and ran the gamut from buffalo steaks and bears' paws *en gelée* to grilled antelope, venison, porterhouse, elk, and mutton. The kitchens must have resembled an aviary, for the bill of fare offered plover, wild doves, quail, partridge, ruffed grouse, teal, mallard duck, sage hen, wild turkey, and game-bird pie in which, presumably, all these found a cozy common nesting place.

If the Windsor was explicit, the Antlers, down the Rio Grande main line at Colorado Springs, was comprehensive in its grandeurs of gastronomy, and without listing them, declared that its chefs were prepared on short notice to produce any dish recognized in the civilized cuisine of any nation. Humorists who demanded sea-lion cutlets and *contre-filets* of giraffe were reminded that these were not conventionally included in the de luxe cuisine of any nation of recognized cultural status.

Aside from its wildlife *sous cloche*, the Windsor was celebrated for its ladies' ordinary, the first public restaurant in the West to solicit the patronage of unescorted women. Nothing but the most eminent respectability was associated with its clientele.

Perhaps the most arresting single figure in the lexicon of luxury in the Rockies was Louis Dupuy, whose Hotel de Paris at Georgetown, then one of the teeming boom towns of the region but today a ghost community, was celebrated on a national scale.

Dupuy was not the true name of this genius of the stewpots (it was Adolphus François Gerard), for he was a deserter from the U.S. Army. But from 1875 until his death in 1900 his premises made culinary history throughout the entire West. Every visiting celebrity from Mme. Franziska de Janauschek, the Bohemian actress on tour in *Bleak House* and *Mary Stuart,* to Lord Dunraven, Eugene Field, and Richard Mansfield made pilgrimages to Georgetown aboard the red-plush coaches of the narrow-gauge Colorado Central (the only means of access), to sample the mushroom omelette, sweetbreads Eugénie, and *cassoulet Toulousain* at the Hotel de Paris. They came also to engage in literary conversation with Louis, an eccentric of engaging dimensions who served only guests enjoying his personal favor. Upon occasion he closed his restaurant, despite the protests of its patrons of the moment, so he might quote Racine and Molière with Mme. Helena Modjeska without interruption. His cellars were phenomenal, not just for their time and place, and his Rainwater Madeira, 1811 cognacs, and vintage Bordeaux were of interest to cultivated oenophilists from France and England, who returned with glowing tales of safaris to Georgetown in search of fine food, rare vintages, and congenial company.

More than one thousand miles to the west of Colorado, San Francisco was busy from the early 1850's establishing the reputation for public opulence and the good life which it enjoys to the present day. The first torrents of tangible wealth that poured in from the Mother Lode after 1848 were supplemented a decade later when the silver bonanzas of the Comstock Lode materialized some two hundred and fifty miles away in the deep mines under Virginia City, Nevada. San Francisco

saw the emergence of a number of public restaurants of more than local celebrity, largely in the tradition of French cuisine, which was brought west with the city's first families, many of whom emigrated from the Deep South. Its first public benefactor in this direction was a magnate named François Pioche, who, feeling that the town lacked culinary talent in keeping with i s station, sent to France and recruited an entire shipload of chefs from the best restaurants of Paris and from the French countryside.

A hotel town from the beginning, San Francisco gloried in the tally of its luxury resorts, including the Russ and Lick Houses, the Grand the Oriental and the Occidental, the early St. Francis, and, eventually, the Palace and Lucky Baldwin's.

Entire books have been written about the Palace, which rose bay-windowed and monstrous in what was still predominantly a shack town in 1875. From its grand opening (in the form of a banquet for General Philip Sheridan) to its present estate as the Sheraton Palace it has been the focal point of San Francisco's public life and most stylish private entertainment, an item of folklore and an article of faith, the scene of more social, political, and financial history than any other single premises in the Golden State.

From the very beginning, every aspect of the Palace was in the grand manner indeed. It was the city's transcendent show place. The Emperor Dom Pedro of Brazil remarked that nothing made him so ashamed of his country as his stay at the Palace.

The hotel's first chef, Jules Harder, whose background embraced Delmonico's and the Grand Union Hotel in Saratoga, set a standard for excellence of cuisine that generations of Palace chefs zealously upheld. A later Palace chef, Fred Mergenthaler, maintained the Harder tradition when he invented oysters Kirkpatrick, a refinement of baked oysters Rockefeller of New Orleans fame, which he diplomatically named for the manager of the hotel. An old Negro, Muffin Tom, made nothing but corn bread and hot egg muffins for generations of San Franciscans, and still another Palace chef, Ernest Arbogast, distinguished himself by inventing California oyster omelette.

Almost as celebrated as the Palace, which was destroyed in the fire and earthquake of 1906 and promptly rebuilt in all its former magnificence by the heirs of Senator William Sharon, who had acquired it in the seventies, was San Francisco's "Cocktail Route" which flourished green-bay-tree-like in its wickedness in the days "Before the Fire." This embraced a number of Bohemian resorts, including Marchand's, the Palace of Art, the Louvre, and, most notoriously, the Poodle Dog and the Pup, respectable family restaurants on their lower floors, but devoted in their more elevated precincts to private apartments where captains of finance might bring ladies who were patently not members of their family circle. Much of the aura of perfumed sin that surrounds the San Francisco legend of the turn of the century derived from these abodes of forbidden romance, and the greatest precautions were taken by patrons and management alike to shroud in anonymity the names of prominent clients. It is said that the Poodle Dog went so far as to install an outsized elevator large enough to accommodate an early automobile, the Apperson Jack Rabbit, and that guests inside their conveyances were wafted to the private dining rooms on the fourth floor. When the fire of 1906 ravished the Poodle Dog, more than a facility of romance was toppled. A way of life in the Old West crashed with it.

The nineties and the years immediately after the turn of the century were also the high-water mark of opulent public dining in the East. In New York, a flood tide of champagne and other vintage potables flowed through some of the most ornate and splendidly maintained restaurants in the world. It was, in Manhattan, the Age of the Lobster Palaces, a category that embraced not only conservative establishments like Sherry's and Delmonico's, but a vast, glittering, red-carpeted, and electrically lit parade of eating places such as Rector's, Shanley's, Bustanoby's, Churchill's, the Knickerbocker Grill, and the Holland House. At some of these establishments, music for dancing was provided, in addition to the staggering menus.

The cream of society and the world of finance furnished the clientele at

Richard Canfield's gambling establishment on 44th Street, almost next door to Delmonico's, dining without charge off canvasback duck and terrapin, Maine lobster and pheasant *sous cloche,* provided by the openhanded management. Canfield's cellar was reported to contain seventy-five thousand dollars' worth of "the finest vintage wines, as well as the more plebeian drinks," and his French chef spent the summer months each year traveling in Europe to acquire new recipes and the secrets of recherché sauces for his master.

After an evening on the town, the more durable playboys ended with late supper or early breakfast, preferably English mutton chops and golden buck rabbits, washed down with a final magnum of White Seal or Mumm's, at Jack Dunstan's chophouse on Sixth Avenue. It was here that the management evolved the celebrated "flying-wedge" of waiters to eject customers who had been overserved in wine.

The Olympus of the era was unquestionably the Waldorf-Astoria, largest hotel in the world, which opened its doors amid great fanfare in 1897, at a cost of some ten million dollars. For blue bloods and *nouveaux riches* alike, lunches, afternoon teas, pre-theatre dinners, and midnight suppers at the Waldorf became *de rigueur.* In its most elaborate restaurant, the Palm Garden, guests were required to wear formal attire, and the waiters all spoke French and German as well as English. The chef reputedly received ten thousand dollars a year.

It was at the Waldorf, in the midst of a national depression in 1897, that Mrs. Bradley Martin played hostess to seven hundred guests, who were asked to attend in costumes of the Louis XV period. In a huge suite decorated à la Versailles, the guests drank more than

A satisfied customer

sixty cases of champagne, ate an opulent supper, danced quadrilles and waltzes, and paid obeisance to Mrs. Martin, who sat on a throne and was dressed, somewhat incongruously, as Mary Stuart.

The newspapers were outraged by the cost of the ball, which was almost ten thousand dollars. Even before the event, public opinion was so stirred up that there were rumors that anarchists intended to bomb the Waldorf.

A few days before the ball, Mrs. Martin met Theodore Roosevelt, then president of the New York City Board of Police Commissioners. "I'm very pleased that you and Mrs. Roosevelt are coming to the ball," Mrs. Martin remarked. "Oh, my wife's going because she's got her costume," replied T. R., "but, as one of the commissioners, I shall be outside looking after the police."

Diamond Jim Brady

DIAMOND JIM BRADY

By Cleveland Amory

In the days of the fifteen-course dinner, he was recognized as Number One eater, the man whom restaurateur George Rector admiringly designated "the best twenty-five customers we had"

You will not find James Buchanan Brady, better known as Diamond Jim, in the *Dictionary of American Biography*—which is certainly the height of something or other, perhaps a virulent form of nineteenth-century academic, anti-celebrity snobbery. But the fact remains that the young man who was born, fittingly enough, the son of a free-lunch-counter-and-saloon operator, whose first job was as a hotel bellboy (he spent, characteristically, as much time eating as working), and who went on to legendary heights as a salesman of railroad equipment—and, as the country's Number One eater, to even more legendary widths—left behind him an enduring name.

When aspersions were cast on the authenticity of his diamonds (his jewel collection, including a thirty-three carat scarf pin, cost him almost two million dollars), Jim was inclined, casually, to scratch his name with them on the doubter's windowpane. When similar skepticism was accorded his gustatory prowess, however, he did not even deign to acknowledge it. Brady, born in 1856, lived in the era of the fifteen-course dinner—and no public dancing, as we know it today, was permitted. In a sense, there was nothing to do *but* eat. And it was thus an era made to order—à la carte, of course—for Diamond Jim. Comparisons with other great gourmets ("Well," a friend once allowed, "he's a kind of combination of gourmand and gourmet") were simply preposterous. Years after his passing, his eating feats were passed on by those who knew him. "One would be willing to match his shade," declared Albert Stevens Crockett, "against the most valiant trenchermen of all time."

For breakfast he would have a full gallon of orange juice—actually, he had several beakers of this at every meal, a fact that was later described as having prolonged his life. Then came, in rapid succession, hominy, eggs, corn bread, muffins, flapjacks, chops, fried potatoes, and a beefsteak.

Breakfast would hold him until about 11:30 A.M., at which time he would have his midmorning snack—one that consisted of two, or sometimes three, dozen clams and oysters. An hour later he was ready for lunch. First, more oysters and clams, then two or three deviled crabs, next a brace of broiled lobsters, followed by a joint of beef, a salad, and several kinds of pie.

During the afternoon came another snack, again a platter heaped skyward with seafood, this time followed by several bottles of lemon soda. (Jim, the son of a saloon man, was a lifelong teetotaler.) Then, records his awed biographer, Parker Morell, "after lying down for an hour or two to gather his forces together for a further assault upon the groaning board, Jim went down to dinner."

It took the late restaurateur George Rector himself to describe the repasts that the rapacious Brady enjoyed for dinner. "I can affirm and testify," he said late in life, "after looking over the books of that dim era, that Diamond Jim was the best twenty-five customers we had." Rector also attested to the truth of Wilson Mizner's observations that at dinner "Jim likes his oysters sprinkled with clams" and "his sirloin steaks smothered in veal cutlets."

First, of course, came the napkin. Jim wore a napkin around his neck. But this was not, according to Rector, "due to lack of etiquette"—rather it was owing "to the conformation of Mr. Brady's topography . . . A napkin on his knee would have been as inadequate as a doily under a bass drum. Diamond Jim's stomach started at his neck and swelled out in majestic proportions, gaining power and curve as it proceeded southward. Therefore the only place where a napkin would have done him any good was around his neck. And there he wore it. It looked like a bookmark in a tome of chins." To begin with, at dinner, came oysters. Diamond Jim would often eat two or three dozen Lynnhaven oysters, each measuring six inches from tip to tail. ("We used to have our oysters shipped up to us from Baltimore daily," George Rector said, "and every second or third shipment would include a barrel of extra large Lynnhavens with the words 'For Mr. Brady' painted on the side of it. Even down in Maryland, the sea food dealers knew about Diamond Jim and saved all the giant oysters for him.") Then would follow half a dozen crabs, claws and all. After the crabs came a brief pause for

green turtle soup—at least two portions
—and then appeared what Rector described as the "deluge" of lobsters. "Six or seven giants," he said, "would suffice." Next came two portions of terrapin, two whole canvasback ducks, and, at long last, a steak and vegetables. Finally, of course, came dessert—which was supplemented by cakes and pastry. "He selected his cakes carefully—in handfuls," Rector recalled. "When he pointed at a platter of French pastry, he didn't mean any special piece of pastry. He meant the platter."

The meal would conclude with Jim ordering a two-pound box of candy, which he would then pass around among his guests. But if any guest actually took any, Jim made a habit of ordering another two-pound box for himself. "They make the food set better," he declared, and they evidently made the theatre set better, too. A devoted first-nighter all his life, Brady was never known to arrive at the theatre without his accompanying box of candy. And he was no mean theatrical critic. "Shaw was more tolerable with bonbons," he explained, "and Ibsen was best with *glacé* fruit."

After the theatre, of course, came supper—not a bird and a bottle, but several birds and several bottles, though for Jim there was never any hard liquor. Once, however, concluding a hard day's eating at Harry Hill's, the famous sporting house, he was challenged to a drinking duel by the pugil-

ist John L. Sullivan. Over a two-hour period, Jim calmly drank some fifteen enormous steins of root beer without visible disaffect, thereby garnering the lifelong admiration of the fighter. "By God, sir, you're a man," exclaimed Sullivan, who had been drinking Pilsener and thought Brady had been, too. "I'm proud to call you my friend! Shake hands again!"

All in all, over a sixteen-hour, 9 A.M. to 1 A.M. span, Diamond Jim consumed a truly incredible amount of edibles. "You must be very proud of your appetite, Mr. Brady," a *grande dame* once said icily as Brady heaved himself up from her elegant table. "And how do you ever know when your appetite is satiated?" "Why, Ma'am, I'll tell you," Brady replied with pristine simplicity, "whenever I sit down to a meal, I always make it a point to leave just four inches between my stummick and the edge of the table. And then, when I can feel 'em rubbin' together pretty hard, I *know* I've had enough."

Most of his eating was done out. "Between Mr. Brady and the Expense Account," records Morell, "it was a case of love at first sight." And Jim, curiously, never married. For ten years he had a liaison with Edna McCauley, a handsome blonde who had been a department-store salesgirl until Diamond Jim picked her up—only to have her, in the end, marry his best friend, Jesse Lewisohn. Ironically, before that time Lewisohn had been the lover of Jim's friend Lillian Russell, who managed to marry four other men in between lovers but was nonetheless fated to go down in history, gustatorily, if not amatorially, with Diamond Jim. For when big Lil was turning down diamonds from legions of swains, it was Diamond Jim who won her heart by teaching her new ways to eat corn on the cob. Lillian liked her dinner ("Another pound or two, what does it matter, Jim?" she would exclaim light-heartedly), and, by that time perhaps the two foremost celebrities of the day, the pair would hold rendezvous where the chief purpose of the assignation seemed to be to see which one could assassinate the most victuals. Brady almost always won, but "for a woman, Nell done damn well."

At a famous eating bout at Bustanoby's in Saratoga, however, the scales were tipped in the other direction when, before the contest, Lillian disappeared. "I'll never forget that night," Bustanoby later said in an interview. "She slipped out to the ladies' room and came out with a heavy bundle under her arm wrapped up in a tablecloth. 'Keep this for me,' Lillian said, 'but don't look.'" That night Lillian won fair 'n' square—what was in the tablecloth, of course, was her corset.

And Brady was, as always, a good sport. Once after an enormous evening repast at Manhattan Beach, he turned beaming to Lillian as, happy after a gargantuan dinner, they were watching the fireworks. "God, Nell," said Diamond Jim, "ain't it grand?"

The double standard of the day was for Jim no more of a problem than the women who could not, for better or worse, lure him from the pleasures of the table. There was, for example, the little matter of Stanford White's Jack-Horner-pie dinner, at which Jim was gustatory guest of honor and also at which girls danced, it was alleged, "in the altogether." At this dinner a mammoth pie was placed in the center of the table, and at a given signal, each of the gentlemen present took hold of a long satin ribbon and tugged. Promptly, the sides of the pie fell apart, and a young lady, clad solely in a satin arm band, danced down the table to Jim. Sitting on Brady's lap, she fed him his dessert as eleven other young ladies came in for the other guests.

On another occasion, White devised a Roman-toga party, at which his guests reclined on Roman sofas and which featured, on swings, young ladies covered only by trays of comestibles across their laps. As the girls swung by the diners the men helped themselves, often grabbing the young ladies instead of dinner. Not so Jim. Beaming with pleasure and rosy with good fellowship, time after time he secured his edible target with the precision of a heron picking off a fish in shallow water —a virtuosity that won him, among other things, no small annoyance from the showgirls in question.

When it came to throwing parties, Jim was no slouch himself. Once, in honor of his race horse, Gold Heels, he invited fifty friends to a dinner on the roof of the Hoffman House in New York. There, between the hours of 4

340

FILLET OF SOLE MARGUERY À LA DIAMOND JIM

"Have 2 flounders filleted. Place bones, skin, and heads in stewpan. Add 1 pound inexpensive fish cleaned and cut into small pieces, ½ cup thinly sliced young carrots, and 1 small chopped leek, 3 sprigs of parsley, 10 whole peppercorns, 1 small bay leaf, 1 sprig of thyme, 1½ quarts cold water. Bring to boiling point very slowly and simmer until liquid is reduced to 1 pint, then strain through fine cheesecloth. Place fillets in buttered baking pan and pour over 1 cup fish stock. Season with sprinkling of salt and pepper, and place in moderate oven (325° F.) 15 to 20 minutes. Carefully lift fillets from pan and arrange on hot ovenproof serving platter. Garnish with 1 dozen poached oysters and 1 dozen boiled shrimps which have been shelled and cleaned. Pour remaining fish stock into baking pan in which fillets were poached and simmer gently until quantity is reduced to 3 or 4 tablespoons, no more. Strain into top part of double boiler and add 4 tablespoons dry white wine, ¼ pound butter. Cook over hot water, stirring until butter is melted. (Have very little water in lower part of double boiler, just enough to create a gentle steam.) Add 4 egg yolks which have been well beaten. Stir constantly until sauce is the consistency of a medium cream sauce. Pour this creamy sauce over fish fillets, oysters, and shrimps, and place under broiler flame until nicely glazed or lightly browned. Allow 1 fillet per serving."

—From Rector's Naughty '90s Cookbook, *by Alexander Kirkland,*
assisted by Muriel Shaffer. Doubleday & Company, Inc., 1949
Copyright © 1949 by Alexander Kirkland and Muriel Shaffer

P.M. and 9 A.M., something in excess of five hundred bottles of champagne were consumed, not to mention innumerable beefsteaks and assorted delicacies. All told, the party set Brady back more than $100,000, including $60,000 worth of baubles for the guests —diamond brooches for the ladies and diamond-studded watches for the men.

For Jim, a restaurateur would go to literally any lengths. There was, for instance, the case of the fillet of sole Marguery à la Diamond Jim. "Diamond Jim had been to Paris and brought home with him glad tidings of a famous dish—fillet of sole Marguery, prepared only in the Café de Marguery," George Rector recalled. Stern measures were obviously called for. In any case, Charles Rector, his father, summoned George from Cornell, where he had been happily immersed in the study of law, and sent him to France with instructions not to return to these shores until the recipe was his, "to return either with the sauce Marguery or in it."

It took him over a year, during which time he served as an apprentice cook, waiter, and busboy before being permitted to "get the hang of the famous sauce." At last, Rector managed "to produce a combination which was voted perfect by a jury of seven master chefs." Finally he returned to America, to be met as his ship docked in Manhattan by an apprehensive father and a bellowing Diamond Jim. "Have you got the sauce?" Brady roared as the gangplank lowered slowly. "I got it," young Rector screeched in reply, and that night, at a private dinner at Rector's attended by Brady, Marshall Field, Victor Herbert, Sam Shubert, and several others, he made good his claim. "George," said Diamond Jim, folding his napkin over what was perhaps the widest waistcoat in the western hemisphere, "that sole was marvelous. I've had nine helpings—and even right now, if you poured some of the sauce over a Turkish towel, I believe I could eat all of it."

"He was," said George Rector in his later years, "the greatest gourmet of his time."

In the end, of course, the strain told. At fifty-six, Jim was taken to Johns Hopkins, where it was discovered, under fluoroscope, that his stomach was six times as large as a normal person's. At first, when his troubles began, Jim was under the impression that he could simply order a new stomach—his preference, he said, was for that of an elephant. But when he had to settle for a new human one, he was willing, on the condition that the doctors wouldn't stop his eating. When told that he could, with care and constant diet, live ten more years, he stoutly refused. "Who wants to live ten years," he said, "if he has to do all them things? I'm gonna go on eatin' what I please as long as I can keep my food down. Then when I cash in my chips it'll be because my number's up anyway."

Five years later, on April 16, 1917, at the Shelburne Hotel in Atlantic City, his number did come up.

DINING OUT

A Picture Portfolio

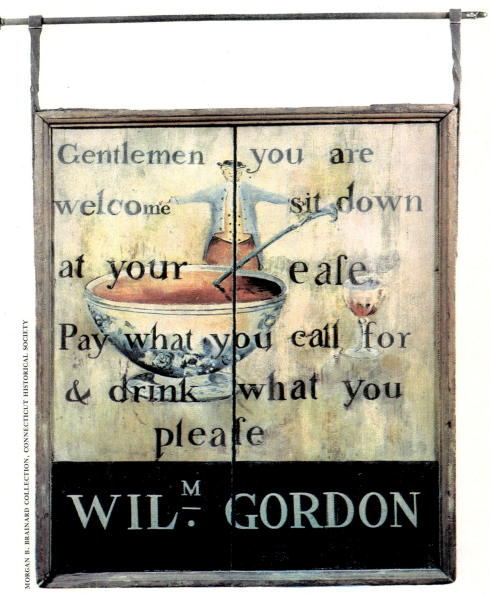

This friendly tavern sign, promising congenial service and surroundings, attracted customers to an early inn at New London, Connecticut.

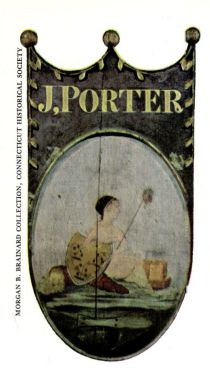

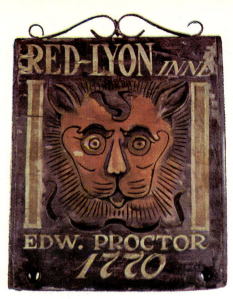

Many weary travelers found solace in the bed, board, and brew promised by these typical tavern signs. (Porter's was in Farmington, Connecticut; the Red-Lyon, in Boston.) The Green Dragon Tavern (right) was a meeting place for the Sons of Liberty who issued invitations to the famed Boston Tea Party.

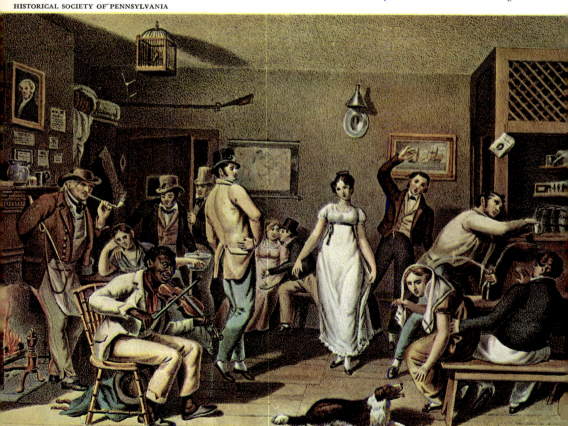

GREEN DRAGON TAVERN

Where we met to plan the Consignment of few Shiploads of Tea.
Dec 16 1773
John Johnson 7 Water Street
Boston Mass. 1773

Inns and Taverns

Early inns and taverns, the humble ancestors of the elegant city hotels, provided more than room and board for travelers. They served, too, as law courts, centers of entertainment, meeting places for revolutionaries, and seminars for students of whistle belly vengeance, cherry bounce, and beer. They were clearinghouses for mail, newspapers, government proclamations, and alarums concerning redcoats. Indeed, about all that the inns did *not* provide were comfortable accommodations and discreet hosts. The consuming curiosity of tavern keepers so annoyed one traveler that "for his tranquillity" he always anticipated the host's inquiries by saying at once, "My name is Benjamin Franklin. I was born in Boston. I am a printer by profession, and am traveling to Philadelphia. I shall have to return at such a time, and I have no news. Now, what can you give me for dinner?"

The nineteenth-century lithograph at left depicts an impromptu dance in a bustling country tavern.

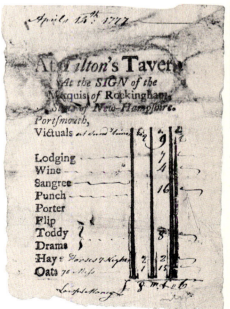

This bill for the room and board of a traveler and his horse dates from the year 1777.

REVERE HOUSE

PARAN STEVENS PROPRIETOR.

DINNER
FOR THE
BOSTON LIGHT INFANTRY,
AT 6 1-2 O'CLOCK.

Wednesday, May 19th, 1852.

BILL OF FARE.

SOUP.

Mock Turtle, | Vegetable.

FISH.

Boiled Salmon, Shrimp Sauce, | Baked Pickerel, Claret Sauce.

BOILED.

Leg South Down Mutton, Caper Sauce,
Turkey and Oysters,
Virginia Ham,
Tongue.

SIDE DISHES.

Mutton Cutlets, Breaded,
Fillet of Beef, with Mushrooms,
Sweetbreads, Larded, with Green Peas,
Veal Cutlets, Tomato Sauce,
Fricassee of Chickens,
Mutton Kidneys, Madeira Sauce,
Timbal of Macaroni, a la Milanaise,
Pattie, a la Financiere,
Calf's Head, Parisian Style,
Turban of Fillets of Chicken, a la Reine.

COLD ORNAMENTAL DISHES.
Galatine of Turkey, Garnished,
Boned Capons, French Style, on
Forms.

COLD ORNAMENTAL DISHES.
Pattie of Liver, in Jelly,
Pattie of Chicken, with Truffles,
Lobster Salad, on Socle.

ROAST.

Sirloin of Beef,
Young Turkey,
Westphalia Ham, Champagne Sauce, | Leg of Lamb, Mint Sauce,
Spring Geese,
Pig.

GAME.

Black Ducks,
Widgeon, | Brant,
Snipe.

Omelette Soufflee, Charlotte Russe, Meringue Baskets,
Jelly, Creams, Pastry, Confectionery.

ORNAMENTS.

DESSERT.

Ice Cream, Fruit, Roman Punch.

COFFEE AND LIQUEUR.

Eastburn's Press.

In 1836, New York's As-
tor House opened and
set new standards of lux-
ury. Its reading room,
painted by Nicolino Cal-
yo, is shown at left. Sev-
en years earlier, the Tremont House, below, had
opened in Boston; it
soon became the proto-
type of modern hotels.

Palaces
for the People

The change from the rustic inns of colonial America
to luxurious hotels, called palaces for the people,
constructed during the nineteenth century, was a
highly dramatic one. The earliest "modern" hotels
could not compare in grandeur with the later public
mansions, but they dazzled even sophisticated city
folk at the time. There were public rooms with marble mosaic floors, carpeted and curtained guest rooms
and corridors, imported carved walnut furniture,
and dining rooms with breath-takingly high ceilings,
marble fireplaces, and menus *(in French!)* that
boasted an unlimited variety of dishes. The New
York *Tribune* called the first hotel bridal chambers
"love bowers where Eve might have whispered love
to Adam after she was expelled from Paradise without regretting the change...."

an Stevens, the "Napoleon of hotel-keep-
" opened Boston's Revere House in 1847
the bill of fare at left). Stevens is often
rred to as the first hotel-chain operator.

TREMONT HOUSE.

BILL OF FARE.

Table D'Hote, August 25, 1844.

Potage au Macaroni.

Boiled Halibut,
" Corned Beef,
" Ham,
" Leg of Mutton,
" Chickens and Pork.

Paté aux huitres,
Fricandeau de veau glacée,
Gigiers de volaille en caisses,
Blanquette de poulets,
Pigeons en compote,
Amourettes de mouton à la tartare,
Poulets grillés à la maitre d'hotel,
Poisson noir au gratin,
Escalope d'huitres,
Beignets de pommes,
Macaroni au beurre,
Cotelettes de mouton panées

Roast Beef,
Pork,
Lamb,
Geese,
Ducks,
Chickens.

PUDDINGS AND PASTRY.

DESSERT.

Eastburn's Press

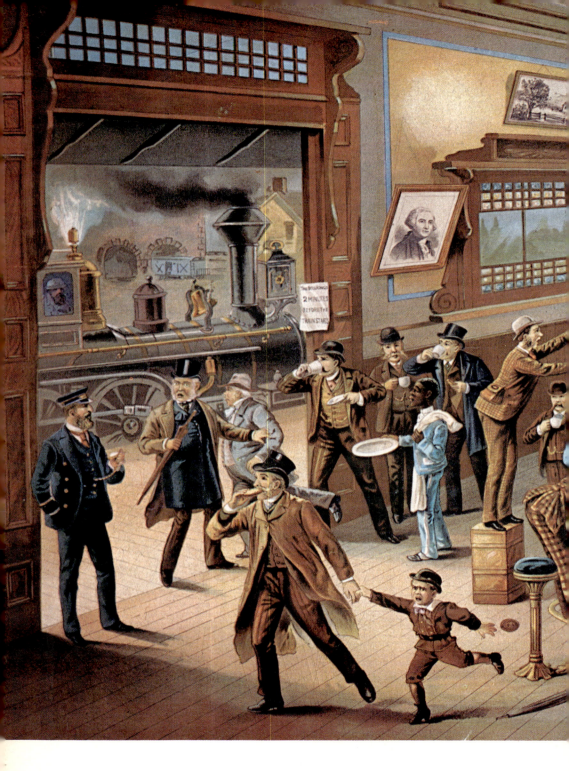

Gobble, Gulp, and — Go!

At times there has been more truth than poetry in the image of the American as a peculiar biped who eats on the run. At first the railroads had no dining cars for coach passengers, and trains stopped for only ten or twenty minutes to permit a quick meal. As this 1886 lithograph shows, dawdling was not encouraged.

349

BILL OF FARE

St. Louis, Cairo, Memphis & New-Orleans Passenger Packet

M. S. MEPHAM

A. H. SHAW
Master

JEWETT WILCOX
Clerk

Printed in oil colors by P. S. Duval, Philad.

Breakfast from 7½ to 9 A.M.

Dinner from 1 to 2½ P.M.

Supper at 6 P.M.

Harvey restaurants such as the one above, in Kansas, made stopover dining more appetizing.

First-class Travel

Gradually, the hurried eating of railroading's early days gave way to more comfortable dining. Luxurious Pullman cars were put into service and, along with the steamships, set a new standard for leisure-class living in the United States. Increasingly, transportation systems ministered to the creature comforts of the rich. By the 1890's, few travelers were likely to be inconvenienced by disasters such as the one Harriet Martineau witnessed on shipboard in 1834. "A sheep had jumped overboard," she wrote, "and so cheated us of some of our mutton."

The steamship menu (left) and the dining-car interior at right show that elegance was readily available to first-class passengers.

Politics in an Oyster House, *by Richard Caton Woodville, shows a typical oyster cellar of the 1840's. Such places often offered all one could eat for six cents, but curbed excesses by slipping a bad oyster onto the plate.*

The Oyster Bar

"Even before the railways annihilated time and space," the dietitian and author Thomas Low Nichols once wrote, "there were oyster expresses from Baltimore across the Alleghenies, which beat the Government mails in speed, and supplied the distant settlements." There was, for a time, something very like a mania for oysters in America. If pedestrians could not stop in at one of the oyster bars that abounded in cities in the nineteenth century, obliging street peddlers filled their needs. A certain Dr. Mackay, an Englishman, became so enamored of American oysters that he snapped up an offer to become New York correspondent for *The Times* of London. In his case, at least, the humble bivalve may be said to have caused a man to forsake his country.

Above, oysters are pan-fried at a fish market. Some fifty thousand oysters were consumed daily in New York's Fulton Fish Market in 1877. In fancier establishments, colorful prints like the one below were displayed to make the customer's mouth water.

10 COURSES FOR 25 Cents.

Full Dinner

Including everything on the Bill
At the extremely low price of
20c. FOR LADIES
AND
25 Cts. for Gentlemen.

At Dunn's,

13 MONTGOMERY PLACE. **13**

This is the ONLY PLACE IN BOSTON, where the following BILL OF FARE can be obtained at the above low prices.

Come Once & you'll Come Again.

DINNER BILL.

Soups, Roast Beef, Roast Lamb
Stuffed Veal, Roast Pork,
Corned Beef, Boiled Ham,
Baked Fish, Vegetables & Fruit
Three Kinds of Pies and Puddings,
Stews and Chowders on Friday,
Tea, Coffee and Milk.

Everything on this Bill for 25 cts.

Meals—4 to 9 A.M. 11 1-2 A.M. to 2 P.M. 5 to 7 1-2 P.M.

The Quick Lunch

As cities grew, working men and women found it cheaper to eat at short-order restaurants than to travel home for lunch. "They swallow, but don't eat; and, like the boa-constrictor, bolt everything, whether it be a blanket or a rabbit..." *Harper's Monthly* stated disdainfully in 1856. But restaurants specializing in low prices and fast service became increasingly popular. In 1877 *Harper's Weekly* reported that a novel Penny Restaurant had just opened in New York (opposite). Bread and butter, baked beans, mush, and a slice of corned beef were among the tasty dishes offered for a cent. Business boomed, for although portions were small, "a fair appetite could be appeased for five cents..."

Ladd's Eating House in Boston (top), offered fast meals "at all hours of the day." Dunn's handbill, above, tempted discriminating diners with ten-course meals for a quarter. The restaurant in the photograph at right made sure that all passers-by were aware of its All-U-Kan-Eat-for-a-nickel dinners.

The First Grand Rush

"ONE CENT! Too Muchee."

"Oh, Mr. Bartender..."

Some nineteenth-century saloons were elegantly appointed, like the one in New York's Hoffman House (left), with its buxom nudes by Adolphe Bouguereau. Others, like the workingman's bar above, were devoid of frills. But all were strictly male institutions, featuring long wooden bars with brass-plated foot-rests, free-lunch counters, and bartenders who were philosophers as well as pourers. The saloon era ended with Prohibition, but many men retained fond memories of hours spent hoisting glasses, laughing at the latest story about the farmer's daughter, and joining friends in a chorus of songs like "Oh, Mr. Bartender, Has My Father Been Here?"

Salty hams and pretzels were offered at the free-lunch counters to whet customers' thirsts.

The James W. Tufts Arctic Soda Water apparatus above was billed as "the most magnificent in the world" when it first appeared in 1876. It lacks some of the rococo charm of The Angelo, two views of which are shown at the top of the opposite page. Designed by the firm of John Matthews, this dexterous contrivance was equipped to dispense seven beverages and sixteen different syrups.

Soda Fountains for the Ladies

"Soda-water is an American drink," *Harper's Weekly* proclaimed chauvinistically in 1891. By that time there were, per capita, more soda fountains (primarily a ladies' institution) than bars in New York City. The origins of the rage may be traced back to 1833, when John Matthews introduced carbonated water. A few years later a Frenchman added syrups, and ice cream was incorporated in 1874, producing that nationally popular concoction, the ice cream soda.

Frigid Cream Soda flowed from the fountain depicted above, which was decorated with statuettes of half-draped beauties, a king, a philosopher, and a spear-carrying maiden. Many ladies who patronized such soda fountains were advocates of Prohibition. At right, a group celebrates adoption of the Eighteenth Amendment by turning one bar into a library.

Above is the courtyard at the Palace. The menu below, engraved on solid silver plates made of ore from the Comstock Lode, was used at a dinner for the silver king William Sharon.

Grandeur West

San Francisco's opulent Palace Hotel cost nearly five million dollars, an astounding figure for the 1870's. Even before the opening, word of the hotel's magnificence got around to humbler communities, moving a writer for a local weekly to speculate: "The statistician of the *News Letter* estimates the ground covered by the Palace Hotel to be . . . equal to the states of Wisconsin and Rhode Island, and the right-hand half of Senegambia . . . All the entrees will be sprinkled with gold dust . . . and every ninth pie will contain a pearl as large as a hen's egg . . . which, of course, belongs to the prettiest girl at that particular table . . . There are thirty-four elevators in all—four for passengers, ten for baggage and twenty for mixed drinks."

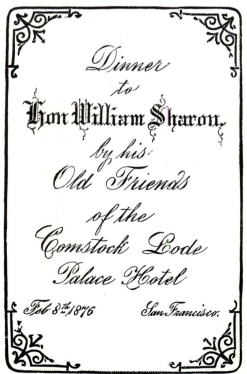

Dinner
to
Hon William Sharon
by his
Old Friends
of the
Comstock Lode
Palace Hotel

Feb 8th 1876   San Francisco.

→ MENU ←
Huitres
Chablis
Consomme Royale
Sherry Isabella
Saumon glace au four à la Chambord
Sauterne
Boudin blanc à la Richelieu
Chateau la Tour
Filet de Boeuf à la Providence
Champagne
Paté de fois Gras
Chateau Yquem
Timbale de Volaille Americaine au Senateur
Clos Vougeot
Côtelettes d'Agneau sautées aux pointes d'Asperges
Sorbet
Becassines au Cresson
Chateau Margeaux
Salade à la Française
DESSERT

In Chef at the Palace Hotel, *painted by Joseph Harrington in 1874, Jules Harder is shown in his working attire. A former employee of Delmorico's in New York, he made gourmets of many San Franciscans. "The most discouraging experience I have," he once said, "is to get up something extra in the way of a sauce or flavor for some big man, and to have . . . it make no more impression than a baked potato."*

...and East

Hotels provided the stage for society in the latter half of the nineteenth century, and throngs of *nouveaux riches* joined the high-toned social life at these "people's palaces." The Waldorf-Astoria became the quintessence of hotel high-life—symbol of New York's power and wealth. In its Men's Café, John Warne "Bet-a-million" Gates allegedly dreamed up the U.S. Steel Corporation; in one of its dining rooms, the Bradley Martins gave a party where only a few of the forty gentlemen guests were not multimillionaires. Along its Peacock Alley a continuous parade of ladies decked out in the latest fashion could be seen; and at the Waldorf "lunching out," the afternoon tea ceremony, and posh pre-theatre dinners were added to the ever-increasing list of Things to Do.

Surely the best-known maître d' in America was Oscar of the Waldorf, pictured above. Oscar contributed to the national cuisine a salad (made originally of apple chunks, celery, and mayonnaise), which for many years seemed as much a part of the American scene as apple pie.

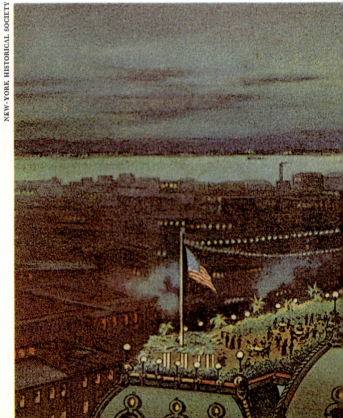

Two of the most fashionable hotels in New York at the beginning of the twentieth century were the Astor and the Knickerbocker. At left are three of the Astor's impeccably dressed maids; below is its roof garden, where guests promenaded along tree-lined walks and sipped drinks under arbors. Above is a dining room at the Knickerbocker with a highly elaborate table setting.

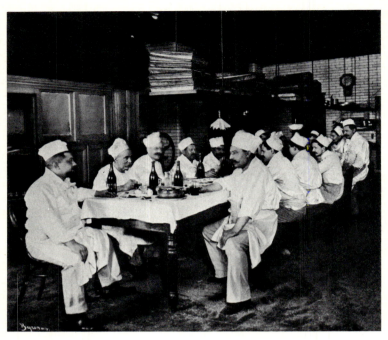

Fifteen of Sherry's chefs sample their own creations, above.

Behind the Scenes

"From vegetable boy to chef, in the kitchen of a Sherry or a Delmonico, is a journey of some twenty years' duration." Pascal Grand, who made that statement in 1902, was one of the men who completed the journey successfully at Sherry's. Another top chef was Charles Ranhofer, who reigned over forty-two assistants in Delmonico's kitchens. Ranhofer was not famous for his modesty; in Grace Mayer's *Once Upon a City* he is quoted as saying, "The culinary art...may be said to be the distinguishing thing of civilization, and in its perfection it is the inspiration of genius...The chef of a large establishment must possess at least two essential qualifications: he must be an epicurean by nature, and this natural gift must be enhanced by long years of training in his profession."

A small army of dishwashers, above, worked in the kitchen of the Hotel Astor. At lower left, a pastry chef at Sherry's decorates a large vase made of sugar. The cooks below are roasting a black bear at the Astor. These three pictures were taken by Joseph and Percy Byron, a famous father-and-son team of photographers.

It's a Great Life

In the last decade of the nineteenth century and the
first of the twentieth, spectacular private parties in restaurants and hotels reached their apogee. Newspapers
were filled with stories about bachelor dinners at which
chorines emerged from pies and danced in the altogether, and about hosts and hostesses who spent thousands of dollars on masquerade balls and other entertainments. But the most unusual affair of all was one
given by the millionaire horse-enthusiast C. K. G. Billings at Louis Sherry's in 1903. To celebrate the opening
of his new stable, Billings invited the members of the
New York Riding Club to Sherry's Grand Ballroom,
which—through the use of scenic backdrops, potted
plants on which real birds perched, and a sodded floor—
had been converted into an idyllic woodland (right).
Up in the freight elevators came a horse for each guest;
the men sat atop the steeds while eating dinner off small
tables attached to the saddles and sipping champagne
from tubes connected to the saddlebags. Needless to say,
fancy troughs were provided for the horses, who dined
as enthusiastically as their riders did.

With vegetation (real and artificial) hanging from the lights, decorating the tables, and adorning the hats of the guests, a ladies' luncheon at Delmonico's in 1902 (left) took on the air of a garden party. At right is a Byron photograph of an elegant dinner held at Delmonico's to celebrate Mark Twain's seventieth birthday.

...If You Don't Weaken

All we know about this event is that it occurred in 1900 or 1901, and that one of the diners was Harrison Grey Fiske. It seems enough, however, to know that America had by that time produced men who could pose straight-faced, after a regal dinner, with laurel wreaths on their heads.

EPILOGUE

By Mark Twain

Touring Europe in 1878, Mark Twain felt nothing but disdain for the food he encountered there. He found the coffee "feeble"; the milk served with it was "what the French call 'Christian' milk,—milk which has been baptized." The butter was "tasteless," the bread "cold and tough, and unsympathetic." "They can't even cook a chicken respectably," he complained, "and as for carving it, they do that with a hatchet." Anticipating his return to the United States and his deliverance from monotonous, unsatisfying meals whose "weary sameness" would "kill the robustest appetite," the chauvinistic Sam Clemens composed the following list:

It has now been many months, at the present writing, since I have had a nourishing meal, but I shall soon have one,—a modest, private affair, all to myself. I have selected a few dishes, and made out a little bill of fare, which will go home in the steamer that precedes me, and be hot when I arrive—as follows:

Radishes. Baked apples, with cream.
Fried oysters; stewed oysters. Frogs.
American coffee, with real cream.
American butter.
Fried chicken, Southern style.
Porter-house steak.
Saratoga potatoes.
Broiled chicken, American style.
Hot biscuits, Southern style.
Hot wheat-bread, Southern style.
Hot buckwheat cakes.

American toast. Clear maple syrup.
Virginia bacon, broiled.
Blue points, on the half shell.
Cherry-stone clams.
San Francisco mussels, steamed.
Oyster soup. Clam soup.
Philadelphia Terapin soup.
Oysters roasted in shell—Northern style.
Soft-shell crabs. Connecticut shad.
Baltimore perch.

Brook trout, from Sierra Nevadas.
Lake trout, from Tahoe.
Sheep-head and croakers, from
   New Orleans.
Black bass from the Mississippi.
American roast beef.
Roast turkey, Thanksgiving style.
Cranberry sauce. Celery.
Roast wild turkey. Woodcock.
Canvas-back-duck, from Baltimore.
Prairie hens, from Illinois.
Missouri partridges, broiled.
'Possum. Coon.
Boston bacon and beans.
Bacon and greens, Southern style.
Hominy. Boiled onions. Turnips.
Pumpkin. Squash. Asparagus.
Butter beans. Sweet potatoes.
Lettuce. Succotash. String beans.
Mashed potatoes. Catsup.
Boiled potatoes, in their skins.

New potatoes, minus the skins.
Early rose potatoes, roasted in the
   ashes, Southern style, served hot.
Sliced tomatoes, with sugar or vinegar.
   Stewed tomatoes.
Green corn, cut from the ear and
   served with butter and pepper.
Green corn, on the ear.
Hot corn-pone, with chitlings,
   Southern style.
Hot hoe-cake, Southern style.
Hot egg-bread, Southern style.
Hot light-bread, Southern style.
Buttermilk. Iced sweet milk.
Apple dumplings, with real cream.
Apple pie. Apple fritters.
Apple puffs, Southern style.
Peach cobbler, Southern style.
Peach pie. American mince pie.
Pumpkin pie. Squash pie.
All sorts of American pastry.

Fresh American fruits of all sorts, including strawberries which are not to be doled out as if they were jewelry, but in a more liberal way. Ice-Water—not prepared in the ineffectual goblet, but in the sincere and capable refrigerator.

Americans intending to spend a year or so in European hotels, will do well to copy this bill and carry it along. They will find it an excellent thing to get up an appetite with, in the dispiriting presence of the squalid table d'hôte.

Foreigners cannot enjoy our food, I suppose, any more than we can enjoy theirs. It is not strange; for tastes are made, not born. I might glorify my bill of fare until I was tired; but after all, the Scotchman would shake his head and say, "Where's your haggis?" and the Fijian would sigh and say, "Where's your missionary?"—*From* A Tramp Abroad

ACKNOWLEDGMENTS

The Editors are especially grateful to these individuals and organizations for their generous assistance and their co-operation: Bernard Katz, for permission to use excerpts from his extensive collection of historical materials concerning food and drink; Mrs. Katharine A. Kellock, for the opportunity to examine material collected by the Writers' Project of the Works Progress Administration for the unpublished volume, *America Eats;* Miss Eleanor Lowenstein of the Corner Book Shop, New York City, for her invaluable assistance; Dr. Don Yoder, Dr. Alfred Shoemaker, and the Pennsylvania Folklife Society, Inc. for permission to quote from various issues of *Pennsylvania Folklife* magazine and others of their publications; Crown Publishers, Inc., for permission to use Shaker recipes from *The Shaker Cook Book,* copyright © 1953 by Caroline B. Piercy; and to the following:

Abby Aldrich Rockefeller Folk Art Collection, Williamsburg, Virginia: Mrs. Richard Black
American Antiquarian Society, Worcester, Massachusetts: Clifford K. Shipton
American Honey Institute
American Meat Institute
American Mushroom Institute
American Spice Trade Association
Armour & Company
Art Institute of Chicago: Marilyn Pokorni
Barker Texas Historical Library: Llerena Friend
L. L. Beans, Trenton, New Jersey
James A. Beard, New York
Berry-Hill Galleries, New York: Henry and Sydney Berry-Hill
Bettmann Archive, Inc.: Robert Jackson
The Book Club of California, San Francisco
Bordeaux Wine Information Bureau
Borden Company
Bourbon Institute
British Travel Association
California Historical Society
California State Library, Sacramento: Allan R. Ottley
Campbell Soup Company
Robert Carlen, Philadelphia
Champagne Producers of France
Mrs. Henry C. Cheves III, Charleston, South Carolina
Chicago Historical Society: Mrs. Paul M. Rhymer
J. H. Chichester, La Cuisinière, Inc., New York
James L. Cogar, Pleasant Hill Community, Kentucky
Corning Museum of Glass, Corning, New York: Paul N. Perrot
Culver Pictures
Daughters of the Republic of Texas Library at the Alamo, Austin: Carmen Perry
Denver Public Library: Mrs. Alys Freeze, Mrs. Opal Harber
Detroit Historical Museum: Margot P. Pearsall
Detroit Institute of Arts
Raymond S. Dey, New Jersey
H. A. Dincalci, Old Print Mart, New York
Edward Eberstadt & Sons, New York
Steven Evans, New York
Mrs. Susan H. Fisher and Mrs. Margaret H. Fisher, Wye Town Farm, Maryland
Fishery Council: John von Glahn
Florida Citrus Commission
General Foods Corporation, New York
Gilcrease Institute of American History and Art, Tulsa, Oklahoma: Dean Krakel
William and Liselotte Glozer, Berkeley, California

Laura Graff, Hermann, Missouri
Douglas Kent Hall, Iowa City
F. Hal Higgins, Davis, California
Historical Society of Montana: Michael Kennedy
Historical Society of York County, Pennsylvania
Laurence Gouverneur Hoes, Virginia
Leonard Huber, New Orleans
Ice Cream Merchandising Institute
Idaho Historical Society: H. J. Swinney
Indiana Historical Society, William Henry Smith Memorial Library: Caroline Dunn
International Association of Ice Cream Manufacturers
IBM
Thomas Jefferson Memorial Foundation, Charlottesville, Virginia: James Bear
Mrs. Evan Jones, New York
Joslyn Art Museum, Omaha: Mildred Goosman
Kansas State Historical Society: Robert Richmond
Kennedy Galleries, Inc., New York: George Schriever
Library of Congress, Prints and Photographs Division: Virginia Daiker, Milton Kaplan
Missouri Historical Society: Mrs. Ruth K. Field
Morristown National Historical Park, New Jersey: Francis S. Ronalds
Mount Vernon Ladies' Association of the Union, Virginia: Charles C. Wall
Museum of the American Indian, Heye Foundation, New York: Dr. Frederick J. Dockstader
Museum of the City of New York: Albert K. Baragwanath
Museum of Fine Arts, Boston: Elizabeth P. Riegel
National Canners Association
National Dairy Council
National Gallery of Art, Index of American Design: Grose Evans
New York Botanical Garden, New York
New-York Historical Society, New York: Geraldine Beard, Arthur Carlson, Betty Ezequelle, Rachel Minick, Caroline Scoon
New York Racing Association, Inc.
New York State Historical Association: Dorothy Barck, Louis Jones, Frederick Rath, Jr.
New York State Library, Albany: Ida M. Cohen
Newport Historical Society, Rhode Island: Mrs. Henry E. Williams
Mrs. Janet Wade Nystrom, Bishop Hill, Illinois
Oakland Art Museum, California: Paul Mills
Old Print Shop, New York: Harry Shaw Newman, Kenneth Newman
Old Salem, Inc., North Carolina: Frank L. Horton
Old Sturbridge Village, Massachusetts: Alexander Wall, Catherine Fennelly, James J. Keeney

Peabody Museum of Archaeology and Ethnology, Cambridge, Massachusetts: Mrs. Katherine B. Edsall
Philadelphia Museum of Art: Mrs. Henry Peter Borie, Hobart Lyle Williams
Helen Ridley, New York
Mrs. Martha G. Robinson, New Orleans
Lawrence B. Romaine, Middleboro, Massachusetts
Christine Sadler, Washington, D.C.
Schwenkfelder Library, Pennsburg, Pennsylvania: Claire Conway
Sealtest Foods
Shaker Museum, Old Chatham, New York: Robert Meader
Barbara Simmons, New York
Sleepy Hollow Restorations, Tarrytown, New York: Saverio Procario, Robert G. Wheeler
Smithsonian Institution: Malcolm Watkins
Watson Smith, Tucson, Arizona
Mrs. Elizabeth Sparks, Winston-Salem *Journal and Sentinel*, North Carolina
State University of Iowa, Iowa City: Ada Stoflet

Mrs. Franz Stumpf, San Antonio, Texas
Sunkist Growers
Swift & Company
J. Walter Thompson Company
United Fruit Company
United States Department of Agriculture: Dr. Wayne Rasmussen
University of the State of New York, State Education Department, Division of Archives and History, Albany: William L. Lassiter
Mrs. George B. Unrath, Iowa City
Valentine Museum, Richmond: Elizabeth J. Dance
Vose Galleries, Boston: Robert C. Vose, Jr.
Wadsworth Atheneum, Hartford, Connecticut
Walters Art Gallery, Baltimore: Edward S. King
Alice Washburn, Perry, Maine
Witte Memorial Museum, San Antonio, Texas: Dr. William A. Burns, Martha Utterback
Irl G. Whitchurch, Denver, Colorado
Elizabeth Woodburn, Booknoll Farm, Hopewell, New Jersey
Wine Institute

PICTURE CREDITS——Front cover: detail from *Fruit in Glass Compote* by Emma Cady; Abby Aldrich Rockefeller Folk Art Collection, Williamsburg, Virginia. Front end paper: banquet table in Alliance, Nebraska, 1900; Denver Public Library. Back end paper: a ladies' tea; Culver Pictures. Page 384: *Kitchen Nymph*, poster; Library of Congress. Line drawings used throughout text, recipe, and menu sections: Culver Pictures; Bella C. Landauer Collection, New-York Historical Society; New York Public Library Picture Collection; Maryland Historical Society; Museum of the City of New York; New York State History Museum; Huntington Library, San Marino, California.

INDEX

The index to Recipes begins on page 630.

A

ABILENE, KAN., 203, 204, 224
ADAMS, ABIGAIL, 87, 310
ADAMS, CHARLES FRANCIS, 91
ADAMS, JOHN, 87, 137, 138, 140
AIKEN, WILLIAM, 126
ALABAMA, 131, 132
ALASKA, 53
ALCOTT, BRONSON, 174
ALE, 18, 22, 150, 159, 207
ALLEN, THOMAS, 233
AMHERST COLLEGE, 174
AMISH, 159, 161, 162, 169, 170-71
ANDOVER, MASS., 84
ANNE, QUEEN, of England, 163
ANTELOPES, 70, 332

ANTLERS HOTEL, Colorado Springs, 332
APPLE BUTTER, 56, 162, 166, 167, 184-85, 187
APPLE PIE, 22, 56, 64, 69, 90-91, 99, 112, 201
APPLES, 56, 62, 69, 90, 112, 113, 137, 161, 166, 187
APPLESAUCE CAKE, 82
APPLESEED, JOHNNY, 55-56
ARBOGAST, ERNEST, 334
ARIZONA, 44
ARMOUR, P. D., 204, 205
ARTICHOKES, 59, 96
ASHCAKES, 13, 129
ASTOR, WILLIAM, 312-13
ASTOR, MRS. WILLIAM, 256, 286, 289, 312-13
ASTOR HOUSE, New York City, 326, 347, 363, 365
AUDUBON, JOHN JAMES, 16, 31, 33

B

BACON, 23, 49, 57, 69, 130, 169, 196, 204
BACON, EDMUND, 137, 139-40
BAGELS, 249
BAGNAL, RICHARD, 87
BAKED BEANS, 81, 92, 93, 101, 354
"BAKERS' RIOT," Boston, 177
BAKING POWDER, 97, 212
BALTIMORE, MD., 125, 238, 338, 353
BANANAS, 153
BANNOCK CAKES, 95
BARBECUES, 130, 218
BARLEY, 207
BARLOW, JOEL, 90
BARNARD, HENRY, 125
BARTRAM, JOHN, 14, 17, 25-28, 33, 43

A KITCHEN NYMPH.

PART 2

Menus and Recipes

OVEN TEMPERATURES

Slow ....300° to 325°
Moderate ....350° to 375°
Moderately hot ....375° to 400°
Hot ....400° to 450°
Very hot ....450° to 500°

WEIGHTS AND MEASURES

LIQUID MEASURE

3 teaspoons = 1 tablespoon
4 tablespoons = ¼ cup
2 cups = 1 pint
2 pints = 1 quart
4 quarts = 1 gallon
1 ounce = ⅛ cup or 2 tablespoons
8 ounces = 1 cup or 16 tablespoons
16 ounces = 1 pint
1 jigger = 3 tablespoons or 1½ ounces
1 pony = 2 tablespoons or 1 ounce
1 gill = ½ cup
1 wineglass = ¼ cup

DRY MEASURE

2 pints = 1 quart
8 quarts = 1 peck
4 pecks = 1 bushel

EQUIVALENTS

DRIED BEANS

White, 1 pound : 2 cups, uncooked = 6 cups, cooked
Kidney, 1 pound : 2⅔ cups, uncooked = 6¼ cups, cooked
Lima, 1 pound : 3 cups, uncooked = 7 cups, cooked

PASTA AND CORN MEAL

Macaroni, 8 ounces : 2 cups, uncooked = 4 cups, cooked
Noodles, 8 ounces : 2½ cups, uncooked = 4 to 5 cups, cooked
Spaghetti, 8 ounces : 2½ cups, uncooked = 4 to 5 cups, cooked
Corn meal : 1 cup, uncooked = 4 cups, cooked

BREAD

1 pound dry bread crumbs = 3½ cups
1 pound bread, crumbled = 9 cups

EGGS

4 to 6 whole eggs, shelled = 1 cup
8 to 10 egg whites = 1 cup

SUGAR

1 pound brown = 2¼ cups, packed
1 pound granulated = 2¼ cups
1 pound confectioners' = 4 to 5 cups

FLOUR

1 pound white all-purpose = 4 cups, sifted
1 pound cake = 4½ cups, sifted
1 pound whole-wheat = 3½ cups

BUTTER

1 ounce = 2 tablespoons (butter the size of a walnut)
2 ounces = 4 tablespoons or ¼ cup (butter the size of an egg)
¼ pound = ½ cup (1 stick) or 8 tablespoons
½ pound = 1 cup (2 sticks)
1 pound = 2 cups

CHEESE

1 pound = 5 cups grated
1 pound = 2⅔ cups cubed

CHOCOLATE

1 ounce = 1 square (unsweetened)
6 ounces = 1 cup (1 package) semisweet chocolate pieces

NUTS

1 pound almonds, unshelled = 1½ cups nut meats
1 pound pecans, unshelled = 2¼ cups nut meats
1 pound walnuts, unshelled = 2 cups nut meats

SHELLFISH

1 pound cooked shrimp, crab,
or lobster meat = 2 cups

A

LONG GRAIN RICE

1 pound, uncooked : 2 cups, uncooked = 6 cups, cooked

THE

KITCHEN COMPANION,

AND

HOUSE-KEEPER'S

OWN BOOK,

CONTAINING ALL THE MODERN, AND MOST APPROVED METHODS IN

COOKERY, PASTRY, & CONFECTIONARY,

WITH AN EXCELLENT COLLECTION OF

VALUABLE RECIPES,

TO WHICH IS ADDED, THE

WHOLE ART OF CARVING, ILLUSTRATED.

Cover of The Kitchen Companion, *a cookbook published in Philadelphia in 1844*

TABLE OF CONTENTS

PART 2

A WORD OF EXPLANATION

How the recipes were selected: We have tried to include in this book recipes for the most delectable and historically interesting dishes prepared in America from the time of its discovery to the beginning of this century. From old cookbooks, hand-written manuscripts, historic menus, and other original sources, these recipes were painstakingly collected. They were adapted for use in today's kitchen, to take full advantage of modern equipment and of current freezing, packaging, and transportation methods, and then tested by trained home economists. All the recipes, we hope, retain the flavor and charm of the originals.

Organization of recipes: To make selection easy, recipes are grouped by course— under Fish, Desserts, and similar headings. Each of these sections contains regional recipes and foreign dishes that became American favorites, as well as traditional recipes enjoyed in all parts of the country. When a recipe is of more than usual historical interest, a note explaining its background appears in brown type. We have also included, in their original form, a few old recipes we found irresistible (the Birds-Nest Salad on page 551 is an example), but since these are just for fun and not something the average cook is likely to prepare, they are also printed in brown ink. The rule of thumb for using the recipe pages, then, is this: practical information for cooking appears in *black* type; historical notes and other comments intended solely for extra reading pleasure appear in *brown*.

Whenever there has been a choice of names for dishes, we tended to favor the old over the new. In some cases, this helps to place the recipe's origins; sometimes not (as with those curious desserts called grunts, fools, and slumps, whose beginnings no one seems certain about). Nomenclature aside, we wish that space permitted inclusion of all the fine old recipes enjoyed by Americans.

Thirty historic menus: On pages 392 to 421 are thirty historical and useful menus, assembled by Mrs. Helen Duprey Bullock, who also contributed a number of recipes to the book. Some of these menus—the Nellie Grant wedding breakfast, for example—were taken from accounts published at the time. Others, such as the Christmas dinner at Mount Vernon, were compiled by Mrs. Bullock after extensive research into writings by and about the persons involved; they are not so much a menu for one specific historical meal as they are a composite, based on expert knowledge of the tastes of the individuals and of the foods available in that time and place. *Asterisks (*) appear beside those dishes in the menus for which recipes are provided in the recipe section.*

Prior to this book's publication, Restaurant Associates, creators of Festival '64/'65—The American Restaurant, learned that the Editors shared their interest in exploring the American culinary heritage. By special arrangement, many of the recipes in this book appear on the menu of Festival '64/'65, located in the Festival of Gas Pavilion at the New York World's Fair.

MENUS

NEW YEAR'S DAY COLLATION

Baked Ham*   **Boned Turkey***   **Daube Glacé***   **Oyster Pan Roast***

Squab in Compote*   **Lobster Salad**   **Chicken Salad***

Watercress or Bread-and-Butter Sandwiches   **Cream Biscuits***

Finger Rolls   **Molded Jellies**

Blancmange*   **Small Cakes**   **New Year's Cookies***

Marzipan in Shapes of Fruits, Vegetables, and Flowers   **Fruits**   **Ices**

Eggnog*   **Champagne**   **Coffee**   **Chocolate**   **Tea**

The custom of paying New Year's calls originated in New York, where the Dutch held open house on New Year's Day and served cherry bounce, *olykoeks* steeped in rum, cookies, and honey cakes. From New York the custom spread throughout the country. On the first New Year's after his inauguration, George Washington opened his house to the public, and he continued to receive visitors on New Year's Day throughout the seven years he lived in Philadelphia. On January 1, 1791, a senator from Pennsylvania noted in his diary: "Made the President the compliments of the season; had a hearty shake of the hand. I was asked to partake of the punch and cakes, but declined. I sat down and we had some chat. But the diplomatic gentry and foreigners coming in, I embraced the first vacancy to make my bow and wish him a good morning."

Eventually, it became *de rigueur* for those who intended to receive company to list in newspapers the hours they would be "at home." It was a disastrous practice: parties of young men took to dashing from house to house for a glass of punch, dropping in at as many of the homes listed in the papers as they could. Strangers wandered in off the streets, newspapers under their arms, for a free drink and a bit of a meal.

The custom of having an open house on the first day of the year survived the assaults of the newspaper readers. The traditional cookies and cakes continued to be served, along with hot toddies, punches, eggnogs, tea, coffee, and chocolate. But public announcements of at-home hours were dropped at the end of the nineteenth century, and houses were open only to invited friends.

A TALBOT COUNTY HUNT BREAKFAST

Bourbon and Branch

*Scrambled Eggs in Cream   Country Sausage with Fried Apple Rings**

Creamed Sweetbreads and Oysters   Capitolade of Chicken*   Kidney Stew**

Bacon and Fried Tomato Slices   Waffles*   Hominy Pudding**

Broiled Salt Roe Herring   Baked Country Ham**

Spoon Bread   Beaten Biscuits*   Buttermilk Biscuits**

Jellies   Apple Butter   Honey   Damson Plum Preserves*

Coffee

Chesapeake bounty

Chesapeake Bay, in Maryland, is one of the most richly endowed areas in the eastern United States. The landed gentry who settled there (in manorial holdings with names like Betty's Love, Lloyd's Landing, Wye House, Fairview, Haphazard, Mary's Delight, Crooked Intention, and Troth's Fortune) dressed their tables with the bay's oysters, fish, and shellfish and with game, fish, and waterfowl from the surrounding tidal rivers and marshes.

Hunt breakfasts were held each spring and fall in Maryland. In the fall, hunters went out for duck and wild goose before sunup and returned to one of the manor houses for breakfast. Preceded by ample quantities of bourbon and other drinks, breakfast was usually served at midday. This menu is typical of breakfasts served in Talbot County, located across the bay from Annapolis.

LA CUISINE CRÉOLE

At the French market

In the New Orleans *Item* for July 8, 1880, Lafcadio Hearn lamented, "We fear that the good old Creole lore is rapidly disappearing. . . . Many of these secrets are kept with something of religious awe. Neither love nor money nor menaces could extort them from the owners. If childless, it is more than likely the secret will die with their owners; if they have children, these generally inherit the mystical power, but hardly ever do they seem in this generation to obtain the success of their fathers and mothers. We have often suggested that all the extant knowledge in regard to Creole cookery and herb medicine, so far as it is possible to obtain it, should be collected and published." Fortunately, in 1885 Hearn listened to his own wisdom and published the first basic book of Creole cookery. At about that same time Charles Gayarré had written in *Harper's* "Good heavens! with what supreme, indescribable contempt would Aunt Henriette or Uncle Frontin have looked down upon the best French *cordon bleu* that had presumed to teach her or him! Sufficient to say that Marc Antony, if he had known a creole cook of the old *régime*, would have given him two or three of his best Asiatic provinces as a reward for feasting Cleopatra." It was in those Saturnian days that meals like the three shown here were common in New Orleans. They include a substantial dinner, an elaborate feast for New Year's Day, and a simple treat of sweet cakes and coffee.

CREOLE FAMILY DINNER

Shrimp with Creole Sauce Remoulade*

Mushroom Bisque

Veal Grillades*

Hominy Pudding*   *Artichokes with Lemon Butter**   *Glazed Baby Carrots**

Salad   *Cheese*

Coconut Custard Pie*   *Demitasse*

LOUISIANA NEW YEAR'S DAY DINNER

Oysters Rockefeller*

Celery   *Radishes*   *Olives*   *Salted Almonds*

Consommé Julienne

Stuffed Baked Fillets Creole*

Roast Stuffed Turkey*   *Cranberry Sauce**   *Green Peas*

Yams with Apples*   *Mashed Potatoes*   *Cauliflower with Brown Butter Sauce*

Daube Glacé*   *Sauce Piquante**

Green Pepper and Tomato Salad with French Dressing*

Toasted Crackers and Cheese

Vanilla Ice Cream* with Bananas Flambé   *Assorted Small Cakes*

Café Brûlot*

COFFEE IN THE VIEUX CARRÉ

Calas*

A Nun's Sigh*   *Crullers*

Café au Lait

PRESCRIPTION FOR A SUCCESSFUL DINNER PARTY

Turtle Soup

Ham Mousse*   *Salmon*

Fillet of Beef or Baby Turkey Bordelaise or Crown Roast of Lamb*

Sweetbreads Toulouse

Pâté en Bellevue*   *Asparagus with Hollandaise Sauce**

Sorbet*

Russian Salad*   *Camembert Cheese with Crackers*

Nesselrode Pudding*   *Demitasse*

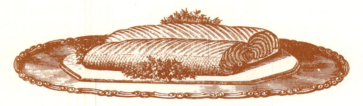

Poached salmon

In the days of Ward McAllister, the self-appointed Boswell of New York's Four Hundred, society was composed of men notable more for their wealth than for their discrimination. Many of McAllister's dicta, therefore, seem to preserve social graces in a setting of disingenuousness ("The highest cultivation in social manners enables a person to conceal from the world his real feelings") and to render truisms as clichés ("A dinner wholly made up of young people is generally stupid. You require the experienced woman of the world, who has at her fingers' ends the history of past, present, and future").

When the chronicler of the Four Hundred presented this menu for a successful dinner party in his *Society As I Have Found It,* he advised, "Success in entertaining is accomplished by magnetism and tact. It is the ladder to social success. If successfully done, it naturally creates jealousy." But, McAllister added, "In planning a dinner the question is not to whom you owe dinners, but who is most desirable. The success of the dinner depends as much upon the company as the cook. Discordant elements—people invited alphabetically, or to pay off debts—are fatal.... So much for your guests."

LINCOLN'S INAUGURAL LUNCHEON

Mock Turtle Soup

Corned Beef and Cabbage*   *Parsley Potatoes*

Blackberry Pie*   *Coffee*

Abraham Lincoln was partial to corn bread, honey, and a good cup of coffee. Aside from these preferences the President seems to have evinced little interest in cuisine—and often to have forgotten altogether about eating. One morning, while the artist Francis B. Carpenter was at the White House painting *The First Reading of the Emancipation Proclamation,* Lincoln heard the clock strike noon and interrupted Carpenter's work with, "I believe, by the by, that I have not yet had my breakfast, —this business has been so absorbing that it has crowded everything else out of my mind."

The conduct of the Civil War preoccupied Lincoln, of course, but his tastes predated his White House years. Leonard Swett, a lawyer who worked with Lincoln in the eighth judicial circuit in Illinois, once said, "I never, in the ten years of circuit life I knew him, heard him complain of a hard bed or a bad meal of victuals." Lincoln's last law partner, William H. Herndon, said more pointedly that Lincoln "filled up and that is all." Noah Brooks, one of Lincoln's friends from Illinois, recalled having been invited to breakfast one morning by Lincoln and noting that "the President would appear to forget that food and drink were needful for his existence, unless he were persistently followed up by some of the servants." Brooks remarked to Lincoln that he was surprised to see that the President preferred milk to coffee for breakfast. Lincoln replied, "eyeing his glass of milk with surprise, as if he had not before noticed what he was drinking, 'Well, I do prefer coffee in the morning, but they don't seem to have sent me in any.'"

Surprisingly enough, Lincoln showed enough interest in his food to plan the above menu. The luncheon was served at Willard's Hotel in Washington at midday on March 4, 1861, immediately following the inaugural ceremonies at the Capitol. After lunch, the Lincoln family went from the hotel directly to the Executive Mansion.

A SOUTHWESTERN DINNER

Meatball Soup*

Baked Avocado Stuffed with Crab Meat*

Refried Beans*   *Summer Squash, Mexican Style**

Chicken Tamales   *Stuffed Beets**

Pineapple-Yam Turnovers*   *Coffee*

The states bordering on Mexico—Texas, New Mexico, Arizona, and California—share a cuisine that is generally called Spanish. In fact, the cuisine is basically that of the American Indians who lived in the Southwest, flavored by additions from the Mexican Indians and from the Spanish conquistadors. The mixing process began in 1519, when the Aztec emperor Montezuma II offered the Spaniards some tomatoes and chilies. The New World was also able to provide the cuisine with three indigenous foods known as the American agricultural triad: corn, beans, and squash. The Spanish contributed their culinary mastery of onions and garlic. In addition to these ingredients, the food of the Southwest makes conspicuous use of seasonings like basil, thyme, rosemary, and oregano.

Two obligatory items in any southwestern dinner are chili peppers and frijoles. Frijoles may refer to a number of different beans, although pinto, or painted, beans are favored. They are served for dinner and for supper and are eaten—warmed-over, or refried—for breakfast (giving rise to the saying, *"Frijoles—frijolitos y frijoles refritos,"* or "Beans—more beans, and warmed-over beans"). Chili peppers provide most of the necessary heat in the cuisine.

Tamales, too, are essential ingredients (and are now commercially packaged). It is said that tamales saved Hernando Cortes and his men from starvation in Mexico. When the Aztecs realized that the Spanish soldiers were not (as had been thought because of their "pure" white skin) high priests from Quetzalcoatl, the god of plenty, they stopped giving the invaders food. Cortes, however, had won the love of a woman named Malinche and told her he would have to leave if his men could not obtain food. Malinche told Cortes to storm the gates of the city on a certain evening. He did, and Malinche led a group of friends who bombarded the Spaniards with tamales.

DINING AT SHAKERTOWN

Shakers at dinner

Shaker Flank Steak*   *Cold Tongue*

Shaker Spinach with Rosemary*   *Fried Tomato Slices**

Shaker Potato Salad*   *Corn Pudding**

Shaker Daily Loaf*   *Blueberry Muffins**   *Graham Gems**   *Buttermilk Biscuits**

Rose Haw Preserves   *Pickles*   *Strawberry Jam*   *Tomato Preserves**

Grape Conserve*   *Pear Marmalade**   *Honey*   *Carrot Pickles**

Mother Ann's Birthday Cake*   *Shaker Cider Cake**

Milk   *Tea*   *Coffee*

The Shaker settlement at Pleasant Hill, in Kentucky's bluegrass country, was organized in 1806. Almost from its beginning, the settlement attracted visitors from neighboring Danville and Harrodsburg. Young couples drove to Pleasant Hill in surreys and carryalls to share (for a modest price) in lavish meals. One Shaker sister wrote in 1866, "As to our fare in general, we have the cream of the earth; plenty of flour, meal, milk and butter . . . strawberries, asparagus, lettuce, radishes, peas, preserves, honey, molasses . . . buttered waffles, fritters, doughnuts, baked dumplings, peach pies, apple pies." The list of comestibles continued to prodigious lengths. Two of the most distinctive parts of Shaker menus were the breads and preserves. In an era when bleaching flour was common practice, the Shakers spoke against killing the "live germ of the wheat." (In an 1871 edition of the Shaker *Manifesto,* an article by Henry Ward Beecher charged that "what had been the staff of life for countless ages had become a weak crutch.") Shaker tables always had an abundance of freshly baked breads and muffins, and jams and jellies.

BETTMANN ARCHIVE

Engraving of Monticello

"Never before," it was said of Thomas Jefferson's eight years in the White House, "had such dinners been given in the President's house, nor such a variety of the finest and most costly wines. In his entertainments republican simplicity was united with epicurean delicacy; while the absence of splendor, ornament and profusion was more than compensated by the neatness, order and elegant simplicity that pervaded the whole establishment."

Jefferson's superb dinners were occasionally equaled by some of his successors in the White House, but they were rarely excelled. All three of the menus given here use foods that were available at Monticello during April, a bountiful month for crops on the plantation. A maigre, or fast day menu, is included (at bottom), since the custom of Friday and Lenten abstinence from meat was well rooted in Virginia and since Jefferson, a deist, had continued his connection with the Anglican church.

Deviled Crab*

Consommé Julienne

Roast Saddle of Lamb* with Brown Gravy   Conserve of Whole Currants

Pilau with Pignon Nuts*

Green Peas with Mint*

Salad of Mixed Garden Stuff* with Monticello Dressing*

Beaten Biscuits* with Assorted Cheese

Crème Brûlée*   Coffee   Fruit   Nuts

Deviled Eggs with Anchovies*

Celery   Radishes   Olives   Small Green Onions

Sorrel Soup*

Standing Ribs of Beef* au Jus   Horse-radish Sauce*

Spinach Timbales*   Scalloped Tomatoes*

Small Roast Potatoes or Macaroni and Cheese Pudding*

Salad

Pots de Crème*   Macaroons   Meringues

Fruit   Coffee   Nuts

Oysters on the Half Shell

Mock Turtle Soup

Baked Shad with Roe Soufflé*

Fresh Asparagus with Virginia Boiled Dressing*   Scalloped Potatoes*

Blancmange* with Brandied Apricots*   Small Cakes

Coffee   Fruit   Nuts

A PENNSYLVANIA DUTCH DINNER

Corn Chowder*

Chicken Potpie* Red Cabbage* Scalloped Potatoes*

Seven Sweets: *Seven Sours:*

Sweet Pickled Peaches* Red-Beet Eggs*

Apple Butter* Pickled Jerusalem Artichokes*

Quince Honey Pickled Yellow Beans

Ginger Pears* Cantaloupe Pickle*

Grape Conserve* Piccalilli

Rhubarb Jam Corn Relish*

Tomato Preserves* Carrot Pickles*

Homemade Bread

Shoo-fly Pie* Applesauce Cake*

Coffee

William Penn, in a pamphlet in 1681, commended the "province of Pennsilvania" with great restraint: "I shall say little in its praise.... This shall satisfie me, that by the Blessing of God, and the honesty and industry of Man, it may be a good and fruitful Land." In 1686, James Harrison, a Quaker minister, was less reserved in his praise of the new land: "The Peach-Trees are much broken down with the weight of Fruit this Year ... Rasberries, Goosberries, Currans, Quinces, Roses, Walnuts and Figs grow well.... Our Barn, Porch and Shed, are full of Corn this year." Dr. Nicholas More wrote in 1686, "We have had admirable English Pease this Summer; every one here is now persuaded of the fertility of the ground, and goodness of the climate, here being nothing wanting, with industry, that grows in England . . . and we have this common advantage above England, that all things grow better, and with less labour." It was in this exceptionally fertile country that the Pennsylvania Dutch nurtured a cuisine that has always reflected the generosity of the land on which they live.

402

Hermann, Missouri, was founded in 1837 by the German Settlement Society of Philadelphia. The purpose of the settlers was to establish a German community in which the language and customs of Germany might be preserved. The site chosen on the banks of the Missouri River was reminiscent of the Rhine Valley; the land was suitable for vineyards, and Hermann became, for a time, the second largest wine-producing center in America. One of the limestone cellars of Hermann's wine company contained the "twelve apostles," casks of 1,500- to 3,000-gallon capacity, carved with likenesses of the apostles.

Winegrowers customarily celebrated in late spring (when the major work in the vineyards had been completed) or in the fall (when the summer sun had done its work and the grapes had been harvested). The May festival became traditional in Hermann after 1844, when the settlers produced their first wine, and the wine drinking was accompanied by dancing, singing, pageants, band concerts, and feasts. Below is a *Maifest* menu, followed by a picnic for the children.

*May Wine Bowl**

*Chicken Fricassee**   *Dumplings**   *Green Peas*   *Fried Mushrooms**

German Rye Bread   *Cheese*   *Coleslaw**   *Pickles*

*Lemon Cheesecake**   *Coffee*   *Sour Cream Raisin Pie**

Spring picnic

*Pink Lemonade**   *Cream Potato Salad**   *Buns with Knackwurst*

*Slices of Brick Ice Cream with Sand Tarts** and Cinnamon Stars**

NELLIE GRANT'S WEDDING BREAKFAST

Soft-Shelled Crabs* on Toast   Chicken Croquettes* with Green Peas

Lamb Cutlets with Tartare Sauce*   Aspic of Beef Tongue

Woodcock and Snipe on Toast   Salad with Mayonnaise

Strawberries with Cream   Orange Baskets Garnished with Strawberries

Charlotte Russe*   Nesselrode Pudding*   Blancmange*

Ice Cream* Garnished with Preserved Fruits   Water Ices

Wedding Cake   Small Fancy Cakes

Roman Punch*   Chocolate   Coffee

A wedding cake

The marriage of Nellie Grant, President Ulysses Grant's only daughter, took place at eleven o'clock on the morning of May 21, 1874. It was the first wedding to be held in the White House in thirty years, since President Tyler married Julia Gardiner. Nellie married a young Englishman, Algernon Sartoris (to whom, at first, her father objected), in an elaborate ceremony in the East Room of the White House. The bride wore a white satin dress, with a white veil and a wreath of white flowers, green leaves, and orange blossoms. The wedding breakfast was served in the state dining room.

Although the press was not admitted, a reporter from the New York *Herald* managed to be present, and it is from his account of the breakfast that the menu is taken. "It is said," the journalist recounted, "by those who have long been frequenters of the White House, nothing to equal it was ever before witnessed."

404

A SYLVAN REPAST

Cream of Celery Soup (Colored Green)

Grilled Trout*

Mushrooms in Cream* on Toast

Roast Rack of Venison*   *Plum Sauce**

Saratoga Chips*   *Green Peas served in Patty Shells*

Salpicon of Fruits*

Quail* in Nests of Puréed Chestnuts*

*English Walnuts and Celery Mixed with Green Mayonnaise
in Cups of Molded Tomato Jelly*

*Small Balls of Cream Cheese, Colored Green to Imitate Birds' Eggs,
in Nests of Shredded Lettuce*

Pistachio Ice Cream Molded in a Ring, Center Filled with Whipped Cream

White Cakes with Green Icing   *Fruits*   *Coffee*

"Of late it has been the fashion to have one prevailing color," Mary Ronald wrote in her *Century Cook Book,* published in 1895. She referred not simply to table decorations, but to the food itself. It was possible, in the 1890's, to find directions for serving a dinner composed almost entirely of foods of a single color. Miss Ronald said, "In many cases this is very suitable as well as complimentary to the guests entertained. For instance, a white dinner to a bride, pink to young people, red to a Harvard company, or yellow to those with Princeton affiliations." Miss Ronald's Sylvan Repast, or "Al Fresco" dinner, an evocation of a woodland scene, was her green dinner. "Of all colors," she said, "green is the easiest to carry out, and perhaps the most pleasing...." The ceiling was decorated to resemble a blue sky dotted with little white clouds. Palms, bay trees, and rubber plants were set about the dining room, and the center of the large round table was filled with ferns, primroses, and moss. Light was provided by green candles covered with green shades. The menu is composed largely of "products of the forest," Miss Ronald said. "The aspect of this dinner was really sylvan."

Turtle Soup

Broiled Salmon Steaks or New England Poached Salmon with Egg Sauce*

Green Peas   Small Boiled New Potatoes in Jackets

Indian Pudding* or Apple Pandowdy*

Coffee   Tea

When John Adams signed the Declaration of Independence, he wrote to his wife, Abigail, that the day of the signing "will be the most memorable epocha in the history of America. I am apt to believe that it will be celebrated by succeeding generations as the great anniversary Festival. It ought to be commemorated, as the day of deliverance by solemn acts of devotion to God Almighty. It ought to be solemnized with pomp and parade, with shows, games, sports, guns, bells, bonfires and illuminations from one end of this continent to the other, from this time forward, forevermore."

Though the Adamses celebrated the Fourth of July each year with enthusiasm, their tastes at the dinner table reflected New England thrift and simplicity. They reflected, too, Mrs. Adams' concern with practical matters. On June 23, 1797, she wrote from Philadelphia to her sister, "To day will be the 5th great dinner I have had, about 36 Gentlemen to day, as many more next week, and I shall have got through the whole of Congress, with their apendages. Then comes the 4 July which is a still more tedious day, as we must have then not only all Congress, but all the Gentlemen of the city, the Govenour and officers and companies, all of whom the late President used to treat with cake, punch and wine. What the House would not hold used to be placed at long tables in the yard. As we are here we cannot avoid the trouble or the expence. . . ."

The Adamses' neighbors in Massachusetts had no such problems on the Fourth of July; they just served the traditional New England dinner of salmon with egg sauce, along with the first new potatoes and early peas. The salmon along the eastern seaboard began to run in late June and were readily available for Independence Day.

The Waldorf-Astoria, 1899

Cape Cod Oysters

Chicken Gumbo Filé*

Celery   Assorted Nuts

Fillet of Flounder, American Style*

Roast Wild Duck*   Currant Sauce*

Wild Rice Sauté   Alligator Pear Salad

Pumpkin Pie* with American Cheese   Coffee

Oscar Tschirky, the maître d'hôtel of the Waldorf-Astoria, was known simply as Oscar—in much the same way (and with similar deference) as one of his contemporaries was referred to as Victoria. Oscar shared his throne with other social arbiters such as Ward McAllister, but in the Palm Garden of the Waldorf-Astoria the greatest measure of recognition a socialite could receive was to have Oscar personally suggest the wines and food for dinner.

Oscar differed from royalty in that he recognized the *nouveaux riches* as equals of the established American "aristocracy." George Boldt, the manager of the Waldorf, would have preferred to cater only to the Four Hundred. But Oscar realized that such people, regardless of their wealth, could not support a large modern hotel, and that such exclusivism was, in any event, obsolescent. Early in this century, Oscar reached beyond the boundaries of the Palm Garden to publish his own cookbook, which became a best seller. Later, he was asked to outline what he considered a dinner typical of American tastes and traditions; his answer was the above menu.

FREE LUNCH

"The Bibulous Loafer," 1882

The Reverend Thomas Dixon, Jr., in an article in *Leslie's Illustrated* of March 3, 1892, declaimed, "All signs seem to point now to the temporary triumph of the saloon over the forces of Christian civilization in America." Speaking of the Hotel Vendôme bar in New York, Reverend Dixon said, "At the extreme end of the room, and separated from the bar by twenty or thirty feet, stands the free-lunch counter, built of African marble and Mexican onyx! It is loaded with the most tempting food cooked by master hands."

The free lunch was an innovation from the West in the early nineteenth century. Throughout the century, as the institution of the free lunch spread across the country, a man could walk into almost any saloon in America and for the price of a drink (or two) help himself to the inexhaustible supplies of the free-lunch counter. The institution reached its zenith between 1890 and 1910, and it was, in those favored years, a boon to the bachelor, the young college student, and the junior clerk, who could dine sumptuously, within their modest means, in the congenial atmosphere of the saloon. This menu (published by The Book Club of California) is taken from San Francisco's Palace of Art, whose proprietor, Ernest Haquette, maintained a lunch counter esteemed as especially generous. The more typical free-lunch counter contained an assortment of salty edibles intended to stimulate thirst. Haquette's spread, although it must have provoked thirst, had some culinary pretensions, too. The Palace of Art was decorated with tasteful oil paintings (its nudes inviting, but modest), a collection of European glass, and ladies. The fact that Haquette admitted ladies to his saloon may account for the special lavishness of his lunch spread.

Yet other free-lunch counters, though they may appear frugal compared with that of the Palace of Art, were no mean affairs of cheese and crackers. In 1896, the New York *Daily Tribune* revealed, "Millions of money are annually expended in this seeming gratuity, and over fifty thousand regulars depend upon what they can gather from our counters for their daily subsistence." Even some of the least distinguished saloons in New York laid out as much as ten thousand dollars per year for their lunches. In 1907, the New York *Herald* reported, in an article giving advice on how a man might live in New York without any money at all: "The man who would live on nothing a year could actually become something of a connoisseur. He could study the cooking of the various chefs and learn where to find the best chicken or salad or roast, fish or oysters, and by carefully selecting his courses he could make an excellent dinner within a radius of a few blocks. . . . he would enjoy the cooking of the best chefs in America."

Radishes   **Crab Salad**   **Celery**

Clam Juice

Pig's Head   **Bolinas Bay Clams**   **Headcheese**

Homemade Sausage, Country Style*   **Beef à la Chili Colorado**

Chili con Carne*   **Honolulu Beans**

Chicken Croquettes*   **Veal Croquettes***   **Terrapin Stew**

Fried Clams   **Sardines**   **Baked Ham***

Saratoga Chips*   **Corned Beef**

Tongue in Spicy Aspic*   **Beef Stew***   **Boston Baked Beans***

Frizzled Beef*   **Smoked Salmon**

Cheese   **Crackers**

Cracked Crab   **Holland Herring**

Almonds   **Popcorn**   **Apples**

A NANTASKET BEACH CLAMBAKE

New England Clam Chowder* or Codfish Chowder*

Baked Clams with Melted Butter Dressing

Baked Blue Fish   Baked Cod*   Fried Perch

Nantasket Chips   Boiled Potatoes   Sweet Potatoes

Clam Fritters*   Corn on the Cob*   Cucumber Salad*

Brown and White Bread

Watermelon   Pie   Tea   Coffee

One of the chief contributions the Indians made to the cuisine of New England was the clambake. Later, New England clambakes, like Kentucky burgoos, were put on to attract voters to election rallies, and became the excuse for innumerable social outings. In the latter half of the nineteenth century, upper Narragansett Bay in Rhode Island was crowded with clambake resorts like Rocky Point and Crescent Park. Bakes were served every day, and fleets of steamboats operating out of Providence and the neighboring area ran excursions to these clambake sites along the shore.

A fire was (and still is—the system used by the Indians on the shores of Rhode Island has not been improved upon) built on a foundation of large stones. When the stones were white-hot, the fire was swept away, and a layer of rockweed was placed on the stones. Clams were placed on the rockweed, then another layer of weed, a layer of potatoes and corn (covered by a layer of husks), then fish enveloped in cloth or paper bags. (The ingredients in a clambake varied somewhat; although not shown on this menu, sausages, lobsters, and even chickens were often added to a bake.) The bake was then blanketed with a wet canvas, which was covered with rockweed and held down at the edges with stones to keep in the steam. The canvas was kept moist throughout the cooking. It took about an hour to heat the stones, and forty-five minutes for the heat from the stones to cook the bake.

The menu here, dating from the late nineteenth century, is taken from the Arlington Hotel at Nantasket Beach, Massachusetts, which advertised this full dinner for fifty cents with "Clams Baked on Heated Rocks . . . No steam pipes are used."

410

BREAKFAST WITH THE AUTOCRAT

Littleneck Clams

Grilled Trout*   *Cucumbers, Sautéed**

Omelette* with Mushrooms in Cream*   *Grilled Plover*

Filet Mignon*   *Potatoes*   *Asparagus with Hollandaise Sauce**

Tomato and Lettuce Salad

Ice Cream*   *Strawberries*   *Cakes*   *Coffee*

"Waiter!"

The opening sentence of Dr. Oliver Wendell Holmes's *The Autocrat of the Breakfast-Table* is characteristic of the book and of the man who spoke with the gentle art—now considered lost—of the conversationalist: "I was just going to say, when I was interrupted . . ."

Dr. Holmes was often interrupted, but it was never a permanent condition. He was considered the poet laureate of both the breakfast and the dinner tables. Holmes was a member of the Saturday Club, founded in Boston in 1855. The club was devoted to the discussion of literature and to monthly banquets which the members unabashedly gave in honor of one another. Holmes's fellow members included Henry Wadsworth Longfellow, Ralph Waldo Emerson, Nathaniel Hawthorne, James Russell Lowell, Louis Agassiz, Richard Henry Dana, Jr., Francis Parkman, John Greenleaf Whittier, William Dean Howells, Henry Adams, and Henry James.

The menu presented here is from a breakfast given in honor of Holmes in 1879.

In the early days of American politics, candidates for office resorted to an eminently successful device to get out the voters: they supplied the electorate with food and drink.

Electioneering—beginning even before 1758, when George Washington served voters rum, punch, beer, wine, cider, and cakes—was always carried on in the midst of great outdoor feasts. Election cannon would roar, banners would fly, and a band would blare an inspiring march as speakers mounted the platform to speak—interrupted only by a midday repast—until well into the evening. In 1840, the rallies reached their zenith in the "Log Cabin and Hard Cider" campaign of William Henry Harrison. At Albany, the Whigs raised a log cabin and feasted on corn bread, cheese, and hard cider. At Columbus, Ohio, there was ginger cake, hoecake, and bacon with the cider. At Wheeling West Virginia, Harrisonites entertained 30,000 at a rally with 360 hams, 26 sheep, 20 calves, 1,500 pounds of beef, 8,000 pounds of bread, over 1,000 pounds of cheese, and 4,500 pies.

George P. Prentice, an editor of a New England magazine who went south to write a biography of Henry Clay, described what he saw of southern politics: "I have just witnessed that strange thing, a Kentucky election. . . . Whiskey and apple toddy flowed in the cities and villages like the Euphrates through ancient Babylon. . . . drunkenness stalked triumphant. . . . Runners, each with a whiskey bottle poking its long, jolly neck from his pocket, were employed in bribing voters, and each party kept half-a-dozen bullies . . . to flog every poor fellow that should attempt to vote illegally; a half-hundredweight of mortar would scarce fill up the chinks in the skulls that were broken."

Year after year Kentucky voters ran the risk of having their skulls broken in order to share in some food and drink and hear an orator. The entry for July 24, 1844, in the diary of Henry Baxter speaks of a Democratic rally in Walnut Lick, Kentucky, which was attended by about two thousand people: "Mr. O'Hara an old Irish lawyer of Owen Co. Ky. followed, and from him we had the whole history of Whiggery and Democracy, from the very beginning of our government until the present time...We then adjourned to dinner which is the first of the kind I ever was at. Here were five or six ditches dug two and a half feet deep, and about as wide, in which had been built fires, which when burned down to the coals, they had put over their quarters of veal and mutton upon spits of wood....Further on was a table about two hundred feet long...strewed from end to end with...meat."

Baxter was, of course, describing a barbecue (from the Spanish *barbacoa,* meaning a "frame"). The Mexican Indians had used frames of green wood to dry and smoke fish, and the Spaniards adapted the method to roast the meat of large animals. Colonists as far north as Pennsylvania used barbecue frames to cook fish, pigs, and sheep, but in Texas, the main feature was always beef, in great quantities. (Westerners distinguish between real barbecues and the lamb barbecues of the sheepherders by calling the latter Basque barbecues, since so many of the sheep farmers were of Basque ancestry.)

A menu adapted from a standard Texas barbecue appears below. With it is a menu built around burgoo, one of the most popular dishes at rallies in Kentucky in the latter half of the nineteenth century.

Barbecued Spareribs*

Four-Bean Salad* ***Buttermilk Biscuits****

Individual Pecan Pies* ***Coffee***

"Hard Cider Triumphant"

Mint Juleps*

Burgoo*

Corn Sticks* ***Coleslaw****

Apple Pie* or **Deep-Dish Blueberry Pie****

Hickory Nut Cake* or **Kentucky Bourbon Cake****

Coffee

Oysters on the Half Shell

Celery   *Radishes*   *Olives*

Consommé

Roast Turkey* with Chestnut Stuffing*   *Giblet Gravy**

Roast Suckling Pig*   *Cranberry Sauce**   *Spiced Crab Apples**

Spinach   *Mashed Potatoes*   *Onions in Cream**   *Brussels Sprouts*

Salad

Mincemeat Pie*   *Pumpkin Pie**   *Vanilla Ice Cream**

Nuts   *Fruits*   *Chocolate Dragées*   *Coffee*

Along with the turkey and other traditional dishes, the Thanksgiving table at Sagamore Hill always featured suckling pig, a favorite food of Roosevelt and his eldest daughter, "Princess Alice." Except for such special occasions, however, the meals at the Roosevelt home were not elaborate. They featured the harvest of the family gardens, orchards, and bayshore; fresh milk, cream, and butter from the dairy herd; and home-baked breads to be eaten with preserves, jams, and jellies. "At Sagamore Hill," Roosevelt once said, "we love a great many things—birds and trees and books, and all things beautiful, and horses and rifles and children and hard work and the joy of life."

Roosevelt dined simply—often content with no more than bread and milk—but he consumed his edibles in great quantities. O. K. Davis recalled, "I have seen him eat a whole chicken and drink four large glasses [of milk] at one meal, and chicken and milk were by no means the only things served." Lloyd Griscom remembered Roosevelt as "stoking up prodigiously, as though he were a machine." And Theodore Roosevelt, Jr., said that his father's coffee cup "was more in the nature of a bathtub." Roosevelt was as fond of sweets (his Thanksgiving dinner is topped here with chocolate candies) as he was of a whole chicken, or half a suckling pig; Richard Henry Dana III once noticed that Roosevelt put as many as seven lumps of sugar in his coffee, "and I bethought me of the humming bird which lives on sweets, and is one of the most strenuously active of vertebrates."

A GENTLEMEN'S DINNER IN THE ROCKIES

Adolphus François Gerard, who was born in Alençon, France, about 1844, spent some time in a French seminary, dissipated a small fortune enjoying the pleasures of Paris, and became a journalist in London and New York. Then, cavalierly, Gerard joined the United States Army and was assigned to a post in Cheyenne, Wyoming. He deserted—and became Louis Dupuy, one of the most famous chefs of the West in the nineteenth century. Dupuy was the proprietor of the Hotel de Paris in Georgetown, Colorado (the second largest city in the state at that time, owing to the silver-mining boom). The rich and renowned from all over the world traveled out of their way to delight in the cuisine at the Hotel de Paris. The dinner below was served in March, 1879; the nine men who had journeyed to Georgetown solely for the purpose of dining at Dupuy's hotel were Jay Gould (who later said it was the best meal he had ever had) and his son George, General Grenville M. Dodge, Sidney Dillon, Russell Sage, Captain G. H. Baker, Oliver Ames, W. A. H. Loveland, and E. K. Berthoud. Together, the nine men represented over two hundred million dollars.

Galantine of pheasants

Oysters on the Half Shell

Soup

Ptarmigan or Pheasant in Casserole*   ***Venison Cutlet***   ***Sauce Piquante****

Sweetbreads Eugénie*

Vegetables   ***Apple Fritters****   ***Salad***

French Bread

Peach Charlotte* with Brandy Sauce*   ***Petits Fours***   ***Coffee***

CULVER PICTURES

Thanksgiving dinner

Haunch of Venison*   *Roast Chine of Pork**

Roast Turkey*   *Pigeon Pasties*   *Roast Goose**

Onions in Cream*   *Cauliflower*   *Squash*

Potatoes   *Raw Celery*

Mincemeat Pie*   *Pumpkin Pie**   *Apple Pie**

Indian Pudding*   *Plum Pudding**

Cider

This menu for a New England Thanksgiving dinner is taken from a letter written in 1779 by Juliana Smith to her "Dear Cousin Betsey." As Thanksgiving Day approached, Grandmother Smith (the great-granddaughter of the Reverend Richard Mather of Dorchester, Massachusetts), "who is sometimes a little desponding of Spirit as you well know, did her best to persuade us that it would be better to make it a Day of Fasting & Prayer in view of the *Wickedness of our Friends & the Vileness of our Enemies,* I am sure you can hear Grandmother say that and see her shake her cap border. . . . But my dear Father brought her to a more proper frame of Mind, so that by the time the Day came she was ready to enjoy it almost as well as Grandmother Worthington did, & she, you will remember, always sees the bright side."

416

While it would be difficult to set forth a single "traditional" Thanksgiving menu, the preparations related by Juliana Smith that went into this dinner were certainly typical of early New England Thanksgivings. "This year it was Uncle Simeon's turn to have the dinner at his house, but of course we all helped them as they help us when it is our turn, & there is always enough for us all to do. All the baking of pies & cakes was done at our house & we had the big oven heated & filled twice each day for three days before it was all done. & *everything was* GOOD, though we did have to do without some things that ought to be used. Neither Love nor (paper) Money could buy Raisins, but our good red cherries dried without the pits, did almost as well & happily Uncle Simeon still had some spices in store. The tables were set in the Dining Hall and even that big room had no space to spare when we were all seated." Apparently roast beef was part of the traditional menu for this family, but "of course we could have no Roast Beef. None of us have tasted Beef this three years back as it all must go to the Army, & too little they get, poor fellows. But, Nayquittymaw's Hunters were able to get us a fine red Deer, so that we had a good haunch of Venisson on each Table." There was an abundance of vegetables on the table, including "one which I do not believe you have yet seen. Uncle Simeon had imported the Seede from England just before the War began & only this Year was there enough for Table use. It is called Sellery & you eat it without cooking." Cider was served instead of wine, with the explanation that Uncle Simeon was saving his cask "for the sick." Juliana added that "The Pumpkin Pies, Apple Tarts & big Indian Puddings lacked for nothing save *Appetite* by the time we had got round to them."

Counting the Reverend Mr. Smith, his wife, two grandmothers, and the six Livingstons from next door, there were forty people at the dinner. "Uncle Simeon was in his best mood, and you know how good that is! He kept both Tables in a roar of laughter with his droll stories of the days when he was studying medicine in Edinborough, & afterwards he & Father & Uncle Paul joined in singing Hymns & Ballads. You know how fine their voices go together. Then we all sang a Hymn & afterwards my dear Father led us in prayer, remembering all Absent Friends . . . We did not rise from the Table until it was quite dark, & then when the dishes had been cleared away we all got round the fire as close as we could, & cracked nuts, & sang songs & told stories. At least some told & others listened. *You know nobody* can exceed the two Grandmothers at telling tales of all the things they have seen themselves, & repeating those of the early years in New England . . ."

A BISHOP HILL SMÖRGÅSBORD

Marinated Salmon   Sardines   Pickled or Smoked Herring

Herring Salad   Pickled Oysters   Crayfish   Shrimp Mayonnaise

Lutfisk   Dill and Mustard Sauce*   Stuffed Celery   Cream Potato Salad*

Aspics Molded and Decorated with Vegetables, Meats, Fish, and Fruits

Smoked or Pickled Tongue   Baked Ham*   Swedish Beans*

Liverwurst Sausages   Swedish Meatballs*   Pickled Pig's Feet

Spiced Crab Apples*   Pâté* and Cheese Balls   Chicken Liver Balls

Janson's Temptation*   Stuffed Cabbage*   Pickled Beets

Swedish Rye Bread*   Crisp Rye Bread   Saffron Bread*

Sharp Wisconsin Cheese   Caraway Seed Cheese   Edam Cheese

Swedish Christmas Cookies   Lingonberry Torte*   Swedish Mints

Coffee   Chocolate

Bishop Hill was founded in the 1840's in Illinois by the prophet Eric Janson and his followers. The prophet had been a purist in Sweden, burning books and calling for a return to the more austere early days of the Church; finally, King Oscar I was moved to contribute to a fund to help the Jansonists leave Sweden for America.

Janson's asceticism, and the rigors of pioneer life, showed in the early cuisine of Bishop Hill, and much of the austerity has persisted. However, as the Jansonists became more settled, the early strictures were softened.

Though Bishop Hill *smörgåsbords* remained coffee-drinking affairs, with none of the *aquavit* and beer and ale found in other Swedish communities in America, the feast gradually came to reflect the riches of the Illinois farm land rather than the privations extolled by the prophet. The menu given here, then, is typical of Swedish *smörgåsbords* throughout the country.

Traditionally, a *smörgåsbord* (meaning "bread and butter table") was only a preliminary to a full meal. Eventually, however, the informal preliminary grew into a buffet meal to be served on holidays.

Love feast in a Moravian Church

Love Feast Buns*   *Christmas Cookies**   *Sugar Cake**

Coffee with Milk

Moravian settlers in Pennsylvania and North Carolina brought with them their old custom of the love feast, a tradition that originated in the agapae, feasts held by early Christians in commemoration of the Last Supper. The custom does not replace holy communion, nor is it considered of equal importance. It is intended merely to rekindle a spirit of love and unity and to remove—at least for a time—all social distinctions. To the accompaniment of singing by the choir, the sweet love feast buns are served from baskets, and a substantial cup of coffee (usually made by brewing the coffee with the sugar and milk) is passed to each participant.

In old Salem, North Carolina, love feasts were celebrated at least five times a year: at New Year's, during Lent, at Christmas, and on August 13 and November 13 (two special Moravian feast days). In 1783, when the community celebrated the Fourth of July for the first time, the observance included a love feast.

In Moravian households, a type of love feast was often held as a quiet celebration of a birthday or as a thank offering to those who had befriended a family in distress or in bereavement. Rather than offering only coffee and the buns, as in the church version, these love feasts included Moravian sugar cake, cheese and biscuits, cookies, and coffee or tea; cider was served when in season.

PUBLIC ARCHIVES OF CANADA

GEORGE   WASHINGTON
PRESIDENT.
1792.

Commemorative medal

An Onion Soup Call'd the King's Soup*

Oysters on the Half Shell   Broiled Salt Roe Herring*   Boiled Rockfish

Roast Beef* and Yorkshire Pudding*   Mutton Chops

Roast Suckling Pig*   Roast Turkey* with Chestnut Stuffing*

Round of Cold Boiled Beef with Horse-radish Sauce*   Cold Baked Virginia Ham

Lima Beans   Baked Acorn Squash*   Baked Celery with Slivered Almonds*

Hominy Pudding*   Candied Sweet Potatoes*

Cantaloupe Pickle*   Spiced Peaches in Brandy*   Spiced Cranberries

Mincemeat Pie*   Apple Pie*   Cherry Pie*   Chess Tarts*

Blancmange*   Plums in Wine Jelly*   Snowballs*   Indian Pudding*

Great Cake*   Ice Cream*   Plum Pudding*

Fruits   Nuts   Raisins

Port   Madeira

Christmas was an especially meaningful holiday at Mount Vernon. George and Martha Washington were married on Twelfth Night in 1759, and throughout their lives they tried to spend the Christmas holiday season together. Even during the Revolution, Martha Washington traveled the winter roads with a military escort to join the General in his winter quarters.

Dinner at Mount Vernon was customarily served at three o'clock in the afternoon—an hour about which the General was altogether precise. He was likely to tell late guests, "Gentlemen ... I have a cook who never asks whether the company has come, but whether the hour has come." (Martha was equally punctual. In 1790, she concluded an evening party promptly at nine o'clock by rising and announcing to her company, "The General always retires at nine, and I usually precede him.")

In the prevailing fashion, dinner was served in three courses and on two tablecloths. One cloth was removed between each course, and the fruit, nuts, and wines were served on the bare table. In the center of the table was an elegant epergne, and handsome platters containing meats and fish were placed symmetrically about the table—with a suitable assortment of vegetables and "corner dishes" of sauces, relishes, and preserves located at other appropriate spots.

Dinners were customarily concluded with toasts around the table. In 1789 William Maclay, a senator from Pennsylvania, was guest at a dinner party with the President and Mrs. Washington, Vice-President and Mrs. Adams, and several others. At the end of the meal, Maclay reported, "the President, filling a glass of wine with great formality drank to the health of every individual name by name round the table. Everybody imitated him, charged glasses, and such a buzz of 'health, sir,' and 'health, madam,' and 'thank you, sir' and 'thank you, madam,' never had I heard before. Indeed, I had liked to have been thrown out in the hurry; but I got a little wine in my glass, and passed the ceremony. The ladies sat a good while, and the bottle passed about; but there was a dead silence almost. Mrs. Washington at last withdrew with the ladies."

The Christmas menu opposite is a composite of meals served at Mount Vernon, made up of dishes that were available there in winter. Visitors to Mount Vernon were given to incomplete accounts, like that of Amariah Frost, who dined with the Washingtons in 1797 and reported, "The dinner was very good, a small roasted pigg, boiled leg of lamb, roasted Fowles, beef, peas, lettice, cucumbers, artichokes, etc. puddings, tarts, etc. etc." In compiling this menu the etceteras have been replaced by recourse to various guests' reports, garden books, farm records, and invoices of goods ordered from merchants.

BEFORE THE SOUP

The cocktail party, with its rounds of drinks and trays of hors d'oeuvres, did not come into vogue until the twentieth century. Previously, guests were invited for dinner rather than just for drinks. Appetizers and canapés were rarely served, except, perhaps, for a half-dozen oysters before the soup. The dishes listed below (with the pages of the recipe section on which they may be found), are especially adaptable for serving at cocktail parties or as appetizers before dinner.

RECIPES

PHILADELPHIA PEPPER POT

During the relentlessly harsh winter of 1777-78, morale was low at Valley Forge, and desertions frequent. According to legend, Washington ordered a good meal to cheer his troops one night—only to be told by his harried cook that there was nothing but tripe, some peppercorns, and useless scraps. Still, an order was an order, and the cook improvised a soup which he called, ex post facto, Philadelphia (in honor of his home town) Pepper Pot. It is said that some Philadelphians still attribute the success of the Revolution to Philadelphia Pepper Pot soup.

3 pounds tripe
1 knuckle of veal with meat left on
2 pounds marrowbone, cracked
2 large onions, sliced
Soup bouquet: several sprigs parsley;
   1 bay leaf; 2 sprigs thyme or ½ teaspoon
   dried thyme; 1 carrot, cut in chunks
½ teaspoon crushed red pepper

1 teaspoon whole allspice
6 whole cloves
4 potatoes, diced fine
2 teaspoons dried marjoram
2 tablespoons chopped parsley
Salt
Pepper
Dumplings (recipe below)

Wash the tripe, put into a kettle with 4 quarts of water, and bring to a boil. Reduce heat, cover, and cook over a low heat for 6 to 7 hours or until the tripe is very soft. Cool in the broth. When cool enough to handle, cut into very small pieces. Pour broth into a container. While tripe is coooking, put veal knuckle in a second kettle with 2 quarts of water. Remove the marrow from marrowbone with a knife or spoon and heat in a saucepan. Toss in onions and sauté until tender. Now combine with the veal knuckle and the de-marrowed bone. Add the soup bouquet, red pepper, allspice, and cloves and cook over a low heat for about 5 hours or until very tender. Cool veal in broth until meat can be handled comfortably, then chop veal in small pieces (discard bones), and add to chopped tripe. Pour broth into a separate container and refrigerate both the meat and the two broths overnight. Next day, remove and discard fat from tripe and veal broth. Combine the two broths and add the chopped tripe and veal, diced potatoes, marjoram, and salt and pepper to taste. Cook over a low heat for about 45 minutes. Add parsley, drop dumplings in broth, and cook as directed. Serves 12.

Dumplings:
1 cup sifted all-purpose flour
2 teaspoons baking powder

¼ teaspoon salt
1 tablespoon shortening
6 tablespoons milk (about)

Sift flour, baking powder, and salt together. Add shortening and pinch it in with your fingers until it is well distributed. Gradually stir in milk with a fork—just enough to make a soft dough. Drop by tablespoons into simmering soup, cover tightly, and cook 15 minutes. Serves 6. The dumplings are limited to 6 servings because your kettle will not accommodate more and they must be cooked, all at one time, in the simmering soup. You can make a second batch of dumplings when you serve the soup on the second day.

CORN CHOWDER

This chowder originated in Massachusetts, but it is also made in the South with tomatoes added to the ingredients below.

3 slices salt pork, cubed
1 large onion, sliced
4 large potatoes, sliced
2 cups water
6 large soda crackers

1 cup milk
2 cups corn (fresh, canned whole kernel,
   or frozen, thawed)
1 teaspoon salt
Dash of paprika

Fry salt pork in a saucepan until crisp and lightly browned. Stir in onion and cook until golden, then add potatoes and water. Continue cooking until potatoes are tender. Crumble soda crackers into a bowl, pour in milk, and soak. Add to the cooked potatoes, then add corn, salt, and paprika. Simmer over a low heat for 8 to 10 minutes. Serves 4.

CHICKEN CORN SOUP

Chicken Corn Soup was a favorite in Lancaster County, Pennsylvania, where it was often served on picnics during the summer.

A 4-pound stewing chicken
1 onion, chopped
4 quarts water
Salt
Pepper
10 ears fresh corn
½ cup chopped celery with leaves

2 hard-cooked eggs, chopped
Rivels:
1 cup flour
Pinch of salt
1 egg
Milk

Cut chicken into pieces and place in a soup kettle. Add onion, water, salt, and pepper. Bring to a boil, then reduce heat, cover, and simmer gently until chicken is tender. Remove chicken from stock and, when cool enough to handle, strip meat from bones. Discard bones and skin, and cut into bite-sized pieces. Return chicken to stock, add corn (cut kernels from cob) and celery. Continue simmering for 30 minutes and prepare *rivels*.

To make the rivels: Combine flour, salt, egg, and enough milk to make a crumbly mixture. Mix with a fork or with your finger tips until crumbs are the size of small peas. Drop *rivels* and chopped eggs into soup. Cook 15 minutes, then season to taste. Serves 6.

PEANUT SOUP

½ cup roasted peanuts
3 cups beef broth
1 cup half-and-half (milk and cream)

½ teaspoon chili powder
½ teaspoon salt

Blend peanuts with *1 cup of the broth* in an electric blender until smooth. Pour into a saucepan and add all remaining ingredients. Bring to a boil, reduce heat to simmer, and cook slowly for 15 minutes. Serve hot with a dab of whipped cream on top, or cold, garnished with thin slices of cucumber or radishes. Serves 4.

BLACK BEAN SOUP

2 cups dried black beans
Ham bone with meat, or ham hock
2 medium onions, chopped
2 carrots, chopped
3 stalks celery, chopped
4 to 5 sprigs parsley
3 whole cloves
Pinch mace or allspice

Pinch thyme
2 bay leaves
1 teaspoon dry mustard
1 tablespoon Worcestershire sauce
¼ cup sherry
2 eggs, hard cooked
Lemon

Soak beans overnight in enough cold water to cover. Drain, add 2 quarts water, ham bone, onions, carrots, celery, parsley, cloves, mace, thyme, bay leaves, dry mustard, and Worcestershire sauce. Bring to a boil, then reduce heat, and simmer gently for 2 to 3 hours or until beans are very tender. Remove ham and bone, cutting any meat into small pieces. Work soup through a sieve or blend in an electric blender. Add diced ham and sherry and season to taste. If soup is too thick (it should look like heavy cream), stir in a little water. Reheat and serve with sliced hard-cooked eggs and thin lemon slices on top. Serves 6.

PUMPKIN SOUP

We have pumpkins at morning, and pumpkins at noon,
If it were not for pumpkins we should be undone.
—From an anonymous poem, circa 1630

Cut half a small pumpkin into wedges, remove seeds and outer skin. Chop pulp into pieces and cook in boiling, salted water until tender when tested with a fork. Drain and work through a sieve. Combine 2 cups pumpkin purée with 3 tablespoons butter, 1 teaspoon sugar, 1 teaspoon salt, and ¼ teaspoon white pepper. Cook over a low heat about 10 minutes. Stir in 3 cups hot milk, a little at a time, and simmer gently for several minutes. Serve with croutons. Serves 4.

SOPA DE ALBONDIGAS
(Meatball Soup)

3 quarts beef broth
¼ cup olive oil
1 small onion, chopped
1 clove garlic, crushed
1 can (8 ounces) tomato sauce
¾ pound beef, ground

¾ pound lean pork, ground
⅓ cup uncooked rice
1 egg, beaten
1½ teaspoons salt
½ teaspoon chili pepper
¼ cup chopped parsley

Use a good rich beef broth, preferably homemade. Heat oil in a soup kettle, stir in chopped onion and garlic, and cook until light gold in color. Stir in tomato sauce and beef broth. Combine ground beef and pork with rice, egg, salt, and chili pepper. Shape into balls the size of a walnut. When broth is boiling briskly, drop in the meatballs, cover, and cook over a moderate heat for 30 minutes. Serve with chopped parsley strewn on top. Serves 4 to 6.

OLD-FASHIONED VEGETABLE SOUP

A 1½-pound shin bone of beef with meat
1½ pounds lean brisket, cubed
3 stalks celery
3 large carrots
2 medium onions
1 can (1 pound, 13 ounce size) tomatoes
½ teaspoon dried basil
½ teaspoon dried thyme
½ teaspoon dried marjoram
½ cup chopped parsley
1½ tablespoons salt
½ teaspoon pepper
½ pound green Lima beans, shelled
½ pound green peas, shelled
3 ears fresh corn

Put the shin bone and the cubed brisket in a large kettle and add enough water to cover them. Cook to the boiling point, then add chopped celery, carrots, and onions. Stir in tomatoes, basil, thyme, marjoram, parsley, salt, and pepper. Cover and cook over a low heat for 2 to 3 hours (timing is not important in vegetable soup—some cooks let it simmer all day long). Thirty minutes or so before serving, add Lima beans, peas, and corn cut off the cob. Before dishing up, skim off all excess fat. Serves 6.

SORREL SOUP

1 pound fresh sorrel
1 medium onion, chopped
¼ cup butter
1 cup light cream
2 egg yolks, beaten
3 cups chicken broth
Salt
Pepper

Chop well-washed and dried sorrel leaves very fine. Cook onion in heated butter until limp, but do not brown. Stir in sorrel and cook over a low heat until wilted—takes about 5 minutes. Blend cream and egg yolks together. Heat chicken broth to a boil, then stir a little into yolk mixture, beating hard. Pour back into broth and heat. Beat constantly and do not allow it to boil. Add sorrel mixture and salt and pepper to taste. Serve hot or refrigerate and serve icy cold. If you like a smoother mixture, blend in the electric blender. Serves 4 to 6.

SPLIT PEA SOUP

1½ cups split peas
Ham bone
1 onion, stuck with 2 cloves
2 or 3 stalks of celery
1 bay leaf
3 or 4 carrots
½ cup heavy cream

Cover the split peas with water and soak overnight or use the quick-cooking variety. Place ham bone, peeled onion stuck with 2 cloves, celery, bay leaf, carrots, and drained split peas in a large kettle. Add 2 to 3 quarts of water, or enough to cover, and bring to a boil. Then lower the heat and simmer gently until the peas are soft and mushy. Lift the ham bone out of the kettle and purée the soup in an electric blender or push through a sieve. Cut off any meat on the bone and cut in slivers. Set aside. Pour soup back into kettle, add cream, and taste for seasoning. Then add slivered ham and bring to a boil, but do not cook further. Serve with a sturdy, crusty bread or croutons. Serves 6.

AN ONION SOUP CALL'D THE KING'S SOUP

This recipe is adapted from *The Lady's Companion*, a cookbook published in 1753, which was owned by Martha Washington.

2 large Bermuda onions, thinly sliced	1½ teaspoons salt
1 quart milk	1 egg yolk
½ teaspoon mace blades	Chopped parsley
½ cup (1 stick) butter	Croutons

Place onions, milk, mace, butter, and salt in a saucepan. Bring to a boil, then reduce heat, and cook slowly for 30 to 40 minutes or until onions are very tender. Pick out mace blades and discard. Beat egg yolk in a small bowl, then add a little of the hot soup, beating constantly. Pour egg mixture into soup and cook a minute or two to thicken slightly. Sprinkle each serving with finely chopped parsley, then add a few croutons. Serves 4.

To make toasted croutons: Toast old firm bread, then cut into tiny squares.

Hot soup at table is very vulgar; it either leads to an unseemly mode of taking it, or keeps people waiting too long whilst it cools. Soup should be brought to table only moderately warm.
—Charles Day, *Hints on Etiquette,* 1844

CRÈME VICHYSSOISE GLACÉ

In 1910, when the roof garden was opened at the Ritz-Carlton on 46th Street and Madison Avenue, chef Louis Diat celebrated by presenting Manhattan society with a new soup. It was one his mother had made— the traditional hot leek-and-potato peasant soup of France, cooled with rich, sweet milk. It was refined by *le maître,* named Vichyssoise after the fashionable French watering spot, Vichy, and was served for the first time to Charles Schwab, the steel magnate.

4 leeks	1 tablespoon salt
1 onion, sliced	2 cups milk
2 tablespoons butter	1 cup light cream
6 medium potatoes, sliced	1 cup heavy cream
1 quart chicken broth or water or combination of both	Chives, chopped fine

Wash leeks very carefully and discard green stalks. Slice the white part, combine with onion, and cook in melted butter until limp but not brown. Add potato slices, chicken broth, and salt. Bring to a boil and boil 35 minutes. Rub through a fine strainer or purée in an electric blender, return to heat, and add milk and light cream. Season to taste and bring to a boil. Do not cook further. Finally, add the heavy cream and chill thoroughly in the refrigerator. Serve in cups with a sprinkling of finely chopped chives on top. Serves 8.

Crayfish

BISQUE D'ÉCREVISSE
(*Crayfish Bisque*)

8 quarts live crayfish
1 tablespoon vinegar
Leaves from 1 bunch celery
4 tablespoons butter
2 large onions
4 cloves garlic
1 cup fine dry bread crumbs
2 tablespoons chopped parsley
1 tablespoon lemon juice
Cayenne
Tabasco
Salt
2 eggs

¾ cup flour
2 carrots, chopped fine
1 parsnip, chopped fine
6 ripe tomatoes, skinned and chopped, or
   1 can (1 pound, 3 ounces) solid-
   pack tomatoes
3 sprigs parsley
2 sprigs (¼ teaspoon dried) thyme
2 sprigs (¼ teaspoon dried) basil
1 bay leaf
Hot steamed rice
4 shallots, chopped fine

Wash the crayfish thoroughly under running water. If the bellies are silty, scrub with a stiff brush. Place in a very large deep kettle, cover with cold water, add 2 or 3 tablespoons of salt, and let stand about an hour. Drain, cover with fresh water, add vinegar and celery leaves. Cover, and cook over a low heat until water boils, then simmer gently for 5 minutes. Strain and reserve the liquid. Crack the tender shell of the tails, pick out the meat, and place in a bowl. Shake the fat from the bodies (or heads) into a second bowl by gently tapping the bottom of the heads. Save about 30 of the largest heads to stuff.

To make the stuffing: Heat *2 tablespoons of the butter* in a saucepan. Toss in *1 onion* and *2 cloves of garlic,* both chopped fine. Cook over a low heat until straw colored. Add half the crayfish fat and all the crayfish tails, coarsely chopped. Cook, stirring constantly, for several minutes. Mix in crumbs, 1 cup of strained liquid in which crayfish cooked, chopped parsley, lemon juice, cayenne, Tabasco, and salt to taste. Continue cooking for about 15 minutes. Remove from heat, beat in eggs thoroughly, and stuff the crayfish heads generously. Save any leftover stuffing. Place stuffed heads on a tray or in a shallow baking dish, dot with butter, and set aside.

To make the bisque: Put flour into a skillet and cook over a moderate heat, stirring constantly, until light brown in color. Cook remaining onion and garlic, both chopped fine, in a large soup kettle with 2 tablespoons of butter and remainder of the crayfish fat until limp. Stir in browned flour until smooth, then add 2 quarts of the strained crayfish liquid, carrots, parsnip, tomatoes, any leftover stuffing, parsley, thyme, basil, bay leaf, additional salt, cayenne, and Tabasco—enough to give a slight bite to the bisque. Simmer over a low heat, without a cover, for 1½ hours, stirring occasionally. Thirty minutes before bisque has finished cooking, bake stuffed crayfish heads in a preheated 350° oven for 15 minutes. Place carefully in the bisque and continue simmering for the final 15 minutes. Serve over steamed rice with a sprinkling of shallots on top. Serves 8.

NEW ENGLAND CLAM CHOWDER

Several centuries ago, in the coastal villages of France, when a fishing fleet came home each man threw a share of his catch into a huge copper pot—*la chaudière*—and the community shared in a feast celebrating the safe return of the fishermen. The tradition found its way to Canada, then drifted down the coast to New England, where *la chaudière* became "chowder"—any concoction made of fish or shellfish or both. The most famous of the American chowders is Clam Chowder, with its two essential ingredients: clams and salt pork or bacon. But "essential" is a prickly word. Every New Englander worth his salty independence has his own version of what is essential to Clam Chowder. The most notable heresy is Manhattan Clam Chowder, which calls for water rather than milk—and tomatoes! Down Easters are so nettled over the Tomato Question that the Maine legislature once introduced a bill to outlaw forever the mixing of clams and tomatoes.

1 quart clams with liquor	3 tablespoons butter
3 cups water	1¾ cups half-and-half (milk and cream)
2 slices salt pork, chopped	1 tablespoon salt
1 medium onion, sliced	Dash of pepper
3 medium potatoes, cut in small cubes	

Combine clams, liquor, and water and cook to a boil. Drain, reserving the broth. Mince the necks and the coarse membranes, chop the rest. Set all aside. Fry the salt pork until lightly browned, stir in onion, and cook until limp but not brown. Add the clam broth and potatoes and cook until potatoes are tender. Then stir in butter, half-and-half, salt, pepper, and clams. Heat but do not boil, pour immediately into large, warmed soup bowls. Serve with crackers. Serves 6 to 8.

MANHATTAN CLAM CHOWDER

½ pound bacon, chopped fine	1 pint clams in liquor
4 medium onions, chopped fine	2 teaspoons salt
4 carrots, chopped fine	¼ teaspoon freshly ground pepper
2 stalks celery, chopped fine	1½ teaspoons dried thyme
2 tablespoons chopped parsley	1 bay leaf
1 can (1 pound, 13 ounce size) tomatoes	3 medium potatoes, diced fine

Fry bacon in a large saucepan or kettle until almost crisp. Toss in onions and cook until they take on color. Next, stir in carrots, celery, and parsley and cook over a low heat for about 8 minutes. Drain tomatoes, putting liquid into a measuring cup. Add tomato pulp to saucepan. Drain clams, mixing the liquor with the tomato liquid. Add enough water to make 1½ quarts of liquid and pour into saucepan. Season with salt, pepper, thyme, bay leaf, and cook to a boil. Reduce heat and simmer gently for 40 minutes. Add potatoes, cover, and cook about 20 minutes. Finally, add the clams, chopped, and simmer 15 minutes longer. Serves 6 generously.

CODFISH CHOWDER

4 pounds fresh cod
2-inch cube of salt pork
1 onion, sliced
6 cups thinly sliced potatoes
4 cups milk

1 tablespoon salt
¼ teaspoon pepper, freshly ground
3 tablespoons butter
8 common crackers, split in half

Have your fish dealer clean and skin the fish. Be sure to ask for the head, tail, backbone, and other trimmings. Cut the cod into 2-inch pieces and set aside. Put head, tail, and all the trimmings in a saucepan with 2 cups of water. Heat to the boiling point, then reduce heat, and cook slowly about 20 minutes. Cut salt pork in small chunks and fry over a low heat until crisp. Stir in onion slices and cook until limp. Parboil potato slices for 5 minutes (use enough boiling water to cover). Drain. Add the potatoes and 2 cups of boiling water to salt-pork mixture. Cook 5 minutes. Add liquid drained from fish bones, then add the cod. Cover and simmer for 10 minutes. Scald milk, pour into fish mixture, and add salt, pepper, butter, and crackers. Heat until piping hot. Serves 6 to 8.

Four tablespoonfuls of onions, fried with pork. One quart of boiled potatoes, well mashed. One and a half pounds sea-biscuit, broken. One teaspoonful of thyme, mixed with one of summer savory. Half-bottle of mushroom catsup. One bottle of port or claret. Half of a nutmeg, grated. A few cloves, mace, and allspice. Six pounds of fish, sea-bass or cod, cut in slices. Twenty-five oysters, a little black pepper, and a few slices of lemon. The whole put in a pot and covered with an inch of water, boiled for an hour, and gently stirred.
—Daniel Webster's chowder recipe, from *The Cook,* 1885

MULLIGATAWNY SOUP

A 3-pound chicken, cut in pieces
¼ cup butter
½ cup chopped carrots
½ cup chopped green pepper
2 greening apples, cored and chopped
1 tablespoon flour
2 teaspoons curry powder

2 quarts chicken broth
2 whole cloves
Pinch mace
Few sprigs parsley, chopped
1 tablespoon sugar
¼ teaspoon pepper
1 tablespoon salt

Sauté chicken pieces in heated butter until well browned. Stir in carrots, green pepper, and apples, and continue cooking, stirring frequently, until mixture is brown. Sprinkle in flour and curry powder. Add broth, a little at a time. Season with all remaining ingredients. Cook to a boil, then reduce heat, cover, and simmer gently until chicken is very tender. Remove chicken from soup and cool until it can be handled comfortably. Strain the soup, working vegetables through a sieve, then return to kettle, and heat. Strip chicken from bones (discard bones and skin) and add to soup. Serve hot with steamed rice. Serves 6 to 8.

BREADS

ANADAMA BREAD

One story that was repeated in Massachusetts in the nineteenth century was of the fisherman who became enraged with his wife. All she gave him for dinner was corn meal and molasses—day after day. One night, when he could no longer control his anger, he tossed flour and yeast into the corn meal and molasses, put it all in the oven, and sat down later to eat a loaf of bread that had no name, mumbling, "Anna, damn her!"

½ cup corn meal	1 package active dry yeast or
3 tablespoons shortening	1 cake compressed
¼ cup molasses	¼ cup warm water
2 teaspoons salt	1 egg, beaten
¾ cup boiling water	3 cups sifted all-purpose flour

Combine corn meal, shortening, molasses, salt, and boiling water in a large bowl. Let stand until lukewarm. Sprinkle yeast over warm water to dissolve, then stir yeast, egg, and *half of the flour* into corn-meal mixture. Beat vigorously. Stir in remaining flour and mix thoroughly until dough forms a soft ball. Use your hand if it seems easier. Transfer to a greased loaf pan, cover with a cloth, and set in a warm place until dough reaches 1 inch above the pan. Sprinkle top with a little corn meal and salt. Bake in a preheated 350° oven for 50 to 55 minutes. Cool before slicing.

SAFFRON BREAD

¼ teaspoon saffron	½ teaspoon salt
2 cups milk	½ teaspoon nutmeg
½ cup melted butter or shortening	6 to 7 cups sifted all-purpose flour
1 package active dry yeast or 1 cake compressed	½ cup candied lemon peel, chopped
1 cup sugar	2 cups currants

Steep saffron in ½ cup boiling water for at least 30 minutes, then strain, saving the saffron liquid. Scald milk, pour into a large mixing bowl, add saffron liquid, and stir in melted shortening. Dissolve yeast in 2 tablespoons warm water and stir into warm (not hot) milk. Add sugar, salt, and nutmeg, then sift in the flour. Add candied lemon peel and currants. Mix thoroughly. Dough should be quite stiff. Cover with a tea towel and let stand in a warm place, away from drafts, until double in size. This takes about 1½ hours. Now punch the dough down with your fist and knead on a floured board until smooth. Divide in half, shape into loaves, and place in 2 greased loaf pans. Let rise a second time until double in size. Bake in a preheated 350° oven about 1 hour. Remove from oven and brush tops of loaves with melted butter. Cool in pans about 10 minutes before turning out. Do not slice until bread has cooled completely. Cut in thin slices and toast, if you wish. Serve with sweet butter.

SHAKER DAILY LOAF

½ package active dry yeast or
  ½ cake compressed
2 tablespoons warm water
1 cup milk

1 tablespoon butter
1 tablespoon sugar
1 teaspoon salt
3½ cups sifted all-purpose flour

Sprinkle yeast over warm water and stir until dissolved. Combine milk, butter, sugar, and salt and heat. Skim off the film and cool to lukewarm, then stir in the yeast. Mix in flour as thoroughly as possible, brush surface with a little melted butter, cover with a tea towel, and set in a warm place until double in size. Transfer to a lightly floured board and knead until satiny smooth. Shape into a loaf and place in a greased loaf pan. Again brush the top with melted butter and let rise a second time until double in size. Bake in a preheated 350° oven for 50 minutes.

SWEDISH RYE BREAD

⅓ cup molasses
1¼ cups water
⅓ cup brown sugar, firmly packed
½ tablespoon aniseed
1 teaspoon salt
1 teaspoon grated orange or lemon rind

1 tablespoon shortening
1 package active dry yeast or
  1 cake compressed
2 cups sifted rye flour
3½ cups sifted all-purpose flour

Combine molasses, water, brown sugar, aniseed, salt, orange or lemon rind, and shortening in a saucepan. Heat to boiling point, then boil 5 minutes. Cool to lukewarm, then stir in yeast until dissolved. Beat in rye flour, cover with a tea towel, and let rise in a warm spot for 4 to 6 hours or overnight. Beat in white flour and knead until thoroughly blended. Let rise in a warm place until double in size. Divide in half, shape into 2 round flat loaves, and place in well-greased 9-inch pie pans. Let rise a third time for 1½ hours. Bake in a preheated 300° oven for 1 hour. Brush crust with melted butter, then cool before cutting.

BOSTON BROWN BREAD

"It was a common saying among the Puritans," Matthew Henry reported in his *Commentaries,* published in the early eighteenth century, "'Brown bread and the Gospel is good fare.'"

1 cup rye flour
1 cup corn meal
1 cup Graham flour
¾ teaspoon baking soda

1 teaspoon salt
¾ cup molasses
2 cups buttermilk
1 cup chopped raisins (optional)

Sift all dry ingredients together, add molasses, buttermilk, raisins. Divide batter and place in 2 buttered 1-quart pudding molds or 3 buttered 1-pound coffee cans, filling them about ¾ full. Molds must be covered tightly, with buttered lids tied and taped so the bread won't force the cover off on rising. Place molds in a pan filled with enough boiling water to reach halfway up the mold and steam for 3 hours, keeping water at the halfway mark. Serve piping hot with butter and Boston Baked Beans (page 527).

SOURDOUGH BREAD

Sourdough may be the oldest of all breads, dating as far back as 4,000 B.C., but—according to one theory—it was unknown in America until Columbus landed with a sourdough starter in the hold of his ship. Sourdough starter is simply a self-perpetuating yeast mixture, made by combining flour, sugar, and water. The bread became identified with America because of the Alaskan sourdoughs—prospectors who carried sourdough starter pots strapped to their packs so that they could make a batch of bread whenever they felt the need, without walking fifty miles to the nearest town for a bit of yeast.

1 cup sourdough starter	6 cups unsifted all-purpose flour
1 package active dry yeast or	2 teaspoons salt
1 cake compressed	2 teaspoons sugar
1½ cups warm water	½ teaspoon baking soda

To make sourdough starter: Mix together 1 cup flour, 1 cup water, and 1 tablespoon sugar and let the mixture stand in a warm place 2 to 3 days or until fermented. Sourdough starter may also be purchased.

Sprinkle yeast over warm water to dissolve. Stir in the sourdough starter, *4 cups of the flour*, salt, and sugar. Stir vigorously for 3 minutes. Transfer to a large greased bowl, cover with a tea towel, and let rise in a warm place until double in size. This takes about 2 hours. Mix baking soda with *1 cup of the remaining flour* and stir into dough. Turn dough onto a floured board and knead in remaining cup of flour (even a little more, if necessary) until dough is smooth and not sticky. Shape it into one large round loaf or 2 oblong loaves and place on a lightly greased cooky sheet. Cover and let rise in a warm place until nearly double in size. Before baking, brush surface with water and score or slash the top diagonally with a sharp knife. Before putting bread in the oven to bake, place a shallow pan of hot water in the bottom of the oven. Bake bread in a preheated 400° oven for 45 to 50 minutes.

OATMEAL BREAD

¾ cup milk	1½ teaspoons salt
1 package active dry yeast or	½ cup dark molasses
1 cake compressed	1 tablespoon butter
1 cup quick-cooking oatmeal	5 cups sifted all-purpose flour
1¼ cups boiling water	

Heat milk until a film forms. Skim surface. Remove from heat and, when lukewarm, stir in the yeast. Put oatmeal in a large bowl. Stir in boiling water, salt, molasses, and butter. Cool to lukewarm, then mix in flour and milk thoroughly. Use your hands because the dough is very heavy. Cover bowl with a clean tea towel and set in a warm spot away from drafts until dough doubles in size (about 1½ hours). Turn out on a floured board and knead lightly for about 3 minutes. Divide in half, shape into 2 loaves, and place in greased loaf pans. Let bread rise a second time until double in size. Bake in a preheated 350° oven for about 1 hour. Remove from oven and brush crust with melted butter. Cool slightly, then remove from pans, and cool completely on a rack. A delicious bread that keeps well.

SALT RISING BREAD

Sometimes called lightnin' bread, Salt Rising Bread was popular at a time when homemade yeasts were both unreliable and troublesome to prepare and keep.

2 cups milk
2 cups white corn meal
1 tablespoon sugar
1 teaspoon salt

½ teaspoon baking soda
8-10 cups sifted all-purpose flour
2 tablespoons shortening

Scald milk, remove from heat, and stir in corn meal, sugar, and salt until smooth. Cover with a tea towel and set in a warm place overnight. The following morning, add 1 cup warm water mixed with baking soda and *about 2½ cups flour* (enough to make a rather stiff batter). Set the bowl of batter in a pan of warm water, cover, and let stand until it foams up (this can take from 2 hours to half a day). Try to keep the water at an even temperature all the time —not too hot, not too cold. If it seems as though the batter is not rising, give it a stir to help it along. Some people object to the odor during this period but, as *Practical Housekeeping* explained, this is "the result of acetous [or sour] fermentation, but the more of that the more sure you are of having sweet bread when baked." When the batter has risen, knead in shortening and more flour (it may take as many as 8 cups) to make a stiff bread dough. Shape into 2 loaves, set in greased loaf pans, and let rise until double in bulk. Bake in a preheated 350° oven for about 1 hour or until light brown in color.

A RISE IN BREAD-STUFFS!—EFFECTS OF EATING AËRATED BREAD.

Magazine cartoon, 1860

435

MORAVIAN SUGAR CAKE

2 medium potatoes
1 package active dry yeast or
  1 cake compressed
½ cup warm water
¼ cup soft butter
½ cup shortening
1 cup sugar

1 teaspoon salt
2 eggs, well beaten
4 cups sifted all-purpose flour (about)
Butter
Brown Sugar
Cinnamon

Pare potatoes and cook in boiling water until tender. Drain (reserve 1 cup of the water) and mash potatoes until smooth. Sprinkle yeast over warm water to dissolve. Combine hot mashed potatoes with butter, shortening, sugar, and salt. Mix thoroughly and, when cooled to lukewarm, stir in 1 cup of potato water and the dissolved yeast. Cover with a tea towel and place in a warm spot until spongy-looking. Beat the mixture with eggs and enough flour to make a soft dough. Cover again and let rise in a warm place until double in size. Divide dough in half and make an even layer in 2 greased 11¼ x 7½ x 1½-inch baking pans. Let rise the third time until light, then with your finger poke holes in the dough, filling the holes with generous amounts of butter and brown sugar. Sprinkle top with cinnamon and bake in a preheated 375° oven for 20 to 30 minutes. Cool and cut into squares to serve.

PHILADELPHIA STICKY BUNS

In the nineteenth century, Sticky Buns—a Philadelphia specialty—were sold fresh every day and were eaten at breakfast, teatime, and dinner.

1 package active dry yeast or
  1 cake compressed
¼ cup lukewarm water
1 cup milk
4½ cups sifted all-purpose flour
½ cup plus 2 tablespoons butter,
  melted

6 tablespoons sugar
2 egg yolks, well beaten
1 teaspoon salt
Grated rind of 1 lemon
1 teaspoon cinnamon
½ cup currants
¾ cup brown sugar

Sprinkle yeast over lukewarm water to dissolve. Scald milk, remove from heat, and cool to lukewarm. Combine milk, yeast, and *1½ cups of the flour* and beat vigorously until smooth. Cover with a tea towel and let stand in a warm place, away from drafts, until light or until mixture has big dimples on the surface. Now add *4 tablespoons of melted butter, 4 tablespoons sugar,* egg yolks, salt, grated lemon, and the remaining 3 cups of flour. Knead the mixture, right in the bowl, until smooth and springy. Cover with a tea towel and let rise in a warm place until double in size—this takes several hours. Transfer dough to a floured board and roll about ¾ of an inch thick in a long rectangular shape (dough is elastic and springs back, but persevere). Brush the surface with *2 tablespoons of melted butter* and sprinkle with remaining 2 tablespoons of sugar, the cinnamon, and currants. Roll tightly and cut in 1-inch slices. Work brown sugar with remaining butter, spreading it over the bottom of a heavy skillet. Place the swirls of dough on top of sugar mixture, spacing them evenly, and let rise again, in a warm place, until double in size. Bake in a preheated 350° oven for 30 minutes or until well browned on top. Invert skillet over cooling rack. Makes 12.

SALLY LUNN

There are several old accounts of the origin of the name "Sally Lunn." One of the more appealing is about an English girl who sold bread on the streets, crying "Solet Lune!" to advertise the buns. The sun and the moon—*soleil-lune,* as it is in French—were the images evoked to describe the golden tops and white bottoms of the buns. By the time *soleil-lune* reached America it had become Sally Lunn and, rather than a bun, was a bread baked in a Turk's-head mold.

1 cup milk	⅓ cup sugar
1 package active dry yeast or	3 eggs
1 cake compressed	4 cups sifted all-purpose flour
½ cup (1 stick) butter	1 teaspoon salt

Heat milk until a film forms. Skim. Cool until lukewarm, then sprinkle in the yeast to dissolve. Meanwhile, work the butter until soft, then add the sugar gradually, and continue working until creamy. Beat the eggs in very hard. Sift flour and salt together. Beat in the flour and the milk mixture alternately. Cover dough with a tea towel and set in a warm place until it doubles in size. Beat very hard and pour into a greased Turk's-head or *gugelhupf* mold or a 10-inch tube pan. Let rise again until double in size, then bake in a preheated 350° oven for 45 to 50 minutes or until nicely browned on top.

PANETTONE

1 cup milk	4 cups all-purpose flour
⅓ cup butter	1 teaspoon salt
1 cup sugar	1 cup currants
4 eggs	2 tablespoons brandy
1 package active dry yeast or	½ cup thinly sliced citron
1 cake compressed	1 teaspoon almond extract
1 tablespoon sugar	Sliced almonds

Scald milk. Remove from heat and cool to lukewarm. While milk cools, work butter until soft, then work in sugar, a little at a time, as thoroughly as possible. Beat in *3 whole eggs and 1 egg yolk* (set aside remaining white to use later). Sprinkle yeast over lukewarm milk, add 1 tablespoon sugar, and stir until well blended. Add to butter mixture, alternating with flour that has been sifted with salt. Beat vigorously. Soak currants in brandy and stir into dough. Add citron and almond extract. Cover bowl with a tea towel and place in a warm spot about 2 to 3 hours or until double in size. Punch down with your fist, turn out on a board sprinkled with ½ cup flour, and knead gently. Place in a greased 10-inch tube pan or Turk's-head mold, patting down the dough. Beat the egg white until it stands in peaks and brush over surface of the dough. Press a layer of thinly sliced almonds on top, cover with a tea towel, and let rise again in a warm place about 1 hour or until double in size. Bake in a preheated 350° oven for 30 to 40 minutes. *Panettone* may be made in two 6-inch molds or in four 1-pound coffee tins, all well greased. When smaller containers are used, reduce the baking time slightly.

PARKER HOUSE ROLLS

The Parker House, established in 1855, is one of Boston's newer institutions. It is also the home of Parker House Rolls, long considered the patrician of American dinner rolls.

1 package active dry yeast or
  1 cake compressed
¼ cup warm water
2 cups milk
2 tablespoons sugar

1 teaspoon salt
3 tablespoons butter
6½ to 7 cups sifted all-purpose flour
1 egg, well beaten

Dissolve yeast in warm water. Combine milk, sugar, salt, and butter in a saucepan, scald, then cool to lukewarm. Stir in yeast and *3 cups of the flour,* beating very hard. Cover with a tea towel and place in a warm spot. Let rise until light and bubbly, then mix in egg and enough of the remaining flour to make a kneadable dough. Knead well, cover again, and let stand in a warm place until double in size. Roll dough about ⅓ inch thick on a lightly floured board (dough will spring back at first). Cut with a 3-inch round cutter. Brush each circle with a little melted butter, crease center with the back of a floured knife, and fold over, pinching the edges together. Place rolls 1 inch apart on ungreased cooky sheets. Let rise again until almost double in size, then bake in a preheated 450° oven for 12 to 15 minutes. Makes about 30.

Butter molds and stamp

MORAVIAN LOVE FEAST BUNS

1 large potato
1 package active dry yeast or
  1 cake compressed
¼ cup warm water
½ cup butter, melted

1 cup sugar
1 teaspoon salt
2 eggs, well beaten
4 cups sifted all-purpose flour (about)

Pare the potato, cut in chunks, and cook in boiling water until tender. Drain, saving ½ cup of the potato water. Mash potatoes until smooth and measure out ½ cup of them. Sprinkle yeast over warm water to dissolve. Combine mashed potato, ½ cup of the reserved potato water, butter, sugar, salt, and eggs. When mixture is lukewarm, stir in yeast. Cover with a tea towel and set bowl in a warm place until mixture is spongy-looking. Then mix in the flour thoroughly. (At this point you should have a soft dough—add more flour, if needed.) Cover and let rise in a warm spot until double in size. Punch dough down and knead on a floured board until smooth. Pinch off pieces of the dough and shape into buns about 3 inches in diameter. Place on a greased cooky sheet and let rise a third time until almost double in size. Bake in a preheated 375° oven for 25 to 30 minutes. When buns begin to turn golden brown, brush tops with cream or melted butter. Cool before serving. Makes 12.

SWEET POTATO ROLLS

1 large yam	3 tablespoons sugar
1 package active dry yeast or	1 tablespoon butter
1 cake compressed	1 cup milk
1 teaspoon salt	3½ to 4½ cups sifted all-purpose flour

Pare yam and cut in several pieces. Add enough water to cover and cook until tender. Drain, saving ¼ cup of the water in which yam was cooked. Cool yam water to lukewarm and dissolve the yeast in it. Mash yam, then beat in salt, sugar, and butter vigorously. Heat milk until a film shines on top, skim, stir into yam mixture, and cool to lukewarm. When right temperature has been reached, add the softened yeast. Stir in flour, a cupful at a time, until dough is thick enough to knead. Lift onto a floured board and knead until smooth and elastic. Place in a greased bowl, cover with a tea towel, and let rise in a warm place until double in size. Punch dough down with your fist. Pinch off pieces the size of a golf ball and put into greased muffin pans. Let rise again until double in size. Bake in a preheated 425° oven for 13 to 15 minutes. Makes about 20.

KOLACHES

When the Bohemians arrived in Nebraska in the 1860's, they brought *kolaches*, often made with prune, apricot, or other fruit filling.

6 tablespoons milk	4 cups sifted all-purpose flour
2 packages active dry yeast or	*Prune Filling:*
2 cakes compressed	1 pound prunes
1 teaspoon salt	1 tablespoon sugar
2 tablespoons sugar	1 tablespoon butter
½ cup soft butter	½ teaspoon cinnamon
4 whole eggs	½ teaspoon vanilla
4 egg yolks	

Heat milk until lukewarm, add yeast, and let stand several minutes to dissolve. Stir in salt and sugar. Put butter in a large mixing bowl, add *1 whole egg and 1 egg yolk*, beating very hard. Continue adding *1 whole egg and additional yolk*, followed each time by hard beating. When all the eggs have been used, mix in yeast and then flour, beating hard. Cover with a tea towel and place in a warm spot until double in size. Pinch off pieces of dough and shape into smooth balls the size of a large walnut. Place 2 inches apart on a buttered baking sheet, cover, and let rise in a warm place for 30 minutes. Press a hollow in the center of each with your thumb and fill the cavity with marmalade, jam, or prune filling. Bake in a preheated 350° oven for 20 minutes. Remove from oven and, when cool, sprinkle tops generously with confectioners' sugar.

To make prune filling: Cook prunes according to package directions. When tender, drain, discard pits, and chop coarsely. Stir in sugar, softened butter, cinnamon, and vanilla. Taste and add sugar if necessary.

QUICK BREADS

Quick breads have one distinctive ingredient—baking powder. Until the end of the eighteenth century, lightness in baked goods could be achieved only by laboriously beating air into dough along with eggs, or by adding yeast or spirits. In the 1790's, pearlash—a refined form of potash that produces carbon dioxide in baking dough—was discovered in America. Pearlash transformed baking methods: 8,000 tons of it were exported to Europe in 1792. Amelia Simmons published several recipes in her *American Cookery* (1796) calling for pearlash.

It was not until the 1850's that baking powder (which worked in the same way as pearlash or saleratus, except that it was new and improved) was commercially produced, first by Preston and Merrill of Boston. In 1857, Professor E. N. Horsford of Harvard developed a formula for phosphate baking powder which moved *Practical Housekeeping* to declare, "Horsford's Bread Preparation saves time, simplifies the whole process of bread-making, saves labor, and reduces the chances of failure to the minimum . . . It is certain that for rolls, biscuits, griddle-cakes, and the whole list of 'Breakfast and Tea Cakes,' the 'Bread Preparation' is superior to yeast or soda."

PECAN BREAD

2½ cups sifted all-purpose flour
1 cup sugar
1 teaspoon salt
2 teaspoons baking powder

2 cups (two 3-ounce cans) pecans, chopped
2 eggs
1 cup milk

Sift the flour, sugar, salt, and baking powder together in a mixing bowl and stir in the pecans. Beat eggs vigorously in a separate bowl until very thick, add the milk, and stir into the flour-nut mixture. Pour into a greased loaf pan and bake in a preheated 350° oven for 1 hour. Turn out of the pan onto a cake rack and cool. Keeps well, wrapped in foil.

BLACK WALNUT BREAD

3 cups sifted all-purpose flour
4½ teaspoons baking powder
½ cup sugar
1 teaspoon salt

1 cup chopped black walnuts
2 eggs
1 cup milk
¼ cup butter, melted

Sift flour, baking powder, sugar, and salt together into a mixing bowl, then stir in the nuts. Beat the eggs, milk, and melted butter, add to flour mixture, and stir until thoroughly blended. Don't attempt to beat out all the lumps. Spoon into a greased loaf pan and bake in a preheated 350° oven for 1 hour. Turn out of pan and cool before serving.

BANANA BREAD

1½ cups sifted all-purpose flour
½ teaspoon baking soda
½ teaspoon baking powder
¼ teaspoon salt
½ cup butter
1 cup sugar
2 eggs

1 teaspoon vanilla
Grated rind of half a lemon
¾ cup mashed ripe bananas
2 tablespoons commercial sour cream
½ cup chopped walnuts or
    Macadamia nuts

Sift together flour, baking soda, baking powder, and salt. Set aside. Work butter until soft, then work in sugar, a little at a time, until smooth. Beat in eggs, one at a time, add the vanilla, grated lemon rind, and bananas. Stir in flour mixture alternately with sour cream. Last of all, mix in the nuts. Pour into a greased loaf pan and bake in a preheated 350° oven for 1 hour or until a toothpick tested in the center comes out dry. Remove from pan and cool on a rack. Cut in thin slices to serve.

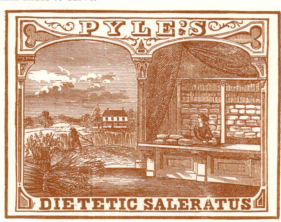

1867 label

CINNAMON FLOP

Topping:
1 cup brown sugar
4 tablespoons softened butter
½ teaspoon cinnamon
Dough:
2 cups sifted all-purpose flour

2 teaspoons baking powder
¼ teaspoon salt
1½ cups sugar
2 tablespoons softened butter
1 egg, well beaten
1 cup milk

Make topping first: Work brown sugar and butter together with your finger tips until well mixed. Then work in cinnamon.

To make dough: Sift flour, baking powder, and salt together and set aside. Mix sugar and butter with your finger tips until butter is well dispersed. Stir in beaten egg thoroughly, then add flour and milk alternately, beginning and ending with flour. Pour into a greased 8-inch square pan, sprinkle the topping over the surface, and bake in a preheated 425° oven for 30 to 35 minutes. Served warm, it makes a delicious breakfast bread.

BISCUITS

The Marquis de Chastellux, traveling through North America in the early 1780's, wrote of a meal he had at the Bullion Tavern in Basking Ridge, New Jersey: "Our supper was very good: only bread was lacking; but inquiring of us what sort we wanted, in an hour's time they served us what we had asked for. This speed will appear less extraordinary if one knows that in America little cakes (*galettes*), which are easily kneaded and baked in half an hour often take the place of bread. Possibly one might . . . tire of them, but I always found them to my taste whenever I met with them." M. Chastellux was describing what Americans commonly call biscuits, which, though rare in most parts of the world, have always been an indispensable ingredient in American cuisine. Recipes for some of the most popular American biscuits, including a few for the cocktail hour, follow.

RICH SHORT BISCUITS

2 cups all-purpose flour or pastry flour
4 teaspoons baking powder
Dash of salt

½ cup (1 stick) butter
Milk

Sift flour, baking powder, and salt into a bowl. Add butter (straight from the refrigerator) cut into 4 or 5 pieces, and work into flour mixture with a pastry blender or two knives until butter is about the size of peas. Add cold milk, a little at a time, stirring it in with a fork. Use only enough milk to hold the dough together. The less you use, the better your biscuits. Now work the dough together with your hands until you've made a ball and all the flour is worked in. Roll dough about ½ inch thick on a lightly floured board, cut with very small biscuit cutter, and place on an ungreased cooky sheet. If you have the time, refrigerate the biscuits for an hour or longer. Bake in a preheated 450° oven for 10 to 12 minutes or until biscuits are lightly browned. Serve hot with fresh, sweet butter. Excellent with cold salads or served with thin slices of Smithfield ham as a cocktail accompaniment. Makes about 20.

CORN MEAL BISCUITS

¾ cup milk
1 cup corn meal
2 tablespoons shortening

¾ teaspoon salt
¾ cup sifted all-purpose flour
4 teaspoons baking powder

Scald milk. Combine corn meal, shortening, and salt in a mixing bowl, then stir in the hot milk until mixture is smooth and shortening has melted. Cool. Sift flour and baking powder together and stir into cold corn-meal mixture. Dump onto a lightly floured board and roll about ¾ inch thick. Cut with a small biscuit cutter, place on ungreased cooky sheet, and bake in a preheated 425° oven for 15 to 20 minutes. The biscuits have a crunchy "bite" to them. Serve hot with butter and, perhaps, maple syrup or honey. Makes about 15.

CREAM BISCUITS

2 cups sifted all-purpose flour
½ teaspoon salt

3 teaspoons baking powder
1 cup heavy cream

Sift flour, salt, and baking powder together in a bowl. In a second bowl, whip the cream until stiff enough to hold a shape. Combine cream and flour mixture with a fork. Place dough on a lightly floured board and knead for about one minute. Pat dough ½ inch thick and cut with a biscuit cutter. Bake in a preheated 450° oven for about 12 minutes. Serve piping hot with plenty of butter. Makes about a dozen medium-sized biscuits.

BUTTERMILK BISCUITS

2 cups sifted all-purpose flour
1 teaspoon baking soda
1 teaspoon baking powder

1 teaspoon salt
1 cup buttermilk or commercial sour cream

Sift flour, baking soda, baking powder, and salt together into a bowl. Add buttermilk or sour cream and blend with a fork until you have a soft dough. Place on a lightly floured board and roll ½ inch thick. Cut with a small biscuit cutter, place on a cooky sheet, and bake in a preheated 425° oven for 12 to 15 minutes or until tipped with gold. Serve piping hot with butter and with honey or strawberry preserves on the side. Makes 12 to 15.

Buttermilk vendor

BENNE SEED COCKTAIL BISCUITS

½ cup benne (sesame) seeds
2 cups sifted all-purpose flour
½ teaspoon salt
1 teaspoon baking powder

½ cup shortening
¼ cup milk (about)
Coarse salt

While you make the dough, toast the benne seeds in a shallow pan in a preheated 350° oven. Sift together flour, salt, and baking powder. Cream shortening until soft, then add the flour mixture, working it in with your hand until it is well combined. Work in the benne seeds. Gradually add milk, stirring with a fork, until dough holds together and has the "feel" of pastry. Roll paper-thin on a lightly floured board and cut with a very small biscuit cutter. Place on a cooky sheet and bake in a 350° oven for 10 to 12 minutes. Sprinkle with coarse salt while they are still hot. Makes about 40 or even more, depending on size of cutter.

BEATEN BISCUITS

In her *New Cookery Book* (1857), Eliza Leslie slighted a southern tradition almost as sanctified as southern belles—Beaten Biscuits. "This is the most laborious of cakes," Miss Leslie said, "and also the most unwholesome, even when made in the best manner. We do not recommend it; but there is no accounting for tastes. Children should not eat these biscuits—nor grown persons either, if they can get any other sort of bread. When living in a town where there are bakers, there is no excuse for making Maryland biscuit. Believe nobody that says they are not unwholesome. . . . Better to live on Indian cakes."

In 1885, Mary Stuart Smith, in her *Virginia Cookery-Book*, replied, "In the Virginia of the olden time no breakfast or tea-table was thought to be properly furnished without a plate of these indispensable biscuits. . . . Let one spend the night at some gentleman-farmer's home, and the first sound heard in the morning, after the crowing of the cock, was the heavy, regular fall of the cook's axe, as she beat and beat her biscuit dough. . . . Nowadays beaten biscuits are a rarity, found here and there, but soda and modern institutions have caused them to be sadly out of vogue."

2 cups flour	1½ teaspoons sugar
½ teaspoon salt	2 tablespoons lard
½ teaspoon baking powder	⅓ to ½ cup water and milk, mixed

Sift dry ingredients together, then cut in lard until mixture appears mealy. Add liquid, a little at a time, to make a stiff dough. Knead thoroughly, then beat with a heavy mallet for half an hour or run several times through the coarse chopper of a meat grinder until dough is elastic. Roll ½ inch thick and cut with small biscuit cutter. Prick tops with fork tines and bake on a cooky sheet in a 325° oven for 35 to 45 minutes or until lightly browned. Makes about 2 dozen.

LOG CABIN CHEESE STRAWS

¼ cup soft butter	Dash cayenne
1 cup grated Cheddar cheese	¾ cup sifted all-purpose flour
¼ cup milk	1½ cups fine soft bread crumbs
¼ teaspoon salt	*Topping:* coarse salt, grated Parmesan
Dash Tabasco	cheese, poppy seeds, or sesame seeds
Dash paprika	

Work butter until creamy, then blend in cheese, milk, salt, Tabasco, paprika, and cayenne. Add flour and bread crumbs, combining thoroughly. Divide mixture in half and refrigerate for several hours or overnight. Roll one portion of the dough at a time, between 2 sheets of wax paper, until quite thin. Work quickly because this very rich pastry will readily soften. With a pastry wheel (called a jagger in old recipes) or knife cut pastry into strips about 5 inches long and ¾ inch wide. Place on a cooky sheet, sprinkle with any one of the suggested toppings, and bake in a preheated 350° oven for 12 to 15 minutes or until delicately browned. Pile log-cabin style on platter. Serve with cocktails or salad. Makes about 40.

CHEDDAR BISCUITS

1 cup sifted all-purpose flour
¼ teaspoon salt

⅓ cup butter
1 cup grated Cheddar cheese

Sift flour and salt together into a bowl. Cut in butter with a pastry blender or two knives, then mix in cheese. Mix lightly with your hand until dough holds together. Roll about ½ inch thick on a lightly floured board. Cut with a small biscuit cutter and prick tops with fork tines. Place on an ungreased cooky sheet and bake in a preheated 350° oven for 12 to 15 minutes. Properly baked, the biscuits should be a rich Cheddar color, not brown. These biscuits taste best cold. Serve with cocktails or as a companion to a simple green salad. They keep well. Makes 22 to 24 biscuits.

Making butter curls

FLASH UN KAS

Flash un Kas is a Pennsylvania Dutch corruption of the German *Fleisch und Käse,* meaning meat and cheese.

2 cups all-purpose flour
Pinch of salt

1 cup (2 sticks) butter
1 package (8-ounce size) cream cheese

Sift flour and salt together in a bowl, then cut in butter and cream cheese with a pastry blender or two knives until mixture appears mealy. Gather into a ball and chill several hours or overnight. Pinch off bits of the pastry and roll as thin as possible on a lightly floured board. Work fast. Cut with a 2-inch round cooky cutter and place on a baking sheet. Spread with any of these fillings: canned liver *pâté* seasoned with a little Worcestershire sauce; ground Smithfield ham highly seasoned with steak sauce and a little ketchup; anchovy paste; caviar. Fold the circles to make a half moon, press edges together, and bake in a preheated 400° oven until delicately browned. Traditionally served with cold beer. Makes 12 to 15.

HOMEMADE CRACKERS

4 cups all-purpose flour
2 tablespoons sugar
1 teaspoon salt

¼ cup butter
1 cup milk

Sift together flour, sugar, and salt. Cut in butter with a pastry blender or two knives until mixture looks mealy. Stir in enough milk to make a stiff dough. Roll about ¼ inch thick on a lightly floured board and cut with a large round cooky cutter. Prick surface in many places with fork tines and brush lightly with milk. Place on an ungreased baking sheet and bake in a 425° oven for 15 to 18 minutes or until light gold in color. Makes several dozen.

POPOVERS

1 cup sifted all-purpose flour
½ teaspoon salt
2 eggs

1 cup milk
1 tablespoon vegetable oil

Grease aluminum or iron popover pans and set them aside or, if custard cups are used, heat in the oven and grease just before filling with batter. Combine all ingredients in a bowl and beat until smooth. Fill pans or cups slightly less than half-full. Bake in a preheated 425° oven about 35 minutes (do not open oven door during baking). Serve immediately to 6.

BLUEBERRY MUFFINS

In 1894, recalling a breakfast in Boston he had had some years earlier with Oliver Wendell Holmes's publisher, James T. Fields, William Dean Howells wrote, "I remember his burlesque pretence that morning of an inextinguishable grief when I owned that I had never eaten blueberry cake before, and how he kept returning to the pathos of the fact that there should be a region of the earth where blueberry cake was unknown." There are those—though Mr. Howells apparently did not share this confusion—who think they have eaten blueberry muffins when, in fact, they have eaten huckleberry muffins. Though the difference is slight, it is one Howells' friend Holmes would have seized upon: the blueberry is a *Vaccinium,* and the huckleberry a *Gaylussacia;* the blueberry has many small seeds, and the huckleberry has ten hard, quite noticeable seeds.

1½ cups sifted all-purpose flour
1½ teaspoons baking powder
¼ teaspoon salt
5 tablespoons softened butter

½ cup sugar
1 egg
½ cup milk
1 cup fresh blueberries

Sift together flour, baking powder, and salt. Set aside. Cream butter, add sugar a little at a time, and continue creaming until mixture is smooth and fluffy. Beat in the egg vigorously. Then stir in flour combination and milk, alternating them and beginning and ending with flour. Fold in blueberries and spoon into a well-greased muffin tin. Bake in a preheated 400° oven for 25 to 30 minutes. Makes 12.

SQUASH GEMS

1½ cups sifted all-purpose flour
¼ teaspoon salt
½ cup sugar
2 teaspoons baking powder

1 egg
¾ cup milk
½ cup frozen squash, thawed
1 tablespoon butter, melted

Sift together flour, salt, sugar, and baking powder. Beat egg vigorously and stir in milk, squash, and butter. Stir into dry ingredients, using as few strokes as possible. Pour into a well-greased muffin tin and bake in a preheated 425° oven for 25 to 30 minutes. Makes 12.

GRAHAM GEMS

1 cup sifted all-purpose flour
¾ teaspoon salt
2 tablespoons brown sugar
3 teaspoons baking powder

1 cup Graham or whole-wheat flour
1 egg
1 cup milk
3 tablespoons shortening, melted

Sift together flour, salt, brown sugar, and baking powder. Stir in Graham or whole-wheat flour thoroughly. Beat egg vigorously in a separate bowl, then stir in milk and melted shortening. Stir into flour mixture until blended—don't attempt to beat out the lumps. Pour into a greased muffin tin and bake in a preheated 400° oven for 15 to 20 minutes or until a toothpick tested in the center comes out dry. Serve warm with butter. Makes 12.

CRANBERRY MUFFINS

2 cups sifted all-purpose flour
2 teaspoons baking powder
3 tablespoons sugar
½ teaspoon salt
1 cup fresh cranberries

½ cup confectioners' sugar
1 egg
1 cup milk
3 tablespoons melted butter

Sift together flour, baking powder, sugar, and salt and set aside. Cut cranberries in half and mix with confectioners' sugar. Beat egg vigorously, then stir in milk, flour combination, and butter. Stir as little as possible—the batter should be lumpy. Fold in the cranberries, spoon into greased muffin tins, and bake in a preheated 400° oven for 20 to 25 minutes or until a toothpick tested in the center comes out dry. Makes 12 to 15.

LAPLANDS

Presenting this recipe for Laplands in her *Virginia Cookery-Book*, Mary Stuart Smith declared, "Nothing in the shape of bread can be more delicate or tempting."

1 cup sifted all-purpose flour
¼ teaspoon salt

3 eggs
1 cup heavy cream

Grease a muffin tin very thoroughly. Sift flour and salt together. Separate eggs and beat the yolks in a small bowl until very thick and creamy. Whip cream until it holds a shape when you lift the beater. Now add the flour and whipped cream to egg yolks alternately, beginning and ending with flour. Finally, whip the egg whites until they stand in peaks. Dump egg batter on top of whites and mix with your hands until all white patches have disappeared. Work quickly. Spoon into muffin tin, filling half-full. Bake in a preheated 375° oven for 20 to 25 minutes. You can prepare the mixture, except for the egg whites, ahead of time. Serve hot with sweet butter. Makes 12.

447

SPICE MUFFINS

2 cups sifted all-purpose flour
½ teaspoon baking soda
1 teaspoon baking powder
½ tablespoon powdered ginger
½ teaspoon ground cloves
½ teaspoon cinnamon
½ teaspoon salt

½ teaspoon white pepper
2 tablespoons shortening
¾ cup sugar
2 eggs, well beaten
⅓ cup molasses
¼ cup buttermilk

Sift together flour, baking soda, baking powder, ginger, cloves, cinnamon, salt, and pepper. Set aside. Work shortening and sugar together in a bowl, beat in eggs vigorously, then stir in the molasses. Stir in flour mixture and buttermilk alternately. Pour batter into a greased muffin tin and bake in a preheated 350° oven for 25 to 30 minutes or until a cake tester or toothpick inserted in the center of one muffin comes out dry. Serve warm with sweet butter. Makes 12.

CORN BREADS

Benjamin Franklin wrote one of the most passionate defenses of the virtues of corn in a letter, signed "Homespun," to the London newspaper *Gazetteer* on January 2, 1766—during the dispute over the Stamp Act. "Vindex Patriae, a writer in your paper," the letter read, "comforts himself, and the India Company, with the fancy, that the Americans, should they resolve to drink no more tea, can by no means keep that Resolution, their Indian corn not affording 'an agreeable, or easy digestible breakfast.' Pray let me, an American, inform the gentleman, who seems ignorant of the matter, that Indian corn, take it for all in all, is one of the most agreeable and wholesome grains in the world . . . and that johny or hoecake, hot from the fire, is better than a Yorkshire muffin . . . Mr. Vindex's very civil letter will, I dare say, be printed in all our provincial news-papers . . . and together with the other kind, polite and humane epistles of your correspondents Pacificus, Tom Hint, etc. etc. contribute not a little to strengthen us in every resolution of advantage, to *our* country at least, if not *yours*."

There are hundreds of varieties of corn in America, all of which are derived from five families: flint, dent, soft, sweet, and popcorn. The two most popular corns for bread are flint and Boone County White, a dent corn. Flint corn is grown throughout the North; in the southern portion of the Corn Belt—from Ohio through southern Tennessee—farmers grow Boone County White, a species originated on the banks of the Wabash River by James Riley, a relative of the poet James Whitcomb Riley. This difference in northern and southern corn has, of course, always made a difference in northern and southern corn breads—it would be inexcusable to make Spoon Bread with northern flint corn.

CORN PONE

William Strachey, in his *Historie of Travell into Virginia Britania*, written in 1612, observed that the Indians "receave the flower in a platter of wood, which, blending with water, they make into flatt, broad cakes . . . they call apones, which Covering with Ashes till they be baked . . . and then washing them in faire water, lett dry with their own heate." Corn Pone, quickly picked up by the white settlers, was usually called pone when kept out of the ashes. Following the Indian tradition, when the same basic corn bread was baked in the hot ashes of an open fire, it was called ashcake.

2 cups white corn meal	4 tablespoons shortening or lard
1 teaspoon salt	¾ cup boiling water
¼ teaspoon baking soda	½ cup buttermilk (about)

Sift together corn meal, salt, and baking soda. Work in fat with finger tips until well blended. Pour in boiling water and continue to work the mixture. Gradually add enough buttermilk to make a soft dough, but one firm enough to be molded or patted into small, flat cakes. Place cakes in a hot well-greased iron skillet and bake in a preheated 350° oven for 35 to 40 minutes. Makes about 12.

CORN STICKS

½ cup sifted all-purpose flour	1½ cups corn meal
2½ teaspoons baking powder	1 egg
½ teaspoon salt	3 tablespoons melted butter
1 tablespoon sugar (optional)	¾ cup milk

Sift together flour, baking powder, salt, and sugar. Then stir in corn meal. In a separate bowl, beat the egg thoroughly, then stir in melted butter and milk. Combine with flour mixture, using as few strokes as possible (the batter will be lumpy). Spoon into greased corn-stick pans or greased muffin tins. Bake in a preheated 425° oven for 20 to 25 minutes or until a toothpick tested in center comes out dry. Makes 15 to 20.

HOECAKE

Hoecake—similar to Corn Pone and ashcake—was baked on a hoe over an open fire. Thoreau wrote of his stay at Walden Pond, "Bread I at first made of pure Indian meal and salt, genuine hoe-cakes, which I baked before my fire out of doors on a shingle or the end of a stick of timber sawed off in building my house; but it was wont to get smoked and to have a piny flavor"

1 cup water-ground white corn meal	1 tablespoon lard, melted
½ teaspoon salt	Boiling water

Combine corn meal and salt, then add lard and enough boiling water to make a dough heavy enough to hold a shape. Form into 2 thin oblong cakes and place in a heavy, hot, well-greased pan. Bake in a preheated 375° oven about 25 minutes. Serve hot.

SPOON BREAD

One of the most famous southern dishes, Spoon Bread traces its origin to the Indian porridge, *suppawn,* and still retains the consistency of a porridge or pudding.

5 tablespoons butter
1 cup water-ground corn meal
1 teaspoon salt

2 cups boiling water
1 cup cold milk
4 eggs

Heat oven to 425°. Put butter in a medium-sized earthenware or glass baking dish and place in oven to melt while you prepare the batter. Combine corn meal and salt in a mixing bowl and stir in boiling water until smooth. Let stand several minutes, then stir in milk. Add the eggs, one at a time, beating hard after each addition. Stir in melted butter last of all. Pour batter into the hot baking dish and bake 25 to 30 minutes. Serve hot, right from the baking dish, with plenty of extra butter. Serves 4.

HOMINY BREAD

½ cup uncooked hominy grits
1 tablespoon butter
3 eggs, separated

½ cup white corn meal
½ teaspoon salt
2 teaspoons baking powder

Stir grits into 2½ cups of boiling, salted water, cover, and cook over a low heat for 30 minutes. Measure out 2 cups of the hot grits and spoon into a mixing bowl. Stir in butter until melted, then add the egg yolks, thoroughly beaten. Sift the corn meal, salt, and baking powder together into the mixture and stir in thoroughly. Beat the egg whites until they stand in peaks and fold into the batter. Pour into a buttered 1½-quart baking dish. Bake in a preheated 350° oven for 1 hour. Serve piping hot with lots of sweet butter. Like Spoon Bread, Hominy Bread is served with meats. Serves 4 to 6.

CRACKLIN' BREAD

Originally Cracklin' Bread was made with cracklings (the crisp bits of pork left after lard has been rendered), salt, corn meal, and water. However, like many old recipes this one has been refined, and now contains eggs and buttermilk.

¾ cup finely diced salt pork
2 cups corn meal
1½ teaspoons baking powder
½ teaspoon baking soda

1 teaspoon salt
2 eggs, well beaten
1 cup buttermilk
2 tablespoons salt-pork drippings

Fry salt pork over a low heat until nicely browned. Drain fat, saving both drippings and cracklings. Sift together corn meal, baking powder, baking soda, and salt. Combine eggs, buttermilk, and drippings. Stir into corn-meal mixture, together with cracklings. Spread dough in a greased 11 x 7 x 1½-inch baking pan and bake in a preheated 400° oven for 25 to 30 minutes.

SPIDER CORNCAKE

Spider Corncake is named for the "spider," an old iron frying pan with legs, which was set right over the hot coals.

1½ cups white corn meal, preferably water-ground
1 tablespoon sugar
1 teaspoon salt

1 teaspoon baking soda
2 eggs, well beaten
2 cups buttermilk
1½ tablespoons melted butter

Start your oven at 450° and put in a 12-inch iron skillet or spider to heat. Sift together corn meal, sugar, salt, and baking soda into a bowl. Combine eggs and buttermilk and stir into corn-meal mixture, keeping it smooth. Last of all, stir in butter. Pour into the hot spider, well greased, and bake (at this same high temperature) for 30 minutes.

"Spider" frying pan and hanging skillet

RHODE ISLAND JOHNNYCAKES

Johnnycakes, originally an Indian food, may first have been known as Shawnee cakes. (Another theory is that they were called journey cakes, since travelers often took packages of them on long trips.) Whatever its origin, the name was gradually battered into "Johnny," and the recipes were jounced through frontier country until no one can agree on the "authentic" ingredients. Today, purists insist that they should not be made with sugar. In Richard Henry Dana's novel *Two Years Before the Mast,* published in 1840, the captain tells his unruly crew, "I'm Frank Thompson, all the way from 'down east.' I've been through the mill, ground, and bolted, and come out a *regular-built down-east johnny-cake,* when it's hot, damned good; but when it's cold, damned sour and indigestible;—and you'll find me so."

1 cup stone-ground white corn meal
1 teaspoon salt

1 teaspoon sugar (optional)
1¼ cups boiling water

Combine corn meal, salt, and sugar. Stir in water until mixture is smooth (batter will be very thick). Drop by tablespoons onto a well-greased griddle and fry over moderate heat for 6 minutes. Turn and cook the second side for 5 minutes. Makes 8 to 10.

VARIATION: If you want thin Johnnycakes, as Rhode Islanders say they should be, thin the batter with ½ cup milk or water. Serve buttered and, if you like, with maple syrup.

451

CREAM WAFFLES

The Dutch introduced waffles to America. It was their custom, when they settled in New York, to give a new bride a waffle iron with her initials and the date of her wedding carved into it.

1 cup sifted all-purpose flour	3 eggs, separated
4 teaspoons baking powder	1 cup heavy cream
¼ teaspoon salt	

Sift together flour, baking powder, and salt. Set aside. Beat yolks vigorously, then add cream, and continue beating hard. Stir in flour combination and beat with a rotary or electric beater until smooth. Fold in stiffly beaten egg whites thoroughly and refrigerate for half an hour. Bake in a preheated waffle iron until crisp and delicately browned. Serve with butter and warm honey or maple syrup. The number of waffles depends on the size of your waffle iron.

STRINGS OF FLATS

Stacks of these griddlecakes were consumed in the old lumbering camps, where they were known both as Flannel Cakes (possibly in honor of the layers of flannel shirts worn by the lumberjacks or because the griddlecakes tasted like flannel) and as Strings of Flats, or Flatcars, presumably for the railroad flatcars that took the lumber to market.

1 cup sifted all-purpose flour	2 eggs
1 tablespoon baking powder	1 cup milk
½ teaspoon salt	2 tablespoons melted butter
2 tablespoons sugar	

Sift flour, baking powder, salt, and sugar into a mixing bowl. In a separate container, beat eggs until light, then stir in milk and melted butter. With as few strokes as possible blend egg mixture in with the dry ingredients. Pour batter onto a hot, greased griddle (griddle is hot enough when a few drops of water tested on it sizzle) and cook until both sides are nicely browned. Serve at once with butter and warm maple syrup or honey.

BUTTERMILK PANCAKES

1½ cups all-purpose flour	1 egg
½ tablespoon baking powder	1¼ cups buttermilk
¼ teaspoon salt	2 tablespoons melted butter
½ tablespoon sugar	

Sift together flour, baking powder, salt, and sugar. Beat egg vigorously, then stir in buttermilk and butter. Combine with flour combination, using as few strokes as possible— overbeating toughens pancakes. Mixture will be lumpy. Drop batter by spoonfuls onto a hot, greased griddle (griddle is right temperature when a few drops of water sprinkled on it sizzle). When large bubbles appear and begin to burst, turn pancakes, then brown on second side. Serve at once.

BUCKWHEAT CAKES

A popular breakfast staple in America's Northwest, Buckwheat Cakes were made famous in London, too, by James McNeill Whistler, who served them at his sophisticated literary breakfasts.

½ package active dry yeast or
  ½ cake compressed
¼ cup lukewarm water
2 cups milk

2 cups buckwheat flour
½ teaspoon salt
1 tablespoon molasses
1 scant teaspoon baking soda

Dissolve yeast in lukewarm water. Scald milk, then cool to lukewarm. Blend together yeast, milk, buckwheat, and salt, beating hard for 2 minutes. Cover with a tea towel and let stand at room temperature overnight. Next day, mix in molasses, baking soda, and ¼ cup warm water. Pour onto a hot greased griddle (griddle is hot enough when several drops of water tested on it sizzle). Brown on both sides. Serve immediately with butter and warm maple syrup.

Label for sacks of buckwheat flour

NEW ORLEANS PAIN PERDU

This recipe for "lost bread," similar to French toast, is adapted from *La Cuisine Creole*. *Pain perdu* was originally flavored with orange-flower water.

Combine 2 eggs with 1 tablespoon confectioners' sugar, a pinch of salt, and ¾ cup milk and beat thoroughly. Stir in grated rind of half a lemon. Dip slices of bread, not too fresh, in the mixture, then fry in plenty of heated butter until crisp and golden brown on both sides. Serve immediately with maple syrup, honey, or a mixture of sugar and cinnamon. This makes enough batter for about 6 slices.

FISH

BAKED SHAD WITH ROE SOUFFLÉ

Shad were so plentiful in colonial days that they were altogether un-fashionable. Edward Eggleston wrote in *Century Magazine* in 1885, "Shad were too plentiful; incredible stories are told of three thousand taken at a haul; they sold for from one to two cents apiece of our present money, and were held so cheap that the salmon were sometimes picked out of a net and the shad rejected. Well-to-do people only ate shad on the sly, lest they should be suspected of not having a good supply of pork." In spite of the commonness of shad, it was the ex-cuse for a number of parties in Washington—in the early days of the republic, senators and representatives sailed down the Potomac nearly every Saturday on parties organized for the sole purpose of eating shad and having a few drinks. George Washington had several fishing stations on the Potomac where shad were caught, and Baked Shad was one of Washington's favorite dishes.

A 5- to 6-pound roe shad
Flour
Salt
Paprika
Lemon juice
Butter
Topping:
1 extra roe
1 tablespoon vinegar
½ teaspoon salt
1 bay leaf

Few sprigs parsley
¼ cup butter
1 medium onion, chopped fine
½ cup flour
1 cup milk
1 cup parsley, chopped
¼ cup white wine
3 eggs, separated
1 teaspoon salt
Juice of 1 lemon

Buy shad split and boned, but *not* cut in half. Set roe aside. Oil skin and place fish, skin down, on a piece of foil. Spread the shad flat, sprinkle with a little flour, salt, paprika, and lemon juice, and dot with butter. Bake in a 350° oven about 1 hour (12 minutes per pound). While shad bakes, prepare topping.

To make the topping: Cover the two shad roe with water. Add vinegar, salt, bay leaf, and parsley. Cook over a low heat about 10 minutes or until the roe is firm. Drain, remove membrane, and separate the eggs with a fork. Melt butter in a saucepan, stir in onion, and cook until limp. Add roe and cook until well coated with butter. Stir in flour until smooth, then add milk, and cook, stirring constantly, until sauce is thick and bubbly. Remove from heat, stir in chopped parsley and wine. Beat egg yolks slightly, stir in some of the hot sauce gradually, then combine with remaining sauce. Season with 1 teaspoon salt and the lemon juice. Beat egg whites until they stand in peaks, then fold into yolk mixture gently. Remove fish from oven and spread roe mixture over the entire shad. Dot with butter and sprinkle with paprika. Return to oven and bake 10 minutes. Place under broiler for a few minutes or until "soufflé" top is delicately browned. Serve at once to 10 or 12.

PLANKED STUFFED SHAD

Shad was known as *elft,* the eleven fish, to the early Dutch settlers in New York. It was on the eleventh of March each year that the first shad were caught and cooked on a plank—a method learned from the Indians.

Buy a 4-pound shad, split and boned, with head, tail, and fins left on. Wash the fish, then rub, inside and out, with sherry, and sprinkle lightly with a mixture of salt, pepper, a little dried thyme, and nutmeg. Stuff with this dressing:

1 cup cooked finnan haddie	1½ teaspoons grated onion
2 cups fresh bread crumbs	Salt
3 tablespoons melted butter	Pepper
¼ cup chopped parsley	Pinch each of nutmeg, thyme, and mace
¼ cup chopped celery leaves	Dry white wine

Prepare the plank by oiling well, then place in a cold oven, and bring the heat up to 400°. Cook finnan haddie as for Creamed Finnan Haddie (page 462).Work through a food grinder. Combine with all ingredients and enough wine to hold the mixture together lightly. Stuff fish and sew the opening together. Reduce heat to 375°. Place shad on the hot plank and bake, allowing 10 to 15 minutes per pound. Baste frequently with melted butter. Shortly before the fish is done, remove the plank from the oven. With a pastry tube, pipe a border of Potatoes Duchesse (page 529) around the edge of the plank. Brush the potatoes with butter, return the plank to the oven, and bake until the fish is done and the potatoes delicately browned. Before serving the planked shad, inside the border of potatoes arrange small bouquets of hot cooked vegetables, such as French green beans, glazed small white onions, asparagus tips with Hollandaise Sauce (page 542), or broiled mushroom caps. Serve with lemon wedges. Serves 6 to 8.

BAKED COD

Cod was once one of the main sources of food for New England. As early as 1640, the cod fishing industry had reached such proportions that in one year New Englanders prepared 300,000 dried codfish for market. So important was the fish—dietarily and economically—for Massachusetts that on March 17, 1784, according to the Journal of the Massachusetts House of Representatives: "Mr. John Rowe moved the House that leave might be given to hang up the representation of a Cod Fish in the room where the House sit, as a memorial of the importance of the Cod Fishery to the welfare of this Commonwealth." In 1798, the four-foot-eleven-inch codfish, called the Sacred Cod, was moved to the new State House and, in 1895, to its present location in the House chamber, opposite the speaker's desk.

Place fillets of cod in a well-oiled baking dish. Sprinkle with salt, pepper, lemon juice, and a little paprika. Dot with butter or cover with buttered crumbs. Bake in a preheated 400° oven until fish flakes easily when tested with a fork. Baking time varies from 12 to 30 minutes, depending on the thickness of the fillets.

LOUISIANA BAKED BLUEFISH

A 4- to 4½-pound bluefish
Salad oil
Salt
Pepper
1 tablespoon finely chopped onion

¾ cup tomato juice
Creole Sauce (page 545)
¾ cup fine fresh bread crumbs
2 tablespoons melted butter

Have fish cleaned, leaving head and tail intact. Lay fish in a shallow, well-oiled baking pan, rub the skin with oil, and sprinkle with salt and pepper. Scatter onion over the fish, then add tomato juice to pan. Bake in a preheated 350° oven for 30 minutes, basting occasionally with the tomato juice. Remove from oven and pour Creole Sauce over fish. Mix bread crumbs with melted butter and sprinkle on top. Slide fish under a preheated broiler, 4 inches from tip of flame, and broil until browned. Serves 6.

FRIED CATFISH

Father Dollier and Father Galinée, members of the American expedition of La Salle, reported on a journey through the Northwest in 1669-70, "Fishing is pretty good. . . . We had only to throw a line in the water to catch forty or fifty fish of the kind called here *barbue* [catfish]. There is none like it in France. Travelers and poor people live on it very comfortably, for it can be eaten, and is very good cooked in water without sauce."

Dip skinned fish (whole or in chunks) in beaten egg yolk. Then coat with dry bread crumbs, cracker crumbs, or corn meal. Preheat deep fat to 370° on a deep-fat thermometer or until a 1-inch cube of bread browns in 60 seconds. Fry fish until crisp and nicely browned. This takes about 3 to 5 minutes, depending on the size of the fish. Drain on paper towels and season to taste with salt and pepper. Serve with Hush Puppies (page 533), Coleslaw (page 548), and pickles.

BROILED SALT ROE HERRING

Herring was the staple fish on the Potomac during the time Washington lived at Mount Vernon. The General had several fishing stations on the river, and one of the managers of his estate recorded, "excellent herring were caught . . . which, when salted, proved an important article of food to the poor. For their accommodation he [Washington] appropriated a station—one of the best he had—and furnished it with all the necessary apparatus for taking herring."

Soak the fish (1 to 2 salt roe herring per person) for 24 hours in enough water to cover. Change the water several times. Place herring, roe side up, on a broiling pan or tray, sprinkle with lemon juice, dot generously with butter, and broil under a low heat for 15 minutes. Serve hot with Corn Sticks (page 449), Spoon Bread (page 450), or hominy grits.

NEW ENGLAND BROILED SCROD

Scrod (a young filleted cod) is strictly a New England dish, and it seems to be always available there. Describing an outing, Benjamin Franklin once wrote: "Being becalm'd off Block Island, our people set about catching cod, and hauled up a great many. Hitherto I had stuck to my resolution of not eating animal food [he had been a vegetarian], and on this occasion I consider'd ... the taking of every fish as a kind of unprovoked murder ... But I had formerly been a great lover of fish, and, when this came hot out of the frying-pan, it smelt admirably well. I balanc'd some time between principle and inclination, till I recollected that, when the fish were opened, I saw smaller fish taken out of their stomachs; then thought I, 'If you eat one another, I don't see why we mayn't eat you.' So I din'd upon cod very heartily ... So convenient a thing it is to be a *reasonable creature,* since it enables one to find or make a reason for every thing one has a mind to do."

Arrange 4 scrod fillets on a well-buttered broiling pan. Sprinkle generously with lemon juice, pour a little melted butter over each fillet, season with salt and a light dusting of paprika. Broil about 4 inches from broiling unit for 6 to 8 minutes or until scrod flakes easily with a fork. Remove to a heated platter with a broad spatula. Serve with Lemon Butter (page 543) and boiled potatoes. Makes 4 servings.

GRILLED TROUT

1 large, freshly caught trout	Pepper
Salt	Melted butter

Cut the cleaned trout so that it will lie flat when opened and remove the backbone. Place, skin side down, in a well-oiled broiling pan. Sprinkle with salt and pepper and brush generously with butter. Broil 3 inches from tip of unit in a preheated 450° broiler 8 to 10 minutes or until fish flakes easily when tested with a fork. Do not overcook.

To grill over hot coals: Use a hinged grill so the fish will stay in place. Make certain grill is hot enough to mark or score the fish. Before grilling, coat fish with flour, then brush thoroughly with oil. During the grilling, brush several times with more oil. For a 4- to 5-pound trout, allow 6 to 8 minutes per side.

FILLET OF FLOUNDER, AMERICAN STYLE

6 fillets of flounder	Corn meal
Flour	Fat for deep-fat frying
2 eggs	Salt
½ cup milk	Pepper

Beat eggs and milk together. Dust fillets with flour, dip in milk mixture, then coat with corn meal. Fry in deep fat preheated to 365° on deep-fat thermometer or until a 1-inch cube of bread browns in 60 seconds. When fillets are crisp and brown, drain on paper towels and season to taste. Serve with Lemon Butter (page 543) or Tartare Sauce (page 543). Serves 4 to 6.

STUFFED BAKED FILLETS CREOLE

4 tablespoons butter
2 tablespoons chopped onion
4 tablespoons chopped celery
2 tablespoons chopped green pepper
2 tablespoons flour
½ cup milk
½ cup fine dry bread crumbs
Pinch each of dried thyme,
   rosemary, and marjoram
1 cup cooked crab meat

1 cup cooked shrimp, cut in pieces
½ cup chopped parsley
¼ teaspoon salt
Dash pepper
1½ teaspoons Worcestershire sauce
Dash Tabasco
4 to 8 fillets of sole or flounder
   (depending on size)
Paprika
Creole Sauce (page 545)

Melt butter in a saucepan. Stir in onion, celery, green pepper and cook until tender. Stir in flour, keeping mixture as smooth as possible. Add milk and cook until thickened. Remove from heat and stir in all remaining ingredients, *except the fillets.* Make a mound of the filling on each of the fillets, roll up ends, and attach with a toothpick. Place in a shallow baking pan, leaving space between fillets. Brush with melted butter and sprinkle with salt and paprika. Bake in a preheated 350° oven for 15 minutes. Then pour Creole Sauce over fish, reduce heat to 325°, and bake 30 minutes longer. Serves 6 to 8.

Fish server

FILLET OF SOLE MARGUERY À LA DIAMOND JIM

2 flounder, filleted
1 pound halibut or cod
½ cup sliced carrots
1 leek, sliced
3 sprigs parsley
10 peppercorns
1 small bay leaf
1 sprig thyme

1½ quarts water
Salt
Pepper
12 oysters, poached
12 boiled shrimp, shelled
¼ cup dry white wine
½ cup (1 stick) butter
4 egg yolks

Ask the fish dealer to give you the heads, tails, and skin from the flounder. Place these trimmings and small chunks of the halibut or cod in a saucepan. Toss in carrots, leek, parsley, peppercorns, bay leaf, and thyme. Add water and cook to a boil, then reduce heat, and simmer gently until liquid is reduced to about 1 pint. Strain through a fine cheesecloth, saving the stock. Arrange fillets in a buttered baking dish and sprinkle with salt and pepper. Add 1 cup of the fish stock and bake in a preheated 325° oven for 15 to 20 minutes. With a broad spatula, carefully transfer fillets to a hot ovenproof serving platter. Arrange oysters and shrimp on top. Set aside. Pour remaining cup of fish stock into pan in which fillets baked. Cook until stock is reduced to about ¼ cup. Strain into top of double boiler, add white wine and butter. Cook over hot water, stirring until butter is melted. Beat egg yolks vigorously, then stir in the butter mixture a little at a time. Pour egg mixture into top of double boiler and cook, stirring constantly, until sauce is the consistency of a medium cream sauce. Pour over fish. Broil in a preheated broiler until golden brown. Serves 4.

NEW ORLEANS BOUILLABAISSE

Bouillabaisse (its name deriving from the instruction, *"Quand ça commence à bouillir—baisse!"*) is one of the most famous of New Orleans dishes. Thackeray, in his *Roundabout Papers* (1891), recalled this New Orleans stew: "At that comfortable tavern on Pontchartrain we had a *bouillabaisse* than which a better was never eaten at Marseilles; and not the least headache in the morning, I give you my word; on the contrary, you only wake with a sweet refreshing thirst for claret and water."

Court bouillon:

Head of a red snapper
1½ quarts boiling water
Bunch of herbs (thyme, parsley, bay leaf)
1 onion, sliced
Bouillabaisse:
6 slices red snapper
6 slices redfish
Salt
Pepper
Cayenne
3 cloves garlic, minced
3 sprigs thyme, chopped, or
  1 teaspoon dried thyme

3 sprigs parsley, chopped
3 bay leaves, crushed
1 teaspoon allspice
2 tablespoons olive oil
3 mild onions, chopped
2 cups dry white wine
6 large ripe tomatoes,
  canned or fresh
½ lemon, thinly sliced
¼ teaspoon saffron
12 slices French bread
½ cup (1 stick) butter

To make the court bouillon: Place the red snapper head in boiling water with the bunch of herbs and the sliced onion. Cook over a low heat, uncovered, until liquid is reduced to about 1 pint. Strain and set liquid aside.

To make the Bouillabaisse: Sprinkle the slices of red snapper and redfish with salt, pepper, and cayenne. Combine garlic, thyme, parsley, bay leaves, allspice and sprinkle over fish slices. Let stand about 30 minutes for flavor to permeate the fish. Heat olive oil in a large heavy kettle, add chopped onions, and cook over a low heat until limp. Lay fish slices on top (do not overlap), cover, and cook slowly for 5 minutes. Turn the slices and cook another 5 minutes. Carefully transfer fish to a platter. Add wine to kettle, then add the tomatoes (sliced, if fresh ones are used), lemon slices, and court bouillon previously set aside. Cook, uncovered, until liquid is reduced by half. Return fish slices to the liquid and simmer gently for 5 minutes. Meanwhile, dissolve the saffron in a little of the hot liquid from the kettle. Set aside. Sauté slices of French bread in melted butter and place on a large deep serving dish. Put a slice of fish on top of each piece of bread and spread the saffron mixture over the fish. Pour the hot broth over all and serve immediately. Serves 12.

VARIATION: To the simmering court bouillon, add ½ pound large uncooked shrimp (in their shells) and 1 pound lobster tails. Cook 5 minutes, then remove from liquid. Shell and clean shrimp (add the shells to the court bouillon). Set shrimp aside. Do the same with the lobster tails. When cooked, cut the lobster meat into small pieces and set aside with the cooked shrimp. In a separate pan, steam open 1 dozen cherry stone clams and ½ pound mussels. Before serving Bouillabaisse, add shrimp and lobster pieces to liquid. Place clams and mussels in the serving dish with the slices of sautéed bread.

POACHED HALIBUT WITH HOLLANDAISE SAUCE

Halibut was at one time so plentiful on the eastern coast that the cod fishermen considered it a nuisance. This recipe was quite common on the menus of nineteenth-century hotels and inns in the East.

Place 4 halibut steaks, 1½ to 2 inches thick and each weighing about half a pound, in a large skillet. Cover almost completely with cold water and season with lemon juice, bay leaf, and salt. Bring to a boil, reduce heat, and simmer for 10 minutes or until fish flakes easily. Do not overcook. Drain thoroughly on a napkin. Place on a hot serving platter, spoon Hollandaise Sauce (page 542) over the fish (or serve the sauce in a warm sauceboat), and garnish with parsley. Serves 4.

POMPANO EN PAPILLOTE

Pompano, which is native to the waters bordering the southern states, is one of the most highly prized fish in the South. This recipe comes from the famous restaurant Antoine's, in New Orleans. The dish was created in honor of a famous balloonist who was visiting New Orleans, and the paper bag—although its main purpose is to retain the flavor of the fish while it cooks—was fashioned to resemble an inflated balloon.

3 medium pompano, filleted, and trimmings	2 tablespoons flour
1 teaspoon salt	3 shallots, chopped
3 cups water	2 cups cooked shrimp, chopped
1 stalk celery, sliced	2 cups cooked crab meat
1 onion, sliced	1 clove garlic, minced
2 cups dry white wine	1 bay leaf, crumbled
6 tablespoons butter	Pinch of dried thyme
	Dash of Tabasco

Have the fish filleted and ask for the trimmings. Place the trimmings (heads and bones) in a kettle, add salt, water, celery, and onion. Bring to a boil, then reduce heat, and continue cooking slowly for 30 minutes. Strain and set aside 1 cup of the stock. Pour remaining stock into a skillet and add ½ cup of the wine. Sprinkle fillets with a little salt and pepper and fold in half. Place in the stock and wine mixture and simmer gently for 8 minutes. Remove from heat and allow fish to cool in the stock. When cool, lift out fillets and drain well. Set aside while you make the sauce.

To make the fish sauce: Melt *2 tablespoons of the butter* in a saucepan, stir in flour until smooth, and cook several minutes. Stir in the cup of fish stock and cook, stirring constantly, until sauce bubbles. Set aside.

Sauté shallots in remaining butter for 5 minutes. Stir in shrimp, crab meat, garlic, bay leaf, thyme, and Tabasco thoroughly. Add remaining wine and cook for 15 minutes, stirring frequently. Blend with the fish sauce and cool. Cut 6 hearts, about 8 inches long and 12 inches wide, from parchment paper. Brush the paper with oil. Place a spoonful of sauce on one side of each heart, then a pompano fillet, and cover with a little sauce. Fold paper hearts over and double fold all surrounding edges to seal securely. Arrange on an oiled baking sheet and bake in a preheated 425° oven for 15 minutes. Serve in the paper to 6.

SHRIMP-STUFFED POMPANO

"We had dinner on a ground-veranda over the water," Mark Twain wrote in *Life on the Mississippi.* "The chief dish [was] the renowned fish called the pompano, delicious as the less criminal forms of sin."

4 pompano (about 1 pound each)	Dash of pepper
1 pound cooked shrimp	3 tablespoons sherry
1 egg, well beaten	1 cup heavy cream
½ teaspoon salt	

Split the cleaned pompano, leaving head and tail intact. Place in an oiled, shallow baking pan. Work shrimp through a food grinder, then combine with egg, salt, pepper, sherry, and *half the cream.* When well blended, stuff fish cavities with the mixture. Pour remaining cream over all and bake in a preheated 350° oven for 40 minutes. Baste occasionally. Serves 4.

NEW ENGLAND POACHED SALMON WITH EGG SAUCE

From the earliest days it has been a tradition all through New England to serve Poached Salmon with Egg Sauce, along with the first new potatoes and early peas, on the Fourth of July. The eastern salmon began to "run" about this time, and the new vegetables were just coming in.

To poach salmon: Take a whole salmon or a 4- to 6-pound piece cut from center of the fish. Wrap the washed, cleaned salmon securely in a piece of cheesecloth, leaving long ends to expedite removing it from the broth when it is cooked. Bring to a boil 2 to 3 quarts of salted water (the amount depends on the amount of fish) containing 3 or 4 peppercorns, a bay leaf, and a couple of slices of lemon. Boil for at least 15 minutes. Reduce heat until liquid is simmering, add the salmon. Turn up the heat until it boils again, then reduce to simmer (it should be barely bubbling) until salmon is cooked. Figure on 6 to 8 minutes per pound. It is cooked perfectly when it flakes easily. Take care not to overcook it. When the salmon is done, lift from the broth and remove the cheesecloth. Place on a hot serving platter and skin very carefully. Garnish with lemon and parsley. While salmon is cooking, make the Egg Sauce.

Sauce:

1 cup milk	3 tablespoons butter
1 cup light cream	3 tablespoons flour
2 small onions, sliced thin	1 teaspoon salt
½ bay leaf	Dash white pepper
1 whole clove	2 hard-cooked eggs

Heat milk and cream together with the onion slices, bay leaf, and whole clove until a film forms. Skim the surface. Melt butter in a saucepan, stir in flour, keeping it smooth, and cook over a very low heat for a few minutes. Pour in scalded milk mixture and cook over a low heat, stirring constantly, until mixture bubbles. Remove from heat, season with salt and pepper, and strain into a saucepan. Add eggs, coarsely chopped, and heat through. Do not cook any further. If the sauce seems too thick, add a little more light cream. Serve separately in a warm sauceboat.

COLD SALMON MOUSSE

1 can (1 pound) red salmon or
   2 cups cooked fresh salmon
2½ tablespoons fresh lemon juice
1 teaspoon salt
Dash cayenne

1 envelope unflavored gelatin
½ cup cold water
3 tablespoons mayonnaise
¼ cup heavy cream

Drain salmon, discard any bones, and mash as smooth as possible with a fork. Combine salmon with lemon juice, salt, and cayenne. Sprinkle gelatin over cold water to soften. Put in a pan of boiling water and stir until gelatin is dissolved. Add to salmon mixture, then add the mayonnaise and the cream, which has been whipped until it holds a shape. Pour into a 1-quart mold and chill until firm. Unmold on a cold platter and garnish with watercress and deviled eggs. Serves 4.

CREAMED FINNAN HADDIE

Finnan Haddie is a Scottish dish, named for Findon, a fishing village in Scotland renowned for its cured haddock. The recipe became common in New England as fishermen began to take haddock off the coast.

1½ pounds finnan haddie
2 tablespoons butter
1 tablespoon flour

1 cup half-and-half (milk and cream)
Dash cayenne

Cut finnan haddie into 1-inch cubes. Cover with boiling water and let stand about 5 minutes. Drain very thoroughly. Heat butter in a saucepan, stir in flour until smooth, then add half-and-half. Season with cayenne and cook, stirring constantly, until smooth. Let the mixture bubble 1 or 2 minutes; stir in finnan haddie. Heat through; do not cook any further. Serves 4.

GEFILTE FISH

5 pounds fish fillets (equal amounts of
   whitefish and pike, and some carp)
   plus trimmings
4 onions, sliced
1 stalk celery, sliced

3 carrots, sliced
Salt
Pepper
3 eggs, well beaten
2 tablespoons matzo meal

Work fish fillets through the finest blade of a food grinder and set aside. Put fish heads, bones, and trimmings in a large kettle along with *3 onions*, celery, carrots, salt, pepper, and enough water to cover. Cook to the boiling point, then simmer. Grate the remaining onion very fine and combine with eggs. Mix thoroughly with the ground fish, adding the matzo meal, a little more salt and pepper, and 4 tablespoons of water. Shape into balls and drop into the simmering fish broth. Make certain broth is barely bubbling, then cover, and cook 2 hours. Cool right in the broth, then transfer to a serving platter. Use the cooked carrots for garnish. Strain the broth and refrigerate until jellied. Serve Gefilte Fish with the jellied broth and horse-radish. Makes 15 to 20 balls.

SCANDINAVIAN FISH PUDDING

1 pound raw ground pike, cod, or haddock
½ cup softened butter
1 tablespoon anchovy paste
1 teaspoon salt
¼ teaspoon white pepper

4 eggs, separated
3 tablespoons flour
1 cup light cream
1 cup heavy cream

Mix the ground fish, butter, anchovy paste, salt, and pepper together. In a separate bowl, beat egg yolks, flour, and light cream vigorously, then beat into fish mixture. Whip the heavy cream until it holds a shape; beat the egg whites until they stand in peaks. Fold or mix both of these into the fish pudding very gently. Pour into a 2-quart baking dish, buttered and dusted with dry bread crumbs, and bake in a preheated 325° oven for 1 to 1¼ hours or until cake tester (or toothpick) inserted in the center comes out clean. Remove from oven, let stand several minutes, then invert and unmold on warm serving platter. Serve with Hollandaise Sauce (page 542) or Mushroom Sauce (page 544). Serves 6.

CODFISH CAKES

1 box (1.6 ounces dehydrated) codfish
3 medium potatoes

1 egg, well beaten
Fat for deep-fat frying

Cover dried codfish with cold water and soak for about 1 hour. Squeeze out as much water as possible and put fish and potatoes (pared and cut in quarters) in a saucepan with enough cold water to almost cover. Cook over a moderate heat until potatoes are tender. Drain thoroughly and mash as smooth as possible. Beat in the egg and drop by tablespoons into hot fat (375° on deep-fat thermometer or until fat browns a 1-inch cube of bread in 60 seconds). Drain on paper towels. Serve with tomato sauce or applesauce. Makes 4 servings.

CIOPPINO

1½ pounds sea bass
1 pound uncooked shrimp in shells
1 live lobster
1 quart clams or mussels
½ cup olive oil
1 large onion, chopped
2 cloves garlic, chopped

1 green pepper, chopped
4 ripe tomatoes, skinned and chopped
½ cup tomato purée
2 cups red wine
½ cup parsley, chopped
1 teaspoon salt
¼ teaspoon pepper

Cut fish into serving pieces, shell shrimp and remove veins. Sever spinal cord of lobster by inserting a knife where tail and body meet, and cut into pieces. Do not remove shells. Scrub the clams or mussels thoroughly and leave in the shells. Arrange fish, shrimp, and lobster in layers in a large kettle. Heat oil in a saucepan, then toss in onion, garlic, and green pepper, and cook about 5 minutes. Now add tomatoes, tomato purée, wine, *half the parsley,* and seasonings. Cover and cook over a low heat for 15 minutes. Pour sauce over layers of fish and shellfish. Cover and simmer slowly for 30 minutes or until bass is tender when tested with a fork. Add the clams or mussels and continue cooking until the shells open. Sprinkle remaining parsley on top and serve with hot garlic bread. Serves 6.

LOBSTER NEWBURG

In the early 1890's, Delmonico's honored one of its best customers, Ben Wenberg, by naming a dish after him: Lobster Wenberg. Shortly thereafter, however, Mr. Wenberg and Mr. Delmonico had a falling-out, and the name of the creation was changed to Lobster Newburg.

1½ cups cooked lobster meat	1 cup heavy cream
4 tablespoons butter	¼ cup Madeira or sherry
Salt	3 egg yolks, lightly beaten
Cayenne	

Cut lobster meat in large chunks. Heat butter in a heavy saucepan, add lobster, season with a little salt and cayenne, and cook for a few minutes. Pour in cream and bring to a boil, then add Madeira or sherry. Pour some of the hot liquid into the egg yolks, a little at a time, beating hard. Pour back into lobster mixture and cook over a very low heat (or in a double boiler), stirring constantly, until slightly thickened. Do not boil. Serve in patty shells or on toast or rice. Serves 2.

BOILED LOBSTER

"Now that we are on marine matters," Captain Frederick Marryat wrote in 1839, "I must notice the prodigious size of the lobsters off Boston coast: they could stow a dozen common English lobsters under their coats of mail. My very much respected friend Sir Isaac Coffin [the Coffins were among the first settlers of Nantucket Island],... once laid a wager that he would produce a lobster weighing thirty pounds. The bet was accepted, and the admiral despatched people to the proper quarter to procure one; but they were not then in season, and could not be had. The admiral, not liking to lose his money, brought up, instead of the lobster, the affidavits of certain people that they had often seen lobsters of that size and weight.... The case was referred to arbitration, and the admiral was cast with the following pithy reply, 'Depositions are not lobsters.' "

A 1- to 1½-pound lobster serves one person. To cook 4 lobsters, bring 4 quarts water to a rolling boil (if sea water is not available, add 4 tablespoons salt to fresh water). Drop live lobsters into the water and bring to a boil again, then cover, reduce heat, and simmer 5 minutes for the first pound, 3 minutes for each additional pound. If overcooked, lobsters will be dry and tough. Remove lobsters immediately from water, lay them on their backs, and split them in half, from end to end, using a large, heavy knife. Remove and discard stomach and intestinal vein. The green liver, or tomalley, is eaten. Hen lobsters yield coral, a pink roe also considered a delicacy. Serve hot with melted butter and lemon wedges or at room temperature with mayonnaise.

To cook lobster in a court bouillon: To 4 quarts water, add 1 cup white vinegar, 1 sliced carrot, 2 large onions (sliced), 6 stalks celery (sliced), 3 bay leaves, 1 teaspoon dried thyme, 1 teaspoon crushed peppercorns, 4 tablespoons salt, and a pinch of caraway. Bring all ingredients to a boil, add lobsters, then cook according to directions above. Cool the lobsters in the court bouillon.

STEAMED CLAMS

In *Cape Cod,* Henry Thoreau speaks of walking with a friend along
the shore of Cape Cod after a storm. "We found some large clams...
which the storm had torn up from the bottom, and cast ashore. I selected
one of the largest, about six inches in length, and carried it along....
We took our nooning under a sand-hill, covered with beach-grass...
I kindled a fire with a match and some paper, and cooked my clam on
the embers for my dinner.... Though it was very tough, I found it
sweet and savory, and ate *the whole* with a relish. Indeed, with the
addition of a cracker or two, it would have been a bountiful dinner."

Scrub steamers with a stiff brush and wash several times until free from sand. Place clams
(about 20 per person) in a large, deep kettle with about a half inch of salted water in the
bottom. Cover the kettle very tightly and steam over moderate heat until the clams open.
This will take from 6 to 10 minutes depending on the size of the clams. Serve at once with
melted butter and cups of the clam broth. Taste the broth first to see if it needs seasoning.

Implement for baking clams

CLAM FRITTERS

John Lawson, visiting the Carolinas in 1709, had a few remarks about
"Man of Noses" (as soft clams, or maninose, were then called) : "Man
of Noses are a Shell-Fish commonly found amongst us. They are valued
for increasing Vigour in Men, and making barren Women fruitful;
but I think they have no need of that Fish; for the Women in *Carolina*
are fruitful enough without their Helps."

2 cups minced clams, fresh or canned
2 eggs, separated
1 cup fine bread crumbs, toasted
1 teaspoon salt
½ teaspoon pepper

½ tablespoon chopped parsley
½ tablespoon chopped chives
⅓ cup milk (about)
Butter or vegetable oil

Clams should be well drained and minced very fine. Beat egg yolks vigorously, then stir in
clams, crumbs, seasonings, chopped parsley, and chives. Add enough milk to make a heavy
batter. Fold in stiffly beaten egg whites. Drop batter from a tablespoon into a skillet containing heated butter or oil. Fry, turning once, until both sides are browned. Serves 4.

AGUACATES RELLENOS CON JAIBA
(Baked Avocado, Stuffed with Crab Meat)

3 firm avocados
Lemon or lime juice
1½ cups crab meat
1 cup thick Cream Sauce (page 542)
Salt

White pepper
Few drops of Tabasco
1 tablespoon capers, drained
6 tablespoons grated Cheddar cheese
(optional)

Cut unpeeled avocados in half lengthwise and remove pits. Sprinkle surfaces generously with lemon or lime juice. Mix crab meat with Cream Sauce, seasonings, and capers. Spoon into avocados and sprinkle with cheese. Place in a shallow baking pan with ½ inch hot water and bake in a preheated 350° oven for 20 to 25 minutes. Serves 6.

MARYLAND DEVILED IMPERIAL CRAB

4 tablespoons butter
1 green pepper, chopped fine
1 small onion, minced
1 tablespoon prepared mustard
1 tablespoon dry mustard

½ teaspoon salt
2 tablespoons good brandy
½ cup Cream Sauce (page 542)
2 tablespoons fine bread crumbs
1 pound crab meat

Melt *2 tablespoons of the butter* in a saucepan, add the green pepper and onion, and cook over a low heat, stirring often, for 10 minutes. Stir in the 2 mustards, salt, brandy, Cream Sauce, and *1 tablespoon of the bread crumbs*. Then add the crab meat. Heat only for a few minutes, stirring gently and taking care not to break up the crab flakes. Spoon into 6 individual baking shells or into a small baking dish that can go to the table. Sprinkle on remaining bread crumbs and dot with remaining butter. Bake in a preheated 400° oven (shells will take about 10 minutes, the baking dish about 25 minutes). Slide under the broiler for a few minutes to brown the tops. Serves 6.

CRAB LOUIS

Crab Louis was created by the chef at the Olympic Club in Seattle, Washington. When the Metropolitan Opera Company played Seattle in 1904, Enrico Caruso kept ordering the salad until none was left in the kitchen.

Dressing:

1 cup mayonnaise
½ cup heavy cream, whipped
¼ cup chili sauce

2 tablespoons grated onion
2 tablespoons parsley, chopped fine
Dash of cayenne

Combine all ingredients and refrigerate. Shred lettuce, arrange on a platter, and heap 1½ pounds lump crab meat, picked over and flaked, on top. Garnish with hard-cooked eggs, fresh tomatoes (peeled and quartered), and slices of avocado or artichoke hearts. Pour the Louis dressing over all. Serves 4.

FRIED SOFT-SHELLED CRABS

Two to three soft-shelled crabs are the usual portion per person. Have them cleaned at the market. Dust lightly with flour, then dip in lightly beaten egg, and, last of all, in fine dry bread or cracker crumbs. Heat fat in a deep frying pan to 350° on deep-fat thermometer or until a 1-inch cube of bread browns in 60 seconds. Add a few crabs at a time and fry about 5 minutes or until golden. Drain on paper towels and sprinkle with salt and pepper. Serve with Tartare Sauce (page 543) or Sauce Remoulade (page 546).

CRAB STEW

2 tablespoons butter
1 small onion, grated
¼ pound mushrooms, sliced thin
2 ripe tomatoes, skinned and chopped
1 pound crab meat
1 teaspoon salt

Dash cayenne
1½ cups heavy cream
Few sprigs parsley, chopped
1 teaspoon chopped chives
¼ cup brandy

Melt butter, stir in grated onion, and cook over a moderate heat for a minute or two. Stir in mushroom slices and cook several minutes. Now add tomatoes and cook about 5 minutes. Stir in crab meat, salt, cayenne, and cream. Heat until mixture comes to a boil—but no longer. Add parsley, chives, and brandy. Serve in soup plates with a heaping tablespoon of cooked rice in the center. Serves 4 to 6.

MARYLAND CRAB CAKES

6 slices white bread
¾ cup olive oil
3 eggs, separated
¼ teaspoon dry mustard
½ teaspoon salt

2 teaspoons Worcestershire sauce
1½ pounds crab meat
Paprika
3 tablespoons butter

Trim crusts from bread and lay slices on a shallow platter. Pour oil over them and let stand until bread is thoroughly saturated. Use forks to break into small pieces. Combine egg yolks with mustard, salt, and Worcestershire sauce. Beat lightly. Stir in bread and crab meat, gently fold in stiffly beaten egg whites, and shape mixture into patties. Sprinkle with paprika and sauté in heated butter until golden on both sides. Serves 6.

FRIED SHRIMP

Remove shells from 1 pound of raw shrimp, leaving tails intact. Mix together 1 egg and 1 tablespoon cold water. Dip the shrimp in this, then coat with fine dry bread or cracker crumbs. Fry in deep fat heated to 350° on deep-fat thermometer (or until a 1-inch cube of bread browns in 60 seconds) until crisp and golden. Drain on paper towels, sprinkle with salt, and serve immediately with Dill and Mustard Sauce (page 543), Sauce Remoulade (page 546), or Tartare Sauce (page 543). Serves 4.

PICKLED SHRIMP

2 pounds raw shrimp
¼ cup mixed pickling spices
Celery leaves (about a handful)
1 cup salad oil
¾ cup white vinegar

1 teaspoon salt
¼ teaspoon black pepper
2 teaspoons celery seed
Few drops of Tabasco
1 large onion, chopped

Combine unshelled shrimp, pickling spices, and celery leaves in a saucepan and add enough water to cover. Cover tightly, bring to a boil, reduce heat, and simmer 3 to 5 minutes. Do not overcook. Cool shrimp in the liquid, then remove the shells. Mix together salad oil, vinegar, salt, pepper, celery seed, and Tabasco. Arrange layers of shrimp and chopped onion in a jar or bowl, add the oil-vinegar mixture, cover, and refrigerate overnight.

SHRIMP CREOLE

¼ cup butter
2 medium onions, chopped fine
1 clove garlic, chopped fine
3 green peppers, coarsely chopped
1 can (1 pound, 3 ounces) tomatoes

2 teaspoons salt
¼ teaspoon pepper
1 teaspoon paprika
1½ pounds raw shrimp
1 teaspoon gumbo filé

Melt butter in a large saucepan. Stir in onions, garlic, green peppers and cook over a low heat until tender. Stir frequently. Pour in the tomatoes and simmer gently for 25 to 30 minutes. Season with salt, pepper, and paprika. While tomato mixture cooks, remove shells and clean shrimp. Add to the sauce and cook 5 minutes longer. Stir in filé. Serve immediately with steamed rice. Serves 6.

SEAFOOD ROYALE

2 tablespoons butter
2 stalks celery, diced
3 medium onions, chopped
1 tablespoon flour
1 cup water
1 teaspoon salt
2 tablespoons chili powder
2 cups canned tomatoes

1 cup cooked peas
1 tablespoon vinegar
1 teaspoon sugar
2 cups cooked, cleaned shrimp
    or combination of shrimp, crab meat,
    scallops, or other shellfish
⅓ cup sherry
3 cups hot cooked rice

Melt butter in a saucepan. Add celery and onions and cook over a moderate heat until onions are limp. Stir in flour until smooth, then add water, salt, and chili powder. Cook, stirring constantly, until mixture thickens. Reduce heat and simmer for about 15 minutes. Then add tomatoes, peas, vinegar, sugar, and shrimp. Cook 10 minutes longer or until shrimp are heated through. Stir in sherry last of all. Serve with hot rice to 6.

OYSTERS

In the nineteenth century, oysters were very much a part of American life. The Lincolns, while they were living in Springfield, Illinois, were often hosts at oyster feasts—affairs at which oysters, and oysters exclusively, were served in every conceivable manner. A few of the variations were: broiled, boiled, deviled, curried, fricasseed, panned, scalloped, pickled, stewed, steamed, pies, omelettes, ketchups, and fritters.

Oysters were consumed in great quantity, by the dozens—a feat all the more remarkable because of the prodigious size of oysters in the nineteenth century. Today it is a rarity to find the enormous six- and eight-inch oysters that were common a hundred years ago. And there is no contemporary story to match that told by a companion of William Makepeace Thackeray, when the British writer visited Boston in 1852. Thackeray was presented with a half-dozen typically large American oysters. "He first selected the smallest one . . . and then bowed his head as though he were saying grace. Opening his mouth very wide, he struggled for a moment, after which all was over. I shall never forget the comic look of despair he cast upon the other five over-occupied shells. I asked him how he felt. 'Profoundly grateful,' he said, 'as if I had swallowed a small baby.' "

SCALLOPED OYSTERS

1 pint oysters	½ cup (1 stick) butter, melted
¼ cup oyster liquor	Salt
2 tablespoons light cream	Freshly ground pepper
½ cup day-old bread crumbs	Paprika
1 cup cracker or rusk crumbs	

Drain oysters, reserving ¼ cup of the liquor. Combine oyster liquor and cream and set aside. Mix both kinds of crumbs together with the melted butter and sprinkle a thin layer on bottom of a buttered 1-quart casserole. Cover with *half of the oysters, half of the liquor and cream mixture,* and a light sprinkling of salt and pepper. Cover with a second layer of crumbs, remaining oysters, remaining liquor and cream, and more salt and pepper. Finish off the dish with the last of the crumbs and sprinkle with paprika. *Note:* Never make more than two layers of oysters in a scallop because the middle layer will remain uncooked. Bake in a preheated 425° oven for 30 minutes. Serves 4.

TO FATTEN OYSTERS

Mix one pint of salt with thirty pints of water. Put the oysters in a tub that will not leak, with their mouths upwards and feed them with the above, by dipping in a broom and frequently passing over their mouths. It is said that they will fatten still more by mixing fine meal with the water.

—From *Housekeeping in Old Virginia,* 1877

LA MÉDIATRICE

The oyster loaf, popular throughout America in the nineteenth century, was known in the Vieux Carré of New Orleans as *la médiatrice,* or the mediator. It was the one thing a man felt might effectively stand between his enraged wife and himself when he came home after spending an evening carousing in the saloons of the French Quarter. A man bought his mediators for pennies, just before going home, in the French market.

Take small French rolls, cut off the tops, and scoop out most of the center. Brush the cut side of the tops and the hollowed-out center of the rolls with melted butter. Place both tops and rolls in a 425° oven until toasted to a very light brown. Meanwhile, sauté the oysters in hot butter until they plump up and the edges curl (takes 2 to 3 minutes). Add salt, pepper, 2 or 3 drops of Tabasco, and, if you like, a little hot cream. Fill the hot rolls and cover with crusty tops. Allow about 3 oysters to one roll. Serve hot.

OYSTER PAN ROAST

½ cup (1 stick) butter
1 pint of oysters
Salt
Freshly ground pepper

2 tablespoons ketchup
1 tablespoon Worcestershire sauce
Big squeeze of lemon juice

Melt butter in a skillet, then add the drained oysters, salt, pepper, and all remaining ingredients. Cook over a moderate heat, stirring constantly, until oysters plump up (1 to 2 minutes). Serve on toast. Makes 4 servings.

GRAND CENTRAL OYSTER STEW

One reassuring oasis of stability in the ever-changing city of New York is the Oyster Bar that opened in Grand Central Station on May 22, 1912, and continues to serve an Oyster Stew made according to its original recipe.

2 cups milk
2 cups light cream
1 quart oysters and liquor
2 tablespoons butter

Salt
Pepper
Celery salt
Paprika (optional)

This recipe is prepared quickly; heat soup bowls before you start. Scald milk and cream together but do not boil. Drain oyster liquor into a saucepan and bring to a boil. Heat oysters in a separate saucepan with 2 tablespoons of the oyster liquor and the butter until the oysters are plump and the edges begin to curl. Remove from heat immediately. Combine hot milk and cream, hot oysters, and hot oyster liquor. Add salt, pepper, and celery salt. Ladle into soup bowls, sprinkle with paprika, and serve with oyster crackers. Serves 6 to 8.

OYSTERS FARCIS

3 dozen oysters
½ cup (1 stick) butter
1 cup shallots, chopped fine
1 cup parsley, chopped fine
½ cup celery, chopped fine
1 tablespoon flour

¾ cup dry bread crumbs
Salt
Cayenne
1 egg, well beaten
6 large oyster shells

Heat oysters in their liquor until edges begin to curl. Drain and cut into small pieces. Set aside. Melt butter in a saucepan. Stir in shallots, parsley, and celery and cook over a low heat until limp. Blend in flour until smooth, then add ½ cup of the bread crumbs and the chopped oysters. Remove from heat, season with salt and cayenne, and stir in the egg. Cool, then spoon into shells. Sprinkle with remaining crumbs and dot with additional butter. Just before serving, place in a preheated 450° oven 8 to 10 minutes or until brown. Serves 6.

OYSTERS ROCKEFELLER

Oysters Rockefeller originated in 1899 at Antoine's, the celebrated restaurant founded in New Orleans by M. Antoine Alciatore. The recipe was named, according to legend, when one of the customers tasted it and cried, "Why, this is as rich as Rockefeller!"

6 tablespoons butter
6 tablespoons raw spinach, chopped fine
3 tablespoons parsley, chopped fine
3 tablespoons celery, chopped fine
3 tablespoons onion, chopped fine
5 tablespoons fine dry bread crumbs

Few drops of Tabasco
½ teaspoon salt
½ teaspoon Pernod or anisette
36 oysters on the half shell
Rock salt

Melt butter in a saucepan and stir in all ingredients *except oysters and rock salt*. Cook over a low heat, stirring constantly, for 15 minutes. Work through a sieve or food mill and set aside. Make a layer of rock salt in pie tins and place oysters on top. Put a teaspoonful of the vegetable mixture on each oyster. Broil under a preheated 400° broiler 3 to 5 minutes or until topping begins to brown. Serve immediately in the pie tins. Serves 6.

DEVILED OYSTERS

1 tablespoon dry mustard
12 oysters
1 egg, beaten

1 cup fresh bread crumbs
2 tablespoons melted butter

Mix mustard and a little water to a smooth paste in a small saucepan. Add freshly opened oysters and cook for 2 minutes, stirring with a gentle hand. Oysters should be thoroughly coated with the mustard. Remove from stove and, when cool, dip them, one by one, in beaten egg, then coat with fresh bread crumbs. Place in a buttered pan, sprinkle tops with melted butter, and broil quickly in a preheated broiler to brown both sides. Serves 2.

POULTRY & GAME

CHICKEN À LA KING

There are innumerable stories about the origin of Chicken à la King—all of them equally authoritative. One version says it was created by Foxhall Keene, suggested to Delmonico's, and first served in that restaurant as Chicken à la Keene. Another authority insists that it was created by the chef at Claridge's Hotel in London in 1881 for the sportsman J. R. Keene (Foxhall's father), whose horse Foxhall had won the Grand Prix in Paris. There are other well-substantiated stories that the dish originated in Florida, on Long Island, and at the Waldorf.

4 tablespoons butter
1 cup fresh mushroom slices
1 green pepper, sliced thin
½ cup dry sherry
2 cups Cream Sauce (page 542)
1 teaspoon salt

Dash cayenne
4 egg yolks
½ cup cream
3 cups boiled chicken, cut in large chunks
1 tablespoon chopped pimiento

Heat butter in a saucepan, add mushrooms, and sauté about 5 minutes or until lightly browned. Stir in green pepper and simmer a few more minutes. Add sherry, Cream Sauce, salt, and cayenne. Heat to a boil, stirring constantly. Combine egg yolks with cream, then stir into mushroom mixture. Add the chicken and heat through, but do not boil. Just before serving, add the pimiento. Serve on toast triangles with rice or in patty shells. Serves 6.

MARYLAND FRIED CHICKEN

6 strips bacon
Butter or vegetable oil
¾ cup flour (about)
1 teaspoon salt

¼ teaspoon pepper
A 3- to 3½-pound frying chicken
2 tablespoons flour
2 cups half-and-half (milk and cream)

Fry bacon in a large skillet until brown on both sides. Remove bacon, drain on paper towels, and set aside. Add enough butter or oil to bacon drippings to make 1 inch of fat in skillet. Dump ¾ cup flour, salt, and pepper into a paper bag and shake it well. Drop in the chicken pieces and shake to coat the chicken. When fat is bubbling hot (but not brown), add chicken pieces and fry until browned on all sides. Now cover skillet, reduce heat, and cook over a low heat for about 25 minutes or until tender when tested with a fork. Transfer chicken to a hot platter and keep warm. Pour off all but 4 tablespoons of the fat, stir in the 2 tablespoons of flour, and cook a few minutes. Then pour in the half-and-half. Cook, stirring constantly, until sauce is smooth and thick. Season to taste. Pour sauce over the hot chicken and garnish with bacon strips. Serves 4.

CAPITOLADE OF CHICKEN

Capitolade—a hash—was served at Monticello. Annette, a French governess for Jefferson's family, suggested, "This dish is for breakfast."

2 tablespoons chopped onion
2 tablespoons melted butter
1 tablespoon shallots, chopped fine
1 clove garlic, crushed
1 cup sliced mushrooms

1 tablespoon flour
⅓ cup white wine
1 cup stock or leftover chicken gravy
2 cups cooked chicken, diced
Chopped parsley

Cook onions in melted butter until limp. Stir in shallots, garlic, and mushrooms. Cook over a low heat about 5 minutes, then stir in flour until smooth. Add wine and stock. Cook until sauce bubbles, then reduce heat and simmer gently for 10 minutes. Stir in diced chicken and season to taste. Spoon into serving dish and sprinkle with chopped parsley.

CHICKEN HASH À LA RITZ

Created by Louis Diat, the chef at the old Ritz-Carlton in New York, Chicken Hash à la Ritz came into existence at about the time the Ritz opened in 1910.

Hash:
3 cups cooked chicken
1½ cups light cream
1½ tablespoons butter
1½ tablespoons flour
1½ teaspoons salt
¾ cup milk

Sauce:
1 cup milk
4 tablespoons butter
2 tablespoons flour
1 medium onion, sliced
¼ teaspoon salt
3 egg yolks
3 tablespoons grated Parmesan cheese

To make the hash: Mince chicken. Combine with cream and cook, over a very low heat, until cream is reduced to about half the original amount. Melt butter in a separate saucepan, add flour and salt, stir until smooth, and cook a minute or two. Add milk slowly and cook over a low heat, stirring constantly, until sauce bubbles. Stir into chicken mixture and pour into a shallow baking dish. Keep the hash hot while you make the sauce.

To make the sauce: Heat milk until a film appears. Skim surface. Do not boil. Melt *2 tablespoons of the butter* in a saucepan and stir in flour until smooth. Cook a minute or so. Gradually add the hot milk, stirring all the while. Add sliced onion and salt and cook over a low heat for about 15 minutes, stirring frequently. Beat egg yolks slightly, then add the hot sauce very slowly, stirring constantly. Mix in remaining 2 tablespoons butter and the cheese last of all. Spoon this mixture over the chicken and broil 4 to 5 inches from broiling unit, in a preheated broiler, until surface is golden. Serves 4.

This hash is usually served with a border of puréed peas, prepared as follows: Cook frozen peas according to package directions, drain thoroughly, and purée in an electric blender. Spoon the hot purée, seasoned with salt and pepper, around the edge of the baking dish after it comes from the broiler.

BURGOO

Burgoo apparently originated in the mid-eighteenth century as a thick porridge, one of the mainstays of a ship's mess. As developed in America, it came to be associated with Kentucky, and to be even thicker by virtue of including hens, squirrels, beef, hogs, lambs, and a wide assortment of vegetables and seasonings. It was made in enormous quantities (800 pounds of beef, 240 pounds of chicken, a ton of potatoes) and served at picnics, horse sales, church suppers, and on Derby Day.

5 tablespoons bacon fat or vegetable oil
2 pounds lean shin bones of beef with meat
1 pound shoulder of veal
2 medium-sized chickens, quartered
4 quarts water
1 tablespoon salt
4 cups onions, chopped
1 clove garlic, chopped
2 cups potatoes, diced
1 bunch celery with tops, diced
1 quart skinned ripe tomatoes or
   2 cans (1 pound, 3-ounce size) tomatoes
6 carrots, diced
2 large green peppers, chopped

1 pint fresh butter beans or
   1 package frozen butter beans
1 small pod red pepper or
   ¼ teaspoon crushed red pepper
1 small onion, stuck with 4 cloves
1 bay leaf
¼ cup dark brown sugar
½ teaspoon freshly ground pepper
2 cups okra, sliced, or 1 package frozen okra
6 ears corn (cut kernels from cob) or
   2 packages frozen corn
½ cup (1 stick) butter
1 cup flour
1 cup parsley, chopped

Heat *3 tablespoons bacon fat or oil* in a large kettle. Add beef and veal and brown well. Add chickens, water, and salt, and cook over a low heat, covered, until very tender. Remove meat and chicken to a tray and, when cool enough to handle, remove and discard all bones and the chicken skin. Cut meat and chicken into sizable pieces, then return to broth. Cook onions in remaining 2 tablespoons bacon fat or oil until limp. Add to broth, along with garlic, potatoes, celery, tomatoes, carrots, green peppers, butter beans, red pepper, onion stuck with cloves, bay leaf, brown sugar, and ground pepper. Cook slowly for about 2 hours, stirring occasionally. Then add okra and corn and cook 15 minutes longer. Before serving, combine butter and flour, working the mixture until well blended. Stir into Burgoo and cook, stirring constantly, until Burgoo has thickened slightly. Taste for seasoning. Before serving, sprinkle with chopped parsley. Serves 20, but recipe can successfully be cut in half.

CHICKEN CROQUETTES

1 cup thick Cream Sauce (page 542)
2 egg yolks, lightly beaten
2 cups cooked chicken, finely chopped
2 tablespoons chopped parsley
½ teaspoon nutmeg
¼ teaspoon grated onion

1 teaspoon Worcestershire sauce
Flour
1 egg, well beaten
Dry bread crumbs
Fat for deep-fat frying

While Cream Sauce is still hot, stir it, a little at a time, into the egg yolks. Add chicken, parsley, nutmeg, grated onion, and Worcestershire sauce and blend thoroughly. Chill in a shallow baking dish. Divide mixture into 12 sections and shape into balls. Dip into flour, then into beaten egg, and finally into dry bread crumbs. Preheat deep fat to 375° to 385° or until a 1-inch cube of bread browns in 60 seconds. Fry croquettes, a few at a time, for 2 to 3 minutes or until golden. Drain on paper towels. Serve with creamed peas or Mushroom Sauce (page 544). Serves 4 to 6.

VARIATION I: Dust 1 cup chicken livers with a mixture of flour, salt, and pepper. Sauté in heated butter until well browned. Place a chicken liver in the center of each croquette.

VARIATION II: Season 12 medium-sized mushrooms with salt and pepper. Sauté in heated butter for several minutes. Shape each croquette around a mushroom.

VARIATION III: Substitute 2 cups of chopped, cooked sweetbreads for cooked chicken.

VARIATION IV: Substitute 2 cups chopped leftover roast veal for cooked chicken.

BRUNSWICK STEW

Brunswick County, North Carolina, has for years been attempting to lay claim to Brunswick Stew. The best-documented case, however, is held by Brunswick County, Virginia, which argues that in 1828 Dr. Creed Haskins of Mount Donum, a member of the Virginia state legislature, wanted something special for a political rally he was sponsoring. Haskins had eaten a squirrel stew created by Jimmy Matthews, and he turned to Matthews for a new variation on that stew. Squirrels gradually disappeared from the recipe for Brunswick Stew, and chicken is now accepted as its major ingredient, but it remained for many years—in its original form—one of the principal attractions of political rallies conducted by the Whigs and Democrats, and of cockfights, family reunions, tobacco curings, and other Virginia gatherings.

Two 3-pound chickens, cut in pieces	2 onions, sliced
2 pounds shin bone of beef or veal	4 cups skinned tomatoes, chopped
1 ham bone from baked Virginia	2 cups celery with tops, chopped
or country ham	2 cups butter beans or small green
1 squirrel, cut in pieces (optional)	Lima beans (fresh or frozen)
3 quarts water	4 cups corn (fresh or frozen)
½ cup sugar	½ cup (1 stick) butter
1 bay leaf	1 pod red pepper, crushed
1 teaspoon basil	1 teaspoon coarse black pepper
2 tablespoons parsley, chopped	4 large potatoes, pared and boiled until tender

Put chickens, beef or veal bone, ham bone, squirrel, water, sugar, bay leaf, basil, and parsley in a large soup kettle. Cook over a low heat until meat is tender enough to fall from bones. Remove meat from broth and cool. To the broth add onions, tomatoes, celery, and beans. Continue cooking slowly until beans are tender. Stir frequently. Remove meat from bones and cut into pieces. Add to stew, then add corn. Simmer for 10 minutes, then stir in butter, red pepper pod, and black pepper. Add salt to taste. Work potatoes through a ricer or blend in an electric blender and stir into stew. Stir constantly for 15 minutes or until mixture is the consistency of mush. Serves 20.

CHICKEN FRICASSEE

A 4- to 5-pound chicken
1 cup water
1½ teaspoons salt
Dash pepper
¼ cup butter

½ pound mushrooms, sliced
1 cup cream
¼ teaspoon mace
Few sprigs parsley

Cut the chicken into serving pieces, place in a Dutch oven or heavy saucepan with a tight-fitting lid, add water, salt, and pepper, and cook to a boil. Lower the heat, cover tightly, and cook very slowly for about 1½ hours or until chicken is extremely tender when pierced with a fork. Melt butter in a saucepan, add mushrooms, and sauté for about 5 minutes. Combine with chicken, then add the cream and mace. Cook, still over low heat, for 10 to 15 minutes longer. Arrange chicken pieces on a hot serving platter, spoon sauce over the top, and sprinkle with finely chopped parsley. Serves 4.

A Dutch oven

CHICKEN PIE, COUNTRY STYLE

1 large chicken
1 carrot
1 onion, stuck with 2 cloves
1 stalk celery
Several sprigs parsley
Salt
Pepper
2 tablespoons butter
2 tablespoons chicken fat

5 tablespoons flour
½ cup cream
Pastry:
2 cups sifted all-purpose flour
½ teaspoon salt
4 teaspoons baking powder
5 tablespoons butter
4 tablespoons solid chicken fat
5 tablespoons milk (about)

To make the filling: Place chicken in a large kettle and pour in enough water to almost cover the bird. Add carrot, onion, celery, and parsley. Season with salt and pepper. Cook over a low heat for about 1½ hours or until the bird is very tender when tested with a fork. Let cool in the stock until the chicken can be handled comfortably. Discard skin and bones, leaving meat in large pieces. Strain the broth, skim off the fat, and refrigerate fat until firm. (You will need 3 cups of broth and 6 tablespoons of chicken fat to make the pie.) Pour 1½ cups of chicken broth over chicken pieces. Heat butter and 2 tablespoons of chicken fat in the top of a double boiler, stir in flour, keeping mixture smooth, and cook a minute or two. Add the remaining 1½ cups of chicken broth and cook, stirring constantly, until sauce is smooth and thick. Stir in cream last of all and taste for seasoning.

To make the pastry: Sift flour, salt, and baking powder together. Cut in butter and chicken fat with two knives or a pastry blender until mixture looks mealy. Add milk gradually (just enough to hold pastry together) and knead on a lightly floured board for half a minute. Refrigerate for 30 minutes. Divide pastry in half and roll one half into a large circle. Line bottom and sides of a round 1½-quart baking dish. (This is an exceptionally rich pastry, so if it breaks at any time, simply patch it.) Drain the chicken pieces, lay all of them in the baking dish, and add the cream sauce. Cover with remaining pastry, rolled thin and slashed in several places. Pinch edges together to seal securely and bake in a preheated 450° oven for 25 minutes or until top crust is golden. Serves 4 to 6.

CHICKEN POTPIE

A 4-pound chicken
1 stalk celery
1 carrot
1 onion, stuck with 2 cloves
1 tablespoon salt

2 cups sifted all-purpose flour
½ teaspoon salt
2 eggs
2 to 3 tablespoons water
4 medium potatoes, sliced
6 to 7 sprigs parsley, chopped

Cut chicken into serving pieces, place in kettle along with celery, carrot, clove-studded onion, salt, and enough cold water to cover. Bring to a boil, then reduce heat, cover, and cook over a low heat for about 40 minutes or until tender when tested with a fork. Remove vegetables and discard them.

To make the dough: Sift flour and salt into a bowl. Dig a small well in the center, drop in eggs, and blend the mixture to make a stiff dough. Add 2 to 3 tablespoons water if needed. Roll as thin as possible on a lightly floured board and cut into 1-inch squares with a pastry wheel or sharp knife. Drop potato slices and pastry potpies into the boiling broth, cover, and cook over a moderate heat for 20 minutes. Sprinkle in the chopped parsley and serve in hot soup plates to 6.

COUNTRY CAPTAIN

According to Miss Eliza Leslie's *New Cookery Book,* Country Captain is an East Indian dish that was probably first introduced to the British by a captain of the sepoys, the native East Indian troops. Miss Leslie's story notwithstanding, Georgians claim this dish as their own, insisting that the mysterious captain drifted into Savannah via the spice trade and entrusted his recipe to southern friends. The recipe is, in any case, flavored with Indian spices.

A 2½-pound chicken (broiler or fryer)
¼ cup flour
1 teaspoon salt
¼ teaspoon pepper
4 to 5 tablespoons butter
⅓ cup onion, chopped fine
⅓ cup green pepper, chopped fine

1 clove garlic, crushed
1½ teaspoons curry powder
½ teaspoon dried thyme
1 can (1 pound) stewed tomatoes
3 tablespoons dried currants
Blanched, toasted almonds
Chutney

Mix together flour, salt, and pepper. Cut chicken in serving pieces and coat. Heat *4 table-spoons of the butter* in a large, heavy skillet until very hot. Add chicken and brown well on both sides. If all the fat is absorbed before chicken is browned, add remaining tablespoon of butter. Remove chicken and set aside. Add onion, green pepper, garlic, curry powder, and thyme to skillet and cook for a few minutes over a low heat, stirring in all the brown particles. Then add the stewed tomatoes. Put the chicken, skin side up, back into the skillet, cover, and cook slowly for 20 to 30 minutes or until tender when pierced with a fork. Last of all, stir in the currants. Serve to 4 with almonds and chutney on the side.

PLYMOUTH SUCCOTASH

Plymouth Succotash is distinguished from the more familiar form by the addition of meats. It was served in a number of Plymouth households once a year, on December 21, in celebration of the date on which the Pilgrims landed.

1 pint pea beans	4 quarts water
A 3-pound chicken	3 cooked potatoes, sliced
2½ pounds corned beef	1 small yellow turnip, cooked and cubed
½ pound salt pork	1½ quarts whole hominy

Soak beans overnight. Drain, cover with fresh water, and cook about 2 hours or until very tender. Drain and work through a sieve or blend in an electric blender. While the beans are cooking, put chicken (cut into serving pieces), corned beef, salt pork, and water in a large kettle. Cook about 2 to 2½ hours or until beef is tender. Stir in bean purée, sliced potatoes, diced turnips, and hominy. Serves 10.

POACHED STUFFED CHICKEN WITH LEMON SAUCE

A 5- to 5½-pound chicken	1 onion, stuck with 2 cloves
3½ cups bread, crumbled fine	1 large bay leaf
Salt	Few sprigs parsley
Pepper	1½ teaspoons salt
1 generous teaspoon thyme	4 peppercorns, crushed
4 to 5 tablespoons butter, melted	*Sauce:*
Giblets and neck	1 cup chicken broth
2 carrots, cut in chunks	2 egg yolks
3 stalks celery with tops, sliced	Juice and rind of ½ lemon

Prepare the stuffing by crumbling enough old bread to make about 3½ cups. Mix in salt and pepper to taste, and the thyme. Then mix in the melted butter until it is well distributed. Stuff the cavity of the bird with mixture. So that liquid will not seep into stuffing, place a small piece of foil inside the bird just above the tail. Lap the loose skin over the foil and skewer securely. Pull the tail up, push inside the bird, and skewer. Truss the legs with soft string and fold the tips of the wings under the chicken. Place stuffed chicken in a large, deep kettle with all the remaining ingredients, add enough cold water to cover, and bring slowly to a boil. Reduce heat to simmer, cover, and poach until chicken is tender, about 1 hour. Take care not to overcook or the bird will lose its shape. Lift chicken from broth, remove all strings, skewers, and foil. Tuck a feather of celery tops or parsley in its tail, place on warm serving platter, and keep it warm while you make the sauce. Serves 4 to 5.

To make the sauce: Strain the broth into a heavy saucepan. Beat egg yolks until very thick and light. Add a little of the hot broth to the beaten eggs, then combine the two. Add the lemon juice and cook over a very low heat, stirring constantly, until sauce is somewhat thicker than heavy cream. Watch carefully because overcooking will curdle the sauce. Just before pouring into a warm sauceboat, add the grated lemon rind. Small white onions steamed in butter go well with this unusually flavored chicken. Use the strained broth for soup, or bottle and refrigerate it to use later.

CHICKEN SALAD

There are innumerable ways to prepare and serve Chicken Salad. Essentially, it is cold chicken (either poached or the remains of roast chicken) usually combined with chopped celery and moistened with either boiled dressing or mayonnaise.

VARIATION I: To make Breast of Chicken Salad, poach 4 chicken breasts in stock until tender when pierced with a fork. When cool enough to handle, remove skin, bone, and all gristle. Cut the meat into ¾-inch chunks, sprinkle with fresh lemon juice, then combine with enough Virginia Boiled Dressing (page 543) or mayonnaise to bind lightly. Arrange on salad greens, garnish with capers and the yolks of 2 hard-cooked eggs forced through a sieve. Serves 4 to 6.

VARIATION II: To make Breast of Chicken Salad with grapes, add ½ to ¾ cup of green seedless grapes to above recipe and eliminate both capers and hard-cooked eggs. Serves 4.

VARIATION III: To make Chicken Salad with celery, add to every 2½ cups cooked chicken, cut in large chunks, 1 cup chopped raw celery. Blend with Virginia Boiled Dressing or mayonnaise to taste. Arrange on a bed of lettuce and garnish with any or all of the following: quartered tomatoes, capers, pimiento strips, stuffed olives. Serves 4.

VARIATION IV: To make Chicken Salad with toasted nuts, follow directions above, replacing celery with same amount of chopped toasted almonds, walnuts, filberts, or pecans. Serves 4.

CHICKEN PUDDING

This recipe is from the family cookbook of President James Monroe.

A 4- to 4½-pound chicken
½ cup flour
1 teaspoon salt
¼ teaspoon pepper
⅓ cup butter

Batter topping:
1¼ cups sifted all-purpose flour
½ teaspoon salt
3 eggs
1 cup milk
2 tablespoons melted butter

Cut chicken into serving pieces. Put the neck, giblets, and backbone in a pan, pour in enough water to cover, and add 1 onion (cut in half), 1 stalk of celery (cut in chunks), a few sprigs of parsley, 1 teaspoon salt, ¼ teaspoon pepper, and ½ teaspoon dried thyme. Cook over a low heat about 45 minutes. Strain and reserve the broth. Combine flour, salt, and pepper in a paper bag. Drop in pieces of chicken and shake until evenly coated. Heat butter in a skillet (one with a tight-fitting lid), add chicken, and sauté until nicely browned on all sides. Add broth, cook to a boil, cover tightly, and simmer gently for 1 to 1¼ hours or until chicken is tender when tested with a fork. Transfer chicken to an 8-inch square baking dish that can be used for serving. Reserve the broth.

To prepare the batter topping: Sift together flour and salt. Set aside. Beat eggs soundly, pour in milk and butter. Stir in flour mixture until smooth. Pour over the chicken, covering it evenly with the batter. Bake in a preheated 450° oven for 15 minutes. Reduce oven temperature to 350° and continue baking 20 to 25 minutes. Topping will puff up and brown around the edges like Yorkshire Pudding.

While the pudding bakes, make a smooth paste with 1 or 2 tablespoons of flour and water. Stir into chicken broth and cook, stirring constantly, until slightly thickened. Serve immediately, with the gravy in a separate dish. Serves 4 to 6.

CHICKEN WITH SMITHFIELD HAM

A 3½- to 4-pound chicken
1 teaspoon salt
1 onion, stuck with 2 cloves
Few sprigs of parsley
2 stalks celery
Sauce:
2 tablespoons butter
2 tablespoons flour
2 cups light cream
¼ teaspoon salt

Dash of nutmeg
Stuffing:
2 cups fresh bread crumbs, finely crumbled
1 small onion, minced
2 tablespoons parsley, chopped
1 teaspoon dried summer savory
¼ teaspoon salt
Dash of pepper
6 thin slices Smithfield ham

To prepare the chicken: Cut chicken in quarters and place in a large saucepan. Toss in salt, onion stuck with cloves, parsley, celery, and enough water to almost cover. Bring to a boil, cover tightly with a lid, and simmer for an hour or two or until tender. Cool in the broth until comfortable to handle, then strip meat from bones in sizable pieces, and discard bones and skin. Arrange chicken pieces in a medium-sized baking dish. Strain broth and save.

To make the sauce: Melt butter in a saucepan, stir in flour until smooth, and cook a minute or two. Pour in cream and cook, stirring constantly, until slightly thickened. Season with salt and nutmeg and pour over chicken.

To make the stuffing: Combine bread crumbs, onion, chopped parsley, summer savory, salt, and pepper in a bowl. Mix in just enough broth to hold stuffing together. Place some stuffing in the center of each slice of ham and roll ham around it (save about two tablespoons of stuffing to use later). Arrange the ham rolls around the chicken in the baking dish, then sprinkle the top with remaining stuffing. Bake in a preheated 350° oven for 30 minutes.

Potato masher

ROAST GOOSE WITH POTATO STUFFING

Although Catharine Beecher suggested this potato stuffing for roast goose in her *Domestic Receipt-Book*, it is also appropriate to use an oyster or chestnut stuffing, or wild rice.

Potato Stuffing:
2 cups hot mashed potatoes
1½ cups bread crumbs
1 medium onion, chopped fine
2 eggs, lightly beaten

1½ teaspoons salt
1 teaspoon sage
½ cup chopped celery leaves
¼ cup chopped parsley

Combine mashed potatoes with all remaining ingredients. Singe and remove all pinfeathers from an 8- to 9-pound goose. Rub the cavity and skin with a cut lemon and salt. Stuff and truss the goose. Place on a rack in a roasting pan (breast side up), toss a cut clove of garlic and a stalk of celery with leaves into the pan, and roast in a preheated 350° oven for 18 to 20 minutes per pound. Prick the skin, around the wings and legs, with a fork to release the fat. Baste occasionally with pan drippings. When goose is tender and the skin brown and crisp, place on a heated platter and garnish with watercress. Serve with applesauce.

TO DRESS DUCKS WITH ORANGE

This recipe for roast duck with orange sauce is adapted from Mary Randolph's *Virginia Housewife*.

1 large duck	¼ cup orange liqueur
Salt	Grated rind of 1 orange
Pepper	¼ cup orange peel, cut in thin strips
½ cup sugar	Fresh lemon juice (optional)
1 tablespoon red wine vinegar	Parsley
Juice of 2 oranges	

Rub cavity of cleaned duck with salt and pepper, then truss securely. Prick the skin around the thighs, back, and lower breast to allow fat to escape. Place in a 350° oven and roast for 1 hour and 40 minutes. Do not baste. When the leg moves easily or the flesh of the leg feels soft when pressed, the duck is done. While the duck roasts, remove excess fat with a baster. When duck is properly roasted, remove trussing strings, place duck on a hot platter, and keep it warm. Sprinkle lightly with salt. Skim off excess fat from roasting pan. Cook sugar and vinegar in a heavy pan over a moderately high heat until mixture has caramelized. Remove from heat, add orange juice, orange liqueur, and the grated orange rind. Put back on the stove and simmer, stirring constantly, until caramel has dissolved completely. Add this to juices left in roasting pan, bring to a boil, and cook for a few minutes, stirring constantly, scraping down the sides of the pan to incorporate all the rich brown particles. Next add the orange peel, then taste. If the sauce seems to lack sharpness, add a squeeze of fresh lemon juice. Pour sauce over duck, arrange orange sections along the backbone down the full length of the duck, and tuck a bouquet of parsley into the tail. Serves 4.

ROAST DUCK

1 large duck	*Sauce:*
Pinch mace	1 medium onion, chopped
Few celery leaves	1 tablespoon butter
3 sprigs parsley	1½ cups giblet broth
1 small onion, chopped	1 teaspoon arrowroot or cornstarch
½ teaspoon dried sage	1 teaspoon grated lemon rind
½ teaspoon salt	1 tablespoon sweet pickles, chopped
½ teaspoon pepper	

Cook duck giblets and neck with 2 cups water, mace, celery leaves, parsley, and a pinch of salt until tender. Strain (save broth). Chop giblets extremely fine and set aside. Combine onion, sage, salt, and pepper and stuff into duck cavity. Place bird on a rack in roasting pan and roast in a preheated 350° oven for 1¼ to 1½ hours. To serve, cut into quarters with kitchen shears, place on platter, and keep duck warm while you make sauce. Serves 2 to 3.

To make the sauce: Chop onion very fine and sauté in heated butter until golden. Pour in almost all of the giblet broth (if there isn't enough to make 1½ cups, add dry red wine). Stir enough of the broth into the arrowroot or cornstarch to make a smooth paste and add to the giblet mixture. Cook over a moderate heat, stirring constantly, until sauce bubbles and thickens. Add lemon rind, sweet pickles, and, last of all, the chopped giblets. Bring to a boil again and pour into gravy boat.

PÂTÉ

2 tablespoons butter
½ pound chicken livers
2 hard-cooked eggs
2 packages (3-ounce size) cream cheese
2 or 3 truffles, coarsely chopped

¾ teaspoon salt
Dash freshly ground pepper
Cognac to taste (about 3 tablespoons)
Canned jellied consommé

Melt butter in a saucepan. Add chicken livers and cook, stirring frequently, until tender (about 8 to 10 minutes). Work liver and eggs through a food grinder or blend in an electric blender. If you use the latter method, do a small quantity at a time. Work the cream cheese until soft, then combine with the ground liver mixture. If you have a blender, put it all back in the container and give it another whirl to make it as smooth as possible. Then stir in truffles, salt, pepper, and cognac. Makes 1½ cups.

To prepare Pâté en Bellevue: Line a small mold (2-cup size) with jellied consommé or aspic, decorate with strips of truffles and the whites of hard-cooked eggs. Cover these with a second layer of consommé. Chill thoroughly. Fill center with the chicken liver *pâté* and cover with another layer of consommé. Chill thoroughly again. Unmold and serve with toast.

THE TURKEY

In *The Physiology of Taste*, Brillat-Savarin—gastronomy's Marquis of Queensbury—wrote: "The turkey is surely one of the noblest gifts which the Old World has received from the New. Superlatively knowing persons maintain that the *Romans* were addicted to the turkey, that it was served at *Charlemagne's* wedding-feast, and that therefore it is false to praise the Jesuits for this most savoury of imports. Let us silence such dealers in paradox with a twofold refutation: 1) The French name of the bird, which, being *coq d'Inde*, clearly betrays its origin; for at first *America* was always known as the *Western Indies;* 2) The appearance of the bird, which is clearly outlandish. A scholar could make no mistake about it."

The origin of the name "turkey" has been variously explained; among the most reasonable speculations is that the word is a corruption of *furkee*, an Indian name for the bird. Americans, of course, rarely think of turkey without thinking of the first Thanksgiving, which the Pilgrims shared with Massasoit and his tribe. As Edward Winslow described that occasion in 1621: "Our harvest being gotten in, our governor sent four men on fowling, that so we might, after a special manner, rejoice together after we had gathered the fruit of our labors. They four in one day killed as much fowl as, with a little help beside, served the company almost a week."

Benjamin Franklin once wrote his daughter, Sarah Bache: "I wish the Bald Eagle had not been chosen as the Representation of our Country; he is a Bird of bad moral Character, like those among men who live by sharpening and robbing, he is generally poor and often very lousy.... The turkey is...a much more respectable bird, and withal a true original Native of America."

DIRECTIONS FOR ROASTING TURKEY

Wash the turkey thoroughly, remove any pinfeathers, and singe any hairs along the edges of the wings and around the legs. Rub the cavity with the cut side of a half lemon and stuff the bird lightly with any of the suggested stuffings (pages 486-87). Close the opening by skewering or sewing it and truss the bird well. Rub the turkey with butter and season with salt and pepper. Place in a large roasting pan and cover with several layers of cheesecloth soaked in butter. Do not add water to the pan. Roast in a preheated 325° oven. Baste several times during roasting period, right through the cheesecloth. Remove the cheesecloth during the last half hour of cooking to allow the turkey to brown. To test whether it is done, move the leg joint up and down—it should give readily—or take several layers of paper towels and squeeze the fleshy part of the drumstick—if properly cooked, it should feel soft. To roast an 8- to 10-pound stuffed turkey, allow 4 to 4½ hours; for a 12- to 14-pound stuffed turkey, allow 5 to 5¼ hours; and for a large stuffed turkey, 18 to 20 pounds, allow 6½ to 7½ hours.

TO PREPARE A TURKEY FOR CHRISTMAS DINNER

The turkey should be cooped up and fed some time before Christmas. Three days before it is slaughtered, it should have an English walnut forced down its throat three times a day, and a glass of sherry once a day. The meat will be deliciously tender, and have a fine nutty flavor.
—Mrs. Stephen J. Field,
Statesmen's Dishes and How to Cook Them, 1890

TURKEY GIBLET GRAVY

Cover the giblets and the neck with water and dry white wine (2 parts of water to 1 of wine). Add a teaspoon of salt, 3 or 4 peppercorns, a sprig of parsley, 1 onion stuck with 2 cloves, and 1 carrot. Bring to a boil and boil for 1 minute. Skim, cover the pan, and lower the heat. Cook gently for 1 hour. Strain the broth, cook it down to 1 cup, and season to taste. Chop giblets and set aside. When the turkey is done, add the juices from the roasting pan to the giblet broth. If you wish a slightly thicker sauce, stir in a little arrowroot, or knead together about 2 tablespoons of butter with the same amount of flour and drop in little balls into the hot liquid. Stir the sauce until thick and well blended. Add chopped giblets before serving.

DEVILED TURKEY

Blend, according to taste, a marinade of cayenne, salt, dry mustard, grated lemon rind, lemon juice, sherry, and Worcestershire sauce. Carve nice slices of cold, cooked turkey and spread each slice with a light coating of softened butter. Arrange in a large, flat baking dish and cover with the marinade. Let stand for about 1 hour. Then bake in a preheated 300° oven for 20 minutes or until hot.

BRAISED GUINEA HEN

The guinea hen, a native of West Africa, was introduced to Europe
in the sixteenth century and became popular in colonial America.

1 guinea hen	¼ teaspoon dry mustard
2 tablespoons butter	1 clove garlic, crushed
1 tablespoon vinegar	Dash cayenne
1 teaspoon salt	½ cup chicken broth
¼ teaspoon pepper	

Cut the guinea hen into quarters and sauté in heated butter on all sides until nicely
browned. Mix together all remaining ingredients, pour over bird, cover, and simmer for
30 minutes or until almost tender. Remove cover, turn up the heat, and continue cooking
until liquid is almost evaporated. Wild rice is an excellent accompaniment. Serves 4.

To roast guinea hen: Have the butcher wrap the breasts in large pieces of salt pork and tie
them securely (like pheasant, which it resembles in flavor, guinea hen is inclined to be dry).
Stuff as you would a chicken (cook the giblets and use them in the stuffing). Roast in a
preheated 400° oven for 40 minutes, basting occasionally. Then remove the pork from the
breasts, return to oven, and roast 10 minutes, at same temperature, to brown.

Quail

Guinea hen

PHEASANT IN CASSEROLE

The pheasant came to America by way of England from China and the
shores of the Black Sea. Richard Bache, an Englishman who married
Benjamin Franklin's only daughter, was the first to attempt to raise
pheasants in this country—on his estate in New Jersey.

A 2½- to 3-pound pheasant	2 medium-sized truffles, sliced
Salt	1 can (7½ ounces) beef gravy
2 strips larding pork	¾ cup Madeira wine
6 tablespoons butter	¼ cup cognac

Truss legs and wings of pheasant close to the body and rub skin with a little salt. Cover
breast of bird with strips of larding pork, since pheasant is inclined to be dry. Place in a
roasting pan along with *4 tablespoons of the butter* and roast in a preheated 425° oven for
45 minutes. A few minutes before the bird is done, heat the remaining 2 tablespoons butter
in a heavy casserole with a tight-fitting lid. Add truffles and sauté for a few minutes. Remove pheasant from oven, discard pork, and cut off cord. Place bird in casserole. Skim
fat from pan and discard. Add the gravy and Madeira to remaining pan juices. Bring to
a boil, stirring constantly until smooth. Then stir in cognac. Pour this sauce over the
pheasant, cover, return to oven, and continue roasting at the same high temperature 15
minutes. Serves 2 to 3.

ROAST WILD DUCK

In the Gay Nineties, an entree of wild duck was almost *de rigueur* at any fashionable dinner. "The Canvasback is superior in flavor to any other species of wild duck, and is much esteemed..." Mary Ronald wrote in *The Century Cook Book* in 1895. "Wild ducks should be very rare and served very hot, on hot plates."

Rub the cavity of the dressed, cleaned duck with salt, then insert one of the following: a few sprigs of parsley; a few juniper berries; apples (pared, cored, and quartered); 2 or 3 small peeled onions; or 1 or 2 teaspoons of currant jelly. Skewer the opening. Place duck or ducks on a rack, breast side up, and rub generously with soft butter. For rare duck, roast the bird in a preheated 500° oven for 18 to 20 minutes, basting every few minutes with melted butter. For well-done duck, roast in a preheated 350° oven, allowing 15 minutes per pound. Baste frequently with melted butter. Serve with fried hominy or wild rice, currant jelly, and a bottle of dry red wine.

SMALL GAME BIRDS, ROASTED

4 small game birds	Beef broth or sherry
2 slices dry firm bread	Salt
4 tablespoons butter	Pepper
1/4 cup pecans, chopped	

Clean birds and set aside. Crumble bread into fine crumbs and cook in *2 tablespoons of the butter* for a minute or two. Combine with pecans, adding just enough broth or sherry to moisten. Season with salt and pepper. Stuff birds until plump, then close the cavities with small skewers or toothpicks. Truss legs and wings close to the bodies with string and place in shallow baking pan. Add just enough boiling water to cover bottom of pan. Brush birds with remaining butter, melted, and bake in a preheated 425° oven for 30 minutes. Baste frequently with melted butter. Serve birds immediately on buttered croutons. Serves 4.

SQUAB IN COMPOTE

This French recipe, a favorite of Jefferson's, is taken from his records at Monticello.

6 plump squabs	1/2 teaspoon salt
2 tablespoons butter	2 slices bacon, diced
1 cup onion, chopped fine	1/4 pound mushrooms, sliced
1 carrot, diced fine	1/3 cup sherry or Madeira

Ask your butcher to truss the squabs. Melt butter in a casserole (one with a tight-fitting lid), add squabs along with onion, carrot, and salt. Sauté until delicately browned on all sides, turning the birds frequently. Next add the bacon, mushrooms, and sherry or Madeira. Cover tightly and simmer gently for 40 to 45 minutes or until tender when tested with a fork. Take care not to overcook or they will fall apart. To serve, place on large croutons (traditionally used as a "mount" for small game birds) and spoon some of the sauce around.

FORCEMEATS

Forcemeats, as they were generally called in old cookbooks, are nothing more than seasoned mixtures used to stuff meats, fish, and fowl. Forcemeat derives from the French *farcir,* "to stuff." Today, they are generally called stuffings or dressings. The stuffings given here are taken from seventeenth- and eighteenth-century cookbooks.

CHESTNUT STUFFING

2 pounds chestnuts
1½ cups (3 sticks) butter
2 cups onion, chopped fine
2 cups thinly sliced celery
9 cups fine dry bread crumbs

2 teaspoons salt
1 teaspoon dried thyme
1 teaspoon dried marjoram
1 teaspoon dried savory

Make a gash in the flat side of each chestnut, place them in a saucepan with boiling water to cover, and simmer for about 5 minutes. While nuts are still hot, remove shells and inner brown skins. Cover chestnuts with more boiling water and cook slowly for 20 to 30 minutes or until tender. Drain and chop coarsely. Melt butter in a saucepan, add onions and celery, and sauté until limp. Add bread crumbs to vegetable-butter combination and mix thoroughly. Then add salt, thyme, marjoram, and savory, mixing them in well. Add the chestnuts. This is enough stuffing for a 12- to 15-pound turkey.

CORN BREAD STUFFING

1½ cups corn meal
2 cups all-purpose flour
2 tablespoons sugar
1 teaspoon salt
4 teaspoons baking powder
2 eggs
2 cups milk
4 tablespoons bacon drippings

1 pound sausage meat
4 medium onions, chopped fine
4 stalks celery, chopped fine
½ teaspoon dried sage
½ teaspoon dried thyme
1 teaspoon salt
Dash pepper

To make the corn bread: Grease two 9-inch square pans. Sift the corn meal, flour, sugar, salt, and baking powder together into a mixing bowl, then stir in lightly beaten eggs, milk, and bacon drippings until well mixed. Spread in baking pans and bake in a preheated 450° oven for 30 minutes. Cool, then crumble.

To make the stuffing: Fry the sausage meat over a low heat until lightly browned, then break it in pieces with a fork. Add the crumbled corn bread and mix together. Remove from heat. Cook the chopped onions in a little bacon fat until limp. Add to the mixture, then add the chopped celery and all remaining ingredients, mixing well. Makes enough stuffing for a 12- to 15-pound turkey.

ALMOND STUFFING

2 cans (4½-ounce size) blanched almonds
6 eggs, separated
1 cup light cream
¼ teaspoon nutmeg (freshly ground, if possible)

1½ pounds (about 1½ loaves) white bread, crumbled fine
½ cup (1 stick) butter, melted
Salt
Pepper

Chop almonds quite fine and toast in a preheated 300° oven until golden, stirring occasionally to brown them evenly. Set aside. In a large bowl beat egg yolks with cream and nutmeg. Add bread crumbs, almonds, butter, and a little salt and pepper. In a separate bowl beat egg whites until they stand in peaks. Spoon on top of the crumb mixture and mix together lightly with your hand. Makes enough stuffing for a 12- to 15-pound turkey.

OYSTER STUFFING

1 pound loaf firm white bread
1 cup (2 sticks) butter
1 large onion, chopped
1 stalk celery, chopped

¼ cup parsley, chopped
2 teaspoons salt
¼ teaspoon pepper
1 pint oysters in liquor

Crumble the bread quite fine. Melt butter in a saucepan, add onion and celery, and cook until onions take on a gold color. Stir into bread crumbs, then add parsley, salt, and pepper. Drain liquor from oysters and heat the liquor to the boiling point. Cut oysters in half, add to hot liquid, and cook until the edges begin to curl. Drain and stir oysters into stuffing. Makes enough stuffing for a 12- to 15-pound turkey.

PECAN STUFFING

1 turkey liver
½ cup (1 stick) butter
1 onion, minced
Toasted bread (enough to make 9 cups)
½ pound fresh mushrooms, chopped fine
1 teaspoon salt
½ teaspoon pepper
1 teaspoon celery seed

1 teaspoon dried thyme
1 tablespoon chopped parsley
½ nutmeg, grated
¼ teaspoon mace
6 eggs, hard-cooked
2 cups salted pecans, coarsely chopped
½ cup dry sherry

Cook the liver in boiling, salted water until tender, then mince. Melt *2 tablespoons of the butter*, add minced onion, and cook until soft. Add the turkey liver and sauté until lightly browned. Toss in the mushrooms and cook very briefly. Crush the toast into fine crumbs (it must be well toasted and dry), combine with the remainder of the butter (melted), the salt, pepper, celery seed, thyme, parsley, nutmeg, and mace. Put the hard-cooked eggs through a ricer and mix in thoroughly. Finally, combine the liver and herb mixtures, and add the pecans and sherry. Makes enough stuffing for a 12- to 15-pound turkey.

MEATS

TO ROAST STANDING RIBS OF BEEF

This recipe is taken from Mary Ronald's *Century Cook Book* (1895).

"To roast beef on a spit before the fire is unquestionably the best method of cooking it; but as few kitchens are equipped for roasting meats, baking them in the oven is generally practised, and has come to be called roasting. Beef should be well streaked with fat, and have a bright-red color. Place the meat to be baked on a rack which will raise it a little above the bottom of the pan. Dredge the whole, top and sides, with flour. Place in a corner of the pan a half teaspoonful of salt and a quarter teaspoonful of pepper. Do not let them touch the raw meat, as they draw out the juices. Put into the pan also two tablespoonfuls of drippings. Place it in a very hot oven for fifteen or twenty minutes, or until the meat is browned; then shut off the drafts and lower the temperature of the oven, and cook slowly until done; baste frequently; do not put water in the pan, as it makes steam, and prevents browning. A roast has a better appearance if the ribs are not too long."

By suggesting that you start the roast at a high temperature, and then lower it, the author follows the French, or searing, method of roasting. Preheat the oven to 450°, then lower it to 325°. The beef should be brought to room temperature before roasting. To cook a rib roast rare, allow 16 to 18 minutes per pound; medium rare, 18 to 22 minutes per pound; well done, 23 to 28 minutes per pound. Do not baste. Salt and pepper the meat after it has finished roasting and stand on a warm platter 10 to 15 minutes before carving. This helps the juices to settle and makes the meat easier to carve.

Thermometer method of roasting: Insert thermometer in the fleshiest part of the roast, making sure it does not touch the bone. Place roast in a preheated 325° oven and roast, without basting, until thermometer reaches 140° for rare; 160° for medium; 170° for well done.

To roast rolled ribs of beef: Place the roast, fat side up, on a rack in the roasting pan and roast as you would a standing rib. Allow an additional 5 to 10 minutes per pound since the bone in a standing rib roast transmits heat and, consequently, the meat roasts more quickly.

YORKSHIRE PUDDING

2 eggs
1 cup milk
1 cup flour (scant)

Salt
Beef drippings

Heat an 8 x 10-inch baking pan in the oven, then pour in ¼ cup beef drippings. Move the pan back and forth until the bottom is well covered. Beat the eggs until very light and fluffy, then beat in the milk and flour, a little at a time. Add a generous pinch of salt and 2 tablespoons beef drippings. Pour the egg mixture into the prepared baking pan and bake in a preheated 450° oven for 10 minutes. Reduce heat to 350°, and bake 10 to 15 minutes longer or until pudding is puffy and delicately browned. Serve immediately to 4.

WESTERN POT ROAST

A 4-pound pot roast
2 teaspoons salt
¼ teaspoon pepper
Dash ginger
3 tablespoons shortening or oil
2 cloves garlic, chopped fine

3 onions, chopped fine
1½ cups prunes
1 cup pitted ripe olives
1 can (6-ounce size) mushrooms or
    1 cup sliced fresh mushrooms

Rub the pot roast with a mixture of salt, pepper, and ginger. Rub it in well. Heat shortening or oil in a Dutch oven, add beef, and brown on all sides. When nicely browned, add garlic, onions, and ½ cup water. Cover tightly and cook over a low heat for about 1½ hours, turning the roast occasionally. As roast is cooking, soak prunes in 1½ cups water. At the end of the cooking period, add prunes and liquid to meat, then add sliced olives and mushrooms (if canned, drain well). Cover and cook gently for another hour or until pot roast is very tender when pierced with a fork. To serve, place beef in the center of a hot serving platter and surround with the fruit mixture. Serves 6 to 8.

One day we were at dinner at head-quarters; an Indian entered the room, walked round the table, and then stretching forth his long tattooed arm seized a large joint of hot roast beef in his thumb and fingers, took it to the door, and began to eat it. We were all much surprised, but General Washington gave orders that he was not to be interfered with, saying laughingly, that it was apparently the dinner hour of this Mutius Scaevola of the New World.

—Chevalier de Pontigibaud,
A French Volunteer of the War of Independence, 1898

BOEUF BOUILLI

This recipe for boiled beef is adapted from one prepared by Étienne Lemaire, Jefferson's steward in Washington.

4 to 5 pounds lean beef (first cut brisket,
    bottom round, or plate beef)
1 large onion, stuck with 6 cloves
3 carrots, cut in chunks
3 to 4 stalks celery with leaves

1 white turnip, quartered
1 parsnip, cut in chunks (optional)
Parsley
4 to 5 peppercorns
1 tablespoon salt

Place the meat in a heavy kettle, then add all the ingredients *except the salt.* Cover with water, bring to a boil, and boil for 5 minutes. Skim off froth, then add salt. Cover, lower the heat, and simmer 2 to 2½ hours or until meat is very tender when pierced with a fork. Potatoes and cabbage are especially compatible with boiled beef and may be cooked separately or added to the meat for the last hour. When meat is tender, lift from the broth, place on warm platter, and surround with cooked vegetables. Serve *Boeuf Bouilli* with Horse-radish Sauce (page 546) or tomato sauce with horse-radish added to taste. Serves 6.

BREAKFAST STEW OF BEEF

This breakfast stew, when presented in slightly different form by Marion Harland in her *Common Sense in the Household,* was one of a number of recipes marked by a cross. Miss Harland noted: "I do not claim for these greater merit than should of right be accorded to many others. I merely wish to call the attention of the novice to them as certainly safe, and for the most part simple. . . . Most of them are in frequent, some in daily, use, in my own family."

2 tablespoons butter	½ teaspoon savory
1 medium onion, chopped	½ teaspoon marjoram
2 pounds lean beef, cubed	1 teaspoon Worcestershire sauce
2 tablespoons flour	1 teaspoon prepared mustard
1 cup beef broth	Juice of ½ lemon
¾ teaspoon salt	Few sprigs parsley, chopped
¼ teaspoon pepper	

Melt butter in a saucepan, add onion, and cook until wilted. Dust beef cubes with flour, add them to the onion, and sauté until well browned on all sides. Stir in broth, salt, pepper, savory, and marjoram. Cover and cook over a low heat for about 1½ hours or until very tender. Before serving, stir in remaining ingredients. Serve over toast, hot grits, steamed rice, or with boiled potatoes. Serves 4.

Meat broiler

SWISS CREAM STEAK

2 pounds round steak	2 medium onions, thinly sliced
Salt	½ cup beef broth or 1 beef bouillon cube
Pepper	dissolved in ½ cup boiling water
½ teaspoon dried marjoram	½ cup commercial sour cream
Flour	2 tablespoons grated Parmesan cheese
¼ cup butter	

Sprinkle both sides of steak with salt, pepper, marjoram, and flour. Pound in, using the rim of a heavy plate. Heat butter in a large skillet (one with a tight-fitting lid), toss in onion slices, and cook until straw colored. Lift out onions with a slotted spoon and set aside. Add steak to hot fat and fry on both sides, over a brisk heat, until well browned. Add beef broth mixed with the sour cream, grated cheese, and cooked onions. Cover tightly and cook over a very low heat for about one and one half hours or until meat is tender when tested with a fork. Serves 6.

SHAKER FLANK STEAK

3 pounds flank steak
2 tablespoons flour
2 tablespoons butter
1 teaspoon salt
¼ teaspoon pepper
1 stalk celery, chopped

1 carrot, chopped fine
½ green pepper, chopped fine
2 medium onions, chopped fine
Juice of ½ lemon
½ cup ketchup

Cut or score both sides of the steak diagonally and dust with flour. Sauté in heated butter until well browned on both sides. Season with salt and pepper, then add all the chopped vegetables. Last of all, add lemon juice and ketchup. Cover tightly and simmer very gently for 1 to 1½ hours or until the steak is tender when tested with a fork. The vegetables cook down to a rich sauce to be served with the meat. Serves 6.

PAN-FRIED STEAK

One of Mark Twain's favorite foods was porterhouse steak with mushrooms, pan fried as in the recipe below.

Choose a porterhouse steak at least 1½ inches thick. Score the fat so the steak will not curl during cooking. If there is sufficient fat or suet on the steak, cut off a few bits and melt in a large heavy frying pan. In lieu of sufficient fat, use about a tablespoon of butter. Place over a high heat and cook 5 minutes on each side. Make an incision near the bone with a sharp knife. If it is too rare, cook a bit longer. Salt and pepper lightly and serve with lemon wedges. Serve, with Mushrooms in Cream (page 520), to 4 or 6.

FILET MIGNON

4 *filets mignons* (about ⅓ pound each)
2 tablespoons melted butter
Salt
Pepper

Small piece of salt pork or bacon
8 large mushrooms
1 cup tiny peas

Have the butcher lard the *filets*. Bring to room temperature before cooking. Brush with butter and sprinkle with salt and pepper. Place the salt pork or bacon in the bottom of a small roasting pan. Arrange a rack on top and place *filets* on the rack. Bake in a preheated 500° oven for 20 to 30 minutes. Transfer meat to hot serving platter. Sauté mushroom caps in a little butter for 5 minutes, then fill with hot, drained, and buttered peas. Remove salt pork or bacon from pan and discard. Stir in the finely chopped stems of the mushrooms and sauté over a brisk heat for a minute or two. Pour in a little water (about ¼ cup) and boil rapidly to concentrate the flavors. Pour over beef. Garnish the platter with the mushrooms, grilled tomatoes, Potatoes Duchesse (page 529), and watercress. Serves 4.

HAMBURGERS

The name for the hamburger sandwich is derived from Hamburg, Germany, a city that once enjoyed prosperous commerce with the Baltic Provinces in Russia, where shredded raw meat (we now know it as steak tartare) comprised a large part of the cuisine. It is from them that Hamburg developed an appreciation of "hamburger," though it was left to Americans to place the meat in a bun and create what is now considered an American specialty. Americans have eaten hamburger without buns, of course. Salisbury steak came into being at the turn of the century, promoted by the physician and food faddist J. H. Salisbury, who recommended eating ground steak three times a day for the relief of colitis, pernicious anemia, asthma, bronchitis, rheumatism, tuberculosis, gout, and hardening of the arteries.

SWEDISH MEATBALLS

2 pounds round or chuck steak, ground
1 pound lean pork, ground
2 eggs, well beaten
1 cup mashed potatoes
1 cup dry bread crumbs
1 teaspoon brown sugar
1 teaspoon freshly ground pepper
2 teaspoons salt

½ teaspoon ground ginger
½ teaspoon ground cloves
½ teaspoon allspice
1 cup milk
Flour
¼ cup shortening
2 cups light cream

Mix together, in a very large bowl, ground beef and pork, eggs, mashed potatoes, bread crumbs, brown sugar, all the seasonings and spices, and the milk. Blend thoroughly and shape into balls the size of a large walnut. The mixture should be soft. Coat the meatballs with flour. Heat the shortening, add a few meatballs at a time, and brown on all sides over a moderate heat. Do not crowd the pan. Transfer the browned meatballs to a large casserole, pour cream over them, and bake in a preheated 325° oven for 40 minutes. Serves 8.

INDIAN CORN STEW

2 tablespoons butter
1 pound beef, ground
1 onion, chopped fine
1 clove garlic, chopped fine
1 green pepper, coarsely chopped
3 cups corn, fresh or frozen

3 ripe tomatoes, skinned and coarsely
   chopped
1 tablespoon Worcestershire sauce
2 teaspoons sugar
1½ teaspoons salt

Melt butter in a large skillet, add beef, and sauté over a high heat until brown. Stir in onion, garlic, green pepper, and cook about 5 minutes. Add corn, tomatoes, and seasonings. Cover and simmer gently for about 30 minutes. Serves 4 to 6.

STEAK TARTARE

Ask the butcher for beef that is free of fat. As a main dish, about 1¼ pounds ground meat will be needed for two people. If served as a first course, allow about ¼ pound per person. Make a mound of the meat on individual plates. In the center of the mound make a small well and drop in the yolk of one egg. Take great care not to break the yolk. To serve, mix the yolk into the meat with one or more of the following: fine-chopped onions, fine-chopped parsley, drained capers, salt, freshly ground pepper. Serve with sweet butter and pumpernickel bread.

Meat chopper

HAMBURGER ROLL WITH MUSHROOM SAUCE

To prepare meat:
2 pounds lean beef, ground
Grated rind of 1 lemon
1 egg
2 tablespoons melted butter
Few sprigs parsley
1 teaspoon salt
¼ teaspoon pepper
½ teaspoon onion juice
Dash nutmeg

Sauce:
1 can (6-ounce size) mushrooms or
   1 cup fresh mushrooms
¼ cup butter
1½ teaspoons lemon juice
¼ cup flour
1½ cups beef broth
½ teaspoon salt
Dash pepper

Mix ground beef thoroughly with grated lemon rind, egg, melted butter, parsley (chopped fine), salt, pepper, onion juice, and nutmeg. Shape into a neat roll about 10 inches long and 2 inches thick. Wrap the roll in brown paper, brush the paper with melted fat, and tie securely with a cord to keep the roll in shape. Place on a rack in baking pan. Bake in a preheated 350° oven for 30 minutes, basting several times, right through the paper, with a mixture of ¼ cup butter melted in 1 cup boiling water. Remove from oven, pull paper off the roll with care, and return meat to oven for 10 minutes more. Serves 6.

To make the Mushroom Sauce: Drain canned mushrooms well and discard liquid, or wash fresh mushrooms in cold water, wipe dry, and cut in quarters (stem and all). Melt butter in a saucepan, add mushrooms and lemon juice, and cook about 5 minutes or until nicely browned. Stir in flour, keeping it as smooth as possible. Remove from heat. Measure drippings from roasting pan and add enough beef broth to make 2 cups. Pour into mushroom mixture and cook over a low heat, stirring frequently, until bubbly. Season with salt and pepper. To serve, slice hamburger roll and spoon sauce over slices. Garnish with parsley.

493

CHILI CON CARNE

Among the lesser disputes that have raged along the Rio Grande is the one over chili. Mexicans claim it as Mexican; Texans claim it as Texan.

4 cans (1 pound, 4 ounce size) kidney beans
   or 1 pound dried red or pinto beans
1 onion, chopped
2 pounds round (top or bottom) of beef
2 tablespoons shortening
2 tablespoons flour

2 cloves garlic, crushed
1 teaspoon dried oregano
¼ teaspoon ground cumin
1 tablespoon salt
1 tablespoon chili powder

If you use dried beans, soak them overnight, then cook several hours until tender. Brown onion in heated shortening. Add meat, cut into very small cubes, and cook until well browned. Stir in flour, cook a minute or two, then add canned, undrained kidney beans (or home-cooked red beans plus 2 cups of the liquid in which they cooked) and all remaining ingredients. Cook over a low heat, stirring frequently, for about 1 hour or until beef is tender. Taste and add more chili if you wish. Serves 8.

NEW ENGLAND BOILED DINNER

Americans have often gone to great lengths to "dress up" their menus by giving French names to American dishes. One of the more outlandish examples of this tendency comes from Grover Cleveland's administration. He told a friend that while he was dining in the White House on refined dishes, he smelled the odor of corned beef and cabbage coming from the servants' quarters and asked to trade his dinner for that of the servants. Cleveland dined on the traditional New England Boiled Dinner and then exclaimed that it was "the best dinner I had had for months . . . this *Boeuf corné au cabeau!*"

4 to 5 pounds corned beef
6 carrots
6 medium potatoes

1 medium yellow turnip
1 small head green cabbage
1 small crookneck or butternut squash

Place beef in a large kettle and cover with cold water. Bring to a boil, then reduce heat, and simmer gently for 3 to 4 hours or until tender when pierced with a fork. While beef simmers, scrape carrots and leave whole; pare potatoes and leave them whole, too; pare turnip and cut in sixths; cut cabbage head in sixths; peel squash, remove seeds and membrane, and cut in large, even chunks. The trick to cooking a good boiled dinner is to have all the vegetables done at the same time. Carrots, potatoes, and turnips take about 30 to 35 minutes to cook. The cabbage and squash will cook in 15 to 20 minutes. As you drop each batch of vegetables into the liquid, increase the heat so the broth continues to bubble. To serve, place the beef in the center of a large heated platter and surround it with all the vegetables. Traditional accompaniments are freshly cooked beets dressed with vinegar, and johnnycake, with apple pie for dessert.

THE HOT DOG

The hot dog reputedly came to America from Frankfurt, Germany. It is said that Antoine Feuchtwanger, a Bavarian, introduced it to St. Louis in the 1880's. He sold hot "franks," along with cotton gloves to prevent customers from burning their fingers. In *Happy Days*, H. L. Mencken intimates that the frankfurter's American debut may date even earlier. "I devoured hot-dogs in Baltimore 'way back in 1886," Mencken said, "and they were then very far from new-fangled . . . They contained precisely the same rubbery, indigestible pseudo-sausages that millions of Americans now eat, and they leaked the same flabby, puerile mustard. Their single point of difference lay in the fact that their covers were honest German *Wecke* made of wheat-flour baked to crispness, and not the soggy rolls prevailing today, of ground acorns, plaster-of-Paris, flecks of bath-sponge, and atmospheric air all compact."

Whoever may have introduced hot dogs to America, it was Harry M. Stevens, a concessionaire at the Polo Grounds in New York, who popularized them, telling his vendors to get out in the stands one cold day and yell, "Red hots! Red hots!" Still, they were not known as hot dogs until T. A. "Tad" Dorgan, a cartoonist, characterized the "red hot" as an elongated bun containing a dachshund.

TAMALE PIE

Many Mexican dishes are not Spanish so much as Indian. The Aztecs served *tamalli* to Cortes when he arrived in Tenochtitlán (Mexico City). Long before they became part of American cookery in the Southwest, they had worked their way toward the Northeast. In 1612, Captain John Smith described them as they were made by Indians in Virginia: "Their corne they rost in the eare greene, and bruising it in a morter of wood with a Polt, lappe it in rowles in the leaves of their corne, and so boyle it for a daintie."

3½ teaspoons salt	1 small green pepper, chopped
1 cup corn meal	1 pound chuck steak, ground
3 tablespoons shortening	½ teaspoon chili powder
1 medium onion, chopped	4 medium tomatoes

Bring 3 cups of water and *1½ teaspoons of the salt* to the boiling point. Then slowly add corn meal in a steady stream, stirring constantly. Cook over a low heat, stirring frequently, for 10 minutes. Remove from heat. Melt shortening in a frying pan, add onion and green pepper, and cook over a low heat until limp but not brown. Add the ground chuck and keep cooking until it is brown. Stir in chili powder and remaining salt. Remove from stove. Cut tomatoes in slices. Spread half the cooked corn meal over the bottom of a medium-sized casserole, cover with a layer of tomatoes, then all the meat mixture. Add a second layer of corn meal and top that with the remaining tomato slices. Bake in a preheated 375° oven for 25 minutes. Serves 4.

DAUBE GLACÉ

This Creole recipe is based, in part, on one found in *La Cuisine Creole,* thought to have been written by Lafcadio Hearn.

4½- to 5-pound beef round
2 bay leaves, crushed
¼ teaspoon sage
1 clove garlic, crushed
½ teaspoon thyme
½ teaspoon marjoram

6 slices bacon
1½ teaspoons salt
¼ teaspoon pepper
3 tablespoons shortening
1 small onion, chopped

Cut 6 deep slits in beef. Combine bay leaves, sage, garlic, thyme, and marjoram and sprinkle equal amounts of the mixture over each slice of bacon. Roll the bacon into small, tight rolls and stuff one in each of the slits. Place the beef in a large deep bowl while you prepare the marinade.

Marinade:
2 cups dry red wine
¾ cup wine vinegar
1 cup water

1 clove garlic, crushed
2 bay leaves
Dash of cayenne
1 teaspoon allspice

To make the marinade: Mix all ingredients together, pour over beef, and refrigerate overnight. The next day, drain beef (save the marinade) and pat dry with paper towels. Sprinkle with salt and pepper. Melt shortening in a large skillet and brown beef on all sides over high heat. Discard all excess fat. Add chopped onion and 1½ cups of the marinade. Bring to a boil, then cover, and simmer for 3 hours or until beef is very tender. Remove from heat and cool in marinade.

Aspic:
3½ pounds veal shank, cracked
2½ pounds pigs' feet, cracked
2 teaspoons salt
Dash of pepper
Dash of cayenne
5 cups water

1 cup dry sherry
4 carrots
4 stalks celery
1 small green pepper
4 sprigs parsley
1 small onion, chopped
2 slightly beaten egg whites plus shells

To make the aspic: Combine all ingredients *except egg whites and shells* and cook over a low heat for 3 hours or until meat is extremely tender. Remove from heat and, when cool enough to handle, strip meat from bones and cut into small pieces. Skim all excess fat from broth, then boil with egg whites and shells for 5 to 10 minutes (this clarifies the broth). Strain through a flannel-lined sieve.

To mold or glacé *the beef:* Pour 1 cup of the liquid aspic into a loaf pan large enough to hold the meat comfortably. Place in the refrigerator and chill until slightly thickened. Garnish the surface with slices of stuffed olives, pimiento cutouts, toasted almonds, or any other suitable accompaniment. Chill until firm. Combine remaining liquid aspic with chopped veal and pig's feet. Place the piece of beef in pan on top of garnish and trim off any meat that does not fit. Pour the aspic-meat mixture around sides and on top. Refrigerate overnight or until firm. To serve, cut in slices. Serves 10 to 12.

OXTAIL STEW

2 oxtails, cut in pieces
2 tablespoons shortening or salad oil
2 teaspoons chili powder
2 teaspoons dry mustard
2 teaspoons cornstarch
2 teaspoons salt
1½ cups orange juice

2 tablespoons lemon juice
Dash of Worcestershire sauce
½ cup seedless raisins
1 jar (4-ounce size) pimientos, cut in strips
1 cup ripe olives, coarsely chopped
3 stalks celery, thinly sliced

Heat shortening or oil in a Dutch oven or heavy kettle, add meat, and brown on all sides. Make a smooth paste of the chili powder, mustard, cornstarch, salt, fruit juices, and Worcestershire sauce. Add this mixture and the raisins to the meat and cook to the boiling point. Reduce heat, cover tightly, and simmer for 2½ hours. Then add pimientos, olives, and celery. Continue cooking for 30 minutes. Serve with rice to 6.

Meat-pie mold

BEEFSTEAK AND KIDNEY PIE

Pastry for a 1-crust pie (page 580)
4 small veal kidneys
1 cup dry red wine
1½ pounds round (top or bottom) of beef
Flour
4 tablespoons shortening

1 medium onion, chopped
1 bay leaf
5 sprigs parsley, chopped
5 sprigs celery tops, chopped
½ teaspoon dried marjoram
¼ pound mushrooms, sliced

Prepare the pastry and refrigerate it while you make the filling. Trim all fat and membrane from kidneys, sprinkle with a little salt, and cover with wine. Set aside. Cut beef into thin strips and sprinkle with flour, pounding it in thoroughly. Fry onion in heated shortening for several minutes, then add beef, and cook over a brisk heat, stirring frequently, until nicely browned. Lift kidneys from wine marinade (save marinade) and separate the kidney clusters. Dust with flour, add to beef, and cook, stirring carefully, until browned. Pour in ½ cup water and season with bay leaf, parsley, celery tops, and marjoram. Cover and cook over a very low heat until meat is tender when tested with a fork (takes about 1 hour). When tender, stir in mushrooms and the wine marinade. Pour into a 2-quart casserole or baking dish that can go to the table. Cover top with thinly rolled pastry, slashed in several places to allow steam to escape, and seal the edges securely. Bake in a preheated 450° oven for 25 to 30 minutes or until crust is perfectly browned. Serves 6 to 8.

TONGUE IN SPICY ASPIC

1 smoked beef tongue
Cayenne
½ teaspoon cinnamon
½ teaspoon allspice
½ teaspoon white pepper

¼ teaspoon ground cloves
¼ teaspoon mace
Several sprigs of parsley, chopped fine
3 tablespoons vinegar

Cover beef tongue with cold water and cook over a gentle heat for 2 to 3 hours or until very tender when pierced with a fork. Lift tongue from broth. Boil broth over a high heat until it is reduced to about 1 pint. Meanwhile, skin the tongue and trim the root. Cut the meat in small cubes and season with a dash of cayenne, spices, and parsley. Pack the mixture into a bowl or mold. Mix 3 tablespoons of vinegar into the hot broth, then pour over the meat. Refrigerate overnight. Unmold and cut in slices to serve. Serves 8.

FRIZZLED BEEF

One of the most formidable problems faced by American pioneers was the preservation of meat. The most widely practiced methods of preservation were salting, pickling, and drying. The Indians had a method of drying both game and beef which they taught the white man; meat dried in this manner was called jerky. These strips of salted, peppered, and dried meat were carried by trappers and cowboys, who sometimes sustained themselves for days by chewing on them. Under more civilized circumstances, jerky was usually creamed and served on biscuits or on fried corn-meal mush.

2 tablespoons butter
¼ pound dried beef, shredded
3 tablespoons flour

2 cups milk
Dash of pepper, freshly ground

Heat butter in a saucepan, add dried beef, and fry over a moderate heat until edges begin to look crisp. Sprinkle in flour and continue cooking 3 to 4 minutes, stirring constantly. Pour in milk and cook, still stirring, until mixture bubbles. Season with a dash of pepper. Serve over toast, biscuits, or Fried Corn Meal Mush (page 532). Makes 4 servings.

CORNISH PASTIES

Pastry:
2 cups sifted all-purpose flour
1 teaspoon salt
⅔ cup shortening
4 tablespoons cold water (about)
Filling:
1 pound round steak, ground

½ pound lean pork, ground
1 cup potatoes, diced fine
½ cup onion, diced fine
½ cup parsley, chopped
1 teaspoon salt
¼ teaspoon pepper

Sift flour and salt together. Cut in shortening with a pastry blender or two knives until mixture resembles corn meal. Mix in the water with a fork. Then, using your hands, gather the pastry together in a mass. Refrigerate while you make the filling. Combine both meats, the potatoes, onion, parsley, and seasonings. Divide the pastry into 8 portions. Roll one portion at a time on a lightly floured board, making a circle about the size of a saucer. Put a heaping tablespoon of filling on half the pastry, fold over the other half, and seal edges with fork tines dipped in flour. Place on a cooky sheet and bake in a preheated 450° oven for 10 minutes. Reduce heat to 350°, and continue baking 50 minutes or until pastry is a tempting brown.

RED FLANNEL HASH

There are several stories purporting to explain the origin of Red Flannel Hash. One states that it was created in the Green Mountains of Vermont, where it was popular with Ethan Allen and his Green Mountain Boys.

3 medium beets, cooked	Pepper
1 large potato, cooked	½ cup (1 stick) butter
1 pound chuck steak, ground	1 medium onion, chopped
Salt	1 tablespoon cream

Chop the beets and potato, mix with ground chuck. Add salt and pepper. Melt *4 tablespoons of the butter* in a large skillet, add the chopped onion, and cook until limp. Stir in the meat-vegetable mixture and cook over a low heat for 10 minutes, stirring occasionally. Lift mixture into a medium-sized baking dish. Melt remaining butter and combine with cream. Spoon this over the hash. Place under a preheated broiler, 3 inches from unit or tip of flame, for 5 minutes or until hash has a rich, brown crust. May be served with poached eggs on top. Serves 4.

STUFFED CABBAGE

1 head green cabbage	⅓ cup milk (about)
1 pound ground beef	1 cup tomato juice
½ pound pork, ground	1 cup beef broth
2 eggs, beaten	¼ cup cider vinegar
1 medium onion, chopped	2 tablespoons sugar
½ cup cooked rice	1 bay leaf
2 teaspoons salt	¼ teaspoon pepper
¼ teaspoon pepper	

Leave cabbage head whole but ream out some of the solid core. Cover with boiling water and cook about 10 minutes. Drain cabbage carefully and pull off 16 to 18 of the largest outer leaves. Trim off some of the thick center ribs. Combine beef, pork, eggs, onion, rice, salt, pepper, and just enough milk to make a loose mixture. Put a heaping tablespoon of the filling in the center of each cabbage leaf, roll up and tuck in the ends, making a neat package. Place side by side in a shallow baking dish and pour in a mixture of tomato juice and all remaining ingredients. Cover and bake in a preheated 350° oven for about 1 hour. Serves 6.

VEAL GRILLADES

2 pounds round of veal
2 tablespoons flour
3 tablespoons butter
2 small onions, chopped
1 clove garlic, chopped
1 stalk celery, chopped
½ green pepper, chopped
1 bay leaf

½ teaspoon dried thyme
1 teaspoon salt
¼ teaspoon pepper
Dash cayenne
2 tablespoons tomato paste
2 cups beef broth
Chopped parsley

Cut veal into slices about ½ to ¾ inch thick and dust with flour. Sauté in heated butter over a high heat until nicely browned on both sides. Add onions, garlic, celery, green pepper, bay leaf, and all the seasonings. Cook until vegetables are slightly limp. Combine tomato paste with broth and add to veal mixture. Cover and cook over a low heat for 35 to 45 minutes or until grillades are tender. At serving time, transfer meat to a hot platter, pour sauce over all, and sprinkle generously with chopped parsley. Serve with steamed rice, Hominy Pudding (page 531), or new potatoes. Serves 4.

Butcher's advertisement

VEAL BIRDS

12 thin slices veal cutlet
½ cup (1 stick) butter
1 medium onion, chopped
2 cups fine bread crumbs
½ cup chopped parsley
½ teaspoon salt
¼ teaspoon pepper
½ teaspoon dried thyme

½ teaspoon dried marjoram
½ teaspoon dried basil
2 to 3 tablespoons milk
Flour
1½ cups beef broth
Bay leaf
Several celery tops
Several sprigs parsley

Veal slices should be pounded as thin as for Veal Scallopini. Melt *half the butter*, stir in onion, and cook several minutes. Combine with bread crumbs and chopped parsley, salt, pepper, and the three herbs. Add just enough milk to moisten the stuffing (it should not be wet). Spread equal amounts of the stuffing on each slice of veal, making it into a small roll and attaching the end with a toothpick. Dust the rolls lightly with flour. Heat remaining half of the butter in a skillet. Add veal birds and brown over a moderate heat. Pour in meat stock, add bay leaf, celery tops, and parsley. Cover tightly and simmer slowly for 30 to 40 minutes or until meat is tender. Serve with pan gravy. Serves 4 to 6.

VEAL CHOPS EN PAPILLOTE

This recipe is adapted from Practical Housekeeping, 1895.

6 veal chops
Salt
Pepper
Flour
4 tablespoons butter
1 tablespoon onion, minced
12 mushroom caps, thinly sliced

½ cup boiled ham, minced
½ cup cooked chicken or veal, minced
3 truffles, thinly sliced (optional)
1 tablespoon parsley, minced
½ cup dry sherry
1 can (7½-ounce size) beef gravy

Slash the fat on edges of chops to keep them from curling. Season with salt and pepper and dust lightly with flour. Melt *2 tablespoons of the butter* in a large, heavy skillet, add the chops, and sauté over medium heat for 25 minutes or until nicely browned and well done. Turn once. Remove chops from skillet and keep them hot. Add remainder of the butter to the same skillet, toss in onion, and cook a few minutes. Then add the mushrooms and cook about 5 minutes longer. Add the ham, chicken or veal, truffles, and parsley. Turn the mixture a few times. Finally, pour in the sherry and beef gravy. Bring to a boil, scraping bottom and sides of the skillet to loosen the rich brown particles. Reduce heat to simmer, and cook a few more minutes. Taste for seasoning. Meanwhile, cut 6 heart-shaped pieces of parchment paper, large enough to overlap each chop by 2 inches or slightly more all around. Butter one side of the paper with softened butter. Place a chop on buttered side of each "heart" and spoon some of the stuffing on top. Divide the mixture evenly among the six. Fold the paper over the chops and roll the edges as you would a hem, sealing the package so that steam and juices cannot escape. Place in a buttered, shallow baking dish and bake in a preheated 400° oven until the paper browns slightly and swells up like a small balloon. This takes only a short time. Serve in the paper packages.

VEAL IN SOUR CREAM

2 pounds veal steak, cut in 1½-inch cubes
3 tablespoons butter
2 tablespoons flour
1 cup commercial sour cream

1 tablespoon minced onion
½ pound mushrooms
2 tablespoons butter
1 teaspoon salt

Melt 3 tablespoons butter in heavy frying pan and sauté meat over high heat until lightly browned on all sides. Do not crowd in the pan; rather do a few pieces at a time. Place meat in baking dish or casserole that has a cover. Add flour to fat remaining in frying pan, and stir until smooth. Then stir in the sour cream thoroughly. Remove from heat. In a separate pan, melt 2 tablespoons butter and cook minced onion until slightly golden, then add mushrooms (if large, slice thin; if small, leave whole), and simmer over low heat for about 5 minutes. Combine mushrooms with sour cream mixture and salt. Pour over veal, cover, and bake in a 325° oven for 1 hour or until meat is tender when pierced with a fork. Serve with steamed rice. Serves 4.

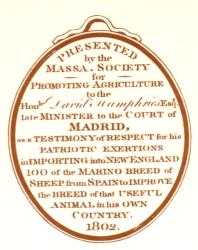

Medal presented to David Humphrey for importing Merino sheep

LAMB SHANKS

6 lamb shanks or chops
1 egg, slightly beaten
1 cup fine dry bread crumbs
Few sprigs parsley, chopped
¼ teaspoon dried thyme
¼ teaspoon dried marjoram

¼ teaspoon dried savory
½ teaspoon salt
½ teaspoon grated lemon rind
3 tablespoons butter
Sherry

Dip the shanks in egg, then coat with a mixture of crumbs, parsley, thyme, marjoram, savory, salt, and lemon rind. Heat butter in a skillet. Add shanks and sauté over a low heat until nicely browned on both sides. Add sherry to pan gravy and serve over shanks. Serves 4.

CROWN ROAST OF LAMB WITH SARATOGA CHIPS

In *The American Frugal Housewife,* published in 1836 and "Dedicated to Those Who Are Not Ashamed of Economy," Lydia Maria Child wrote: "That part of mutton called the rack . . . is cheap food. It is not more than four or five cents a pound; and four pounds will make a dinner for six people. . . . If your family be small, a rack of mutton will make you two dinners. . . ."

Buy as much of the rack of lamb as you will need (they range in size from 12 to 16 chops) and have the butcher make it into a crown roast. Place it in a shallow roasting pan, stuffing the center with foil so the crown will keep its shape. Put bits of salt pork on the tips of the bones or wrap the ends in foil to prevent charring. Roast in a preheated 300° oven for 1½ hours. Season with salt and pepper and place on a hot platter. Remove foil and fill the center of roast with Saratoga Chips (page 528) which have been heated in the oven. Or, if you prefer, fill center with Puréed Chestnuts (page 516). The number it will serve depends on the size of the crown. To serve the crown in proper style, put paper frills around the tips of the bones.

502

MINT-STUFFED BARBECUED LAMB

A 7-pound leg of lamb, boned
2 cups fresh mint leaves
Sauce:
1½ cups cider vinegar

½ cup (1 stick) butter
1 tablespoon Worcestershire sauce
Red pepper to taste
1 or 2 garlic cloves, crushed

Stuff the boned lamb with mint leaves that have been washed and dried. Pack them into the cavity as tightly as possible, then skewer and tie the meat securely. Wrap in foil and allow to stand in the refrigerator for several hours (preferably overnight) so that the flavor of the mint can permeate the meat. Bring to room temperature before cooking. To roast over charcoal, place lamb on a rack 4 inches from bed of coals (which have been prepared ahead of time). Brush the meat frequently with the barbecue sauce and turn occasionally during the entire cooking period. It will take about 1½ to 1¾ hours for rare, and better than 2 hours for well done. To roast in the oven, place the lamb in a roasting pan on a rack, pour the barbecue sauce over the meat, and roast in a preheated 325° oven for 1¼ to 1½ hours for rare; 2 to 2½ hours for well done. Baste frequently with the sauce, using either a brush or baster. Although the mint contributes enormously to the flavor of the lamb, one does not eat it. Serve with new potatoes steamed in butter.

To make the barbecue sauce: Combine vinegar, butter, Worcestershire sauce, red pepper, and crushed garlic in a saucepan. Bring to a boil, then simmer for about 20 minutes.

Lamb chop frill

IRISH LAMB STEW

2 pounds boned shoulder of lamb
1 cup sliced raw potatoes
¼ small head cabbage, shredded
2 leeks, sliced thin
2 medium onions, sliced
1 stalk celery, sliced
1½ teaspoons salt
¼ teaspoon freshly ground pepper

1 bay leaf
1 clove garlic, crushed
¼ teaspoon dried thyme
8 small onions
4 carrots
2 white turnips, quartered
1 pound green peas, shelled
Few sprigs parsley

Have meat cut into 2-inch cubes. Arrange alternate layers of lamb and the mixed sliced vegetables in a casserole or baking dish. Season with salt, pepper, bay leaf, garlic, and thyme. Cover with water and bring to a boil on top of the stove. Cover casserole, place in a preheated 350° oven, and bake for 1½ hours or until meat is tender. Cook onions, carrots, turnips, and peas—each separately—until tender. Drain. Lift meat out of casserole onto a plate and keep it warm. Strain liquid from stew and reserve. Work vegetables (from stew) through a sieve, ricer, or in a blender, then combine with the strained liquid, the whole cooked vegetables, and the meat. Taste and adjust seasoning. Serve hot with parsley, chopped fine, sprinkled on top. Serves 4.

HAM

Shortly after President James K. Polk left office in 1849, he visited New Orleans and, after looking over the French dishes offered in one restaurant, "asked a servant in a low tone if he could give me a piece of cornbread and boiled ham." Polk was born in North Carolina, which is considered part of Smithfield ham country. Quite a number of southern states—Tennessee, Georgia, and Kentucky among them—claim to produce the best ham; but Smithfield, Virginia, has long enjoyed the most prestigious reputation for its product. As early as 1639 (the town of Smithfield was not founded until 113 years later), settlers in Virginia were exporting pork and bacon to New England. Over a century ago, Queen Victoria placed an order for six hams a week to come from Smithfield.

In 1818, the New England poet Henry C. Knight wrote of life in Virginia in his book *Letters from the South and West:* "A meat-house is one of the first houses built; hung on all sides with chines, middlings, joles, and hams; perhaps finer flavoured for having run wild [and fed on the peanuts grown in Virginia]. One of the common petty larcenies of the slaves, is breaking into the smoke-house. It is remarked that, north of the Potomac, one may find good beef, and bad bacon; and south of the Potomac, good bacon and bad beef."

Smithfield hams have been so highly esteemed that several other parts of the country have attempted to raise imitations. In 1926, in order to protect its industry and its traditions, the General Assembly of Virginia placed a statute in its books: "Genuine Smithfield hams [are those] cut from the carcasses of peanut-fed hogs, raised in the peanut-belt of the State of Virginia or the State of North Carolina, and which are cured, treated, smoked, and processed in the town of Smithfield, in the State of Virginia."

TO COOK AGED, COUNTRY-CURED HAMS

Soak the ham overnight (at least 12 to 18 hours) in enough water to cover it entirely. Drain, cover meat again with fresh cold water, and bring to the simmering point only. Do not boil. Simmer the ham for just 2 hours, regardless of the size or weight, then remove from stove, and allow ham to cool in the liquor. When ham is cold, cut off the rind, score, stud with cloves, and glaze with one of the following:

Brown Sugar Glaze: Mix 1 cup brown sugar with 1 teaspoon dry mustard and ½ teaspoon ground cloves. Add a little of the fat from the pan (just enough to make a stiff paste) and spread this mixture over the fat.

Honey Glaze: Spoon honey over the fat.

Apricot Jam Glaze: Spoon apricot jam over the fat.

Bake in a preheated 400° oven for 30 minutes. Serve cut in paper-thin slices, hot or cold.

TO BAKE MODERN HAMS

These hams do not require boiling as country-cured hams do. Put ham, skin side up, in roasting pan. Place in a preheated 300° oven and bake approximately 20 to 22 minutes per pound for a 10- to 12-pound ham; 18 to 20 minutes per pound for a 12- to 15-pound ham; 15 to 18 minutes per pound for a ham 15 pounds or over. If you use a meat thermometer, insert it in the fleshiest part of the ham and bake until thermometer reads 165°. Remove ham from the oven, cut off the rind, and score the fat. Glaze with any of the glazes on page 504, return to a 400° oven, and bake another 15 minutes to set the glaze. Serve hot or cold.

HAM BAKED IN MAPLE SYRUP

Cut off the rind from a slice of ham about 1¼ to 1½ inches thick, and slash the fat in several places to keep it from curling. Mix 2 teaspoons dry mustard with 2 tablespoons cider vinegar until smooth, then add ¾ cup pure maple syrup. Pour over ham (some cooks stud the ham with cloves to add flavor) and place in a 350° oven for 50 to 60 minutes. Baste frequently with the sauce. When ham is cooked, remove from baking pan and place on warm serving platter. Put baking pan, with sauce, on top of stove over high heat and cook the sauce, stirring constantly, until it is a good consistency for gravy. Pour over ham slice or serve separately in a sauceboat. Ham prepared this old-fashioned way is especially good when served with new potatoes and asparagus, broccoli, or cauliflower with Hollandaise Sauce (page 542). Serves 4.

HAM WITH ORANGE

Slash the fatty rim of a nice thick slice of ham to keep it from curling. Sauté in 1 tablespoon melted butter over a low heat until lightly browned on both sides. Place on a hot platter and keep it warm. Pour 1 cup orange juice into pan drippings, stirring until you have mixed in all the rich, brown particles. Add 1 tablespoon of arrowroot or cornstarch, mixed with a little water until smooth, and cook, stirring constantly, until sauce thickens. Last of all, mix in 1 tablespoon honey and the sections from 2 small oranges (be sure to remove all membrane). Heat through, then pour sauce over ham slice, and garnish with parsley. A generous slice should serve 4.

RED-EYE GRAVY

After frying a slice of country ham about ¼ inch thick, drain off any excess fat, add a little water to the drippings and about a tablespoon of strong coffee to give it color. Bring to a boil and serve with the ham and, traditionally, grits and hot biscuits.

BAKED STUFFED HAM PONTALBA

A 14-pound ham, boned
4 cups shelled pecans, ground
3 onions, chopped fine
1 small can truffles, cut in pieces
6 bay leaves
2 sprigs (½ teaspoon dried) thyme
3 teaspoons dried sage

3 teaspoons ground cloves
¼ teaspoon cayenne
½ cup Madeira wine
1 apple
1 cup cane syrup
Brown sugar
Fine dry bread crumbs

Ask your butcher to bone the ham. If a dry smoked ham is used, the ham must be soaked in cold water for 12 hours. When a modern cured ham is used, soaking is unnecessary. To make the stuffing: cut out about ½ pound of ham to make a cavity, and work the ham through a food grinder. Blend thoroughly with the pecans, *1 chopped onion*, truffles, *2 bay leaves (crumbled)*, thyme, *1 teaspoon sage, 1 teaspoon ground cloves,* cayenne, and Madeira to make the stuffing. Pack into ham cavity, sewing or skewering it securely. Put these seasonings on the ham: *1 chopped onion, 2 bay leaves, 1 teaspoon sage, 1 teaspoon cloves.* Sew a cloth securely around ham and place in a large kettle. Add enough water to cover, and the remaining chopped onion, bay leaves, sage, cloves, the whole unpared apple, and the syrup. Bring to a boil, cover, reduce heat, and simmer for about 6 hours or until tender. Allow ham to cool in the liquid. When cool, remove rind, pat ham with a mixture of brown sugar and crumbs, and bake in a preheated 375° oven until surface is well browned and ham is hot.

—————

SCHNITZ-UN-GNEPP

Schnitz means "cut" and, in Pennsylvania Dutch usage, it has come to mean cut dried apples. There are both sweet and sour *Schnitz*: the sour *Schnitz* are used for pies; the sweet apples go into sweet *Schnitz,* served with dumplings *(gnepp)* as in this recipe.

2½- to 3-pound smoked ham with bone
2 cups dried apples

2 tablespoons brown sugar

Cover ham almost completely with cold water. Bring to a boil, reduce heat, cover, and simmer gently for 2 hours. Meanwhile, put dried apples in a bowl and cover with cold water to soak. When ham has been cooked 2 hours, add drained apples and brown sugar. Simmer 1 hour, then lift ham onto a large platter and spoon apples around it. Reserve ham broth.

Dumplings:
1½ cups sifted all-purpose flour
3 teaspoons baking powder
½ teaspoon salt

1 tablespoon butter
¼ cup milk (about)
1 egg, well beaten

Sift together flour, baking powder, and salt into a bowl. Pinch in the butter with your finger tips until well distributed, then stir in enough milk to make a soft dough. Add egg. Drop dumplings from a soup spoon into the boiling ham broth, cover tightly, and simmer 10 to 12 minutes. Arrange dumplings on the platter around the meat and spoon a little broth over them. The liquid may be thickened by stirring in a little flour mixed to a smooth paste with water. Serves 6 to 8.

HAM MOUSSE

In *Society As I Have Found It*, Ward McAllister wrote, "We ask [the chef] for a novelty, and his great genius suggests, under pressure, *mousse aux jambon* [Ham Mousse], which is attractive to the eye, and, if well made, at once establishes the reputation of the artist, satisfies the guests . . . and allays their fears for their dinner."

2 envelopes gelatin
¼ cup sherry
1⅓ cups chicken broth

2 eggs, separated
3½ cups cooked ham, ground
1 cup heavy cream

Sprinkle gelatin over sherry to soften. Heat chicken broth until bubbling. Beat egg yolks slightly, stir in a little heated broth, then pour back into broth. Cook over a low heat, stirring constantly, for a minute or two. Remove from heat, mix in gelatin until dissolved, then add the ham. Fold in stiffly beaten egg whites and stiffly beaten cream. Spoon into a 1-quart mold and refrigerate until firm. Unmold on a platter. Serves 6.

GLAZED HAM AND PORK LOAF

To make the loaf:
2 pounds ham, ground
1½ pounds lean pork, ground
1 teaspoon salt
¼ teaspoon pepper
2 eggs, well beaten
1 cup milk

1 cup cracker crumbs
Glaze:
1½ cups brown sugar, firmly packed
1 tablespoon prepared mustard
½ cup cider vinegar
½ cup water

Combine thoroughly ground ham and pork, salt, pepper, eggs, milk, and crumbs. Shape the mixture into a loaf, place in a shallow baking pan, and bake in a preheated 350° oven for 1½ hours. When loaf goes in the oven, mix brown sugar, mustard, vinegar, and water in a saucepan and cook for about 5 minutes. As the ham loaf browns, baste it with the glaze. Baste frequently during remaining baking time. Serve hot or cold to 6 or 8.

CHARLES COUNTY, MARYLAND, STUFFED HAM

In Charles County, Maryland (named for Charles Calvert, Third Lord Baltimore), ham has been prepared by this method for three centuries.

Cook aged, country-cured ham (page 504) to the point where ham is cooled in the liquor. When meat is cool, remove from liquor and set aside. Heat liquor to the boiling point, then toss in 8 quarts (1 peck) of well-washed, tender spring greens. A favorite combination includes: mustard and turnip greens, spinach or kale, small green onions with their tops, and land cress (not to be confused with watercress). When greens are wilted, drain thoroughly and chop fine. Season with celery seed and freshly ground pepper. With a sharp knife make deep crescent-shaped incisions in the ham, top and bottom, and stuff the openings tightly with the chopped greens. Wrap the ham in unbleached muslin and sew securely. Return ham to liquor and simmer 5 minutes per pound. Remove muslin. May be served hot or cold. If a precooked ham is used, cook greens in boiling water and proceed as above.

STUFFED SPARERIBS

"Many people buy the upper part of the spare-rib of pork," Lydia Maria Child observed in 1836 in *The American Frugal Housewife,* "thinking it the most genteel; but the lower part of the spare-rib toward the neck is much more sweet and juicy, and there is more meat in proportion to the bone."

4 to 5 cooking apples
1 box (1 pound) prunes
2 strips lean spareribs (about 10 inches long)

Salt
Pepper
Brown sugar
Cinnamon

Pare apples, core, and cut into thick slices. Cook in a small amount of water until almost tender. Drain. Cook prunes according to package directions. Drain and remove pits. Place one strip of the spareribs in a shallow roasting pan and sprinkle with salt and pepper. Spread the cooked apples over the ribs evenly. Cover with prunes, then sprinkle with a little brown sugar, cinnamon, and more salt. Place second strip of ribs on top and link edges together, here and there, with skewers. Bake in a preheated 325° oven for about 2 hours or until fork pierces the meat easily. Serves 6.

Political barbecue, 1876

BARBECUED SPARERIBS

Section the ribs from 2 racks of spareribs into easy-to-eat pieces. Sprinkle with salt and pepper and place on a rack in roasting pan. Bake in a preheated 350° oven for 35 minutes, turning them occasionally. Brush lavishly with Barbecue Sauce (page 545), increase oven heat to 400°, and continue baking for another 35 minutes or until well browned. Turn ribs frequently, brushing each time with the sauce. Serves 4 to 6.

To make Barbecued Lamb Riblets: Section 2 racks of lamb breast. Sprinkle with salt and pepper and brush with the Barbecue Sauce (page 545). Roast in a preheated 400° oven for 1 hour, turning occasionally and brushing with sauce each time. Serves 4.

PORK AND APPLE PIE

The cookbook *(La Cuisine Creole)* from which this recipe was adapted advises: "This is a plain and wholesome dish; when the family is large and apples plentiful, it will be an economical way of giving the boys 'apple pie.' "

Pastry for a 2-crust pie (page 580)
4 greening apples
2 pounds lean pork, cubed
½ teaspoon dried thyme
2 tablespoons sugar

1 teaspoon salt
¼ teaspoon pepper
1 tablespoon butter
1 egg, beaten

Line bottom and sides of a deep pie dish with pastry. Pare apples, core, and cut into slices. Arrange alternate layers of pork and apples in the pie shell, sprinkling the layers as you go along with a mixture of thyme, sugar, salt, and pepper. Dot the last layer with butter and cover with pastry. Slash pastry in several places, then brush it lavishly with egg, and bake in a preheated 350° oven for 1½ to 2 hours. Serve either lukewarm or cold—but not chilled, and never hot from the oven. If you do not mind departing from tradition, serve a mixture of freshly grated horse-radish and sour cream with it.

ROAST SUCKLING PIG

Mrs. Leslie's *American Family Cook Book*, from which this recipe is adapted, instructs: "A sucking-pig, like a young child, must not be left for an instant."

1 suckling pig (about 10 to 15 pounds)
2 loaves (1 pound each) white bread
3 cups water
1 large onion, chopped
½ cup butter

1 tablespoon dried sage
1½ teaspoons salt
¼ teaspoon freshly ground pepper
1 tart apple, peeled and grated

Ask the butcher to clean the pig thoroughly. Crumble bread into a large bowl, add water, and set aside to soak. Cook onion in melted butter until limp. Remove from heat and stir in sage, salt, pepper, and apple. Squeeze moisture from bread and combine bread with onion mixture. Fill the pig with this dressing and place in a kneeling position in a roasting pan. Put a block of wood in its mouth and tie the legs in place. Sprinkle skin with salt and cover ears and tail with foil to prevent charring. Pour 1 cup hot water into the pan and roast pig in a preheated 325° oven for 3½ to 4 hours or until tender when tested with a fork. Baste frequently with pan drippings. About 30 minutes before pig has finished cooking, remove foil. To serve, place roasted pig on a hot platter, replace wooden block in mouth with a small red apple, insert cranberries or grapes in eye sockets. Surround with water-cress. Serves 8 to 10.

To carve: Cut at right angles to the backbone, making cuts about one inch apart. Run the knife along the backbone and under meat to loosen, then lift off each piece.

509

GLAZED ROAST PORK

Kitchen stoves, although invented in the late eighteenth century, were not immediately taken up by American housewives. Indeed, they were resisted well into the nineteenth century. One of Eliza Leslie's books giving instructions for fireplace cookery was still being published in 1870. This pork roast, then, was cooked even until that late date in a reflecting oven, a device with its open side facing the fireplace and its curved metal back facing out. The meat was placed on a spit in the reflecting oven and turned by hand. Today the same effect can be achieved in a modern rotisserie.

A 5- to 6-pound loin of pork	*Glaze:*
Flour	1 cup sugar
Salt	⅓ cup cider vinegar
Pepper	1 teaspoon hickory-smoked salt

Score the fat on the roast lightly, then rub the entire surface with flour, salt, and pepper. Place on a rack in a shallow roasting pan. Roast in a preheated 450° oven for 15 minutes, then reduce heat to 350°, and continue roasting 30 to 35 minutes per pound, basting frequently with the glaze. Serves 6.

To make the glaze: Pour sugar in a heavy skillet and cook over a moderate heat until it becomes a rich, golden brown liquid. Pour in half a cup of boiling water, a little at a time (mixture sputters at this point, so stand back), and cook, stirring constantly with a wooden spoon, until all lumps have dissolved. Measure ½ cup of the caramel syrup and combine it with vinegar and hickory-smoked salt.

To roast in a rotisserie: Prepare pork as directed above, start rotisserie at 450°, and revolve slowly for 15 minutes or until meat begins to turn brown. Then reduce heat to 350° and baste, at frequent intervals, with glaze. Allow 30 to 35 minutes per pound.

SCRAPPLE

Scrapple, or *ponhaws* as the Pennsylvania Dutch called it, was originated as a thrifty way to use scraps of pork after hogs had been slaughtered.

1½ pounds pork shoulder	Dash of ground cloves
¼ pound pork liver	¼ teaspoon dried thyme
1 cup yellow corn meal	1 teaspoon dried sage
2 teaspoons salt	1 teaspoon dried marjoram
¼ cup onions, chopped fine	½ teaspoon freshly ground pepper

Combine pork shoulder and liver in a saucepan with 1 quart water and cook, over a moderate heat, for 1 hour. Drain, reserving the broth. Discard all bones and chop meat fine. Blend corn meal, salt, 1 cup water, and 2 cups of the broth in a saucepan. Cook, stirring constantly, until thick. Stir in meat, onions, all the spices and herbs. Cover and simmer gently for about 1 hour over a very low heat. Pour into a 9 x 5 x 3-inch loaf pan and chill until firm. Cut into slices about ½ to ¾ inch thick, dust lightly with flour, and fry in a little heated shortening over a moderate heat until crisp on both sides. Serve at once.

HOMEMADE SAUSAGE, COUNTRY STYLE

Combine 2 pounds of fresh lean pork, coarsely ground, with ½ tablespoon dried thyme or sage, dash of cayenne, ¾ teaspoon freshly ground black pepper, and 1 teaspoon salt. Mix well with your hand. Divide in half and shape into two rolls, wrapping each roll securely in foil. Sausage will keep several weeks under refrigeration.

To fry sausages: Cut off slices about ¾ inch thick. Place in a cold skillet and fry over a low heat until well browned on both sides and thoroughly cooked. Serve with applesauce.

CREOLE SAUSAGE

1 pound lean pork, ground
½ pound pork fat, ground
½ large onion, chopped fine
½ garlic, crushed
½ teaspoon salt
½ teaspoon pepper, freshly ground

¼ teaspoon ground chili pepper
¼ teaspoon cayenne
¼ teaspoon dried thyme
¼ teaspoon allspice
1 small bay leaf, crumbled
1 tablespoon chopped parsley

Combine ground pork and pork fat with onion, garlic, salt, pepper, chili pepper, cayenne, thyme, allspice, bay leaf, and parsley. Shape into a roll, wrap securely in foil, and refrigerate. Keeps well for several weeks. This is a hot, highly seasoned sausage meat. To fry, follow directions for Homemade Sausage, Country Style (above).

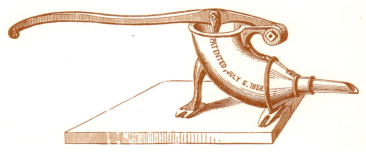

Sausage stuffer

COUNTRY SAUSAGE WITH FRIED APPLE RINGS

Core unpared apples (choose a crisp, tart variety) and cut into rings about ½ inch thick. Allow 2 to 3 rings per serving. Shape sausage meat into patties. Fry in a heavy skillet, over a low heat, until well done but not crisp. Transfer to a heated platter, set aside, and keep warm. Leave about ½ inch of fat in the skillet (pour off the excess) and add as many apple rings as will fit comfortably. Sprinkle lightly with brown sugar and cinnamon and cook, turning frequently (use care so that they do not lose their shape). Cover pan for a few minutes to soften apples, then remove cover, and cook a little longer or until rings have a rich glaze. As you finish cooking each batch, place them on the platter with the sausages.

ROAST RACK OF VENISON

William Byrd, in *Histories of the Dividing Line Betwixt Virginia and North Carolina,* stated: "Our Indian kill'd a Deer, & the other men some Turkeys, but the Indian begg'd very hard that our Cook might not boil Venison & Turkey together, because it wou'd certainly spoil his luck in Hunting, & we shou'd repent it with fasting and Prayer."

A rack of venison weighs 6 to 8 pounds. Bring the meat to room temperature before roasting. Place in a roasting pan, rub generously with butter, or cover with a piece of salt pork, secured with string. If you use butter, baste occasionally during the roasting period. Place in a preheated 325° oven and roast 18 minutes per pound. Do not overcook. Venison should be rare, not well done. Let stand on a warm platter before carving to allow the juices to settle. Salt and pepper to taste. Then serve with Cumberland Sauce (page 544). Puréed Chestnuts (page 516), potatoes, squash, or wild rice are all excellent accompaniments.

CREAMED SWEETBREADS AND OYSTERS

2 pairs sweetbreads
1 tablespoon vinegar
1 stalk celery with leaves
Few sprigs of parsley
4 tablespoons flour
½ teaspoon paprika

4 tablespoons butter
1 cup heavy cream
1 pint oysters in liquor
1 teaspoon salt
Dash of mace or nutmeg
¼ cup dry sherry

Soak sweetbreads in cold salted water for 20 minutes. Drain, add vinegar, celery, parsley, and enough cold water to cover. Cook to the boiling point, then simmer slowly for 15 to 20 minutes, depending on the size of the sweetbreads. Drain and plunge immediately in ice water to blanch. When cold, trim off any tubes and cartilage. Place in a pie dish, cover with wax paper, and put a weight on top. (Pressing the sweetbreads ensures a firm texture.) Separate into small sections with your hands, leaving the tender membrane covering the clusters intact. Coat sweetbreads with flour and paprika. Sauté in heated butter until a delicate golden color. Stir in cream and cook over a low heat, stirring constantly, until smooth and thick. Heat oysters in their liquor until the edges begin to curl. Combine with sweetbreads. Season with salt, mace or nutmeg, and sherry. Serve over crisp hot waffles. Serves 4.

To make Oyster and Sweetbread Pie: Pour into a deep pie dish or casserole (one that can go to the table) and cover with pastry (page 580). Seal edges securely and bake in a preheated 425° oven for 15 to 20 minutes or until nicely browned.

SWEETBREADS EUGÉNIE

Prepare and cook sweetbreads as directed in Creamed Oysters and Sweetbreads. Dip sweetbreads in beaten egg, then in a mixture of flour, salt, and paprika. In a skillet, heat 4 tablespoons butter until it begins to bubble. Add the sweetbreads and sauté over a low heat until golden brown on both sides. Place on a slice of toast, cover with Béchamel Sauce (page 542), and garnish with slices of truffles or lightly sautéed mushrooms. Serves 4.

RABBIT FRICASSEE

"As to their being fresh," Amelia Simmons counseled in speaking of how to buy a good rabbit, "judge by the scent." Though rabbit may seem a frontier food, in recipes like this one it was served at such civilized ménages as Monticello.

1 rabbit	Rind from ¼ lemon
Flour	Few sprigs parsley
¼ cup butter	2 stalks celery with leaves
Salt	1 bay leaf
Pepper	1 tablespoon flour
1 medium onion, chopped fine	1 tablespoon butter
1½ cups red wine	Chopped parsley

Cut rabbit into serving pieces and dust with flour. Heat butter in a skillet with a tight-fitting lid, add rabbit pieces, and sprinkle with salt and pepper. Fry until nicely browned on all sides. Now stir in onion and cook for a few minutes. Next, pour in the wine. Tie lemon rind, parsley, celery, and bay leaf in a little cheesecloth and drop into the skillet. Cover and simmer gently until meat is tender—takes about 1 hour. Lift rabbit onto a hot serving platter. Discard seasoning bag. Work flour and butter together until well blended, then add to liquid, and cook, stirring constantly, until sauce bubbles. Pour over rabbit and sprinkle top with chopped parsley. Serves 4.

The Christians stayed three months in Autiamque, enjoying the greatest plenty of maize, beans, walnuts, and dried plums (persimmons); also rabbits, which they had never had ingenuity enough to ensnare until the Indians there taught them.

—The Gentleman of Elvas, the Lord Inquisitor,
Expedition of Hernando de Soto, 1541

KIDNEY STEW

1 pound small veal kidneys	⅓ cup dry red wine
1 teaspoon salt	2 carrots, diced fine
¼ teaspoon pepper	Flour
2 bay leaves	4 tablespoons butter or bacon drippings
6 peppercorns	¼ pound mushrooms, sliced
1 large onion	

Wash kidneys, trim away any fat, membrane, or connective tissue, and put in a bowl. Add salt, pepper, bay leaves, peppercorns, *2 slices of the onion* (save the rest to use later on), and wine. Cook diced carrots in 2 cups salted water until almost tender. Lift kidneys from bowl (save marinade) and slice in small pieces. Coat generously with flour and fry in heated butter or bacon drippings until nicely browned. Stir in remaining piece of onion, chopped, and continue cooking until onion is limp. Add carrots and the water in which they cooked. Heat, stirring constantly, until sauce thickens. Add mushrooms and cook a few minutes longer. Last of all, stir in the strained marinade. Bring to a boil but do not cook further. May be served from a chafing dish over crisp toast or waffles. Makes 4 to 6 servings.

VEGETABLES

GLAZED PARSNIPS

"Parsnips," Amelia Simmons noted rather enigmatically in *American Cookery,* "are a valuable root, cultivated best in rich old grounds, and doubly deep plowed, late sown, they grow thrifty, and are not so prongy."

6 medium parsnips
3 tablespoons butter, melted
¼ cup brown sugar, firmly packed

½ cup cider
1 teaspoon salt

Peel parsnips, cut in quarters lengthwise, trim out any woody core. Cook in boiling, salted water until tender when tested with a fork. Drain thoroughly. Lay parsnips in a shallow baking dish. Mix together the butter, brown sugar, cider, and salt. Spoon this mixture over the parsnips. Bake 20 minutes in a 400° oven. Baste occasionally with the glaze. Serves 4.

BAKED STUFFED EGGPLANT

1 large or 2 small eggplants
½ cup (1 stick) butter
1 medium onion, chopped fine
1 can (1 pound, 3 ounces) solid-pack
  tomatoes or 6 ripe tomatoes, skinned
1 cup celery, diced

1 teaspoon dried basil
½ teaspoon dried thyme
¾ teaspoon salt
Pepper, freshly ground
1 cup fresh bread crumbs

Cut eggplant in half lengthwise. Remove pulp, leaving the shell about ½ inch thick, and butter inside of shell. Dice the pulp and set aside. Melt *half the butter* in a saucepan. Stir in onion and cook until straw colored. Add diced eggplant, tomatoes, celery, basil, thyme, salt, and pepper. Cook over a moderate heat until mixture is thick and celery is tender. Spoon vegetable mixture into eggplant cavities. Cover with crumbs, lightly sautéed in remaining butter, and place in a shallow baking pan. Pour ½ inch boiling water in the pan. Place in a preheated 325° oven and bake for 15 to 20 minutes. To serve as an entree, substitute 1½ cups cooked shrimp or crab meat for one cup of the eggplant. Serves 4 to 6.

GREEN PEAS WITH MINT

Of the great variety of vegetables Jefferson grew at Monticello, his favorite was the pea. In Albemarle County, Virginia, it was customary for the neighboring gentlemen-farmers to compete each spring for the distinction of serving the first green peas. Jefferson took the honors so frequently that one year he told his children not to speak of the peas in his garden so that his friend George Divers of Farmington might give the annual dinner.

Cook frozen peas according to package directions or shell fresh peas and cook in boiling, salted water. In either case, do not overcook. Dot with butter and sprinkle with fresh chopped mint. Serves 4.

AMBUSHED ASPARAGUS

This recipe is adapted from *Common Sense in the Household*.

Cut the tops from 6 hard dinner rolls (either square or rectangular) and hollow out most of the center. Brush centers with melted butter and place them, along with the tops, in a 300° oven to dry while you prepare the asparagus. Cook 1 pound fresh asparagus (or 1 package frozen) until tender. Drain and cut the spears into small pieces. Set aside. Make 2 cups of well-seasoned Cream Sauce (page 542). Stir in asparagus, season with a dash of nutmeg, then spoon the mixture into the hot, crisp rolls. Cover with tops and put back in the oven for 3 minutes. May be served with crisp bacon for breakfast or lunch.

TURNIP GREENS

Cook 1 pound pork or salt pork in boiling, lightly salted water until tender when tested with a fork. Add water as needed. Wash thoroughly 2 bunches turnip greens and 1 bunch mustard greens. Pare and chop coarsely 4 white turnips. Add greens and turnips to pork and cook over a low heat for 40 to 45 minutes. Drain and serve with Corn Meal Dumplings (page 532) cooked in the pot liquor, Spider Corncake (page 451), or Corn Meal Biscuits (page 442). Serves 4.

MASHED TURNIPS

This recipe is adapted from the *New England Economical House-keeper*, where it was called "Turnip Sauce."

Pare 2 medium-sized yellow turnips (rutabagas) and 2 large potatoes. Cut into chunks of equivalent size. Place in a saucepan, cover with boiling, salted water, and cook until tender. Drain and dry thoroughly, then put through a ricer. Beat in a generous amount of butter, salt and pepper to taste, a big pinch of sugar, and some heavy cream, heated. Continue beating until turnips are very smooth. These can be made ahead of time and kept warm in a double boiler. Serves 4 to 6.

ONIONS IN CREAM

24 small white onions
2 tablespoons butter
2 tablespoons flour
1 cup half-and-half (milk and cream)

½ teaspoon salt
Dash of cloves
¼ cup chopped parsley

Cover peeled onions with cold, salted water and bring to a boil. Reduce heat and cook slowly until onions are tender when tested with a fork. Drain thoroughly. Melt butter in a saucepan, add flour a little at a time, stir until smooth, and cook over a low heat for several minutes. Stir in half-and-half and continue cooking, stirring constantly, until sauce is smooth and bubbly. Remove from heat, stir in salt, cloves, and parsley. Combine with onions. Serves 4.

PLANTATION STRING BEANS

1 pound green beans	1 teaspoon salt
4 slices bacon	¼ teaspoon pepper
4 to 6 scallions	

Snip off ends and slice green beans into thin slivers. Dice bacon and fry until crisp. Scoop out the bits of bacon, drain on paper towels, and set aside. Chop scallions and sauté in bacon fat until limp. Add beans, stir thoroughly, and cook over a moderate heat for about 1 minute. Add 1 tablespoon water, cover tightly, and cook 4 minutes. Remove cover and continue cooking and stirring until beans are tender but still crisp. Before serving, season with salt and pepper and sprinkle the beans with the drained bacon bits. Serves 4 to 6.

GREEN BEANS WITH CHESTNUTS

Take enough cooked chestnuts, chopped coarsely, to make about ⅓ cup. Sauté lightly (only a minute or two) in 6 tablespoons of butter. Add 1 pound cooked green beans and mix well. Taste for seasoning. Serves 4.

In July, when the chestnuts and corn are green and full grown, they half boil the former, and take off the rind; and having sliced the milky, swelled, long rows of the latter, the women pound it in a large wooden mortar, which is wide at the mouth, and gradually narrows to the bottom; then they knead both together, wrap them up in green corn-blades of various sizes, about an inch-thick, and boil them well, as they do every kind of seethed food. This sort of bread is very tempting to the taste, and reckoned most delicious to their strong palates.

—James Adair,
The History of the American Indian, 1775

PURÉED CHESTNUTS

1 pound chestnuts	2 tablespoons butter
1 teaspoon oil	½ teaspoon pepper, freshly ground
1 tablespoon vinegar	2 to 3 tablespoons heavy cream
3 stalks celery, coarsely chopped	Salt
1 small onion, coarsely chopped	

Make a gash in the flat side of each chestnut, place them in a pan with the oil, and shake until well coated. Heat in a preheated 350° oven until the shells and inner skins can be removed easily. Shell the chestnuts, cover with water, and add the vinegar, celery, and onion. Boil until tender. Drain, discard celery and onion, and purée or mash until free of lumps. Beat in the butter, pepper, and cream. Add salt to taste. A rich and delicious accompaniment to venison, game, or turkey.

RUTABAGA PUDDING

Rutabagas were the subject of a bitter dispute that was aired in the New York newspapers in 1818. William Cobbett, the proprietor of a seed store in New York, maintained that he sold the best dollar-a-pound seeds in the City. As a gratuitous jab at his competitor, Grant Thorburn, Cobbett made the additional claim that he had introduced the rutabaga to America. Thorburn retorted by saying that *he* sold the best seed at a dollar a pound—and then devastated his opponent with the facts: "In the year 1796 a large field of these turnips was grown by Wm. Prout on that piece of ground now occupied by the navy yard, at the city of Washington."

2 pounds rutabagas (yellow turnips)	1½ teaspoons salt
½ cup fine dry bread crumbs	Big pinch of sugar
½ cup milk	2 eggs, well beaten
2 tablespoons melted butter	

Peel rutabaga and cut in cubes, then cover with boiling water. Place a lid on the pan and cook vegetable over moderate heat until tender when pierced with a fork. Drain thoroughly. Mash as smooth as possible or put through a ricer, then beat in all remaining ingredients. Spoon into a 1½-quart baking dish or casserole and bake in a preheated 350° oven for 1 hour. Serves 4 to 6.

CHARTREUSE OF VEGETABLES

According to Mary Ronald's *Century Cook Book*, "Chartreuse is a liqueur made by the monks of the French monastery of Grand Chartreuse; but a class of dishes has also been given this name, where two or more foods are used which conceals the others. The story goes that on fast days the monks were thus able to indulge in forbidden food, and savory viands were hidden under cabbage or other severely plain articles." Thomas Jefferson was partial to the chartreuse recipe below, adapted from the Monticello manuscript collection.

6 small kohlrabi	Parsley
8 carrots	Salt
6 small beets or small white turnips	Pepper
2 medium-sized yellow turnips	

Each vegetable must be cooked separately. Peel and slice, rather thin, the kohlrabi, carrots, white turnips (if you use them), and the yellow turnips. The beets are cooked whole in their skins. Drop each vegetable in a pot of boiling, salted water and cook until tender. Drain. Peel and slice the beets. Layer the vegetables, alternating the color, in a 1½-quart mold or the bottom of a double boiler (any deep, straight-sided vessel will do). Sprinkle finely chopped parsley and a dash of salt and pepper between the layers. Place the vessel in a pan of hot water, cover tightly (lacking a cover, use foil), and bake 20 minutes in a 350° oven. Unmold on a warm serving platter and serve with Hollandaise Sauce (page 542). Serves 6.

SQUASH

Indians grew a wide variety of squash long before the first white men reached America. Crooknecks and bush-scallops grew in the Northeast, cushaws and sweet potato squashes in the South, the Boston marrow and autumn turban in New England. Captain John Smith described the squash ("macocks") he found in the early days of Virginia, saying that the Indians "plant amongst their corn pumpions, and a fruit like unto our muskmelon, but less and worse, which they call macocks." Surely the best-known and most popular American squash is the Hubbard, whose history was revealed in a letter by James J. H. Gregory, written in December, 1857, for *The Magazine of Horticulture*. "Of the origin of the Hubbard squash we have no certain knowledge," Mr. Gregory said. "The facts relative to its cultivation in Marblehead are simply these. Upwards of twenty years ago, a single specimen was brought into town, the seed from which was planted in the garden of a lady, now deceased; a specimen from this yield was given to Captain Knott Martin, of this town, who raised it for family use for a few years, when it was brought to our notice in the year 1842 or '43. We were first informed of its good qualities by Mrs. Elizabeth Hubbard, a very worthy lady, through whom we obtained seed from Capt. Martin. As the squash up to this time had no specific name to designate it from other varieties, my father termed it the 'Hubbard Squash.'"

BAKED SQUASH

Wash 2 squash (acorn, Hubbard, etc.) and cut them in half. Spoon out seeds and fibers from the cavity. Put 4 slices of bacon in a shallow baking pan and bake in a preheated 350° oven until crisp. Remove from oven, drain on paper towels, and set aside. Sprinkle squash with salt and pepper and place, cut side down, in the bacon fat. Bake at 350° about 1 hour or until tender when tested with a fork. Just before serving, sprinkle lightly with brown sugar, brush with some of the bacon fat, and drop the bacon, crumbled, into squash cavities. Serves 4.

COLACHE

(Summer Squash, Mexican Style)

4 summer squash	1 small onion, chopped
4 ears of corn	Salt
3 ripe tomatoes	Pepper
¼ cup butter	

Wash squash and cut in small pieces; cut corn kernels from the cob; skin tomatoes and cut in cubes. Heat butter in a saucepan, stir in onion, and cook until limp but not brown. Add squash, corn, tomatoes, salt, and pepper. Cover and cook over a low heat for 30 to 40 minutes, stirring occasionally. Makes 6 servings.

PENNSYLVANIA RED CABBAGE

2 tablespoons shortening or bacon
  drippings
1 large onion, chopped fine
2 apples, pared, cored, and thinly sliced
1 cup water
½ cup red wine vinegar

2 tablespoons sugar
1 teaspoon salt
Dash pepper
1 bay leaf
1 medium-sized head red cabbage
1 tablespoon flour

Heat shortening or bacon drippings in a large, heavy saucepan. Add the onion and sauté 3 to 4 minutes. Toss in apple slices and cook several minutes longer. Stir in water, vinegar, sugar, salt, pepper, and bay leaf and bring to the boiling point. Remove from heat while you shred the cabbage, and stir it into the vinegar mixture. Cover tightly, and cook over a low heat for 40 to 45 minutes, stirring occasionally. Just before serving, add the flour, stirring constantly until mixture thickens slightly. Excellent with pork, goose, duck, suckling pig, or game. Serves 4.

JERUSALEM ARTICHOKES

The roots of Jerusalem artichokes were eaten in this country by the Indians before the arrival of Columbus. They were cultivated in Italy as *girasole* (meaning "a flower that turns toward the sun"), which became "Jerusalem" in English. They are entirely different from the globe, or French, artichoke, which is an edible thistle.

1½ pounds Jerusalem artichokes
⅓ cup melted butter
3 tablespoons fresh lemon juice

½ teaspoon salt
Few sprigs parsley, chopped

Peel artichokes and cook in boiling, salted water until tender. Test with a toothpick after 15 minutes—artichokes should not be overcooked. Drain thoroughly. Dress with a mixture of butter, lemon juice, salt, and chopped parsley. Serves 4 to 6.

GLAZED BABY CARROTS

2 bunches baby carrots
6 tablespoons butter

6 tablespoons sugar
½ teaspoon cinnamon or ginger

Wash carrots, scrape if necessary, and leave whole. Cook in a small amount of boiling, salted water about 12 to 15 minutes or until tender when tested with a fork. The time depends on size and degree of freshness. Drain thoroughly. Combine butter, sugar, and cinnamon or ginger in a large skillet. Cook, stirring constantly, until well blended. Add carrots and cook over a low heat, shaking the pan frequently to glaze carrots on all sides. When shiny and well glazed, serve to 6.

HARVARD BEETS

1 can (1 pound) baby beets
¼ cup sugar
½ teaspoon salt
½ tablespoon cornstarch

¼ cup cider vinegar
1½ tablespoons ginger marmalade
2 tablespoons butter

Drain beets thoroughly and set aside. Combine sugar, salt, and cornstarch in top of a double boiler. Pour in vinegar and cook over direct heat, stirring constantly, until smooth and bubbly. Add beets, ginger marmalade, and butter. Place over simmering water for about 30 minutes. Serves 4.

BAKED CELERY WITH SLIVERED ALMONDS

1 large bunch Pascal celery
4 tablespoons butter
2 tablespoons flour
1 cup milk

½ cup celery water
½ cup blanched, slivered almonds
2 tablespoons dry bread crumbs

Wash celery and cut into slices about ½ inch thick (save a generous handful of the celery tops). Place the celery in a saucepan, cover halfway with boiling, salted water, and lay the celery leaves on top. Cook for 10 to 15 minutes after water has reached the boiling point or until tender. Discard leaves and drain celery thoroughly, saving ½ cup of the celery water. While celery cooks, melt 2 tablespoons of the butter in a saucepan, stir in flour until smooth, add milk. Cook over a low heat, stirring constantly, until smooth and bubbly. Stir in ½ cup celery water and taste to see if more salt is needed. Place a layer of the cooked celery in a shallow baking dish, spoon half the sauce over it, and sprinkle with half the almonds. Add the remaining celery, then the sauce. Sprinkle the top with bread crumbs, dot with the remaining butter, and sprinkle remaining almonds over all. Bake in a preheated 350° oven for 30 minutes. Serves 4.

MUSHROOMS IN CREAM

½ cup (1 stick) butter
¼ cup olive oil
1½ pounds fresh mushrooms
Salt

Pepper, freshly ground
1 teaspoon dried tarragon
¾ cup heavy cream
1 teaspoon fresh lemon juice

Heat butter and oil in a large heavy skillet over a low heat. Meanwhile, wash mushrooms, remove stems, and slice fairly thin. Add to butter-oil mixture and cook about 5 minutes, stirring frequently. Add butter if needed. Sprinkle in salt and a large amount of pepper (more than seems reasonable). The freshly ground pepper adds wonderful flavor. Stir in tarragon, crumbled fine. Continue cooking 5 minutes longer, giving mixture an occasional stir. Add the cream and simmer until sauce has thickened slightly—it should have body but should not be really thick. If sauce seems too thin, stir in a little cornstarch or arrowroot and cook until it reaches a good consistency. Just before serving, add the fresh lemon juice. Serve with steak or over crisp toast as a luncheon dish. Serves 4.

FRIED MUSHROOMS

1 pound fresh small button mushrooms
1 beaten egg

Cracker crumbs
Salt

Wash and dry fresh, firm mushrooms. Dip in beaten egg and cracker crumbs. Preheat fat to 375° on deep-fat thermometer or until a 1-inch cube of bread browns in 60 seconds. Fry mushrooms until brown, then drain on paper towels. Salt to taste. Serves 4 to 6.

SPINACH TIMBALES

4 eggs
1½ cups warm milk or ½ cup heavy cream
    and 1 cup chicken stock
1 teaspoon salt
Dash of pepper

Dash of nutmeg
1 teaspoon lemon juice
1 cup cooked spinach, well drained and
    chopped fine

Beat together eggs, warm milk, salt, pepper, nutmeg, and lemon juice until frothy. Stir in spinach. Pour mixture into 6 to 8 buttered custard cups, depending on size of the cups. Set in a pan of hot water and bake in a preheated 325° oven for 20 to 30 minutes or until a knife tested in the center comes out dry. Unmold onto hot plates and serve plain or with Hollandaise Sauce (page 542).

SHAKER SPINACH WITH ROSEMARY

2 pounds spinach
¼ teaspoon fresh rosemary or
    large pinch of dried rosemary
3 sprigs parsley, chopped

1 green onion, chopped
2 tablespoons butter
Salt
Pepper

Trim thick stems from spinach, wash the leaves several times in cold water. Chop coarsely and pile in a large saucepan with all remaining ingredients. Cook, covered, in its own juices about 5 minutes or until spinach is limp but still bright green. Serves 4.

SAUTÉED OR FRIED CUCUMBERS

Pare 2 medium-sized cucumbers, then cut in slices about ¼ inch thick. Pat with paper towels to remove all moisture.

To sauté: Sprinkle with salt and pepper and coat lightly with flour. Cook in ¼ cup melted butter until golden brown on both sides.

To fry: Dip each slice in fine dry bread crumbs, then in slightly beaten egg, then again in the crumbs. Fry several at a time in deep fat heated to 385° on deep-fat thermometer or until a 1-inch cube of bread browns in 60 seconds. When slices are golden brown, drain on paper towels and season with salt and pepper. Serve at once to 4.

CREOLE TOMATOES

3 large tomatoes
1 green pepper, chopped
1 small onion, chopped
4 tablespoons butter
Salt

Pepper
6 rounds of toast
1 tablespoon butter
1 tablespoon flour
½ cup light cream

Pour boiling water over tomatoes, let stand several minutes, then slip off the skins. Cut tomatoes in half crosswise and place in a flame-proof baking dish. Cover the tops generously with a mixture of green pepper and onion. Dot each tomato with butter and sprinkle with a little salt and pepper. Bake in a preheated 350° oven for 15 to 20 minutes or until tomatoes are very tender. Place each tomato on a round of buttered toast and keep warm. To make the sauce, add the tablespoon of butter to the pan drippings. When it has melted, add the flour and stir until smooth. Then add the cream. Cook, stirring constantly, until sauce thickens. Season to taste. Pour sauce over tomatoes and serve to 6.

A De Bry engraving of Indians transporting vegetables

SCALLOPED TOMATOES

6 ripe tomatoes or 1 can (1 pound,
  3 ounce size) solid-pack tomatoes
1 cup coarse dry bread crumbs
1 teaspoon sugar

Salt
Pepper
3 tablespoons butter

Skin the ripe tomatoes and cut in slices. Combine crumbs, sugar, salt, pepper, and butter. Place a layer of tomatoes in the bottom of a buttered casserole and sprinkle with some of the crumb mixture. Repeat with tomato layers and crumb mixture until dish is filled, then top with remaining crumb mixture. Bake in a preheated 350° oven for 30 minutes. Serves 4 to 6.

VARIATION: To make Scalloped Tomatoes, Southern Style, use the above ingredients, but increase the sugar to ¾ cup. Melt butter in a heavy skillet, add all remaining ingredients, and heat to a boil. Reduce heat and cook very, very slowly about 1 hour. Stir occasionally. When done, the tomatoes should be lightly glazed and most of the liquid absorbed. If they look too dry before they start to glaze, stir in a little more butter.

FRIED TOMATO SLICES

Choose firm, almost ripe tomatoes and cut in slices about ½ inch thick. Plan on 2 to 3 slices per person. Dip each slice of tomato into corn meal seasoned with salt and pepper, coating both sides. Fry some bacon until crisp (allow at least 2 slices per person). Drain on paper towels. Add tomato slices to bacon fat (a thin film of fat is sufficient) and fry several minutes on each side or until coating is crisp. To fry more than one panful of tomato slices, wipe out pan and add more fat before proceeding with second batch.

DELAWARE SUCCOTASH

Originally, succotash—or *misickquatash*, as the Narragansett Indians called it—was made of corn and kidney beans, and cooked in bear grease. One of the early settlers wrote of *misickquatash*, "In Winter [the Indians] esteeme their Corne being boyled with Beanes for a rare dish." Indeed, the Pilgrims probably thought it a rare dish themselves; it may have been one of the first recipes taught by friendly Indians to the settlers at Plymouth Rock, to be made from the sparse materials at hand.

2 thin slices salt pork
1 pint shelled (2 pounds unshelled) Lima beans or 1 package (2 cups) frozen, thawed Lima beans
8 ears corn or 1 package (2 cups) frozen, thawed corn

1 large ripe tomato, skinned and cubed
1 teaspoon salt
¼ teaspoon pepper
Dash of nutmeg

Lay slices of salt pork in bottom of a saucepan and cover with Lima beans. Add enough water to cover, and cook over a low heat until the beans are tender. Cut the kernels from fresh corn and combine with beans, cubed tomato, and seasonings. Cover and continue cooking over a low heat for 10 to 15 minutes. Stir frequently to prevent scorching. Serves 6.

SUCCOTASH

2 cups fresh Lima beans or 2 packages frozen Lima beans
2 cups whole kernel corn (fresh, frozen, or canned)
2 tablespoons butter

1 teaspoon salt
Dash of pepper
1 teaspoon sugar
½ cup water
¼ cup heavy cream

Cook Lima beans in boiling, salted water until tender (if frozen Lima beans are used, cook according to package directions). Mix cooked beans with corn (if fresh, cut from the cob; if canned, drain; if frozen, use straight from the package), butter, salt, pepper, sugar, and water. Cook over a low heat for 10 to 15 minutes. Drain, then add cream. Heat through but do not boil. Serves 4 to 6.

CORN ON THE COB

"Some people take the whole stem," Fredrika Bremer wrote on her visit to America in 1850, "and gnaw [the kernels] out with their teeth : two gentlemen do so who sit opposite . . . myself at table, and whom we call 'the sharks,' because of their remarkable ability in gobbling up large and often double portions of everything which comes to table, and it really troubles me to see how their wide mouths . . . ravenously grind up the beautiful white, pearly maize ears."

Ideally, corn should be husked and cooked within a few minutes from the time it leaves the garden. Since this is not always possible, corn should be refrigerated until ready to use—but never longer than absolutely necessary. To test corn for ripeness, open the husks and pierce a kernel with your fingernail. If it is as young as it should be, it will be milky inside. Fill a large kettle with enough water to cover the corn and bring water to a rolling boil. *Do not add salt* (it tends to toughen the corn). Add instead 1 or 2 teaspoons of sugar. Husk the ears, remove the silk, and plunge into the boiling water. When water comes to a boil again, cook 3 to 5 minutes. Very young tender corn needs only about 3 minutes of boiling. The shorter the cooking time, the better the corn will be. Place corn in a dish lined with a linen napkin and fold it over the corn to hold in the heat. Serve with salt, pepper, and butter.

It is not elegant to gnaw *Indian corn. The kernels should be scored with a knife, scraped off into the plate, and then eaten with a fork. Ladies should be particularly careful how* they *manage so ticklish a dainty, lest the exhibition rub off a little desirable romance.*
—Charles Day, *Hints on Etiquette*, 1844

SHAKER DRIED CORN

Until well into the nineteenth century, drying was the principal means of preserving fruits and vegetables—and the Shakers made a specialty of dried corn. At one time the chief occupation of the Sisters of North Union, Ohio—a Shaker settlement that flourished between 1822 and 1889—was the drying of sweet corn.

1 cup dried corn	½ teaspoon salt
2 cups boiling water	2 tablespoons butter
2 teaspoons sugar	½ cup light or heavy cream

Place corn in a saucepan, pour in boiling water, and let stand at least 1 hour. At the end of this soaking period, stir in sugar, salt, and butter. Cook, uncovered, over a low heat for about 30 minutes. (To prevent scorching, make certain heat is low because the corn will absorb most of the liquid.) Stir in cream and cook 5 minutes longer. Serves 4.

CORN PUDDING

This recipe has been handed down in the family of General Daniel Morgan, a Revolutionary War hero.

2 cups fresh corn or
  1 package frozen corn
3 eggs
¼ cup flour

1 teaspoon salt
½ teaspoon white pepper
2 tablespoons butter, melted
2 cups light cream

Cut corn from the cob or thaw the frozen corn. Beat eggs vigorously, then stir in corn and a mixture of flour, salt, and white pepper. Add butter and cream. Pour into a buttered 1½-quart baking dish or casserole, place in a pan of hot water, and bake in a preheated 325° oven for 1 hour or until a knife tested in center comes out dry. Serves 6 to 8.

CORN CUSTARD WITH TOMATOES

1 cup grated fresh corn
4 eggs
1 small onion, grated
½ teaspoon salt
Dash cayenne
1½ cups milk

4 medium tomatoes
Flour
Salt
4 tablespoons butter
1 cup light cream

Grate corn from cobs into a bowl and measure correct amount. Beat eggs vigorously and stir in onion, salt, and cayenne. Heat milk until a film forms, skim, and stir into corn mixture. Pour into 6 buttered custard cups and place in a shallow pan containing about 1 inch of boiling water. Bake in a preheated 325° oven for 50 to 60 minutes or until a knife inserted in center of custard comes out clean. Shortly before custards are done, cut tomatoes in slices, dust both sides with flour, sprinkle with salt, and sauté in heated butter over a brisk heat. Fry several minutes on each side. Remove from skillet, stir in 1 or 2 teaspoons of flour, and pour in cream. Cook, stirring constantly, until sauce thickens just enough to make a smooth gravy. Taste and add salt if necessary. Remove custards from cups, place on a hot platter, surround with tomatoes, and spoon sauce over tomatoes. Serves 6.

CORN OYSTERS

2 cups grated fresh corn
2 eggs, separated
½ teaspoon salt

Dash pepper
¼ cup flour
¼ cup shortening

Grate corn from cobs into a bowl and measure correct amount. Stir in well-beaten egg yolks, salt, pepper, and flour. Beat egg whites until stiff but not dry. Fold them into corn mixture gently. Heat shortening in a skillet. Drop corn batter from a teaspoon into hot fat and brown quickly on both sides. Serve very hot with chops, a roast, or a cold fowl. Makes 12 to 14.

BRUNA BÖNER
(Swedish Beans)

1¼ cups dry brown beans or kidney beans
1½ quarts cold water
1 tablespoon salt
2 tablespoons cider vinegar

2 tablespoons molasses
1 tablespoon brown sugar
1 tablespoon butter
1 tablespoon cornstarch

Soak the beans overnight in cold water. The following day, cook in the same water, with salt added, for about two hours or until the beans are tender but still hold their shape. (During the cooking period there should always be enough water on the beans so that the water can be seen.) Stir in vinegar, molasses, brown sugar, and butter and continue cooking 10 minutes longer. Make a smooth paste of cornstarch and a little water and stir into the beans. Cook a few minutes longer until the liquid thickens slightly. Serves 6 to 8.

Advertisement for equipment for sorting beans

COWPOKE BEANS

1 pound dried pinto or red beans
Ham bone
1 red chili pepper (optional)
1 teaspoon salt
¼ pound suet, chopped
1 large onion, chopped
1 clove garlic, chopped

4 ripe tomatoes, chopped
½ cup chopped parsley
½ teaspoon ground cumin
½ teaspoon dried marjoram
1½ tablespoons chili powder
1 teaspoon salt

Cover beans with cold water and soak overnight. Next day add the ham bone, red chili pepper, and salt to the undrained beans. Bring to a boil, reduce heat, cover, and simmer gently for several hours or until beans are tender. Drain and save liquid. Toward the end of the cooking period, heat suet in a large skillet, stir in onion and garlic, and cook 5 minutes or until onions take on a little color. Add tomatoes, parsley, 1 cup of the bean liquid, and all remaining ingredients. Cook over a low heat, stirring frequently, for 45 minutes. Combine with beans and continue simmering gently for 20 minutes. Serves 6 to 8.

BOSTON BAKED BEANS

It is for baked beans that Boston is known as Bean Town. The Puritan Sabbath lasted from sundown on Saturday until sundown on Sunday, and baked beans provided the Puritans with a dish that was easy to prepare. The bean pot could be kept in the slow heat of a fireplace to serve at Saturday supper and Sunday breakfast. Housewives too busy with other chores were able to turn the baking of the beans over to a local baker. The baker called each Saturday morning to pick up the family's bean pot and take it to a community oven, usually in the cellar of a nearby tavern. The free-lance baker then returned the baked beans, with a bit of brown bread, on Saturday evening or Sunday morning.

6 cups pea or navy beans
1 pound salt pork
1 tablespoon dry mustard
1 tablespoon salt

1 teaspoon black pepper
1 cup molasses
1 small onion (optional)

Pick over beans, cover with cold water, and soak overnight. In the morning, drain, cover with fresh water, bring to a boil very slowly, then simmer until the skins burst, "which is best determined," wrote Fannie Farmer, "by taking a few beans on the tip of a spoon and blowing on them, when skins will burst if sufficiently cooked." Miss Farmer adds that beans tested this way "must, of course, be thrown away." Drain beans. Scald the salt pork, which should be well streaked with lean, by letting it stand in boiling water for 5 to 10 minutes. Cut off two thin slices, one to place in bottom of pot, the other to be cut into bits. Score rind of the remaining piece with a sharp knife. Mix dry mustard, salt, black pepper, and molasses. Alternate the layers of beans in the pot with the molasses mixture and the bits of pork. If you use an onion, bury it in the middle. When the bean pot is full, push the large piece of pork down into the beans with the rind sticking up. Add boiling water to cover, put the lid on, and bake all day (a minimum of 6 to 8 hours) in a 250° oven. Check from time to time and add boiling water if needed. Uncover pot during last hour of baking so the rind can brown and crisp. To this day many old-timers believe the rich brown goodness of Boston Baked Beans is largely due to the earthenware bean pot, with its narrow throat and big bulging sides. Lacking one of these pots, you can successfully use any deep earthenware casserole that has a cover. Serves 10 to 12.

FRIJOLES REFRITOS
(Refried Beans)

1 can (20 ounces) kidney or Mexican beans
3 tablespoons olive oil or bacon drippings
1 small onion, chopped fine
1 clove garlic, chopped fine

½ green pepper, chopped fine
1 teaspoon chili powder
3 tablespoons hot beef broth

Drain beans (reserve the liquid) and mash thoroughly. Heat oil or drippings in a skillet, add onion, garlic, green pepper, and cook over a low heat until tender. Stir in chili powder mixed with hot beef broth, then add the beans. Cook slowly, stirring continuously. Add bean liquid as needed. Beans are cooked properly when they are completely dry. Serves 6.

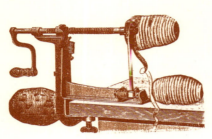

Above: a potato parer. Right: an implement used to make Saratoga Chips.

SARATOGA CHIPS

The invention of Saratoga Chips is usually attributed to George Crum, the chef of Moon's Lake House at New York's fashionable nineteenth-century spa, Saratoga Springs. One of the fussier patrons persisted in returning orders of French fried potatoes to the chef, insisting that they were not thin enough. In a rage, Crum disdainfully sliced some potatoes paper-thin, dropped them into boiling fat, and had his triumphant gibe served to the guest (who loved them).

To make Saratoga, or Potato, Chips: Pare potatoes and slice paper-thin with a vegetable slicer. Soak in cold water for 2 hours. Dry thoroughly and fry in deep fat until crisp and golden. Drain on paper towels and sprinkle with salt.

POTATO OLIVES

Pare 6 large potatoes and cut into balls with a melon-ball cutter. Drop the potatoes into boiling, salted water and cook until almost tender. Drain and cool. Melt ½ cup butter in a saucepan, add potato balls, and cook over a low heat until potatoes are golden on all sides. Shake the pan frequently to brown potatoes on all sides. Serve immediately with a sprinkling of chopped parsley on top. Serves 6.

POTATO PANCAKES

Combine in the blender 2 eggs, 1 slice onion, 1 teaspoon salt, a few sprigs of parsley, 1 cup diced raw potatoes. Turn blender on high, remove cover, and add ¼ cup flour and a second cup of diced potatoes. Do not overblend. Pour onto a hot greased griddle and cook until brown on both sides. This makes a soft pancake, more like a griddlecake. Makes 12.

POTATOES DUCHESSE

2 cups hot mashed potatoes
2 eggs, beaten
1 teaspoon baking powder

½ teaspoon salt
½ teaspoon nutmeg (optional)
Beaten egg or melted butter

Combine potatoes, eggs, baking powder, salt, and nutmeg, beating hard. Form into cakes or shape with a pastry tube and place on a buttered baking sheet. Brush with slightly beaten egg or melted butter. Brown under broiler flame or bake in a preheated 400° oven until golden. The potato mixture may also be dropped by spoonfuls into deep fat preheated to 385° to 395° on deep-fat thermometer or until a 1-inch cube of bread browns in 60 seconds. When well browned, drain on paper towels. May be prepared ahead and reheated in a preheated 425° oven for 8 to 10 minutes.

SCALLOPED POTATOES

Slice pared potatoes as thin as possible. Place a layer of potatoes in a casserole, dust with a little flour, season with salt, pepper, chopped onion (about 1 slice) and dot with butter. Repeat the layers of potatoes, with seasonings between, until the casserole is full. Then add enough milk to reach the top layer. Bake in a preheated 325° oven for 1½ hours. The number it will serve depends, of course, on the size of your casserole.

JANSON'S TEMPTATION

Eric Janson, the Swedish religious reformer who founded Bishop Hill, Illinois, in 1846, preached rigorous asceticism to his followers—no liquor and a diet that barely sustained life. One day, according to legend, a zealous Jansonist discovered the prophet feasting, secretively, on a casserole of anchovies and potatoes, bound together with golden butter and rich milk. The dish became known as Janson's Temptation.

Fine dry bread crumbs
6 medium potatoes
1 medium onion, chopped fine
2 small cans flat anchovy fillets, drained

¼ teaspoon pepper
5 tablespoons butter
2 cups milk

Butter a 2-quart casserole or baking dish and coat bottom and sides with crumbs. Pare potatoes and cut into paper-thin slices. Combine onion, anchovies (cut into pieces), pepper, and butter. Place a layer of potatoes in bottom of dish and sprinkle half the onion mixture over it. Add another layer of potatoes and the rest of the seasonings. Top with remaining potatoes and pour in the milk. Sprinkle top with ⅓ cup of crumbs and dot with butter. Bake in a preheated 350° oven for about 1 hour. Potatoes should be tender when tested with a fork and milk should be largely absorbed. Do not add salt because anchovies contribute all the salt necessary. Makes 6 servings.

CANDIED SWEET POTATOES

Sweet potatoes (the dark orange variety are often called yams) have been grown in this country since at least the early seventeenth century and are associated with southern cooking. Robert Beverley described the sweet potatoes of Virginia in 1705 as "about as long as a Boy's leg, and sometimes as long and big as both the Leg and Thigh of a young Child, and very much resembling it in Shape."

6 sweet potatoes	½ cup water
½ teaspoon salt	4 tablespoons butter
1 cup dark brown sugar	1 tablespoon lemon juice

Cook the sweet potatoes in their jackets in boiling, salted water until nearly tender. Drain, peel, and cut in slices about ½ inch thick. Place in a greased, shallow baking dish and sprinkle with salt. Cook together brown sugar, water, and butter in a separate pan for several minutes. Then stir in lemon juice and pour over potatoes. Bake in a preheated 375° oven for 20 to 25 minutes, basting occasionally with the syrup. Serves 4 to 6.

YAMS WITH APPLES

Bake 4 large yams until tender. Meanwhile, pare 4 tart cooking apples, core, and cut into thin slices. Peel yams, cut into slices about ½ inch thick, and arrange alternate layers of yams and apples in a buttered baking dish. Sprinkle each layer with sugar and a dash of nutmeg. Dot with butter. Cover and bake in a preheated 350° oven for 30 to 35 minutes. The tartness of the apples cuts the sweet flavor of the yams. Serve as an accompaniment for roast duck, game, or ham. Makes 4 to 6 servings.

MACARONI AND CHEESE PUDDING

On February 6, 1802, after dinner with President Jefferson at the White House, Mr. Manasseh Cutler wrote that there was "a pie called macaroni, which appeared to be a rich crust filled with the strillions of onions, or shallots, which I took them to be, tasted very strong, and not agreeable. Mr. Lewis told me there were none in it; it was made of flour and butter, with a particularly strong liquor mixed with them."

2½ cups elbow macaroni	1 teaspoon salt
¼ cup butter	Dash pepper
¼ cup flour	2 cups grated Cheddar cheese
2¼ cups milk	

Cook macaroni according to package directions until tender, then drain thoroughly. While macaroni cooks, melt butter in a saucepan, stir in flour until smooth, and cook a minute or two. Add the milk a little at a time, and cook, stirring constantly, until sauce bubbles. Add salt and pepper. Arrange alternate layers of macaroni and cheese in a medium-sized baking dish or casserole, reserving some of the cheese (about ¼ cup) to sprinkle over top. Pour hot sauce over all, sprinkle with the cheese, and dot with bits of butter. Bake 35 minutes in a preheated 400° oven. Serves 4 to 6.

NOODLES JEFFERSON

Cook 2 cups (1 package) noodles according to package directions. Drain well. Add 1 cup (2 sticks) soft or melted sweet butter and 2 cups freshly grated Parmesan cheese. Toss gently until well mixed. Season with freshly ground pepper to taste. Serves 4.

Advertisement, Collection of F. Hal Higgins

HOMINY PUDDING

Hominy was adopted from the Indians and became an important basic food for American pioneers. It is, simply, hulled corn—the pioneers removed the hulls by soaking the grains of corn in a weak wood lye. Washed and boiled until it was tender, hominy was often served in place of potatoes. It was ground, too, into grits—fragments slightly coarser than corn meal—which have become closely identified with the South. Grits are traditionally eaten for breakfast with butter and milk, or made into breads and puddings. G. W. Featherstonhaugh, an Englishman traveling in the South in 1837, wrote: "Our breakfast was admirable, excellent coffee with delicious cream, and that capital, national dish of South Carolina, snow-white homminy brought hot to table like maccaroni, which ought always to be eaten, with lumps of sweet fresh butter buried in it! this is certainly one of the best things imaginable to begin the day liberally with."

1 cup hominy grits
5 cups boiling water
2 eggs, separated

½ cup light cream
1 teaspoon salt
¼ teaspoon white pepper

Stir grits into boiling water. Cover and cook over a low heat for 25 to 30 minutes. Set aside to cool. Then measure exactly 2 cups of the cooled grits into a bowl and beat until smooth. Beat yolks soundly and stir into grits. Add cream, salt, and pepper. Beat egg whites until they stand in peaks and fold into grit mixture, lightly but thoroughly. Spoon into a well-buttered 1-quart casserole and bake in a preheated 350° oven for 40 minutes or until surface is golden. Serve immediately to 4.

CORN MEAL

FRIED CORN MEAL MUSH

"...how I blush/To hear the Pennsylvanians call thee *Mush*," Joel Barlow wrote in his poem "The Hasty Pudding." The Fried Corn Meal Mush recipe here is, indeed, simply a fried Hasty Pudding. "Nasaump," as Roger Williams described it in 1643 in *A Key into the Language of America*..., is "a kind of meale pottage, unpartch'd. From this," Williams said, "the *English* call their *Samp*, which is the *Indian* corne, beaten and boil'd, and eaten hot or cold with milke or butter ... and which is a dish exceeding wholesome for the *English* bodies."

5 cups boiling water	2 tablespoons milk
1½ cups yellow corn meal	Bread or cracker crumbs
1 teaspoon salt	Butter or bacon fat
1 egg yolk	

Boil water in the top of a double boiler. Then combine corn meal with salt and 1½ cups cold water. Stir into boiling water a little at a time, stirring constantly. Cook over high heat about 3 minutes. Cover and cook over boiling water for 15 minutes. Pour into a greased loaf pan and cool. Cut the firm mush into slices about ¾ inch thick. Beat egg yolk with milk, dip slices in mixture, then coat with fine dry bread or cracker crumbs. Fry in heated butter or bacon fat until crisp and golden. Serve hot with warm maple syrup.

Fath'r and I went down to camp
Along with Captain Goodin,
And there we saw the men and boys
As thick as hasty puddin'.
—Verse from *Yankee Doodle*

CORN MEAL DUMPLINGS

1 cup corn meal	2 eggs
¼ cup all-purpose flour	½ cup milk
1 teaspoon baking powder	1 tablespoon melted butter
½ teaspoon salt	

Sift together corn meal, flour, baking powder, and salt. Beat eggs and milk together, then stir into dry ingredients. Add the melted butter. Drop batter from a spoon into a pot of boiled greens or heated stock. Cover tightly and cook over a low heat for 15 minutes.

532

CHEESE AND CORN MEAL LOAF

1 cup corn meal
1 cup milk
2 cups boiling water
1 teaspoon salt

½ pound Cheddar cheese, cubed
Flour
½ cup shortening

Combine corn meal and milk in a saucepan. Add boiling water and cook over a moderate heat, stirring constantly, until thick. Reduce heat, cover, and cook over a low heat for 10 minutes. Stir occasionally. Remove from heat. Add salt and cheese, stirring until cheese melts. Spoon into a loaf pan and cool. When cold and solid, turn out of pan and cut into slices about ¾ inch thick. Dust slices lightly with flour and fry in heated shortening until crisp and golden on both sides. Serve for breakfast or lunch with fried ham, sausages, or crisp bacon. Serves 4 to 6.

HUSH PUPPIES

According to one old southern legend, the hounds that went along on hunting expeditions were a hungry lot and would start yelping as soon as they caught the smell of fish frying for their masters' dinner. To quiet the hounds, the hunters dropped bits of corn-meal batter into the fish pan and then tossed the tidbits to the dogs with the gentle rebuke, "Hush, puppy!"

1½ cups corn meal
½ cup all-purpose flour
2 teaspoons baking powder
½ teaspoon salt

1 egg, well beaten
¾ cup milk
1 small onion, grated
Fat for deep-fat frying

Sift together corn meal, flour, baking powder, and salt. Mix egg, milk, and onion in a bowl. Combine with dry ingredients and drop from a spoon into hot fat. When Hush Puppies are crisp and golden (about 1 minute), lift from fat with slotted spoon and drain on paper towels. Serve hot. In the South, Hush Puppies are usually served with fried fish. Made bite-sized, they are delicious served with drinks. Makes about 20.

POLENTA

This recipe is adapted from Mary Randolph's *Virginia Housewife*.

1 cup corn meal
1 teaspoon salt
½ cup grated Parmesan cheese

3 tablespoons butter
Paprika

Bring 3 cups of water to a rolling boil. Combine corn meal with 1 cup cold water and salt. Stir into boiling water and cook, stirring frequently, for about 10 minutes. Pour into a loaf pan and refrigerate until firm. Shortly before serving, cut the Polenta into slices about ½ inch thick and place in a shallow baking dish. Sprinkle with Parmesan cheese, dot with butter, and shake paprika over all. Broil about 4 inches from tip of preheated broiling unit until brown—about 4 to 5 minutes. Serves 6.

RICE DISHES

CREOLE JAMBALAYA

Jambalaya (derived from the Spanish word *jamon,* meaning ham) was introduced to New Orleans by the Spanish in the late 1700's. It was made, at first, only with ham; when the Creole cooks took the recipe into their repertoire, they added shrimp from the Gulf waters. Creole Jambalaya, considered one of the classic Creole dishes, can be made with crab, shrimp, chicken, ham, and a variety of other ingredients— one at a time, or all together.

1 tablespoon shortening
1 pound smoked pork sausage or ham,
   cut into ½-inch cubes
½ cup chopped green pepper
1 tablespoon flour
3 cups cooked shrimp, cleaned
3 cups skinned tomatoes, diced
2½ cups water

1 large onion, sliced
1 clove garlic, minced
2 tablespoons parsley, chopped
2 cups uncooked long-grain rice
2 tablespoons Worcestershire sauce
1¼ teaspoons salt
½ teaspoon dried thyme
¼ teaspoon red pepper

Melt shortening in a large skillet, add sausage or ham and green pepper. Cook, stirring frequently, for 5 minutes. Stir in flour until smooth and cook a minute or two longer. Add shrimp, tomatoes, water, onion, garlic, and parsley. Cook to the boiling point, then stir in rice and all remaining ingredients. Cover and cook over a low heat for 30 minutes or until rice is tender and all the liquid is absorbed. Sprinkle with chopped parsley. Serves 8.

WILD RICE AND CHICKEN LIVER PILAU

Technically, wild rice is not a true rice but the seed of a tall aquatic grass native to both North America and eastern Asia. It was such an important food for the Indians that the Sioux and Chippewa fought many battles for better stands.

1 cup uncooked wild rice
½ cup (1 stick) butter
1 medium onion, chopped fine
1 green pepper, chopped fine

16 chicken livers, cut in half
1 teaspoon salt
¼ teaspoon pepper
3 tablespoons brandy

Cook rice in boiling, salted water until tender but still firm. Do not overcook. Drain. Heat *half the butter* in a skillet, add onions and green pepper, and sauté for 5 minutes or until limp. Push vegetables aside and sauté *half the chicken livers* until nicely browned on all sides. Combine vegetable-liver mixture with rice and season with salt and pepper. Set aside, keeping it warm. Heat remaining butter in a saucepan and add remaining chicken livers. Sauté until cooked through. Heat brandy and ignite with a match. Pour over chicken livers, spooning the brandy over them until flame dies. Serve separately with the wild rice mixture. Serves 4.

SOUTH CAROLINA DRY RICE

"The finest rice in the world," Dr. Sturtevant said in his *Notes on Edible Plants*, "is that raised in North and South Carolina." Carolina rice is said to have been first introduced to Charleston in 1694, brought there by a Dutch brig out of Madagascar.

1 cup long-grain rice
1½ cups water
Salt

Juice of ¼ lemon
2 tablespoons butter

Combine all ingredients in a heavy saucepan and heat to a boil. Stir once (no more) with a long-pronged fork. Turn heat down low and cook until all the water has disappeared and rice is dry and flaky—takes about 20 minutes. Serves 4.

HOPPING JOHN

It is said in the South that without a dish of Hopping John on New Year's Day, a year of bad luck will follow. The name may have derived from a custom that children must hop once around the table before the dish is served or may have been the sobriquet of a lively waiter.

½ pound bacon, in one piece
2 cups black-eyed peas, fresh, frozen,
   or dried

1 teaspoon salt
1 cup long-grain rice

If you use dried peas, soak them overnight in cold water. Cook the bacon in 2 quarts water about 1 hour. Then add black-eyed peas and salt. Continue cooking for 30 minutes or until peas are almost tender. Add rice and boil about 15 to 18 minutes longer. Lift out bacon, slice, and set aside, keeping it warm. Drain peas and rice thoroughly, then place in a warm oven for a few minutes or until rice is fluffy. Serve with sliced bacon on top. Serves 6.

RED RICE

4 slices bacon
2 onions, chopped fine
1 can (6-ounce size) tomato paste
1½ cups water
1 tablespoon salt

¼ teaspoon pepper
1 tablespoon sugar
2 cups uncooked rice
½ cup bacon drippings

Fry the bacon in a saucepan until almost crisp. Lift from pan and set aside. Drain off all but 2 tablespoons of the drippings and reserve. Stir onions into the saucepan and cook until wilted, then add tomato paste, water, salt, pepper, and sugar. Cook over a low heat about 10 minutes. There should be 2 cups of sauce. Put rice in a large saucepan or the top of a steamer. Add sauce and ½ cup bacon drippings (if you do not have enough drippings, make up the necessary amount with butter). Cover and steam or cook over a very low heat for 30 minutes. Fork in the crumbled bacon and continue cooking 30 to 45 minutes or until rice is tender and all liquid absorbed. Serves 6 to 8.

GUMBO Z'HERBES

Gumbo z'herbes can be made with almost any greens, seasonings, and herbs. It originated in the Congo and was introduced to New Orleans by Negroes; it was then modified with herbs sold there in the French market by Cherokee and Choctaw Indians.

1 pound salt pork
4 to 5 bunches fresh young greens selected from the following: mustard, radish tops, spinach, lettuce, beet tops, collards, watercress, carrot tops, turnip tops, broccoli, endive
1 head cabbage, kale, or kohlrabi, or 1 box Brussels sprouts
Selection of herbs to taste: dill, tarragon, chives, thyme, parsley, sorrel, dandelion, fennel, leeks, celeriac, sage

1 heaping tablespoon lard
2 tablespoons flour
2 large onions, chopped
4 cloves garlic, chopped fine
2 tablespoons vinegar
1 pod red pepper
Salt
Pepper

Cover salt pork with water and cook until tender. Drain, then chop into small cubes. While meat cooks, trim and wash greens and break cabbage into pieces. Place all greens in a large kettle, add enough water to cover, and cook until very tender. Drain thoroughly, saving water in which greens cooked. Add herbs to greens and chop very fine or blend in an electric blender. Set aside. Heat lard in a deep kettle, stir in flour until smooth, and cook, stirring constantly, until *roux* begins to take on color. Add onions and garlic and cook several minutes. Stir in cubed salt pork and the chopped greens. Cook 5 minutes, stirring constantly. Pour in 1½ quarts of liquid in which greens cooked and simmer until mixture becomes a thick purée. Stir in vinegar and red pepper pod, broken into pieces. Add salt and pepper to taste. Serve hot with rice. Serves 6.

PILAU WITH PIGNON NUTS

Pilau (rice blended with shrimp, chicken, or other ingredients) is of Oriental origin. The dish seems to have been brought to America by early traders. Charleston, a great seaport before the Revolutionary War, may have been the first landing spot for pilau brought from India. Pilau is still associated with the Carolinas.

1 cup long-grain rice
¼ cup pistachio nuts
½ cup pignon nuts or toasted slivered almonds

3 tablespoons butter
2 teaspoons powdered mace

Cook rice. Meanwhile, remove shells and inner skin from pistachios. Leave the nuts whole. Melt butter in a heavy saucepan, toss in both kinds of nuts, and cook several minutes, stirring frequently. Add rice and mace and stir with a fork until heated through. Makes about 6 servings.

536

CHICKEN GUMBO FILÉ

Filé—dried and powdered sassafras leaves—seems to have been made first by Louisiana's Choctaw Indians. It was included in a great number of Creole recipes for thickening stews and soups. As used in these dishes, filé imparted a distinct flavor which, as Dr. Sturtevant stated in *Notes on Edible Plants,* is "much relished by those accustomed to it."

A 3- to 4-pound chicken
1 tablespoon lard
½ pound lean ham, diced
2 tablespoons chopped parsley
1 bay leaf, crumbled
1 sprig (½ teaspoon dried) thyme

1½ dozen oysters in liquor
Salt
¼ pod red pepper
2 tablespoons filé powder
Boiled rice

Cook chicken in boiling water until tender. Remove from saucepan (save the broth), cool, strip meat from bones, and cut into serving pieces. Set aside. Heat lard in a soup kettle, add ham, and cook for 5 minutes, stirring frequently. Stir in parsley, bay leaf, and thyme and cook several minutes longer or until browned. Measure liquor from oysters, add enough chicken broth and boiling water to make 1½ quarts of liquid, and pour into soup kettle. Season with salt and red pepper pod. Simmer for 30 minutes, then add the oysters, and simmer a few minutes until edges begin to curl. Add the chicken. Remove from heat and stir in filé, a little at a time (if filé is cooked, even simmered, it makes the gumbo stringy). Serve immediately in soup plates over boiled rice. Serves 4.

SEAFOOD-OKRA GUMBO

"Shrimps are much eaten here," a visitor to New Orleans in 1805 said, "also a dish called *gumbo.* This last is made of every eatable substance, and especially of those shrimps which can be caught at any time."

1 pound uncooked shrimp in shell
¼ cup butter
1 pound okra, sliced
2 onions, chopped fine
1½ tablespoons flour
1 cup tomatoes
12 oysters in liquor

2 teaspoons salt
1 clove garlic, crushed
Pinch of cayenne or ¼ pod red pepper
Tabasco
Worcestershire sauce
½ pound crab meat
Boiled rice

Shell shrimp and sauté in *2 tablespoons of the butter* for several minutes or until they turn a bright coral color. Set aside. Heat remaining 2 tablespoons butter in a soup kettle, add okra, and cook, stirring frequently, until tender. Stir in onion and cook several minutes, then stir in flour until smooth. Add tomatoes and cook the mixture several minutes longer. Add enough water to the oyster liquor to make 2 quarts of liquid. Stir into okra mixture and add salt, garlic, and cayenne or red pepper pod. Simmer for 1 hour, then add shrimp, and simmer another half hour. Fifteen minutes before serving, add the oysters and cook over a low heat until edges begin to curl. Then add Tabasco, Worcestershire sauce, and crab meat and heat through. Serve gumbo in soup plates over boiled rice. Serves 6 to 8.

Egg carrier

EGGS & CHEESE

OMELETTE

2 eggs
1 tablespoon water
½ teaspoon salt

Dash of pepper
2 tablespoons butter

Beat together eggs, water, salt, and pepper. Melt butter in an omelette pan or skillet until very hot but not brown or smoking. Pour in egg mixture and cook over a medium heat, lifting the edges with a spatula to allow the liquid to run underneath. When omelette is golden brown on the bottom but still creamy on top, fold one half over the other and slide onto a warm platter. May be served with Mushrooms in Cream (page 520) or Creole Sauce (page 545). Spoon sauce around the omelette and garnish with watercress.

HANGTOWN FRY

According to some Californians, Hangtown Fry was created in 1849. A miner from Shirttail Bend hailed into Hangtown with a poke full of nuggets, plunked his fortune down on the counter of Cary House, and said he wanted the finest, most expensive meal they had. When he was told that oysters and eggs were the most expensive items on the menu (in those days whiskey was $1,500 a barrel, turnips a dollar each), he told the cook to put them together and serve up the food. The dish was made, originally, with the small Pacific Coast Olympia oysters.

1 dozen oysters
Flour
9 eggs

Fine cracker crumbs
3 tablespoons butter

Drain oysters on paper towels. Dip each one in flour seasoned with salt and pepper, then in *1 well-beaten egg*, last of all in cracker crumbs. Fry in heated butter for a few minutes or until nicely browned on both sides. Beat remaining 8 eggs with salt and pepper. Pour over oysters and cook until firm on the bottom. Turn with a large spatula and cook the second side a minute or two longer. Serves 4.

WILD ONIONS AND EGGS

4 bunches wild onions or green onions
2 to 3 tablespoons bacon fat

6 eggs
1 teaspoon salt

Wash the onions and chop fine (chop both the bulb and green tops). Cook in heated bacon fat, with 1 tablespoon of water added, until onions are tender. Season eggs with salt and beat until yolks and whites are well blended. Pour over onions and scramble. Serves 4.

538

SISTER ABIGAIL'S BLUE FLOWER OMELETTE

It is not unusual to use flowers—nasturtiums, squash and pumpkin blossoms, rose petals—in cooking. The use of chive blossoms, however, seems peculiarly a Shaker innovation, or perhaps Sister Abigail's.

Break 4 eggs into a bowl. Add 4 tablespoons of water or milk, ½ teaspoon salt, dash of pepper, 1 tablespoon finely chopped parsley, 1 tablespoon chopped chives, and 12 chive blossoms (these can be eliminated if chives are not in blossom). Beat until well blended. Heat 2 tablespoons butter in an omelette pan or skillet. When butter is bubbly but not brown, pour in omelette mixture. Stir with a fork until eggs begin to set, then cook a little longer, without stirring. Loosen sides of omelette with a fork and roll out onto a heated platter. Serve at once to 2.

KENTUCKY SCRAMBLE

1 cup cooked whole-kernel corn (fresh, canned, or frozen)
3 tablespoons butter or bacon drippings
1 green pepper, chopped
Few sprigs of parsley, chopped
2 slices pimiento, chopped
6 eggs
1 teaspoon salt
¼ teaspoon pepper

Drain corn and sauté in heated butter or bacon drippings for several minutes. Stir in green pepper, parsley, and pimiento and continue cooking about 5 minutes longer. Just before serving, beat together the eggs, salt, and pepper, then pour into corn mixture, and scramble until eggs are set but still moist. Serves 4.

WESTERN SANDWICH

The sandwich is generally thought to be an American food, but its inventor was John Montagu, Fourth Earl of Sandwich. Montagu was a renowned British politician, and an even more renowned gambler. His fondness for gambling was so extreme that he neglected lunch, and usually bolted a piece of meat between slices of bread to sustain himself at the poker table. The Western Sandwich was invented by pioneers. It was common for eggs to get "high" after a long haul over hot trails. In order to salvage the eggs, and kill the bad flavor of them, pioneer women mixed eggs with onions and any other seasonings on hand.

¼ pound ham or 4 slices bacon, diced
1 green pepper, chopped
1 medium onion, chopped
4 eggs
Salt
Pepper
Bread or round buns

Fry ham or bacon in a skillet for several minutes. Toss in green pepper and onion and cook until vegetables are almost tender. Beat eggs in a bowl with salt and pepper. Pour over mixture in skillet and cook until eggs are set. Turn with a broad spatula and brown second side lightly. Place between slices of buttered bread or buns. Makes 4 sandwiches.

DEVILED EGGS WITH ANCHOVIES

6 hard-cooked eggs
1 teaspoon prepared mustard
Few sprigs parsley, chopped
½ teaspoon salt
1 tablespoon lemon juice

1 tablespoon salad oil
1 tablespoon capers, drained well
6 rolled anchovy fillets
Watercress

Cut eggs in half lengthwise. Remove yolks and mash until smooth. Stir in mustard, parsley, salt, lemon juice, oil, and capers thoroughly. Pile mixture back into egg whites. Garnish with anchovies and serve on a bed of watercress.

Cheese press

CHEESE BLINTZES

½ cup all-purpose flour
¼ teaspoon salt
2 eggs

½ cup milk
1 cup water
Butter

Sift flour and salt together. Beat eggs in a bowl until frothy, then blend in flour mixture. Add milk, a little at a time, stirring until smooth. Mix in water last of all. Batter should be very thin. Heat a small skillet (6 to 7 inches in diameter), adding just enough butter to coat the bottom. When butter starts to sizzle, pour in a little of the batter (enough to coat bottom of the pan when you tilt it back and forth). Cook blintzes until edges look slightly dry and lacy (these little crêpes are cooked only on one side). Invert skillet over a tea towel and hit side of pan to loosen the crêpe. Do not stack them on top of each other while they are warm.

Cheese Filling:
½ pound farmer cheese
¼ pound small-curd cottage cheese
¼ pound cream cheese
2 egg yolks, slightly beaten

¼ cup sugar
¼ teaspoon salt
½ teaspoon cinnamon
1 tablespoon grated lemon rind

Blend the cheeses together until smooth. Beat in egg yolks and all remaining ingredients. Divide filling evenly among the crêpes, placing it in the center on the cooked side. Fold edges over the filling to make a neat, square package. Melt 2 tablespoons butter in a large skillet. Arrange blintzes in the pan and fry over a moderate heat until golden brown on both sides. Serve very hot with cold sour cream.

WELSH RABBIT

Welsh Rabbit was reputedly improvised when a Welsh chieftain ran out of game for his banquet table and asked his cook to devise something from whatever stores were on hand. The cook produced this cheese dish, which he named—presumably not to call the guests' attention to the fact that the meat supply had vanished—"rabbit." It persisted as Welsh Rabbit in most American kitchens (though some befuddled cookbook writers have "corrected" matters by referring to the dish as "rarebit"). This recipe is adapted from one given in Sarah Josepha Hale's *New Cook Book*.

1 pound sharp natural Cheddar cheese
2 teaspoons Worcestershire sauce
½ teaspoon dry mustard

Dash of cayenne
Dash of paprika
½ cup ale or beer

Shred the cheese and set aside. Mix all remaining ingredients in a saucepan and place over a very low heat until ale or beer is hot. Add the cheese and stir until it has melted. Pour over hot toast triangles. Serves 4 to 6.

CAILLETTE

Large head green cabbage
1 cup milk
3 cups dry bread crumbs
2 eggs, lightly beaten
1 cup grated Cheddar or Swiss cheese

Salt
Pepper
Dash of nutmeg
Chicken or beef broth

Remove 12 to 14 large outer leaves from cabbage and cut off some of the thick rib. Cover with boiling water to soften. Heat milk and pour over crumbs. Mix in eggs, cheese, salt, pepper, and nutmeg thoroughly. Put a heaping tablespoon of the mixture on each drained cabbage leaf, folding in sides and ends to make a neat package. Fasten with toothpicks or tie with string and drop into gently boiling broth. Cook for 30 minutes or until cabbage is tender. Lift from broth and serve immediately. Serves 4 to 6.

LIEDERKRANZ CANAPÉS

Liederkranz, one of the few native American cheeses, was discovered by accident in 1892 by Emil Frey, a young Swiss who was working as an apprentice cheese maker in a factory in Monroe, New York. Frey's boss took a sample of the new cheese to some of his friends at the Liederkranz Club in New York. Their response was enthusiastic, and the cheese was immediately named Liederkranz.

Combine 1 cake of Liederkranz cheese with 2 tablespoons softened butter and several drops of Tabasco and mash until very smooth. Mix in a sprinkling of chopped chives, about 2 green onions (chopped very fine), and freshly ground pepper. Spread on thin slices of rye or pumpernickel bread and cut into small squares or triangles.

SAUCES

CREAM SAUCE

1 cup milk
1 slice onion
1 sprig parsley
2 tablespoons butter
2 tablespoons flour

2 tablespoons heavy cream
Salt
White pepper
Nutmeg

Scald a mixture of the milk, onion, and parsley. Melt butter in a saucepan, stir in flour until smooth, and cook over a low heat for several minutes. Do not brown. Strain hot milk into butter-flour combination and continue cooking over a low heat, stirring constantly, until sauce bubbles. Then simmer gently for several minutes. Stir in cream and season to taste with salt, pepper, and nutmeg. Makes 1 generous cup.

BÉCHAMEL SAUCE
(White Sauce)

2 tablespoons butter
2 tablespoons flour
1 cup milk

Salt
White pepper
Nutmeg (optional)

Melt butter in a saucepan. Stir in flour until smooth and cook over a low heat for several minutes. Do not brown. Stir milk into mixture and continue cooking over a low heat, stirring constantly, until sauce bubbles. Cook very gently for several minutes until sauce has thickened. Season with salt, pepper, and, if you wish, a pinch of nutmeg. Makes 1 cup.

HOLLANDAISE SAUCE

½ cup (1 stick) butter
1 tablespoon lemon juice
2 egg yolks

½ teaspoon salt
Dash of cayenne

Divide the butter into three equal parts. Place one portion in top of double boiler, add lemon juice and egg yolks. Cook over hot water, stirring constantly with a wire whisk. When butter has melted, add second portion, and, as mixture begins to thicken, add the third. Remove from heat and stir in salt and cayenne. *Do not let the water under the saucepan boil at any time.* Serve at once or keep sauce warm over hot water. Makes about ¾ cup.

VIRGINIA BOILED DRESSING

4 egg yolks
2 tablespoons cold water
2 tablespoons cider vinegar
1 teaspoon dry mustard

1 teaspoon sugar
1 teaspoon salt
1 cup commercial sour cream

Mix together egg yolks, cold water, vinegar, mustard, sugar, and salt in the top of a double boiler. Cook over boiling water, stirring constantly, until thick. Cool, then fold in sour cream. Makes about 1½ cups.

DILL AND MUSTARD SAUCE

2½ tablespoons dry mustard
5 tablespoons sugar
½ teaspoon salt
2 tablespoons olive oil

1 tablespoon vinegar
½ cup commercial sour cream
2 tablespoons chopped fresh dill or
  1 tablespoon dill weed

Blend together mustard, sugar, and salt. Add the oil and vinegar alternately. Stir slowly until blended, then beat hard. Fold in sour cream and dill. Serve with cold fish and shellfish. Makes about 1 cup.

LEMON BUTTER

To make Lemon Butter, melt butter (about 2 to 3 tablespoons per person) and add fresh lemon juice to taste. Especially good with fish.

TARTARE SAUCE

1 cup mayonnaise
1 teaspoon fresh tarragon, chopped fine, or
  ⅓ teaspoon dried tarragon
1 tablespoon onion, chopped fine

1 tablespoon parsley, chopped fine
1 tablespoon capers, drained
1½ tablespoons sour pickle, chopped fine

Combine all the ingredients thoroughly and let stand an hour or two to develop flavor. Makes about 1¼ cups.

OYSTER SAUCE

Season 1 cup of Cream Sauce (page 542) with 1 teaspoon Worcestershire sauce. Before serving, heat to a boil, then stir in 3 tablespoons chopped parsley and 1 cup finely chopped or ground oysters with their liquor. Serve with roast turkey or chicken or as a sauce for poached fish.

MUSHROOM SAUCE

¼ pound mushrooms
2 tablespoons butter
½ teaspoon salt
¼ teaspoon white pepper

2 tablespoons flour
2 cups cream
1 tablespoon dry sherry

Cut mushrooms in half or slice (depending on the size) and sauté in heated butter for about 5 minutes. Sprinkle in salt, pepper, and flour, then stir until smooth. Add cream and cook, stirring constantly, until sauce bubbles and thickens. Continue simmering for another 5 to 8 minutes. Just before serving, stir in sherry. Add salt to taste.

CUMBERLAND SAUCE

2 oranges
2 lemons
½ cup red currant jelly

1 cup port wine
1 tablespoon arrowroot
1 tablespoon Grand Marnier (optional)

Peel the rind of *1 orange and 1 lemon* with a vegetable peeler, then shred, and set aside. Squeeze the juice from both oranges and lemons and strain. Combine with the jelly in a saucepan, bring slowly to a boil, and simmer about 3 minutes. Add the port. Mix arrowroot with 1 tablespoon water until smooth and stir into the boiling liquid. Cook for a few minutes until sauce has thickened slightly. Add the rind and, if you like, the Grand Marnier. This sauce improves if made a day ahead and then reheated. Serve with ham, duck, or game.

MINT SAUCE

Strip leaves from enough fresh mint to make about ½ cup when packed tightly. Chop fine and place in a small, sturdy jar or in a mortar and pestle if you have one. Add 2 table-spoons sugar and ¼ teaspoon salt. Pound with the handle of a wooden spoon until leaves are bruised thoroughly. Stir in ⅓ cup cider vinegar and the same amount of water. Prepared in this way, Mint Sauce keeps its fresh flavor for a long time when refrigerated in a sealed jar. Good with any cold meat except beef but especially good with lamb, hot or cold.

CURRANT SAUCE

Combine 1 cup currant jelly or whole currant preserves with 1 cup port wine in the top of a double boiler. Heat over boiling water until ingredients are thoroughly blended. Serve hot.

SAUCE PIQUANTE

Heat 1 can (7½-ounce size) brown gravy and blend with 1 tablespoon each of lemon juice, finely chopped onion, chopped green pepper, drained capers or chopped sour pickles, and a dash of cayenne.

544

PLUM SAUCE

Wash 1 pound Damson plums, cut in half, and remove pits. Combine fruit with ½ cup sugar in a saucepan. Add 1 stick cinnamon, 1 teaspoon whole mace, and 1 teaspoon whole cloves tied together with cheesecloth. Bring to a boil, reduce heat, and simmer gently until sauce has the consistency of jam. Remove spices and chill sauce. Makes 1 cup.

Straining sauce

CREOLE SAUCE

4 cups canned or fresh tomatoes, skinned
2 tablespoons butter
1 clove garlic, chopped fine
¼ teaspoon dried thyme
1 bay leaf, crumbled

1 teaspoon salt
Dash pepper
Dash cayenne
1 tablespoon flour

Combine tomatoes, *1 tablespoon of the butter,* garlic, thyme, bay leaf, salt, pepper, and cayenne in a saucepan. Cook over a moderate heat, stirring occasionally, until quantity has been reduced to about half. Melt remaining 1 tablespoon butter in a small saucepan. Stir in flour and cook until lightly browned. Add to tomatoes and cook a few minutes longer. Remove from heat and strain through a fine sieve or blend in an electric blender. Sautéed onions, green and red peppers, and mushrooms may be added. If this is done, do not strain or blend.

BARBECUE SAUCE

1 can (1 pound, 3 ounce size) tomatoes
1 medium onion, chopped
1 clove garlic, chopped
1 tablespoon brown sugar
1 tablespoon butter
½ cup ketchup

½ cup Worcestershire sauce
½ cup vinegar
1 teaspoon salt
¼ teaspoon pepper
Dash cayenne
¼ teaspoon dry mustard

Pour tomatoes into a saucepan, breaking up the large chunks with a fork. Add all remaining ingredients, cook to boil, then reduce heat, and simmer slowly for about 45 minutes.

SAUCE FOR COLD MEAT

Combine a few sprigs of parsley (minced fine) with a pinch of dried thyme (or, if available, a sprig or two of fresh thyme), 3 or 4 stems of fresh chives (chopped fine), 6 tablespoons dry bread crumbs, ½ teaspoon salt, and a big pinch of freshly ground pepper. Place this mixture over thinly sliced cold lamb, cold veal, or cold chicken, and sprinkle with a bit of tart French Dressing (page 553).

SAUCE REMOULADE

1¼ cups mayonnaise
¼ cup chopped sour pickles
¼ cup chopped capers, drained

2 tablespoons chopped parsley, chives, or
  fresh tarragon
½ teaspoon anchovy paste

Combine all ingredients and serve cold. Excellent with cold fish or shellfish.

CREOLE SAUCE REMOULADE

3 hard-cooked eggs
½ teaspoon dry mustard
2 teaspoons cold water
½ clove garlic, minced fine
Salt

Cayenne
1 tablespoon tarragon or wine vinegar
3 tablespoons olive oil
1 raw egg yolk
Juice of ½ lemon

Separate whites from yolks of hard-cooked eggs. Work whites through a coarse sieve and set aside. Put yolks in a bowl and mash thoroughly. Add mustard (blended to a paste with water), minced garlic, salt, cayenne, and vinegar. Mix until smooth. Beat in oil, drop by drop, then add raw egg yolk and lemon juice. Taste and beat in more oil or vinegar, if needed. Use the shredded egg whites as a garnish. Serve with shrimp, lobster, or other cold, cooked fish.

HORSE-RADISH SAUCE

½ teaspoon dry mustard
6 tablespoons freshly ground horse-radish
1 teaspoon salt

½ teaspoon white pepper
½ cup heavy cream, whipped

Mix mustard with 1 tablespoon cold water, stir until smooth, then combine with horse-radish, salt, and pepper. Allow to stand for 10 minutes. Fold thoroughly into the whipped cream. Excellent with hot or cold meats, especially beef or tongue. Makes 1 cup.

SALADS

OKRA SALAD

Cook a box of frozen whole okra according to package directions. Drain and chill. Shortly before serving, garnish with sliced fresh tomatoes and season with a tart French Dressing (page 553). Serves 3 to 4.

GREEN BEAN SALAD

1 pound green beans	2 sprigs summer savory
2 cups shredded lettuce	or ¼ teaspoon dried savory
2 scallions, chopped	French Dressing (page 553)

Trim ends from whole green beans. Cook in a little boiling, salted water until tender but still crisp. Drain thoroughly and cool. Shortly before serving, toss beans with all remaining ingredients. Use only enough French Dressing to coat the various ingredients lightly. The Shakers, who conceived this excellent summer salad, tossed in "6 nasturtium leaves" and "12 nasturtium pods." Serves 4.

BOHEMIAN SALAD

8 medium potatoes	1 herring (cleaned, boned, and chopped
1 onion, chopped fine	coarsely)
2 tart apples (pared, cored, and	2 tablespoons capers, drained
coarsely diced)	½ to ¾ cup French Dressing (page 553)
½ cup thin strips boiled ham	1 can flat anchovy fillets
½ cup thin strips roast veal or chicken	4 hard-cooked eggs
½ cup thin strips of smoked tongue	1 cup baby beets
	Lettuce and watercress

Cook potatoes in their jackets in boiling, salted water until tender. When cool, peel and cut into thin slices. Place in a large salad bowl. Add onion, diced apples, ham, veal or chicken, tongue, herring, and capers. Pour French Dressing over all (start with a small amount, then add more if potatoes absorb it quickly) and toss gently. Add salt and pepper, if needed. Let stand at room temperature about 30 minutes before serving. Garnish the salad as follows: arrange drained anchovy fillets, spoke-fashion, on top. Separate yolks from whites of eggs and work separately through a coarse sieve. Spoon alternate mounds of these between anchovies. Marinate beets in a little vinegar to which several cloves have been added; when they are tart, arrange beets in a garland around the salad bowl. Garnish with tufts of lettuce and watercress. Serves 6.

RED-BEET EGGS

1 teaspoon dried mustard
2 tablespoons sugar
1 teaspoon salt

½ cup cider vinegar
1 can (1 pound) baby beets
4 eggs, hard cooked

Mix together mustard, sugar, salt, and vinegar and cook to the boiling point. Pour over well-drained beets and set aside to cool. When cool, add the shelled hard-cooked eggs and refrigerate overnight. Shake container occasionally so eggs will pick up the beet color all over. Serve beets as a salad on watercress. The pickled eggs may be used as a garnish for the salad or served separately. Makes 4 servings.

COLESLAW

The Dutch word for salad, *sla*, was quickly absorbed into the American language. Concerning cabbage, Amelia Simmons noted: "The . . . small tight heads, are best for slaw."

1 small head green cabbage
½ cup heavy cream or commercial
　　sour cream
2 tablespoons sugar

1 teaspoon salt
¼ teaspoon pepper
2 tablespoons cider vinegar

Shred cabbage very fine (1 head should make about 1 quart when shredded). Mix cream with all remaining ingredients, add the cabbage, and toss gently until coated. Serve immediately, otherwise salad will become limp and soggy. Serves 4.

FOUR-BEAN SALAD

2 cups canned kidney beans, heated
2 cups whole cooked green beans (fresh,
　　canned, or frozen)
2 cups cut cooked Italian green beans
　　(fresh or frozen)
2 cups cooked baby Lima beans
　　(fresh or frozen)

1 cup French Dressing (page 553)
1 cup celery hearts and leaves, chopped
Crisp lettuce
2 cups Sour Cream Salad Dressing (page 552)
1 large Bermuda onion
1 large green pepper
12 large stuffed olives

Rinse and drain kidney beans, then mix with whole green beans, cut Italian green beans, and baby Lima beans. While still warm, toss with French Dressing. Allow to marinate an hour or two, then add celery. Arrange lettuce in a large salad bowl. Combine beans with *1 cup Sour Cream Salad Dressing* and pile on top of lettuce. Garnish with rings of Bermuda onion, rings of green pepper (remove the seeds), and sliced stuffed olives. Serve with remaining Sour Cream Salad Dressing in a separate bowl. Serves 8 to 10.

BETABEL RELLENO
(Stuffed Beets)

6 medium-sized cooked beets
2 celery stalks, with leaves, chopped fine
1 green onion (scallion) with top

½ cup cooked peas or other leftover vegetable
Mayonnaise

Scoop out centers of beets. Chop the centers quite fine and mix with the celery, onion, and vegetable. Season with salt and pepper. Add just enough mayonnaise to bind the vegetables together. Fill the cavities of the beets. Serve on a bed of shredded lettuce. Serves 6.

WALDORF SALAD

Although Oscar Tschirky, known as Oscar of the Waldorf, was the maître d' rather than the chef at the Waldorf-Astoria (and once said, "my job is the serving of food, never the cooking"), he did create the Waldorf Salad. The original recipe called only for equal parts of raw apples, cut in small pieces, and celery, moistened with mayonnaise and served on lettuce leaves. Later someone added coarsely chopped walnuts, and it is this version that has become famous.

GAZPACHO SALAD

In *The Virginia Housewife*, Mary Randolph identifies *gazpacho* as Spanish in origin. Although one of Mrs. Randolph's competitors suggests that it "is a kind of raw soup, eaten with a spoon," Mrs. Randolph's recipe is more like a salad.

Arrange in a glass or crystal bowl alternate layers of unpeeled and very thinly sliced cucumbers, skinned and thinly sliced tomatoes, very thinly sliced Bermuda onions, coarse crumbs of dry French bread. Pour a tart French Dressing (page 553) over all and refrigerate until icy cold.

RUSSIAN SALAD

Naming the proper dishes for a dinner party in *Society As I Have Found It*, Ward McAllister punctiliously noted that a Russian Salad "is a pleasing novelty at times."

Cook equal amounts of the following vegetables separately: finely diced carrots, finely diced potatoes, green beans cut into ½-inch pieces, and shelled peas. When tender but still firm, drain and place in a bowl. Drain and dice an equal amount of canned beets and combine with all the other vegetables. Add 1 or 2 chopped scallions, then enough French Dressing (page 553) to moisten the salad. Marinate for 1 hour. Just before serving, drain off excess dressing and add enough mayonnaise to hold the vegetables together. Season to taste. Arrange in a salad bowl with a garnish of greens.

SAUERKRAUT SALAD

Sauerkraut, a Pennsylvania Dutch staple, has been celebrated in sermons, songs, poetry, and quite a few tired old jokes. It has been so famous that, according to a note by the editor of *The Guardian* in 1869, "when General Lee took possession of Chambersburg on his way to Gettysburg, we happened to be a member of the Committee representing the town. Among the first things he demanded for his army was twenty-five barrels of Saur-Kraut."

1 can (1-pound size) sauerkraut	1 cup chili sauce
1 green pepper, chopped fine	⅓ cup brown sugar
1 small onion, chopped fine	1 teaspoon paprika
3 stalks celery, chopped fine	3 tablespoons fresh lemon juice

Drain sauerkraut and place in a salad bowl. Toss in green pepper, onion, and celery. Set aside. Blend together chili sauce, brown sugar, paprika, and lemon juice. Pour over salad mixture and toss well. Serves 4 to 6.

SOUTHERN SALAD

1 package frozen black-eyed peas	French Dressing (page 553)
1 cup celery, chopped fine	Watercress
1 cup diced tomatoes, drained	Sweet onion

Cook peas according to directions on the package. Drain and cool. Add celery, tomatoes, and enough French Dressing to flavor the salad (about 4 to 5 tablespoons). Toss lightly and serve on a bed of watercress with a garnish of onion rings. Serves 4.

PERSIMMON AND GRAPEFRUIT SALAD

Native American persimmons drew comments from early explorers—many of them, since the discoverers had not taken the time to ripen the fruit, were negative. But the plumlike fruit gradually became popular for a variety of recipes. Francis Peyre Porcher wrote in 1869 that it made a good drink when fermented; it was used for beer, bread, puddings, and salads. The Japanese persimmon is possibly more popular in America than the country's own variety. Commodore Perry brought it to America in 1855, when he returned from his expedition to Japan.

Cut ripe, peeled persimmons in long slices and arrange on a salad plate alternating with sections of fresh grapefruit. Garnish with watercress and dress lightly with a tart French Dressing (page 553), preferably made with lemon juice rather than vinegar.

CUCUMBER SALAD

"We recommend," Mrs. Leslie said in *The American Family Cook Book*, "the eaters to be mindful of the duty of mastication, without the due performance of which, all undressed vegetables are troublesome company for the principal viscera, and some are even dangerously indigestible." Mrs. Leslie notwithstanding, General Ulysses S. Grant was inordinately fond of cucumbers. As General Horace Porter remarked in an article, "Campaigning with Grant," the General "often made his entire meal upon a sliced cucumber and a cup of coffee."

2 cucumbers	¾ teaspoon salt
1 small onion	¼ teaspoon pepper
½ cup commercial sour cream	3 tablespoons sugar
⅓ cup vinegar	¼ teaspoon dry mustard

Slice unpared cucumbers very thin, then combine with the onion, sliced equally thin. Mix all remaining ingredients in a bowl and stir until smooth. Just before serving, pour the dressing over the cucumbers and onion and toss gently. If dressing is added too far in advance, the salad will become too soggy. Serves 6.

BIRDS-NEST SALAD

Rub a little green coloring paste into cream cheese, giving it a delicate color like birds' eggs. Roll it into balls the size of birds' eggs, using the back or smooth side of butter-pats. Arrange on a flat dish some small well-crimped lettuce leaves; group them to look like nests, moisten them with French dressing, and place five of the cheese balls in each nest of leaves. The cheese balls may be varied by flecking them with black, white, or red pepper.

—From *The Century Cook Book*, 1895

SALAD OF MIXED GARDEN STUFF

Salads were usually served at the principal meals at Monticello; Jefferson's fondness for them is reflected in an inventory of his garden, which included nineteen varieties of lettuce alone.

1 head Bibb lettuce	1 small head chicory
1 bunch watercress	Few sprigs tender spinach leaves
1 small head endive	1 tablespoon chopped chives or scallions
1 small head iceberg lettuce	

Wash the salad greens in ice water, drain, and pat completely dry. Tear apart (do not cut) and place in the refrigerator to crisp. To serve, toss with Monticello Dressing (page 553).

SHAKER POTATO SALAD

Cook 6 medium potatoes in their jackets in boiling, salted water until tender when pierced with a fork. When cool enough to handle, peel and cut into thin slices. Dice 3 slices of bacon and fry until crisp. Stir in 1 medium-sized onion, chopped, and cook a few minutes longer. Take care not to brown the onion. Stir in 1 teaspoon salt, dash of pepper, 1 tablespoon of sugar, and ½ cup vinegar mixed with the same amount of water. Heat to a boil, pour over potatoes, and toss gently. Serve with finely chopped parsley on top. Serves 6.

Nor do I say, that it is filthy to eat potatoes. I do not ridicule the using of them as sauce. What I laugh at is, the idea of the use of them being a saving; of their going further than bread; of the cultivation of them in lieu of wheat adding to the human sustenance of a country. . . . As food for cattle, sheep or hogs, this is the worst of all the green and root crops; but of this I have said enough before; and therefore, I now dismiss the Potatoe with the hope, that I shall never again have to write the word, or see the thing.

—William Cobbett, *A Year's Residence in the United States of America*, 1819

CREAM POTATO SALAD

6 large potatoes	¼ teaspoon pepper
¾ cup heavy cream (about)	1 medium onion, sliced thin
4 tablespoons cider vinegar	8 red radishes, sliced thin
1 tablespoon salad oil	Salad greens
1½ teaspoons salt	

Cook potatoes in their jackets in boiling, salted water until tender when pierced with a fork. Peel and dice. Combine the cream, vinegar, oil, salt, and pepper. Pour over warm potatoes and toss gently. Potatoes should absorb almost all the cream. Add onion slices, separated into rings, and the radishes. Mellow at least 30 minutes, then garnish with greens, and serve at room temperature. Serves 6.

SOUR CREAM SALAD DRESSING

1 cup mayonnaise	1 tablespoon chives or green
1 cup commercial sour cream	onion tops, chopped
	1 teaspoon dill weed (optional)

Combine mayonnaise with sour cream. Stir in chives or onion and dill. Makes 2 cups.

FRENCH DRESSING

Basic French Dressing is a mixture of good wine vinegar, good oil, salt, pepper, and, if you wish, fresh green herbs and mustard. Lemon juice may be used in place of vinegar. The correct proportions are 1 of vinegar to 3 of oil, with salt and freshly ground pepper to taste. As is true of so many things, French Dressing is always best when freshly made.

HOT CREAM DRESSING

4 slices bacon	1 tablespoon water
3 tablespoons vinegar	1 teaspoon flour
2 tablespoons commercial sour cream	1 tablespoon sugar
1 egg yolk	½ teaspoon salt

Fry bacon until crisp. Remove from pan, drain, and set aside. Pour off all but 2 tablespoons of bacon fat and stir in vinegar and sour cream. Mix together egg yolk, water, and flour until smooth. Stir into pan mixture and cook over a very low heat, stirring constantly, until dressing thickens. Remove from heat and stir in sugar and salt. Pour the hot dressing over fresh, washed greens (either dandelion, endive, lettuce, or spinach or a combination of them) and scatter the crumbled bacon over the top.

RUSSIAN DRESSING

Blend ½ cup mayonnaise with ¼ cup chili sauce, 1 tablespoon finely chopped green pepper, 1 tablespoon finely chopped pimiento, and 1 teaspoon finely chopped chives. Makes ¾ cup.

MONTICELLO DRESSING

Jefferson took a great interest in developing benne (sesame) oil for salad dressings as a substitute for the olive oil imported from Europe. On January 6, 1808, he wrote from Monticello to John Taylor of South Carolina: "The African negroes brought over to Georgia a seed which they called Beni, & the botanists Sesamum. I lately received a bottle of the oil, which was eaten with sallad by various companies. all agree it is equal to the olive oil. a bushel of seed yields 3. gallons of oil. I propose to cultivate it for my own use at least."

Combine 1 small clove of garlic (crushed), 1 teaspoon salt, ½ teaspoon white pepper, ⅓ cup olive oil, ⅓ cup sesame oil, ⅓ cup tarragon or wine vinegar. Place in a covered jar and shake well before pouring over salad.

SUN-COOKED STRAWBERRY JAM

Choose brightly colored berries that are not too ripe. It is difficult to prepare more than 4 to 5 quarts at a time. Wash, then drain very thoroughly. Remove hulls and slice small berries in half, large ones in quarters. Weigh the fruit, place in a large kettle, and add sugar. For each pound of fruit allow ¾ pound sugar. Stir until all berries are coated with sugar. Bring to a rolling boil and boil *exactly 3 minutes*. Pour immediately into flat glass, enamel, or china dishes to a depth of ½ inch—the fruit should lie flat in the syrup. Cover completely with panes of glass and place outside in unobstructed sunlight. Turn glass covers each time enough moisture accumulates on top to pour off (this may be every few minutes for an hour or two, with intervals longer after that). Stir occasionally with a spoon to expose all surfaces of berries and syrup to the action of the sun. Strawberries are "cooked" when syrup forms jellied ridges or waves when container is tilted at one end. This usually takes about 1½ days of full sunshine. Bottle immediately. A paraffin cover is not necessary. (If rainy or cloudy weather should interfere, bring dishes, still covered tightly, inside. Strawberries will keep safely for several days if fruit has cooked 4 or 5 hours.)

GRAPE CONSERVE

4 pounds Concord grapes
Grated rind and juice of 2 oranges
5 cups sugar

Dash of salt
1 cup seedless raisins
1 cup walnuts, finely chopped

Wash grapes, pluck from stems, and pinch skins from pulp, putting skins into a bowl and pulp into a saucepan. Cook pulp over a low heat for about 5 to 8 minutes to loosen the seeds, then work through a sieve. Return purée to saucepan, stir in grated orange rind and juice, the sugar, salt, and raisins. Cook over a low heat, stirring constantly, until the sugar has dissolved. Increase heat and boil until mixture thickens, stirring constantly. Add skins and continue boiling 5 minutes longer or until conserve is quite thick. Stir in walnuts, pour into sterilized 6-ounce jelly glasses, and seal securely. Makes 8 glasses.

PEAR MARMALADE

4 pounds ripe pears
1 lemon

1 large orange
3 pounds sugar

Wash pears, cut in half, and remove cores. Wash lemon and orange, cut off ends, and quarter. Work all the fruit through a food grinder. Put into a kettle and stir in sugar thoroughly. Cook to boil, then reduce heat, and continue cooking over a low heat for 35 to 40 minutes or until shiny and almost transparent. Stir frequently. Spoon into sterilized jars and seal. Makes about 3 pints.

CANDIED CRANBERRIES

Cranberries may have been known at first as "crane berries," since cranes living in the New England bogs ate the berries. They were early recognized as a good preventive of scurvy, and ships putting out to sea from Down East ports always carried casks of this "bogland medicine" in their stores. Though they are now commercially grown in Wisconsin, Washington, Oregon, and New Jersey, cranberries were associated first with Massachusetts. John Josselyn, visiting New England in 1663, wrote: "The *Indians* and *English* use them much, boyling them with Sugar for Sauce to eat with their Meat, and it is a delicate Sauce." In Josselyn's day they were known, too, as "bounce berries," since they were, and still are, tested for ripeness by their ability to bounce.

Wash 2 cups of fresh cranberries and spread an even layer on the bottom of a shallow baking dish. Sprinkle with 1 cup of sugar, cover tightly, and bake in a preheated 350° oven for 1 hour. Give them an occasional stir during baking period. Chill before serving. Serve with meat or fowl.

"The Jelly wont Jell."— illustration from *Success with Small Fruits* (1881)

CRANBERRY SAUCE

Pick over and wash 4 cups of cranberries. Combine 2 cups sugar with 1½ cups water, bring to a boil, and cook for 10 minutes. Add the cranberries, cover, and cook until they stop popping. Skim off froth. Cool before serving. Add a dash of cognac if you wish.

SPICED CRAB APPLES

4 pounds crab apples
4½ cups sugar
1 quart vinegar

2 sticks cinnamon
½ tablespoon whole cloves

Choose firm, ripe crab apples, free from blemishes. Do not pare; leave the stems attached. In a kettle large enough to contain the fruit, combine sugar, vinegar, and spices. Bring slowly to a boil and cook for 5 minutes. Add fruit, again bring to a boil, then turn down heat, and cook slowly until apples are tender. Allow fruit to stand in syrup overnight. The next day, drain off the syrup and cook it until it is the consistency of honey. Pack fruit into 1-pint sterilized jars and fill with syrup. Seal. Makes 6 jars.

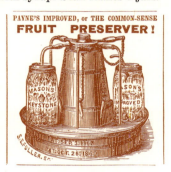

Advertisement, *Harper's Weekly*

APPLE BUTTER

Apple Butter has always been associated with the Pennsylvania Dutch, and it has a special meaning for the Schwenkfelders. Every September for the last 226 years, the Schwenkfelders have held *Gedaechtnisz Tag*—a thanksgiving service. The Schwenkfelders began their arduous voyage to America in July, 1734. Christopher Schultz, a sixteen-year-old orphan, kept a diary during the trip and, on September 21, 1734, he recorded "it was again calm, and the anchor was dropped near New Castle, and we obtained our first *fresh water* out of the river today. The captain rowed over and brought back a bag of *apples*." With rolls that were provided, the Schwenkfelders had a meal of fresh food, the first after their long voyage. Their traditional thanksgiving— water, bread, butter, Apple Butter—commemorates that fact each year.

3 quarts sweet cider
8 pounds ripe, well-flavored apples
2½ cups brown sugar, firmly packed
2 teaspoons cloves

2 teaspoons cinnamon
1 teaspoon allspice
½ teaspoon salt

Cook cider over a high heat, uncovered, about 30 minutes or until it is reduced to half. Wash, quarter, and core unpeeled apples, add to cider, and cook over a low heat until very tender. Stir frequently. Work apple mixture through a sieve, returning the purée to the kettle. Stir in sugar, all the spices, and salt. Cook over a very low heat, stirring almost continuously, until Apple Butter thickens. Pour into sterilized pint jars and seal securely. Makes 4 jars.

APPLESAUCE

In *American Cookery,* Amelia Simmons strongly urged Americans to plant their own apple trees, "excepting in the compactest cities." She argued that many otherwise useless spots might be turned into orchards, and cautioned families to "preserve the orchard from the intrusions of boys, &c. which is too common in America." Miss Simmons concluded that the "net saving would in time extinguish the public debt."

Pare, core, and slice thin 10 greening apples. Add 1 cup water and cook over a low heat, covered, for 15 minutes, stirring occasionally. Remove from heat and rub apples through a sieve or, preferably, blend in an electric blender to make a smooth sauce. Add 1 cup granulated sugar, return to a brisk heat, and cook about 5 minutes longer. Cool, but do not chill, and serve with cold heavy cream. Makes 5 to 6 cups, depending on the size of the apples.

ALBEMARLE PEACH CHUTNEY

Chutney (from the Hindu *catni*) was probably introduced to America by schooner captains plying the Indian spice trade.

7 pounds firm fresh peaches	¼ cup scraped ginger root or
1 pint cider vinegar	3 tablespoons ground ginger
2 pounds dark brown sugar	1½ tablespoons salt
½ cup grated onion	2 tablespoons paprika
2 boxes (1-pound size) seedless raisins	1 tablespoon cumin powder
5 apples, pared and diced	Grated rind and juice of 2 lemons
2 tablespoons white mustard seed	

Peel and cut peaches (enough to make about 4 quarts) in slices about ¾ inch thick. Cover with vinegar and brown sugar. Set aside. Combine all remaining ingredients and cook over a low heat, stirring constantly, until the mixture is thoroughly blended. In a separate saucepan, cook the peach mixture for several minutes or until peaches are tender but still hold their shape. Combine both mixtures and cook together for a few minutes. Pour into sterilized jars and seal securely. Makes about 5 quarts.

SWEET PICKLED PEACHES

6 pounds firm fresh peaches	½ teaspoon whole cloves
3 cups cider vinegar	½ teaspoon whole allspice
3 cups sugar	½ teaspoon mace

Pour boiling water over peaches and let stand several minutes, then drain and skin. (Some varieties resist this method and must be pared with a knife.) Cut each peach in half, remove the pit, and pack into 2 or 3 sterilized quart jars (the size of the peaches and the way in which they are packed is the determining factor). Bring vinegar and sugar to the boiling point. Add all the spices and continue boiling for 5 minutes. Pour over the peaches immediately and seal securely. Makes 2 to 3 jars.

CANTALOUPE PICKLE

Peel a large unripe cantaloupe, remove seeds and membrane, cut into small pieces. Cover with white vinegar, then pour off all the vinegar and measure it. To every pint of vinegar add 1¾ cups of brown sugar (firmly packed), 8 whole cloves, ½ teaspoon cinnamon, and ¼ teaspoon mace. Bring the mixture to a boil. Add melon and cook over a low heat until tender and almost transparent. With a slotted spoon, transfer cantaloupe to a bowl. Continue to boil pickling liquid for about 12 minutes. Pour over melon. Cool completely before using. Makes about 1 quart.

CORN RELISH

2 packages frozen corn or	¼ cup sugar
4 cups fresh corn	1 tablespoon salt
¼ head cabbage, shredded	1 tablespoon dry mustard
1 sweet red pepper, chopped fine	½ cup white vinegar
5 stalks celery, thinly sliced	½ cup water

Cook corn until tender. Drain and set aside. Combine cabbage, red pepper, and celery in a saucepan. Add about 1 cup of water, cover, and cook 5 minutes. Drain and combine with corn. Mix together sugar, salt, and dry mustard. Then stir in vinegar and water. Pour over vegetables, heat to a boil, then continue cooking 15 minutes longer. Stir occasionally. Pour into sterilized pint jars and seal, or refrigerate and use immediately. Makes 2 jars.

GINGER PEARS

2 pounds hard late pears	2 pounds sugar
Juice and rind of 1 lemon	2 ounces ginger root or crystallized ginger
½ cup water	

Pare, quarter, core, and cut pears into thin slices. Squeeze lemon juice, then cut rind into thin slices. Combine both rind and juice with water, sugar, and small chunks of ginger. Cook over a low heat for 45 minutes or until mixture is clear and syrupy. Add pears and continue simmering for 45 minutes (the pears should be transparent and the syrup quite thick). Pour into sterilized jars and seal. Makes 3 to 4 half-pint jars.

CARROT PICKLES

4 cups sliced, uncooked carrots	¼ teaspoon ginger
2 medium onions, sliced	¼ teaspoon cloves
¾ cup sugar	¼ teaspoon celery seed
¾ teaspoon salt	1 tablespoon salad oil
½ teaspoon cinnamon	2 cups vinegar

Cook carrot and onion slices in 1 cup of water over a low heat for 10 minutes. Drain, add all remaining ingredients, and simmer gently for 15 minutes. Ladle into 4 sterilized pint jars and seal securely.

YANKEE TOMATO RELISH

2 cups skinned and chopped tomatoes
½ cup onion, chopped fine
1 cup chopped celery
¼ cup green pepper, chopped fine

6 tablespoons sugar
1 tablespoon mustard seed
½ cup cider vinegar

Before measuring tomatoes, squeeze out most of the juice, then combine tomatoes with all remaining ingredients. Pour into a sterilized jar, cover, and let stand for at least 24 hours before using. Makes about 1 quart.

TOMATO KETCHUP

Get them quite ripe on a dry day, squeeze them with your hands till reduced to a pulp, then put half a pound of fine salt to one hundred tomatoes, and boil them for two hours. Stir them to prevent burning. While hot press them through a fine sieve, with a silver spoon till nought but the skin remains, then add a little mace, 3 nutmegs, allspice, cloves, cinnamon, ginger and pepper to taste. Boil over a slow fire till quite thick, stir all the time. Bottle when cold. One hundred tomatoes will make four or five bottles and keep good for two or three years.
—Mrs. Samuel Whitehorne, *Sugar House Book*, 1801,
Collection of Newport Historical Society

TOMATO PRESERVES

5 large ripe tomatoes
3½ cups sugar

Juice and rind of 1½ lemons
½ cup crystallized ginger, chopped

Pour boiling water over tomatoes, let stand for several minutes, then slip off the skins. Chop tomatoes in small cubes. Cover with sugar and allow to stand for 1 hour. Squeeze juice from lemons and cut rind in fine slivers. Combine with tomato mixture and crystallized ginger. Cook over a low heat, stirring frequently, until preserves thicken. A good test is to spoon some into a saucer; if the liquid turns syrupy thick on cooling, preserves are done. Makes about 1½ pints.

PICKLED JERUSALEM ARTICHOKES

2 pounds Jerusalem artichokes
1 cup white vinegar
1 cup water

1 cup sugar
5 whole cloves
½ teaspoon salt

Peel artichokes and cook whole in boiling, salted water until tender. Start testing with a toothpick after about 15 minutes. Do not overcook. Drain thoroughly. Combine all remaining ingredients and cook to a boil. Pour over artichokes and let stand at least 8 hours before using. Makes about 1 quart.

DESSERTS

NEW ORLEANS CALAS
(*Rice Cakes*)

Vendors used to sell *calas* on the streets in the French Quarter of New Orleans with the cry, *"Belles calas! Calas tout chaud!"*

½ cup uncooked rice
3 cups boiling water
1 package active dry yeast or
   1 cake compressed
3 eggs, well beaten
¼ cup flour (about)

½ cup sugar
½ teaspoon salt
Dash of nutmeg
Fat for deep-fat frying
Confectioners' sugar

Cook rice in boiling water until very tender. Drain and set aside to cool. Dissolve yeast in 2 tablespoons warm water. Mix with cold rice and let stand in a warm spot overnight. The following day, beat in eggs, flour, sugar, salt, and nutmeg, adding more flour, if necessary, to make a thick batter. Heat fat to 370° on deep-fat thermometer or until a 1-inch cube of bread browns in 60 seconds. Drop batter from tablespoons into hot fat and fry until golden brown. Drain on paper towels and sprinkle with confectioners' sugar. Serve hot.

A NUN'S SIGH

These *Beignet Soufflés*—as light as a nun's sigh—are made of chou paste, the base for cream puffs and éclairs. The recipe was adapted from *French Dishes for American Tables* by Pierre Caron, *chef d'entremets* at the old Delmonico's.

1 cup sifted all-purpose flour
Pinch of salt
1 tablespoon sugar
1 cup water
⅓ cup butter

4 eggs
1 teaspoon vanilla
Fat for deep-fat frying
Confectioners' sugar

Sift together flour, salt, sugar, and set aside. Heat water and butter together until butter melts. Add flour combination all at once, and stir rapidly with a wooden spoon until dough leaves sides of pan and forms a lump. Remove from heat and beat in eggs, one at a time, beating hard after each addition. When dough is no longer slippery-looking, stir in vanilla. Scoop up a heaping teaspoon of the dough and, with a second teaspoon, push it off into preheated fat (350° on deep-fat thermometer or until a 1-inch cube of bread browns in 60 seconds). When puffed and golden brown, drain on paper towels. Sprinkle with confectioners' sugar and serve hot. Makes several dozen.

FRUIT FRITTERS

1 cup sifted all-purpose flour
¼ teaspoon salt
2 tablespoons sugar
2 eggs, separated
⅔ cup milk

1 tablespoon melted butter
1 teaspoon fresh lemon juice
2 cups cubed fruit
Fat for deep-fat frying
Cinnamon

Sift together the flour, salt, and sugar. Set aside. Combine egg yolks and milk, then beat in butter and lemon juice. Stir in flour mixture with as few strokes as possible and gently fold in stiffly beaten egg whites. If you use canned fruit, drain on paper towels. Heat deep fat to 350° or until a 1-inch cube of bread browns in 60 seconds. Drop a piece of fruit into batter, drain slightly, and fry in hot fat until golden brown on each side. Drain on paper towels and sprinkle with a mixture of granulated sugar and a little cinnamon. Serves 8.

Deep-fat fryers

DOUGHNUTS

1 cup sugar
3½ teaspoons baking powder
½ teaspoon cinnamon
½ teaspoon nutmeg
½ teaspoon salt

4 cups all-purpose flour (about)
2 eggs
1 cup milk
3 tablespoons melted butter
Fat for deep-fat frying

Sift together sugar, baking powder, cinnamon, nutmeg, salt, and flour. Beat eggs thoroughly, then stir into dry ingredients. Add the milk and melted butter. Roll about ⅓ inch thick on a floured board and cut with a doughnut cutter (lacking this, use a biscuit cutter and make a hole in the center with a large thimble). Fry several at a time in hot fat (375° on deep-fat thermometer or until a 1-inch cube of bread browns in 60 seconds) until nicely browned. Drain on paper towels. Dust with granulated or confectioners' sugar. Makes 2 dozen.

TRIFLE

The Trifle was brought to America by the British colonists. In this country, the wine-soaked cake was also known as Tipsy Squire and Tipsy Parson.

Place a layer of spongecake in a crystal bowl. Saturate it with sherry, rum, or brandy. Stud with ½ cup toasted almonds, then refrigerate until serving time. Make custard according to directions given in Snow Eggs (page 571). Combine 1 cup heavy cream with 1 tablespoon confectioners' sugar and 1 teaspoon vanilla, then beat until stiff. Before serving, pour custard over spongecake, then pile whipped cream on top. Jam may be spread over the cake before the custard and cream are added. Serves 6 to 8.

EMPAÑADAS DE CAMOTE CON PIÑA
(Pineapple-Yam Turnovers)

Filling:
1 cup cooked yam, mashed
½ cup crushed pineapple, drained
1 tablespoon lime or lemon juice
¼ teaspoon salt
1 egg, beaten
½ cup light brown sugar
½ cup blanched almonds, chopped
½ teaspoon cinnamon

Pastry:
2 cups sifted all-purpose flour
2 tablespoons sugar
2 teaspoons baking powder
½ teaspoon salt
⅔ cup shortening
5 or 6 tablespoons ice water

To make the filling: Combine mashed yam with pineapple and all remaining ingredients for the filling. Set aside.

To make pastry: Sift together flour, sugar, baking powder, and salt. Cut in shortening with a pastry blender or two knives until mixture looks mealy. Add water, just enough to hold pastry together when kneaded lightly. Roll as thin as pie pastry on a lightly floured board and cut into circles, 3 to 4 inches in diameter. Spoon filling on one half of the circle, wet edge of pastry with a little water, then fold other half of pastry over, and press edges together with fork tines. Prick pastry tops. Bake in a preheated 375° oven for 15 to 20 minutes or until delicately browned. Serve at room temperature. Makes 15.

OLYKOEKS
(Raised Doughnuts)

In his *History of New York...by Diedrich Knickerbocker,* Washington Irving wrote of a large "dish of balls of sweetened dough fried in hog's fat, and called dough nuts or oly koeks." The Dutch introduced doughnuts—they called them oily cakes—to the New World.

1 cup milk
1 package active dry yeast or
  1 cake compressed
¼ cup lukewarm water
1 cup brown sugar, firmly packed
6 cups sifted all-purpose flour

1 teaspoon salt
1 teaspoon cinnamon or nutmeg
2 eggs, well beaten
1 cup softened butter
Fat for deep-fat frying

Scald milk, then cool to lukewarm. Sprinkle yeast over lukewarm water to dissolve. Sift together sugar, flour, salt, and cinnamon or nutmeg. Combine milk and yeast in a large bowl. Stir in the flour with your hands (the dough will be very heavy), then stir in beaten eggs. Cover and let rise in a warm place until double in size. Punch down the dough, then work in the butter with your hands until dough is smooth and well blended. Roll about ½ inch thick on a lightly floured board and cut with a doughnut cutter. Place doughnuts on a tray lined with wax paper, cover again, and let rise in a warm place until light and puffy. Drop several at a time into deep fat preheated to 375° on deep-fat thermometer or until a 1-inch cube of bread browns in 60 seconds. Fry until nicely browned on both sides. Lift from fat, drain on paper towels, and sprinkle with confectioners' sugar, granulated sugar, or a mixture of granulated sugar and a little cinnamon. Makes about 40.

FASTNACHTS

These Pennsylvania Dutch doughnuts were served traditionally on Fastnacht Day (Shrove Tuesday)—a last sweet treat before the Lenten season began.

1 package active dry yeast or
  1 cake compressed
¼ cup warm water
2 cups milk
1 teaspoon sugar
6 to 7 cups sifted all-purpose flour

2 eggs
4 tablespoons butter, melted
¾ cup sugar, plus 2 tablespoons
1¼ teaspoons salt
Fat for deep-fat frying
Confectioners' sugar

Sprinkle yeast over warm water to dissolve. Scald milk, remove from heat, and cool. Add *1 teaspoon of the sugar, 3 cups of the flour,* and the yeast, and stir thoroughly. Cover and let stand in a warm place until double in size. Beat eggs vigorously and combine with butter, sugar, salt, and remaining flour. When the dough rises, stir in the egg mixture. At this point, mixture should be stiff enough to roll. Add more flour, if needed. Cover and let rise in a warm place a second time until double in size. Punch down with your fist, then roll about ½ inch thick on a lightly floured board. Cut into 2-inch squares, making a slit in the middle. Cover and let rise a third time. Fry several at a time in deep fat preheated to 350° on deep-fat thermometer or until hot enough to brown a 1-inch cube of bread in 60 seconds. Drain on paper towels and sprinkle with confectioners' sugar.

PANNEQUAIQUES

Jefferson seems to have delighted as much in the spelling as in the recipes of his steward in Washington, Étienne Lemaire. The President once wrote his daughter : "I enclose you Lemaire's receipts. The orthography will be puzzling and amusing but the receipts are valuable." Among Jefferson's favorites was this recipe for *Pannequaiques*—now called crêpes.

1 cup sifted all-purpose flour
1 tablespoon sugar
¼ teaspoon salt
2 eggs

2 additional egg yolks
1¾ cups milk
2 tablespoons melted butter
1 teaspoon rum or cognac

Combine all ingredients in a mixing bowl and beat with a rotary or electric beater until smooth. If you prefer to use a blender, put all ingredients in the container and blend until as thick as heavy cream. Heat a 6-inch skillet until a drop of water tested on the bottom sizzles. Grease the skillet, then add a generous tablespoonful of the batter. Tip the pan back and forth so there will be a thin coating of batter over the bottom of the pan. When crêpe is brown on the bottom, turn and brown the other side. Lift out of skillet and place on wax paper. Sprinkle each pancake as it comes from the pan with confectioners' sugar, then stack on top of each other, keeping them warm. Place on dessert platter and cut in wedges, or spread currant jelly between each layer and sprinkle confectioners' sugar on top.

STRAWBERRY SHORTCAKE

Roger Williams, founder of Providence in 1636, wrote in his *Key into the Language of America*...that the strawberry "is the wonder of all the Fruits growing naturally in those parts.... In some parts where the *Natives* have planted, I have many times seen as many as would fill a good ship, within few miles compasse." Williams went on to say: "The *Indians* bruise them in a Morter, and mixe them with meale and make Strawberry bread." From the time the colonists first discovered strawberries, a proliferation of Strawberry Shortcake recipes has sprung up.

2 cups sifted all-purpose flour	½ cup milk (about)
1 tablespoon baking powder	1 quart strawberries
¼ teaspoon salt	Sugar
½ cup softened butter	3 tablespoons butter

Sift together flour, baking powder, and salt. Add butter, working it thoroughly into the flour mixture. Using a fork, lightly mix in the milk—just enough to make a soft dough. Divide in half and pat each portion on the bottom of an inverted 8-inch cake pan. Prick surface with fork tines. Bake in a preheated 400° oven for about 15 minutes or until golden. While shortcakes bake, wash and hull berries. Crush half the berries and sprinkle generously with sugar. Sugar remaining whole berries. Take shortcakes from oven and, while still hot, dot surfaces with butter. Drain crushed berries (save the juice) and spoon on one layer, cover with second shortcake, and place drained whole berries on top. Return to oven for about 5 minutes, then pour fresh strawberry juice over the top and serve warm with plain or whipped cream.

Strawberry vendor

BLUEBERRY SHORTCAKE

3½ cups sifted all-purpose flour	1 egg
1 tablespoon baking powder	¾ cup milk (about)
½ teaspoon salt	1 pint blueberries
½ cup (1 stick) butter	½ cup sugar

Sift together flour, baking powder, and salt. Cut in butter with a pastry blender or two knives until mixture resembles corn meal. In a separate bowl, beat egg thoroughly, then stir in milk. Stir this lightly into the flour combination with a fork. Divide dough in half and roll one portion to fit in the bottom of a 9-inch pie pan. Cover with blueberries, then sprinkle with sugar. Cover with remaining dough rolled into a circle. Bake in a preheated 400° oven for 30 minutes or until dough takes on a golden tone. Serve warm with butter and sugar or cream. Serves 6.

PLUMS IN WINE JELLY

1 can (1 pound, 13 ounce size) plums   2 envelopes unflavored gelatin
Red or white wine

Drain plums, measure the syrup, and pour it into a saucepan. Pit the plums and place in a bowl. If you choose greengage plums, use a light white wine such as Chablis; if you use red or purple plums, then select a not-too-dry red wine. Measure wine (the wine plus the syrup should equal 1 pint). Pour the wine over the plums. Sprinkle gelatin over ½ cup cold water to soften. Heat plum syrup and stir in gelatin until dissolved. Combine with plums and wine and pour into a mold. Refrigerate until firm. Turn out of mold onto serving plate. Serves 4 to 6.

AMBROSIA

Ambrosia, the food eaten by Greek gods to preserve their immortality, is familiarly known to Americans as a combination of oranges and coconut—a very popular dessert in the South. In some sections, it is traditionally served for Christmas dinner.

Cut rind and white membrane from juicy oranges, then cut crosswise into thin slices, discarding the seeds. Put a generous layer of orange slices in a crystal bowl, sprinkle with sugar, and cover with a layer of shredded coconut. Continue layering with oranges, sugar, and coconut, ending with the coconut. Chill several hours before serving. Today other fruits are frequently added, such as pineapple, bananas, grapes, even berries—but the orange and coconut remain as the base.

FROZEN PLUM PUDDING

½ cup chopped candied cherries   2 cups milk
½ cup chopped citron   2 cups heavy cream
¼ cup sherry   ¼ cup macaroon crumbs
1 cup sugar   ¼ cup chopped blanched almonds
Dash salt   ¾ cup heavy cream, whipped
¾ teaspoon ground cardamom seed   1 tablespoon sugar
2 eggs, beaten

Soak cherries and citron in sherry for an hour or two. Combine sugar, salt, and cardamom in a saucepan. Stir in eggs and milk. Cook over a low heat, stirring constantly, until mixture coats a wooden spoon. Cool, then stir in 2 cups heavy cream. Pour into ice cream freezer and freeze until mushy. Then add the sherry-flavored cherries and citron, the macaroon crumbs, and almonds. Continue cranking the freezer until mixture is firm. Pack into a 6-cup plum-pudding or gelatin mold and cover securely. Place in freezer compartment of refrigerator overnight to mellow. Unmold on a serving platter and return to freezer an hour or two or until firm. Frost the pudding with whipped cream sweetened with sugar. Return to freezer until whipped cream is firm. Serves 12 to 15.

SALPICON OF FRUITS

Combine 1 cup rum and 1 cup sugar in a saucepan. Bring to a boil, then pour over 4 cups cut fruit (oranges, bananas, grapes, pineapple, etc.). Let stand until cold. Chill in refrigerator or freeze in ice cube tray for several hours, stirring occasionally.

POACHED SECKEL PEARS

The Seckel pear, the finest and best known of all American pears, is named for the farmer who first grew this variety on his farm outside Philadelphia, shortly after the Revolution.

1½ cups water
1½ cups sugar
2 pounds Seckel pears

2 tablespoons chopped crystallized ginger
Heavy cream

Combine water and sugar in a saucepan and cook over a moderate heat until syrup begins to thicken. Wash pears (do not peel) and drop them into the hot syrup. Cook over a low heat, basting occasionally, for about 30 minutes or until tender when pierced with a fork. Remove from stove and stir in crystallized ginger. Serve slightly warm or cool, not chilled, with a pitcher of cream or unsweetened whipped cream. Serves 6.

BANANAS FLAMBÉ

Remove skins from 4 green-tipped bananas and cut in half lengthwise. Heat ½ cup (1 stick) butter in a chafing dish, add bananas, and sprinkle with ¾ cup sugar and 4 tablespoons lemon or lime juice. Cook until lightly browned, turning occasionally. To *flambé*, warm ⅓ cup cognac, pour over bananas, and ignite. Spoon sauce over fruit until flame dies out.

SPICED PEACHES IN BRANDY

12 large whole spiced peaches, canned
12 cloves
1 blade mace

1 stick cinnamon
1 cup brandy

Stick one clove in each peach and place in saucepan with the juice. Add cinnamon and mace and simmer gently until heated through. With a skimmer, remove the peaches to a large stone crock or wide-mouthed glass jar which has been scalded with boiling water. Add one cup of brandy and cover. Simmer remaining peach juice until it is reduced to half its original volume, then pour it into the crock. Cover tightly and store in a cool place for at least 3 days before serving. If stored for a longer time, add brandy as needed to keep the fruit covered with liquid. Apricots may be substituted for peaches.

HAZELNUT BAVARIAN CREAM

1 envelope unflavored gelatin
¼ cup cold water
½ cup milk
4 egg yolks
¼ cup sugar

Pinch of salt
¾ cup hazelnuts or walnuts, ground
2 tablespoons dark rum
2 cups heavy cream

Sprinkle gelatin over cold water to soften. Combine milk, egg yolks, sugar, and salt in the top of a double boiler. Cook over boiling water, stirring constantly, until mixture will coat a wooden spoon. Stir in gelatin until dissolved, then add ground nuts and rum. Refrigerate until the consistency is that of raw egg whites. Fold in stiffly beaten cream and pour into a 1½-quart mold or bowl. Chill until firm. Serves 6 to 8.

BLANCMANGE

½ pound blanched almonds
¼ cup water
¼ cup milk
1 tablespoon unflavored gelatin

1 cup heavy cream
½ cup sugar
1 tablespoon flavoring (kirsch, orgeat, rum, or maraschino)

Pound almonds in a mortar until very fine or blend in an electric blender. Stir in water and milk, allow to stand for 10 to 15 minutes, then strain through cheesecloth. The mixture will be very heavy and will take time to drip through; make certain every last bit of liquid is extracted. Sprinkle gelatin over ¼ cup water to soften. Scald cream, then stir in gelatin and sugar until both are dissolved. Add almond liquid and flavoring. Pour into a small mold or bowl and refrigerate for several hours until firm. Serve with whipped cream to 4.

CAPE COD BERRY GRUNT

1 pint berries
1 cup water
½ cup sugar
1½ cups sifted all-purpose flour

1 tablespoon baking powder
¼ teaspoon salt
1 tablespoon butter
¼ cup milk (about)

Cook the washed berries in water and sugar until soft (about 5 to 10 minutes, depending on the kind of berries and degree of ripeness). If you use frozen berries, mix the thawed fruit with ½ cup sugar (do not cook). Sift together flour, baking powder, and salt. Pinch in the butter with your finger tips until well dispersed, then stir in enough milk to make a soft dough. Place berries in bottom of a 1½-quart mold or ovenproof bowl, spoon dough on top, and cover tightly with a lid or a piece of foil. Place in a deep kettle and pour in enough boiling water to reach the halfway mark. Cover the kettle and simmer slowly for 1½ hours. Turn out of mold and serve hot with cream or New England Nutmeg Sauce (page 579). Serves 6.

PEACH COBBLER

⅔ cup sugar
1 tablespoon flour
3 cups fresh peach slices
4 tablespoons butter
¾ teaspoon cinnamon

1½ cups all-purpose flour
1 tablespoon baking powder
¼ teaspoon salt
3 tablespoons butter
½ cup milk (about)

Combine sugar and flour in a saucepan. Add peaches and cook over a low heat, stirring constantly, until fruit is tender (takes about 5 minutes, depending on the variety and quality of the fruit). Pour into an 8-inch square pan, dot with butter, and sprinkle with cinnamon. Set aside. Sift together flour, baking powder, and salt. Pinch in butter with your finger tips until well distributed. With a fork, stir in milk (just enough to make a soft dough), transfer to a lightly floured board, and knead a second or two. Roll into a 9-inch square about ½ inch thick. Place on top of the peaches, pinching dough to rim of pan. Bake in a preheated 425° oven for 25 to 30 minutes or until nicely browned. Serve warm, with or without cream.

LOUISA MAY ALCOTT'S APPLE SLUMP

The author of *Little Women* was so fond of this New England dessert that she named her house in Concord, Massachusetts, Apple Slump.

6 cups apples, pared, cored, and sliced
1 cup sugar
1 teaspoon cinnamon
½ cup water

1½ cups sifted all-purpose flour
¼ teaspoon salt
1½ teaspoons baking powder
½ cup milk (about)

Combine apple slices, sugar, cinnamon, and water in a saucepan with a tight-fitting lid. Heat to the boiling point. Sift together flour, salt, baking powder. Stir in enough milk to make a soft dough. Drop dough from a tablespoon onto apple mixture. Cover tightly and cook over a low heat for 30 minutes. Serve warm with New England Nutmeg Sauce (page 579) or rich cream. This dessert can be made with various fresh or frozen berries. Serves 6.

DOWN EAST APPLE BROWN BETTY

1½ cups dry bread crumbs
¼ cup melted butter
4 medium apples, peeled and sliced
¾ cup brown sugar, firmly packed
Pinch of salt

1 teaspoon cinnamon
¼ teaspoon nutmeg
¼ teaspoon ground cloves
1 teaspoon grated lemon rind
Juice of 1 lemon

Work bread crumbs and butter together and pat a third of the mixture on the bottom of a buttered baking dish. Cover with *half the apples*. Mix together sugar, salt, cinnamon, nutmeg, cloves, and lemon rind. Sprinkle half the mixture over the apple. Add *half the lemon juice* and 1 tablespoon of water. Add another layer of crumbs. Repeat with apples, sugar mixture, lemon juice, and water. Sprinkle remaining crumbs on top, cover, and bake in a preheated 350° oven for 40 minutes. Remove cover and continue baking at 400° for 10 minutes. Serve warm with cream, vanilla ice cream, or Lemon Sauce (page 579). Serves 6.

APPLE PANDOWDY

Pastry:
1½ cups flour
Dash of salt
½ cup shortening
Ice water
¼ cup melted butter (about)
Filling:
½ cup sugar

½ teaspoon cinnamon
¼ teaspoon salt
¼ teaspoon nutmeg
10 large apples
½ cup light molasses or maple syrup
3 tablespoons melted butter
¼ cup water

Sift flour and salt together into a bowl, then blend in the shortening with a pastry blender or two knives until mixture is mealy. Sprinkle a little ice water over the mixture, just enough to hold the dough together. Roll the pastry out, brush with butter, and cut it in half. Place the halves on top of each other and cut in half again. Repeat last step two more times, each time brushing the pastry with butter. Pile the pieces (there will be 16) on top of each other and chill at least 1 hour. Then roll the pastry and divide in half, using one portion to line a deep medium-sized baking dish. Reserve the other portion for the top. Refrigerate both while you make the filling.

To make the filling: Mix together sugar, cinnamon, salt, and nutmeg. Peel and core apples, then cut in thin slices. Mix thoroughly with sugar-spice combination and pile into pastry-lined baking dish. Combine molasses or maple syrup with melted butter and water. Pour over the apples. Cover with pastry and seal. Place in a preheated 400° oven for 10 minutes, then reduce heat to 325°. At this point, "dowdy" the dessert by cutting the crust into the apples with a sharp, sturdy knife. Return to oven and bake for 1 hour. Serve hot with thick cream or ice cream. Serves 6.

PERSIMMON PUDDING

Early settlers found that the native American persimmon could "drawe a man's mouth awrie with much torment" if not properly ripe. Some dismissed the "pessemmins" as "a good kind of horse plomb," but they gradually became welcome ingredients for puddings, especially in the Middle West and the Carolinas.

2 to 3 very ripe persimmons
¾ cup brown sugar, firmly packed
1 cup milk
¼ cup butter, melted
1 cup sifted all-purpose flour

2 teaspoons baking powder
¼ teaspoon salt
¼ teaspoon cinnamon
Heavy cream

Peel persimmons and work through a sieve or blend in an electric blender. Measure one cup persimmon pulp and combine with brown sugar, milk, and butter. Sift together flour, baking powder, salt, and cinnamon and stir into persimmon pulp until smooth. Pour into a buttered 1½-quart baking dish and bake in a preheated 325° oven for about 1 hour or until pudding pulls away from sides of dish (surface should be soft). Serve warm or cold with whipped cream. Serves 4 to 6.

INDIAN PUDDING

In February, 1809, Mrs. Samuel Harrison Smith, a prominent figure in Washington society, recorded in a letter to her sister-in-law that one of her guests, a Mr. Hauto, "to our great entertainment, had some difficulty in making way with his indian pudding and molasses, but when I assured him that this dish was immortalized by the greatest poet of our country [Joel Barlow], he made out to mortalize it."

¼ cup corn meal
2 cups hot milk
¼ cup sugar
⅛ teaspoon baking soda
½ teaspoon salt
½ teaspoon ground ginger

½ teaspoon ground cinnamon
¼ cup molasses
1 cup cold milk
Whipped cream
Nutmeg

Stir corn meal, a little at a time, into the hot milk and cook over low heat or in the top of a double boiler, stirring constantly, for 15 minutes or until thick. Remove from heat. Mix together sugar, baking soda, salt, ginger, and cinnamon, then stir into the corn-meal mixture. Add molasses and cold milk, mixing thoroughly. Pour into a 1-quart casserole and bake in a preheated 275° oven for 2 hours. Serve warm with whipped cream and a light sprinkling of freshly grated nutmeg. Serves 6 to 8.

Nineteenth-century egg beater

CHARLOTTE RUSSE

The origin of the Charlotte Russe is fairly obscure, but it is generally thought to have been the creation of the famous French chef Carême. It was served at a banquet given at the White House during Van Buren's Presidency and was a popular dessert in the 1800's.

1 cup milk
1 envelope unflavored gelatin
2 tablespoons cold water
4 egg yolks
½ cup sugar

¼ teaspoon salt
Grated rind of 1 lemon
¼ cup lemon juice
6 ladyfingers, split
1 cup heavy cream

Scald milk. Sprinkle gelatin over cold water to soften. Mix together egg yolks, sugar, and salt. Pour hot milk, a little at a time, over the yolk mixture, beating hard all the time. Cook over a low heat, stirring constantly, until mixture is smooth and slightly thickened. Remove from heat, add gelatin, and stir until dissolved. Stir in lemon rind and juice, then refrigerate until cold but not set. Line a 1-quart mold or bowl with ladyfingers, placing some on the bottom and the remainder upright around the sides. Some of the ladyfingers may have to be cut to make them fit. Beat heavy cream until it holds a shape, fold into gelatin mixture gently, and pour into mold. Chill 2 to 3 hours or until firm. To serve, unmold on a crystal or silver platter or cake stand. Serves 6.

PLUM PUDDING

3 cups fine bread crumbs, one day old
½ teaspoon salt
¾ teaspoon ground cinnamon
½ teaspoon ground nutmeg
¼ teaspoon ground cloves
⅔ cup brown sugar, firmly packed
¾ cup milk, scalded
6 eggs, well beaten
⅓ pound suet, ground

1½ cups raisins
½ cup currants
¼ cup candied orange peel, chopped
¼ cup candied lemon peel, chopped
¼ cup candied citron, chopped
¼ cup dates, chopped
½ cup tart apples, chopped
¼ cup rum, brandy, or cider

Combine crumbs with salt, spices, and brown sugar. Stir in the scalded milk and cool. Mix in eggs and suet, then add all the fruits and rum, brandy, or cider. Work mixture with your hands to distribute fruit evenly. Place in a greased 2-quart mold. Seal securely with lid or foil and stand on a rack in the bottom of a kettle. Add enough boiling water to cover the mold halfway. Cover kettle tightly and steam over a low heat for 5 to 6 hours. Add more boiling water when necessary. Serve warm with Hard Sauce (page 579). Makes 12 servings.

SNOW EGGS

Oeufs à la neige, or Snow Eggs, as they were referred to at Monticello, are best known in this country as Floating Island. Jefferson's cook James used rose or orange-flower water in this recipe rather than the almond extract indicated here.

1 cup milk
1 cup light cream
3 egg whites
Dash of salt
½ cup sugar

1 teaspoon almond extract
4 egg yolks
½ cup sugar
½ teaspoon vanilla

Heat milk and cream in a shallow pan. Meanwhile, beat the egg whites with a dash of salt until they stand in peaks. Beat in the sugar a little at a time, then add the almond extract. With a dessert spoon, scoop out egg-shaped portions of the meringue. Remove milk from heat and drop the meringue "eggs" into the hot milk. (Cook only a few at a time.) Return pan to very low heat. Poach meringues for 2 to 4 minutes, turning them once with great care. With a slotted spoon lift the firm snow eggs out of the milk and onto a tea towel.

To make the custard: Beat the egg yolks with sugar until well mixed. Flavor with vanilla. Then add the cream-hot-milk mixture in a thin, steady stream, stirring constantly. Place over boiling water and cook, stirring constantly, until custard is thick enough to coat a wooden spoon. Takes about 15 minutes. Chill.

To serve, pour custard into a crystal bowl and arrange the snow eggs on top. Serves 4.

VARIATION: To make Snow Eggs in the Victorian manner, make the custard in the recipe above but do not poach the meringue eggs. Instead, after beating the egg whites until they stand in stiff peaks, beat in, a little at a time, about ⅓ cup of raspberry or strawberry preserves. Spoon little mounds of the mixture onto the chilled custard.

CRÈME BRÛLÉE

This recipe is adapted from one used by Julien, Thomas Jefferson's French cook in Washington. At that time, before broilers came into general use, the crust was glazed by passing a hot shovel or a salamander (shown at right) over it.

2 cups heavy cream
1 inch of vanilla bean

4 egg yolks, well beaten
Maple or brown sugar

Pour cream into a saucepan, add vanilla bean, bring slowly to the boiling point, and boil for one minute *exactly*. Remove from heat, take out vanilla, and pour cream into the well-beaten egg yolks, stirring constantly with a whisk. Pour into double boiler and cook, stirring constantly, over simmering water for 5 minutes, or until custard coats a wooden spoon (pan should not touch water). Pour into a greased baking dish and refrigerate. When thoroughly chilled and firm, cover the entire surface with a layer of sugar to a depth of ⅓ inch. Place under preheated broiler, leaving door open, until the sugar has melted and formed a hard crust. Chill again before serving. Serves 4.

POTS DE CRÈME

2 cups light cream
½ pound sweet chocolate, grated
Dash of salt

6 egg yolks, slightly beaten
1 tablespoon cognac or rum

Combine cream, chocolate, and salt in a saucepan. Cook over a low heat, stirring constantly, until mixture is thoroughly blended and cream is scalded. Pour this hot mixture, a little at a time, into the egg yolks, beating hard. Pour into mousse pots or into a large crystal or silver dessert bowl and place in the refrigerator for several hours or until firm. Serves 6 to 8.

SISTER ABIGAIL'S STRAWBERRY FLUMMERY

The Shakers were unusually attentive to the needs of their elders, and they developed a special diet, and special dishes, for the aged. This recipe is among the more popular of those dishes.

3 cups milk
⅓ cup cornstarch
5 tablespoons sugar
¼ teaspoon salt

1 egg, well beaten
½ teaspoon rose water or vanilla
1 quart fresh strawberries, raspberries,
    loganberries, or blueberries

Scald 2¼ *cups of the milk*. Mix cornstarch, sugar, and salt in a bowl, then add remaining milk, a little at a time. When smooth, combine with scalded milk and cook over a moderate heat, stirring constantly, until thick and bubbly. Remove from heat and gradually beat a small amount into the egg. Blend with remaining mixture, add rose water or vanilla, and cook over a low heat for 2 minutes, stirring constantly. Pour into a 1-quart mold and chill until firm. Unmold on serving platter and surround with sweetened berries. Serves 4 to 6.

PEACH CHARLOTTE

2 envelopes unflavored gelatin
2 cups milk
4 eggs, separated
½ cup sugar
¼ teaspoon salt

1 cup heavy cream
Ladyfingers
Fresh or brandied peach halves
Brandy Sauce (page 579)

Sprinkle gelatin over ¼ cup cold water to soften. Scald milk in the top of a double boiler. Beat egg yolks vigorously, adding sugar and salt a little at a time. Pour in a little of the hot milk, beating constantly. Pour back into milk and cook over boiling water until thick enough to coat a wooden spoon. Remove from heat and stir in gelatin until dissolved. Cool, then fold in stiffly beaten egg whites and whipped cream. Line a greased 1½-quart mold with ladyfingers, pour in the charlotte mixture, and chill until firm. Turn out onto serving platter and garnish with fresh or brandied peach halves. Serve with Brandy Sauce to 6.

BAKED HONEY CUSTARD

Refined, white sugar was a scarce and high-priced commodity on the American frontier, and many families substituted tree-sweetenin', bee-sweetenin', and molasses. Sugar and syrup were made from maple trees, and honey came from beehives, which were common around frontier households. Honeybees were unknown in the New World until the early 1600's, but they soon became indispensable and gave rise to dessert recipes like this one.

2 cups milk
4 tablespoons honey
3 eggs

¼ teaspoon salt
Sprinkle of mace or nutmeg

Scald milk, then stir in the honey. Beat eggs and salt together, then slowly beat in a little of the hot milk mixture. Combine the two and pour into 6 custard cups, scattering a little mace or nutmeg on top of each. Set cups in a pan of hot water and bake in a preheated 375° oven for 30 to 40 minutes. When a knife inserted in center comes out dry, the custard is cooked. Remove cups from water immediately and serve cold. Serves 6.

GOOSEBERRY FOOL

1 quart ripe gooseberries, strawberries,
   blackberries, or raspberries
1 cup sugar

1½ teaspoons grated lemon rind
1½ cups heavy cream
½ cup crumbled macaroons

Combine the berries with ¼ cup of water in a saucepan. Cook over a low heat until fruit is extremely tender. Remove from heat and work through a sieve to make a smooth purée. While hot, stir in sugar and lemon rind. Set aside to cool. Whip cream until it holds a shape, then fold into the cool fruit purée. Spoon into a serving bowl, sprinkle surface with macaroon crumbs, and chill thoroughly. Serves 6.

SNOWBALLS

Pastry for a 2-crust pie (page 580)
6 large apples
Orange marmalade
¼ cup soft butter
½ cup brown sugar

4 teaspoons cinnamon
1 teaspoon allspice
1 teaspoon nutmeg
Hard Sauce (page 579)

Prepare pastry and roll out thin on a floured board. Cut into 6 squares large enough to cover the apples. Pare apples, leave whole, but remove the core. Fill each cavity with orange marmalade. Make a smooth paste of butter, brown sugar, and the three spices. Spread this paste over each apple. Wrap apples in pastry squares, pricking surface here and there with a fork. Bake in a preheated 425° oven for 15 minutes, then reduce heat to 350°, and continue baking 40 to 45 minutes. Serve warm with Hard Sauce.

ICE CREAM

What is perhaps the first written comment on ice cream in America comes from a letter written in 1744 by William Black, a guest of Thomas Bladen, proprietary governor of Maryland. Black wrote, "You saw a plain proof of the Great Plenty of the Country, a Table in the most Splendent manner set out with Great Variety of Dishes, all serv'd up in the most Elegant way, after which came a Dessert no less Curious; Among the Rarities . . . was some fine Ice Cream which, with the Strawberries and Milk, eat most Deliciously."

Ice cream is believed to be a Chinese invention. Originating as "water ices" some 3,000 years ago, it was brought to the West by Marco Polo. Its lineage and literature are imposing. In America, George Washington made it; Mrs. Alexander Hamilton served it; Dolley Madison popularized it. Ice cream was often served at elaborate dinners as the *pièce de résistance;* at Madison's second inaugural ball, in 1812, the climactic moment was marked by the serving of ice cream. The cream came from the President's dairy at Montpelier, and strawberries from Mrs. Madison's garden topped the dish.

By the early 1900's, millions of Americans ate ice cream in cones, sodas, sundaes, and out of bucket freezers. The old pot freezer (in which the ingredients were beaten by hand and then shaken up and down in a pan of ice and salt until frozen) disappeared in 1846 when Nancy Johnson invented the hand-cranked portable ice cream freezer. In 1851, Jacob Fussell, a milk dealer in Baltimore, set up the first large wholesale ice cream business. In 1874, according to legend, the ice cream soda was introduced at the semicentennial of the Franklin Institute in Philadelphia; the ice cream cone reputedly was originated at the St. Louis fair in 1904. The sundae (originally an ice cream soda without soda) came into being to skirt a law prohibiting the sale of "stimulating beverages" on Sunday.

VANILLA ICE CREAM

¾ cup light cream
¼ cup sugar
Dash of salt

2 egg yolks
1 tablespoon vanilla
1 cup heavy cream

Refrigerator method: Scald the light cream, remove from heat, stir in sugar and salt. Beat egg yolks lightly, then beat in a little of the hot cream. Pour back into cream and cook over a low heat, stirring constantly, until the custard will coat a wooden spoon (cooking the custard in the top of a double boiler is less tricky). Remove from heat, stir in vanilla, and cool. When cool, fold in stiffly beaten heavy cream and pour into an ice cube tray. Set temperature control at coldest point and freeze until firm. Serves 4.

Freezer method: Double, triple, or even quadruple the ingredients (depending on the size of your freezer). Prepare custard as above, then cool. Stir in vanilla and *unbeaten* heavy cream. Follow usual freezing technique.

VARIATION I: To make strawberry ice cream, omit vanilla. Instead add 1 cup crushed fresh strawberries or 1 package frozen strawberries, thawed, drained, and crushed. Fold into cream before mixing with custard. Any fresh fruit may be substituted for the strawberries.

VARIATION II: To make chocolate ice cream, melt 1 square (1 ounce) unsweetened chocolate in the light cream when you make the custard.

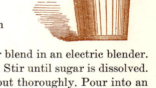

GREENGAGE ICE CREAM

1 can (1 pound, 3 ounce size) greengage plums
Juice of 1 lemon
1 cup sugar

¼ teaspoon salt
1 cup milk
1 cup heavy cream

Drain plums, remove pits, and work the fruit through a sieve or blend in an electric blender. Combine the plum purée with lemon juice, sugar, salt, and milk. Stir until sugar is dissolved. Beat cream until stiff, then fold into the plum mixture gently but thoroughly. Pour into an ice cube tray and freeze until firm but not solid. Serves 4 to 6.

CRANBERRY ICE

Outlining his prescription for a successful dinner party in *Society As I Have Found It,* Ward McAllister recommended serving a sorbet, or ice, as a refreshing diversion between courses. This ice can also be served as a dessert after smaller dinners.

Cook 2 cups fresh cranberries in 1 quart water until the berries pop. Then work through a sieve. Measure out 1½ quarts of liquid, add 2 cups of sugar, and cook until sugar has dissolved. Remove from heat and stir in 1 teaspoon unflavored gelatin which has been soaked in ¼ cup cold water. Pour into two ice cube trays and freeze until sherbet is mushy. Spoon into a bowl and beat with a rotary or electric beater until smooth. Pour back into ice trays and freeze until firm. Serves 8.

NESSELRODE PUDDING

This dessert was, according to legend, created by the chef to the Comte de Nesselrode. A number of different versions of it have been popular in this country; this one is similar to Ward McAllister's.

1 pint light cream
4 egg yolks
½ cup sugar
Chestnut purée (below) or
   1 can (8¾-ounce size) chestnut purée
¼ cup Malaga or sherry

½ cup currants
¼ cup seedless raisins
½ cup sugar
½ cup water
¾ cup heavy cream

Scald light cream. Beat egg yolks in a bowl, then beat in ½ cup sugar, a little at a time. Add scalded cream gradually and pour back into saucepan. Cook over a very low heat, stirring constantly, until custard will coat a wooden spoon. Remove from heat, then stir in chestnut purée and Malaga or sherry. Freeze the mixture (preferably in an ice cream freezer—if the mixture is not firmly frozen, the fruit, when added, will sink to the bottom). Cook currants, raisins, sugar, and water together over a moderate heat until the fruit becomes plump and the syrup thickens. Beat heavy cream until stiff. Stir the fruit and whipped cream into the frozen custard. Pack mixture into a melon or charlotte mold, cover, seal securely, and freeze until firm. This can be done in a freezer or the mold can be placed in a container of ice and salt (4 to 6 parts ice to 1 part rock salt). Unmold on a platter and serve well chilled. The pudding may be garnished with *marrons glacés* and whipped cream. Serves 6 to 8. Chopped candied fruit may be substituted for raisins and currants.

To make chestnut purée: Remove shell and inner brown skin from 20 plump chestnuts. Cook in a mixture of 1½ cups water, ½ cup sugar, and about 1 inch of vanilla bean. When tender, drain off most of the syrup and purée in a blender or work through a sieve.

Nineteenth-century mousse and pudding molds

MAPLE MOUSSE

½ cup pure maple syrup
2 eggs, separated

Pinch of salt
1 cup heavy cream

Heat maple syrup over a low heat until beads appear around the edge of the syrup. Separate eggs and place yolks in the top of a double boiler. Beat yolks vigorously, then add the heated syrup, a little at a time, beating hard all the while. Place over simmering water and cook, beating constantly with a rotary or electric beater, until the mixture will coat a wooden spoon, about 8 to 10 minutes. Cool completely. While maple combination cools, beat egg whites, with a pinch of salt added, until they stand in peaks. Beat heavy cream until stiff. Combine maple mixture, egg whites, and cream, folding gently until well blended. Pour into an ice cube tray and freeze about 1½ hours or until firm but not solid. Serves 6.

BAKED ALASKA

The idea of encasing ice cream in hot pastry was current long before the "Alaska"—as it was called on the menu at Delmonico's—was known. In 1802, a guest of President Jefferson's wrote that dessert at a White House dinner consisted of "Ice-cream very good, crust wholly dried, crumbled into thin flakes." And Benjamin Thompson, the American-born scientist who later became Count Rumford in England, laid claim to the creation of a meringue-topped ice cream, stating that his "omelette surprise" was the by-product of investigations in 1804 into the resistance of stiffly beaten egg whites to the induction of heat. As the idea of combining ice cream with warm pastry or meringue spread, and variations on the dessert were developed, it became known at first as Alaska-Florida, and later as Baked Alaska. George Augustus Sala, an Englishman who visited Delmonico's in the 1880's, reported: "The 'Alaska' is *a baked ice.* . . . The nucleus or core of the *entremet* is an ice cream. This is surrounded by an envelope of carefully whipped cream, which, just before the dainty dish is served, is popped into the oven, or is brought under the scorching influence of a red hot salamander. . . . So you go on discussing the warm cream *soufflé* till you come, with somewhat painful suddenness, on the row of ice. E'en so did the Shepherd in Virgil grow acquainted with love, and find him a native of the rocks."

Cover a thick plank, such as a bread board or chopping board, with a piece of heavy paper. Place a layer of spongecake or poundcake, cut at least 1 inch thick, on the paper. Then place a solid 1-quart brick of ice cream in the center of the cake. The cake should be large enough to extend at least ½ inch beyond the ice cream all around. Cover completely with a thick coating of meringue. Place in a preheated 500° oven for 3 to 5 minutes or until meringue is touched with gold. Serve at once to 6 or 8.

To make the meringue: Beat 4 egg whites with a dash of salt until they hold a soft shape. Add 1 cup sugar, a little at a time, and continue beating until meringue stands in peaks.

A DISH OF SNOW

3 egg whites
3 tablespoons confectioners' sugar, sifted
1 cup heavy cream

1 tablespoon rose water
1 fresh coconut, grated, or
   2 cans (4-ounce size) coconut

Beat the egg whites until they stand in peaks, then beat in the sugar, a tablespoon at a time (if not sweet enough, sift in a little more sugar). Beat cream in a separate bowl until very stiff, then mix in the rose water. Gently combine egg whites and whipped cream, making certain they are well mixed. This must be done at the very last minute—the mixture won't stand up for any length of time. Heap the coconut in the center of a silver or crystal bowl and "ornament," as they used to do, "with fine leaves such as peach or honeysuckle." Spoon the sauce over the coconut and serve at once.

MINNEHAHA SAUCE

4 tablespoons butter
⅔ cup brown sugar

¼ cup heavy cream
Grated rind and juice of 1 lemon

Blend together, in the top of a double boiler, the butter, brown sugar, heavy cream, and lemon rind and juice. Cook over boiling water, beating constantly, until sauce is a creamy froth. Serve with a simple dessert. Makes about 1½ cups.

STRAWBERRY SAUCE

Beat 1 egg white until it stands in peaks. Add 1 cup mashed strawberries (fresh or frozen), and continue beating until mixture looks fluffy. Gradually beat in 1 cup confectioners' sugar and 2 tablespoons butter, beating until sauce is light and airy. Serve over a simple, not-too-sweet dessert or use as a topping for shortcake. Makes about 2 cups.

MAPLE PECAN SAUCE

Cook ¾ cup maple syrup over a moderate heat for 6 to 8 minutes or until syrup thickens slightly. Remove from heat and stir in ½ cup coarsely chopped pecans or walnuts. Serve warm over ice cream. Makes about 1 cup.

BUTTERSCOTCH SAUCE

Melt ⅓ cup butter over low heat. Stir in 1 cup brown sugar (firmly packed), 2 tablespoons light corn syrup, and ½ cup heavy cream. Cook to the boiling point. Remove from heat and cool slightly before serving. Serve over ice cream or with unfrosted cakes or plain custards.

CARAMEL SAUCE

Combine ½ pound caramel candies with 1 cup heavy cream in top of double boiler. Cook over hot water, stirring frequently, until well blended. Makes 1½ cups.

CHOCOLATE NUT SAUCE

Heat ¼ cup butter in a heavy skillet, add 1 cup coarsely chopped nuts (walnuts, pecans, cashews, peanuts, slivered Brazil nuts, or filberts), and sauté until well browned. Remove from heat and stir in 1 package (6-ounce size) semi-sweet chocolate pieces until melted. Serve warm over vanilla or coffee ice cream. Makes 1¼ cups.

LEMON SAUCE

Mix ⅓ cup sugar and 1 tablespoon cornstarch together in a saucepan. Add 1 cup water and cook, stirring constantly, until mixture bubbles. Simmer gently for a few minutes, then remove from heat. Stir in 3 tablespoons butter, ½ teaspoon grated lemon rind, 1½ tablespoons fresh lemon juice, and a pinch of salt. Serve hot with pudding.

NEW ENGLAND NUTMEG SAUCE

Mix together 1 cup sugar and 1 tablespoon flour. Stir in 1 cup boiling water and cook, stirring constantly, until sauce bubbles and thickens slightly. Add 1 tablespoon butter and simmer gently for 5 minutes. Remove from heat and stir in 1 teaspoon nutmeg. Serve hot.

HARD SAUCE

Cream ⅓ cup of butter until soft. Add, a little at a time, 1 cup confectioners' sugar and either 1 teaspoon of vanilla or 2 tablespoons cognac or rum, stirring until smooth. Serve cold with steamed puddings or on apple pie.

BRANDY SAUCE

½ cup milk	2 tablespoons sugar
½ cup heavy cream	Dash of salt
2 eggs, separated	3 tablespoons brandy

Scald milk and cream together in the top of a double boiler. Beat egg yolks until light in color, then beat in sugar, a little at a time, and salt. Add milk-cream mixture gradually, beating constantly. Pour back into double boiler and cook over boiling water until sauce thickens enough to coat a wooden spoon. Remove from heat, stir in brandy, then pour over stiffly beaten egg whites, beating vigorously. Cool before serving.

SAUCE MELBA

1 cup raspberries (fresh or frozen)	1 tablespoon cornstarch
½ cup sugar	1 tablespoon water
½ cup currant jelly	Slivered almonds

If fresh berries are used, wash and drain; if frozen, thaw. Place berries and sugar in a saucepan, mash with a fork, add the currant jelly, and cook over a low heat until mixture begins to bubble. Combine cornstarch with water to make a smooth paste. Stir into berries and cook until clear and slightly thickened. Strain and cool. Spoon over ice cream and strew with toasted slivered almonds.

To make Peach Melba: Cut peaches in half, and fill each half with vanilla ice cream. Spoon some of the sauce over them.

PIES

PASTRY FOR PIE CRUST

2 cups all-purpose flour	⅔ cup shortening
1 teaspoon salt	5 to 6 tablespoons ice water

Sift flour and salt together in a bowl. Cut in shortening with a pastry blender or two knives until mixture looks mealy. Sprinkle water over mixture (the less water you use, the better your pastry). Mix lightly with a fork, then work the pastry with your hands until it can be formed into a ball. Chill thoroughly. Divide in half and roll one portion at a time on a lightly floured board. Using light strokes, start in the center and roll toward the edge. When dough is about ⅛ inch thick, line a 9-inch pie pan, pressing pastry to bottom and sides. Refrigerate both parts while you prepare the filling.

To make pastry for a 1-crust pie: Follow directions given above, cutting the ingredients in half. To prepare a baked pastry shell, line a 9-inch pie pan with the pastry and bake in a preheated 450° oven for 12 to 15 minutes.

LEMON MERINGUE PIE

Pastry for a 1-crust pie (above)	1 tablespoon butter
1 cup sugar	Grated rind of 1 lemon
Dash of salt	¼ cup lemon juice
¼ cup flour	*Meringue:*
3 tablespoons cornstarch	3 egg whites
2 cups water	¼ teaspoon cream of tartar
3 egg yolks, beaten	6 tablespoons sugar

Prepare pastry, line a 9-inch pie pan, and bake in a preheated 450° oven for 12 to 15 minutes. Cool. Mix sugar, salt, flour, and cornstarch in a saucepan, stir in water, a little at a time, and cook over a low heat, stirring constantly, until mixture is thick and bubbly. Stir a little into egg yolks, very gradually, continuing to beat hard. Combine with the hot mixture and cook over a very low heat for about 2 minutes. Remove from heat and stir in butter, lemon rind, and juice. Cool for about 10 minutes, then pour into baked pastry shell, and cool completely. Pile the meringue on the cool lemon filling, spreading it until it touches rim of pastry all around the edge. Bake in a preheated 425° oven for 5 to 7 minutes or until top is lightly browned.

To make meringue: Beat egg whites until frothy, then add cream of tartar, and continue beating until whites hold a soft shape. Beat in the sugar, a little at a time, beating vigorously until meringue is satiny and stiff enough to stand in peaks.

KEY LIME PIE

Condensed milk was first manufactured in 1858, and after the Civil War it was a godsend to the devastated South. In Key West, Florida, it was not only a sorely needed food but the inspiration for this famous pie recipe.

Pastry for a 1-crust pie (page 580)
3 eggs, separated
1 can condensed milk

¾ cup fresh lime juice
6 tablespoons sugar

Line a 9-inch pie pan with pastry. Bake in a preheated 450° oven for 12 to 15 minutes, then cool. Beat egg yolks and condensed milk together, then beat in lime juice until smooth. Pour this uncooked filling into baked pie shell. Beat egg whites until they hold a shape, then beat in sugar, a little at a time, until meringue stands in peaks. Spoon meringue over top of filling, spreading it to the edge of the pastry all around. Bake in a preheated 425° oven for 5 to 7 minutes or until meringue is touched with gold. Cool before serving. Do not refrigerate. Some people prefer whipped cream to the meringue, in which case the pie should not be baked.

PEACH CRAB LANTERN

A writer in 1801 stated: "Had some peaches stewed in order to make Crab Lanterns for dinner." Crab Lanterns was the common name for fried peach pies, shaped like half-moons.

3 fresh peaches
½ cup sugar
½ cup water
½ teaspoon ground cinnamon
1 cup sifted all-purpose flour
2 tablespoons sugar
2 teaspoons baking powder

¼ teaspoon salt
¼ cup butter
1 egg yolk
3 tablespoons milk (about)
Fat for deep-fat frying
Confectioners' sugar

Skin peaches (skin will slip off easily if you let peaches stand in boiling water a few minutes), remove pits, and cut in slices about ½ inch thick. Cook sugar and water together for several minutes, then add peach slices and cinnamon. Continue cooking about 2 minutes, shaking the pan back and forth almost constantly. Remove from heat and cool. Sift together flour, sugar, baking powder, and salt into a bowl. Cut in butter with a pastry blender or two knives. Mix egg yolk and milk together, then stir into flour combination with a fork, adding only enough liquid to hold the dough together. Turn out on a floured board, divide in half, and roll, one portion at a time, about as thick as pie pastry. Cut into circles the size of a large coffee cup. Drain peach slices and place several slices on half the circle. Fold over the other half; then, with fork tines, seal edges and prick tops. Refrigerate. Heat fat to 350° on deep-fat thermometer or until a 1-inch cube of bread browns in 60 seconds. Fry the pies until they are a light, tempting brown. Drain on paper towels and sprinkle with confectioners' sugar. Applesauce (page 557), Mincemeat (page 585), Prune Filling (see Kolaches, page 439), stewed fruits, or preserves may be substituted for the peach filling. Makes 12.

APPLE PIE

An immigrant living in Beloit, Wisconsin, wrote on November 29, 1851, to friends back in Norway: "Strawberries, raspberries, and blackberries thrive here. From these they make a wonderful dish combined with syrup and sugar, which is called *pai*. I can tell you that is something that glides easily down your throat; they also make the same sort of *pai* out of apples or finely ground meat, with syrup added, and that is really the most superb." A hundred years earlier, in 1758, a Swedish parson named Dr. Acrelius had written home: "Apple-pie is used through the whole year, and when fresh apples are no longer to be had, dried ones are used. It is the evening meal of children. House-pie, in country places, is made of apples neither peeled nor freed from their cores, and its crust is not broken if a wagon wheel goes over it."

Apple Pie is what some things are as American as, and it has, in various forms, been eaten for breakfast, for an entree, and for dessert. Some of the first orchards in New England were planted by William Blaxton, a clergyman who owned, for a time, a farm on Beacon Hill. He moved to Rhode Island in 1635 and raised what is now called the Sweet Rhode Island greening—the first apple, as a distinct type, to be grown in the United States.

Pastry for a 2-crust pie (page 580)	½ teaspoon cinnamon (optional)
4 large greenings (peeled, cored, and sliced very thin)	Grated rind of ½ lemon
	1 tablespoon lemon juice
1 cup sugar	Butter
¼ teaspoon salt	Cream

Prepare the pastry. Divide in half, line a 9-inch pie pan with one portion, and save the remainder for the top. Refrigerate both while you make the filling. Measure the sliced apples. You should have about 4 cups. Mix apple slices with sugar, salt, cinnamon (if you use it), lemon rind, and lemon juice. Arrange a row inside chilled pastry shell, about one-half inch from edge, and work toward center until shell is covered. Pile remaining slices on top. Dot with butter and cover with top crust, slashed in several places. Seal edges securely and crimp. Bake in a preheated 450° oven for 10 minutes. Reduce heat to 350° and bake 30 to 35 minutes. Five minutes before pie has finished baking, brush top with cream and sprinkle generously with sugar. Serve warm or at room temperature with Cheddar cheese or ice cream.

MARLBOROUGH TART

Pastry for a 1-crust pie (page 580)	Grated rind and juice of 1 lemon
½ cup Applesauce (page 557)	¼ cup sherry
½ cup sugar	3 eggs, well beaten
⅔ cup light cream	

Line a 9-inch pie pan with pastry. Refrigerate while you make the filling. Combine applesauce with sugar, cream, lemon rind, lemon juice, and sherry. Stir in the well-beaten eggs and pour into chilled pastry shell. Bake in a preheated 400° oven for 10 minutes. Reduce oven heat to 325° and bake 45 minutes. The filling will not become firm until the pie cools.

APPLE PIE WITH CHEDDAR PASTRY

But I, when I undress me
Each night, upon my knees
Will ask the Lord to bless me
With apple-pie and cheese.
—Eugene Field, "Apple-Pie and Cheese"

1⅔ cups sifted all-purpose flour
¼ teaspoon salt
1 cup grated Cheddar cheese,
  loosely packed

½ cup shortening
¼ cup ice water
Filling for Apple Pie (page 582)

Sift flour and salt together, then work in the cheese thoroughly with a fork. Work in the shortening, then add the water, sprinkling it over the surface of the mixture. Stir lightly with a fork until pastry holds together. Divide pastry in half and line a 9-inch pie pan with one portion, saving the other for the top crust. Refrigerate both while you make the Apple Pie filling. Bake as directed for Apple Pie.

MARK TWAIN'S MUSH APPLE PIE

Pour cold Applesauce (page 557) into an unbaked 9-inch pastry shell (page 580), cover with thinly rolled pastry slashed in several places, seal edges securely, and crimp neatly. Bake in a preheated 450° oven for 20 minutes. Then reduce heat to 375° and bake 25 minutes or until crust is nicely browned. Serve warm with, if you wish, whipped or sweet cream.

COCONUT CUSTARD PIE

Pastry for a 1-crust pie (page 580)
Filling:
3 cups milk
1 cup sugar
4 tablespoons cornstarch
4 egg yolks
¼ cup butter
1½ cups grated coconut (fresh or canned)

1½ teaspoons vanilla
Meringue:
4 egg whites
½ teaspoon salt
¼ cup sugar
½ teaspoon vanilla
½ cup grated coconut (fresh or canned)

Line a 9-inch pie pan with pastry and bake in a preheated 450° oven 12 to 15 minutes. Pour coconut filling into chilled pastry shell. Cover with swirls of meringue and sprinkle ½ cup grated coconut on top. Bake in a preheated 425° oven for 5 to 6 minutes or until meringue is lightly browned.

To make the filling: Scald milk. Blend sugar and cornstarch together in the top of a double boiler. Pour in hot milk, a little at a time, and stir until smooth. Beat egg yolks in a bowl, then add the milk mixture, a little at a time. Pour back into top of double boiler and cook over boiling water, stirring constantly, until as thick as mayonnaise. Remove from heat and stir in butter, coconut, and vanilla. Cool.

To make meringue: Beat egg whites and salt together until they hold a soft shape. Beat in sugar, a little at a time, until meringue is smooth and stands in peaks. Stir in vanilla.

RHUBARB PIE

Setting forth her recipe for Rhubarb Pie in *The American Frugal Housewife,* Lydia Child cautioned: "These are dear pies, for they take an enormous quantity of sugar."

Pastry for a 2-crust pie (page 580)
3 cups sliced rhubarb
1½ cups sugar
2 tablespoons flour

¼ teaspoon salt
1 tablespoon lemon juice
2 egg yolks

Line a 9-inch pie pan with half the pastry. Save remaining pastry for top crust. Chill both while you prepare the filling. Cut rhubarb in slices about ½ inch thick and place in pie shell. Make a smooth paste of sugar, flour, salt, lemon juice, and slightly beaten egg yolks. Spoon on top of rhubarb and cover with top crust, slashed in several places. Bake in a preheated 400° oven for 20 minutes. Reduce heat to 350° and continue baking about 20 minutes or until pastry takes on a rich gold color. In some sections of the country rhubarb is known as pie plant.

PUMPKIN PIE

"Pumpkin pie," according to *The House Mother,* "if rightly made, is a thing of beauty and a joy—while it lasts.... Pies that cut a little less firm than a pine board, and those that run round your plate are alike to be avoided. Two inches deep is better than the thin plasters one sometimes sees, that look for all the world like pumpkin flap-jacks. The expressive phrase, 'too thin', must have come from these lean parodies on pumpkin pie. With the pastry light, tender, and not too rich, and a generous filling of smooth spiced sweetness—a little 'trembly' as to consistency, and delicately brown on top—a perfect pumpkin pie, eaten before the life has gone out of it, is one of the real additions made by American cookery to the good things of the world. For the first pumpkin pie of the season, flanked by a liberal cut of creamy cheese, we prefer to sit down, as the French gourmand said about his turkey: 'with just two of us; myself and the turkey!'"

Pastry for a 1-crust pie (page 580)
2 cups cooked pumpkin (fresh, canned,
    or frozen)
⅔ cup brown sugar, firmly packed
2 teaspoons cinnamon
½ teaspoon ginger

½ teaspoon salt
¾ cup milk
2 eggs, well beaten
1 cup heavy cream
¼ cup brandy

Prepare pastry, line a 9-inch pie pan, and refrigerate while you make the filling. Combine pumpkin, sugar, spices, and salt in a mixing bowl. Then beat in milk, eggs, cream, and brandy with a rotary beater or an electric mixer. Pour into unbaked pastry shell and bake in a preheated 325° oven for 1 hour or until a knife inserted in center comes out dry. Cool. Serve plain, or with Cheddar cheese or whipped cream mixed with ginger (use 1 cup heavy cream and 2 tablespoons chopped crystallized ginger).

SUNNYSIDE MINCEMEAT PIE

This recipe is from the cookbook of Catherine Richardson, the daughter of Marion McLinden, who was in charge of the family kitchen at Sunnyside, Washington Irving's New York home.

2 pounds lean beef, ground
1 pound suet, ground
2 pounds sugar
5 pounds tart apples (pared, cored, and chopped)
2 pounds muscat raisins
1 pound currants
1 pound sultana raisins
½ pound citron, chopped

½ pound orange peel, chopped
1 tablespoon salt
1 teaspoon cinnamon
1 teaspoon allspice
1 teaspoon mace
1 quart boiled cider (about)
Brandy
Pastry for a 2-crust pie (page 580)

Mix beef, suet, sugar, fruit, salt, spices, and cider in a large kettle. Cover and simmer, stirring frequently, for 2 hours. Add cider if needed. Stir in brandy to taste. Pack into sterilized 1-quart jars, seal securely, store in a cool place, and allow to mellow at least 1 month before using. Makes 5 jars.

To make the pie: Line a 9-inch pie pan with pastry. Spoon in enough mincemeat to fill the pan and cover with remaining pastry, rolled thin. Seal securely and slash top in several places so steam can escape. Bake in a preheated 450° oven for 30 minutes. Serve warm.

SHOO-FLY PIE

There are many types of Pennsylvania Dutch Shoo-fly Pie. Those who dunk prefer a dry version like the recipe here. Others prefer what is called wet-bottom Shoo-fly. All varieties contain molasses, and the presence of molasses is responsible for one widely held theory about the way Shoo-fly Pie was named—that flies are partial to molasses and have to be chased away while the cook is making the pie.

Pastry for a 1-crust pie (page 580)
Crumb mixture:
1½ cups all-purpose flour
½ cup brown sugar, firmly packed
Pinch of salt
½ teaspoon cinnamon
Big pinch each ginger and nutmeg
¼ cup soft butter

Filling:
½ teaspoon baking soda
½ cup molasses
½ cup boiling water
⅔ of crumb mixture

Line an 8-inch pie pan with pastry. Refrigerate while you prepare the crumb mixture and filling. Combine flour with brown sugar, salt, and spices. Pinch in the butter until the mixture looks mealy. Set aside. Stir baking soda and molasses into boiling water. Add two-thirds of the crumb mixture and pour into the unbaked pie shell. Sprinkle top with remaining crumbs and bake in a preheated 375° oven for 30 to 40 minutes or until crust and crumbs are golden brown.

585

CHERRY PIE

Pastry for a 2-crust pie (page 580)
4 cups tart red cherries
2⅔ tablespoons quick-cooking tapioca
1¼ cups sugar

1 tablespoon lemon juice
¼ teaspoon almond extract
1½ tablespoons butter

Prepare pastry and line a 9-inch pie pan. Save remaining pastry for top and refrigerate both while you make the filling. Pit cherries and toss thoroughly with tapioca, sugar, lemon juice, and almond extract. Let stand about 10 minutes, then pour into unbaked pie shell, and dot with butter. Cover with top crust (or make a lattice top) and seal edges. Bake in a preheated 450° oven for 10 minutes. Reduce heat to 350° and continue baking 40 to 45 minutes.

To keepe Cherries yt [so that] you may have them for tarts at Christmas without Preserving: Take ye fayrest cherries you can get, fresh from ye trees, wth out bruising, wipe them one by one with a linnen cloth, yn [then] put ym [them] into a barrel of hay & lay them in ranks, first laying hay on the bottom, & then cherries & yn hay & yn cherries & then hay agayne, stop them close up yt noe ayre get to ym. then set them under a fether bead where one layeth continually for ye warmer they are kept ye better it is soe they be neere no fire. Thus doeing you may have cherries any time of ye yeare. You allsoe May keep Cherries or other fruits, in glasses close stopt from ayre.

—From Martha Washington's cookbook,
Collection of the Historical Society of Pennsylvania

VINEGAR PIE

Pastry for 1-crust pie (page 580)
¼ cup flour
½ teaspoon nutmeg
½ teaspoon cinnamon
½ teaspoon allspice
½ teaspoon cloves
Dash of salt
4 egg yolks

2 egg whites
1 cup sugar
1 cup commercial sour cream
3 tablespoons melted butter
3 tablespoons cider vinegar
1 cup coarsely chopped walnuts or pecans
1 cup raisins

Prepare pastry and line a 9-inch pie pan. Chill while you make the filling. Sift together flour, spices, and salt. Set aside. Beat egg yolks thoroughly. Wash and dry the beater, then beat the 2 whites until they stand in peaks. Gently fold sugar into egg whites and stir into yolks. Add flour mixture alternately with the sour cream. Combine butter, vinegar, nuts, and raisins and stir into the filling. Pour into pie shell and bake in a preheated 450° oven for 10 minutes. Reduce heat to 400° and bake 5 minutes. Then turn heat to 350°, and continue baking for about 15 minutes or until filling is set. Cool. May be served with whipped cream.

CHESS TARTS

Pastry for a 2-crust pie (page 580)
3 eggs
¾ cup sugar

Pinch of salt
2 tablespoons melted butter
Grated rind and juice of 1 lemon

Line 12 small fluted tart shells with pastry. Refrigerate while you make the filling. Beat the eggs vigorously, then add sugar and salt, beating until smooth. Stir in the butter, lemon rind, and juice. Spoon into chilled tart shells (fill them almost to the top of the pastry) and bake in a preheated 350° oven for 30 to 35 minutes or until tops are a pale gold color. Remove from oven and cool. The filling will sink slightly when tarts are completely cold.

BLACKBERRY PIE

Blackberries are cultivated in no other part of the world and, indeed, were not thought worth cultivating in this country until the 1830's. To the pioneers, blackberries were a nuisance, a weed spoken of in polite conversation only in terms of how it might best be removed. It crept hesitantly into the early cookbooks, frequently as a fruit for medicinal purposes ("Blackberry Syrup, for Cholera and Summer Complaint"). It was listed, however, as an alternate fruit to be used in some recipes, and gradually the weed became quite popular.

Pastry for a 2-crust pie (page 580)
4 cups fresh blackberries
3 tablespoons flour

1 tablespoon lemon juice
1 tablespoon butter

Line a 9-inch pie pan with half the pastry. Save remaining pastry for top crust. Chill both while preparing the blackberries. Combine berries with flour and lemon juice. Spoon into pie shell and dot with butter. Cover with top crust slashed in several places. Bake in a preheated 450° oven for 15 minutes. Reduce heat to 350° and bake 35 to 40 minutes or until browned.

DEEP-DISH BLUEBERRY PIE

1 quart blueberries
1 cup sugar
3 tablespoons flour
1 tablespoon lemon juice

2 tablespoons butter
Pastry for a 1-crust pie (page 580) or
Cream Biscuit dough (page 443)

In a deep pie dish, about 8 inches in diameter, toss berries with sugar and flour. Sprinkle with lemon juice and dot with butter. Cover with pastry or Cream Biscuit dough. Bake in a preheated 400° oven for 10 minutes, then reduce heat to 325°, and continue baking 15 to 20 minutes. Serve warm—either plain, with cream, or with vanilla ice cream.

SOUR CREAM RAISIN PIE

Pastry for a 1-crust pie (page 580)
2 eggs
¾ cup sugar
¼ teaspoon salt
1 teaspoon cinnamon

½ teaspoon nutmeg
¼ teaspoon cloves
1 cup commercial sour cream
1 cup seeded raisins

Prepare pastry and line an 8-inch pie pan. Refrigerate it while you make the filling. Beat eggs lightly, then stir in sugar, salt, cinnamon, nutmeg, and cloves. Stir in sour cream and raisins and pour into chilled pastry shell. Bake in a preheated 450° oven for 10 minutes, then reduce heat to 350°, and bake 30 minutes longer or until a knife inserted in center comes out dry. Serve warm.

CRANBERRY PIE

"I said my prayers and ate some cranberry tart for breakfast."
—From the diary of William Byrd, 1711

Pastry for a 2-crust pie (page 580)
3 cups fresh cranberries
1 cup raisins
2 tablespoons flour

1¼ cups sugar
½ cup water
1 teaspoon vanilla

Prepare pastry and line a 9-inch pie pan. Save remaining pastry for the top. Refrigerate both while you make the filling. Chop cranberries coarsely. Combine with raisins and all remaining ingredients. Place in chilled pie shell, cover with top crust (slashed in several places) and crimp edges together securely. Bake in a preheated 450° oven for 10 minutes. Then reduce oven temperature to 350° and continue baking a half hour longer. Cool before serving.

PECAN PIE

Pastry for a 1-crust pie (page 580)
3 eggs
¼ teaspoon salt
¾ cup sugar

½ cup melted butter
1 cup dark corn syrup
1½ cups pecan halves (about)

Prepare pastry, line a 9-inch pie pan, and bake in a preheated 450° oven for 5 minutes. Cool. Beat eggs and salt until very light and lemon colored. Beat in sugar a little at a time. With a wire whisk, fold in melted butter and syrup. Pour into partially baked shell and arrange pecan halves on top, broken side down. Bake for 10 minutes in a preheated 425° oven, reduce heat to 325°, and bake for 30 minutes. Serves 6 to 8. This pie can be baked in small fluted foil pans to make 8 to 10 individual pies. Reduce baking time slightly (bake until crust is golden).

SWEET POTATO PIE

Pastry for a 1-crust pie (page 580)
1¼ cups cooked, mashed sweet potatoes
½ cup brown sugar, firmly packed
½ teaspoon salt
¼ teaspoon cinnamon

2 eggs, well beaten
¾ cup milk
1 tablespoon melted butter
Pecan halves (optional)

Prepare pastry and line an 8-inch pie pan. Chill while you make the filling. Combine sweet potatoes, brown sugar, salt, and cinnamon in a bowl. Mix together eggs, milk, and butter and stir into sweet-potato mixture thoroughly. Pour into chilled pastry shell and arrange a circle of pecans around the edge. Bake in a preheated 400° oven for 45 minutes or until a knife comes out dry when inserted in the center.

CONCORD GRAPE TART

The grape has been the subject of more horticultural experiments than any other fruit in America: more than two thousand varieties had been introduced to America by the end of the nineteenth century. Possibly the most famous and most valuable of all varieties was the Concord grape, first planted in Concord, Massachusetts, by Ephraim W. Bull in 1849. In the century following its introduction, more Concord grapes were sold in the United States than all other species combined.

2 cups sifted all-purpose flour
½ teaspoon salt
¼ teaspoon baking powder
1 cup sugar
½ cup (1 stick) butter

4 cups Concord grapes
3 tablespoons flour
1 tablespoon lemon juice
2 egg yolks
1 cup commercial sour cream

Sift together flour, salt, baking powder, and *2 tablespoons of the sugar*. Pinch in butter with your finger tips until it appears mealy. Lift into an 8-inch square baking pan and press an even layer on bottom and about two-thirds of the way up the sides. Refrigerate until filling is prepared. Pinch off grape skins, separating pulp from skins. Cook pulp over a low heat for 7 minutes. Remove from heat and work thoroughly through a sieve (this is an easy way to remove the seeds). Combine pulp purée with grape skins, flour, remaining sugar, and lemon juice. Pour into prepared pastry and bake in a preheated 400° oven for 15 minutes. Mix egg yolks and sour cream together, then pour over the surface, and continue baking 25 to 30 minutes. Serve at room temperature. Serves 6.

OLD-FASHIONED SEEDCAKE

2 cups sifted all-purpose flour
¼ teaspoon salt
¼ teaspoon nutmeg
1 cup (2 sticks) butter
1 cup sugar

2 teaspoons caraway seeds
6 eggs, separated
2 tablespoons brandy
Caraway comfits (sugared caraway seeds) or
    lump sugar, crushed

Sift together the flour, salt, and nutmeg. Set aside. Work butter until creamy, then gradually work in the sugar until mixture looks and feels fluffy. Stir in caraway seeds and beat in egg yolks, one at a time, beating hard after each addition. Add flour and brandy, alternately, and fold in the stiffly beaten egg whites, gently but thoroughly. Spoon batter into a greased and lightly floured 9-inch tube pan. Sprinkle caraway comfits or coarsely crushed lump sugar on top. Bake in a preheated 350° oven for 1 hour or until cake pulls away from sides of pan. Cool in pan about 10 minutes, then turn out onto cake rack, and cool completely. A day or two of mellowing, with the cake tightly wrapped, develops the delicious caraway flavor.

HONEY UPSIDE DOWN CAKE

Topping:
½ cup honey
¼ cup butter
4 to 5 cooking apples
Maraschino cherries
Cake batter:
1½ cups sifted all-purpose flour
1 teaspoon baking powder
¼ teaspoon baking soda
¼ teaspoon cinnamon

½ teaspoon nutmeg
Dash ginger
½ cup (1 stick) soft butter
¾ cup honey
1 egg
½ cup milk
Sauce:
½ cup honey
½ cup (1 stick) butter

To make the topping: Put honey and butter in a heavy 10-inch skillet (one that can go into the oven). Cook over a low heat until butter has melted. Core unpared apples and slice about ½ inch thick. Arrange enough of these slices in the honey mixture to fit comfortably. Simmer gently, turning once, until apples are partly cooked. Put a cherry in the center of each apple ring. Set aside for a moment.

To make the batter: Sift flour with baking powder, baking soda, cinnamon, nutmeg, and ginger. Set aside. Beat butter and honey together vigorously. Add the egg and beat thoroughly. Stir in flour mixture and milk alternately. Pour over apple rings and bake in a preheated 350° oven for 40 to 45 minutes or until a toothpick inserted in the center comes out dry. Turn upside down on a large platter and serve hot or cold with the sauce on the side.

To make the sauce: Combine honey with butter and heat until butter has melted. Do not boil.

KENTUCKY BOURBON CAKE

¾ pound (3 sticks) butter
2 cups white sugar
2¼ cups light brown sugar, firmly packed
6 eggs
5½ cups sifted all-purpose flour

¼ teaspoon salt
1 teaspoon mace
2 cups bourbon whiskey
3½ cups (1 pound) pecan meats

Cream butter until soft in your largest mixing bowl. Combine white and brown sugar thoroughly. Gradually work half the sugar mixture into butter, keeping it as smooth as possible. In a separate bowl beat eggs until light and fluffy. Then gradually beat in remaining sugar until you have a smooth, creamy mixture. Stir into butter mixture thoroughly. Sift flour, salt, and mace together. Add flour combination and whiskey to batter, alternating them and beginning and ending with flour. Break pecans into pieces and stir into batter. Pour into a well-greased 10-inch tube pan (batter should almost fill the pan) and bake in a preheated 300° oven for 1½ to 1¾ hours or until cake shrinks slightly from pan. Allow cake to cool in the pan about 15 minutes, then turn out onto cake rack, and cool completely. Bourbon Cake improves with age. It should be well-wrapped in foil and stored in the refrigerator. Do not freeze.

THE QUEEN OF ALL CAKES

This recipe is adapted from *Practical Housekeeping*, where it is called Ice-Cream Cake. The filling is made, the author explains, from thick sweet cream, beaten "until it looks like ice-cream." This elegant deception, the reader is instructed, "is the queen of all cakes."

½ cup sifted cake flour
¼ teaspoon salt
3 eggs, separated
1 teaspoon cider vinegar
½ cup sugar
¼ teaspoon almond extract

Filling:
1 can (3½ ounces) blanched almonds
¾ cup heavy cream
¼ cup sugar
½ teaspoon vanilla

Grease a jelly-roll pan, line with wax paper, and grease the wax paper. Sift flour and salt together and set aside. Beat egg yolks with an electric beater for 10 minutes. Wash the blades of the beater, then beat egg whites until frothy. Add vinegar and beat in the ½ cup sugar, a little at a time, until it becomes a satiny mixture that stands in peaks. Stir in almond extract, then fold into yolks gently. Sift flour over the surface and fold in until batter is well blended. Pour into pan and bake in a preheated 350° oven for 12 to 15 minutes or until cake begins to pull away from the sides of the pan. Do not overbake. Invert on a tea towel sprinkled lightly with confectioners' sugar and carefully pull off wax paper. Beginning with the broad side of the cake, roll it up. Keep towel around the cake as it cools, to hold the shape.

To make the filling: Chop almonds coarsely and toast in a 350° oven until golden. Beat cream until stiff, then stir in sugar, vanilla, and almonds. Unroll the cooled cake, spread the cream filling over the surface, and reroll. Chill before serving, then cut into slices.

VARIATION: To make an old-fashioned Jelly Roll, substitute jelly for cream filling.

GENERAL ROBERT E. LEE CAKE

This recipe is adapted from one used by Mrs. Robert E. Lee. The Lee
Cake was especially popular in the nineteenth century, when a number
of variations on the original recipe were published in cookbooks.

2 cups sifted all-purpose flour
½ teaspoon cream of tartar
1½ teaspoons baking powder
8 eggs, separated

2 cups sugar
Grated rind and juice of 1 lemon
Dash of salt

To make the cake: Grease and flour four 9-inch cake pans. Sift together flour, cream of
tartar, and baking powder four times. Beat egg yolks with a rotary or electric beater until
very thick, light, and creamy. Add the sugar, a few tablespoons at a time, and continue
beating until mixture is smooth and pale yellow. (This is a spongecake, essentially, so
thorough beating is imperative.) Stir in lemon rind and lemon juice. Beat egg whites and
salt until they stand in peaks. Fold into egg-yolk mixture alternately with the flour until
well mixed. Spoon into cake pans and bake in a preheated 325° oven 20 to 25 minutes or
until cake begins to pull away from sides of pans. Loosen edges with a knife and turn out on
cake racks to cool while you prepare the filling and frosting.

Lemon Jelly Filling:
6 egg yolks
2 cups sugar

Grated rind of 2 lemons
Juice of 4 lemons
½ cup butter

To make the filling: Mix egg yolks with sugar, lemon rind, and lemon juice and cook over
boiling water, stirring constantly, until sugar dissolves. Add butter and continue cooking,
stirring constantly, for 20 minutes or until filling is smooth and very thick. Cool, then
spread between layers of cooled cake.

Lemon-Orange Frosting:
¼ cup butter
6 cups confectioners' sugar, sifted
1 egg yolk

2 tablespoons lemon juice
3 to 4 tablespoons orange juice
Grated rind of 1 lemon
Grated rind of 2 oranges

To make the frosting: Beat or work butter until it has the appearance of thick cream, stir
in confectioners' sugar, a little at a time, and continue working until mixture is very smooth.
Beat in egg yolk and lemon juice. Stir in enough orange juice to make a spreadable frosting,
then add grated lemon and orange rinds. Spread on sides and top of cake.

GLAZED COCONUT CAKE

1¾ cups sifted all-purpose flour
¼ teaspoon salt
2½ teaspoons baking powder
½ cup (1 stick) butter
1 cup sugar
2 eggs
⅔ cup milk

1 teaspoon almond extract

Glaze:
6 tablespoons melted butter
6 tablespoons brown sugar
3 tablespoons heavy cream
½ cup grated or flaked coconut

Sift together flour, salt, and baking powder. Set aside. Cream butter until soft, add sugar, a little at a time, beating until smooth. Add eggs, one at a time, beating hard after each addition. Add milk and flour mixture, alternating them and beginning and ending with flour. Stir in almond extract and pour into an 8-inch square cake pan. Bake in a 350° oven for 45 minutes or until cake pulls away slightly from sides of pan. Turn out of pan and spread, while still warm, with glazed coconut.

To make the glaze: Mix together melted butter, brown sugar, heavy cream, and grated or flaked coconut. Spread on top of cake and place about 4 inches from broiling unit for several minutes or until nicely browned. Watch carefully because it takes only 3 to 4 minutes for the glaze to turn the right color.

HARTFORD ELECTION CAKE

A recipe for Election Cake—one of the first foods to be identified with American politics—was published as early as 1800 in Amelia Simmons' *American Cookery*. The cake was served at election time and, in the 1830's, this recipe became popularly known as Hartford Election Cake.

1 medium-sized potato	½ package active dry yeast or
1 cup milk	½ cake compressed
1 teaspoon salt	1 egg, well beaten
1½ tablespoons sugar	3½ to 4 cups sifted all-purpose flour
2 tablespoons shortening	

Cook potato in boiling water until tender. Drain, peel, and work through a sieve or ricer, then set aside. Scald milk. Pour into a large bowl and stir in salt, sugar, shortening, and potato. When lukewarm, stir in yeast until dissolved. Add egg, then flour, a little at a time, to make a soft but still manageable dough. Turn out on a floured board and knead until smooth and elastic. Place in a greased bowl, brush with a little melted butter, cover with a tea towel, and put in a warm spot to rise. Let rise until a little more than double in size.

Ingredients for second step:	1 teaspoon ground cinnamon
¾ cup (1½ sticks) softened butter	¼ teaspoon ground cloves
1 egg	¼ teaspoon ground allspice
1¼ cups light brown sugar, firmly packed	¼ teaspoon ground mace
½ cup sherry	¼ teaspoon grated nutmeg
1 cup seedless raisins, chopped	1 teaspoon salt
1 cup sifted all-purpose flour	Milk Frosting (page 606)

When yeast dough has risen sufficiently, push down the dough with your fist and work in butter thoroughly. Then, using your hand as the mixer, stir in the egg, sugar, sherry, raisins (toss them, first, in 2 tablespoons of the flour), and remaining flour sifted with the spices and salt. Pour into a large greased Turk's-head or *gugelhupf* mold or a 10-inch tube pan, filling pan only two-thirds full. Cover with a tea towel and let rise about 1 to 1½ hours in a warm place. Bake in a preheated 325° oven for 50 to 60 minutes. Cool about 10 minutes, then turn out of the pan, and cool completely before frosting.

LINGONBERRY TORTE

4 squares (4 ounces) unsweetened chocolate
1 cup milk
1 cup flour
½ teaspoon salt
2½ teaspoons baking powder
4 eggs, plus 1 egg yolk

1½ cups sugar
2 teaspoons almond extract
Lingonberry jam (if unavailable, substitute currant or whole cherry preserves)
Butter Cream Frosting, coffee variation (page 606)

Combine chocolate and milk in the top of a double boiler. Cook over hot water until chocolate melts. Stir frequently. Cool. Sift flour, salt, and baking powder together and set aside. Beat the eggs and additional egg yolk with a rotary or electric mixer until light and thick. Add sugar gradually and continue beating hard until mixture is very smooth (hard beating at this point is imperative). Stir in almond extract, then the chocolate-milk mixture. Sift flour mixture on top and fold in gently but thoroughly. Pour batter into 2 greased 9-inch cake pans and bake in a preheated 350° oven for 10 minutes. Reduce heat to 325° and continue baking 25 to 30 minutes longer or until a toothpick inserted in the center comes out dry. Cool several minutes, then invert on a cake rack to cool completely. Spread lingonberry jam between layers. Frost the top with Butter Cream Frosting, coffee variation.

MOTHER ANN'S BIRTHDAY CAKE

Ann Lee, founder of the Shakers, was born on February 29, 1736. To commemorate her birthday, each year on March 1 the Shakers held an afternoon meeting, followed by a supper at which this cake was served. The original recipe advises, "Cut a handful of peach twigs which are filled with sap at this season of the year. Clip the ends and bruise them and beat the cake batter with them. This will impart a delicate peach flavor to the cake."

3 cups sifted all-purpose flour
½ cup cornstarch
1 tablespoon baking powder
1 teaspoon salt
1 cup (2 sticks) butter
2 cups sugar

1 cup milk
2 teaspoons vanilla
12 egg whites
Peach jam
Butter Cream Frosting (page 606) or White Mountain Frosting (page 607)

Sift together flour, cornstarch, baking powder, and salt. Set aside. Cream butter until soft, then add sugar, a little at a time, and continue working until mixture is as smooth as possible. Add flour combination and milk alternately, beginning and ending with flour. Stir in vanilla, then fold in stiffly beaten egg whites very gently and thoroughly. Pour into 3 well-greased and lightly floured 9-inch cake pans. Bake in a preheated 350° oven for 25 to 30 minutes or until cake pulls away from sides of pan. Let stand several minutes before turning out onto cake racks. When cold, spread peach jam between layers and frost sides and top.

LEMON CHEESECAKE

2 tablespoons butter
¾ cup zwieback crumbs
¼ cup confectioners' sugar
4 eggs
1 cup granulated sugar
¼ cup all-purpose flour

¼ teaspoon salt
1 teaspoon grated lemon rind
3 tablespoons lemon juice
½ teaspoon vanilla
2 cups well-drained cottage cheese
1 cup heavy cream

Grease bottom and sides of an 8-inch spring-form pan with the butter. Blend zwieback crumbs and confectioners' sugar together, reserving 2 tablespoonfuls for the top of the cake. Sprinkle remaining crumb mixture on bottom and around sides of pan. Beat together eggs, granulated sugar, and flour thoroughly. Stir in salt, lemon rind, lemon juice, and vanilla. Mix in cottage cheese and heavy cream thoroughly. Pour into the crumb-lined pan, sprinkle with remaining crumb mixture, and bake in a preheated 325° oven for 1 hour. Cool in the pan, then chill. Makes 6 to 8 servings.

BURNT SUGAR CAKE

Caramel syrup:
½ cup sugar
½ cup boiling water
Batter:
2¼ cups sifted all-purpose flour
2½ teaspoons baking powder
Pinch salt
½ cup (1 stick) butter
1½ cups sugar
3 eggs, separated

4 tablespoons caramel syrup
1 cup milk
Frosting:
1½ cups sugar
4 tablespoons water
2 tablespoons caramel syrup
½ teaspoon cream of tartar
2 egg whites
½ teaspoon almond extract

To make caramel syrup: Pour sugar in a heavy skillet. Place over a moderate heat until sugar has melted and turned a rich caramel brown. Add boiling water (there will be a lot of sputtering, so stand back) and cook a minute or two longer until syrup is slightly thickened. Set aside and cool. This caramel syrup makes enough to use for both batter and frosting.

To make the batter: Sift together flour, baking powder, and salt. Set aside. Work butter until soft, then add ¾ *cup sugar*, a little at a time, and continue working the mixture until smooth. In a separate bowl, beat egg yolks thoroughly, then beat in remaining ¾ cup sugar until creamy. Stir yolk mixture into creamed butter along with the 4 tablespoons caramel syrup. Mix in flour combination, alternating with milk and beginning and ending with flour. Last of all, fold in egg whites beaten until they stand in peaks. Divide batter into 2 well-greased and floured 8-inch cake pans. Bake in a preheated 375° oven for 20 to 25 minutes or until cake shrinks from sides of pan. Remove from pans and cool on cake rack.

To make frosting: Put all ingredients, except almond extract, in the top of a double boiler and mix well. Place over rapidly boiling water and cook, beating constantly with a rotary or electric beater for *exactly* 7 minutes. Remove from heat, add almond extract, and beat until frosting is thick enough to spread. When cake is cold, spread frosting between layers, around sides, and over the top. Makes enough frosting to spread generously.

GINGERBREAD LOAF

John Adams once said—apparently in reference to the Molasses Act passed by the British Parliament in 1733—"Molasses was an essential ingredient in American independence." Molasses and ginger are inextricably linked with early American cooking; Amelia Simmons' *American Cookery* contained a recipe for molasses gingerbread.

2 cups sifted all-purpose flour	½ cup brown sugar, firmly packed
½ teaspoon salt	2 eggs, separated
1 teaspoon ground ginger	½ cup commercial sour cream
1 teaspoon baking soda	½ cup molasses
½ cup (1 stick) butter	

Sift together flour, salt, ginger, and baking soda. Set aside. Cream butter until soft. Add sugar, a little at a time, beating until smooth. Beat egg yolks vigorously and stir into butter-sugar mixture. Combine sour cream and molasses and add to the mixture, alternating with the flour combination. Finally, fold in stiffly beaten egg whites and pour into a greased loaf pan. Bake in a preheated 350° oven for 50 to 60 minutes or until a toothpick inserted in center comes out dry. Serve warm or cool, plain or with sweet butter, whipped cream, sweetened sour cream, or vanilla ice cream.

PRUNE CAKE

Plums were grown throughout America in colonial days, but the idea of raising them on a large scale for the purpose of making prunes came along late in the country's history. Pierre Pellier, a Frenchman, introduced Agen plums to California in 1856. Named for a district in France that is famous for its prunes, Agen plums are one of the oldest varieties under cultivation and excellent for prune making. The Santa Clara Valley, owing to Pellier's work, became a center for prunes in the late 1850's and has remained an important source.

⅔ cup prune pulp	½ cup shortening
1½ cups sifted all-purpose flour	1½ cups sugar
½ teaspoon cinnamon	2 eggs
½ teaspoon nutmeg	⅔ cup buttermilk
½ teaspoon allspice	⅓ cup chopped walnuts
¼ teaspoon salt	Sherry Frosting (page 606)
½ teaspoon baking soda	

Chop unsweetened cooked prunes, measure correct amount, and set aside. Sift together flour, all the spices, salt, and baking soda. Set this aside, too. Cream shortening until soft, then work in sugar, a little at a time, as thoroughly as possible. Add eggs and beat very hard, then stir in the prune pulp. Stir in flour combination and buttermilk, alternating them, and beginning and ending with flour. Last of all, stir in the nuts. Pour into a greased 10-inch tube pan and bake in a preheated 350° oven for 50 to 60 minutes or until cake pulls away from the sides of the pan. Cool about 10 minutes before turning out of pan. Cool completely before covering with Sherry Frosting.

MAPLE GINGERBREAD

2⅓ cups sifted all-purpose flour
1 teaspoon baking soda
1½ teaspoons powdered ginger
½ teaspoon salt
1 egg

1 cup maple syrup
1 cup sour cream
4 tablespoons melted butter
Maple Frosting (page 607)

Sift together flour, baking soda, ginger, and salt. Set aside. In a separate bowl beat egg vigorously, then stir in maple syrup, sour cream, and butter. Mix in the flour combination and pour into a greased and lightly floured 11 x 7 x 1½-inch baking pan. Bake in a 350° oven for 30 minutes or until cake pulls away from the sides of the pan. When cool, frost the top with Maple Frosting.

TWO-SPICE CAKE

1 cup butter
2¼ cups sugar
5 eggs
3 cups sifted all-purpose flour
1 tablespoon ground cloves

1 tablespoon cinnamon
Pinch of salt
1 cup buttermilk
1 teaspoon baking soda
Confectioners' sugar

Grease a 10-inch tube pan. Cream butter until soft and light, then gradually work in sugar until mixture is very light and fluffy. In a separate bowl beat eggs thoroughly and add to creamed mixture. Mix well. Sift flour with cloves, cinnamon, and salt. Beat about one-third of the flour combination into the batter, then stir in *half the buttermilk*. Add another third of the flour-spice combination and mix thoroughly. Stir baking soda into remaining half cup buttermilk and mix into batter along with the remaining flour. Pour into cake pan and bake in a preheated 350° oven 45 to 55 minutes or until cake tester comes out dry. Cool 10 minutes, then turn out on a cake rack, and cool completely. Sift confectioners' sugar over the top.

BISHOP'S BREAD

1¼ cups sifted all-purpose flour
1 teaspoon salt
1¼ cups (½ pound) mixed candied
    fruit, chopped
1¼ cups almonds or pecans, chopped

3 eggs
½ cup sugar
1 teaspoon vanilla
1 teaspoon orange extract

Sift flour and salt together and mix with candied fruit and nuts. Set aside. Beat eggs vigorously, then add sugar a little at a time, and continue beating hard until mixture is smooth and very thick. Stir in vanilla, orange extract, and flour combination. Pour into a greased and lightly floured loaf pan. Bake in a preheated 325° oven for 50 to 60 minutes or until toothpick inserted in center comes out dry. Remove from pan and cool on a cake rack. Cut in thin slices to serve. A cup (1 package) chocolate pieces may be added with the fruit and the nuts.

BOSTON CREAM PIE

Cake:
1½ cups sifted cake flour
2 teaspoons baking powder
¼ teaspoon salt
⅓ cup butter
1 teaspoon vanilla
¾ cup sugar
2 eggs
½ cup milk

Filling:
1 cup half-and-half (milk and cream)
¼ cup sugar
3 tablespoons flour
Dash of salt
1 egg, slightly beaten
½ teaspoon vanilla

To make the cake: Sift together flour, baking powder, and salt. Set aside. Work butter and vanilla together until creamy, then work in sugar, a little at a time, until smooth. Beat in eggs one at a time, beating hard after each addition. Stir in milk and flour combination alternately. Pour batter into 2 greased 8-inch round cake pans and bake in a preheated 375° oven for 25 minutes or until cake pulls away from sides of pan. Cool.

To make the filling: Scald half-and-half. Combine sugar, flour, and salt in a bowl and stir in the hot milk until smooth. Add to egg very slowly, beating constantly. Cook over boiling water, stirring constantly, until custard thickens. Remove from heat, stir in vanilla, and cool. When both cake and filling are cool, spoon filling between the layers and sprinkle top with confectioners' sugar, or frost with Chocolate Frosting (page 606).

VARIATION: To make Washington Pie, put raspberry jam or jelly between the layers in place of the custard, and shower the top with confectioners' sugar.

═══════════════════════════

PLUMB CAKE

Four pounds flour, four pounds currants, four pounds butter, four pounds sugar, four pounds citrion, one half an ounce mace, one half pint brandy, forty eggs. Will make a devilish good wedding cake such as I had.
—Oliver Hazard Perry,
Collection of Newport Historical Society

═══════════════════════════

SHAKER CIDER CAKE

3 cups sifted all-purpose flour
½ teaspoon baking soda
¼ teaspoon salt
½ teaspoon nutmeg

½ cup (1 stick) soft butter
1½ cups sugar
2 eggs, well beaten
½ cup cider

Sift together the flour, baking soda, salt, and nutmeg. Set aside. Work butter and sugar together as thoroughly as possible (mixture is never really smooth) and beat in the eggs. Stir in flour mixture and cider, alternating them and beginning and ending with flour. Spoon into a greased loaf pan and bake in a preheated 350° oven for about 1 hour or until toothpick inserted in the center comes out dry. Cool. To serve, cut in thin slices.

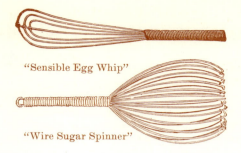

"Sensible Egg Whip"

"Wire Sugar Spinner"

LADY BALTIMORE CAKE

When Owen Wister chose Charleston for the setting of a novel, he made Mrs. Alicia Rhett Mayberry—one of the city's former belles—his central character. Mrs. Mayberry had created a cake called Lady Baltimore, which Wister duly described and made the title of his book, and, when *Lady Baltimore* was published in 1906, Mrs. Mayberry's cake became one of the most popular of American confections.

Cake batter:
2¾ cups sifted cake flour
4 teaspoons baking powder
¾ teaspoon salt
¾ cup butter
1½ cups sugar
4 egg whites
1 cup milk
1 teaspoon almond extract

Syrup:
1 cup sugar
½ cup water
½ teaspoon almond extract
Filling:
White Mountain Frosting (page 607)
2 cups pecans or walnuts, coarsely chopped
1 cup (6 or 8) figs, coarsely chopped
½ cup raisins
Brandy and sherry (optional)

To make the cake: Sift together flour, baking powder, and salt several times. Set aside. Cream butter until very soft, then work in *1 cup of the sugar,* a little at a time, until mixture is light and fluffy. Add flour and milk alternately, starting with *one-fourth of the flour.* Stir only until mixed, then stir in *one-third of the milk.* Follow this procedure, ending with flour. Beat egg whites until they stand in peaks, then beat in remaining sugar, a little at a time, making sure you incorporate all the sugar into the meringue. Fold meringue into batter, gently but thoroughly, until all white patches have disappeared. Mix in almond extract. Grease and coat with flour three 9-inch cake pans. Pour batter into pans, dividing it equally. Bake in a preheated 350° oven for 25 to 30 minutes or until cake pulls away from sides of pan or a toothpick inserted in center comes out dry. Cool for 5 minutes, then turn out on cake racks.

To make the syrup: While cake bakes, make a thick syrup with sugar and water. Bring slowly to a boil, then boil for 6 or 7 minutes. Flavor with almond extract. Spoon this syrup over the cake while it is still hot. Then cool the cake.

To make the filling: Prepare White Mountain Frosting and divide in half. Chop nuts, figs, and raisins (they may be soaked overnight in brandy or sherry) and add to half of the frosting.

To finish cake: Place bottom layer on a very large, flat cake plate, spread with half the nut-fruit filling, cover with second layer and the remainder of the filling. Place third layer on top. Frost sides and top with remainder of White Mountain Frosting.

ANGEL CAKE

Angel Cake was one of the favorite desserts of President Hayes's wife.

1 cup sifted cake flour	1 teaspoon cream of tartar
1½ cups egg whites (about 12)	1½ cups sugar
¼ teaspoon salt	1 teaspoon almond extract

After measuring flour, sift it three times and set aside. Put egg whites into your largest mixing bowl, add salt, and beat with a rotary or electric beater until foamy. Sprinkle cream of tartar over the eggs and continue beating until they stand in peaks. Sprinkle in the sugar, three or four tablespoons at a time, and fold it in gently but thoroughly. Use as few strokes as possible. When you add the last of the sugar, stir in the almond extract. Sift about ¼ *of the flour* over the entire surface of the batter and fold it in gently with a rubber spatula or with your hands. Continue sifting and folding until all flour is used. Do not overmix but make certain it is well mixed and all patches of flour have disappeared. Pour batter into an ungreased 10-inch tube pan and bake in a preheated 375° oven for 35 to 40 minutes or until cake springs back when pressed gently. To serve, tear apart with two forks. Do not cut with a knife.

TRADITIONAL POUNDCAKE

As cupcakes were named for having their ingredients measured by the cupful, so the ingredients of poundcake were first measured by the pound ("one pound sugar, one pound butter, one pound flour, one pound . . . eggs," as Amelia Simmons instructed). Poundcakes are of British origin, but they have enjoyed wide popularity in America.

3 cups sifted all-purpose flour	2 cups (4 sticks) butter
¼ teaspoon salt	2 cups sugar
1 teaspoon baking powder	9 eggs, separated
1 teaspoon mace	2 tablespoons cognac

Grease a 10-inch tube pan and coat lightly with flour. Sift together flour, salt, baking powder, and mace. Set aside. Cream butter until soft, then work in sugar a little at a time, and continue creaming until mixture is smooth. Beat egg yolks thoroughly and stir into creamed mixture. Add flour combination a little at a time, stirring until batter is free of lumps. Beat egg whites until they stand in peaks and fold into the batter along with the cognac. Mix only until all white patches have disappeared, working with a light hand. Pour into cake pan and bake in a preheated 350° oven for 35 minutes. Reduce oven heat to 325° and continue baking 25 minutes or until cake tester comes out dry. Let stand at least 10 minutes before turning out on a cake rack.

VARIATION I: You can substitute ½ teaspoon each of almond extract, lemon extract, and rose water, eliminating both the mace and cognac. Add the flavorings to butter when you cream it. The English often top poundcake with Almond Paste (page 607) and Milk Frosting (page 606). Cool the cake thoroughly before frosting.

VARIATION II: To make Lemon Poundcake, add grated rind of 2 lemons when you combine egg yolks and creamed mixture. Then add 6 tablespoons lemon juice, alternating with flour and beginning and ending with the flour. No other flavorings are necessary.

COCONUT POUNDCAKE

3 cups sifted all-purpose flour
¼ teaspoon salt
2 teaspoons baking powder
1 cup softened butter
1 pound (3½ cups) confectioners' sugar

1 teaspoon vanilla
4 eggs, well beaten
½ cup milk
1 can (4 ounces) grated coconut
Grated rind of 1 lemon

Sift together flour, salt, and baking powder. Set aside. Work butter until creamy, then add confectioners' sugar, a little at a time, beating until smooth. Beat in vanilla and the well-beaten eggs. Mix in flour combination and milk, alternating them and beginning and ending with flour. Finally, stir in coconut and lemon rind. Pour into a buttered and lightly floured 10-inch tube pan. Bake in a preheated 350° oven for 35 minutes. Reduce oven heat to 325° and continue baking 35 minutes longer or until cake pulls away from the sides of the pan. Cool about 10 minutes, then remove from pan, and cool completely on a cake rack. Serve cake without frosting, cut in very thin slices. This cake keeps well wrapped in foil.

CANDY CAKE

½ cup (1 stick) butter
½ cup sugar
3 eggs, well beaten
½ cup molasses
1½ teaspoons vanilla

1½ cups all-purpose flour
Pinch salt
1 cup (4-ounce can) black walnuts
Confectioners' sugar

Work butter until soft, then gradually work in the sugar until mixture is well blended. Beat in eggs, molasses, and vanilla. Mix in flour thoroughly. Add pinch of salt, then the nuts. Pour into a greased 11¼ x 7½ x 1½-inch baking pan and bake in a preheated 350° oven for 30 minutes or until a toothpick comes out dry. Sprinkle with confectioners' sugar and cut into thin fingers when cold.

HICKORY NUT CAKE

2 cups all-purpose flour
1 teaspoon baking soda
1 teaspoon cinnamon
1 teaspoon nutmeg
½ cup (one stick) butter
1 cup sugar

3 eggs, separated
1 teaspoon lemon juice
1 cup seedless raisins
2 cups coarsely chopped hickory nuts
3 tablespoons bourbon whiskey
½ teaspoon salt

Sift together flour, baking soda, cinnamon, and nutmeg and set aside. Cream butter until soft, then cream in sugar, a little at a time, until mixture is smooth. Beat egg yolks hard and add to mixture, then add lemon juice. Mix raisins and nuts with flour combination and add to batter alternating with the whiskey. Beat egg whites and salt together until they stand in peaks, then fold into batter gently but thoroughly. Pour into 2 well-greased loaf pans and bake in a preheated 250° oven for 2 to 2½ hours or until cake pulls away from the sides of pan.

MARTHA WASHINGTON'S GREAT CAKE

"Take 40 eggs & divide the whites from the youlks," reads the original recipe, now in the archives at Mount Vernon, "& beat them to a froth." Beating the whites of forty eggs to a froth with a little bundle of twigs would give any modern cook pause. This adaptation calls only for the ingredients available to Mrs. Washington, including "frensh" brandy. The cake was served at Mount Vernon on Christmas, Twelfth Night, and other "Great Days."

1 pound golden raisins
1 box (11 ounces) currants
1 cup (8 ounces) candied orange peel
¾ cup (6 ounces) candied lemon peel
1 cup (8 ounces) citron
⅓ cup (3 ounces) candied angelica
⅓ cup (3 ounces) candied red cherries
⅓ cup (3 ounces) candied green cherries
½ cup brandy

4½ cups sifted all-purpose flour
1 teaspoon mace
½ teaspoon nutmeg
1 pound (4 sticks) softened butter
2 cups sugar
10 eggs, separated
2 teaspoons fresh lemon juice
⅓ cup sherry

Pick over raisins and currants and soak them in water overnight. Chop orange and lemon peel quite fine; do the same with the citron, angelica, and both kinds of cherries. Pour brandy over fruit, cover, and allow to stand overnight. The following day, sift together flour, mace, and nutmeg. Set aside. Work butter until creamy, then add *1 cup sugar*, a little at a time, beating until smooth. Beat egg yolks until thick and light, then beat in remaining cup of sugar, a little at a time, and the lemon juice. Combine with butter-sugar mixture. Add flour and sherry alternately. Stir in all the fruit and, last of all, fold in stiffly beaten egg whites. Pour the batter into a well-greased and floured 10-inch tube pan, a 10-inch Turk's-head mold, or 2 large loaf pans. Place pan of hot water in the bottom of a preheated 350° oven. Place cake pans in oven and bake 20 minutes. Reduce heat to 325° and continue baking 1 hour and 40 minutes for large cake; 40 minutes for loaf cakes. Cakes are done when a toothpick, inserted at the center, comes out dry. Turn out on rack to cool, then wrap in cheesecloth soaked in sherry (or brandy), and store in an airtight crock or tin for a month or more. If, during this mellowing period, the cheesecloth dries out, soak it again with the same spirits and rewrap the cake. Recipe makes about 11 pounds of Great Cake.

STACK CAKE

This recipe is identified with the Smoky Mountain region, where the principal sweetening ingredient in use was—and still is—molasses. This cake resembles gingerbread, with applesauce between the layers.

4 cups sifted all-purpose flour
1 teaspoon salt
2 teaspoons baking powder
½ teaspoon baking soda
¾ cup shortening
1 cup sugar

1 cup molasses
3 eggs
1 cup milk
Applesauce (page 557)
 or canned applesauce
Confectioners' sugar

Sift together flour, salt, baking powder, and baking soda. Set aside. Work shortening until soft. Add sugar a little at a time while creaming the mixture. Mix in molasses thoroughly, then beat in the eggs, one at a time. Stir in flour combination and milk alternately. Spoon a thin layer of batter, about ⅓ inch, in greased 9-inch cake pans. Bake in a preheated 350° oven for 15 to 20 minutes or until cake pulls away from sides of pan. There will be six or seven thin layers of cake. When all layers are baked and cooled, stack with a generous amount of lightly spiced applesauce between each layer. Sprinkle confectioners' sugar on top.

BLACK FRUITCAKE

This recipe is of English origin and is known variously as Dark Fruit-cake, English Fruitcake, Black Fruitcake, and Merry Christmas Cake.

¼ pound candied citron
⅛ pound candied lemon peel
⅛ pound candied orange peel
½ pound candied cherries
1 pound candied pineapple
1 pound golden raisins
½ pound seeded raisins
¼ pound currants
½ cup dark rum, cognac, sherry, or Madeira
¼ pound blanched shelled almonds

¼ pound shelled walnuts or pecans
2 cups sifted all-purpose flour
½ teaspoon mace
½ teaspoon cinnamon
½ teaspoon baking soda
½ cup (1 stick) butter
1 cup sugar
1 cup brown sugar, firmly packed
5 eggs
1 tablespoon milk
1 teaspoon almond extract

The fruits and nuts should be prepared a day ahead as follows: sliver the citron, lemon, and orange peel into very thin strips; cut the cherries in half and the pineapple in thin wedges. Set aside. Pick over the raisins and currants to eliminate stray stems or seeds, add rum, cognac, sherry, or Madeira, and soak overnight. Chop the almonds and the walnuts or pecans coarsely. Set them aside, too. The following day, prepare the pan. Grease a 10-inch tube pan, four 1-pound coffee cans, or 2 bread pans, measuring 9 x 5 x 3 inches. Line with brown paper.

To make the cake: Mix *½ cup of the sifted flour* with all the fruits and nuts in a large bowl. Sift remaining flour with spices and baking soda. Cream butter until soft, then work in granulated sugar and brown sugar, a little at a time, until mixture is smooth. Stir in the eggs, milk, almond extract, and, finally, the flour mixture. Mix thoroughly. Pour over the fruit and nuts and work together, with your hands, until batter is very well mixed. Lift the batter into the pan or pans and press it down firmly to make a compact cake when cooked. Bake in a preheated 275° oven. A tube pan that uses all the batter will take 3¼ hours; the bread pans, which will each hold half the batter, 2¼ hours; the coffee cans, which each hold one-fourth of the batter, 2 hours. Remove cakes from oven, let stand half an hour, then turn out onto cake racks. Peel off the brown paper very carefully. The four small, round cakes make attractive Christmas presents.

To age fruitcakes: Allow at least four weeks. Wrap each cake in several layers of cheesecloth well soaked in rum, cognac, sherry, or Madeira. Place in an airtight container, such as a large crock or kettle, and cover tightly. If cheesecloth dries out, moisten it with a little of the wine or spirits. Do not overdo it. The cakes should be firm, not soft, at the end of the aging period. This will make them easy to slice in neat, compact slices. If you wish to frost fruitcakes after they have been properly aged, cover the top first with Almond Paste (page 607), then with Milk Frosting (page 606). To decorate, make a garland of candied cherries, slivered angelica, and blanched whole almonds around the edge of the cake.

MARBLE CAKE

Get out all ingredients for both cakes, measure them accurately, and grease and flour a 10-inch tube pan. Set the oven at 350°, and follow the directions below.

To make white cake:
2½ cups sifted cake flour
2 teaspoons baking powder
¼ teaspoon salt
½ cup (1 stick) softened butter
1 teaspoon vanilla
1 cup sugar
½ cup milk
4 egg whites
To make dark cake:
2 cups sifted cake flour

1 teaspoon baking soda
¼ teaspoon salt
1 teaspoon cinnamon
1 teaspoon cloves
½ teaspoon nutmeg
½ cup shortening
1 cup brown sugar, firmly packed
4 egg yolks, beaten
½ cup molasses
1 cup buttermilk
Chocolate Frosting (page 606)

First make the white cake: Sift flour, baking powder, and salt together. Work butter until creamy, stir in vanilla, then gradually beat in the sugar. Beat until mixture is as smooth as possible. Stir in milk and flour mixture alternately. Last of all, fold in stiffly beaten egg whites, gently but completely. Set batter aside.

To make the dark cake: Sift flour, baking soda, salt, cinnamon, cloves, and nutmeg together. Set aside. Work shortening until soft. Gradually work in the brown sugar. When mixture is as smooth as possible, beat in egg yolks and molasses. Then stir in buttermilk and flour mixture alternately.

To fill the pan: Put a heaping tablespoon of white batter next to same amount of dark batter all around the bottom of the pan. Make a second layer with white batter on top of dark batter. Follow this pattern until all batter is used. Work quickly. Bake in a preheated 350° oven for 60 to 65 minutes or until cake tester comes out dry when inserted into center of cake. Cool completely before covering sides and top with Chocolate Frosting.

BROWNSTONE-FRONT CAKE

2 cups sifted all-purpose flour
1 teaspoon baking soda
Dash salt
1 cup boiling water
2 squares (2 ounces) unsweetened
   chocolate

½ cup (1 stick) butter
1¾ cups brown sugar, firmly packed
2 eggs
½ cup commercial sour cream
1 teaspoon vanilla
Chocolate Frosting (page 606)

Sift together flour, baking soda, and salt. Set aside. Pour boiling water over chocolate and let stand until cool. Cream butter until soft, then work in brown sugar, a little at a time, until smooth. Beat eggs vigorously and stir into sugar combination. Add flour mixture and sour cream alternately, beginning and ending with flour. Finally, stir in the chocolate-water mixture and vanilla. Pour batter into a greased 9 x 5 x 3-inch loaf pan and bake in a 325° oven 50 to 60 minutes or until cake begins to shrink away from sides of pan. Cool for a few minutes, then turn out on a cake rack. When completely cooled, frost with Chocolate Frosting.

APPLESAUCE CAKE

1½ cups sifted all-purpose flour
1 teaspoon baking soda
Pinch of salt
1 teaspoon cinnamon
1 teaspoon cloves
½ cup shortening

¾ cup brown sugar, firmly packed
1 egg
1 cup applesauce
1 cup nuts, chopped
1 cup raisins
½ cup pitted dates, chopped

Sift together flour, baking soda, salt, cinnamon, and cloves. Set aside. Work shortening until soft, then stir in sugar, a little at a time, working the mixture until smooth. Beat in the egg vigorously. Alternately stir in flour mixture and applesauce. Then add nuts, raisins, and dates. Pour batter into a greased loaf pan and bake in a preheated 350° oven for 50 to 60 minutes or until cake pulls away from sides of pan. Cool several minutes before turning out onto a cake rack.

CINNAMON CUPCAKES

1½ cups sifted all-purpose flour
2 teaspoons baking powder
Pinch of salt
1 tablespoon cinnamon
½ cup (1 stick) butter

1 cup sugar
2 eggs
½ cup milk
Whipped Cream Frosting,
    cinnamon variation (page 607)

Sift together flour, baking powder, salt, and cinnamon. Set aside. Work butter until soft, then gradually work in sugar as thoroughly as possible. Beat in eggs, one at a time, beating hard after each addition. Stir in the flour combination and milk alternately. Spoon into greased muffin pans and bake in a preheated 350° oven for 25 minutes or until a toothpick inserted in center comes out dry. Frost with Whipped Cream Frosting, cinnamon variation. Makes 18.

NAPLES BISCUITS

This recipe for Naples Biscuits, or Ladyfingers, is adapted from Mary Randolph's *Virginia Housewife*.

3 eggs, separated
⅓ cup confectioners' sugar
⅓ cup flour

Pinch salt
½ teaspoon vanilla

Beat egg yolks long and hard, preferably with an electric mixer. Wash blades of mixer, dry thoroughly, then beat egg whites until they hold a soft shape. Add sugar, a little at a time, and continue beating until mixture stands in peaks. Fold into yolks gently, then sift flour and salt over the top and fold in, then add the vanilla. Shape into thin fingers with a spoon or decorating tube on a cooky sheet lined with brown paper. Bake in a preheated 350° oven for 10 to 12 minutes. Cool on a cake rack and sprinkle with a little confectioners' sugar. Makes 16 to 18.

CHOCOLATE FROSTING

2 squares unsweetened chocolate
2 tablespoons softened butter
½ teaspoon vanilla
Pinch of salt

1 cup confectioners' sugar
1 egg
¼ cup milk

Melt chocolate over hot, not boiling, water. Combine butter, vanilla, and salt in a bowl. Stir in confectioners' sugar, a little at a time, until smooth, then beat in egg, milk, and the melted chocolate. Beat hard until creamy and stiff enough to spread.

BUTTER CREAM FROSTING

½ cup softened butter
1½ cups confectioners' sugar

2 tablespoons milk
½ teaspoon vanilla

Combine all ingredients and beat with an electric beater at high speed until smooth and thick. If the frosting is too thin, add additional confectioners' sugar.

VARIATION I: To make Coffee Butter Cream Frosting, substitute 1 teaspoon instant coffee for vanilla.

VARIATION II: To make Chocolate Butter Cream Frosting, melt ½ cup semi-sweet chocolate pieces over hot, not boiling, water. Beat frosting, then stir in melted chocolate.

SHERRY FROSTING

Combine ⅓ cup softened butter, 1 egg white, 1 tablespoon sherry, and 2 cups confectioners' sugar in a bowl. Beat with a rotary or electric beater until frosting is smooth and of a spreading consistency, then stir in 1 tablespoon orange rind grated fine.

MILK FROSTING

Combine 1½ cups sugar, ½ cup milk, and 1 teaspoon butter in a saucepan. Cook, stirring constantly, until mixture begins to boil. Then boil, without stirring, until a few drops tested in cold water form a soft ball. Remove from heat, stir in ½ teaspoon vanilla, and beat until frosting is of a spreading consistency. Spread over top of cake, letting it dribble down the sides. If frosting becomes too stiff to spread, melt in top of double boiler over boiling water, then beat again.

WHIPPED CREAM FROSTING

Combine 1 cup heavy cream with ¼ cup sugar. Chill in refrigerator at least two hours, then beat with a rotary or electric beater until stiff. Flavor with vanilla, almond extract, orange extract, etc.

VARIATION I: To make Cocoa Whipped Cream Frosting, substitute ¼ cup brown sugar, firmly packed, for the sugar and add ¼ cup cocoa.

VARIATION II: To make Cinnamon Whipped Cream Frosting, add ½ teaspoon cinnamon.

MAPLE FROSTING

2 cups confectioners' sugar   3 tablespoons maple syrup
Pinch of salt   1 tablespoon heavy cream
1 tablespoon softened butter

Combine all ingredients. Beat until mixture is smooth and of a spreading consistency.

WHITE MOUNTAIN FROSTING

3 cups sugar   3 egg whites
1 cup water   Dash of salt
¼ teaspoon cream of tartar   Flavoring (vanilla, orange extract, etc.)

Cook together sugar, water, and cream of tartar until candy thermometer reaches 238° or until syrup spins a long thread when dripped from a spoon. Pour a thin, slow stream of the syrup into stiffly beaten egg whites, beating constantly until frosting stands in peaks. Stir in salt and flavoring to taste.

ALMOND PASTE

1 pound blanched almonds   1 teaspoon almond extract or
1 pound confectioners' sugar, sifted   2 teaspoons rose water
3 egg whites

Work almonds through a food grinder or blend in an electric blender. Thoroughly mix in confectioners' sugar. Beat egg whites slightly, then stir into the almond mixture. Add almond extract or rose water, using your hands to blend the heavy mixture.

COOKIES

NEW YEAR'S COOKIES

Christmas and New Year's have always called for special recipes, and the Dutch New Year's *koekjes,* traditionally baked in molds that produced the design of an eagle or the name of a famous person like Washington, were once among the most ornate. In 1808, Washington Irving's *Salmagundi: Or, The Whim-Whams and Opinions of Launcelot Langstaff, Esq., and Others* claimed: "These notable cakes, hight [called] new-year-cookies . . . originally were impressed on one side with the burly countenance of the illustrious Rip [Van Winkle]."

3 cups sifted all-purpose flour	2 eggs
1 tablespoon baking powder	1 cup sugar
½ teaspoon salt	1 cup heavy cream
1 teaspoon nutmeg	1½ tablespoons caraway seeds

Sift together flour, baking powder, salt, and nutmeg. Set aside. Beat eggs until very light, beat in sugar, a little at a time, and then the cream. Stir in flour combination and caraway seeds. Refrigerate for several hours until dough is firm enough to handle. Roll about ¼ inch thick on a lightly floured board and cut with a small cooky cutter. Sprinkle tops with sugar and bake on greased cooky sheets in a preheated 350° oven for about 10 minutes. Makes about 8 dozen.

APEES

These cookies, especially popular at Christmastide in Pennsylvania, were probably named for Ann Page, a famous nineteenth-century Philadelphia cook. In his *Annals of Philadelphia,* published in 1830, J. F. Watson wrote: "Philadelphia has long enjoyed the reputation of a peculiar cake called the apee . . . Ann Page, still alive . . . first made them, many years ago, under the common name of cakes. . . . On her cakes she impressed the letters A. P., the letters of her name."

1 cup (2 sticks) butter	2⅓ cups sifted all-purpose flour
1 teaspoon vanilla	¼ teaspoon cream of tartar (scant)
1⅓ cups sugar	¼ teaspoon salt
2 eggs	⅔ cup commercial sour cream

Work butter and vanilla until soft, then work in sugar a little at a time, and continue mixing until very smooth. Add eggs, one at a time, beating hard after each addition. Sift together flour, cream of tartar, and salt. Stir into mixture, alternating with sour cream. Drop by teaspoonfuls onto a greased cooky sheet and bake in a preheated 375° oven for 10 minutes. Cookies should be very pale. Makes about 6 dozen.

CINNAMON STARS

1 pound unblanched almonds	2 cups sifted confectioners' sugar
5 egg whites	2 teaspoons cinnamon
Dash of salt	1 teaspoon grated lemon rind

Work almonds through a nut grinder or blend in an electric blender. Set aside. Beat egg whites and salt until they hold a shape. Beat in confectioners' sugar, a little at a time, and continue beating until the mixture stands in peaks. Stir in the cinnamon and grated lemon rind. Transfer about one third of the mixture to another bowl to use later as a glaze. Fold ground almonds into remaining mixture and blend thoroughly. Pat half the mixture at a time on a board or pastry cloth lightly sprinkled with additional confectioners' sugar. Pat about ⅓ inch thick, dusting the palm of your hand frequently with confectioners' sugar if mixture seems sticky. Cut with a small star or round cutter and place on a greased cooky sheet. Brush tops with reserved egg-white mixture and bake in a preheated 300° oven for 20 minutes or until edges begin to firm (the color remains the same). Makes about 5 dozen.

SAND TARTS

2 cups sifted all-purpose flour	1 cup sugar
½ teaspoon salt	1 egg
1 teaspoon baking powder	1 egg yolk
½ cup (1 stick) butter	1 teaspoon cinnamon
½ teaspoon vanilla	3 tablespoons sugar

Sift together flour, salt, and baking powder. Cream butter and vanilla until soft, then add the sugar a little at a time. Work the mixture until light and fluffy. Add unbeaten egg and extra egg yolk, beating well. Mix in the flour mixture and beat hard. Chill dough in refrigerator for several hours or, preferably, overnight. Divide the dough into portions and roll one portion at a time on a sugar-sprinkled board until paper thin. If possible, use a pastry cloth and a rolling pin in a knitted sleeve. If dough becomes too soft to handle easily, return to refrigerator and chill. Cut with cooky cutters, place on an ungreased cooky sheet, and brush tops with a little milk. Mix the sugar and the cinnamon together and sprinkle on each cooky. Bake in a preheated 350° oven for 8 to 10 minutes or until edges of cookies turn a delicate brown. Makes about 3 dozen.

ANISE CAKES

½ cup (1 stick) butter	1 teaspoon aniseed
1½ cups sugar	3 cups sifted all-purpose flour
3 eggs	½ cup blanched almonds

Cream butter until soft, then gradually add sugar, and continue working until well blended. Add eggs, one at a time, beating hard after each addition. Stir in aniseed and flour. Drop batter from a teaspoon onto greased cooky sheet and place an almond on top. Bake in a preheated 350° oven for 10 to 12 minutes or until bottoms of cookies turn a golden brown. The tops should be pale. The cakes improve in flavor if allowed to ripen in an airtight container for several days before serving. Makes 3 to 4 dozen.

THE BUTTER DROP

The Butter Drop, forerunner of the Toll House Cooky, appears in a great number of old cookbooks, beginning with *American Cookery* by Amelia Simmons.

1 cup plus 2 tablespoons sifted
    all-purpose flour
½ teaspoon salt
½ teaspoon baking soda
½ cup (1 stick) butter

6 tablespoons brown sugar
6 tablespoons granulated sugar
1 egg
½ teaspoon vanilla

Sift together flour, salt, and baking soda and set aside. Work butter until soft, then add both kinds of sugar, a little at a time, beating until creamy. Beat in egg and vanilla vigorously. Then stir in flour combination. Drop batter from a teaspoon onto a greased cooky sheet, allowing plenty of room for expansion. Bake in a preheated 375° oven for 8 to 10 minutes. Makes about 48.

To make Toll House Cookies: Stir in 1 cup chocolate pieces and ½ cup coarsely chopped nuts before you spoon batter onto the baking sheet.

CREOLE KISSES

3 egg whites
2 cups confectioners' sugar

1 teaspoon vanilla
½ cup chopped pecans

Beat egg whites with a rotary or electric beater until they stand in peaks. Beat in the sugar and vanilla a little at a time. Stir in pecans. Cover a cooky sheet with brown wrapping paper. Drop the Kisses from a teaspoon onto the ungreased paper and bake in a preheated 350° oven for 15 to 20 minutes. Makes about 45.

SNICKERDOODLES

New England cooks had a penchant for giving odd names to their dishes—apparently for no other reason than the fun of saying them. Snickerdoodles come from a tradition of this sort that includes Graham Jakes, Jolly Boys, Brambles, Tangle Breeches, and Kinkawoodles.

3¼ cups sifted all-purpose flour
½ teaspoon salt
1 teaspoon baking soda
1 teaspoon cinnamon
1 cup (2 sticks) butter

1½ cups sugar
3 eggs, well beaten
1 cup hickory nuts or walnuts, coarsely chopped
½ cup currants
½ cup raisins, chopped

Sift together flour, salt, baking soda, and cinnamon. Set aside. Work butter until creamy, then add sugar, a little at a time, beating until smooth. Beat in eggs thoroughly. Stir in flour combination, nuts, currants, and raisins. Drop from a teaspoon onto a greased cooky sheet about 1 inch apart, and bake in a preheated 350° oven for 12 to 14 minutes. Cookies keep well in an airtight container. Makes about 10 dozen.

EDENTON TEA PARTY CAKES

On October 25, 1774, fifty-one ladies of Edenton, North Carolina, met at the behest of one Penelope Barker, in the home of Elizabeth King, to express their indignation over the British tax on tea. They resolved at this tea party (with tea made from dried raspberry leaves) : "We the Ladys of Edenton do hereby solemnly engage not to conform to the pernicious practice of drinking tea." At this gathering cookies, made according to this recipe of Penelope Barker's, were served.

3½ cups sifted all-purpose flour	1 teaspoon vanilla
1 teaspoon baking soda	2 cups brown sugar, firmly packed
½ teaspoon salt	3 eggs
¾ cup butter	

Sift together flour, baking soda, and salt. Set aside. Work butter and vanilla until soft, then add the sugar, a little at a time, while continuing to cream the mixture. Beat in eggs, one at a time, and stir in flour combination thoroughly. Divide dough in half, wrap each half in wax paper, and chill for several hours or until firm enough to handle easily. Roll out one portion at a time as thin as possible on a lightly floured board and cut with a cooky cutter. Place several inches apart on a greased cooky sheet and bake in a preheated 400° oven for 7 to 9 minutes. Makes 6 dozen cookies when a 2½-inch cooky cutter is used.

BENNE CAKES

Benne (sesame) seeds, brought to the South by African slaves, were thought to bring good luck. The seeds were planted as a border around cotton fields and were used in desserts, candies, and cookies.

Dough:	Grated rind of 1 orange
3 cups sifted all-purpose flour	1 egg
2 teaspoons baking powder	½ cup milk
½ teaspoon salt	*Glaze:*
½ teaspoon nutmeg	2 tablespoons butter
¾ cup butter	¾ cup honey
½ cup sugar	3 tablespoons benne (sesame) seeds

Sift together flour, baking powder, salt, and nutmeg. Cream the butter until soft, then work in sugar, a little at a time, until light and fluffy. Finally, stir in orange rind. Beat egg and milk together slightly. Mix into sugar-butter combination alternately with the flour mixture. Dust your hands with a little flour, pinch off pieces of the dough, and roll into small balls the size of a walnut. Bake on ungreased cooky sheets in a preheated 350° oven for 10 minutes or until lightly browned. Cool on a rack. Makes about 5 dozen.

To make the glaze: Cook butter, honey, and benne seeds until a few drops tested in cold water separate into threads that are hard but not brittle (290° on a candy thermometer). Cool until foam settles. Dip the top of each cooky in the glaze. Work quickly. If the glaze hardens, reheat over hot water. Stir the glaze occasionally to keep seeds from floating on top. These cookies are best when fresh.

MUSTER DAY GINGERBREAD

Muster Day, or Training Day, Gingerbread is named for a New England tradition. Before the Civil War, the first Tuesday of every June was set aside as Training Day for all men from ages eighteen to forty-five. This military training began at nine o'clock in the morning, and the men were usually accompanied by wives, children, cousins, aunts, uncles, sisters, grandfathers, and friends. It became, of course, an occasion for festivity, and this Gingerbread was one of the indispensable ingredients of the day.

⅔ cup brown sugar, firmly packed
⅔ cup molasses
1 teaspoon ginger
1 teaspoon cinnamon
½ teaspoon cloves

¾ tablespoon baking soda
⅔ cup butter
1 egg
5 cups all-purpose flour

Heat brown sugar, molasses, ginger, cinnamon, and cloves to the boiling point. Remove from heat, add baking soda, and pour over butter in a mixing bowl. Stir until butter has melted, then stir in the egg and flour thoroughly. Knead for a few minutes, then gather dough into a ball. Refrigerate dough until firm enough to roll easily, then roll on a lightly floured board, and cut with fancy cooky cutters. Place on greased cooky sheet and bake in a preheated 325° oven for 8 to 10 minutes.

CASHEW SHORTBREAD

2 cups sifted cake flour
½ teaspoon baking powder
1 cup (2 sticks) butter

½ cup confectioners' sugar
1 cup salted cashews, chopped

Sift flour and baking powder together and set aside. Cream butter until soft, then work in sugar with your hands until smooth. Stir in flour and, last of all, the cashews. Chill in refrigerator for at least 1 hour. Divide dough in half and roll one portion at a time about ⅓ inch thick on a lightly floured board. Refrigerate other half until needed. Work fast. Cut into 1½-inch squares and place on an ungreased cooky sheet. Bake in a preheated 375° oven for 15 minutes. Makes about 4 dozen.

COCONUT JUMBLES

⅔ cup butter
1 cup sugar
1 egg, well beaten

1 cup flour
1 can (4-ounce size) grated coconut

Cream butter, then work in sugar, a little at a time, and continue working until well blended. Stir in egg thoroughly. Mix in flour and coconut with your hands. The batter will be very stiff. Drop from a teaspoon onto a greased cooky sheet, allowing plenty of room for expansion. Bake in a preheated 425° oven for 10 to 12 minutes. Makes about 40.

GINGERSNAPS

These Gingersnaps, Miss Harland instructed in *Common Sense in the Household*, "will keep for weeks, *if locked up.*"

¾ cup butter
¾ cup shortening
2¾ cups sugar
2 eggs
½ cup molasses

4 cups sifted all-purpose flour
2 teaspoons baking soda
2 teaspoons cinnamon
2 teaspoons cloves
2 teaspoons ginger

Cream the butter and shortening until soft and light, then add *2 cups of the sugar,* a little at a time, and continue creaming until mixture is very fluffy. Beat in the eggs and molasses thoroughly. Sift together all the dry ingredients and mix, little by little, with the creamed batter, beating hard. The batter will be quite soft. Roll pieces of the dough into balls about 1 inch in diameter, then roll each ball in the remaining sugar. Place on greased baking sheet about 3 inches apart to allow for spreading and bake in a preheated 375° oven for 12 to 15 minutes. After you take Gingersnaps from the oven, let them stand a minute before cooling on a wire rack. Makes about 100. Do not make these in hot, humid weather because they will remain soft.

MORAVIAN CHRISTMAS COOKIES

½ cup brown sugar, firmly packed
¾ teaspoon baking soda
½ teaspoon salt
¾ teaspoon ginger
¾ teaspoon cloves
¼ teaspoon nutmeg

¾ teaspoon cinnamon
¼ teaspoon allspice
1 cup molasses
½ cup shortening
4 cups sifted all-purpose flour

Sift together the brown sugar, baking soda, salt, and all the spices. Heat molasses just to the boiling point but *do not boil.* Stir in the shortening until absolutely smooth. Cool slightly, then beat in the sugar-spice mixture. Now knead in the flour with your hands until dough holds together. Shape into a big ball and chill in the refrigerator until firm. This dough will keep for weeks so you can bake as many cookies as you want at a time. Break off pieces of the dough and roll paper-thin on a lightly floured board. Cut into circles, place on a greased cooky sheet, and bake 6 to 8 minutes in a preheated 375° oven. Makes about 10 dozen.

BROWNIES

2 squares (2 ounces) unsweetened chocolate
½ cup butter
1 cup sugar
2 eggs, well beaten

1 teaspoon vanilla
½ cup sifted all-purpose flour
Pinch of salt
½ cup chopped walnuts

Melt chocolate over hot water. Work butter until soft, then gradually beat in sugar. When mixture is as smooth as possible, beat in eggs and vanilla. Stir in flour, salt, melted chocolate, and chopped nuts. Pour into a greased 8-inch square cake pan and bake in a preheated 350° oven for 25 to 30 minutes (brownies should remain soft). Cut in squares.

CANDY

PECAN NOUGAT

1½ cups coarsely chopped pecans   2 tablespoons fresh lemon juice
2 cups sugar

Spread pecans over a shallow baking pan and toast in a 350° oven about 10 to 15 minutes. Combine sugar and lemon juice in a heavy skillet. Cook over a low heat, stirring constantly with a wooden spoon, until melted sugar has a deep golden color. Stir in pecans and pour into a large, oiled pan or on a marble slab. Work fast, spreading the nougat with an oiled spatula as thin as possible. Cool until solid, then break into pieces.

HONEY POPCORN BALLS

3 quarts popcorn, popped   1 cup sugar
1 cup honey   Pinch of salt

Pop the corn and measure correct amount into a large bowl. Cook honey, sugar, and salt in a saucepan over medium heat until syrup reaches 245° on candy thermometer or until a few drops tested in cold water form a firm ball which does not flatten when removed from the water. Pour over popcorn in a very thin, steady stream. (Fork the syrup through the popcorn thoroughly while you pour.) When mixture is cool enough to handle, butter your hands and shape it into balls, pressing it together firmly. Makes about 2 dozen.

DOTTY DIMPLE'S VINEGAR CANDY

Rebecca Sophia Clarke (Sophie May) of Norridgewock, Maine, wrote more than forty books for children, including the six-volume series, published from 1867 to 1869, called the *Dotty Dimple Stories*. Miss Clarke's books were distinguished by their lack of plot, overweening presence of moralizing, cute naughtiness, and baby talk. They were distinguished, too, by talk of this candy, which became as popular with children as did the books and was, unlike the stories, enduringly cherished by children.

Combine 3 cups sugar with 1½ cups vinegar and cook over a low heat, stirring constantly, until sugar is dissolved. Continue cooking until syrup reaches the soft-crack stage (270° to 290° or until a few drops tested in cold water separate into threads which are hard but not brittle). Pour onto a large buttered platter and let cool until candy can be handled comfortably. Butter your hands and pull the taffy until it is white and almost firm. Stretch into a rope about 1 inch in diameter and snip off pieces with scissors.

614

VASSAR FUDGE

Fudge was popular in the late nineteenth century in women's colleges. Sometimes cooked over the gaslight which hung from the center of the ceiling, it was used as the excuse for parties after "lights-out." These fudge recipes were given by Maria Parloa in a booklet distributed by Walter Baker & Co. in 1905.

2 cups sugar
2 squares (2 ounces) unsweetened
  chocolate

1 cup light cream
1 tablespoon butter

Combine sugar, coarsely chopped chocolate, and cream. Cook over a moderate heat, stirring only until sugar and chocolate have melted. Continue cooking until mixture reaches 238° or until a few drops tested in cold water form a soft ball. Remove from heat, add butter, and cool slightly. Beat until fudge begins to harden, then transfer to a buttered platter. Cut into squares before the fudge is absolutely firm. Makes a little more than 1 pound.

VARIATION: To make Wellesley Fudge, add ½ pound of marshmallows when the candy is removed from the heat.

SMITH COLLEGE FUDGE

1 cup granulated sugar
1 cup brown sugar, firmly packed
¼ cup molasses
½ cup light cream

2 squares (2 ounces) unsweetened chocolate
¼ cup butter
1½ teaspoons vanilla

Combine the 2 sugars, molasses, cream, and coarsely chopped chocolate in a saucepan. Cook over a moderate heat, stirring until sugar and chocolate have melted. Continue cooking, without stirring, until mixture reaches 238° or until a few drops tested in cold water form a soft ball. Remove from heat, stir in butter and vanilla, cool slightly, then beat until fudge begins to harden. Pour onto a buttered platter and cut into squares before the fudge is completely hard. Makes about 1¼ pounds.

SECRETS

Take glazed paper of different colours, and cut into squares of equal size, fringing two sides of each. Have ready, burnt almonds, chocolate nuts, and bonbons or sugar-plums of various sorts; and put one in each paper with a folded slip containing two lines of verse; or what will be much more amusing, a conundrum with the answer. Twist the coloured paper so as entirely to conceal their contents, leaving the fringe at each end.

—Eliza Leslie, *Directions for Cookery*, 1837

PEANUT BRITTLE

2 cups sugar
1 cup light corn syrup
½ cup water
2 cups peanuts

1 tablespoon butter
1 teaspoon vanilla
2 teaspoons baking soda

Combine sugar, syrup, and water in a heavy skillet. Cook over a low heat until mixture reaches 230° or until it spins a thread about 2 inches long when dropped from a spoon. Stir in peanuts and continue cooking to 300° or until a few drops tested in cold water separate into threads which are hard and brittle. Remove from heat and stir in remaining ingredients. Pour onto a greased platter, spreading as thin as possible. When cold, break into pieces.

PRALINES

Pralines were named for the French diplomat César du Plessis-Praslin, later Duc de Choiseul. It is said that Praslin's butler advised him that almonds coated with sugar would not cause indigestion. In Louisiana, the Creoles adapted Pralines, substituting native pecans for almonds and brown sugar for white.

3 cups light brown sugar, firmly packed
¼ cup water

1 tablespoon butter
1 cup pecan meats

Combine sugar, water, and butter in a saucepan. Cook over a low heat until candy thermometer indicates 238° or until a little syrup dropped into cold water forms a soft ball which flattens when taken out of the water. Add pecans and stir until mixture adheres to the nuts. Remove from heat and continue stirring until candy is thick and opaque. Drop from a tablespoon onto wax paper, making small patties. Makes about 2 dozen.

CREAM PRALINES

1½ cups sugar
⅓ cup light molasses
1 cup light cream

1 tablespoon butter
Dash of nutmeg
1½ cups pecan meats, coarsely chopped

Combine sugar, molasses, cream, butter, and nutmeg in a large saucepan. Bring to a boil and cook over medium heat, stirring occasionally, until mixture reaches 240° on candy thermometer or until a little syrup dropped in cold water forms a firm ball. This takes from 35 to 40 minutes. Remove from heat and let stand 3 minutes, then add the nuts, and drop from a teaspoon onto wax paper or foil. Makes about 2½ dozen.

SALT WATER TAFFY

This famous candy is sold all along the Boardwalk at Atlantic City and, it is claimed, is made with sea water.

1 cup sugar
1 tablespoon cornstarch
⅔ cup white corn syrup
1 tablespoon butter
½ cup water

¼ teaspoon salt
Food coloring
Flavoring extracts (vanilla, almond, orange, peppermint, etc.)

Mix sugar and cornstarch in a saucepan. Stir in corn syrup, butter, water, and salt. Cook over a moderate heat until mixture reaches 254° or until a few drops tested in cold water form a ball which holds its shape. Remove from heat, add a few drops of food coloring and flavoring extract, and pour onto a buttered platter. Cool until it can be handled comfortably. Butter your hands and pull the taffy until it is light in color and firm enough to hold a shape. Stretch into a roll about 1 inch in diameter and snip off bits with kitchen shears. Wrap each piece in wax paper.

Taffy pull

SUGARED NUTS

Measure out 2 cups of nut meats (walnuts, black walnuts, hickory nuts, pecans, etc.), place in a saucepan, and warm the nut meats slightly. Combine 1 cup sugar with ½ cup water and cook, stirring constantly, until sugar is dissolved. Continue cooking until syrup reaches 238° or until a little syrup, dropped into cold water, forms a soft ball which flattens when taken out of the water. Remove from heat and pour very slowly over the warm nuts, shaking the nuts back and forth vigorously. The intended result is a relatively even coating of sugar over all the nuts.

DRINKS

COBBLERS

In *The Bon-Vivant's Companion,* Jerry Thomas wrote, "Like the julep, this delicious potation is an American invention, although it is now a favorite in all warm climates. The 'cobbler' does not require much skill in compounding, but to make it acceptable to the eye, as well as to the palate, it is necessary to display some taste in ornamenting the glass after the beverage is made."

Fill a tall glass with shaved ice, add 2 jiggers (3 ounces) spirits (whiskey, applejack, brandy, or rum) or wine (sherry, Rhine wine, Bordeaux, or sauterne) and 1 teaspoon sugar dissolved in a little water. Stir well. Add 2 or 3 orange slices and serve with a straw.

VARIATION I: To make Cobblers with champagne, fill four tall glasses ⅓ full with shaved ice, then add 1 teaspoon sugar dissolved in a little water. Fill glasses with champagne and decorate each glass with a piece of orange or lemon peel.

TODDIES AND SLINGS

Toddies and Slings are essentially the same. The word "toddy" is derived from *tari,* a Hindu word, and means fresh or fermented sap from various species of palm trees. When "toddy" was adopted by traders, it became a specific potion made by man rather than by nature. "Sling"—originally English slang for any drink or draught— also came to mean a particular drink. During the summer, according to John Bernard's *Life in the Old Dominion,* a southern gentleman would "rise about nine, when he exerted himself to walk as far as his stables to look at the stud he kept for the races; at ten he breakfasted on coffee, eggs, and hoe-cake, concluding it with the commencement of his diurnal potations—a stiff glass of mint sling. . . . He then sought the coolest room and stretched himself on a pallet in his shirt and trousers. . . . Between twelve and one his throat would require another emulsion, and he would sip half a pint of some mystery termed bumbo, apple toddy, or pumpkin flip." The Mint Sling and Apple Toddy Bernard speaks of are variations on the more traditional Slings and Toddies given here.

To make a hot Whiskey Toddy: Dissolve 1 lump of sugar in a glass half full of boiling water. Add 1 jigger of whiskey and a small twist of lemon peel. Sprinkle with nutmeg.

VARIATION I: To make a Whaler's Toddy, dissolve 1 teaspoon sugar in a small mug half full of boiling water. Add ½ slice lemon, 3 whole cloves, 1 small piece of cinnamon, and ¼ cup rum. Stir with a spoon, then sprinkle with grated nutmeg.

VARIATION II: To make a Kentucky Toddy, dissolve 1 lump of sugar in a little water, then combine with 1 jigger bourbon and a twist of lemon peel. Add an ice cube and stir well.

MINT JULEP

Although versions of the Julep (called *julab* in Arabic and *gulab* in Persian) can be traced back as far as 1400 A.D., the drink is now identified with the southern United States. "I must...descant a little upon the mint-julep," Captain Frederick Marryat wrote in his diary while traveling through the South in 1838, "as it is, with the thermometer at 100°, one of the most delightful and insinuating potations that ever was invented, and may be drunk with equal satisfaction when the thermometer is as low as 70°."

The Julep has been made with rum, brandy, bourbon, and other potent liquors. It is generally agreed, however, that the classic Julep is the one made with bourbon, which has been popularized in Kentucky. There are two principal unresolvable arguments about the Mint Julep: whether the mint in a Julep should be crushed or not, and whether or not a Julep drinker should use a straw or bury his nose in the mint. Such arguments notwithstanding, Julep drinkers do agree, as Charles Dickens noted during his travels through the American South in 1842, "that...the mounds of ices, and the bowls of mint-julep and sherry cobbler they make in these latitudes, are refreshments never to be thought of afterwards, in summer, by those who would preserve contented minds."

To make a Kentucky Mint Julep: Chill silver mugs or goblets or heavy cut-crystal tumblers on ice in the refrigerator for as long as possible. Dissolve sugar (allow 1 lump per mug) in a little water. Fill each mug with finely crushed ice, add enough bourbon to cover the ice, and stir until the outside of the mug is heavily frosted. Then stir in the sugar syrup to taste. Tuck 5 or 6 sprigs of fresh mint into the ice so that they protrude above the rim.

VARIATION I: To make a Georgia Mint Julep, substitute equal amounts of cognac and peach brandy for the bourbon.

VARIATION II: To make a Louisiana Mint Julep, substitute rum for bourbon.

VARIATION III: To make a Major Bailey, muddle 1 teaspoon confectioners' sugar, 4 dashes fresh lime juice, and 6 mint leaves in a tall goblet. Fill with shaved ice, then add 1 jigger of gin. Stir until outside of glass is frosted. For other variations, see pages 132-33.

CLARET CUP

3 tablespoons sugar
Grated rind of 1 lemon
3 slices of lemon
1 tablespoon Angostura bitters
1 strip cucumber peel

½ jigger each of brandy, maraschino, and white curaçao
1 quart soda water, chilled
2 bottles red wine, chilled
Mint leaves

Combine all ingredients *except soda, wine, and mint,* cover, and let stand for about one hour. When ready to serve, place a block of ice in a chilled punch bowl. Strain punch into bowl, add wine, and garnish with mint leaves.

COCKTAILS

There are a number of theories concerning the origin of the word "cocktail" and, although none is completely reliable, one story from New Orleans seems quite plausible. Monsieur A. A. Peychaud arrived in New Orleans in 1793, opened an apothecary shop, and dispensed—according to a secret family formula—a tonic he called "bitters." Occasionally, for customers suffering severely from a malady, Peychaud would serve a mixture of cognac and bitters, presented to customers in an eggcup, or *coquetier,* as it was called in French. It is said that Americans—who soon insisted on having bitters with other combinations of liquors—slurred *coquetier* into "cocktail." Among the earliest references to such a mixed drink is one in a periodical called *The Balance,* dated May 13, 1806, describing the cocktail as "a stimulating liquor composed of spirits of any kind, sugar, water, and bitters. It is vulgarly called *bitter sling,* and is supposed to be an excellent electioneering potion."

Virtuoso at the bar

THE MARTINI, 1862

Jerry Thomas, author of *The Bon-Vivant's Companion,* claims to have originated the Martini while tending bar at San Francisco's Occidental Hotel between 1860 and 1862. Thomas called it the Martinez, and later chroniclers have said it was named for a chilly traveler on his way to Martinez, California.

1 dash of bitters
2 dashes of maraschino
1 jigger of gin

1 wineglass of vermouth
2 small lumps of ice

Shake thoroughly and strain into a large cocktail glass. Put ¼ slice lemon in the glass and serve. To make the cocktail very sweet, add 2 dashes syrup.

OLD-FASHIONED WHISKEY COCKTAIL

The Old-Fashioned Whiskey Cocktail is said to have been invented by the bartender at the Pendennis Club in Louisville, Kentucky.

Mix together ¼ lump of sugar and 2 teaspoons water. Add a dash of Angostura bitters, 1 jigger whiskey, and 1 piece lemon peel. Add ice and stir.

―――――――

NEW ORLEANS SAZERAC

"The planter 'takes a drink' a dozen times in the forenoon," Nathaniel Parker Willis wrote from New Orleans in 1852, "but he does not *drink* it. He seldom calls for it when alone. It is with him a matter of etiquette. Wherever he meets friend or acquaintance, there is a drinking saloon near by—and he would feel as much at a loss to exchange the compliments of the day, without stepping in to do it over a glass, as to bow to a lady without his hat, or manage an interview without mention of health or weather." It seems likely that the planter in New Orleans most often exchanged the compliments of the day over Sazerac, which originated in the Vieux Carré and was one of the most famous New Orleans drinks.

Muddle 1 lump sugar with 1 teaspoon water, a dash each of Angostura and orange bitters, 3 dashes of absinthe or Pernod. Then add 1 jigger bourbon, 1 ice cube, and a twist of lemon peel. Stir, then strain into an old-fashioned glass and serve.

―――――――

RAMOS GIN FIZZ

Henry C. Ramos arrived in New Orleans in 1888 and purchased the Imperial Cabinet saloon, where this famous drink was served. The drink requires such a great deal of shaking—at least five minutes—that one of the distinctive features of Ramos' establishment was its corps of young boys who did nothing but stand behind the bar to attend to shaking Gin Fizzes. During the Mardi Gras of 1915, the corps reached the prodigious size of thirty-five lads.

1 tablespoon confectioners' sugar
3 to 4 drops orange-flower water
Juice of ½ lime
Juice of ½ lemon
1 jigger dry gin

1 egg white
1 jigger rich milk or cream
1 squirt Seltzer water
2 drops vanilla (optional)

Put all the ingredients, in the order given, in a cocktail shaker. Fill with crushed ice (the ice should not be too fine since lumps are needed to whip the egg white and cream to a froth). Shake long and steadily until mixture thickens. Strain into a tall, thin highball glass.

FLIP

Flips were originally hot drinks concocted in the winter and were warmed by thrusting an iron flip dog or loggerhead into the mug, which produced a pleasant sizzle and a burnt taste. Gradually they became cold drinks, and the flip dogs that hung by the fireplace were of no use except for poking large logs. A Yard of Flannel is a hot Flip which, when properly made, looks fleecy. In the eighteenth century, Myles Arnold reported the drink to be a favorite with the riders on the Boston Post route: "and indeed, 'tis said they sometimes wrap themselves warmly with it."

To make a Yard of Flannel: Heat 1 quart ale in a saucepan. Beat 4 eggs with 4 tablespoons sugar and 1 teaspoon grated nutmeg or ginger, then add ½ cup dark rum. Pour into a pitcher. When ale is almost boiling, pour it into another pitcher. To combine the two mixtures, pour hot ale, a little at a time, into egg mixture, stirring briskly to prevent curdling. Then pour the contents of the two pitchers back and forth until the mixture is as smooth as cream.

To make a cold Flip: dissolve 1 teaspoon confectioners' sugar in a little water in a cocktail shaker. Add 1 jigger spirits or 2 jiggers wine, 1 egg, and 2 or 3 lumps of ice. Shake thoroughly and serve with a little grated nutmeg on top.

SHRUBS AND BOUNCES

Shrubs and Bounces belong to the same family—both are made with a fruit base and brandy or rum—and they are part of the heritage of colonial America. There seems to be little rationale for their names (although "shrub" may derive from the Arabic *shurb*, meaning drink), but, then, there is little rationale for many old colonial drinks, like the Mam, Meridian, the Bogus, Bombo, Rombo, Rumbullion, and Rattle-Skull, the Tiffs and Toddies, Sampsons and Stone Fences, and Whistle Belly Vengeance. The Indians had a rum drink called Coow-woow, which some said was their customary war whoop. The recipes here are eminently palatable, in contradistinction to many of the quaint-sounding old potions.

To make Lime Rum Shrub: Dissolve 1½ cups sugar in 2½ cups water, then combine with 1 quart dark rum and 1 cup fresh lime juice. Mix well, bottle, and let stand in a cool place at least 7 days before using.

To make Orange Brandy Shrub: Dissolve 2 cups sugar in 2½ quarts fresh orange juice. Add 1 quart brandy. Mix well, bottle, and let stand in a cool place at least 7 days before using.

To make Cherry Bounce: Mash 5 pints cherries and crack the stones. Pour 1 quart dark rum over them and let the mixture stand at least 7 days. Strain through several layers of cheesecloth, then sweeten to taste with brown sugar. Mix well, bottle, and let stand at least another week before using.

To serve a Shrub or a Bounce, pour into a highball glass filled with shaved ice or ice cubes.

STONE FENCE

In 1809, Washington Irving, in his *History of New York...by Diedrich Knickerbocker*, told how the Dutch "lay claim to be the first inventors of the recondite beverages, *cock-tail*, *stone-fence*, and *sherry-cobbler*." The first Stone Fence appears to have been made with sweet cider and applejack; it was later made with sweet cider and bourbon.

Pour ¼ cup bourbon into a highball glass, add 2 or 3 ice cubes, and fill the glass with sweet cider.

BENJAMIN FRANKLIN'S ORANGE SHRUB

To a Gallon of Rum two Quarts of Orange Juice and two pound of Sugar—dissolve the Sugar in the Juice before you mix it with the Rum —put all together in a Cask & shake it well—let it stand 3- or 4-Weeks & it will be very fine & fit for Bottling—when you have Bottled off the fine pass the thick thro' a Philtring paper put into a Funnell—that not a drop may be lost. To obtain the flavour of the Orange Peel paire a few Oranges & put it in Rum for twelve hours—& put that Rum into the Cask with the other—For Punch thought better without the Peel.
— From the Franklin Papers,
American Philosophical Society

SANGAREE

The essential characteristic of Sangaree (from the French *sang*, meaning "blood") is its deep red color, derived from red wine. In colonial days, this mild drink was valued as a bracer.

To make Peach Sangaree: Combine ½ cup sliced peaches, 2 tablespoons lemon juice, pinch of salt, 3 tablespoons sugar, pinch of cinnamon, 1 whole allspice, and ½ cup red Bordeaux wine. Mix well and chill for one hour. Strain into a tall glass and fill with sparkling water.

To make Strawberry Sangaree: Combine ½ cup crushed strawberries, 2 tablespoons sugar, 1 teaspoon lemon juice, and ½ cup red Bordeaux wine. Mix well and chill for one hour. Strain into a tall glass and fill with sparkling water.

To make Pineapple Sangaree: Combine ½ cup diced pineapple, 2 tablespoons sugar, 1 whole allspice, 1 tablespoon orange juice, 1 teaspoon lemon juice, and ½ cup red Bordeaux wine. Mix well and chill one hour. Strain into a tall glass and fill with sparkling water.

To make Orange Sangaree: Combine ¼ cup orange juice, 2 tablespoons lemon juice, 2 tablespoons sugar, 1 clove, 2 whole allspice, and ½ cup red Bordeaux wine. Mix well and chill for one hour. Strain into a tall glass and fill with sparkling water.

HAYMAKER'S SWITCHEL

In the haying season farmers used to take their "nooning" (midday dinner) with them, which included a jug of Switchel to wash the meal down. Although a Switchel was usually straight, farmers have been known to spike it with hard cider, or even brandy, which Down Easters used to say got the hay in the barn in half the time.

To make Haymaker's Switchel: Combine 1 cup brown sugar, ½ teaspoon ginger, ½ cup molasses, ¾ cup vinegar, and 2 quarts of water. Mix together, add ice, and chill.

MAY WINE BOWL

2 quarts white wine, well chilled
3 sprays fresh (1 ounce dried) woodruff

½ cup fine granulated sugar
1 cup small strawberries

Sprinkle sugar over woodruff and let stand in a tightly covered glass jar for several hours. Add *2 cups of the wine* to the woodruff, cover again, and let stand overnight. Place a large lump of ice in a punch bowl. Add woodruff and the wine in which it soaked. Pour the remaining cold wine over the ice and stir. Garnish with strawberries. Fills 20 punch cups.

There's a little place just out of town,
Where, if you go to lunch,
They'll make you forget your mother-in-law
With a drink called Fish-House Punch.
— From The Cook, *1885*

FISH HOUSE PUNCH

This punch is the specialty of Philadelphia's famed fishing and social club, the State in Schuylkill, which was founded in 1732, during the reign of George II, by a group of amateur anglers and cooks. When William Black visited Philadelphia in 1744, he reported in his journal that he and his company were welcomed at Gray's Ferry with a bowl of punch large enough to have "swimm'd half a dozen young geese."

¾ to 1 pound sugar
1 quart lemon juice (scant)
2 quarts Jamaica rum

1 quart cognac
½ cup peach brandy

Dissolve the sugar in the smallest possible amount of cold water, then stir in the strained lemon juice. Pour this mixture over a large solid lump of ice, then add the rum, cognac, and peach brandy, in that order. Allow the mixture to mellow for several hours, giving it an occasional stir.

ROMAN PUNCH

It was customary, in the nineteenth century, to serve an ice or sherbet mixed with liquor just after the roast. At some of the formal banquets given by President Grant as many as thirty courses were served, and such middle-course fortification was no doubt necessary. This Roman Punch was the favorite "cup" of the period. During the administration of President Hayes, his wife forbade any liquor to be served at dinners at the White House. As long as Mrs. Hayes was hostess, there were no wineglasses, no fragrance of bourbon, no champagne coolers in evidence at state dinners. Mrs. Hayes's singlehanded temperance movement was not generally appreciated; Secretary of State Evarts stated he would not permit the diplomatic corps to have their annual dinner at the White House if there was to be no wine. At a dinner party given by the Hayeses some of the company eventually noticed that platters of oranges were being consumed with dispatch. They would then try an orange and discover it contained what they thought was Roman Punch. But President Hayes wrote in his diary: "The joke of the Roman punch oranges was not on us but on the drinking people. My orders were to flavor them strongly with the same flavor that is found in Jamaica rum. This took! There was not a drop of spirits in them!"

To make Roman Punch: Mix quickly 1 quart lemon sherbet with 1 cup Jamaica rum. Spoon into chilled punch glasses or scooped-out oranges and serve at once.

An orange filled with Roman Punch

PLANTER'S PUNCH

Dissolve 1 tablespoon sugar in the juice of 1 lime. Add 2 jiggers (½ cup) rum and cracked ice. Shake well. Strain into a tall glass half filled with finely cracked ice and decorate with a maraschino cherry, a sliver of fresh pineapple, and half a slice of orange.

PINK LEMONADE

3 lemons
¾ cup sugar
12 to 14 ice cubes

3 cups cold water
½ bottle maraschino cherries and juice

Scrub lemons, trim off ends, and cut into very thin slices, discarding seeds. Place slices in a bowl, add sugar, and press hard with the back of a wooden spoon until all sugar is dissolved. Add ice cubes, water, and cherry juice. Strain into glasses and garnish with whole maraschino cherries. Makes 6 to 8 servings.

OLD-FASHIONED EGGNOG

Eggnog is descended from the English sack posset, a hot drink made with ale or with dry Spanish wine called sack. Like posset, Eggnog was originally made with ale ("nog" is an English word for a strong ale), but—as it was adopted by Americans—it came to be made with more typical American liquors, like rum, bourbon, and even cider. The earliest American cookbooks relegated Eggnogs to a section of recipes for the sick and the weak. An Eggnog-type milk punch given in *American Practical Cookery Book* was accompanied by the note: "This must be used only with advice."

12 eggs, separated
1 cup sugar
1 quart milk
2 cups bourbon

1 cup Jamaica rum
1 quart heavy cream, whipped
Nutmeg

Beat egg yolks slightly, add sugar, a little at a time, and continue beating until smooth. Pour in milk, bourbon, and Jamaica rum. Beat egg whites until they stand in peaks. Fold egg whites and whipped cream into yolk mixture, gently but thoroughly. Serve cold with freshly grated nutmeg on top. Serves 25 to 30.

BALTIMORE EGGNOG

The Bon-Vivant's Companion, from which this was adapted, notes: "Egg Nog made in this manner is digestible, and will not cause headache. It makes an excellent drink for debilitated persons, and a nourishing diet for consumptives."

16 eggs, separated
¾ cup sugar
⅔ of a whole nutmeg, freshly grated

1 cup brandy or rum
1 cup Madeira
3 quarts half-and-half (milk and cream)

Beat egg yolks until very thick and creamy, then thoroughly beat in the sugar, a little at a time. Beat in the nutmeg, then mix in the brandy or rum and Madeira. Beat egg whites until they stand in peaks, then fold into the yolk mixture. Stir in the half-and-half. Serve in a chilled punch bowl. Serves 20 to 30.

KENTUCKY EGGNOG

24 egg yolks
1½ cups sugar
1½ cups Jamaica rum

2 bottles (fifths) bourbon
1 quart heavy cream, whipped
1 quart vanilla ice cream

Beat egg yolks until light, then beat in sugar, and continue beating steadily for 20 minutes. Stir in the rum and allow the mixture to stand at least 1 hour or until rum has "cooked" the eggs. Then add bourbon. Just before serving, stir in the whipped cream and ice cream. Pour into a well-chilled punch bowl. Serves 30 to 35.

SYLLABUB

Syllabub is closely related to Eggnog. The name is derived from wine that came from Sillery in the Champagne region of France, and from "bub," an Elizabethan slang word for bubbling drink. Although Eggnog called for strong liquors, Syllabub has always been made with wine—some men eschewed this weak potation, considering it a lady's drink. Traditionally a Christmas drink, Syllabub was often made "under the cow"—as shown in a recipe from Richard Brigg's *New Art of Cookery*, published in Philadelphia in 1792, which instructed that a bowl filled with wine be placed under a cow, and the cow milked "till [the Syllabub] has a fine froth at the top."

2 cups white wine	3 cups milk
5 tablespoons grated lemon rind	2 cups light cream
⅓ cup lemon juice	4 egg whites
1½ cups sugar	Nutmeg

Combine wine, lemon rind, and juice. Stir in *1 cup of the sugar* and let stand until sugar dissolves. Combine milk and cream, add wine mixture, and beat with rotary beater until frothy. Beat egg whites until stiff, add remaining ½ cup sugar, a little at a time, beating constantly until whites stand in peaks. Pour wine mixture into punch bowl, top with puffs of egg white, and sprinkle whites with nutmeg. Traditionally served with New Year's Cookies (page 608). Syllabub is so mild, children are allowed to share it. Makes 16 punch cups.

Barroom brawl

CAFÉ BRÛLOT

Brûlot, literally translated, means burnt brandy. In Louisiana, and particularly in New Orleans, *Café Brûlot* was frequently served with the room in darkness, as, according to Lafcadio Hearn, "The crowning of a grand dinner . . . the *pièce de résistance*, the greatest *pousse-café* of all."

Brew three large cups of strong, drip coffee and keep it very hot. Heat, by rinsing in boiling water, a *brûlot* bowl, earthenware bowl, or chafing dish, and a silver ladle. Place 2 very thin strips of lemon rind and the same amount of orange rind in the bowl. Add 4 whole allspice, 2 whole cloves, 1 small stick of cinnamon, 8 small lumps of sugar, and 1½ cups of brandy. Ladle out several lumps of sugar and a little of the brandy. Ignite this ladleful and, when blazing well, slide contents back into the bowl. Keep ladling mixture in and out of bowl while brandy flames. Add the hot coffee, a little at a time, and continue to ladle the mixture until the flame dies. Serve at once in demitasse cups.

HOT BUTTERED RUM

Nicholas Cresswell wrote in his journal in 1777 that the people of New England "import large quantities of Molasses from the West Indies, which they distill and sell to Africa and the other Colonies, which goes by the name of Yankee Rum or Stink-e-buss." Rum had become an important part of the American economy by the early seventeenth century, and the passage of the Molasses Act by the British Parliament in 1733 had done much to lay the foundation for revolution.

Once independence was won, rum found its way into domestic politics. It was used by politicians to influence voters, a practice once dubbed by Theodorick Bland, Jr., as "swilling the planters with bumbo." The honored tradition of feasting voters on food and drink originated quite early in the history of America. When George Washington ran for the legislature in 1758—though a Virginia statute expressly forbade the treating of voters and declared all elections obtained in this manner illegal—Washington's agent supplied the voters of Frederick County, Virginia, with 160 gallons of rum, beer, wine, and cider, or about a quart and a half per voter. The list included 28 gallons of rum, and 50 gallons of rum punch. After the election, Washington wrote his agent, "My only fear is that you spent with too sparing a hand."

Warm a heavy tumbler. Combine 1 teaspoon confectioners' sugar, ¼ cup boiling water, ¼ cup dark rum, and 1 tablespoon butter in the tumbler, fill with boiling water, and stir until well mixed. Serve immediately with freshly grated nutmeg on top.

TOM AND JERRY

The Tom and Jerry has been such a popular American drink that many a bartender, up to the present century, laid claim to inventing or naming it. Pierce Egan, the great dean of British boxing, wrote a book in 1821 called *Life in London, or the days and Nights of Jerry Hawthorne and his Elegant Friend Corinthian Tom,* from which some authorities insist the Tom and Jerry received its name. Egan, it is said, popularized the drink to such an extent that taprooms became known as Tom and Jerries.

It is often alleged in America that the originator of the drink was Professor Jerry Thomas, author of *The Bon-Vivant's Companion* (from which this recipe is taken) and bartender for a time at San Francisco's El Dorado bar. As is so often the case in saloon discussions, solid historical documentation has become somewhat befogged. What can be said with certainty is that the Professor at the El Dorado did popularize the drink in America.

Use 1 egg for each drink. Separate the eggs and beat the whites until frothy. Then beat in 1 heaping teaspoon sugar for each egg white and continue beating until whites stand in peaks. Beat egg yolks separately until thick and lemon-colored. Mix the two together with a pinch of baking soda. Place 2 tablespoons of the egg mixture in each mug. Add ½ jigger brandy and ½ jigger rum, then fill to the top with hot milk, cream, or boiling water. Give it a stir, then grate a little nutmeg on top.

BLUE BLAZER

However dubious the claim that Professor Jerry Thomas invented the Tom and Jerry, it is certain that he was responsible for the Blue Blazer. While keeping bar at San Francisco's El Dorado, the Professor was confronted by a miner who was burdened down with a brace of pistols, several months' worth of gold dust, and a rambunctious thirst. When the miner demanded a drink that would compensate for his many months away from civilization, Thomas asked him to come back in an hour. The Professor then called upon all his experience and inventiveness and, when the miner returned, took down from behind the bar two silver mugs that had been put on a special rack only for show. At this signal all the El Dorado patrons gathered around the bar. Thomas put whisky and boiling water into one of the mugs, set a match to it, and tossed the flaming mixture back and forth between the two mugs, quashing the blue flame after about ten seconds. It is reported that the miner missed three days of civilization after quaffing the Blue Blazer. In *The Bon-Vivant's Companion,* the Professor cautions, "The novice in mixing this beverage should be careful not to scald himself. To become proficient in throwing the liquid from one mug to the other, it will be necessary to practise for some time with cold water."

Put 1 wineglass Scotch whisky and 1 wineglass boiling water in a mug. Ignite the liquid and, while it is blazing, pour ingredients 4 or 5 times from one mug to the other. Properly done, this will have the appearance of a continuous stream of liquid fire. Sweeten with 1 teaspoon pulverized white sugar. Serve in a small bar tumbler with a piece of lemon peel.

Mixing a Blue Blazer

INDEX TO RECIPES

The index to the Illustrated History appears in Part 1, on page 373.

C